What's New in this Edition

Linux Unleashed, Second Edition offers you quite a few changes over the first edition, as well as the latest release of Slackware's Linux CD-ROM. The book's text has been expanded considerably with many new chapters added, including segments on how to deal with Linux as a server on the Internet and how to improve system administration. We've also updated chapters to reflect changes in Linux since our first book. In some cases, these were minor revisions, but some topics—such as installation and configuration—have changed dramatically.

We've also taken the opportunity to add extra details demanded by readers of the first edition. In most cases, these were clarifications or additional examples. Hopefully, these changes will make this edition's material more accurate and useful for you.

With this book, not only do you get a CD-ROM with the latest Slackware Linux, which contains many significant changes to Linux software and utilities, you also get several hundred new pages of material. Some of these changes include the following :

- Up-to-date information on installing and using the new Slackware 3.0 kernel.
- Up-to-date information on installing and using the XFree86 version 3.1.1. software.
- More information on applications for solving mathematical problems using Linux.
- An introduction to database systems under Linux.
- Updated information on getting your printer services working under Linux.
- More information on the Linux HOWTO documents and where to get more information.
- An introduction to languages and tools for software development under Linux.

Linux

UNLEASHED
SECOND EDITION

Kamran Husain, Timothy Parker, Ph.D; et al.

SAMS
PUBLISHING

201 West 103rd Street
Indianapolis, IN 46290

This edition is dedicated to the memory of my father Dr. Bilal Riaz Husain. —Kamran Husain

This one is for my brothers Jeremy and Joshua. Scientia est potentia. —Tim Parker

Copyright © 1996 by Sams Publishing

SECOND EDITION

International Standard Book Number: 0-672-30908-4

Library of Congress Catalog Card Number: 95-72332

99 98 97 96   4 3 2

Interpretation of the printing code: the rightmost double-digit number is the year of the book's printing; the rightmost single-digit, the number of the book's printing. For example, a printing code of 96-1 shows that the first printing of the book occurred in 1996.

Composed in AGaramond and MCPdigital by Macmillan Computer Publishing

Printed in the United States of America

Trademark

Publisher	Richard K. Swadley
Acquisitions Manager	Greg Wiegand
Development Manager	Dean Miller
Managing Editor	Cindy Morrow
Marketing Manager	Gregg Bushyeager
Assistant Marketing Manager	Michelle Milner

Acquisitions Editor
Rosemarie Graham

Development Editor
Angelique Brittingham

Software Development Specialist
Wayne Blankenbeckler

Production Editor
James Grass

Copy Editor
Marla Reece

Technical Reviewers
Justin Bell
Christopher Dent
John Fleming
John Groenveld
Rob Pfister
Stephen Tallon

Editorial Coordinator
Bill Whitmer

Technical Edit Coordinator
Lynette Quinn

Formatter
Frank Sinclair

Editorial Assistant
Sharon Cox

Cover Designer
Nathan Clement

Book Designer
Alyssa Yesh

Production Team Supervisor
Brad Chinn

Production
Gina Brown, Mona Brown, Charlotte M. Clapp, Cheryl Dietsch, Michael Dietsch, Terri Edwards, Jason Hand, George Hanlin, Louisa Klucznik, Ayanna Lacey, Clint Lahnen, Paula Lowell, Erika Millen, Ryan Oldfather, Steph Mineart, Beth Rago, Erich J. Richter, Bobbi Satterfield, Craig Small, Laura A. Smith, SA Springer, Andrew Stone, Tim Taylor, Susan Van Ness, Mary Beth Wakefield, Mark Walchle, Colleen Williams, Jeff Yesh

Overview

Contents

Part III Editing, Typesetting, and More

Part V   Linux for Programmers

Part VIII   Advanced Programming Topics

Part IX Appendixes

Acknowledgments

As usual, my wife, Uzma, has been a tremendous help and has provided support and time for this book. With a pair of three-year-old twins to look after and a job of her own, she has given up a lot to see this book come to completion.

Of course, my mom, Saleha Husain got me started in this endeavor and kept me going to finish this book.

Obviously, I cannot forget those individuals whose comments, flames, and downright blunt remarks made me wonder why I wrote this book in the first place! No, really, your comments helped me nail some problems with the first edition. I am sure that you nerds will find more things to add, edit, delete and/or tweak. Send me e-mail and we'll see what we can do.

Finally, the development staff has to be thanked for their patience as deadlines went by and blood pressures went up. Hey, we did it!

Thank you, everyone, for your help.

Now if you'll excuse me, I'd like to go to the mail box to look for my fat royalty check, which I will promptly use to go on a vacation with my wife. You can rest assured that as I bask in the sunlight off a tropical island, I will be thinking of you folks who are now going to be tied to your computers as you work with Linux. Thinking, yes, …and smiling as I sit as far away as possible from any computer. ;-).

Kamran Husain

The second edition of *Linux Unleashed* was inspired by the kind souls who took the time to comment on the first edition and what they would like to see added. With the release of a new version of Slackware Linux, we undertook this project with enthusiasm and feel the result is a much better book.

As mentioned in the first edition, writers seldom work in a vacuum. Instead, they are guided (and yes, even hassled) by the editors and production people who try their hardest to ensure the project remains on time and on topic.

The first edition of this book was a concerted effort by five authors. This version was developed by Kamran and I, and a dedicated group of editors at Sams, led by Acquisitions Editor Rosemarie Graham. The authors would like to extend thanks to all the staff at Sams for their fine work, and for producing yet another book we are proud of.

Thanks to Rosemarie Graham at Sams for getting us going, and to Jim Grass and Angelique Brittingham for handling the tough chore of managing the production of this book once we finished with it. The technical editors did a marvelous job with this edition, and we thank them for their efforts. Thanks again to Yvonne for understanding why I spent those late evenings at the computer, and to my parents for tolerating yet another delay in a long-overdue visit. Finally, thanks to Grace Buechlein for her tolerance and good humor as another of her books got pushed back to make way for this one.

Tim Parker

About the Authors

Kamran Husain is a software consultant with experience in Windows UNIX system programming. He has dabbled in all sorts of software for real-time systems, applications, telecommunications, seismic data acquisition and navigation, X Window/Motif and Microsoft Windows applications. He refuses to divulge any more of his qualifications. Kamran offers consulting services and teaches training classes through his company, MPS Inc., in Texas. He is an alumnus of the University of Texas at Austin. You can reach Kamran through Sams Publishing, Web http://www.ikra.com, or via e-mail at khusain@ikra.com or mpsi@aol.com.

Tim Parker is a consultant and technical writer based in Ottawa, Canada. He is Technical Editor for *SCO World Magazine*, and Contributing Editor for *UNIX Review, Advanced Systems Magazine*, and *Canadian Computer Reseller*. He has written more than 800 feature articles and two dozen books. When not writing, Tim is a private pilot, scuba diver, white-water kayaker, and general adrenaline junkie.

Uzma Husain is an alumna of the New Jersey Institute of Technology, where she received her masters in computer science. Her work experience is in the financial software and MIS arena.

Peter MacKinnon is a software developer with Bell-Northern Research in Ottawa, Canada. He has a degree in mathematics from Dalhousie University and a computer science degree from the Technical University of Nova Scotia. His current work involves the development of reverse-engineering tools.

Rick McMullin is a computer consultant with Brierly, Doucette, and Simpson Consulting Ltd. of Ottawa, Canada. He specializes in object-oriented systems development and computer security. Rick has been teaching UNIX courses for several years and has been a strong enthusiast and supporter of Linux since its early releases.

Ed Treijs is a technical writer and consultant based in Toronto, Canada. When not writing technical manuals, Ed tinkers with his three classic Firebirds.

Rob Pfister is a software engineer specializing in very large database applications. He holds a degree in computer science from the University of Maine. Rob has been a Linux enthusiast since he installed version 0.96 in early 1992.

Introduction

If imitation is the most sincere form of flattery, UNIX should be proud indeed. The Linux project began several years ago as a public domain version of the popular UNIX operating system—the most widely used operating system in the world. Linux made it possible for anyone to obtain a full-featured version of UNIX for their own pleasure and education, with a minimum of monetary outlay. (With commercial versions of UNIX costing many hundreds of dollars, this was a very important aspect of Linux's popularity.)

Although begun by a single programmer, Linux quickly blossomed into a project organized by people around the world, each contributing ideas, code, and effort for the good of the project and no recompense. The environment, in many ways, recalled the excitement and dedication the nascent personal computer industry experienced years ago.

This book was an interesting project right from the start. It combined the expertise of several veteran UNIX and Linux users with a complete Slackware distribution version of Linux supplied on CD-ROM. This is, essentially, one-stop shopping for a Linux system. The CD-ROM coupled with the installation chapters of this book help you install the complete Linux system software on your PC. Then you can read through the subjects that interest you in the book, working through with the examples on your machine.

For those who have never used Linux (or UNIX) before, you will find the operating system both engrossing and confusing. UNIX has a long and evolved history, leading inevitably to some idiosyncrasies with the operating system. On the other hand, UNIX and Linux are a powerful multitasking operating system that can take your PC far beyond the limitations of the DOS operating system.

Conventions Used in This Book

The following typographic conventions are used in this book:

- Code lines, commands, statements, variables, and any text you type or see on the screen appears in a `computer` typeface. When lines of input and output are shown together, **`bold computer`** typeface is often used to show the user's input.
- Placeholders in syntax descriptions appear in an *`italic computer`* typeface. Replace the placeholder with the actual filename, parameter, or whatever element it represents.
- *Italics* highlight technical terms when they first appear in the text and are sometimes used to emphasize important points.
- Pseudocode, a way of explaining in English what a program does, also appears in *italics*.

■ A special icon ➥ is used before a line of code that is really a continuation of the preceding line. Sometimes a line of code is too long to fit as a single line in the book, given the book's limited width. If you see the ➥ before a line of code, remember that you should interpret that "line" as part of the line immediately before it.

We sincerely hope you enjoy reading this book, and that you find the information useful, educational, and beneficial. The book covers many aspects of Linux, not all of which you will care about. However, we set out to create the most complete introduction to Linux that we could, and we think we've accomplished that task. Enjoy!

IN THIS PART

I

PART

Introduction

Introduction to Linux

1

by Kamran Husain

IN THIS CHAPTER

Welcome to Linux.

This book is about Linux, a clone of the UNIX operating system that runs on Intel 80x86-based machines, where x is 3 or higher.

This first chapter will acquaint you with the features of Linux. This chapter doesn't go into a large amount of detail or cover any advanced topics. Instead, it is intended to give you, a new Linux user, an introduction to what Linux is about, what features you can expect from it, and what sources of information are available.

Don't be afraid to experiment. The system won't bite you. You can't destroy anything by working on the system. UNIX has some amount of security built in to prevent "normal" users (the role that you will now assume) from damaging files that are essential to the system.

The worst thing that can happen is that you'll delete all of your files, and you'll have to go back and reinstall the system. So, at this point, you have nothing to lose.

One note of caution when reading this chapter: At times we will delve into topics that may seem very alien to you, especially if you are new to UNIX and Linux. Don't despair. As we go through this book, you will become more and more familiar with the topics introduced here. Linux is not an easy system to pick up in one day, so don't try to do it. There is no substitute for experience, so relax and learn Linux at your own pace.

What This Book Is Not

This book makes several assumptions about you, the reader. I hope that we can safely assume that you have some working knowledge of PCs and Microsoft's Disk Operating System (MS-DOS). (In some Linux documentation, MS-DOS is also referred to as *messy-dos,* but I'll let you be the judge of that!) If you are not familiar with DOS or computers in general, now would be a good time to pick up a book for beginning with PCs. Still, you should be able to follow this book without needing any extra material.

Most readers of this book will probably be experienced UNIX users. Unfortunately, in the case of readers who are not familiar with UNIX, the ordering of chapters in this book may seem awkward. If you are new to UNIX, please refer to the list of other reference books from Sams Publishing, found in Appendix A, "Linux FTP Sites and Newsgroups." We will attempt to cover some of the basics of UNIX in Part II, "Using Linux," of this book. Whatever small amount is left over, you can get from these reference books, and from slugging it out with Linux.

One last item before we begin. Even though this book attempts to cover a lot of topics on Linux, we cannot guarantee that it will cover precisely *all* the topics you are looking for. However, this book will give you an idea of where to look next, and this book shall provide you with a good starting point. After a little hand holding, you should be able to work with Linux on your own. Enough said.

Now let's get started with Linux.

What Is Linux?

Linux is a free UNIX clone designed for the Intel 80386- and 80486-class processors on PCs. Linux also works with Pentium-class computers.

Linux supports a wide range of software such as TeX, X Window systems, the GNU C/C++ compiler, and TCP/IP. It's a versatile, very UNIX-like implementation of UNIX, freely distributed by the terms of the GNU General Public License. (See Appendix E, "Copyright Information.") Linux is also very closely compliant with the Posix.1 standard, so porting applications between Linux and UNIX systems is a snap.

New users of UNIX and Linux may be a bit intimidated by the size and apparent complexity of the system before them. There are many good books on using UNIX out there, for all levels of expertise ranging from novice to expert. However, few (if any) of these books specifically cover the topic of using Linux.

Although 95 percent of using Linux is exactly like using other UNIX systems, the most straightforward way to get going on your new system is with a book tailored for Linux. This book will get you started. We could list the 5 percent differences, but as it's stated in most of my text books (which bail out of a hard answer with similar phrase): "this is so d**n obvious that we have left it as an exercise for the reader."

How to Pronounce Linux

Pronouncing the word *Linux* is one of the great mysteries of the Linux world. Americans pronounce the name *Linus* with a long *i* sound, as in *style*. However, because Linux was originally based on a small PC-based implementation of UNIX called *Minix* (pronounced with a short *i*), the actual pronunciation of Linux preserves this characteristic: It's LIH-nucks.

Linux Versus UNIX

Linux is not a trademark and has no connection to the trademark UNIX. UNIX is a trademark of Novell.

UNIX is one of the most popular operating systems worldwide because of its large support base and distribution. It was originally developed as a multitasking system for minicomputers and mainframes in the mid-1970s, but has since grown to become one of the most widely used operating systems anywhere, despite its sometimes confusing interface and lack of central standardization.

UNIX is a multitasking, multiuser operating system. This means that many people can be using one computer at the same time, running many different applications. (This differs from MS-DOS, in which only one person can use the system at a time.)

Under UNIX, for users to identify themselves to the system, they must log in, which entails two steps: entering your login name (the name by which the system identifies you), and entering your password, which is your personal secret key to logging into your account. Because only you know your password, no one else can log into the system under your user name.

In addition, each UNIX system has a host name assigned to it. It is this host name that gives your machine a name, and gives it character, class, and charm. The host name is used to identify individual machines on a network, but even if your machine isn't networked, it should have a host name. In Chapter 42, "Networking," we'll cover setting your system's host name.

Versions of UNIX exist for many systems, ranging from personal computers to supercomputers. Most versions of UNIX for personal computers are quite expensive and cumbersome. So where does Linux fit in? Well, Linux is free (which solves the expensive part). Linux is free because the programmers who put the code together did so from scratch and did not impose any requirements for payments. With a true altruistic spirit, they put their code in shareware. The authors can get paid for it, and do retain authorship, but let you use their product without cost. It is also very powerful, and easy to install and maintain by an individual (so much for the cumbersome part).

So What Do I Get with a Linux System?

Linux is a freely distributable version of UNIX developed primarily by Linus Torvalds at the University of Helsinki in Finland. Linux was further developed with the help of many UNIX programmers and wizards across the Internet, giving the ability to develop and change the system to anyone with enough know-how and gumption to hack a custom UNIX kernel.

UNIX and its clones have long been perceived as large, resource-hungry, disk-chomping systems. Linux is not such a beast. Linux is small, fast, and flexible.

Linux has been publicly available since about November of 1991. Version 0.10 went out in November of 1991, and Version 0.11 followed in December of 1991. There are very few small bugs now, and in its current state, Linux is most useful for people who are willing to port code and write new code. Because Linux is very close to a reliable/stable system, Linus decided that Version 0.13 will be known as Version 0.95. Believe it or not, the whole story started with two processes that printed AAAA... and BBBB... on a dumb terminal. Linus then expanded on this simple task-switching mechanism and, with the help of many avid supporters, developed and released a stable, working version of Linux.

So, what are some of the important features of Linux that make it so unique? Here are a few:

- ■ **Full multitasking and 32-bit support.** Linux, like all other versions of UNIX, is a real multitasking system, enabling multiple users to run many programs on the same system at once. The performance of a 50 MHz 486 system running Linux is comparable to many low- to medium-end workstations running proprietary versions of UNIX. Linux is also a full 32-bit operating system, utilizing the special protected-mode features of the Intel 80386 and 80486 processors.

- ■ **The X Window System.** The X Window System is the de facto industry standard graphics system for UNIX machines. A complete version of the X Window System, known as *XFree86,* is available for Linux. The X Window System is a very powerful graphics interface, supporting many applications. For example, you can have multiple login sessions in different windows on the screen at one time. Other examples of X Window applications are xtetris, xvier, xlander, and x11perf.

■ **TCP/IP (Transmission Control Protocol/Internet Protocol) support.** This is the set of protocols that links millions of university and business computers into a worldwide network known as the Internet. With an Ethernet connection, you can have access to the Internet or to a local area network from your Linux system. Using SLIP (Serial Line Internet Protocol), you can access the Internet over the phone lines with a modem.

■ **Virtual memory and shared libraries.** Linux can use a portion of your hard drive as virtual memory, expanding your total amount of available RAM. Linux also implements shared libraries, allowing programs that use standard subroutines to find the code for these subroutines in the libraries at runtime. This saves a large amount of space on your system, because each application doesn't store its own copy of these common routines.

■ **The Linux kernel uses no code from any other proprietary source.** Much of the software available for Linux is free. In fact, a large number of utilities in Linux are developed by the GNU project at the Free Software Foundation in Cambridge, Massachusetts. However, Linux enthusiasts, hackers, programmers, and recently even commercial companies from all over the world, have contributed to the growing pool of Linux software.

■ **Linux supports (almost) all of the features of commercial versions of UNIX.** In fact, some of the features you find in Linux may not be available on other proprietary UNIX systems.

■ **GNU software support.** Linux supports a wide range of free software written by the GNU Project, including utilities such as the GNU C and C++ compiler, `gawk`, `groff`, and so on. Many of the essential system utilities used by Linux are GNU software.

■ **Linux is closely compatible with the IEEE POSIX.1 standard.** Linux has been developed with software portability in mind, thus supporting many important features of other UNIX standards.

■ **Virtual memory support.** Linux also utilizes all of your system's memory, without memory limits or segmentation, through the use of a virtual memory manager.

■ **The Linux system runs exclusively in 32-bit mode.** This is a major step up from a 16-bit integer limitation in MS-DOS.

■ **Linux has built-in support for networking, multitasking, and other features.** You'll see this touted as "New Technology" in systems such as Windows NT. In fact, UNIX (and now, Linux) has implemented this "New Technology" for well over 15 years.

■ **Linux requires and uses fewer resources and less memory or disk space than many MS-DOS or Microsoft Windows systems.** This includes large applications (such as Microsoft Word or Lotus 1-2-3).

■ **Linux is in a constant state of development.** It's hard to keep up with the revisions that come up on a daily basis on the FTP sites on the Internet.

■ **Linux is cheaper to get than most commercially available UNIX systems and UNIX clones.** If you have the patience and access to the Internet, the only price you pay for Linux is your time. Linux is freely available on the Internet. For a nominal fee of anywhere from US $30 to US $90, you can save yourself some time and get CD-ROM or floppy disk distributions from several commercial vendors. See Chapter 2, "Types of Linux Available."

Quite arguably, the most important advantage of using Linux is that you get to work with a real kernel. All of the kernel source code is available for Linux, and you have the ability to modify it to suit your needs. Looking at the kernel code is an educational experience in itself.

The development of Linux has been so rapid because of the availability of the source code. Also, with an ever-expanding group of hackers who want to get their hands dirty with their own system, Linux has grown steadily into the fully packed operating system that it is today.

NOTE

Linux uses the 386 chip protected-mode functions extensively, and is a true 32-bit operating system. Linux simply will not run on an 8086, 8088, or 80286 computer.

So, how reliable is Linux anyway? Surprisingly, Linux is a very stable operating system. The only real bugs are with alpha drivers (that's why they're alpha) and with some parts of the TCP/IP code. For 99 percent of applications, however, Linux is very robust. Sometimes you'll find that running X Window on Linux is faster on a 486-33 than on some Sun workstations, with the same amount of RAM, running SunOS.

The Downside of Linux and the Reason for This Book

Linux is a hacker's kernel. This hacker attitude can be a daunting experience for someone not familiar with UNIX.

Plus, help is generally not available, nor is it a phone call away as with a commercial version of UNIX. You can get help from the Internet newsgroups and other members of the Linux community via e-mail. However, when it's midnight and your system just won't boot like the README file said it would, you do feel a sense of despair. So, when using Linux, remember that it is truly a hacker's operating system, developed by, and for, UNIX hackers.

There is a huge distinction between commercial versions of UNIX and Linux: Commercial versions of UNIX are designed for customers, and will work out of the box; Linux is not guaranteed to work at all on your system. You are indeed on your own.

Actually, the only problem for new users is a lack of basic UNIX system administrative knowledge. Setting up and running your own UNIX system is something that most UNIX users never get to do, even after years of experience. Yes, you get to do it yourself, but it isn't that easy. You might actually consider being nice to your local UNIX system administrator after installing Linux for the first time.

Here are some other parts of Linux that you should be warned about:

- Some of the features on your favorite UNIX system may not be available for your Linux system. Your choice in this matter is to either write the application yourself, convince someone else to write it, or find an alternative process (the easiest way out in most cases).

- As with software, some of the hardware in your machine may not be supported by Linux. Again, your choices are to either write the driver software yourself, or get it from somewhere else. Please see the end of this chapter for an *in*complete list of supported hardware.

- You do have to spend some time managing your Linux machine. It does take time and effort to manage your own Linux system.

You develop a knack for fixing problems from experience. However, only with experience can you learn to recognize common problems and find or develop solutions.

Even with standard Linux distributions, sometimes little quirks need to be fixed by hand in order for everything to work correctly. If you have previous UNIX experience, it should be easy to find these problems. However, if you're new to UNIX, it would serve you well to read up on using and running a UNIX system before you dive in.

To reiterate, Linux isn't for everyone. Many users can get in over their heads when starting with Linux. To keep your head above water, I strongly encourage you to read a good book on UNIX system administration, such as *UNIX System V, Release 4 Administration,* Second Edition (Sams Publishing, 1991).

About Linux's Copyright

Ah, yes, that old topic of copyrights. Compared to death and taxes, Linux copyrights are a mere annoyance. Linux is *NOT* public domain software.

Actually, Linux is copyrighted under the GNU General Public License, sometimes called the GPL or copyleft (instead of *right*). This copyleft license was developed by the Free Software Foundation to allow programmers to write "free software," with "free" referring to freedom, not just cost. The GPL provides for the protection of such free software in a number of ways:

- It allows the original author to retain the software's copyright.

- It allows others to take the software and modify it, or even base other programs on it.

- It allows others to redistribute or resell the software, or modified versions of the software. Note that you can even resell the software for profit. However, in reselling or redistributing the software, you cannot restrict any of these rights from the party you're selling it to.

NOTE

If you sell the software, you have to be able to provide at no cost the full source code, so that others can modify the software and resell it if they so desire. You cannot hold back the source of your modifications.

The original authors of the Linux software may never see a dime of these revenues. This is allowed by the GNU GPL because the point of free software isn't to make money. This is simply an understanding between the authors of the software and those who are using it or selling it.

Another point is that free software, as covered by the GNU GPL (which includes Linux), comes with absolutely no warranty. However, individual vendors may provide support for the software, which usually includes a warranty. However, unless you purchase such support, the assumption is that the software comes with no such warranty; so, if you use a piece of free software that goes haywire and wipes out everything on your system, neither the authors nor those that distributed the software to you are liable.

Free software as covered by the GPL is not shareware, nor is it in the public domain. Neither of these terms correctly describes what free software really is. The complete GNU GPL is in Appendix E. To sum it all up, you can freely distribute Linux as much as you like, and you can even modify it and distribute your own version of Linux. But, in doing so, you can't take away those rights from others. In short, you must attribute the original authors of the work. The original author will always hold copyrights to what she or he has done.

> **CAUTION**
>
> Please note that there are absolutely no warranties with any of the software you get with Linux. If an application goes awry and wipes your disk for you, you have no one's neck to wring. Unless someone explicitly gives you a warranty in writing for the software, do NOT assume any warranty whatsoever.

Hardware Requirements

Now that you know a little about the good and bad points of Linux, let's see what's required in terms of hardware.

Unlike some other versions of UNIX for the PC, Linux is very small. You can run an entire system from a single, high-density 5.25-inch floppy. However, to run a complete Linux system, there are other hardware requirements.

Linux, by its very nature, is continuously expanding, and more features are added every day. However, hardware compatibility is limited to the hardware that the developers themselves have access to. For instance, if none of the Linux developers has access to the WhizBang Slice-O-Matic T3222 Ethernet card from a no-name manufacturer, chances are it isn't supported.

Fortunately, there are many *generic* drivers for the IDE disk driver for Linux. These generic drivers should work with all IDE hard drives and adapters. Most internal tape drives are supported, but external tape drives that run off the parallel printer port are generally not supported.

A good place to look on the CD-ROM is in the /docs directory for the Hardware-HOWTO file. This file lists a lot of the supported hardware for Linux.

If your favorite peripheral isn't supported by Linux, all that's required is to write a kernel driver for it. This may be easy or difficult, depending on the hardware and the technical specifications that are available. For example, some hardware devclopers prefer to write their own drivers for MS-DOS and Windows, and not release specifications for third parties to write their own. Therefore, writing drivers for Linux can be difficult, if not impossible.

The following is a rough guideline of some hardware requirements for Linux. You do not have to follow them exactly, but this list should give you a general idea of what is required.

TIP

If you're in the market for a new system, you should heed the following recommendations.

■ An Intel 80386- or 80486-based system. You don't need a math coprocessor, although I strongly recommend that you have one. If you have an 80386 chip, 80387 math coprocessors are available separately, and are installed in a socket on your motherboard. If you have a 80486 processor, the math coprocessor is on the 486 chip itself. (The exception is the 80486SX, which is a 486 chip with the coprocessor disabled.)

If you don't have a math coprocessor, the Linux kernel emulates floating-point math for you. If you do have one, however, floating point math is handled by the hardware, which is a real plus in speed for some applications.

The 386SX, 486SX, and the accelerated 486DX and 486DX2 chips are all reported to work without any problems. It is suggested that you have a genuine Intel processor, instead of a clone. Look for the *Intel Inside* logo on the machine. The Intel Pentium chip works with Linux without any changes.

■ Your system must be either an ISA, EISA, or local bus architecture machine. These terms specify how the CPU communicates with hardware, and are a characteristic of your motherboard. Most existing systems use the ISA bus architecture.

If your machine uses local bus, it is strongly recommended that it complies with the VESA Local Bus standard (most local bus systems do). Pentiums with PCI bus video cards do not pose any problems either.

The EISA bus is a newer form of the ISA bus, which is reportedly faster on some machines. Local bus architecture is often the fastest of the three because it allows the CPU to communicate directly to video and drive adapters.

NOTE

MicroChannel architecture (MCA) machines, such as the IBM PS/2 line, are *not* currently supported.

■ At least 4MB of RAM. Technically, Linux is capable of running on a system with only 2MB; however, some distributions of Linux require 4MB for installation.

Memory is speed, so if you have more physical RAM, you'll thank yourself for it later. If you're a "power user," 8MB should be more than enough for most applications. More than 8MB of RAM definitely speeds up some applications. In fact, if you want to use X Window, at least 8MB of RAM is required.

NOTE

Linux uses the first 640KB for kernel text, kernel data, and buffercache. Your motherboard may eat up 384KB because of the chipset. Moreover, there are init/login, a shell, and possibly other daemons. Then, while compiling, there are make and gcc (2.57 ~770KB). So, you don't have enough real memory and have to resort to paging contents of memory to and from disk.

■ An AT standard–compatible hard drive controller. This includes MFM, RLL, ESDI, and IDE controllers. Many SCSI controllers are also supported. These terms specify the means used to communicate with the hard drive through the controller card; most controllers are either IDE or SCSI.

Disk Space Requirements

You need a hard drive with space available for installing Linux. The amount of space required depends on the amount of software you're installing, and how much free space you want to leave yourself.

If you install only a small amount of software, less than 10MB is required. However, if you install a number of optional software packages, including the X Window System, perhaps 100MB or more (including space for users) will be required.

In addition, you probably want to set aside some amount of space on your drive as a swap partition, used for virtual memory.

In general, you should look for about 100MB of disk space for your use, and an additional 16MB or so of disk space for a swap space. The swap space is an area on the disk that is a repository in which Linux can store images of running programs when memory is tight.

Linux supports almost all hard drive/controller combinations that are register-compatible with a Western Digital WD1003 MFM disk controller. This controller was the *original* and most common PC-AT disk controller. Most AT MFM, RLL, ESDI, and IDE setups look like this. IDE and MFM drives seem to work with no problem. Linux also works for some ESDI drives, and for almost all SCSI devices, with no problems. As before, the docs/Hardware-HOWTO file on the CD-ROM lists the latest compatible hardware.

There is an alpha driver for the XT disk controller, but in general it's best to have an AT controller.

Generally, the rule is this: If you have the disk configured into the CMOS setup of your machine, it will work—if the BIOS is talking to a WD 1003–compatible board, Linux will too.

> **CAUTION**
>
> There are problems with some MAXTOR drives on high-speed machines. I have seen some messages about problems with very high-speed memory (under 60ns) on fast machines (a 100 MHz 486DX2). The solution was to turn off the *turbo* mode and slow down the machine.

> **CAUTION**
>
> During testing with Linux, I have found that mixing two different types of SIMMs (70ns and 100ns) caused the PC to behave very strangely, with crashes during the installation process. The solution was to use the same speed memory. These SIMMs were the 9, not the 3, chip version. Generally speaking, it's *never* a good idea to mix RAM chips of different speeds on a single motherboard.

You need a Hercules, CGA, EGA, VGA, or Super VGA video card and monitor. In general, if your video card and monitor work under MS-DOS or Microsoft Windows, Linux should be able to use them without any problem. However, if you're going to use the X Window System, certain hardware configurations are not yet supported. The list of such requirements can be found in the /docs/ XFree86-HOWTO file on the CD-ROM.

Other Hardware Requirements

Linux also runs on a number of laptop machines. (Some laptops use certain software interrupts to power the memory, and Linux doesn't work well with these systems to date.) The best way to find out whether Linux will run on your hardware is to just try it out.

> **NOTE**
>
> At the time of this writing, Linux didn't run on an IBM PS/2 computer. Stay tuned to the Internet for details.

Other hardware drivers currently are under development for Linux. However, to use these drivers, you usually have to patch them into your kernel code, which assumes that you already have a running Linux system. A kind of chicken-or-the-egg problem if you haven't already installed Linux, isn't it? In such cases, you can install whatever Linux you happen to have, and then apply the patches with the Linux patch command.

There is also the issue of tape drives for Linux. There is a working QIC-02 device driver for Linux, supporting Everex/Wangtek cards. There are additional patches for the QIC-02 to support Archive SC402/499R. You can find them in the `/pub/linux/alpha/qic-02` directory at `tsx-11.mit.edu` `server`. (There have been reports of some bugs in the driver, but you can back up and restore.)

Most of the newer tape drivers are for SCSI drives; so if you have a SCSI tape drive, chances are good that it is supported.

Special Requirements for X Window Systems

Your 4MB of RAM will make X run very slowly. You should have at least 8MB of RAM for running and compiling programs in X. You need another 6MB to 10MB of disk space for the GCC compiler, in addition to the X Window System.

Another important point with running X is the support for VGA cards. Most chipsets and VGA cards are supported with the et3000, et4000, GVGA, PVGA1, WD890c00, TRIDENT, CIRRUS, NCR, COMPAQ. The monochrome version of the X server is called the X386mono. This server supports generic VGAs and Hercules cards.

Here is a quick list of the types of supported cards:

- 8514 ATI graphics ULTRA, ATI graphics Vantage should work with any VESA standard 8514/A register compatible card. Courtesy Kevin Martin (`martin@cs.unc.edu`).

- Scott Laird (`lair@quads.uchicago.edu`) writes: I uploaded a new version of the X8514 X Server to sunsite and tsx-11. It is in

  `/pub/Linux/X11/X-servers/X8514/X8514scale.tar.Z`

  on `sunsite.unc.edu`.

  This version is linked with Version 4.2 of the jumptable libraries. It includes TCP/IP support, support for compressed bitmap fonts, and Type 1 and Speedo scaleable fonts. There's a README file in the same directory that answers more questions.

- XS3 S3 chipset server (`jon@robots.ox.ac.uk`). Get the FAQ on `ftp.robots.ox.ac.uk` (`pub/linux/S3` check sunsite).

- Xega Generic 640×480×16 compatible server (originally for laptops). This requires a Microsoft mouse at `/dev/mouse` for now, and it does not use Xconfig; use environment variables to define the font path and so on in `.xinitrc`:

  ```
  export
  FONT_PATH=/usr/lib/X11/fonts/misc:/usr/lib/X11/fonts75dpi
  ```

  This command works better with Courier fonts, so add something like the following to `.Xresources`:

  ```
  *Font: -*-courier-medium-r-*--10*
  ```

- A link kit is available at tsx-11 (you need gcc2.2.2 or better) in `pub/linux/ALPHA/Xega/` `Xega.T.Z`.

CAUTION

Do not try to bring up an X server that does not support your hardware. There have been cases in which damage has resulted from pushing the monitor (especially a fixed-frequency monitor) beyond its specs.

As far as "mice" go, Linux supports both serial and Bus varieties. For the serial mice, you can use Logitech, Microsoft, MouseSystems, or compatibles. For Bus mice, the following are known to work: Logitech, Microsoft, ATI_XL, PS/2 (aux).

NOTE

If you are unsure whether you have a bus mouse, check to see whether your mouse card has a selection for a sample rate switchable between 30Hz and 60Hz (or possibly 25/50Hz). If it does not, it's *not* a true bus mouse. (InPort mice, for example, won't work with this driver.)

There you have it, a brief introduction to an operating system that could very well change the way you program. Now, how to get yourself ready for Linux.

Before You Get Started

Assuming that you have hardware compatible with Linux, obtaining and installing the system is not difficult. But, be prepared to be a bit frustrated at first, especially if you are new to UNIX or Linux.

The two best defenses against frustration with using Linux are as follows:

- Get organized.
- Educate yourself about Linux and UNIX.

TIP

Experience with my bad memory has forced me to keep an indexed log of all the bugs, quirks, and symptoms in Linux. I have a dog-eared notebook of all the weird features of Linux. As you work with Linux, you might want to keep a personal log of your misadventures with it.

The CD-ROM

The CD-ROM enclosed in this book has lots of useful documentation. Unfortunately, this is the classic chicken-and-egg problem. You need the documentation to install the Linux software, but you have to access the CD-ROM to get more information about how to install the software!

Right now, in this chapter, it's way too early to worry about reading the contents from the CD-ROM. The next two chapters will step you through the installation process. So please don't worry if you do not know how to look for this documentation.

> **NOTE**
>
> If you are anxious to get this information, you can borrow a DOS machine or UNIX workstation and look at the /doc directory of the CD-ROM.

> **TIP**
>
> You can look at all the files and directories on the CD-ROM from an MS-DOS machine. The problem is that UNIX filenames that do not follow the DOS style of filenames may appear garbled. You can, however, print or read the text files on the CD-ROM by accessing them from within DOS.

In the next chapter, we will cover some of the files that you can look at in the CD-ROM after you have installed Linux. You can skip ahead to Chapter 2 and see how to read the CD-ROM directory tree for the documentation.

> **NOTE**
>
> Please see Chapter 15, "Using the Linux Documentation," to find out where to get more information on Linux.

The Linux Hardware Compatibility List

The Hardware Compatibility List lists some of the hardware that is known to work with Linux. However, much of the hardware is not on this list; for example, all IDE drives should work with Linux, so all makes and models are not listed there. The Hardware Compatibility List is in this file:

```
sunsite.unc.edu:/pub/Linux/docs/HARDWARE.
```

Because you do not yet have access to the CD-ROM, it's a good idea to review the following list to see whether your system matches the "known to work" items. Keep in mind that if your hardware is not listed here, it does not mean that your hardware will not work. Absence from the list may simply mean that your hardware is not supported, and that you are on your own in terms of getting more help about your hardware should you run into problems. See Listing 1.1 for some supported hardware.

Listing 1.1. The `Hardware-HOWTO` file for Linux.

```
Linux Hardware Compatibility HOWTO
  FRiC (Boy of Destiny), frac@pobox.com
  v6969, 16 July 1995
  This document lists most of the hardware supported by Linux and helps you locate
any necessary drivers.
  1.  Introduction
  1.1.  Welcome
Welcome to the Linux Hardware Compatibility HOWTO. This document lists most
 of the hardware supported by Linux, now if only people would read this first
 before posting their questions on Usenet.
Subsections titled Others list hardware with alpha or beta drivers in varying
 degrees of usability orother drivers that aren't included in standard kernels
 Note that some drivers only exist in alpha kernels, so if you see something
 listed as supported but isn't in your version of the Linux kernel, upgrade
.The latest version of this document can be found on the net at the usual
 sites where the Linux HOWTO's are kept. If you know of any Linux hardware
 (in)compatibilities not listed here please let me know. Send mail (note my
 new e-mail address) or find me on IRC. Thanks.
  1.2.  System architectures
  This document only deals with Linux for Intel platforms, for other platforms
check the following:
  o  Linux/68k      <http://www-users.informatik.rwth-aachen.de/~hn/linux68k.html>
  o  Linux/MIPS     <http://www.waldorf-gmbh.de/linux-mips-faq.html>
  o  Linux/PowerPC      <ftp://sunsite.unc.edu/pub/Linux/docs/ports/Linux-PowerPC-
FAQ.gz>
  o  Linux for Acorn     <http://www.ph.kcl.ac.uk/~amb/linux.html>
  o  MacLinux     <http://www.ibg.uu.se/maclinux/>
  2.  Computers/Motherboards/BIOS
  ISA, VLB, EISA, and PCI buses are all supported.
  PS/2 and Microchannel (MCA) is not supported in the standard kernel.
  Alpha test PS/2 MCA kernels are available but not yet recommended for beginners
or serious use.
  2.1.  Specific systems
  o  Compaq Deskpro XL     <http://www-c724.uibk.ac.at/XL/>
  o  IBM PS/2 MCA systems     <ftp://invaders.dcrl.nd.edu/pub/misc/>
  3.  Laptops
  Some laptops have unusual video adapters or power management,
  it is  not uncommon to be unable to use the power management features.
  PCMCIA drivers currently support all common PCMCIA controllers,
 including Databook TCIC/2, Intel i82365SL, Cirrus PD67xx, and
 Vadem  VG-468 chipsets. Motorola 6AHC05GA controller used in some Hyundai
 laptops is not supported.  (Read the PCMCIA HOWTO.)
  o  APM     <ftp://tsx-11.mit.edu/pub/linux/packages/laptops/apm/>
  o  PCMCIA     <ftp://cb-iris.stanford.edu/pub/pcmcia/>
  o  non-blinking cursor     <ftp://sunsite.unc.edu/pub/Linux/kernel/patches/
```

continues

18

Listing 1.1. continued

```
console/noblink-1.5.tar.gz>
   o  power savings (WD7600 chipset)
       <ftp://sunsite.unc.edu/pub/Linux/system/Misc/low-level/pwrm-1.0.tar.Z>
   o  other general info
       <ftp://tsx-11.mit.edu/pub/linux/packages/laptops/>
   3.1.  Specific laptops
   o  Compaq Contura Aero      <http://domen.uninett.no/~hta/linux/aero-faq.html>
   o  IBM ThinkPad       <http://peipa.essex.ac.uk/tp-linux/tp-linux.html>
   o  NEC Versa M and P       <http://www.santafe.edu:80/~nelson/versa-linux/>
   o  Tadpole P1000      <http://peipa.essex.ac.uk/tadpole-linux/tadpole-linux.html>
   o  Linux, X, and the WD90C24A2 video chipset      <http://www.castle.net/~darin/>
   4.  CPU/FPU
   Intel/AMD/Cyrix 386SX/DX/SL/DXL/SLC, 486SX/DX/SL/SX2/DX2/DX4, Pentium.
   Basically all 386 or better processors will work. Linux has built-in
   FPU emulation if you don't have a math coprocessor.
   Linux does not support SMP yet. Multi-processor systems will run Linux
   but only the first processor will be used. There's some work being done
   right now, check the Linux Project Map for details.A few very early AMD
   486DX's may hang in some special situations. All current chips should be
   okay and getting a chip swap for old CPU's should not be a problem.
   ULSI Math*Co series has a bug in the FSAVE and FRSTOR instructions that
   causes problems with all protected mode operating systems. Some older IIT
   and Cyrix chips may also have this problem. There are problems with TLB
   flushing in UMC U5S chips. Fixed in newer  kernels.
   o  enable cache on Cyrix processors
       <ftp://sunsite.unc.edu/pub/Linux/kernel/patches/CxPatch030.tar.z>
   o  Cyrix software cache control
       <ftp://sunsite.unc.edu/pub/Linux/kernel/patches/linux.cxpatch>
   5.  Video cards
   Linux will work with all video cards in text mode, VGA cards not listed
   below probably will still work with mono VGA and/or standard VGA drivers.
   If you're looking into buying a cheap video card to run X, keep in mind
   that accelerated cards (ATI Mach, ET4000/W32p, S3) are MUCH  faster than
   unaccelerated or partially accelerated (Cirrus, WD) cards.
   S3 801 (ISA), S3 805 (VLB), ET4000/W32p, and ATI Graphics Wonder (Mach32)
   are good low-end accelerated cards. "32 bpp" is actually 24 bit color
   aligned on 32-bit boundaries. It does NOT mean the cards are capable of
   32-bit color, it's still 24-bit color (16,777,216 colors). 24-bit packed
   pixels modes are not supported in XFree86, so cards that can do 24-bit
   color modes in other  OS's may not able to do this in X. These cards
   include Mach32, Cirrus  542x, S3 801/805, ET4000, and others.
   5.1.  Diamond video cards
   Most recent Diamond cards ARE supported by the current release of XFree86
   Early Diamond cards are not supported by XFree86, but there are ways
   of getting them to work.
   o  Diamond support for Xfree86      <http://www.diamondmm.com/linux.html>
   o  Diamond FAQ (for older cards)  <ftp://sunsite.unc.edu/pub/Linux
   /X11/Diamond.FAQ>
   o  Diamond Disgruntled Users Page (for older cards)      <http://
   gladstone.uoregon.edu/~trenton/diamond/>
   5.2.  SVGALIB
   o  VGA
   o  EGA
   o  ATI Mach32
   o  Cirrus 542x
   o  OAK OTI-037/67/77/87
```

```
o  Trident TVGA8900/9000
o  Tseng ET3000/ET4000/W32
5.3.  XFree86 3.1.1, Accelerated


o  ATI Mach8
o  ATI Mach32 (16 bpp - does not work with all Mach32 cards)
o  ATI Mach64 (16/32 bpp)
o  Cirrus Logic 5420, 542x/5430 (16 bpp), 5434 (16/32 bpp), 62x5
o  IBM 8514/A
o  IBM XGA, XGA-II
o  IIT AGX-010/014/015/016
o  Oak OTI-087
o  S3 911, 924, 801, 805, 928, 864, 964, Trio32, Trio64, 868, 968
o  see Appendix A for long list of supported cards
o  Tseng ET4000/W32/W32i/W32p
o  Weitek P9000 (16/32 bpp)
o  Diamond Viper VLB/PCI
o  Orchid P9000
o  Western Digital WD90C31/33


5.4.  XFree86 3.1.1, Unaccelerated
o  ATI VGA Wonder series
o  Avance Logic AL2101/2228/2301/2302/2308/2401
o  Chips & Technologies 65520/65530/65540/65545
o  Cirrus Logic 6420/6440
o  Compaq AVGA
o  Genoa GVGA
o  MCGA (320x200)
o  MX MX68000/MX68010
o  NCR 77C22, 77C22E, 77C22E+
o  Oak OTI-067, OTI-077
o  Trident TVGA8800, TVGA8900, TVGA9xxx (not very fast)
o  Tseng ET3000, ET4000AX
o  VGA (standard VGA, 4 bit, slow)
o  Video 7 / Headland Technologies HT216-32
o  Western Digital/Paradise PVGA1, WD90C00/10/11/24/30/31/33


5.5.  Monochrome
o  Hercules mono
o  Hyundai HGC-1280
o  Sigma LaserView PLUS
o  VGA mono


5.6.  Others
o  EGA (ancient, from c. 1992)      <ftp://ftp.funet.fi/pub/OS/Linux/BETA
/Xega/>
5.7.  Works in progress
o  Compaq QVision
o  Number Nine Imagine 128
No, I do not know when support for these cards will be finished, please
don't ask me. If you want support for these cards now get  Accelerated-X.
5.8.  Commercial X servers
Commercial X servers provide support for cards not supported by  XFree86,
and might give better performances for cards that are supported by XFree86.
In general they support many more cards than  XFree86, so I'll only list
cards that aren't supported by XFree86 here. Contact the vendors directly
or check the Commercial HOWTO for more info.
```

continues

Listing 1.1. continued

```
5.8.1.  Accelerated-X 1.2
o  ARK Logic
o  Chips & Technologies 82C45x, 82C48x, F655xx
o  Compaq QVision 2000
o  Matrox MGA-I, MGA-II
o  Number Nine I-128
o  S3 Trio32 (732), Trio64 (764), 866, 868, 968
o  Weitek P9100
$199, X Inside, Inc. <info@xinside.com>.
Accel-X supports most cards in 16 and 32 bpp modes and it also supports
24-bit packed pixel modes for cards that have these modes, including ATI
Mach32, Mach64 (1280x1024@24bpp), ET4000/W32p,  S3-866/868/968, and more.
Accel-X also supports XVideo (Xv) extensions (on Matrox Comet, Marvel-  II,
and SPEA ShowTime Plus), PEX, and XIE.
5.8.2.  Metro-X 2.3.2
$149, Metro Link <sales@metrolink.com>.


Metro-X supports more boards than XFree but less than Accel-X, however
I don't have much more information as I can't seem to view the
PostScript files they sent me. Mail them directly for more info.
6.  Controllers (hard drive)
Linux will work with standard IDE, MFM and RLL controllers. When using
MFM/RLL controllers it is important to use ext2fs and the bad block checking
options when formatting the disk.
Enhanced IDE (EIDE) interfaces are supported. With up to two IDE interfaces
and up to four hard drives and/or CD-ROM drives.
ESDI controllers that emulate the ST-506 (that is MFM/RLL/IDE) interface
will also work. The bad block checking comment also applies  to these
controllers.
Generic 8 bit XT controllers also work.
7.  Controllers (SCSI)
It is important to pick a SCSI controller carefully. Many cheap ISA SCSI
controllers are designed to drive CD-ROM's rather than anything else.
Such low end SCSI controllers are no better than IDE. See the  SCSI HOWTO
and look at performance figures before buying a SCSI card.
7.1.  Supported
o  AMI Fast Disk VLB/EISA (BusLogic compatible)
o  Adaptec AVA-1505/1515 (ISA) (Adaptec 152x compatible)
o  Adaptec AHA-1510/152x (ISA) (AIC-6260/6360)

o  Adaptec AHA-154x (ISA) (all models)

o  Adaptec AHA-174x (EISA) (in enhanced mode)

o  Adaptec AHA-274x (EISA) / 284x (VLB) (AIC-7770)

o  Adaptec AHA-294x (PCI) (AIC-7870)

o  Always IN2000

o  BusLogic (ISA/EISA/VLB/PCI) (all models)

o  DPT PM2001, PM2012A (EATA-PIO)


o  DPT Smartcache (EATA-DMA) (ISA/EISA/PCI) (all models)
```

o DTC 329x (EISA) (Adaptec 154x compatible)

o Future Domain TMC-16x0, TMC-3260 (PCI)

o Future Domain TMC-8xx, TMC-950

o NCR 53c7x0, 53c8x0 (PCI)

o Pro Audio Spectrum 16 SCSI (ISA)

o Qlogic / Control Concepts SCSI/IDE (FAS408) (ISA/VLB/PCMCIA)
   PCMCIA cards must boot DOS to init card

o Seagate ST-01/ST-02 (ISA)

o SoundBlaster 16 SCSI-2 (Adaptec 152x compatible) (ISA)

o Trantor T128/T128F/T228 (ISA)

o UltraStor 14F (ISA), 24F (EISA), 34F (VLB)

o Western Digital WD7000 SCSI

7.2. Others

o AMD AM53C974, AM79C974 (PCI) (Compaq, Zeos onboard SCSI)
   <ftp://sunsite.unc.edu/pub/Linux/kernel/patches/scsi/AM53C974-0.3.tgz>

o Adaptec ACB-40xx SCSI-MFM/RLL bridgeboard
   <ftp://sunsite.unc.edu/pub/Linux/kernel/patches/scsi/adaptec-40XX.tar.gz>

o Adaptec APA-1460 SlimSCSI (PCMCIA)
   <ftp://cb-iris.stanford.edu/pub/pcmcia/>

o Acculogic ISApport / MV Premium 3D SCSI (NCR 53c406a)
   <ftp://sunsite.unc.edu/pub/Linux/kernel/patches/scsi/ncr53c406-0.10.patch.gz>

o Always AL-500
   <ftp://sunsite.unc.edu/pub/Linux/kernel/patches/scsi/al500_0.1.tar.gz>

o BusLogic (ISA/EISA/VLB/PCI) (new beta driver)
   <ftp://ftp.dandelion.com/BusLogic-1.0-beta.tar.gz>

o Iomega PC2/2B
   <ftp://sunsite.unc.edu/pub/Linux/kernel/patches/scsi
   /iomega_pc2-1.1.x.tar.gz>

o New Media Bus Toaster PCMCIA
   <ftp://lamont.ldeo.columbia.edu/pub/linux/bus_toaster-1.5.tgz>

o Qlogic (ISP1020) (PCI)
   <ftp://sunsite.unc.edu/pub/Linux/Incoming/>

o Ricoh GSI-8
   <ftp://tsx-11.mit.edu/pub/linux/ALPHA/scsi/gsi8.tar.gz>

continues

Listing 1.1. continued

```
o  Trantor T130B (NCR 53c400)
   <ftp://sunsite.unc.edu/pub/Linux/kernel/patches/scsi/53c400.tar.gz>




7.3.  Unsupported


o  Parallel port SCSI adapters

o  Non Adaptec compatible DTC boards (327x, 328x)


8.  Controllers (I/O)

Any standard serial/parallel/joystick/IDE combo cards.  Linux supports
8250, 16450, 16550, and 16550A UART's.

See National Semiconductor's "Application Note AN-493" by Martin S.
Michael. Section 5.0 describes in detail the differences between the
NS16550 and NS16550A. Briefly, the NS16550 had bugs in the FIFO
circuits, but the NS16550A (and later) chips fixed those. However,
there were very few NS16550's produced by National, long ago, so these
should be very rare. And many of the "16550" parts in actual modern
boards are from the many manufacturers of compatible parts, which may
not use the National "A" suffix. Also, some multiport boards will
use 16552 or 16554 or various other multiport or multifunction chips
from National or other suppliers (generally in a dense package
soldered to the board, not a 40 pin DIP). Mostly, don't worry about it
unless you encounter a very old 40 pin DIP National "NS16550" (no A)
chip loose or in an old board, in which case treat it as a 16450 (no
FIFO) rather than a 16550A. - Zhahai Stewart <zstewart@hisys.com>


9.  Controllers (multiport)

9.1.  Supported


o  AST FourPort and clones

o  Accent Async-4

o  Bell Technologies HUB6

o  Boca BB-1004, 1008 (4, 8 port) - no DTR, DSR, and CD

o  Boca BB-2016 (16 port)

o  Boca IO/AT66 (6 port)

o  Boca IO 2by4 (4S/2P) - works with modems, but uses 5 IRQ's

o  Cyclades Cyclom-8Y/16Y (8, 16 port)
```

o PC-COMM 4-port

o STB 4-COM

o Twincom ACI/550

o Usenet Serial Board II

9.2. Others

o Comtrol RocketPort (8/16/32 port)
  <ftp://tsx-11.mit.edu/pub/linux/packages/comtrol/>

o DigiBoard COM/Xi
  contact Simon Park <si@wimpol.demon.co.uk>

o DigiBoard PC/Xe (ISA) and PC/Xi (EISA)
  <ftp://ftp.digibd.com/drivers/linux/>

o Specialix SIO/XIO (modular, 4 to 32 ports)
  <ftp://sunsite.unc.edu/pub/Linux/kernel/patches/serial/sidrv0_5.taz>

o Stallion EasyIO (ISA) / EasyConnection 8/32 (ISA/MCA)
  <ftp://sunsite.unc.edu/pub/Linux/kernel/patches/serial
  /stallion-0.1.9.tar.gz>

o Stallion EasyConnection 8/64 / ONboard (ISA/EISA/MCA) / Brumby /
  Stallion (ISA)
  <ftp://sunsite.unc.edu/pub/Linux/kernel/patches/serial
  /stallion-0.1.9.tar.gz>

10. Network adapters

Ethernet adapters vary greatly in performance. In general the newer
the design the better. Some very old cards like the 3C501 are only
useful because they can be found in junk heaps for $5 a time. Be
careful with clones, not all are good clones and bad clones often
cause erratic lockups under Linux. Read the Ethernet HOWTO for full
detailed descriptions of various cards.

10.1. Supported

10.1.1. Ethernet

o 3Com 3C501 - "avoid like the plague"

o 3Com 3C503, 3C505, 3C507, 3C509/3C509B (ISA) / 3C579 (EISA)

o AMD LANCE (79C960) / PCnet-ISA/PCI (AT1500, HP J2405A,
  NE1500/NE2100)

continues

Listing 1.1. continued

o   AT&T GIS WaveLAN

o   Allied Telesis AT1700

o   Ansel Communications AC3200 EISA

o   Apricot Xen-II

o   Cabletron E21xx

o   DEC DE425 (EISA) / DE434/DE435 (PCI)

o   DEC DEPCA and EtherWORKS

o   HP PCLAN (27245 and 27xxx series)

o   HP PCLAN PLUS (27247B and 27252A)

o   Intel EtherExpress

o   Intel EtherExpress Pro

o   NE2000/NE1000 (be careful with clones)

o   New Media Etherne

o   Racal-Interlan NI5210 (i82586 Ethernet chip)

o   Racal-Interlan NI6510 (am7990 lance chip) - doesn't work with more
    than 16 megs RAM

o   PureData PDUC8028, PDI8023

o   SEEQ 8005

o   SMC Ultra

o   Schneider & Koch G16

o   Western Digital WD80x3

o   Zenith Z-Note / IBM ThinkPad 300 built-in adapter

10.1.2. Pocket and portable adapters

o   AT-Lan-Tec/RealTek parallel port adapter

o   D-Link DE600/DE620 parallel port adapter

10.1.3. Slotless

13.2. Unsupported

o   Emerald and Tecmar QIC-02 tape controller ca
    <insom@math.ucr.edu>
o   Drives that connect to the parallel port (eg

o   Some high speed tape controllers (Colorado T(

o   Irwin AX250L/Accutrak 250 (not QIC-80)

o   IBM Internal Tape Backup Unit (not QIC-80)

o   COREtape Light

14. CD-ROM drives

14.1. Supported

o   SCSI CD-ROM drives
    (From the CD-ROM HOWTO) Any SCSI CD-ROM drive
    512 or 2048 bytes should work under Linux; th
    majority of CD-ROM drives on the market.

o   EIDE (ATAPI) CD-ROM drives

o   Aztech CDA268, Orchid CDS-3110, Okano/Wearnes

o   GoldStar R420

o   LMS Philips CM 206

o   Matsushita/Panasonic, Kotobuki (SBPCD)

o   Mitsumi

o   Optics Storage Dolphin 8000AT

o   Sanyo H94A

o   Sony CDU31A/CDU33A

o   Sony CDU-535/CDU-531

o   Teac CD-55A SuperQuad

14.2. Others

o   LMS/Philips CM 205/225/202
    <ftp://sunsite.unc.edu/pub/Linux/kernel/patches

o   SLIP/CSLIP/PPP (serial port)

o   EQL (serial line load balancing)

o   PLIP (parallel port) - using "LapLink cable" or bi-directional
    cable

10.1.4. ARCnet

o   works with all ARCnet cards

10.1.5. Token Ring

o   IBM Tropic chipset cards

10.2. Others

10.2.1. Ethernet

o   3Com Vortex Ethercards (3C590, 3C595 (100 mbps)) (PCI)
    <http://cesdis.gsfc.nasa.gov/pub/linux/drivers/vortex.html>

o   DEC 21040/21140 "Tulip" / SMC PCI EtherPower 10/100
    <http://cesdis.gsfc.nasa.gov/linux/drivers/tulip.html>

10.2.2. ISDN

o   Diehl SCOM card
    <ftp://sunsite.unc.edu/pub/Linux/kernel/patches/network
    /isdndrv-0.1.1.tar.gz>
o   ICN ISDN card
    <ftp://ftp.franken.de/pub/isdn4linux/>

o   Teles ISDN card
    <ftp://ftp.franken.de/pub/isdn4linux/>

10.2.3. Amateur radio cards

o   AX.25 networking
    <ftp://sunacm.swan.ac.uk/pub/misc/Linux/Radio/>

o   Ottawa PI/PI2

o   Most generic 8530 based HDLC boards

o   No support for the PMP/Baycom board

continues

Listing 1.1. continued

The ASP chip on Sound Blaster 16 series a
AWE32's onboard MIDI synthesizer is not s
never be supported.

Sound Blaster 16's with DSP 4.11 and 4.12
causes hung/stuck notes when playing MIDI
same time. The problem happens with eithe
or MIDI devices attached to the MIDI port

12.   Hard drives

All hard drives should work if the contro

(From the SCSI HOWTO) All direct access S(
of 256, 512, or 1024 bytes should work. O·
work (Note that this can often be fixed by
sector sizes using the MODE SELECT SCSI c(

Large IDE (EIDE) drives work fine with new
partition must lie in the first 1024 cylir
limitations.

Some Conner CFP1060S drives may have probl
The symptoms are inode errors during e2fsc
Conner has released a firmware upgrade to
Conner at 1-800-4CONNER (US) or +44-1294-3
microcode version (found on the drive labe
call.

Certain Micropolis drives have problems wi·
cards, contact the drive manufacturers for
suspect problems.

o   Multiple device driver (RAID-0, RAID-1)
    <ftp://sweet-smoke.ufr-info-p7.ibp.fr/pu

13.   Tape drives

13.1.   Supported

o   SCSI tape drives
    (From the SCSI HOWTO) Drives using both ·
    blocks smaller than the driver buffer lei
    distribution sources) are supported. Vir·
    work. (Send mail if you know of any incor

o   QIC-02

o   QIC-117, QIC-40/80 drives (Ftape)
    <ftp://sunsite.unc.edu/pub/Linux/kernel/t
    using the floppy controller should work.
    details. Various dedicated QIC-80 control
    Iomega Tape Controller II) are also suppo

Listing 1.1. continued

o   NEC CDR-35D (old)
    <ftp://sunsite.unc.edu/pub/Linux/kernel/patches/cdrom/linux-
    neccdr35d.patch>

o   Sony SCSI multisession CD-XA
    <ftp://tsx-11.mit.edu/pub/linux/patches/sony-multi-0.00.tar.gz>

14.3.   Notes

PhotoCD (XA) is supported.

All CD-ROM drives should work similarly for reading data. There are
various compatibility problems with audio CD playing utilities.
(Especially with some NEC drives.) Some alpha drivers may not have
audio support yet.

Early (single speed) NEC CD-ROM drives may have trouble with currently
available SCSI controllers.

15.   Removable drives

All SCSI drives should work if the controller is supported, including
optical drives, WORM, CD-R, floptical, and others. Iomega Bernoulli
and Zip drives, and SyQuest drives all work fine.

Linux supports both 512 and 1024 bytes/sector disks.

16.   Mice

16.1.   Supported

o   Microsoft serial mouse

o   Mouse Systems serial mouse

o   Logitech Mouseman serial mouse

o   Logitech serial mouse

o   ATI XL Inport busmouse

o   C&T 82C710 (QuickPort) (Toshiba, TI Travelmate)

o   Microsoft busmouse

o   Logitech busmouse

o   PS/2 (auxiliary device) mouse

16.2. Others

o Sejin J-mouse
   <ftp://sunsite.unc.edu/pub/Linux/kernel/patches/console
/jmouse.1.1.70-jmouse.tar.gz>

o MultiMouse - use multiple mouse devices as single mouse
   <ftp://sunsite.unc.edu/pub/Linux/system/Misc/MultiMouse-1.0.tgz>

16.3. Notes

Those pad devices like Glidepoint also work, so long they're
compatible with another mouse protocol.

Newer Logitech mice (except the Mouseman) use the Microsoft protocol
and all three buttons do work. Eventhough Microsoft's mice have only
two buttons, the protocol allows three buttons.

The mouse port on the ATI Graphics Ultra and Ultra Pro use the
Logitech busmouse protocol. (See the Busmouse HOWTO for details.)

17. Modems

All internal modems or external modems connected to the serial port.

A small number of modems come with DOS software that downloads the
control program at runtime. These can normally be used by loading the
program under DOS and doing a warm boot. Such modems are probably best
avoided as you won't be able to use them with non PC hardware in the
future.

PCMCIA modems should work with the PCMCIA drivers.

Fax modems need appropriated fax software to operate.

o Digicom Connection 96+/14.4+ - DSP code downloading program
   <ftp://sunsite.unc.edu/pub/Linux/system/Serial/smdl-
   linux.1.02.tar.gz>

o ZyXEL U-1496 series - ZyXEL 1.4, modem/fax/voice control program
   <ftp://sunsite.unc.edu/pub/Linux/system/Serial/ZyXEL-1.4.tar.gz>

18. Printers/Plotters

All printers and plotters connected to the parallel or serial port
should work.

continues

Listing 1.1. continued

```
o  HP LaserJet 4 series - free-lj4, printing modes control program
   <ftp://sunsite.unc.edu/pub/Linux/system/Printing/free-
   lj4-1.1p1.tar.gz>

o  BiTronics parallel port interface
   <ftp://sunsite.unc.edu/pub/Linux/kernel/misc/bt-ALPHA-0.0.1.tar.gz>


18.1.  Ghostscript

Many Linux programs output PostScript files. Non-PostScript printers
can emulate PostScript Level 2 using Ghostscript.

o  Ghostscript
   <ftp://ftp.cs.wisc.edu/pub/ghost/aladdin/>


18.1.1.  Ghostscript supported printers


o  Apple Imagewriter

o  C. Itoh M8510

o  Canon BubbleJet BJ10e, BJ200

o  Canon LBP-8II, LIPS III

o  DEC LA50/70/75/75plus

o  DEC LN03, LJ250

o  Epson 9 pin, 24 pin, LQ series, Stylus, AP3250

o  HP 2563B

o  HP DesignJet 650C


o  HP DeskJet/Plus/500

o  HP DeskJet 500C/520C/550C/1200C color

o  HP LaserJet/Plus/II/III/4

o  HP PaintJet/XL/XL300 color

o  IBM Jetprinter color

o  IBM Proprinter

o  Imagen ImPress

o  Mitsubishi CP50 color

o  NEC P6/P6+/P60
```

o   Okidata MicroLine 182

o   Ricoh 4081

o   SPARCprinter

o   StarJet 48 inkjet printer

o   Tektronix 4693d color 2/4/8 bit

o   Tektronix 4695/4696 inkjet plotter

o   Xerox XES printers (2700, 3700, 4045, etc.)

18.1.2. Others

o   Canon BJC600 and Epson ESC/P color printers
    <ftp://petole.imag.fr/pub/postscript/>

19. Scanners

o   A4 Tech AC 4096
    <ftp://ftp.informatik.hu-berlin.de/pub/local/linux/ac4096.tgz>

o   Fujitsu SCSI-2 scanners
    contact Dr. G.W. Wettstein <greg%wind.UUCP@plains.nodak.edu>

o   Genius GS-B105G
    <ftp://tsx-11.mit.edu/pub/linux/ALPHA/scanner/gs105-0.0.1.tar.gz>

o   Genius GeniScan GS4500 handheld scanner
    <ftp://tsx-11.mit.edu/pub/linux/ALPHA/scanner/gs4500-1.3.tar.gz>

o   HP ScanJet, ScanJet Plus
    <ftp://ftp.ctrl-c.liu.se/unix/linux/wingel/>

o   HP ScanJet II series SCSI
    <ftp://sunsite.unc.edu/pub/Linux/apps/graphics/scanners
    /hpscanpbm-0.3a.tar.gz>

o   Logitech Scanman 32 / 256
    <ftp://tsx-11.mit.edu/pub/linux/ALPHA/scanner/logiscan-0.0.2.tar.gz>

o   Mustek M105 handheld scanner with GI1904 interface
    <ftp://tsx-11.mit.edu/pub/linux/ALPHA/scanner/scan-
    driver-0.1.8.tar.gz>

o   UMAX SCSI scanners
    contact Craig Johnston <mkshenk@u.washington.edu>

20. Other hardware

continues

Listing 1.1. continued

```
20.1.  VESA Power Savings Protocol (DPMS) monitors

20.2.  Joysticks


o  Joystick driver                                          ʹ
   <ftp://sunsite.unc.edu/pub/Linux/kernel/patches/console
   /joystick-0.7.3.tgz>

o  Joystick driver (module)
   <ftp://sunsite.unc.edu/pub/Linux/kernel/patches/console/joyfixed.tgz>


20.3.  Video capture boards


o  FAST Screen Machine II
   <ftp://sunsite.unc.edu/pub/Linux/apps/video/ScreenMachineII_1.1.tgz>

o  ProMovie Studio
   <ftp://sunsite.unc.edu/pub/Linux/apps/video/PMS-grabber.tgz>

o  VideoBlaster, Rombo Media Pro+
   <ftp://sunsite.unc.edu/pub/Linux/apps/video/vid_src.gz>

o  WinVision video capture card
   <ftp://sunsite.unc.edu/pub/Linux/apps/video/fgrabber-1.0.tgz>


20.4.  UPS


o  APC SmartUPS
   <ftp://sunsite.unc.edu/pub/Linux/system/UPS/apcd-0.1.tar.gz>

o  UPS's with RS-232 monitoring port (unipower package)
   <ftp://sunsite.unc.edu/pub/Linux/system/UPS/unipower-1.0.0.tgz>

o  various other UPS's are supported, read the UPS HOWTO


20.5.  Miscellaneous


o  Analog Devices RTI-800/815 ADC/DAC board      contact Paul
   Gortmaker<gpg109@anu.edu.au>

o  HP IEEE-488 (HP-IB) interface        <ftp://beaver.chemie.fu-berlin.de/pub/
   linux/IEEE488/>

o  Maralu chip-card reader/writer       <ftp://ftp.thp.uni-koeln.de/pub
   /linux/chip/>

o  Mattel Powerglove       <ftp://sunsite.unc.edu/pub/Linux/apps
   /linux-powerglove.tgz>
```

o   Reveal FM Radio card   <ftp://magoo.uwsuper.edu/pub/fm-radio/>

o   Videotext cards   <ftp://sunsite.unc.edu/pub/Linux/apps/video
    /videoteXt-0.5.tar.gz>

21. Related sources of information

o   Cameron Spitzer's hardware FAQ archive   <ftp://rahul.net/pub/cameron
    /PC-info/>

o   Computer Hardware and Software Vendor Phone Numbers   <http://
    mtmis1.mis.semi.harris.com/comp_ph1.html>

o   Guide to Computer Vendors   <http://www.ronin.com/SBA/>

o   System Optimization Information   <http://www.dfw.net/~sdw/>

22. Acknowledgments

Thanks to all the authors and contributors of other HOWTO's, many
things here are shamelessly stolen from their works; to Zane Healy and
Ed Carp, the original authors of this list; and to everyone else who
sent in updates and feedbacks. Special thanks to Eric Boerner and lilo
(the person, not the program) for the sanity checks. And thanks to Dan
Quinlan for the original SGML conversion.

23. Appendix A. S3 cards supported by XFree86 3.1.1.

CHIPSET	RAMDAC	CLOCKCHIP	BPP	CARD
801/805	AT&T 20C490		16	Actix GE 32
				Orchid Fahrenheit 1280+
801/805	AT&T 20C490	ICD2061A	16	STB PowerGraph X.24
805	S3 GENDAC		16	Miro 10SD VLB/PCI
				SPEA Mirage VLB
805	SS2410	ICD2061A	8	Diamond Stealth 24 VLB
928	AT&T 20C490		16	Actix Ultra
928	Sierra SC15025	ICD2061A	32	ELSA Winner 1000 ISA/VLB/EISA
928	Bt485	ICD2061A	32	STB Pegasus VL
928	Bt485	SC11412	16	SPEA Mercury VLB
928	Bt485	ICD2061A	32	#9 GXE Level 10/11/12
928	Ti3020	ICD2061A	32	#9 GXE Level 14/16
864	AT&T 20C498	ICS2494	32	Miro 20SD (BIOS 1.x)
864	AT&T 20C498/	ICD2061A/	32	ELSA Winner 1000 PRO VLB/PCI
	STG1700	ICS9161		MIRO 20SD (BIOS 2.x)
864	STG1700	ICD2061A	32	Actix GE 64 VLB
864	AT&T 20C498/	ICS2595	16	SPEA Mirage P64 DRAM
				(BIOS 3.x)
	AT&T 21C498			
864	S3 86C716 SDAC		32	ELSA Winner 1000 PRO
				Miro 20SD (BIOS 3.x)
				SPEA Mirage P64 DRAM (BIOS 4.x)
				Diamond Stealth 64 DRAM
864	ICS5342	ICS5342	32	Diamond Stealth 64 DRAM (some)

continues

Listing 1.1. continued

864	AT&T 20C490	ICD2061A	32	#9 GXE64
864	AT&T 20C498-13	ICD2061A	32	#9 GXE64 PCI
964	AT&T 20C505	ICD2061A	32	Miro Crystal 20SV PCI
964	Bt485	ICD2061A	32	Diamond Stealth 64
964	Bt9485	ICS9161A	32	SPEA Mercury 64
964	Ti3020	ICD2061A	8	ELSA Winner 2000 PRO PCI
964	Ti3025	Ti3025	32	#9 GXE64 Pro VLB/PCI
				Miro Crystal 40SV
764	(Trio64)		32	SPEA Mirage P64 (BIOS 5.x)
				Diamond Stealth 64 DRAM
				#9 FX Vision330
				STB PowerGraph 64
				(all Trio64 based cards)
868			32	ELSA Winner 1000AVI
968	TVP3026		32	ELSA Winner 2000PRO/X
				Diamond Stealth 64 Video VRAM

As you can see from the preceding listing, Linux does support a variety of hardware devices.

Summary

In this chapter, you learned about Linux and some of its more prominent features, including the following:

- UNIX is a trademark of Novell. Linux is not a trademark and has no connection to trademark UNIX.

- Linux is designed to run on Intel 80386, 80486, and Pentium computers. Linux supports the 387 math coprocessor chip.

- Linux has most of UNIX's features and applications built into it. These features include a Virtual File System (VFS), networking, multitasking, and multiuser capabilities, along with a host of applications such as XFree86, TeX, and the GNU utilities.

- You will learn a lot about operating systems when working with Linux.

- Linux is copyrighted under the GNU copyleft agreement. See Appendix E.

- The hardware requirements for Linux include at least a 80386 (or better still 80486) processor, about 100MB to 120MB of disk space, 4MB of RAM, and a 3.5-inch high-density floppy drive.

- The more memory you have, the faster Linux will run.

- The swap space on Linux is an area on the disk used by Linux as a scratch area when working with lots of processes.

- You need 8MB of RAM to get X Window systems to run with an acceptable degree of performance.

- You need to educate yourself a little on Linux and UNIX before you start the installation procedure. This is especially important if you are new to UNIX.

■ There are several ways to find help on topics in Linux: the Linux Documentation Project, FAQs, INFO-SHEETS, and from the files in the CD-ROM itself.

■ The Hardware-HOWTO document contains a lot of information about all the devices supported by Linux.

■ It's best to check the Linux Hardware Compatibility List on the CD-ROM before starting your installation process or buying anything for your PC.

Types of Linux Available   2

*by Kamran
Husain*

IN THIS CHAPTER

This chapter will cover the many types of Linux systems and distributions available. I strongly recommend that you read this chapter at least once before starting the installation process. This chapter covers the following topics:

- The various distribution types in Linux
- The types of disk sets for each distribution
- What distribution sets are important for you
- How to look for files on the CD-ROM
- How to get Linux from FTP sites
- How to get Linux from BBS sites
- How to find FTP sites where you can get Linux updates

Linux Releases

There are many independent releases of Linux with their own lists of unique features. Some of these releases are available free of charge if you have access to the Internet. Some releases are available for a nominal fee ($20 to $90) for distribution on CD-ROM or disks. Typically, the CD-ROM versions are cheaper and are easier to use than the floppy disk distributions because the cost of one CD-ROM is less than the cost of 30 or more floppy disks. Another plus for the CD-ROM is the convenience of having everything on one source media. It beats swapping disks!

What's a Linux Release?

A Linux *release* is a set of files for a complete Linux system. Various changes made by the Linux community are incorporated into each release.

Linux releases are identified by numbers. These numbers are of the form *X.YY.ZZ*, where *X* is 0 or 1, and *YY* and *ZZ* are numbers between 0 and 99. At the time I wrote this, the release number was 1.2.13. Generally, the higher the number, the newer the release. Some release numbers also include *pNN*, where *NN* is a number between 1 and 20. These refer to patches to a specific Linux version (a *patch* is a fix or an update to the software). For example, 0.99p15 would mean the fifteenth patch to the Linux release 0.99.

A release consists of several components called *series of disks*, or a collection of disks. For example, the X Window series of disks comes on 10 disks. Each series is referred to by its name. A name generally tells you who put the software together and what its date is.

Some of the releases of Linux are as follows:

- Slackware 2.3.

  The Slackware 2.3 is the Linux release on the CD-ROM included with this book. I will cover this distribution in great detail in the section "More on the Slackware Distribution" later in this chapter. You can get future versions of this release on CD-ROM from various vendors for about $25.

The primary distributor for this release is Patrick Volkerding, who can be reached at `volkerdi@mhd1.moorhead.msus.edu`.

■ The Red Hat Software Inc. release.

A commercial release of Linux from Red Hat Software Inc. Its latest version is 2.1. What you are paying for with the "commercial" part is the full service support that you get from Red Hat Software for its software. The installation package has a very snappy installation program complete with 3-D buttons, scrolling lists, icons, and so on.

The highlight of the installation package is the Red Hat Packet Manager (RPM). Using the RPM enables you to safely install and uninstall packages. By far, the uninstall capability of the package is the best feature because most upgrades to critical packages require a complete Linux installation. RPM can even let you install packages straight from an FTP site (such as `$ rpm -iv ftp://ftp.site.com/foobar.rpm`).

One more feature is that the RPM recognizes configuration files that you may have modified. If the new file and the installed file are the same, RPM copies the new file over the installed file. If they are not, the installed file is saved as `filename.rpmsave` for you to compare with the new file. This way you do not have to remember what files you modified. Neat.

Finally, the Glint package enables you to build and debug packages and their contents. With a graphical interface, it's easy to view, install, and uninstall packages.

Contact them at:

Red Hat Software Inc.
25 Sylvan Rd. South
Westport, CT 06880
`info@redhat.com` or `www.redhat.com`
800 454-5502

Or, download a boot disk and two root disks from `ftp.pht.com/pub/linux/redhat` and the installation scripts provided on these disks will take care of downloading the rest.

■ The Softlanding Linux System release (SLS).

The SLS release is available from:

Softlanding Software
910 Lodge Ave.
Victoria, B.C.
Canada V8X-3A8
(604) 360-0188

This release consists of about 23 disks for Linux and 10 for X11. The nice thing about this release is that you can pick and choose which disks and packages you want to install. The first disk (`a1`) must be "rawritten" (using `rawrite.exe`, discussed in Chapter 3, "Installing Linux") on floppies, and the rest of the images must be put onto DOS formatted floppies using the DOS `copy` command. This release contains all the software package(s) you need to get started with Linux and, for newcomers, is easy to install.

The SLS release can also be found at `tsx-11.mit.edu` in the directory `/pub/linux/packages/SLS` `sunsite.unc.edu` in the directory `/pub/Linux/SLS`.

▪ The TAMU (Texas A&M University) Linux release.

The TAMU release supposedly is like the SLS release but has some different software packages and a different installation procedure than SLS. The installation procedure is the main difference from SLS. A single boot diskette, which boots directly into an automated installation program, is used. This installation program asks a few questions about the desired configuration and sets up everything, including your file systems, booting from the hard drive with LILO (see Chapter 5, "Odds and Ends") and a simplified X Window configuration.

This release is a full-featured package, including X Window, `emacs`, networking tools, boot utilities, and a list of sources for all installation programs without any use restrictions. TAMU.99p12+ is available from `sc.tamu.edu` in `pub/free_unix/TAMU.99p4`.

▪ H.J. Lu's bootable rootdisk.

This is a release of the Linux kernel and basic binaries on a single floppy. It, along with HLU's `gccdisk`, `libdisk`, and so on, is good for upgrading or installing a basic Linux system by hand. It's not recommended for newcomers, because there's no real install script; it's mostly meant as an upgrade of the basic system software. Beginners should install SLS or MCC-interim (see the next item) instead.

H.J. Lu's bootable rootdisk release is found at `tsx-11.mit.edu:` in the directory `/pub/linux/packages/GCC`.

▪ The Manchester Computing Centre Interim release.

This is the fabled MCC-Interim Linux release, which was originally the *de facto* standard Linux distribution. A new version has recently appeared for Linux 1.0. This release has almost all of the important Linux software, such as Slackware, but does not contain `emacs` or X Window.

MCC-Interim can be found on `sunsite.unc.edu` in the directory `/pub/Linux/distributions/MCC/1.0+` and also at `ftp.mcc.ac.uk` in the directory `/pub/linux/mcc-interim/1.0+`.

▪ Trans-Ameritech release.

Trans-Ameritech is the most comprehensive release in terms of the software it offers. It is available only on CD-ROM. The CD-ROM is quite helpful because it offers a complete, uncompressed, bootable Linux file system. This feature has two distinct advantages: You have instant access to the file of your choice without having to uncompress or unzip any archives, and it saves the disk space that you would use uncompressing these archives.

The CD-ROM is based on the Slackware distribution of Linux with all the source code, an uncompressed file system, and NetBSD source and binary distribution. The current Trans-Ameritech distribution is the Slackware 2.3 release and is available for $49.95.

To minimize the possibility of hardware conflicts, many extra kernels are provided for different configurations. They are usable for installation and normal use. Many online documents are provided for quick reference, including the Linux Documentation Project files in source, dvi, and ps formats. This distribution also includes the HylaFAX (previously known as Flex FAX), a package that enables you to send and receive faxes on either class 1 or class 2 fax-modems.

To help first-time Linux users, many of the provided documentation files are readable from DOS even before Linux is installed.

All source files for Linux are available on the CD-ROM. The most often needed source code files are uncompressed and can be used directly from CD-ROM. An uncompressed Linux file system is available for reference and disk space conservation. You can run programs directly from CD-ROM. There is a large information directory, including many man pages, for online reference.

For a hacker's reference, an uncompressed FreeBSD source tree is provided. You can order by phone (408) 727-3883.

■ The Linux Support Team Erlang Distribution (LST).

This release is for you if you speak German. The menus, manuals, and installation instructions are in German. You can get this release from `ftp.uni-erlangen.de` under `/pub/Linux/LST.distribution`.

NOTE

There are several other vendors where you can get Linux. The complete distribution can be found in the file `Distribution-HOWTO` on the CD-ROM at the back of this book.

■ Yggdrasil.

Yggdrasil Plug-and-Play Linux is a complete CD-ROM distribution of the Linux operating system. It includes a great deal of software covering nearly every package that you would expect to find on a complete UNIX system. A complete file list is available via FTP from `yggdrasil.com`.

They also offer The Linux Bible, a full library of Linux and UNIX documentation, including three books from the Linux Documentation Project, their Yggdrasil installation manual, and the complete set of Linux HOWTO guides.

Yggdrasil's Plug-and-Play Linux is named for *plug-and-play operation,* which means that you can place a floppy in drive A, turn the computer on, and answer all the questions. That's all there is to installation. The reality is a little more complicated, because you have to know whether your hardware is compatible before you begin.

The login screen lists a number of preconfigured user names, including `install`, which installs the system, giving paragraphs of explanation about every question it asks the user.

The install script even searches for a modem, and on finding it, configures mail and UUCP so that mail sent to an Internet address is transparently delivered through a bulletin board system at Yggdrasil. Some people might not like this, so don't say that I didn't warn you!

The X Window configuration is automated, too, with forms to fill in as you run X for the first time, as well as a graphical control panel that enables additional forms for configuration of networking, SLIP, outgoing UUCP, the printer, and so on. You can call them, toll-free, in the U.S. at 800 261-6630 or e-mail them at `info@yggdrasil.com`.

Yggdrasil Computing, Incorporated
4880 Stevens Creek Blvd., Suite 205
San Jose, CA 95129-1034

■ InfoMagic Developer's Resource CD-ROM kit.

The InfoMagic Linux Developer's Resource is a complete snapshot of the `sunsite.unc.edu` and `tsx-11.mit.edu` archives. It also includes the complete GNU software collection (in source form). The following Linux distributions are included on the discs: Slackware, Debian, SLS, TAMU, MCC, and JE (Japanese Extensions).

The Linux HOWTO documents have been formatted for use with the Microsoft Multimedia Viewer (which is included) to enable browsing and full text search under Microsoft Windows. You can contact them at 800 800-6613 or via e-mail at `Orders@InfoMagic.com`.

The contents of the CDs can also be found at the site `ftp.InfoMagic.com` in the directory `/pub/vendor/Infomagic` or `ftp.uu.net` in the directory `/vendor/InfoMagic/cd-roms/linux`.

There you have it. This list of locations where you can get Linux from is incomplete. In fact, I should apologize to the folks whose company names didn't get listed here. There was not enough time for me to fully review all the distributions before this book went to press. If you would like a more complete list, please look at the newsgroups `comp.os.linux.announce` and `comp.os.linux.misc`.

The document `Distribution-HOWTO` is archived on a number of Linux FTP sites, including `sunsite.unc.edu` in `pub/Linux/docs/HOWTO`.

Other Linux Information Sources

If you like magazines, you will love *The Linux Journal* (LJ), a monthly publication covering the Linux community. Most material in LJ is new (that is, derived from a bunch of USENET newsgroup topics). Each issue includes columns and articles on Linux programming, GNU, Free Software Foundation issues, systems administration, questions and answers, interviews, and more. This is a darn good magazine. You can reach the publishers at

The Linux Journal
P.O. Box 85867
Seattle, WA 98145-1867
(206) 527-3385

If you want to keep up-to-date with the latest releases of Linux, try to get quarterly updates to your Linux system via a subscription to Morse Telecommunication, Inc.'s *Linux Quarterly CD-ROM*. Each CD contains the complete contents of `tsx-11.mit.edu`. This is one of the most popular Internet Linux sites. It provides both source and binary files of major Linux distributions, utilities, source code, and documentation. This quarterly update includes Slackware, SLS, MCC, and Debian releases of Linux. Get information through e-mail from `Order@morse.net`.

Lastly, the Linux Systems Labs (`dirvin@vela.acs.oakland.edu`) also can provide commercial software for Linux, including manuals, database applications, and other applications software not in the shareware or public domain. You can contact Linux Systems Labs at 800 432-0556.

Finding Linux Updates on the Internet

As I mentioned earlier, a CD-ROM is not the only place for you to get Linux or information about Linux. After all, you might not have a CD-ROM reader. If you don't, you aren't out of luck. You can still get Linux goodies from the Internet sites in the following listing. The catch is that you have to be on the Internet.

So why am I showing you how to get Linux from the Internet when you already have it on a CD?

Well, some of the files on the CD might be different a year from now. In fact, some of the locations you see listed here might be different too. By showing you how to find out more, you can use the `archie` method at a later time to locate updates to Linux and more information easily.

If you want to learn more about the Internet and `archie`, read *The Internet Unleashed* (Sams Publishing, 1994).

I used the `telnet` program to log into `archie.internic.net`, a good site from which to use the `archie` program. The `archie` program is a searching utility for locating files on the Internet by specifying keywords. I logged in with the name `archie` and didn't have to provide a password. (See Listing 2.1.)

The `archie>` prompt is where I issued the `find Linux` command. The `search type of sub` means that we'll ask `archie` to search for all strings in its database with the word *Linux* anywhere in it.

The output from Listing 2.1 shows only a few files. I have edited it to fit in the book. Your listing won't match.

Listing 2.1. Using Archie to find Linux.

```
$ telnet archie.internic.net
...
login: archie

*******************************************************************

        Welcome to the InterNIC Directory and Database Server.

*******************************************************************
# Bunyip Information Systems, 1993, 1994

# Terminal type set to 'vt100 24 80'.
# 'erase' character is '^?'.
# 'search' (type string) has the value 'sub'.
archie> find Linux
# Search type: sub.
# Your queue position: 1
```

continues

Listing 2.1. continued

```
# Estimated time for completion: 16 seconds.
working...

Host unix.hensa.ac.uk     (129.12.43.16)
Last updated 23:37 22 Nov 1994

    Location: /pub/sunsite/pub
        DIRECTORY    drwxr-xr-x    1024 bytes  21:32 16 Nov 1994  Linux


Host unix.hensa.ac.uk     (129.12.43.16)
Last updated 23:37 22 Nov 1994

    Location: /pub/walnut.creek/XFree86/binaries
        DIRECTORY    drwxr-xr-x    1536 bytes  20:26 13 Nov 1994  Linux

Host romulus.ucs.uoknor.edu    (129.15.10.20)
Last updated 18:31 16 Nov 1994

    Location: /
        FILE     -rwxrwxrwx      13 bytes  15:05 12 Nov 1994  Linux

Host ftp.germany.eu.net    (192.76.144.75)
Last updated 23:39  6 Nov 1994

    Location: /pub/os
        DIRECTORY    drwxrwxr-x     512 bytes  01:44  5 Nov 1994  Linux

Host csc.canberra.edu.au    (137.92.1.1)
Last updated 03:23  6 Nov 1994

    Location: /pub/ise
        DIRECTORY    drwxr-xr-x    1024 bytes  18:49 31 Oct 1994  Linux

Host power.ci.uv.es    (147.156.1.3)
Last updated 21:12 23 Nov 1994

    Location: /pub/linux/docs/faqs
        FILE     -r--r--r--   96319 bytes  16:25 30 Oct 1994  Linux-FAQ


Host ftp.ncsa.uiuc.edu    (141.142.20.50)
Last updated 20:06 11 Nov 1994

    Location: /HDF/contrib
        DIRECTORY    drwxrwxr-x     512 bytes  01:02 30 Oct 1994  Linux
[24;1H[K:[24;1H[24;1H[K

Host romulus.ucs.uoknor.edu    (129.15.10.20)
Last updated 18:31 16 Nov 1994

    Location: /mirrors/Linux/docs/faqs
        FILE     -rwxrwxrwx      15 bytes  00:56 30 Oct 1994  Linux-FAQ

Host monu1.cc.monash.edu.au    (130.194.1.101)
Last updated 21:27 17 Oct 1994
```

```
    Location: /pub/linux/docs/faqs
       FILE    -rw-r--r--   96568 bytes  23:39 21 Sep 1994  Linux-FAQ


Host dutiws.twi.tudelft.nl    (130.161.156.11)
Last updated 03:10 23 Nov 1994

    Location: /pub
       DIRECTORY   drwxrwxr-x     512 bytes  10:31 29 Aug 1994  Linux


Host telva.ccu.uniovi.es    (156.35.31.31)
Last updated 22:27 23 Nov 1994

    Location: /uniovi/mathdept/src
       DIRECTORY   drwxr-xr-x    1024 bytes  10:36 28 Jul 1994  Linux


Host neptune.ethz.ch    (129.132.101.33)
Last updated 17:38 15 Nov 1994

    Location: /pub/Oberon
       DIRECTORY   drwxrwxr-x     512 bytes  07:31 22 Jul 1994  Linux


Host ftp.germany.eu.net    (192.76.144.75)
Last updated 23:39  6 Nov 1994

    Location: /pub/os/Linux/Local.EUnet/Kernel/Linus/net-source
       DIRECTORY   drwxr-xr-x     512 bytes  04:23 19 Jul 1994  Linux


archie> find LDP
# Search type: sub.
# Your queue position: 1
# Estimated time for completion: 16 seconds.
working...

Host hpcsos.col.hp.com    (15.255.240.16)
Last updated 18:49 13 Nov 1994

    Location: /mirrors/.scsi0/linux/docs
       FILE    -rwxr-xr-x      17 bytes  20:42  4 Nov 1994  LDP


Host romulus.ucs.uoknor.edu    (129.15.10.20)
Last updated 18:31 16 Nov 1994

    Location: /mirrors/Linux/docs
       FILE    -rwxrwxrwx      17 bytes  23:14 24 Oct 1994  LDP


Host mcsun.eu.net    (192.16.202.2)
Last updated 20:32 10 Nov 1994

    Location: /os/linux/doc
       FILE    -rwxrwxrwx      12 bytes  14:22 18 Sep 1994  LDP

archie>quit
```

Getting Slackware from the Internet

The Slackware release of Linux may be found on any number of FTP sites worldwide. The Linux META-FAQ lists several of the Linux FTP sites. To reduce net traffic, I suggest that you try to find the software on the FTP site nearest you. However, two of the major Linux FTP sites are `sunsite.unc.edu` and `tsx-11.mit.edu`.

CAUTION

Make sure that you use binary mode when you download any Linux installation disk set files from the Internet. You can do this by typing `set binary` at the FTP prompt.

The Slackware release also may be found on the following FTP sites:

`sunsite.unc.edu:/pub/Linux/distributions/slackware`

`tsx-11.mit.edu:/pub/linux/packages/slackware`

`ftp.cdrom.com:/pub/linux/slackware`

`ftp.cdrom.com` is Slackware's home site.

TIP

If you don't find this version at these sites, use `archie` to search for the word *slackware*.

Before you download from your nearest FTP site and put it on floppies, keep in mind what you want from each release. Note that some releases only give you the kernel and a few utilities, and others give you everything you need (including X11, GCC, and more).

In the latter case, you must download more than 50 big files.

NOTE

If you're new to the UNIX world, Linux (as with any UNIX clone) is difficult to understand at first. There isn't a lot of real documentation out there. Linux was never meant to be the hugely popular free UNIX that it has become, and the lack of documentation doesn't bother UNIX wizards who can figure it out from just poking around.

More on the Slackware Distribution

Now you should have enough information to be able to obtain future releases of Linux in your sleep. Let's get on with the matter of the Linux CD-ROM included with this book.

The Slackware distribution is the release on the CD-ROM. This release is also available on floppy disks as *sets*. Each set is a collection of floppy disks containing related software. The following disk sets are available on the CD-ROM for Linux:

■ Disk Set A.

This set is the base system for Linux. These disks contain enough to get you up and running and have elvis and communication programs available. They are based around the 1.2.13 Linux kernel and the file system standard (FSSTND).

> **NOTE**
>
> Disk Set A is known to fit on 1.2MB disks, although the rest of Slackware won't. If you have only a 1.2MB floppy, you can still install the base system, download other disks you want, and install them from your hard drive.

■ Disk Set AP.

This set contains the applications you will most likely use on Linux. It includes various applications and add-ons, such as the man pages, groff, ispell (GNU and international versions), term, joe, jove, ghostscript, sc, bc, and the quota patches.

■ Disk Set D.

This set is referred to as the *program development.* This set contains the distribution for GCC/G++/Objective C version 2.7.0, make (GNU and BSD), byacc and GNU bison, flex, the 5.0.9 C libraries, gdb, SVGAlib, ncurses, clisp, f2c, p2c, m4, perl, and rcs.

■ Disk Set E.

This set contains the GNU emacs (version 19.29 for this CD-ROM) editor.

■ Disk Set F.

This set contains the latest collection of FAQs and other documentation. Usually, it is created when the release is put together. This set contains a lot of useful information.

■ Disk Set K.

This set contains the Linux kernel source versions 1.2.13 and 1.3.20 libraries. If you plan to use the Cor C++ compiler or expect to compile a custom kernel, you will need to install this package.

■ Disk Set N.

This set contains all the files you will need for networking with Linux. The packages include TCP/IP, UUCP, mailx, dip, deliver, elm, pine, smail, cnews, nn, tin, and trn.

■ Disk Set Q.

This set contains the source files for the Linux kernel and images (it currently contains the alpha version of Linux 1.3.18).

- Disk Set T.

  This set contains the `TeX` and `LaTeX2` text formatting systems. `TeX` is an extremely sophisticated typesetting package for mathematical expressions.

- Disk Set TCL.

  This set contains the `Tcl`, `Tk`, `TclX`, `blt`, and `itcl` families of program development tools. You can use `Tcl` and `Tk` to develop X Window applications by writing simple scripts.

- Disk Set X.

  This set contains the base XFree86 3.1.2 system from MIT. This set includes `libXpm` and the Freeware Window managers, such as `fvwm` 1.23b.

- Disk Set XAP.

  This set includes the binary files for X applications: X11 `ghostscript`, `libgr13`, `seyon`, `xfilemanager` `0.5`, `xv` 3.10, GNU `chess` and `xboard`, `xfm` 1.3.2, `ghostview`, and various X games.

- Disk Set XD.

  This is the full X11 R 6 program development kit. This set includes all X11 libraries, server link kit, and PEX support.

- Disk Set XV.

  This is a window manager for the X Window system. The release included on the CD-ROM is "Xview 3.2/p1-X11R6," which contains the XView libraries and the Open Look virtual and nonvirtual window managers.

- Disk Set IV.

  This set contains the Interviews libraries, include files, and the documentation and drawing applications. The Interviews package is a C++ object-oriented graphical user interface development package.

- Disk Set OI.

  ParcPlace generously has made available Object Builder 2.0 and Object Interface Library 4.0. Linux developers may use these programs according to the terms in the "copying" notice found in these directories.

- Disk Set Y.

  Perhaps the most important set of all, this contains the Games collection for Linux. Yes, it does include Tetris for terminals.

You do not have to install all these sets for a Linux distribution. As a bare minimum you will require the A, AP, D, and F sets to get started. If you plan to run X Window, you have to install all of the X and XAP disks. Obviously, if you want to develop applications on your system, you will need the D series disk set, and for X Window, you will need the XD series set. The rest of the disk sets are optional. If you can spare the disk space, you should install them and see if you like them.

Common Extensions for Filenames

Table 2.1 is a list of common filename extensions for the files you will see in Linux archives. The fname in the following table implies the filename with which you want to work.

Table 2.1. File extensions used in Linux releases.

Extension	Used By
.Z	compress/uncompress. Use uncompress fname foo.Z to uncompress the file, where fname is the name of the file that was uncompressed.
.z, .gz, .gzip	gzip is now used by many archive sites instead of compress. If you don't have gzip on your system, get it! To uncompress one of these files, use gzip -d fname.z. .gz is the new gzip extension.
.tar	Tar file. Use tar xvf fname.tar to unpack it. Or you can use tar tvf fname.tar to get an index listing of the tar file.
.taz	Compressed tar file. You can do something such as zcat fname.taz ¦ tar xvf - or tar xvfz fname.taz to unpack it (some versions of tar don't have the z option).
.tpz, .tgz	gzipped tar file. If you have gzip, zcat is linked to it, so you can do zcat foo.tpz ¦ tar xvf to unpack it.
.tpz	The old extension. All gzipped tar files should now end in .tgz instead.

Most distributions use gzipped tar files with the tgz extension.

The Location of Disk Sets on the CD-ROM

The disk sets on the CD-ROM can be found in the /slakware directory. (In DOS, this will be the SLAKWARE directory.) See Listing 2.2 for a directory listing of all the packages on the CD-ROM at the back of this book.

Listing 2.2. The distribution on the CD-ROM in this book.

```
$ ls -l /cdrom/slakware
total 2466
-r--r--r--   2 root     root          527 Sep  5 05:41 00_index.txt
-r--r--r--   2 root     root        19915 Oct 23 02:15 CHECKSUMS
-r--r--r--   2 root     root        43463 Oct 23 01:13 FILE_LIST
-r--r--r--   2 root     root      2233113 Oct 23 02:07 MANIFEST
-r--r--r--   2 root     root          409 Mar 21  1995 README
drwxr-xr-x   2 root     root         4096 Oct 31 13:32 a1/
drwxr-xr-x   2 root     root         2048 Oct 31 13:32 a2/
drwxr-xr-x   2 root     root         2048 Oct 31 13:32 a3/
drwxr-xr-x   2 root     root         2048 Oct 31 13:32 a4/
```

continues

Listing 2.2. continued

```
drwxr-xr-x   2 root      root           2048 Oct 31 13:32 a5/
drwxr-xr-x   2 root      root           4096 Oct 31 13:32 ap1/
drwxr-xr-x   2 root      root           2048 Oct 31 13:32 ap2/
drwxr-xr-x   2 root      root           2048 Oct 31 13:32 ap3/
drwxr-xr-x   2 root      root           2048 Oct 31 13:32 ap4/
drwxr-xr-x   2 root      root           2048 Oct 31 13:32 ap5/
drwxr-xr-x   2 root      root           2048 Oct 31 13:32 d1/
drwxr-xr-x   2 root      root           2048 Oct 31 13:32 d10/
drwxr-xr-x   2 root      root           2048 Oct 31 13:32 d2/
drwxr-xr-x   2 root      root           2048 Oct 31 13:32 d3/
drwxr-xr-x   2 root      root           2048 Oct 31 13:32 d4/
drwxr-xr-x   2 root      root           2048 Oct 31 13:32 d5/
drwxr-xr-x   2 root      root           2048 Oct 31 13:32 d6/
drwxr-xr-x   2 root      root           2048 Oct 31 13:32 d7/
drwxr-xr-x   2 root      root           2048 Oct 31 13:32 d8/
drwxr-xr-x   2 root      root           2048 Oct 31 13:32 d9/
drwxr-xr-x   2 root      root           2048 Oct 31 13:32 e1/
drwxr-xr-x   2 root      root           2048 Oct 31 13:32 e2/
drwxr-xr-x   2 root      root           2048 Oct 31 13:32 e3/
drwxr-xr-x   2 root      root           2048 Oct 31 13:32 e4/
drwxr-xr-x   2 root      root           2048 Oct 31 13:32 e5/
drwxr-xr-x   2 root      root           2048 Oct 31 13:32 e6/
drwxr-xr-x   2 root      root           2048 Oct 31 13:32 f1/
drwxr-xr-x   2 root      root           2048 Oct 31 13:32 f2/
drwxr-xr-x   2 root      root           2048 Oct 31 13:32 k1/
drwxr-xr-x   2 root      root           2048 Oct 31 13:32 k2/
drwxr-xr-x   2 root      root           2048 Oct 31 13:32 k3/
drwxr-xr-x   2 root      root           2048 Oct 31 13:32 k4/
drwxr-xr-x   2 root      root           2048 Oct 31 13:32 k5/
-r--r--r--   1 root      root          14480 Aug 28 23:45 makeflop
drwxr-xr-x   2 root      root           4096 Oct 31 13:32 n1/
drwxr-xr-x   2 root      root           2048 Oct 31 13:32 n2/
drwxr-xr-x   2 root      root           2048 Oct 31 13:32 n3/
drwxr-xr-x   2 root      root           2048 Oct 31 13:32 n4/
drwxr-xr-x   2 root      root           2048 Oct 31 13:32 q1/
drwxr-xr-x   2 root      root           2048 Oct 31 13:32 q10/
drwxr-xr-x   2 root      root           2048 Oct 31 13:32 q11/
drwxr-xr-x   2 root      root           2048 Oct 31 13:32 q12/
drwxr-xr-x   2 root      root           2048 Oct 31 13:32 q13/
drwxr-xr-x   2 root      root           2048 Oct 31 13:32 q14/
drwxr-xr-x   2 root      root           2048 Oct 31 13:32 q15/
drwxr-xr-x   2 root      root           2048 Oct 31 13:32 q2/
drwxr-xr-x   2 root      root           2048 Oct 31 13:32 q3/
drwxr-xr-x   2 root      root           2048 Oct 31 13:32 q4/
drwxr-xr-x   2 root      root           2048 Oct 31 13:32 q5/
drwxr-xr-x   2 root      root           2048 Oct 31 13:32 q6/
drwxr-xr-x   2 root      root           2048 Oct 31 13:32 q7/
drwxr-xr-x   2 root      root           2048 Oct 31 13:32 q8/
drwxr-xr-x   2 root      root           2048 Oct 31 13:32 q9/
drwxr-xr-x   2 root      root           6144 Oct 31 13:32 t1/
drwxr-xr-x   2 root      root           4096 Oct 31 13:32 t2/
drwxr-xr-x   2 root      root           2048 Oct 31 13:32 t3/
drwxr-xr-x   2 root      root           2048 Oct 31 13:32 t4/
drwxr-xr-x   2 root      root           2048 Oct 31 13:32 t5/
drwxr-xr-x   2 root      root           2048 Oct 31 13:32 t6/
drwxr-xr-x   2 root      root           2048 Oct 31 13:32 t7/
```

```
drwxr-xr-x  2 root     root          2048 Oct 31 13:32 t8/
drwxr-xr-x  2 root     root          2048 Oct 31 13:32 t9/
drwxr-xr-x  2 root     root          2048 Oct 31 13:32 tcl1/
drwxr-xr-x  2 root     root          2048 Oct 31 13:32 x1/
drwxr-xr-x  2 root     root          2048 Oct 31 13:32 x10/
drwxr-xr-x  2 root     root          2048 Oct 31 13:32 x11/
drwxr-xr-x  2 root     root          2048 Oct 31 13:32 x12/
drwxr-xr-x  2 root     root          2048 Oct 31 13:32 x13/
drwxr-xr-x  2 root     root          2048 Oct 31 13:32 x14/
drwxr-xr-x  2 root     root          2048 Oct 31 13:32 x15/
drwxr-xr-x  2 root     root          2048 Oct 31 13:32 x16/
drwxr-xr-x  2 root     root          2048 Oct 31 13:32 x2/
drwxr-xr-x  2 root     root          2048 Oct 31 13:32 x3/
drwxr-xr-x  2 root     root          2048 Oct 31 13:32 x4/
drwxr-xr-x  2 root     root          2048 Oct 31 13:32 x5/
drwxr-xr-x  2 root     root          2048 Oct 31 13:32 x6/
drwxr-xr-x  2 root     root          2048 Oct 31 13:32 x7/
drwxr-xr-x  2 root     root          2048 Oct 31 13:32 x8/
drwxr-xr-x  2 root     root          2048 Oct 31 13:32 x9/
drwxr-xr-x  2 root     root          2048 Oct 31 13:32 xap1/
drwxr-xr-x  2 root     root          2048 Oct 31 13:32 xap2/
drwxr-xr-x  2 root     root          2048 Oct 31 13:32 xap3/
drwxr-xr-x  2 root     root          2048 Oct 31 13:32 xap4/
drwxr-xr-x  2 root     root          2048 Oct 31 13:32 xd1/
drwxr-xr-x  2 root     root          2048 Oct 31 13:32 xd2/
drwxr-xr-x  2 root     root          2048 Oct 31 13:32 xd3/
drwxr-xr-x  2 root     root          2048 Oct 31 13:32 xv1/
drwxr-xr-x  2 root     root          2048 Oct 31 13:32 xv2/
drwxr-xr-x  2 root     root          2048 Oct 31 13:32 xv3/
drwxr-xr-x  2 root     root          2048 Oct 31 13:32 y1/
drwxr-xr-x  2 root     root          2048 Oct 31 13:32 y2/
drwxr-xr-x  2 root     root          2048 Oct 31 13:32 y3/
drwxr-xr-x  2 root     root          2048 Oct 31 13:32 y4/
```

This listing shows the contents of the CD-ROM distribution disks directory. Examine the output from Listing 2.2 carefully. You will see that the A set consists of five disks: a1, a2, a3, a4, and a5. Similarly, the AP set also consists of five disks: ap1, ap2, ap3, ap4, and ap5.

NOTE

Slackware does not maintain a complete list of disk space requirements for each disk set. You need at least 7MB of hard disk space just to install just the A series of disks; a very rough estimate of the required disk space would be 2 or 2.5MB per disk for all other sets.

So, to install the minimum set of A, AP, and F sets, you will use about 7MB for the A set, plus 10MB for the AP and 2MB for the F set, requiring you to have at least 19MB on your hard drive. With the price of hard drives falling these days, it should not be difficult to find a fairly cheap 100MB to 200MB drive.

You will see similar directory structures on the FTP sites. This style of distribution is very helpful in the cases where you might have a bad distribution disk and would have to download from only one directory.

If you want to install Slackware from floppies instead of the hard drive, you'll need to have one blank, DOS-formatted floppy for each Slackware disk that you want to work with.

The A disk set (disks A1 through A3) may be either 3.5- or 5.25-inch floppies. However, the rest of the disk sets must be 3.5-inch disks.

You do not need to modify or uncompress the files on the disks; just copy them to DOS floppies. The Slackware installation procedure takes care of uncompressing the files for you at the time of installation.

What's in a Package in a Disk Set?

One way to tell whether you need a package is to look in the contents directory on the CD-ROM. This directory contains descriptions of all the packages and their files. For example, look at the files in the D package's first disk, d1. (See Listing 2.3.)

Listing 2.3. Checking the contents of a Linux package.

```
$ ls -al /cdrom/slakware/xd1
total 1356
drwxr-xr-x   2 root      root          2048 Oct 31 13:32 ./
drwxr-xr-x  94 root      root         12288 Oct 31 13:33 ../
-rw-r--r--   2 root      root            54 Sep  5 05:40 00_index.txt
-rw-r--r--  94 root      root           551 Aug  4 23:04 diskxd1
-rw-r--r--   1 root      root          1037 Aug  4 22:53 maketag
-rw-r--r--   1 root      root            69 Aug  4 22:54 tagfile
-rw-r--r--   1 root      root            69 Oct  1 19:41 tagfile.org
-rw-r--r--   1 root      root       1362357 Aug  4 22:23 xd_lkit.tgz
```

The xd1 disk contains the file xd_lkit.tgz, among others. I would like to know more about this package; the name xd_lkit.tgz doesn't tell me much. So what do I do? The way to look at a file description is to look at the diskxd1 file. Here are the lines of this diskxd1 file. (See Listing 2.4.)

Listing 2.4. Looking at the description of a package.

```
$ cat /cdrom/slakware/xd1/diskxd1

CONTENTS: xd_lkit1
xd_lkit1: XFree86 3.1.2 Linkkit (part one)
xd_lkit1:
xd_lkit1: If you want or need to rebuild an XFree86 3.1.2 server you need this
xd_lkit1: package in addition to the base configuration and the programmers kit.
xd_lkit1: It is not needed for other X program development.
xd_lkit1:
xd_lkit1: When rebuilding all the servers (including PEX) you will typically
xd_lkit1: need an additional 10MB of disk space.  If you are building just a
xd_lkit1: single server you will need 2 MB (2.5 MB with PEX) of space.
xd_lkit1:
xd_lkit1:
$
```

You can find similar descriptions for all the packages. This makes it easier for you to identify and install only the packages you need.

> **TIP**
>
> If you are going to mail order, order a CD-ROM version of the Linux distribution. Not only will you pay less in shipping, but the CD-ROM media is very robust compared to disk. The time saved in installing from CD-ROM instead of floppies may indeed be worth the purchase of a CD-ROM drive.

Obtaining Linux from BBSs

A *bulletin board system* (BBS) enables you to transfer messages and files via your phone line. All you need is a computer with communications software and a modem. Some BBSs transfer messages among each other, forming large computer networks similar to Usenet. The most popular of these in the United States are FidoNet and RIME.

Linux is available from various BBSs worldwide. Some of the BBSs on FidoNet carry `comp.os.linux` as a FidoNet conference.

> **NOTE**
>
> While you are installing Linux, you might get the error `You may have inserted the wrong disk` when you insert the next disk in a series.
>
> Each disk has a small file on it that contains the name of the disk. For example, the SLS a3 disk has a file on it called `diska3`. If it doesn't exist, or is named something else (such as `diska3.z`), create it or rename it. If you copied the files to the SLS floppies using `copy *.*`, you probably missed the `diska3` file because it doesn't have an extension in the filename.
>
> Also, the last disk in a series (for example, the a4 or b5 disk) has a file on it called `install.end`. You need this file as well. These files are used by the installation programs to keep track of when to stop installing a package.

Accessing DOS Files from Linux

Linux supports several features that you can use to access your DOS files from Linux. With the `mtools` package, included with most distributions of Linux, you can use commands such as `mcopy` and `mdir` to access your DOS files. Another option is to mount a DOS partition or floppy directly under Linux, which gives you direct access to your files by way of the DOS file system.

You will find the `mtools` package indispensable if you have to swap files between DOS and Linux. When you first start Linux from a DOS machine, it's comforting to know that you can transfer files easily between two machines that are running different operating systems, so don't worry; you will not have to give up your familiar DOS environment.

Why use `mtools` if you can just mount a DOS drive? `mtools` is good if you want to do something quickly—for example, if you want to get directories on a bunch of floppies. The mount procedure requires you to mount the drive, get a directory, and then `umount` it. With `mtools` you can get the directory with one command.

`mtools` also comes with the Slackware release of Linux and is available in source code form on most Linux FTP sites. This `mtools` source tree can prove to be interesting reading, especially if you are a programmer.

There is also a DOS Emulator available for Linux, and work is beginning on a Microsoft Windows emulator to run under the X Window System. The DOS Emulator isn't perfect, so don't expect to play DOOM (Id Software) on this emulator. Dosemu is still in development stages. You can use it to run some standard applications such as WordPerfect 5.1, Quicken, and Lotus 1-2-3. At the time I wrote this, Dosemu was slow and crashed frequently. However, you can work with it for some quick tasks.

Summary

This chapter has given you a whirlwind tour of what's actually available for Linux. You also learned about Linux releases and how to interpret the release numbers.

I covered the Slackware release in greater detail than other Linux releases. This preferential treatment results from the fact that the Slackware release is included on the CD-ROM that comes with this book.

Each Linux release consists of several disk sets. Each disk set contains a lot of files. Some of these files are just labels, and some are called packages. A *package* is generally a compressed tar archive containing binary files and directory trees. You now know how to determine what types of files are stored in each disk set.

You also know how to get Linux from lots of other sources, including mail order companies, BBSs, and other CD-ROM vendors.

Finally, for DOS fans, Linux provides a host of tools to read or write DOS disks and files. There is even an experimental DOS emulator for you to run DOS programs under Linux. Any DOS partitions can be mounted to appear as directory trees, so you can still work with your data on DOS disks.

Installing Linux

3

by Kamran Husain

IN THIS CHAPTER

The types of available root disks are found in the `rootdsks` directory. I suggest that you use the `color` version and if that does not work, use the `text` version.

Table 3.2 lists the root images available.

> **NOTE**
>
> The `color` version of the install system has some known bugs:
>
> ■ You will see the cancel selection for certain options. This selection only cancels the current package you are installing, not the entire installation process.
>
> ■ This version looks pretty with its colored boxes and other features, but it's not particularly forgiving of extra keystrokes entered between screens. If you are not patient, use the `text` version.

Table 3.2. Root images for 1.44MB drives.

Filename	Description
color	A root install disk which uses the new full-screen, color-install program. Be patient as you use this particular installation.
text	A root install disk for text-based installations. No fancy graphics, just a dumb terminal version of the install program.
umsdos	A version of `color144` used to install UMSDOS, a file system that enables you to install Linux into a directory on an existing MS-DOS partition. Not as fast as `ext2` or `xiafs`, but it works, and you don't have to repartition your drive.
tape	An experimental (at the time of writing) disk designed to support installation from tape.
pcmcia	For laptop installation with PCMCIA cards.
rescue	A bare root disk with utilities such as `vi`, `lilo`, and `e2fsck`. Use this root image if you have trouble getting into a misconfigured system.

Creating Boot and Root Floppies

You must create floppies from the boot and root disk images on the CD-ROM or on the ones you downloaded. This step must be done no matter what type of installation you will eventually be doing.

There are two ways to create the floppies: using a Microsoft Windows interface or using an MS-DOS interface. The Windows interface is much easier to deal with than the MS-DOS interface. However, you may be limited in disk space on your DOS partition to accommodate Windows, or you may not have access to Windows.

TIP

You will need a total of three pre-formatted disks for the installation process. During the creation process, you will use two of these disks—one for root and one for boot. During installation, the install program will prompt you to use the third disk for temporary data storage.

Creating Boot and Root Floppies with Windows

This section is for those Linux installations from Slackware that are different from the one on the CD at the back of this book. Please skip this section if you don't have the Slackware Distribution Version 3.0 or later four-CD release.

From the File Manager run the D:\LININST\LININST.EXE program. (Substitue the D: for whatever your drive letter is for your CD-ROM drive). You will be presented with a screen as shown in Figure 3.1. Check the items you want and click OK.

The program will prompt you for the correct discs. Swap them when prompted.

FIGURE 3.1.

The Windows installation main screen.

Using MS-DOS to Create the Boot and Root Floppies

This is where you use the MS-DOS program RAWRITE.EXE to write the images to the floppy disks. Although the boot images are not compressed on the CD-ROM, the root images are compressed in a .gz format. These root images should not be decompressed prior to using RAWRITE since the kernel will automatically do this when it loads the image into ramdisk from the floppy.

CAUTION

Your boot sequence in the CMOS on your PC must be A: first, then C:. Otherwise, you will not be able to boot up from floppy disks.

Then you will use RAWRITE.EXE to write the boot and root disk images to the floppies. For example, if you're using the scsi boot disk, issue the commands

```
D:\> cd install
D:\INSTALL> rawrite
RaWrite 1.3 - Write disk file to raw floppy diskette

Enter source file name: d:\bootdsks.144\scsi
Enter destination drive: a
Please insert a formatted diskette into drive A: and press -Enter- : <Enter>
Writing image to drive A:  Press ^C to abort.
Track: 33  Head: 0  Sector: 10
Done.
```

RAWRITE copies the file, block-by-block, directly to the floppy. Then use RAWRITE for the root disk image (such as COLOR) for the next floppy.

```
D:\> cd install
D:\INSTALL> rawrite
Enter source file name: d:\rootdsks\color.gz
Enter destination drive: a
Please insert a formatted diskette into drive A: and press -Enter- : <Enter>
Writing image to drive A:  Press ^C to abort.
Track: 29  Head: 0  Sector: 4
Done.
```

Now you should have two floppy disks, one with a boot image and one with a root image. Note that these two floppies are no longer readable by MS-DOS.

TIP

Be sure you're using brand-new, error-free floppies. The floppies must have no bad blocks on them. Using brand-new, formatted floppies will work in your favor.

NOTE

You do not need to be running MS-DOS in order to install Slackware. However, running MS-DOS makes it easier to create the boot and root floppies, and it makes it easier to install the software because you can install directly from an MS-DOS partition on your system and create the floppies. If you are not running MS-DOS on your system, you can use someone else's MS-DOS system to create the floppies and then install.

Creating Boot Floppies on a UNIX System

You don't need to use GZIP.EXE and RAWRITE.EXE under MS-DOS to create the boot and root floppies. You can use the gzip and dd commands on a UNIX system to do the same job. For this, you will need a UNIX workstation with a floppy drive. For example, on a Sun workstation with the floppy drive on device /dev/rfd0, you can use the following command:

```
% dd if=bare of=/dev/rfd0 obs=18k
```

The `dd` command writes the file `bare` to the floppy disk. The `obs` parameter is required to specify the output block size argument.

Using Floppy Disks

If you wish to install Slackware from floppies instead of from the hard drive or CD-ROM, you'll need to have one blank, MS-DOS, high-density, 3.5-inch, 1.44MB formatted floppy for each Slackware disk that you downloaded.

To make the disks, use the MS-DOS `COPY` command to copy the files from each Slackware directory onto an MS-DOS formatted floppy. You do not have to use `rawrite` to write the rest of the files (that is, other than the A1 and root disk). The rest of the disks are readable by MS-DOS. The following command

```
> COPY \DISTRIBU\SLACKWAR\D1\*.* A:
```

copies the contents of the D1 disk to the floppy in Drive A:. You should repeat this for each disk that you downloaded.

You do not need to modify or uncompress the files on the disks; you need to copy them to MS-DOS floppies. The Slackware installation procedure takes care of uncompressing the files for you.

Partitioning Your Hard Drive

For most Linux installations, you need at least two partitions: one for swap space (used as virtual memory) and another for your "root file system" (that is, the actual Linux software). You can also make separate partitions for your `/usr filesystem…`. If you have UNIX experience, you'll be able to figure out how to divide software between multiple partitions. If you are new to UNIX, you should work with one partition only. For most installations, having one root file system and one swap partition is the best way to go.

The first thing you need to do is resize the existing partitions (if any) on your drive to make space for Linux. For example, if you have a DOS partition taking up all of your drive, you need to use MS-DOS `FDISK` to delete the partition and re-create a smaller version. Of course, in so doing, you can lose everything on that DOS partition. Back up the files first and reinstall them after you've re-created and reformatted the partition.

> **CAUTION**
>
> Once you delete a partition, you will lose all the data on that partition. So be careful how you resize your partitions. Always make a backup of your directory tree before modifying the hard disk partition table.

> **CAUTION**
>
> In Chapter 3, "Installing Linux," during the discussion on the installation process, I recommended that you install LILO and have the setup program configure it for you. If you have already done so, the only reason why you should be running this is if you have created a new kernel or added a new hard drive or another operating system.

If this is the first time you are installing LILO, or you are about to add a new partition, you will have to start with a new header. This program is very easy to use and asks several questions about your system. The sheer number of possibilities cannot be completely covered here, but here are the terms with which you must be familiar:

- `/dev/hda` and `/dev/hdb` refer to both IDE hard drives 1 and 2 on your system. Individual partitions on each hard drive are referred to as `/dev/hda1`, `/dev/hda2`, `/dev/hda3`, and so on for drive 1. Similarly `/dev/hdb1` and so on for drive 2.

- SCSI hard drives are referred to as `/dev/sda` and `/dev/sdb` for drives 1 and 2, respectively. Individual SCSI partitions are also referred to in a similar manner as for the IDE drives: `/dev/sda1`, `/dev/sda2`, are the first and second partitions of the first SCSI drive.

- The *Master Boot Record* (MBR) is the first boot sector of your drive that contains the partitioning information and bootstrap code. LILO will change this sector and make it incompatible with DOS. The DOS MBR program simply loads MS-DOS from the boot sector, which in turns loads `command.com`.

> **NOTE**
>
> LILO's boot program can only be stored on the first hard drive.

After the `liloconfig` program has run, it will create a file called `lilo.conf` for you in the `/etc` directory. (See Listing 4.2.) If you already have this file in your `/etc` directory, you can edit it too. Of course, depending on how your system is set up, the contents of your Linux installation may vary.

Listing 4.2. The `/etc/lilo.conf` file.

```
#
# LILO configuration file
# generated by 'liloconfig'
#
# Start LILO global section
boot = /dev/hda
```

```
#compact        # faster, but won't work on all systems.
# delay = 50
vga = normal    # force sane state
ramdisk = 0     # paranoia setting
# End LILO global section
# Linux bootable partition config begins
image = /vmlinuz.cd
  root = /dev/hda2
  label = CDlinux
image = /vmlinuz
  root = /dev/hda2
  label = Bare
# Linux bootable partition config ends
# DOS bootable partition config begins
other = /dev/hda1
  label = DOS
  table = /dev/hda
# DOS bootable partition config ends
```

TIP

Please read the file INCOMPAT in the LILO release for compatibility notes.

In this lilo.conf file, you can see three different kernels that can be booted from /dev/hda. There is no /dev/hdb in this system. The first image will be the default image into which you will boot. This image is called vmlinuzcd and has the label "CDlinux". The other two images are labeled "Bare" for a test kernel on the same hard-drive partition, and "DOS" for the DOS partition.

If you uncomment the delay line, LILO will wait five seconds for you to make a choice. A delay of 0 will cause LILO to wait forever for you to make a decision.

If you are really stingy about disk space, uncomment the compact button. There is a risk, though, that the compact version will not work with your system. Normally this line should be commented out.

Now run the QuickInst.new shell script, which will install LILO for you. After the installation is over, you have to restart the machine with the command: /sbin/shutdown -r now.

NOTE

QuickInst can only be used for first-time installations or to entirely replace an existing installation, **not** to update or modify an existing installation of LILO. Be sure you've extracted LILO into a directory that doesn't contain any files of other LILO installations.

Command-Line Arguments

The /sbin/lilo command installer accepts several command-line options. Some of the usual ones are listed here. Check the README file with your installation package for more details.

- ■ -C <config_file>. Specifies the configuration file that is used by the map installer. If -C is omitted, /etc/lilo/config is used. In this example, you would use /etc/lilo.conf.

- ■ -q. Lists the currently mapped files.

- ■ -r <root_directory>. Changes the directory to the specified directory before doing anything else. This is useful when running the map installer while the normal root file system is mounted somewhere else, for example, when recovering from an installation failure with an install disk.

- ■ -t. Test only. Performs the entire installation procedure without replacing the map file or writing the modified boot sector. This can be used in conjunction with the -v option to verify that LILO will use sane values.

- ■ -v. Be verbose about what it's doing. If you don't do this, the installation process will not display any messages or status information.

- ■ -u [boot device]. Restores the backup copy of the specified boot sector. The name is normally derived from its present name.

- ■ -V. Prints the version number and exits.

There are also many command-line options that correspond to configuration variables. (See Table 4.1.)

Table 4.1. Command-line options for LILO.

Command-line option	Configuration variable
-b <boot_device>	boot=<boot_device>
-c	compact
-d <tsecs>	delay=<tsecs>
-i <boot_sector>	install=<boot_sector>
-f <disktab_file>	disktab=<disktab_file>
-l	linear
-m <map_file>	map=<map_file>
-P fix	fix-table
-P ignore	ignore-table
-s <save file>	backup=<save file>
-S <save file>	force-backup=<save file>
-v ...	verbose=<level>

Configuration Parameters

The /etc/lilo.conf file can have the following parameters. All of these can be set from the command line, but storing them in a configuration file is more reliable. The following options are available to you:

- boot=<boot_device>   Sets the name of the device that contains the boot sector. If boot is omitted, the boot sector is read from (and possibly written to) the device that is currently mounted as root.

- compact   Tries to merge read requests for adjacent sectors into a single read request. This drastically reduces load time and keeps the map smaller. Use compact when booting from a floppy disk. Remember, it may not work on some hard drives.

- delay=<tsecs>   Specifies the number of tenths of a second LILO should wait before booting the first image. This is useful on systems that immediately boot from the hard disk after enabling the keyboard. LILO doesn't wait if delay is omitted.

- linear   Generates linear sector addresses instead of sector/head/cylinder addresses. Linear addresses are translated at runtime and do not depend on disk geometry. Note that boot disks, where linear is used, may not be portable.

- install=<boot_sector>   Installs the specified file as the new boot sector. If install is omitted, /etc/lilo/boot.b is used as the default.

- disktab=<disktab_file>   Specifies the name of the disk parameter table. The map installer looks for /etc/lilo/disktab if disktab is omitted.

- map=<map_file>   Specifies the location of the map file. If map is omitted, the file /etc/lilo/map is used.

- message=<message_file>   Specifies a file containing a message that is displayed before the boot prompt. No message is displayed when waiting for a Shift key after printing "LILO." The FF character ([Ctrl-L]) clears the local screen. The size of the message file is limited to 65,535 bytes. The map file has to be rebuilt if the message file is changed or moved. The default file for messages is the /etc/boot.message file. Use this file to display boot options for your LILO configuration.

- verbose=<level>   Turns on lots of progress reporting. Higher numbers give more verbose output.

- backup=<backup_file>   Copies the original boot sector to <backup_file> (which may also be a device, such as /dev/null) instead of /etc/lilo/boot.<number>.

- force-backup=<backup_file>   Like backup, but overwrites an old backup copy if it exists. backup=<backup_file> is ignored if force-backup appears in the same configuration file.

- prompt   Forces entering the boot prompt without expecting any prior key-presses. Unattended reboots are impossible if prompt is set and timeout isn't.

- timeout=<tsecs>   Sets a timeout (in tenths of a second) for keyboard input. If no key is pressed for the specified time, the first image is automatically booted. Similarly, password input is aborted if the user is idle for too long. The default timeout is infinite.

Depending on the kernel configuration, some special configuration options for nonstandard hardware might be recognized as well. Some of these boot prompts include:

- For a Panasonic CD-ROM with SoundBlaster support, use: `sbpcd=0x340,SoundBlaster`.
- For a bus mouse, use `bmouse=irq`.
- For reserving ports from being autoprobed by device drivers in special hardware device conflict situation, you can use `reserve=port,size`. For example, `reserve=0x200,8` will reserve 8 ports starting at 0x200 from being probed by device drivers.
- Ethernet cards usually take parameter from the `ether=x,x,x,...` comamnd. The actual parameters sent depend on the type of card.
- For Mitsumi CD-ROM, use `mcd=port,irq`. For example, `mcd=0x340,11`.
- If your Ethernet card is not recognized, try `ether=10,0x340` to probe for it at port 0x340 using interrupt 10. Note that the interrupt number here is given before the port number given for the Mitsumi CD-ROM driver.

The parameters for each type of device will come with their documentation, so do not assume anything. Use only specified values. If you do follow instructions, you may wind up causing irrecoverable errors which may lead to a corrupt file system.

> **TIP**
>
> Remember that all hex numbers to the boot prompt MUST be entered with a 0x in front of them. The default interpretation is that of decimal digits.

Updating LILO

When updating to a new version of LILO, the initial steps are the same as for a first-time installation: extract all files, configure the `makefile`, run make to build the executables, and run `make install` to move the files to `/etc/lilo`.

The old versions of `boot.b`, `chain.b`, and similar files are automatically renamed to `boot.old`, `chain.old`, and so on. This is done to ensure that you can boot even if the installation procedure does not finish. `boot.old`, `chain.old`, and the others can be deleted after the map file is rebuilt.

Because the locations of `boot.b`, `chain.b`, and the like have changed and because the map file format might be different too, you have to update the boot sector and the map file. Run `/etc/lilo/lilo` to do this.

Updating the Kernel

Whenever any of the kernel files that are accessed by LILO are moved or overwritten, the map has to be rebuilt. (It is advisable to keep a second, stable kernel image that can be booted if you forget to update the map after a change to your usual kernel image.) Run `/etc/lilo/lilo` to do this. The kernel has a `make target zlilo` that copies the kernel to `/vmlinuz` and runs `/etc/lilo/install`.

Uninstalling LILO

In order to keep LILO from being invoked when the system boots, its boot sector has to be either removed or disabled. All other files belonging to LILO can be deleted after removing the boot sector, if desired.

LILO 0.14 (and newer) can be de-installed with the `lilo -u` command.

If LILO's boot sector has been installed on a primary partition and is booted by the standard MBR or some partition-switching program, it can be disabled by making a different partition active. MS-DOS's FDISK, Linux's fdisk, or LILO's activate can do that.

If LILO's boot sector is the master boot record (MBR) of a disk, it has to be replaced with a different MBR, typically MS-DOS's standard MBR. When using MS-DOS Version 5.0 or above, the MS-DOS MBR can be restored with FDISK /MBR. This only alters the boot loader code, not the partition table. LILO automatically makes backup copies when it overwrites boot sectors. They are named /etc/lilo/boot.<nnnn>, with <nnnn> corresponding to the device number, that is 0300 is /dev/hda, 0800 is /dev/sda, and so on. Those backups can be used to restore the old MBR if no easier method is available.

The commands are

```
dd if=/etc/lilo/boot.0300 of=/dev/hda bs=446 count=1
```

or

```
dd if=/etc/lilo/boot.0800 of=/dev/sda bs=446 count=1
```

respectively.

> **WARNING**
>
> Some Linux distributions install boot.<nnnn> files from the system where the distribution was created in /etc/lilo. Using those files might yield unpredictable results. Therefore, the file creation date should be carefully checked.

> **NOTE**
>
> Some other operating systems (such as MS-DOS 6.0) appear to modify the MBR in their install procedures. It is therefore possible that LILO will stop to work after such an installation and Linux has to be booted from floppy disk. The original state can be restored by either re-running /etc/lilo/lilo (if LILO is installed as the MBR) or by making LILO's partition active (if it's installed on a primary partition).
>
> Typically, the new operating system then has to be added to LILO's configuration (and /etc/lilo/lilo has to be re-run) in order to boot it.

Table 4.2. BIOS error codes.

Code	Value
0x00	Internal error. This code is generated by the sector-read routine of the LILO boot loader whenever an internal inconsistency is detected. This might be caused by corrupt files; try rebuilding the map file.
0x01	Illegal command. This shouldn't happen.
0x02	Address mark not found. This usually indicates a media problem. Try again several times.
0x03	Write-protected disk. This shouldn't happen.
0x04	Sector not found. This typically indicates a geometry mismatch. If you're booting a raw-written disk image, verify whether it was created for disks with the same geometry as the one you're using. If you're booting from a SCSI disk, you should check whether LILO has obtained correct geometry data from the kernel or whether the contents of your /etc/lilo/disktab file correspond to the real disk geometry. Removing compact may help too.
0x06	Change line active. This should be a transient error. Try booting a second time.
0x08	DMA overrun. This shouldn't happen. Try booting again.
0x09	DMA attempt across 64KB boundary. This shouldn't happen. Try omitting the c option.
0x0C	Invalid media. This shouldn't happen and might be caused by a media error. Try booting again.
0x10	CRC error. A media error has been detected. Try booting several times, running the map installer a second time (to put the map file at some other physical location or to write good data over the bad spot), mapping out the bad sectors/tracks, and, if all else fails, replacing the media.
0x20	Controller error. This shouldn't happen.
0x40	Seek failure. This might be a media problem. Try booting again.
0x80	Disk timeout. The disk or the drive isn't ready. Either the media is bad or the disk isn't spinning. If you're booting from a floppy, you might not have closed the drive door. Otherwise, trying to boot again might help.

> **TIP**
>
> Read the README file in the LILO distribution for more excruciating details on LILO.

BOOTLIN

The BOOTLIN package is used for using DOS MBR to boot off the hard drive. To install this package, you must take the following steps:

1. From within Linux, copy a bootable kernel to your DOS partition.
2. Edit config.sys on the DOS partition to include two files: BOOT.SYS and BOOTLIN.SYS. The README files for these packages tell you how.
3. Reboot.

Now when you reboot, the BOOT.SYS and BOOTLIN.SYS files will boot into Linux for you.

To get back to running only DOS, remove the BOOTLIN.SYS and BOOT.SYS from your config.sys file.

The disadvantage of this approach is that you are limited to having DOS on your hard drive. What a repulsive thought. Ugh.

Restoring the MBR

If you want to restore the MBR to the original DOS MBR, you can use the following procedure:

1. Boot from a DOS floppy.
2. Run fdisk /MBR from the DOS prompt. (You can also use the command SYS C:.)
3. Reboot.

Summary

In this chapter we covered the topic of installing, configuring, and using LILO. We also covered some of the basic errors you can face and how to set up LILO using the liloconfig utility. The information you have learnt from this topic should get you started in setting up LILO to boot Linux on your machine off the hard drive.

Odds and Ends

5

*by Kamran
Husain*

of any packages by using the spacebar. Press Enter when you are done or select the Cancel button if you want to bail out now.

The *installpkg* Utility

The `installpkg` utility creates `*.tgz` packages for distributing Linux files. This program has four modes of operation:

- `installpkg package_name`. By itself, it will install the `*.tgz` package you specified in the system. For example, `installpkg flex.tgz` will install `flex` on your system for you.
- `installpkg -warn package_name`. This will not do the installation process, but simply tells you what it's about to do.
- `installpkg -r package_name`. This recursively installs the files in the root directory from your current directory.
- `installpkg -m package_name`. This will make a package for you given all the files in the directory you happen to execute this is in.

Information about all of the installed packages on your system is stored in `/var/adm/packages`. Any related script files are stored in `/var/adm/scripts`.

The `removepkg` utility is used to remove packages that are listed in the `/var/adm/packages` directory. There is a `-warn` option that tells you what files will be removed but are not actually removed yet. Do not use the `removepkg` utility unless you are absolutely sure that the files in this package are not used elsewhere.

Generating a New Kernel

You will have to install a new kernel if:

- After installation, the Linux kernel does not have the features that the boot disk kernel had. For example, when you used the boot disk, you could access your CD-ROM, but the kernel on the hard disk does not recognize it!
- You want to add more features to the kernel. See Chapter 52, "Working with the Kernel."
- The kernel Linux installed for you is very big and you want a leaner, meaner kernel that uses less memory.

To reboot after installation, you have to compile a custom kernel for your hardware. Follow these steps:

1. If you haven't installed the C compiler and kernel source, do that.
2. Use the `bootkernel` disk you created at the time you installed Linux. At the LILO prompt, enter `mount root=/dev/hda1`. Ignore any error messages as the system starts up.
3. Change to `root`.
4. Go to `/usr/src/linux`.

5. Run the command `make config`.

6. Choose your drivers and so on.

7. These four commands will build and install the new kernel to work with LILO:

```
# make dep
# make clean
# make zlilo
# rdev -R /newkernel 1
```

Setting the Default Video Mode

You don't have to recompile the kernel to set the default video mode. Just use `rdev` with the `-v` switch to set the video mode in the kernel (either on your hard drive or on your boot floppy). For example, to change the kernel in `/vmlinuz` to prompt for the video mode on bootup, type the following:

```
rdev -v /vmlinuz -3
```

To change the kernel on your boot floppy, type

```
rdev -v /dev/fd0 {video-mode}
```

The valid video-mode options for the kernel are:

-3 Prompt the user for a response every time
-2 Extended VGA
-1 Normal VGA

The `rdev` program resides in `/sbin`. `rdev` is very handy and also is used to set the root and swap partitions, ramdisk size, and more in a compiled kernel. It means you don't have to recompile the kernel to make these changes. Use `rdev -?` for a list of options.

Accessing DOS Files

You can always mount the DOS directories and disks to get to DOS files. There is a set of tools called `mtools` that expedites this procedure. Look at the man pages for a complete description of this handy toolset. The following commands are available for Linux:

`mattrib`	Changes MS-DOS file attribute flags
`mcd`	Changes MS-DOS directory.
`mcopy`	Copies MS-DOS files to/from UNIX.
`mdel`	Deletes an MS-DOS file.
`mdir`	Displays an MS-DOS directory.
`mformat`	Adds an MS-DOS file system to a low-level formatted diskette.
`mlabel`	Makes an MS-DOS volume label.
`mmd`	Makes an MS-DOS subdirectory.

mrd	Removes an MS-DOS subdirectory.
mread	Low-level reads (copy) an MS-DOS file to UNIX.
mren	Renames an existing MS-DOS file.
mtype	Displays the contents of an MS-DOS file.
Mwrite	Low-level writes (copy) a UNIX file to MS-DOS.
mtools	A public domain collection of programs that enable UNIX systems to read, write, and manipulate files on an MS-DOS file system (typically a disk). Each program attempts to emulate the MS-DOS equivalent command.

Configuring *mtools*

An entry in the file /etc/mtools contains the following fields: drive, device, fat, cylinders, heads, sectors, and offset. Two examples of entries from /etc/mtools are

```
A /dev/fd0 12 80 2 15
C /dev/hda1 16 0 0 0
```

which define the DOS disk in drive A as accessible through the device /dev/fd0, having a 12-bit FAT, 80 cylinders, 2 heads, and 15 sectors per track; DOS disk in drive C is accessible through the device /dev/hda1, has a 16-bit FAT, and its geometry is simply that of the hard disk where it lives. The last three numbers can be zero if you wish; this enables mtools to try to figure out the disk's geometry itself, and perhaps to fail. A 12-bit FAT is common for floppies but might occur in small hard-disk partitions. A 16-bit FAT is common for hard disks.

This is an extract of my /etc/mtools file:

```
A /dev/fd0 12 0 0 0     # 3.5  1.4 Meg (autodetect)
B /dev/fd1 12 0 0 0     # 5.25 1.2 Meg (autodetect)
C /dev/hda1 16 0 0 0    # 1st partition of my Disk
```

There are two detailed README files in the mtools.n2 distribution. These files treat compiling and using mtools. There is a file README.mtools that treats only using mtools, which is a part of the MCC interim version of Linux.

> **TIP**
>
> If you want to get to the MS-DOS files the hard way, you can use
>
> ```
> mount -t msdos /dev/hda1 /msdos
> ```
>
> to mount the partition /dev/hda1 as an MS-DOS file system on the directory /msdos.

Handling Multiple CD-ROMs

Use the following shell script to mount the CD-ROM drive:

```
#
# This should be run while root"
```

```
# uncomment the next line to see what's happening
echo "Execute:  mount -t iso9660 /dev/cdrom /cdrom"
#
mount -t iso9660 /dev/cdrom /cdrom
```

> **CAUTION**
>
> Don't pull the CD-ROM out if it's already mounted; use umount /cdrom before swapping disks.

Identifying Bad Blocks on Your Hard Disk

Unfortunately, the -c option on mkefs does not work. The mkefs program cannot detect bad blocks on a hard drive. So if you create a file system over a part of your hard drive with bad blocks, things will eventually go wrong. What you need is a "bad block list" (in a file); use the -l option on mkefs so it will flag those blocks when making a file system.

> **WARNING**
>
> Do not check for bad blocks on a mounted system. Doing a check on a mounted file system will cause irreparable damage and/or loss of data. Unmount the file system first. If you have to check on the root file system, boot off floppy disk, unmount the file system, and then check for bad blocks.

mke2fs and mkxfs correctly flag bad blocks, so this only applies to mkfs and mkefs. This is also only needed for older RLL and MFM drives. SCSI and IDE drives have bad block logic on board, so you are safe there.

How do you generate a bad block list? As this is only needed for older drives and older file system types (such as Minix and extfs). Your best bet is to use mke2fs or mkxfs anyway.

Patching the Kernel

This section contains brief information from the README file in the tar file called lmscd0.4.tar.gz. This tar file has the patches for installing an alpha driver to the kernel. The purpose of this section is to provide you with enough information on how to patch your kernel with updates as they arrive in the Internet archives.

Obviously, each patch will contain its own specific information and instructions. However, you can get an idea of what is involved in applying patches to a kernel. The tar file contains these files: lmscd0.4.diff and a README file.

> **CAUTION**
>
> You MUST read the README file in detail when you download this file. The driver is in development, and the README file will contain more up-to-date infor-mation.

> **CAUTION**
>
> This driver supports neither 205MS drives, nor 206 drives, or any configuration differing from CM250 HA with a 205 drive.

The lmscd0.4 package is an experimental driver for the LMS/Philips CD-ROM CM 205 connected to the CM 250 adapter. It has several enhancements and speed ups versus the 0.2 version of the driver. The 0.4 version runs stable on many machines and is designed for Linux 1.2. It supports the kernel mechanism for allocating I/Os and IRQs.

> **NOTE**
>
> There is no audio support for the Philips driver.

Unpacking and Applying the Patches

First unpack the .tar.gz file. Now apply the changes into your kernel source using the patch command:

```
        # cd /usr/src/linux
# make mrproper
# zcat lmscd0.4.tar.gz ¦ gtar xfv -
# patch -p1 <lmscd0.4.diff (or the needed patch)
```

You should see no error messages. If you do, either fix them manually or accept the fact that this driver will not work.

It also has debugging information, which can be compiled into the driver. By default, most of it is turned off. To turn on some of the debug messages, change the values of DLEVEL, CLEVEL, and DFUNC.

DLEVEL defines the four debugging levels:

#define DLEVEL 0	Prints very few messages.
#define DLEVEL 1	Prints some messages whenever an error occurs.
#define DLEVEL 2	Prints most actions taken that are running.
#define DLEVEL 3	Very verbose.

CLEVEL supports the following levels:

```
#define CLEVEL 0        Turns all integrity checks off.
#define CLEVEL 1        Does a lot of tests that really should not fail.
#define CLEVEL 2        Reports strange bugs only.
```

I did get this driver to work with an old Philips drive; however, it did not work with a newer version of a 205 drive.

Recompile Your Kernel

You have to configure your kernel again to ensure that the CD-ROM driver is really included. Type the following commands as root:

```
# cd /usr/src/linux
# make mrproper
# make config
# make depend
# make zImage
```

When asked about the configuration, answer yes to the questions about the "LMS/Philips CD-ROM driver support" and the "ISO9660 CD-ROM file system support." After "make depend," use your favorite options to compile a kernel. For further information, such as installing your newly compiled kernel, refer to the FAQ.

> **TIP**
>
> When compiling the kernel, if you have 8MB RAM or less, get out of the X Window system. It will notably, perhaps drastically, reduce your compile time.

While running make config, answer the LMS question about your hardware configuration with Y. Also, enter the correct number (3, 4, 5, or 6) for the interrupt number. Other interrupts are also allowed. For the I/O address, enter the index number and not the port address itself. If you do not enter 2 (0x300), 3 (0x310), or 4 (0x330), the default is 0x340.

After recompiling and installing your new kernel, you have to reboot. To access the drive, you have to create an entry for it in the /dev file. Type the following lines:

```
# mknod /dev/lmscd b 24 0
# chown root:disk /dev/lmscd
# chmod 444 /dev/lmscd
```

To mount a disc in the CD-ROM use the command:

```
mkdir /cdrom
mount -t iso9660 /dev/lmscd /cdrom
```

When changing a disc in the CD-ROM, always unmount it first, then press the eject button. Use the following command to unmount:

```
umount -t /dev/lmscd
```

Please contact the author, Kai Petzke at `wpp@marie.physik.tu-berlin.de` for compliments, bug reports, and comments.

Adding New File Systems

Although this may not seem to be the appropriate place in the book for the topic of creating file systems to expand your files system space, it is. After you have worked with Linux for a while, you will want extra space for all the files you accumulate. If you are not familiar with the way files work in Linux, you might want to familiarize yourself with Chapter 8, "The Linux File System."

In most cases, you will want to expand the /usr partition to allow for more programs. Most programs wind up under the /usr partition by default and it's easy to run out of room. A key point to keep in mind is that you do not have to have your entire file structure on the same drive or under the / (root) directory. The major restriction is that /:, /sbin, /bin, /lib, /dev, and /conf have to exist on the root drive for Linux to boot. Any other file systems, including /usr, can be mounted afterwards.

Let's start with the example of adding a new physical drive to your system. You can just as easily extend this example to that of creating new partitions on your existing drive and creating a file system on them.

My example here deals with the hard drive on an IDE controller, so my first drive is addressed as /dev/hda and the second as /dev/hdb. If you have a SCSI controller, you will have /dev/sda and /dev/sdb for the first and second drives, respectively.

You have to do the next operation as root, so read the instructions here carefully and be careful when deleting files. The usual check and balance system of confirming permissions on deleting important files does not apply to the superuser.

Create a new partition on your new disk as we did in Chapter 3, "Installing Linux." You can run fdisk /dev/hdb to run fdisk directly on the second partition. As a summary, you will use the n command to create a new partition, specify the size in +Megabytes, and assign a type 83 for Linux native type of partition. After you have created the new partition, it's a good idea to reboot. Most of the documentation I have read on Linux says that it's not necessary, but I am of the old school of thought of being safe and not sorry.

On your return from the reboot, you will create the extended file system with the mke2fs command. The extended file system is the preferred file system because it allows for clean boots without having to worry about a file system check every time you reboot. The syntax for this command to create a file system is

```
mke2fs -c partition size-in-blocks
```

Therefore, to create your new file system with 480,000 blocks, you would use the command:

```
# mke2fs -c /dev/hdb1 4800000
```

where the /dev/hdb1 is the first partition on drive B, the -c flag checks the newly created blocks for errors, and the size is 480,000 blocks. Be prepared for an onslaught of messages about inodes, blocks, and so forth. This process may take a while, so be patient.

Now you can mount this new file system with the mount command. First, create an empty directory in your root directory, let's call it /data.

```
# cd /
# mkdir data
# mount -t ext2 /dev/hdb1 /data
```

The mount command shown above will mount the file system in the second drive as /data. The -t option specifies what type of file system exists on the new partition. You can now copy files into this new /data partition. Now you can use this partition for extra space.

The problem is that this mount is valid only for the duration while your machine is running. If you want this to be mounted automatically at boot time, you should edit the /etc/fstab file and add the following line:

```
/dev/hdb1    /data ext2  defaults
```

The line will cause init, the boot process for Linux, to mount the /dev/hdb1 partition on to the /data directory as an extended file system using the default mount parameters.

Linux Loadable Modules

The Linux kernel (since version 1.2.0) also supports loadable modules. Using loadable modules enables you to build a minimal kernel and add or remove modules to this kernel without requiring a kernel rebuild. A module could be support for a kernel function; for example, the Point to Point Protocol (PPP) support module is a loadable module. Only a few loadable modules exist for the Linux kernels at this time, including the sysv, ppp, or slhc (required for ppp) modules.

To see what modules exist in your system use the lsmod command. To install a module, use the insmod command. Some modules may require other modules. To check the dependencies, use the depmod command. To install a module (and its dependant modules) use the depmod command.

Summary

It's hard to summarize this chapter except to say that this has been a grab-bag of all the things that did not fit anywhere else.

You should now be able to administer the packages on your system, generate a new kernel if necessary, and set the default video mode of your display. This is your first step toward being the superuser you have always dreamed of becoming.

You can still access your old favorite DOS files with the `mtools` package and configure it to suit your system.

In most of this chapter, though, we covered some topics of installing, configuring, and using Linux. These topics did not fit anywhere else in the book, but are important enough to be included here.

PART

IN THIS PART

Using Linux

Getting Started with Linux

6

by Ed Treijs

IN THIS CHAPTER

Congratulations! Now that you have successfully installed Linux, you can start using it. In this chapter we will look at the steps you need to take to begin working with Linux, including the following:

- Starting and stopping Linux
- Logging in and out
- Creating a new user with `adduser`
- Changing your password
- Using virtual terminals
- Displaying system users with `who`

Starting (and Stopping!) Your Linux System

Depending on the setup you chose during Linux installation and configuration, either Linux starts automatically when you power on your computer, or it requires you to type something (such as `Linux`) to specify that you want to boot Linux.

As your Linux system starts up, you see quite a few Linux initialization messages scroll through your screen. When Linux has completed its startup, you should see the following prompt:

```
Welcome to Linux 1.2.13.
darkstar login:
```

WARNING

A Linux system must always be shut down properly. Improper shutdown, such as simply turning off your system, can cause serious damage to your Linux system! When you are finished using your Linux system, you must shut it down properly, as described in the next section. If you start to boot Linux, and then change your mind, you should let the system start up fully and then follow the shutdown procedure.

Because you know how to start Linux, it's even more important to know how to shut it down properly. Like many UNIX systems, if Linux is not powered down properly, damage to files can result. The easiest way to ensure a proper shutdown is to press the Ctrl, Alt, and Delete keys simultaneously. (This is the famous Ctrl-Alt-Delete "three-finger salute" used in DOS.)

Pressing Ctrl-Alt-Delete causes a number of advisory messages and Linux shutdown messages to be displayed. You must wait until the Linux shutdown procedure has finished, at which point your monitor shows the initial "power-on" screen, before turning your computer off.

What's This About "Logging In?"

Linux waits for a login. A login is simply the name that you supply to Linux to identify yourself to the operating system. Linux keeps track of which names are permitted to log in or access the system, and only allows valid users to have access.

> **NOTE**
>
> If you supplied a name to your system when installing Linux, the system name is used at the prompt. In the login shown earlier, the system has been called `darkstar`. The system name enables you to identify your machine to others when using networks or modem connections. Don't worry if you didn't name your system yet, because you can change the system's name at any time.

Every login name on the system is unique. Normally, a password is assigned to each login, too. This secret password is like the identification number you use with your bank card to prove that you really are who you say you are. Also, the things you can do with your login—the login's privileges— are controlled by Linux; different logins have different levels of privileges.

> **NOTE**
>
> Usually, login names reflect a person's real name. Although you can't have two identically named logins on your system, you can easily create logins for users with the same (real) name by having one or two characters different. So, for example, the login names `suej` and `suek` are treated by Linux as completely separate logins.
>
> Conversely, there is no reason that one human being (for instance, yourself) can't have two, three, or a dozen login names. In fact, because you will be the system administrator of your Linux system, you will have one or more administrative logins, and one or more regular user logins.

At the login prompt, try typing your name, your dog's name, or any other random name that occurs to you. None of these are valid logins (at least not yet). The system asks you for a password; it won't matter what you type, so just press Enter or type a random string of characters. Because the logins are not valid on the system, Linux won't let you in. It displays the message `Login incorrect` to tell you that either the name or the password you entered is not valid.

The only valid login on your Linux system after installation is the most powerful and dangerous login Linux offers: `root`. In the section "Creating a New Login," later in this chapter, we will create a safe login for you to use. This login can have your name, your dog's name, or whatever else you choose.

> **NOTE**
>
> The login prompt is actually produced by a program called `login` whose only task is to accept your user ID and password, verify it, and then display a message preventing your access or letting you through to the next program that starts your user session.

Why You Shouldn't Use the *root* Login

You will have to use the root login from time to time. Some things simply cannot be done on the Linux system without logging in as root. You should not, however, use the root login as your regular login. This is especially true if you are exploring the system, poking around, and trying out new commands that may not do what you thought they would!

Linux, as you already know, is a multiuser, multitasking operating system. Multiuser means that several people can be using Linux at the same time (of course, you have to add some additional terminals to your system, or it will get very crowded around the keyboard). Multitasking means that Linux can do more than one thing at a time. For example, you can spell-check a document while downloading information from some remote system. (Multiuser implies multitasking, because all users must be able to do their own work at the same time.) Linux, therefore, is very good at juggling all these tasks, keeping them from interfering with each other, and providing safeguards so that you cannot damage the system or another user's work.

WARNING

The root login does not restrict you in any way. With one simple command, issued either on purpose or by accident, you can destroy your entire Linux installation. For this reason, use the root login only when necessary. Avoid experimenting with commands when you do log in as root.

When you log in as root, you *become* the system. The root login is also sometimes called the *superuser* login, and with good reason. To use an analogy, instead of being a passenger on an airplane, you suddenly have all the privileges of the flight crew, the mechanics, and the cabin crew. "Hmm, what does this do?" becomes an extremely dangerous phrase when logged in as root.

One of the oldest stories in UNIX lore tells of new users who log in as root and, in ten keystrokes, destroy their system completely and irrevocably. But if you're careful to follow the steps given here, and stop and take a moment to think about the commands you are giving, none of the "How many new users does it take to nuke a system?" jokes will apply to you!

NOTE

System administrator is another term you will see often. A *system administrator* is the actual person who sets up and maintains the Linux system. The amount of work involved in system administration varies from system to system. A full-time system administrator may be required in an office for powerful machines that have many users, peripheral units such as printers and tape drives, and are connected to a network. Your Linux system will not require that level of dedication!

System administration, because it deals with sensitive matters such as creating or deleting logins, requires superuser privileges. These privileges are provided by the root login. So, the system administrator is an actual person wielding superuser powers gained by logging in as root.

Your First Login

After all the cautions about using the root login, we're going to have you log in as root. Because root is the only authorized login on a newly installed Linux system, this is unavoidable. Also, we will be performing a couple of important procedures that require root privileges. However, after this first login, we will create a user ID that can prevent accidental damage to the operating system.

At the login prompt

```
darkstar login:
```

type

```
root
```

and press the Enter key. After installation, the root login has no password, so you are not prompted for one.

> **NOTE**
>
> Linux is *case-sensitive* (as are all UNIX versions). A capital R is, to Linux, a completely different letter from a lowercase r. When you type Linux commands, you must use the proper case or Linux will not understand them. The majority of Linux commands are typed in lowercase. This includes the login root; if you type Root or rOoT, Linux will reject the login.
>
> There is a curious exception, though. If you type the login IN ALL CAPITALS, the system will accept it—but from then on, everything on your screen will be in capital letters! This is left over from the days when some terminals only had uppercase letters. Although these terminals are now all gone or in museums, the login program retains this historical curiosity.

After you have logged in as root, the system starts up a user session for you. At this point you should see the following on your screen:

```
darkstar login: root
Last login: Sun Dec 11 17:26:18 on tty1
Linux 1.2.13.
You have mail.

If it's Tuesday, this must be someone else's fortune.
darkstar:~#
```

Linux tells you when the login for this user was last recorded (although this information may not appear the very first time you log in), and then provides you with some version information. Linux also tells you that this login has a mail message waiting to be read. Finally, if games were installed on your system, Linux gives you a witty saying or aphorism.

It is always good practice to scan the line that starts with Last login, and check that the time given is correct. This is especially important if your Linux system is accessed by other users or connected

Quite often you find yourself doing something, perhaps in a long and complicated program, and realize that you should have done something else first. Flip to another virtual terminal and do whatever it is.

Another handy use of virtual terminals is when, through experimentation or otherwise, your screen locks up or starts typing in strange symbols. From a different virtual terminal, you can try to fix things, or restart the system if necessary.

Linux also comes with a very powerful multitasking windowing environment called X. Installing and running X Window systems is described in Chapter 21, "Installing X Window on Linux."

Commands and Programs

"Run the who command" and "Run who" are much more common ways of saying "Type who at the prompt and press Enter." We will use the shorter expressions wherever their meaning is clear. Sometimes people familiar with Linux drop the word "run," so that one user might tell another, "I tried who but didn't see anything unusual." It's understood by the context that when they "tried who," they actually ran it.

Something else you will notice if you are reading carefully is that there seem to be both Linux *programs* and Linux *commands*. A command is what you type at the shell prompt. For this reason, the combination of the shell prompt and what you type after it is often called a *command line*. When you press the Enter key, Linux takes the command you've entered and tries to perform it. The Linux system has built-in responses to some commands; for other commands it finds the appropriately named program on your hard disk and executes that program.

In the strictest sense, then, the command is what you type, and the program is what performs your command. However, very simple programs with straightforward results, such as who, are often referred to as commands, although there is actually a who program on your hard disk. More complicated programs, usually interactive such as adduser, or open-ended such as a text editor, are called programs. So you might hear one experienced user tell another, "The adduser program worked fine. I tried the who command 15 minutes later and the new user had logged in already."

Summary

In this chapter, we assigned a password to the root login and created a new user ID to be used in the next few chapters. We tried out Linux multitasking, and we learned some useful Linux terminology tips that will serve us well in the future (we will try to avoid seeing too many error messages, though). At this point, you can either ensure that you have logged out of all virtual terminals, or move on to the following chapters.

In the next two chapters, we will become more familiar with using Linux. In Chapter 7, "Basic Linux Commands and Utilities," we try out a variety of Linux commands as we exercise our Linux muscles. In Chapter 8, we learn more about how Linux stores its programs and data, and explore some of the interesting terrain on your hard drive.

Basic Linux Commands and Utilities

7

by Ed Treijs

IN THIS CHAPTER

In this chapter, we will discover the following:

- How to modify the basic function of Linux commands by using command options
- How to run two or more Linux commands in tandem by using input and output redirection
- How to use parameters, such as filenames, with Linux commands
- How to read and understand the notational shorthand used in Linux and UNIX documentation
- How to use Linux online man pages and help facilities
- How to use wildcards that fill in for one or more filenames
- How to check your environment variables
- How to list processes running on the Linux system
- How to kill processes
- How to temporarily become another user
- How to use grep (and understand what grep means!)

How Linux Commands Work

Most Linux commands are very flexible. When you enter a Linux command, there are several ways to tailor the basic command to your specific needs. We will look at the two main ways used to modify the effect of a command:

- Specifying or redirecting a command's input and output
- Using command options

A simple way to picture what a Linux command does is to imagine that it's a black box that is part of an assembly line. Items come down a conveyor belt, enter the black box, get processed in some way, come out of the black box, and are taken away on another conveyor belt. Command options let you fine-tune the basic process happening inside the black box. Command redirection lets you specify which conveyor belt will supply the black box with items and which conveyor belt will take away the resulting products.

Once you understand how redirection and command options work, you will be able to (at least in principle) use any Linux or UNIX command. This is because UNIX was based on a few simple design principles. Commands, therefore, should work in consistent ways. Of course, UNIX has grown and changed over the years, and the design principles can sometimes get buried under all the changes. But they still make up the foundation, so that UNIX-based systems such as Linux are quite coherent and consistent in how they work.

> **TIP**
>
> Pressing Ctrl-U at any point, right up to before you press Enter, lets you clear everything you've typed on the command line. You can use this whenever you spot an error at the very beginning of your typing, or when you decide you don't want to run a particular command after all. You can also use the Backspace key to "back up" by erasing characters (in fact, it can be almost a reflex action), but it's usually faster to just erase the whole command line and start again.
>
> Perhaps the most powerful keys to use at the command prompt are the arrow keys. The left and right arrows move the cursor non-destructively. If you make a typo early in the line, you can left-arrow your way to the character and type in a correction. Additionally, the up and down arrows enable you to jump through a list of the last several commands used (similar to DOS's DOSKEY utility).

Command Options

You can use command options to fine-tune the actions of a Linux command. Quite often, a Linux command will do almost—but not quite—what you want it to do. Instead of making you learn a second command, Linux lets you modify the basic, or default, actions of the command by using options.

The ls command is an excellent, and useful, example of a command that has a great many options. The ls command lists the files found on the Linux system's hard drive. This sounds simple enough, doesn't it? Try entering the command

```
darkstar:~$ ls
darkstar:~$
```

Well, nothing much seemed to happen.

Now try typing ls -a. Type it exactly as listed. The space between ls and -a is necessary, and there must be no space between the - and the a.

```
darkstar:~$ ls -a
./             .bash_history  .less          .term/
../            .kermrc        .lessrc
```

What you have done is modified what ls does by adding a command option—in this case, -a. By default, ls lists only files whose names don't begin with a period. However, -a tells ls to list all files, even ones that begin with a period. (These are usually special files created for you by Linux.) At present, all the files in your directory start with a period, so ls by itself does not list any files; you must add -a to see the files you have at present.

The ls command has many more options. You can use more than one option at a time. For example, try typing ls -al:

```
darkstar:~$ ls -al
total 10
drwxr-xr-x   3 fido     users        1024 Dec 21 22:11 ./
```

```
drwxr-xr-x   6 root      root         1024 Dec 14 01:39 ../
-rw-r--r--   1 fido      users         333 Dec 21 22:11 .bash_history
-rw-r--r--   1 fido      users         163 Dec  7 14:31 .kermrc
-rw-r--r--   1 fido      users          34 Jun  6 1993 .less
-rw-r--r--   1 fido      users         114 Nov 23 1993 .lessrc
drwxr-xr-x   2 fido      users        1024 Dec  7 13:36 .term/
```

You now get a listing with many more details about the files. (These will be explained in Chapter 8, "The Linux File System.") The l option can be used by itself; ls -l will give detailed descriptions of files that don't begin with a period. Sometimes filenames are so long they don't fit on a single line. Linux simply wraps the remainder to the next line.

<hr>

NOTE

Strictly speaking, the dash (-) is not part of the command option. The dash simply tells Linux to understand each letter immediately following it as a command option. There *must* be a space before the dash, and there *must not* be a space between the dash and the letter or letters making up the command option. There *must* be a space after the command option if anything else is to be entered on the command line after it.

You can type more than one command option after the dash, as we did with ls -al. In this case, we are specifying both the a and the l options. The order you specify options in usually doesn't matter; ls -al will give the same results as ls -la. Combining options doesn't work with all Linux commands, and then only with those that use a single letter to specify each option.

Multiple options can also be specified individually, with each option preceded by a dash and separated from other options by spaces—for example, ls -a -l. This is usually done only when a particular option requires a further parameter.

<hr>

By default, ls lists files in alphabetical order. Sometimes you might be more interested in when a file was created or last modified. The t option tells ls to sort files by date instead of alphabetically by filename, showing the newest files first. Therefore, typing ls -alt gives

```
darkstar:~$ ls -alt
total 10
drwxr-xr-x   3 fido      users        1024 Jan  2 13:48 ./
-rw-r--r--   1 fido      users         333 Dec 21 22:11 .bash_history
drwxr-xr-x   6 root      root         1024 Dec 14 01:39 ../
-rw-r--r--   1 fido      users         163 Dec  7 14:31 .kermrc
drwxr-xr-x   2 fido      users        1024 Dec  7 13:36 .term/
-rw-r--r--   1 fido      users         114 Nov 23 1993 .lessrc
-rw-r--r--   1 fido      users          34 Jun  6 1993 .less
```

The r option tells ls to produce a reverse output. This is often used with the t option. The following is an example of what you might get if you entered ls -altr:

```
darkstar:~$ ls -altr
total 10
-rw-r--r--   1 fido      users          34 Jun  6 1993 .less
```

```
-rw-r--r--   1 fido     users         114 Nov 23  1993 .lessrc
drwxr-xr-x   2 fido     users        1024 Dec  7 13:36 .term/
-rw-r--r--   1 fido     users         163 Dec  7 14:31 .kermrc
drwxr-xr-x   6 root     root         1024 Dec 14 01:39 ../
-rw-r--r--   1 fido     users         333 Dec 21 22:11 .bash_history
drwxr-xr-x   3 fido     users        1024 Jan  2 13:48 ./
```

Many other options can be used with ls, although we have now tried the most commonly used ones. The important thing to remember is that you can usually customize a Linux command by using one or more command options.

NOTE

As with basic Linux commands, case is important! For instance, ls has an R option (*recursive:* show files in subdirectories, too) that gives much different results from the r option.

TIP

You can think of a as the "all files" option, l as the "long list" option, t as the "sort by time" option, r as the "reverse sort" option, and so on. In fact, most options in Linux are *mnemonic*—the option letter stands for a word or phrase. Some option letters mean the same thing in many different Linux commands. For instance, v often means *verbose*—in other words, "Give me lots of detail."

However, do not assume that, on any unfamiliar command, certain options will work in the "usual" way! For instance, r is the recursive option for many Linux commands; however, in the case of ls, reverse sort is more commonly used, and therefore it gets the easier-to-type lowercase r, while recursive is left with the capital R. It might seem like not much extra effort to press the Shift key to get the capital letter, but try typing a string of four or five options, one of which is capitalized!

NOTE

You can easily find out which options are available for any Linux command by using the man command. See the section "The Linux Man Pages" later in this chapter.

Other Parameters

Linux commands often use parameters that are not actual command options. These parameters, such as filenames or directories, are *not* preceded by a dash.

For instance, by default `ls` lists the files in your current directory. You can, however, tell `ls` to list the files in any other directory simply by adding the directory to the command line. For instance, `ls /bin` will list everything in the `/bin` directory. This can be combined with command options, so that `ls -l /bin` gives you detailed listings of the files in `/bin`. Try this. You will be impressed by the number of files in the `/bin` directory!

You can also specify `ls` to list information about any particular file by entering its filename. For instance, `ls -la .lessrc` gives detailed information only about the `.lessrc` file.

Input and Output Redirection

Many Linux commands let you specify which file or directory they are to act upon, as we saw with the example `ls -l /bin` earlier.

You can also "pipe" the output from a command so that it becomes another command's input. This is done by typing two or more commands separated by the ¦ character. (This character normally is found on the same key as the \ character. You must hold down the Shift key or you will get \ instead of ¦). The ¦ character means "Use the output from the previous command as the input for the next command." Therefore, typing `command_1¦command_2` does both commands, one after the other, before giving you the results.

Using our assembly-line metaphor, we are processing items through two black boxes instead of just one. When we use piping, it's like hooking up the first command's output conveyor belt to become the input conveyor belt for the second command.

> **TIP**
>
> Although Linux doesn't care whether ¦ is set off by spaces, if `command_1 ¦ command_2` is easier for you to read and understand than `command_1¦command_2`, by all means use spaces around ¦.

You will have noticed that the output of `ls -l /bin` is many lines long, so that much of the information scrolls off the screen before you can read it. You can pipe this output to a formatting program called `more`, which displays information in screen-sized chunks. When you enter `ls -l /bin ¦ more`, you will see the following:

```
darkstar:~$ ls -l /bin ¦ more
total 1611
-rwxr-xr-x   1 root     bin          1248 Sep 17 04:25 arch*
-rwxr-xr-x   1 root     bin        295940 Sep  5 01:45 bash*
-rwxr-xr-x   1 root     bin          4840 Nov 24  1993 cat*
-rwxr-xr-x   1 root     bin          9220 Jul 20 12:06 chgrp*
-rwxr-xr-x   1 root     bin         13316 Jul 20 12:06 chmod*
-rwxr-xr-x   1 root     bin         13316 Jul 20 12:06 chown*
lrwxrwxrwx   1 root     root            17 Dec  7 13:37 compress -> /usr/bin/comp
ress*
-rwxr-xr-x   1 root     bin         21508 Jul 20 12:06 cp*
-rwxr-xr-x   1 root     bin         41988 May  1  1994 cpio*
lrwxrwxrwx   1 root     root             4 Dec  7 13:40 csh -> tcsh*
```

```
-rwxr-xr-x  1 root     bin          5192 Nov 24  1993 cut*
-rwxr-xr-x  1 root     bin         19872 Mar 23  1994 date*
-rwxr-xr-x  1 root     bin         17412 Jul 20 12:06 dd*
-rwxr-xr-x  1 root     bin         13316 Jul 20 12:06 df*
-rwxr-xr-x  1 root     bin         66564 Jun  9  1994 dialog*
-rwxr-xr-x  1 root     bin          1752 Sep 17 04:25 dmesg*
lrwxrwxrwx  1 root     root            8 Dec  7 13:37 dnsdomainname -> hostname
*
-rwxr-xr-x  1 root     bin         13316 Jul 20 12:06 du*
-rwxr-xr-x  1 root     bin          3312 Mar 23  1994 echo*
-rwxr-xr-x  1 root     bin         36684 May  4  1994 ed*
-rwxr-xr-x  1 root     bin           326 Mar 23  1994 false*
--More--
```

The --More-- at the bottom of the screen tells you that there's more text to come. To go to the next screen of text, press the spacebar. Every time you press the spacebar, more displays another screenful of text. When the last screenful of text has been displayed, more returns you to the Linux prompt.

TIP

The more command can do many other things. For instance, to move back one screen at a time, type b for "back." Another useful command is q for "quit." This lets you leave immediately, without having to go through all the remaining screens of text.

While in more, type h for "help." This will list the commands available within more.

NOTE

The Linux system sometimes uses the command less instead of more. One difference you will notice is that, unlike more, less requires you to type q to return to the command line, even if you're at the end of the text to be displayed. This might seem cumbersome, but it prevents you from accidentally exiting the program by pressing the spacebar once too often.

The name less is a play on more. Originally, less was designed to have many features that more lacked. The version of more included in your Linux system has most of these features, however.

The Linux man program, discussed later, uses less to display text. Most other UNIX systems use more by default. Don't get confused. Remember to type q to exit from less!

Another thing you can do in Linux is to send output to a file instead of the screen. There are many different reasons why you might want to do this. You might want to save a "snapshot" of a command's output as it was at a certain time, or you might want to save a command's output for further examination. You might also want to save the output from a command that takes a very long time to run, and so on.

To send output to a file, use the > symbol (found above the period on your keyboard). For instance, you can place the output of the ls -l /bin command into a file called test by typing `ls -l /bin > test`. Again, spaces around > are optional and not strictly necessary, but they do make the command much more readable.

If you now do an `ls` or `ls -l`, you will see that you've created a new file called `test` in your own directory.

To see the contents of a file, you can again use the `more` command. Just specify the name of the file you want to look at. In this case, you would type `more test`.

WARNING

Be careful! When you use >, you completely overwrite the previous contents of the file you specify to take the output (if that file existed). For example, if we already had a file called `test` in our directory, its old contents would be completely replaced by the output from `ls -l /bin`. Linux *will not* warn you that you are about to do this!

Be particularly careful if you're not in your usual directory, or if you're logged in as root. You could, for instance, accidentally clobber the Linux program `test`, which exists as a file named `test`—fortunately, not in the directory where we created our `test` file! It's a good idea to check if the output file already exists before using >. In our example, we could have typed `ls -l test` beforehand. If no information is displayed, the file does not exist.

You can specify that you want to add your output to the end of the file, rather than replace the file's contents, by using >>. Type `who >> test` to add the output of the `who` command to the end of the text already in the file `test`.

You can examine the results by using either `more` or `less` and paging through to the end of the file, or by using the Linux command `tail`, which displays the last few lines of the specified file. In this case, you would type `tail test` to see the last few lines of the file `test`. Try using `tail`!

NOTE

For a more detailed discussion of redirection and piping, see Chapter 10, "Using `bash`."

Notational Conventions Used to Describe Linux Commands

There is a set of accepted notational conventions used to describe, in a concise and consistent way, the correct syntax for any given Linux command. This specifies what options or parameters you must use, what options or parameters you can use or not use, and so on. Sometimes this set of conventions is used to give a complete and exhaustive listing of a command's syntax, showing every possible command and parameter. Sometimes it is used to make a particular example more general and the command's basic usage clearer.

If you remember the following five basic rules, you will be able, in principle, to understand the syntax of any Linux or UNIX command.

Six Basic Rules of Linux Notation

1. Any text standing by itself, and not within [ ], <>, or {}, must be typed exactly as shown.

2. Any text within square brackets ([ ]) is optional. You can type it or not type it. For instance, the syntax ls [-l] means you must type ls (per the first rule), while adding -l is optional, but not necessary. Do not type the square brackets themselves! In our example, type ls or ls -l. Don't type ls [-l].

3. Angle brackets (<>) and the text within them must be replaced by appropriate text (usually a name or value). The text within the brackets usually indicates the nature of the replacement. For instance, the syntax more *<filename>* means that you should replace *<filename>* with the name of the file you wish to examine using more. If you want to look at the file test, you would type more test. Remember, do not use the angle brackets when you actually type the command!

4. Curly braces ({}) indicate that you must choose one of the values given within the braces. The values are separated by ¦ (which in this case means *or*, not *pipe!*). For example, the syntax command -{a¦b} means you must enter either command -a or command -b.

5. An ellipsis (…) means "and so on." They are normally used with parameters such as filenames, as described later.

6. The sixth basic rule states that the brackets can be combined as necessary. For instance, you don't have to type a filename with the more command. This would be indicated as more [*<filename>*]. The outer set of square brackets makes the entire parameter optional. If you do decide to use the parameter, replace the inner set of angle brackets with the appropriate value. Because the more command enables one or more filenames to be specified, the syntax becomes more [*<filename>*…]. The ellipsis means you can have as many *<filenames>* as you wish.

Online Help Available in Linux

Linux has help facilities available online. If you forget the exact use of a command, or you're looking for the right command to use, the answer might be available straight from Linux. The two help facilities we will try out are the bash shell's help command, and the man command, which is available on almost all UNIX systems, including Linux.

NOTE

If you have not installed the man pages package, you should do so now. Although it is possible to get by without man pages, they are a very valuable resource for both novice and expert Linux users.

The Linux Man Pages

The "man" in "man pages" stands for "manual." (As usual, the creators of UNIX shortened a long but descriptive word to a shorter, cryptic one!) Typing man <command> lets you view the manual pages dealing with a particular command.

Try typing man passwd to see what the Linux manual has to say about the passwd command.

The general layout of a man page is as follows:

```
COMMAND(1)              Linux Programmer's Manual         COMMAND(1)

NAME
       command - summary of what command does

SYNOPSIS
       <complete syntax of command in the standard Linux form>

DESCRIPTION
       More verbose explanation of what "command" does.

OPTIONS
       Lists each available option with description of what it does

FILES
       lists files used by, or related to, command

SEE ALSO
       command_cousin(1), command_spouse(1), etc.

BUGS
       There are bugs in Linux commands??

AUTHOR
       J. S. Goobly (goobly@hurdly-gurdly.boondocks)

Linux 1.0               22 June 1994                      1
```

The man page for passwd is actually quite understandable. Be warned, however, that man pages are often written in a very formal and stylized way that sometimes bears little resemblance to English. This is done not to baffle people, but to cram a great deal of information into as short a description as possible.

For example, try man ls. Notice how many options are available for ls and how long it takes to explain them!

Although it can take practice (and careful reading!) to understand man pages, once you get used to them, the first thing you'll do when you encounter a strange command is call up the man page for that command.

Finding Keywords in Man Pages

Sometimes you know what you want to do, but you don't know which command you should use to do it. You can use the keyword option by typing man -k <keyword>. The man program will return the name of every command whose name entry (which includes a very brief description) contains that keyword.

For instance, you can search on manual:

```
darkstar:~$ man -k manual
man (1)                 - Format and display the on-line manual pages
whereis (1)             - Locate binary, manual, and or source for program
xman (1)                - Manual page display program for the X Window System
```

You have to be careful to specify your keyword well, though! Using directory as your keyword isn't too bad, but using file will give you many more entries than you will want to wade through.

NOTE

You might have noticed that commands seem to be followed by numbers in brackets, usually (1). This refers to the manual section. Back in the days when UNIX manuals came in printed, bound volumes, normal commands were in Section 1, files used by administrators were in Section 5, programming routines were described in Section 3, and so on.

Therefore, some man pages are not about commands at all, but rather about files or system calls used in Linux!

If a particular entry shows up in more than one section, man will show you the lowest-numbered entry by default. You can see higher-numbered entries by specifying the section number. For instance, Section 5 has a manual entry on the passwd file. To see this rather than the manual entry for the passwd command type man 5 passwd.

In general, man *<n>* *<entry>* will find the man page for *<entry>* in Section *<n>*.

The *bash* Shell *help* Facility

When you type a command at the prompt, the shell program takes what you've written, interprets it as necessary, and passes the result to the Linux operating system. Linux then performs the actions requested of it. Many Linux commands require Linux to find and start up a new program. However, the shell itself can perform a number of functions. These functions can be simple, often-used commands, so that the overhead of starting up separate programs is eliminated, or they can be facilities that make the shell environment friendlier and more useful. One of these facilities is the help command, which provides information on the bash shell's built-in functions.

Type help at the prompt. You will see at least some of the following:

```
GNU bash, version 1.14.15(1)
Shell commands that are defined internally. Type 'help' to see this list.
Type 'help name' to find out more about the function 'name'.
Use 'info bash' to find out more about the shell in general.

A star (*) next to a name means that the command is disabled.
```

```
%[DIGITS ¦ WORD] [&]              . [filename]
:                                [ arg... ]
alias [ name[=value] ... ]       bg [job_spec]
bind [-lvd] [-m keymap] [-f filena break [n]
builtin [shell-builtin [arg ...]] case WORD in [PATTERN [¦ PATTERN].
cd [dir]                         command [-pVv] [command [arg ...]]
continue [n]                     declare [-[frxi]] name[=value] ...
dirs [-l]                        echo [-neE] [arg ...]
enable [-n] [name ...]           eval [arg ...]
exec [ [-] file [redirection ...]] exit [n]
export [-n] [-f] [name ...] or exp fc [-e name] [-nlr] [first] [last
fg [job_spec]                    for NAME [in WORDS ... ;] do COMMA
function NAME { COMMANDS ; } or NA getopts optstring name [arg]
hash [-r] [name ...]             help [pattern ...]
history [n] [ [-awrn] [filename]] if COMMANDS; then COMMANDS; [elif
jobs [-lnp] [jobspec ...] ¦ jobs - kill [-s sigspec ¦ -sigspec] [pid
let arg [arg ...]                local name[=value] ...
logout                           popd [+n ¦ -n]
pushd [dir ¦ +n ¦ -n]            pwd
read [-r] [name ...]             readonly [-n] [-f] [name ...] or r
return [n]                       select NAME [in WORDS ... ;] do CO
set [—abefhknotuvxldHCP] [-o opti shift [n]
source filename                  suspend [-f]
test [expr]                      times
trap [arg] [signal_spec]         type [-all] [-type ¦ -path] [name
typeset [-[frxi]] name[=value] ... ulimit [-SHacdmstfpnuv [limit]]
umask [-S] [mode]                unalias [-a] [name ...]
unset [-f] [-v] [name ...]       until COMMANDS; do COMMANDS; done
variables - Some variable names an wait [n]
while COMMANDS; do COMMANDS; done { COMMANDS }
```

You will have to pipe the output of `help` to `more` (`help ¦ more`) to keep the first part from scrolling off your screen.

Wildcards: * and ?

In many a late-night card game, jokers are shuffled into the deck. The jokers are *wildcards* that can become any card of your choice. This is obviously very useful! Linux has wildcards also. They are, if anything, more useful than jokers in a card game.

Linux has several wildcards. Wildcards are used as a convenient and powerful shortcut when specifying files (or directories) that a command is to operate on. We will briefly look at the two most popular wildcards: * and ?.

The most commonly used wildcard is *, which stands in for any combination of one or more characters. For example, c* will match all filenames that begin with c. You can see this for yourself by typing `ls /bin/c*`.

What happens if you type `ls /bin/c*t`? How about `ls /bin/*t`?

The ? wildcard is more restrictive than *. It only stands in for any *one* character. You can see this by comparing `ls/bin/d*` with `ls/bin/d?`.

NOTE

Wildcards can only be used to match filenames and directory names. You can't, for example, type pass* at the Linux prompt and expect Linux to run the passwd program for you.

WARNING

Be very careful when using wildcards with dangerous commands, such as the ones used to permanently delete files! A good check is to run ls with the wildcards you plan to use and examine the resulting list of files to see if the wildcard combination did what you expected it to do. Also double-check that you typed everything correctly *before* pressing the Enter key!

Environment Variables

When you log in, Linux keeps a number of useful data items in the background ready for the system to use. The actual data is held in something called an *environment variable,* whose name is often descriptive or mnemonic. In fact, this is no different from the way you and I remember things. We know that there always is a piece of information called "day of the week" (the environment variable); however, we change the data in this variable, from Monday to Tuesday to Wednesday, and so on, as days go by.

To see the list of *exported* environment variables, type env. The environment variable's name is on the left, and the value held by the variable is on the right.

The most important variable to note is the PATH, whose value is your *search path*. As we will see in the next chapter, when you type a command, Linux will search every place listed in your search path for that command.

A longer list of environment variables, consisting of several new variables in addition to the ones you saw earlier, is displayed by the command set. The new variables are local: they have not been marked for export. For more information on exporting variables, see Chapter 10. You can think of local variables as items of information you need for only a certain time or location. For instance, remembering the variable "what-floor-am-I-on" becomes an unnecessary piece of information once you leave the building!

Processes and How To Terminate Them

In the previous chapter, we learned about the who command, which shows you the usernames of everyone who is logged into the system. The who program actually gets its information from the Linux system, which maintains and updates the list of the system's current users.

In fact, Linux keeps much more detailed records about what is happening on the system than just who is logged in. Because Linux is a multitasking system, in which many programs or program threads may be running simultaneously, Linux keeps track of individual tasks or *processes*.

Although these processes are usually well behaved and well managed by Linux, sometimes they might go out of control. This can happen if a program hits a bug or a flaw in its internal code or supplied data, or if you accidentally enter the wrong command or command option.

Being able to identify these misbehaving processes, and then being able to terminate or *kill* them, is an essential piece of knowledge for *all* Linux/UNIX users. (Obviously the world was a less kind and gentle place when the kill command was developed and named.) When you are your own system administrator, as in our case, it's doubly important!

The Process Status Command: *ps*

To find out what processes are running, we use the ps command. ps stands for "process status," not the "post script" you would write at the end of a letter.

Typing ps by itself gives you a concise listing of your own processes:

```
darkstar:~$ ps
  PID TTY STAT  TIME COMMAND
   41 v01 S     0:00 -bash
  134 v0l R     0:00 ps
```

The information in the first column, headed PID, is important. This is the Process ID number, which is unique, and which Linux uses to identify that particular process. You must know a process's PID to be able to kill it.

The TTY column shows you which terminal the process was started from.

The STAT column gives the status of the process. The two most common entries in the status column are S for *sleeping* and R for *running*. A sleeping process is one that isn't currently active. However, don't be misled. A sleeping process might just be taking a very brief catnap! In fact, a process might switch between sleeping and running many times every second.

The TIME column shows the amount of system time used by the process. Clearly, neither of our processes are taking up any appreciable system time!

Finally, the NAME column contains the name of the program you're running. This will usually be the command you typed at the command line. However, sometimes the command you type starts one or more *child* processes, and in this case, you would see these additional processes show up as well, without ever having typed them yourself. Your login shell will have a - before it, as in -bash in the previous example. This helps to distinguish this *primary* shell from any shells you might enter from it. These will not have the - in front.

If you are logged in as root, you will see a list of *all* processes on the system. This is because the root username, being the superuser, owns everything that happens on the Linux system.

If you are an "ordinary" user, but have also logged in on another terminal (including another virtual terminal you have selected by pressing Alt-F*n* as discussed in Chapter 6, "Getting Started with Linux"), you will see the processes you are running on the other terminal (or terminals) as well.

One useful option with ps is u. Although it stands for "user," as in "List the username as well," it actually adds quite a few more columns of information in addition to just the username:

```
darkstar:~$ ps -u
USER    PID %CPU %MEM SIZE  RSS TTY STAT START   TIME COMMAND
fido     41  0.1  6.8  364  472 v01 S    23:19   0:01 -bash
fido    138  0.0  3.3   72  228 v01 R    23:34   0:00 ps -u
```

In addition to the username in the USER column, other interesting new items include %CPU, which shows you what percentage of your computer's processing power is being used by the process, and %MEM, which shows you what percentage of your computer's memory is being used by the process.

If you want to see all processes running on the system, and not just the processes started by your own username, you can use the a command option. (The root login sees everyone's processes automatically and does not have to use a, so root can get the following output by simply typing ps.)

```
darkstar:~$ ps -a
 PID TTY STAT  TIME COMMAND
  62 v03 S     0:00 /sbin/agetty 38400 tty3
  63 v04 S     0:00 /sbin/agetty 38400 tty4
  64 v05 S     0:00 /sbin/agetty 38400 tty5
  65 v06 S     0:00 /sbin/agetty 38400 tty6
 330 v02 S     0:00 -bash
 217 v01 S     0:00 -bash
 217 v01 S     0:00 ps -a
```

As you can see, quite a few "other" processes are happening on the system! In fact, most of the processes we see here will be running whether or not anyone is actually logged into the Linux system. All the processes listed as running on tty psf are actually system processes, and are started every time you boot up the Linux system. Processes of the form /sbin/agetty 38400 tty6 are login processes running on a particular terminal waiting for your login.

It can be useful to combine the a and u options (if you're not root).

```
darkstar:~$ ps -au
USER     PID %CPU %MEM SIZE  RSS TTY STAT START   TIME COMMAND
root      72  0.0  3.6  390  532 v01 S    17:55   0:01 -bash
root      74  0.0  1.5   41  224 v03 S    17:55   0:00 /sbin/agetty 38400 tty3
root      75  0.0  1.5   41  224 v04 S    17:55   0:00 /sbin/agetty 38400 tty4
root      76  0.0  1.5   41  224 v05 S    17:55   0:00 /sbin/agetty 38400 tty5
root      77  0.0  1.5   41  224 v06 S    17:55   0:00 /sbin/agetty 38400 tty6
```

```
root          78  0.0  1.5   56   228 s00 S    17:55   0:00 gpm -t mman
root          98  0.0  1.5   41   224 v02 S    18:02   0:00 /sbin/agetty 38400 tty2
root         108 18.8  3.6  384   528 pp0 S    18:27   0:01 -bash
```

A more technical l option can sometimes be useful:

```
darkstar:~$ ps -l
  F   UID  PID  PPID PRI NI SIZE  RSS WCHAN      STAT TTY    TIME COMMAND
  0   501   41     1  15  0  364  472 114d9c      S   v01   0:00 -bash
  0   501  121    41  29  0   64  208 0           R   v01   0:00 ps -l
```

The interesting information is in the PPID column. PPID stands for "Parent Process ID"—in other words, the process that started the particular process. Notice that the ps -l command was started by -bash, the login shell. In other words, ps -l was started from the command line. Notice also that the PPID for the login shell is PID 1. If you check the output from ps -au above, you will see that the process with PID of 1 is init. The init process is the one that spawns, or starts, all other processes. If init dies, the system crashes!

> **NOTE**
>
> The Linux ps command has some quirks when it comes to options.
>
> First of all, the dash before the options is not necessary. In the earlier example, ps l would work the same as ps -l. Because most Linux commands *do* require the use of dashes with their command options, and other versions of UNIX might require dashes when using ps, it's best to use the dash anyway.
>
> Second, the order in which you enter the options does matter, especially if you try to combine the l and u options! Try typing ps -lu, and then ps -ul. This behavior is not covered in the ps man page. The moral is twofold: First, use the minimum possible number of command options. Second, the man pages are, alas, not always correct and complete.

The Process Termination Command: *kill*

The kill command is used to terminate processes that can't be stopped by other means.

> **NOTE**
>
> Before going through the following procedure, if it's a program you're stuck in, make sure you can't stop or exit it by typing Ctrl-C or some other key combination.

1. Switch to another virtual console and log in as root.
2. Run ps -u and identify the offending process. You will use its PID in the next step.
3. Use the kill program by typing kill <PID>, where PID is the Process ID you wish to kill. Make sure that you have correctly identified the offending process! As root, you can kill any user process, including the wrong one if you misread or mistype the PID.

4. Verify that the process has been killed by using `ps -u` again. You can type `ps -u <PID>`, which shows you the status of only the specified PID. If there's a null result and you're just given the Linux prompt again, the PID is dead, so go to step 8. However, it's best to look at the complete `ps -u` list if it's not too long. Sometimes the offending process reappears with a new PID! If that is the case, go to step 6.

5. If the process is still alive and has the same PID, use `kill`'s 9 option. Type `kill -9 <PID>`. Check it as in step 4. If this does not kill the process, go to step 7. If the process is now dead, go to step 8.

6. If the offending process has reappeared with a new PID, that means that it's being created automatically by some other process. The only thing to do now is to kill the parent process, which is the true offender! You might also have to kill the parent process when `kill -9` does not work.

7. Use `ps -l` to identify the troublesome process's PPID. This is the PID of the parent process. You should check the parent's identity more closely by typing `ps -u <Parent PID>` before going ahead and killing it as described in step 3, using the PID of the *parent* in the `kill` command. You should follow through with step 4 and, if necessary, step 5, making sure the parent process has been killed.

8. The process is killed. Remember to log off. You should not leave `root` logged in on virtual consoles, because you will forget that the `root` logins are there!

NOTE

Sometimes processes are simply unkillable! In this case, you're best off shutting down the Linux system and rebooting.

Linux keeps ordinary users (as opposed to root) from killing other users' processes (maliciously or otherwise). For instance, if you are an ordinary user and you try to kill the `init` process, which always has PID=1, you will see

```
darkstar:~$ kill 1
kill:  (1) - Not owner
```

Actually, not even `root` can kill the `init` process, although there is no error message. The `init` process is one of those "unkillable" processes discussed earlier, because it's such a key process. That's all for the best!

Becoming Someone Else: The *su* Command

Usually, when you want to temporarily become a different user, you will simply switch to another virtual terminal, log in as the other user, log out when you're done, and return to your "home" virtual terminal. However, there are times when this is impractical or inconvenient. Perhaps all your virtual terminals are already busy, or perhaps you're in a situation (such as logged on via a telephone and modem) in which you don't have virtual terminals available.

In these cases, you can use the su command. "su" stands for "super user." If you type su by itself, you will be prompted for the root password. If you successfully enter the root password, you will see the root # prompt, and you will have all of root's privileges.

You can also become any other user by typing su *<username>*. If you are root when you type su *<username>*, you are not asked for that user's password since in principle you could change the user's password or examine all the user's files from the root login anyway. If you are an "ordinary" user trying to change to another ordinary user, you will be asked to enter the password of the user you are trying to become.

> **NOTE**
>
> Although su grants you all the privileges you would get if you logged on as that user, be aware that you won't inherit that login's exact environment or run that login's startup files (if any). This means that su is not really suited to doing extended work, and it's quite unsuitable for troubleshooting problems with that login.

The *grep* Command

"What on earth does grep mean?" you ask.

This is a fair question. grep must be the quintessential UNIX acronym, because it's impossible to understand even when it's spelled out in full!

grep stands for *Global Regular Expression Parser*. You will understand the use of this command right away, but when "Global Regular Expression Parser" becomes a comfortable phrase in itself, you should probably consider taking a vacation.

What grep does, essentially, is find and display lines that contain a pattern that you specify. There are two basic ways to use grep.

The first use of grep is to filter the output of other commands. The general syntax is *<command>* ¦ grep *<pattern>*. For instance, if we wanted to see every actively running process on the system, we would type ps -a ¦ grep R. In this application, grep passes on only those lines that contain the pattern (in this case, the single letter) R. Note that if someone were running a program called Resting, it would show up even if its status were S for sleeping, because grep would match the R in Resting. An easy way around this problem is to type grep " R ", which explicitly tells grep to search for an R with a space on each side. You must use quotes whenever you search for a pattern that contains one or more blank spaces.

The second use of grep is to search for lines that contain a specified pattern in a specified file. The syntax here is grep *<pattern>* *<filename>*. Be careful. It's easy to specify the filename first and the pattern second by mistake! Again, you should be as specific as you can with the pattern to be matched, in order to avoid "false" matches.

Summary

By this point you should have tried enough different Linux commands to start getting familiar (if not yet entirely comfortable) with typical Linux usage conventions.

It is important that you be able to use the man pages provided online by Linux. A very good exercise at this point is to pull up man pages for all the commands we have looked at in the past two chapters: login, passwd, who, adduser, and so on. If some of the commands listed under "See also:" look interesting, by all means take a look at their man pages too!

> **NOTE**
>
> Some man pages, such as the one for bash, are *extremely* long. Do not plan to read them all in one sitting!

In Chapter 8, we head out from "home" and poke around in the Linux filesystem. As system administrators, we should know what our hard drives contain! For instance, there are special "administrator-only" directories crammed with goodies.

Several more "essential" commands will be introduced. By the end of the next chapter, you will have seen and tried most of the important "user" Linux commands and will have had a taste of some of the "administrator" commands.

The Linux File System

8

by Ed Treijs

In this chapter, you learn about:

- Files: what they are, types of files, filenames
- Directories: what they are, parent directories and subdirectories, directory names, your home directory
- Absolute and relative file and directory names
- Moving between directories using the cd command
- Using the cat command to create a new file
- Creating directories
- Moving and copying files
- Removing files and directories
- File and directory ownership, using chown and chgrp to change ownership
- File and directory permissions, using chmod to change permissions
- Using the gunzip command to uncompress .gz files compressed by gzip
- The tar command
- The standard Linux directories and directory structure

To understand how Linux works, and to use the system beyond a superficial level, you must be familiar with the Linux notion of files and the file system into which they are organized.

Files: An Overview

The most basic concept of a file, and one you may already be familiar with from other computer systems, defines a *file* as a distinct chunk of information that is found on your hard drive. *Distinct* means that there can be many different files, each with its own particular contents. To keep files from getting confused with each other, every file must have a unique identity. In Linux, you identify each file by its name and location. In each location or *directory,* there can be only one file by a particular name. So, for instance, if you create a file called novel, and you get a second great idea, you will either have to call it something different, such as novel2, or put it in a different place, to keep from *overwriting* the contents already in your original novel.

Common Types of Files

Files can contain various types of information. The following three types will become the most familiar to you:

- User data: Information that you create and update. The very simplest user data is plain text or numbers. You learn to create these simple files later in this chapter. More complicated user data files might have to be *interpreted* by another program to make sense. For instance, a spreadsheet file looks like gibberish if you look at it directly. To work with a spreadsheet, you have to start up the spreadsheet program and read in the spreadsheet file.

- System data: Information, often in plain text form, that is read and used by the Linux system—to keep track of which users are allowed on the system, for instance. As a system administrator, you are responsible for changing system data files. For instance, when you create a new user, you modify the file /etc/passwd, which contains the user information. Ordinary users of the system are usually not concerned with system data files, except for their private startup files.

- Executable files: These files contain instructions that your computer can perform. This set of instructions is often called a *program*. When you tell the computer to perform them, you're telling it to *execute* the instructions given to it. To human eyes, executable files contain meaningless gibberish—obviously your computer doesn't think the way you do! Creating or modifying executable files takes special tools. You learn how to use these programming tools in Part V, "Linux for Programmers."

Filenames

Linux allows filenames to be up to 256 characters long. These characters can be lower- and upper-case letters, numbers, and other characters, usually the dash (-), the underscore (_), and the dot (.).

They can't include reserved *metacharacters* such as the asterisk, question mark, backslash, and space, because these all have meaning to the shell. We met some metacharacters when we discussed wildcards in the previous chapter. Other metacharacters will be introduced in the Linux shell chapters.

Directories: An Overview

Linux, like many other computer systems, organizes files in *directories*. You can think of directories as file folders and their contents as the files. However, there is one absolutely crucial difference between the Linux file system and an office filing system. In the office, file folders usually don't contain other file folders. In Linux, file folders *can* contain other file folders. In fact, there is no Linux "filing cabinet"—just a huge file folder that holds some files and other folders. These folders contain files and possibly other folders in turn, and so on.

Parent Directories and Subdirectories

Imagine a scenario in which you have a directory, A, that contains another directory, B. Directory B is then a *subdirectory* of directory A, and directory A is the *parent directory* of directory B. You will see these terms often, both in this book and elsewhere.

The Root Directory

In Linux, the directory that holds all the other directories is called the *root directory*. This is the ultimate parent directory; every other directory is some level of subdirectory.

From the root directory, the whole structure of directory upon directory springs and grows like some electronic elm. This is called a *tree structure* because, from the single *root* directory, directories and subdirectories branch off like tree limbs.

How Directories Are Named

Directories are named just like files, and they can contain upper- and lowercase letters, numbers, and characters such as -, ., and _.

The slash (/) character is used to show files or directories within other directories. For instance, usr/bin means that bin is found in the usr directory. Note that you can't tell, from this example, whether bin is a file or a directory, although you know that usr must be a directory because it holds another item—namely, bin. When you see usr/bin/grep, you know that both usr and bin must be directories, but again, you can't be sure about grep. The ls program shows directories with a following /—for example, fido/. This notation implies that you could have, for instance, fido/file; therefore, fido must be a directory.

The root directory is shown simply by the symbol / rather than mentioned by name. It's very easy to tell when / is used to separate directories and when it's used to signify the root directory. If / has no name *before* it, it stands for the root directory. For example, /usr means that the usr subdirectory is found in the root directory, and /usr/bin means that bin is found in the usr directory and that usr is a subdirectory of the root directory. Remember, by definition the root directory can't be a subdirectory.

The Home Directory

Linux provides each user with his or her own directory, called the *home* directory. Within this home directory, users can store their own files and create subdirectories. Users generally have complete control over what's found in their home directories. Because there are usually no Linux system files or files belonging to other users in your home directory, you can create, name, move, and delete files and directories as you see fit.

> **WARNING**
>
> Your home directory does not provide privacy! Normally, any user can go into another's home directory and read (and copy!) the files stored there (although he can't delete or change the files). When Linux creates your home directory, it in effect provides you with an open office cubicle whose desk and filing cabinet drawers are unlocked.
>
> You *must* lock up everything you want to keep private. (This topic is covered in the section "File Permissions and Ownership.") It is generally considered rude or nosy to poke around in someone else's home directory, just as it's rude or nosy to poke around in someone's office while they're away from their desk, but the world is full of nosy and rude people, so you must take precautions!
>
> Note that anyone logged in as root can read and manipulate *all* the files on the system, including files that users have locked up. If you can't trust the system administrator (who usually has the root password), don't use the system!

The location of a user's home directory is specified by Linux and can't be changed by the user. This is both to keep things tidy and to preserve system security.

Navigating the Linux File System

Fortunately, navigating the Linux file system is simple. There are only two commands to be learned, and one of them has absolutely no options or parameters!

The *pwd* Command: Where Am I?

Type pwd at the Linux command prompt. You see

```
darkstar:~$ pwd
/home/fido
darkstar:~$
```

This tells you that you're currently in the directory /home/fido. (If you are logged in under a different user name, you will see that name in place of fido.) This is your home directory. When you log in, Linux always places you in your home directory.

The letters "pwd" stand for "print working directory." Again, a command's name or function has been cut down to a few easy-to-type characters. (You will often see the term *current directory* used in place of *working directory*.)

You might be wondering what "working directory" or "being in a directory" really means. It simply means that Linux commands, by default, perform their actions in your working directory. For instance, when you run ls, you are shown only the files in your working directory. If you want to create or remove files, they will be created or removed in your working directory.

Absolute and Relative Filenames

If you specify only the name of a file, Linux looks for that file in your working directory. For example, more myfile lets you read the contents of the file myfile. But myfile must be in your current working directory, or the more command won't find it.

Sometimes you want to specify a file that isn't in your current directory. You would then specify the name of the directory the file is in, as well as the name of the file itself.

If, for instance, your current directory has a subdirectory called novel, which contains a file called chapter_1, you could type more novel/chapter_1, which tells more that it should look in the subdirectory novel for the file chapter_1. This is called a *relative filename.* You are specifying the location of chapter_1 *relative* to where you are now, in the subdirectory novel, which is found in your current directory. If you changed your working directory, the relative filename would no longer work.

Two special directory specifications are ".￼" and "..". "." always stands for the directory you are currently in, and ".." stands for the parent directory of your current directory. (You see how "."

Creating and Deleting Files

Linux has many ways to create and delete files. In fact, some of the ways are so easy to perform that you have to be careful not to accidentally overwrite or erase files!

Return to your home directory by typing cd. Make sure you're in your /home/<user> directory by running pwd.

In the last chapter, you created a file by typing ls -l /bin > test. Remember, the > symbol means "redirect all output to the following filename." Note that the file test didn't exist before you typed this command. When you redirect to a file, Linux automatically creates the file if it doesn't already exist.

What if you want to type text into a file, rather than some command's output? The quick and dirty way is to use the command cat.

cat: That Useful Feline

The cat command is one of the simplest, yet most useful, commands in Linux. It certainly does more than any living feline!

The cat command basically takes all its input and outputs it. By default, cat takes its input from the keyboard and outputs it to the screen. Type cat at the command line:

```
darkstar:~$ cat
```

The cursor moves down to the next line, but nothing else seems to happen. Now cat is waiting for some input:

```
hello
hello
what
what
asdf
asdf
```

Everything you type is repeated on-screen as soon as you press Enter!

How do you get out of this? At the start of a line, type ^D (Ctrl-D). (In other words, hold down the Ctrl key and press D.) If you're not at the beginning of a line, you have to type ^D twice. ^D is the Linux "end of file" character. When a program such as cat encounters a ^D, it assumes that it has finished with the current file, and it goes on to the next one. In this case, if you type ^D by itself on an empty line, there is no next file to go on to, and cat exits.

> **NOTE**
>
> When you say that a program *exits,* you mean that it has finished running and that you are back at the Linux command prompt. It might seem odd to talk about the *program* exiting when, from your point of view as a user, you have exited the program. This turn of phrase goes back to the early days of UNIX, when it was coined by the people who were programming the system. They looked at things from the program's point of view, not the user's!

So how do you use cat to create a file? Simple! You redirect the output from cat to the desired filename:

```
darkstar:~$ cat > newfile
Hello world
Here's some text
```

You can type as much as you want. When you are finished, press ^D by itself on a line; you will be back at the Linux prompt.

Now you want to look at the contents of newfile. You could use the more or less commands, but instead, let's use cat. Yes, you can use cat to look at files simply by providing it with a filename:

```
darkstar:~$ cat newfile
Hello world
Here's some text
darkstar:~$
```

Neat! You can also add to the end of the file by using >>. Whenever you use >>, whether with cat or any other command, the output is always *appended* to the specified file. (Note that the ^D character does not appear on-screen. I show it in the examples for clarity.)

```
darkstar:~$ cat >> newfile
Some more lines
^D
darkstar:~$ cat newfile
Hello world
Here's some text
Some more lines
darkstar:~$
```

To discover what cat actually stands for, let's first create another file.

```
darkstar:~$ cat > anotherfile
Different text
^D
darkstar:~$
```

Now, try this:

```
darkstar:~$ cat newfile anotherfile> thirdfile
darkstar:~$ cat thirdfile
```

```
Hello world
Here's some text
Some more lines
Different text
darkstar:~$
```

cat stands for *concatenate*; cat takes all the specified inputs and regurgitates them in a single lump. This by itself would not be very interesting, but combine it with the forms of input and output redirection available in Linux and you have a powerful and useful tool.

Sometimes you want to change just one line of a file, or perhaps you are creating a large and complicated file. For this you should use one of the editing programs available in Linux. They are discussed in Chapter 16, "Text Editors."

Creating Directories

To create a new directory, use the mkdir command. The syntax is mkdir *<name>*, where *<name>* is replaced by whatever you want the directory to be called. This creates a subdirectory with the specified name in your current directory:

```
darkstar:~$ ls
anotherfile     newfile       thirdfile
darkstar:~$ mkdir newdir
darkstar:~$ ls
anotherfile     newdir/       newfile       thirdfile
```

> **TIP**
>
> The mkdir command is already familiar to you if you have used MS-DOS systems. In MS-DOS, you can abbreviate mkdir as md. You might think that md would work in Linux, because, after all, most of the commands we've seen have extremely concise names. However, Linux doesn't recognize md; it insists on the full mkdir.
>
> If you frequently switch between Linux and MS-DOS, you might want to use mkdir for both systems. However, be warned that you might start typing other Linux commands in MS-DOS—for example, typing ls instead of dir!

Moving and Copying Files

You often need to move or copy files. The mv command moves files, and the cp command copies files. The syntax for the two commands is similar:

```
mv <source> <destination>
cp <source> <destination>
```

As you can see, mv and cp are very simple commands. Here's an example:

```
darkstar:~$ ls
anotherfile     newdir/       newfile       thirdfile
```

```
darkstar:~$ mv anotherfile movedfile
darkstar:~$ ls
movedfile    newdir/        newfile         thirdfile
darkstar:~$ cp thirdfile xyz
darkstar:~$ ls
anotherfile    newdir/        newfile        thirdfile        xyz
```

You can use cat (or more or less) at any time to verify that anotherfile became movedfile, and that the contents of file xyz are identical to the contents of thirdfile.

It can get more confusing if you're moving or copying files from one directory to another. This is because a file's *real* name includes its absolute path—for instance, /home/fido/newfile. However, Linux lets you leave off parts of the file's name, because it's more convenient to refer to newfile rather than /home/fido/newfile.

For instance, suppose you want to move newfile into the newdir subdirectory. If you want the file to keep the same name, you type

```
darkstar:~$ mv newfile newdir/newfile
```

However, it's much more common to type

```
darkstar:~$ mv newfile newdir
```

Here, because you have typed a directory name for the destination, Linux assumes that you want the file to be placed in the specified directory.

You could also use cd to change to the directory you want to move the file to:

```
darkstar:~$ cd newdir
darkstar:~newdir$ copy ../newfile .
```

This example is a bit less intuitive than the first two! You specify that the source is ../newfile, which means "the file newfile in the current directory's parent directory." The destination you simply specify as ".", which is short for "the current directory." In other words, you're telling mv to "go up one level, grab newfile, and move it to right here." Because this is less intuitive, you might find yourself automatically *pushing* a file from your current directory to another directory rather than *pulling* a file from another directory into your current directory.

You can also change the name of the file while moving or copying it to another directory. The following is just one possible way:

```
darkstar:~$ cp newfile newdir/anothername
```

This would create a copy of newfile in the directory newdir and name the copied file anothername.

WARNING

When moving or copying files between directories, you should always double-check that the file's destination directory exists and verify the directory's name. Otherwise, the results of your command can be unexpected, as the following two examples show.

1 or - -x: execute

6 or rw-: read and write

5 or r-x: read and execute

3 or -wx: write and execute (rare)

7 or rwx: read, write, and execute

> **NOTE**
>
> Anyone who has permission to read a file can then copy that file. When a file is copied, the copy is owned by the person doing the copying. He or she can then change ownership and permissions, edit the file, and so on.

> **WARNING**
>
> Removing write permission from a file doesn't prevent the file from being deleted! It does prevent it from being deleted accidentally, since Linux asks you whether you want to override the file permissions. You have to answer y, or the file will not be deleted.

Changing File Permissions

To change file permissions, use the chmod (change [*file*] mode) command. The syntax is chmod *<specification> file*.

There are two ways to write the permission specification. One is by using the numeric coding system for permissions:

```
darkstar:~$ ls -l myfile
-rw-r--r--  1 fido     users          114 Dec  7 14:31 myfile
darkstar:~$ chmod 345 myfile
darkstar:~$ ls -l myfile
--wxr--r-x  1 fido     users          114 Dec  7 14:31 myfile
darkstar:~$ chmod 701 myfile
darkstar:~$ ls -l myfile
-rwx----x  1 root     users          114 Dec  7 14:31 myfile
```

This method has the advantage of specifying the permissions in an absolute, rather than relative, fashion. Also, it's easier to tell someone "Change permissions on the file to seven-five-five" than to say "Change permissions on the file to read-write-execute, read-execute, read-execute."

You can also use letter codes to change the existing permissions. To specify which of the permissions to change, type u (user), g (group), o (other), or a (all). This is followed by a + to add permissions or a - to remove them. This in turn is followed by the permissions to be added or re-moved. For example, to add execute permissions for the group and others, you would type

```
darkstar:~$ chmod go+r myfile
```

Other ways of using the symbolic file permissions are described in the chmod man page.

Changing Directory Permissions

You change directory permissions with chmod, exactly the same way as with files. Remember that if a directory doesn't have execute permissions, you can't cd to it.

> **WARNING**
>
> Any user who has write permission in a directory can delete files in that directory, whether or not that user owns or has write privileges to those files.
>
> Most directories, therefore, have permissions set to drwxr-xr-x. This ensures that only the directory's owner can create or delete files in that directory.
>
> It is especially dangerous to give write permission to all users for directories!

Miscellaneous File Commands

There are many Linux commands to manipulate files, directories, and the entire file system. Many of these commands are used only by system administrators. You will touch on a few that are also used by ordinary users. These and other important system administrator commands are further detailed in Chapter 37, "System Administration Basics."

Fear of Compression: The Zipless File

Most Linux files are stored on the installation CD-ROM in compressed form. This allows more information to be stored.

When you installed Linux, the installation program uncompressed many of the files it transferred to your hard drive. However, if you look, you will be able to find compressed files!

Any file ending in .gz—for example, squashed.gz—is a compressed file. To uncompress this par-ticular type of file, type gunzip *<file>*. For this example, you would type gunzip squashed.gz. The gunzip program creates an uncompressed file and removes the .gz extension. Therefore, you would wind up with a normal file called squashed.

To compress a file, use the gzip command. Typing gzip squashed would compress squashed and rename it squashed.gz.

Another type of compressed file you might see ends with the extension .zip. Use `unzip` to uncompress these files. To create files of this type, use `zip`.

How to *tar* Without Feathering

In almost any location with several Linux or UNIX systems, sooner or later you will hear someone say, "Put that in a `tar` file and send it over."

They are referring to the output created by the `tar` program. Although `tar` stands for *tape archive,* it can copy files to floppy disk or to any filename you specify in the Linux file system. The `tar` command is used because it can archive files and directories into a single file and then recreate the files and even the directory structures later. It's also the easiest way to place Linux files on a floppy disk.

To create a tar file, you typically type `tar cvf <destination> <files/directories>`, where `files/directories` specifies the files and directories to be archived, and `destination` is where you want the `tar` file to be created. If you want the destination to be a floppy disk, you usually type `/dev/fd0` as the destination. This specifies your primary floppy drive (A: in MS-DOS). You can use a floppy disk that's been formatted under MS-DOS.

WARNING

When `tar` archives to a floppy disk, all the data already on the disk is destroyed. You have to reformat it to use it with MS-DOS again.

To extract a tar file, you typically type `tar xvf <tar file>`. For instance, to pull files from a floppy disk, you would type `tar xvf /dev/fd0`.

NOTE

Unlike `zip` and `gzip`, `tar` doesn't remove, delete, or rename the files it puts into the archive. However, when `tar` extracts archived files, it overwrites existing files with files of the same name from the archive.

Important Directories in the Linux File System

Most of the directories that hold Linux system files are "standard." Other UNIX systems will have identical directories with similar contents. This section summarizes some of the more important directories on your Linux system.

/

This is the root directory. It holds the actual Linux program, as well as subdirectories. Do not clutter this directory with your files!

/home

This directory holds users' home directories. In other UNIX systems, this can be the /usr or /u directory.

/bin

This directory holds many of the basic Linux programs. bin stands for *binaries*, files that are executable and that hold text only computers could understand.

/usr

This directory holds many other user-oriented directories. Some of the most important are described in the following sections. Other directories found in /usr include

docs	Various documents, including useful Linux information
man	The man pages accessed by typing man *<command>*
games	The fun stuff!

/usr/bin

This directory holds user-oriented Linux programs.

/usr/spool

This directory has several subdirectories. mail holds mail files, spool holds files to be printed, and uucp holds files copied between Linux machines.

/dev

Linux treats *everything* as a file! The /dev directory hold *devices*. These are special files that serve as gateways to physical computer components. For instance, if you copy to /dev/fd0, you're actually sending data to the system's floppy disk. Your terminal is one of the /dev/tty files. Partitions on the hard drive are of the form /dev/hd0. Even the system's memory is a device!

A famous device is /dev/null. This is sometimes called the *bit bucket*. All information sent to /dev/null vanishes—it's thrown into the trash.

/usr/sbin

This directory holds system administration files. If you do an `ls -l`, you see that you must be the owner, root, to run these commands.

/sbin

This directory holds system files that are usually run automatically by the Linux system.

/etc

This directory and its subdirectories hold many of the Linux configuration files. These files are usually text, and they can be edited to change the system's configuration (if you know what you're doing!).

Summary

You should now feel more comfortable working in Linux. Understanding and being able to navigate the Linux file system is very important, since Linux really does consist simply of some files organized in a fairly standard way.

You still might find yourself stumped by certain file or directory problems. Remember that the online man pages can assist you. Linux gives you a lot of flexibility in creating files, specifying absolute or relative names, and setting permissions. Don't be afraid to experiment (as an ordinary user, in your home directory). There are too many different ways to perform tasks to list or exhaustively describe here. Don't cling to rigid recipes written on a piece of paper. You learn by trying!

You should go on to Chapters 9, "Introduction to the GNU Project Utilities," through 12, "Using tcsh," especially if you want to create programs or macros from system command files or learn more about the built-in user interface features in Linux shells. Chapter 16 has some very useful information about editing text files.

Once you are familiar with shells and have had some practice manipulating files and directories, you can move on to the advanced topics in Part III, "Editing, Typesetting, and More," through Part VIII, "Advanced Programming Topics," of this book.

Introduction to the GNU Project Utilities

9

by Peter MacKinnon

IN THIS CHAPTER

```
history [-r¦w¦a¦n] [filename]
```

In this form, the -r option tells the history command to read the contents of the history file and use them as the current history list. The -w option will cause the history command to write the current history list to the history file (overwriting what is currently in the file). The -a option appends the current history list to the end of the history file. The -n option causes the lines that are in the history file to be read into the current history list.

All of the options for the second form of the history command can use the filename option as the name of the history file. If no filename is specified, the history command will use the value of the HISTFILE shell variable.

The fc command can be used in two different ways to edit the command history. In the first way, the fc command would be entered using the following command-line syntax:

```
fc [-e editor_name] [-n] [-l] [-r] [first] [last]
```

where all options given in braces are optional. The -e editor name option is used to specify the text editor to be used for editing the commands. The first and last options are used to select a range of commands to take out of the history list. first and last can refer either to the number of a command in the history list or to a string that fc will try to find in the history list.

The -n option is used to suppress command numbers when listing the history commands. The -r option lists the matched commands in reverse order. The -l command lists the matched commands to the screen. In all cases except when the -l command option is used, the matching commands will be loaded into a text editor.

NOTE

The text editor used by fc is found by taking the value of editor name if the -e editor name option is used. If this option was not used, fc uses the editor specified by the variable FCEDIT. If this variable does not exist, fc will use the value of the EDITOR variable. Finally, if none of these variables exists, the editor that will be chosen is vi, by default.

Aliases

Another way that bash makes life easier for you is by supporting command aliases. *Command aliases* are commands that the user can specify. *Alias commands* are usually abbreviations of other commands, designed to save keystrokes.

For example, if you are entering the following command on a regular basis, you might be inclined to create an alias for it to save yourself some typing:

```
cd /usr/X11/lib/X11/fvwm/sample-configs
```

Instead of typing this command every time you wanted to go to the `sample-configs` directory, you could create an alias called `goconfig` that would cause the longer command to be executed. To set up an alias like this you must use the `bash` `alias` command. To create the `goconfig` alias, enter the following command at the `bash` prompt:

```
alias goconfig='cd /usr/X11/lib/X11/fvwm/sample-configs'
```

Now, until you exit from `bash`, the `goconfig` command will cause the original, longer command to be executed as if you had just typed it.

If you decide after you have entered an alias that you did not need it, you can use the `bash` `unalias` command to delete the alias:

```
unalias goconfig
```

There are a number of useful aliases that most users find helpful. These can be written in a file that you execute when you log in, to save you from typing them each time. Some aliases that you might want to define are the following:

- `alias ll='ls -l'`
- `alias log='logout'`
- `alias ls='ls -F'`

If you are a DOS user and are used to using DOS file commands, you can use the `alias` command to define the following aliases so that Linux behaves like DOS:

- `alias dir='ls'`
- `alias copy='cp'`
- `alias rename='mv'`
- `alias md='mkdir'`
- `alias rd='rmdir'`

NOTE

When defining aliases, you can't include spaces on either side of the equal sign, or the shell can't properly determine what you want to do. Quotation marks are necessary only if the command within them contains spaces or other special characters.

If you enter the `alias` command without any arguments, it will display all of the aliases that are already defined on-screen. The following listing illustrates a sample output from the `alias` command:

```
alias dir='ls'
alias ll='ls -l'
alias ls='ls -F'
alias md='mkdir'
alias net='term < /dev/modem > /dev/modem 2> /dev/null&'
alias rd='rmdir'
```

Input Redirection

Input redirection is used to change the source of input for a command. When a command is entered in bash, the command is expecting some kind of input in order to do its job. Some of the simpler commands must get all of the information that they need passed to them on the command line. For example, the rm command requires arguments on the command line. You must tell rm the files that you want it to delete on the command line, or it will issue a prompt telling you to enter rm -h for help.

Other commands require more elaborate input than a simple directory name. The input for these commands can be found in a file. For example, the wc (word count) command counts the number of characters, words, and lines in the input that was given to it. If you just type wc <enter> at the command line, wc waits for you to tell it what it should be counting. There will be a prompt on the command line asking for more information, but because the prompt is sometimes not easily identifiable, it will not necessarily be obvious to you what is happening. (It might actually appear as though bash has died, because it is just sitting there. Everything that you type shows up on-screen, but nothing else appears to be happening.)

What is actually occurring is that the wc command is collecting input for itself. If you press Ctrl-D, the results of the wc command will be written to the screen. If you enter the wc command with a filename as an argument, as shown in the following example, wc will return the number of characters, words, and lines that are contained in that file:

```
wc test
11 2 1
```

Another way to pass the contents of the test file to wc is to redirect the input of the wc command from the terminal to the test file. This will result in the same output. The < symbol is used by bash to mean "redirect the input to the current command from the specified file." So, redirecting wc's input from the terminal to the test file can be done by entering the following command:

```
wc < test
11 2 1
```

Input redirection is not used all that often because most commands that require input from a file have the option to specify a filename on the command line. There are times, however, when you will come across a program that will not accept a filename as an input parameter, and yet the input that you want to give exists in a file. Whenever this situation occurs, you can use input redirection to get around the problem.

Output Redirection

Output redirection is more commonly used than input redirection. *Output redirection* enables you to redirect the output from a command into a file, as opposed to having the output displayed on-screen.

There are many situations in which this can be useful. For example, if the output of a command is quite large and will not fit on the screen, you might want to redirect it to a file so that you can view it later using a text editor. There also may be cases where you want to keep the output of a command to show to someone else, or so you can print the results. Finally, output redirection is also useful if you want to use the output from one command as input for another. (There is an easier way to use the output of one command as input to a second command. This is shown in the "Pipelines" section in this chapter.)

Output redirection is done in much the same way as input redirection. Instead of using the < symbol, the > symbol is used.

> **NOTE**
>
> The best way to remember which symbol is input or output redirection is to think of the < as a funnel that is funneling input into the command (because the command receiving the input will be on the left-hand side of the <) and the > as a funnel that is funneling the output from the command into a file.

As an example of output redirection, you can redirect the output of the `ls` command into a file named `directory.out` using the following command:

```
ls > directory.out
```

Pipelines

Pipelines are a way to string together a series of commands. This means that the output from the first command in the pipeline is used as the input to the second command in the pipeline. The output from the second command in the pipeline is used as input to the third command in the pipeline, and so on. The output from the last command in the pipeline is the output that you will actually see displayed on-screen (or put in a file if output redirection was specified on the command line).

You can tell `bash` to create a pipeline by typing two or more commands separated by the vertical bar or pipe character, ¦. The following example illustrates the use of a pipeline:

```
cat sample.text ¦ grep "High" ¦ wc -l
```

This pipeline would take the output from the `cat` command (which lists the contents of a file) and send it into the `grep` command. The `grep` command searches for each occurrence of the word High in its input. The `grep` command's output would then consist of each line in the file that contained the word High. This output is then sent to the `wc` command. The `wc` command with the `-l` option prints the number of lines contained in its input.

To show the results on a real file, suppose the contents of `sample.text` was

```
Things to do today:
Low: Go grocery shopping
High: Return movie
High: Clear level 3 in Alien vs. Predator
Medium: Pick up clothes from dry cleaner
```

The pipeline would return the result 2, indicating that you had two things of high importance to complete today:

```
cat sample.text ¦ grep "High" ¦ wc -l
2
```

Prompts

bash has two levels of user prompt. The first level is what you see when bash is waiting for a command to be typed. (This is what you normally see when you are working with bash.)

The default first-level prompt is the $ character. If you do not like the $ character as the prompt, or you would prefer to customize your prompt, you can do so by setting the value of the PS1 bash variable. For example:

```
PS1="Please enter a command"
```

sets the bash shell prompt to the specified string.

The second level of prompt is displayed when bash is expecting more input from you in order to complete a command. The default for the second level prompt is >. If you want to change the second-level prompt, you can set the value of the PS2 variable, as in

```
PS2="I need more information"
```

In addition to displaying static character strings in the command prompts (as in the two preceding examples), you can also use some predefined special characters. These special characters place things such as the current time into the prompt. Table 10.1 lists the most commonly used special-character codes.

Table 10.1. Prompt special character codes.

Character	Meaning
\!	Displays the history number of this command.
\#	Displays the command number of the current command.
\$	Displays a $ in the prompt unless the user is root. When the user is root, it displays a #.
\\	Displays a backslash.
\d	Displays the current date.
\h	Displays the host name of the computer on which the shell is running.
\n	Prints a newline character. This will cause the prompt to span more than one line.
\nnn	Displays the character that corresponds to the octal value of the number nnn.
\s	The name of the shell that is running.
\t	Displays the current time.

Character	Meaning
\u	Displays the user name of the current user.
\W	Displays the base name of the current working directory.
\w	Displays the current working directory.

These special characters can be combined into several useful prompts to provide you with information about where you are. (They can be combined in very grotesque ways, too!) Several examples of setting the PS1 prompt are:

```
PS1="\t"
```

This would cause the prompt to have the following appearance (there would not be a space after the prompt):

```
02:16:15
```

The prompt string

```
PS1=\t
```

would cause the prompt to have the following appearance:

```
t
```

This shows the importance of including the character sequence in quotation marks. The prompt string

```
PS1="\t\\ "
```

will cause the prompt to look like this:

```
02:16:30\
```

In this case, there would be a space following the prompt because there was a space within the quotation marks.

Job Control

Job control refers to the ability to control the execution behavior of a currently running process. Specifically, you can suspend a running process and cause it to resume running at a later time. bash keeps track of all of the processes that it started (as a result of user input), and you can suspend a running process or restart a suspended one at any time during the life of that process.

Pressing Ctrl-Z suspends a running process. The bg command restarts a suspended process in the background, whereas the fg command restarts a process in the foreground.

These commands are most often used when a user wants to run a command in the background but by accident starts it in the foreground. When a command is started in the foreground, it locks the shell from any further user interaction until the command completes execution. This is usually no problem because most commands only take a few seconds to execute. If the command you are running is going to take a long time, though, you would typically start the command in the background so that you could continue to use bash to enter other commands in the foreground.

For example, if you started the command find / -name "test" > find.out (which will scan the entire filesystem for files named test and store the results in a file called find.out) in the foreground, your shell may be tied up for many seconds or even minutes, depending on the size of the filesystem and the number of users on the system. If you had issued this command and wanted to continue executing in the background so you could use the system again, you would enter the following:

```
control-z
bg
```

This would first suspend the find command, then restart it in the background. The find command would continue to execute, and you would have bash back again.

Customizing *bash*

Many ways of customizing bash have already been described in this chapter. Until now, the changes that you made affected only the current bash session. As soon as you quit, all of the customizations that you made will be lost. You can make the customizations more permanent by storing them in a bash initialization file.

You can put any commands that you want to be executed each time bash is started into this initialization file. Commands that are typically found in this file are alias commands and variable initializations.

The bash initialization file is named profile. Each user who uses bash has a .profile file in his home directory. This file is read by bash each time it starts, and all of the commands contained within it are executed.

The following code shows the default .profile file. This file is located in the /etc directory and is read when you start bash. If you want to add your own customizations to bash, you must copy this file into your home directory (if it is not already there) and call it .profile.

> **NOTE**
>
> Some setup programs make a copy of the .profile file in your home directory for you automatically when they create your login. However, not all routines do this, so you should check your home directory first. Remember that all files starting with a period are hidden and can only be displayed with the ls -A or ls -a command.

```
# commands common to all logins
export OPENWINHOME=/usr/openwin
export MINICOM="-c on"
```

```
export MANPATH=/usr/local/man:/usr/man/preformat:/usr/man:/X11/man:/usr/openwin
/man
export HOSTNAME="`cat /etc/HOSTNAME`"
PATH="$PATH:/usr/X11/bin:$OPENWINHOME/bin:/usr/games:."
LESS=-MM
# I had problems using 'eval test' instead of 'TERM=', but you might want to
# try it anyway. I think with the right /etc/termcap it would work great.
# eval 'tset -sQ "$TERM"'if [ "$TERM" = "" -o "$TERM" = "unknown"]; then
TERM=linux
fi
#PS1='`hostname`:`pwd`# '
if [ "$SHELL" = "/bin/pdksh" -o "$SHELL" = "/bin/ksh" ]; then
 PS1="! $"
elif [ "$SHELL" = "/bin/zsh" ]; then
 PS1="%m:%~%# "
elif [ "$SHELL" = "/bin/ash" ]; then
 PS1="$ "
else
PS1='\h:\w\$ '
fi
PS2='> '
ignoreeof=10
export PATH DISPLAY LESS TERM PS1 PS2 ignoreeof
umask 022
# set up the color-ls environment variables:
if [ "$SHELL" = "/bin/zsh" l; then
  eval 'dircolors -z'
elif [ "$SHELL" = "/bin/ash" l; then
  eval 'dircolors -s'
else
  eval 'dircolors -b'
fi
echo
fortune
echo
export TAPE="/dev/nftape"
```

bash Command Summary

Here are some of the most useful commands built into the bash shell:

> alias: Used to set bash aliases (command nicknames that can be defined by the user).
>
> bg: Background command. Forces a suspended process to continue to execute in the background.
>
> cd: Change working directory. This command changes the current working directory to the directory specified as an argument.
>
> exit: Terminates the shell.
>
> export: Causes the value of a variable to be made visible to all subprocesses that belong to the current shell.
>
> fc: Fix command. Used to edit the commands in the current history list.
>
> fg: Foreground command. Forces a suspended process to continue to execute in the foreground.

help: Displays help information for bash built-in commands.

history: Brings up a list of the last *n* commands that were entered at the command prompt, where *n* is a configurable variable specifying the number of commands to remember.

kill: Used to terminate another process.

pwd: Print working directory. Prints the directory in which the user is currently working.

unalias: Used to remove aliases that have been defined using the alias command.

bash has many more commands than are listed here, but these are the most frequently used ones. To see the other commands bash offers and for more details of the commands listed, refer to the bash man page (type man bash).

bash Variables

Here are some of the most useful bash variables, including the variable name and a brief description:

EDITOR, FCEDIT: The default editor for the fc bash command.

HISTFILE: The file used to store the command history.

HISTSIZE: The size of the history list.

HOME: The HOME directory of the current user

OLDPWD: The previous working directory (the one that was current before the current directory was entered).

PATH: The search path that bash uses when looking for executable files

PS1: The first-level prompt that is displayed on the command line

PS2: The second-level prompt that is displayed when a command is expecting more input

PWD: The current working directory

SECONDS: The number of seconds that have elapsed since the current bash session was started

bash has many more variables than are listed here, but the most commonly used ones are shown. To find out what other variables bash offers, call the man page with the command man bash.

Summary

In this chapter you looked at some of the useful features of the Bourne Again Shell, bash. You have seen how command completion, aliasing, and job control can all combine to make you more productive and efficient when working with bash.

In the next chapter you will look at another popular Linux shell, the Public Domain Korn Shell (pdksh). It offers many useful features, too, providing you with a choice of shells.

Using *pdksh*

11

by
Rick McMullin

IN THIS CHAPTER

```
bind '^XC'=forward-char
bind '^XD'=backward-char
```

The following list gives some of the most useful editing commands that you can use for binding keys, along with the default binding and a description of each. You can get a listing of all of the editing commands that pdksh supports by typing the bind command without any arguments.

abort (^G) is used to abort another editing command. It is most commonly used to stop a history list search.

backward-char (^B) moves the cursor backward one character. This command is often bound to the left arrow key.

backward-word (^[b) moves the cursor backward to the beginning of a word.

beginning-of-line (^A) moves the cursor to the beginning of the command line.

complete (^[^[) tells pdksh to try to complete the current command.

copy-last-arg (^[_) causes the last word of the previous command to be inserted at the cursor position.

delete-char-backward (ERASE) deletes the character that is to the left of the cursor.

delete-char-forward deletes the character to the right of the cursor.

delete-word-backward (^[ERASE) deletes the characters to the left of the cursor back to the first white space character that is encountered.

delete-word-forward (^[(d) deletes the characters to the right of the cursor up to the first character that occurs after a whitespace character.

down-history (^N) moves down one line in the history list. This command is often bound to the down arrow key.

end-of-line (^E) moves the cursor to the end of the current line.

forward-char (^F) moves the cursor forward one character. This command is often bound to the right arrow key.

forward-word (^[F) moves the cursor forward to the end of a word.

kill-line (KILL) deletes the current line.

kill-to-eol (^K) deletes all of the characters to the right of the cursor on the current line.

list (^[?) causes pdksh to list all of the possible command names or filenames that can complete the word in which the cursor is currently contained.

search-history (^R) searches the history list backward for the first command that contains the inputted characters.

transpose-chars (^T) exchanges the two characters on either side of the cursor. If the cursor is at the end of the command line it switches the last two characters on the line.

up-history (^P) moves up one command in the history list. This command is often bound to the up arrow key.

Customizing Your *pdksh*

Many ways of customizing pdksh have been described in this chapter. Until now, though, the changes that you made only affected the current pdksh session. As soon as you quit pdksh, all of the customizations that you made are lost. There is a way of making the customizations more permanent.

This is done by storing all of your customizations in a pdksh initialization file. Users can put commands into this file that they want to be executed each and every time pdksh is started. Examples of commands that are typically found in this file are aliases and initializations of variables (such as the prompts).

In order to set up your customization file, you must tell pdksh where to look for the initialization file. This is different than with bash. The bash shell automatically knew where to look for its customization file. To tell pdksh where to look for the customization file, you must create a file in your home directory called .profile. This file is read and all of the commands in the file are executed each time you log into the system.

A sample of the commands that you should place in your .profile file are as follows:

```
export ENV=$HOME/.kshrc
EDITOR=emacs
```

The first line in the .profile file sets the ENV variable. This is the variable that pdksh looks at to find the initialization file that it should use. If you plan to customize pdksh, you should tell pdksh to look for a file in your home directory. The filename .kshrc is often used as the pdksh initialization filename, but you can pick another name if you want.

If you are not planning to customize pdksh, you can set the ENV variable to be equal to the system default pdksh initialization file. This file is in the /etc directory, and is called ksh.kshrc.

The second line in the .profile file sets the EDITOR variable. This is used by the .kshrc initialization file to determine what type of command-line editing commands to use for your session. If you prefer to use vi command-line editing, you can set this variable to be equal to vi.

Listing 11.1 shows most of what is contained in the system default ksh.kshrc file. If you want to add your own customizations to pdksh, you should copy this file into your home directory and then add the customizations that you want to your own copy of the file.

TIP

Instead of copying the file to your home directory, you can create a new file in your home directory that calls the system default file, and then add customizations afterward.

■   tcsh Variables

The last two chapters introduced you to the Bourne Again Shell (bash) and the Public Domain Korn Shell (pdksh). This chapter introduces a third shell, tcsh. This chapter shows you how tcsh supports the following:

■   Command-line completion
■   Command history and aliases
■   Input and output redirection
■   Pipelines
■   Changing your prompts
■   Job control
■   Key bindings
■   Spelling correction

In addition to these topics, we will see how you can customize tcsh to suit your tastes. You will also be introduced to several important tcsh commands and variables.

Rounding out the chapter is a section on neat little features that tcsh provides that are not available in any of the other shell programs we have discussed.

An Introduction to *tcsh*

tcsh is a modified version of the C shell (csh). It is fully backward-compatible with csh, but it contains many new features that make user interaction much easier. The biggest improvements over the csh are in the areas of command-line editing and history navigation.

Command Completion

Just like pdksh and bash, tcsh supports command-line completion. You invoke command-line completion in tcsh exactly the same way as you do in bash: by pressing the Tab key at any point while you are typing a command.

When you press the Tab key, tcsh tries to complete the command by matching what has been typed with any file in the directory that the command is referring to. For example, assume that you typed the following command and then pressed the Tab key:

```
emacs hello
```

Here, tcsh will try to match the letters hello with any file (or subdirectory) in the current directory. If there is a single file in the current directory that begins with the letters hello, tcsh fills in the rest of the filename for you. Now assume that you typed the following command and then pressed the Tab key:

```
emacs /usr/bin/hello
```

In this case, tcsh would try to match the letters hello with any file in the /usr/bin directory. From these examples, you can see that you must give tcsh something to go on before asking it to complete the command for you.

Another example of using command-line completion is as follows: Assume that the directory that you are currently in contains these files:

```
News/ bin/ mail/ sample.txt testfile ttd.txt
```

If you want to print the sample.txt file, you could type the following command:

```
lpr sample.txt
```

Using command-line completion, you could get away with typing the following command and then pressing the Tab key:

```
lpr s
```

At this point, tcsh attempts to complete the command and finds that the only file that can possibly match what was typed so far is the sample.txt file. tcsh would then complete the command by putting the following text on the command line:

```
lpr sample.txt
```

You can now either confirm that this is the intended command by pressing the Enter key, or you can edit the command if it isn't what you intended.

Wildcards

tcsh enables you to use wildcards in your commands. It supports the same three wildcards as bash and pdksh:

> * matches any character or any number of characters.

> ? matches any single character.

> [...] matches any single character contained within the brackets.

The * wildcard can be used to perform some of the same functions as command-line completion. If you entered a command like

```
cd t*
```

and only one subdirectory in the current directory begins with the letter t, this command would behave the same as if you had used command-line completion by pressing the Tab key.

The * matches any character or any number of characters, so the shell will replace the t* with the file in the directory that matches the wildcard pattern.

This will work reliably only if there is one file in the directory that starts with the letter t. If more than one file in the directory starts with the letter t, the shell will try to replace t* with the list of filenames in the directory that match the wildcard pattern, and the cd command will make the first directory in this list the working directory. This will end up being the file that comes first alphabetically and may or may not be the intended file.

A case that is more suited to using the * wildcard is if you want to perform the same operation on a number of files that have similar filenames. For example, assume the current directory contains the following files:

```
Mail/ atc1.stk atc2.stk bin/ borl.stk cdrom.txt lfi.stk temp/
```

If you want to print both of the files that start with atc and end with the .stk extension, you could do so by typing

```
lpr a*.stk
```

This command will do the job, because there are no other files in the directory that start with the letter a and have the .stk extension.

Using the ? wildcard, the following command will accomplish the same thing:

```
lpr atc?.stk
```

Using the [...] wildcard, you could enter the following command to get the same files to print:

```
lpr atc[12].stk
```

Command History

The tcsh shell provides a mechanism for accessing the command history that is similar to ones provided with bash and pdksh. The shell remembers the last history commands that have been entered into the shell (where history is a user-definable tcsh variable).

tcsh stores the text of the last history commands in a history list. When you log into your account, the history list is initialized from a history file. The default filename for the history file is .history, but you can change it using the histfile tcsh variable. This file is located in your home directory. Notice that the file begins with a period. This means that the file is a hidden file and will appear in a directory listing only if you use the -a or -A options of the ls command.

> **NOTE**
>
> In order for the history list to be saved in the history file, you must make sure that the savehist variable is set to the number of commands that you want to be saved. Refer to the .login file listing in the "Customizing tcsh" section of this chapter for an example of setting this variable.

The simplest way of using the history list is to use the up and down arrow keys to scroll through the commands that were entered earlier. Pressing the up arrow key will cause the last command entered to appear on the command line. Pressing the up arrow key again will put the command before that on the command line, and so on. If you move up in the command buffer past the command that you wanted, you can move down the history list one command at a time by pressing the down arrow key.

The command that is on the command line can be edited. You can use the left and right arrow keys to move along the command line, and you can insert text at any point. You can also delete text from the command line by using the Backspace or Delete keys. Most users should find these simple editing commands sufficient, but for those who do not, tcsh also supports a wide range of equivalent emacs and vi editing commands. See the "Key Bindings" section of this chapter for more information on vi and emacs command-line editing.

Another method of using the history file is to display and edit the history list using a number of other editing commands that tcsh provides. The history command can be invoked by any one of three different methods. The first method has the following command-line syntax:

```
history [-hr] [n]
```

This form of the history command displays the history list to the screen. The n option is used to specify the number of commands to display. If the n option is not used, the history command will display the entire history list. The -h option causes history to remove the command numbers and timestamps that are usually present in the output of the history command. The -r option tells history to display the commands in reverse order, starting with the most recent command. The following command displays the last five commands that were entered:

```
history 5
```

The second method of invoking the history command is used to modify the contents of the history file or the history list. It has the following command-line syntax:

```
history -S ¦ -L ¦ -M [filename]
```

The -S option writes the history list to a file. The -L option appends a history file to the current history list. The -M option merges the contents of the history file with the current history list and sorts the resulting list by the timestamp contained with each command.

NOTE

All of the options for the second form of the history command use the *filename* option as the name of the history file. If no filename is specified, the history command will use the value of the histfile variable. If the histfile variable isn't set, it will use the ~/.history (home directory) file.

The history command using the -c option clears the current history list.

In addition to the history command and its options, tcsh also contains many history navigation and editing commands. The following commands are used to navigate through the history list:

- !*n* re-executes the command with the history number of *n*.
- !-*n* re-executes the command that is *n* commands from the end of the history list.
- !! re-executes the last command that was entered.
- !c re-executes the last command in the history list that begins with the letter c.
- !?c? re-executes the last command in the history list that contains the letter c.

The history editing commands enable you to replace words and letters in previously entered commands as well as add words to the end of previously entered commands. More information on these editing commands can be found by referring to the tcsh man page. You can view this man page by entering the following command at the shell prompt:

```
man tcsh
```

Aliases

Command aliases are commands that you can specify and execute. Alias commands are usually abbreviations of other Linux commands. You tell tcsh to execute a Linux command whenever it encounters the alias. For example, if you entered the following alias command:

```
alias ls 'ls -F'
```

the ls -F command would be substituted for the ls command each time the ls command was used.

If you decide after you enter an alias that you don't need or want that alias to exist any longer, you can use the tcsh unalias command to delete that alias:

```
unalias cd
```

After you use the unalias command to remove an alias, the alias will no longer exist, and trying to execute that alias will cause tcsh to return a command not found error message.

Some aliases that you might want to define are:

- alias ll 'ls -l'
- alias ls 'ls -F'

If you are a DOS user and are accustomed to using DOS file commands, you might also want to define the following aliases:

- alias dir 'ls'
- alias copy 'cp'
- alias rename 'mv'

- alias md 'mkdir'
- alias rd 'rmdir'

> **NOTE**
>
> When you define aliases, quotation marks are necessary only if the command within them contains spaces or other special characters.

If you enter the `alias` command without any arguments, it will print to the screen all of the aliases that are already defined. The following listing illustrates sample output from the `alias` command:

```
alias ls 'ls -F'
alias dir 'ls'
alias ll 'ls -l'
alias md 'mkdir'
alias rd 'rmdir'
```

Input and Output Redirection

The standard input and output of a command can be redirected using the same syntax that is used by `bash` and `pdksh`. The < character is used for input redirection, and the > character is used for output redirection. The following command redirects the standard input of the `cat` command to the `.cshrc` file:

```
cat < .cshrc
```

In practice, input redirection isn't used very often because most commands that require input from a file support passing the filename as an argument to the command.

Output redirection is used much more frequently. The following command redirects the standard output of the `cat` command to the file named `cshenv` (which has the effect of storing the contents of the `.cshrc` and `.login` files in one file named `cshenv`):

```
cat .cshrc .login > cshenv
```

> **CAUTION**
>
> The file to which output is being redirected is created if it does not exist and is overwritten without warning if it already exists.

Pipelines

`tcsh` pipelines, just like `bash` and `pdksh` pipelines, are a way to string together a series of Linux commands. This means that the output from the first command in the pipeline is used as the input to the second command in the pipeline. The output from the second command in the pipeline is used as input to the third command in the pipeline, and so on. The output from the last command in the pipeline is the output that the user will actually see. This output will be displayed to the screen (or put into a file if output redirection was specified on the command line).

You can tell tcsh to create a pipeline by typing two or more commands separated by the ¦ character. The following command illustrates an example of using a tcsh pipeline:

```
cat file1 file2 ¦ wc -l
```

The cat command in this pipeline appends file2 to the end of file1 and passes the resulting file to the wc command. The wc command prints to the screen the total number of lines contained in the resulting file.

Prompts

tcsh has three levels of user prompt. The first-level prompt is what you see when tcsh is waiting for you to type a command. The default prompt is the % character . This prompt can be customized by assigning a new value to the prompt tcsh variable:

```
set prompt="%t$"
```

This example would change the first-level prompt to the current time followed by a dollar sign.

The second-level prompt is displayed when tcsh is waiting for input when in a while or for loop (used in shell programming, discussed in Chapter 13, "Shell Programming"). The default for the second-level prompt is %R?, where %R is a special character sequence that displays the status of the parser. You can change the second-level prompt by setting the value of the prompt2 tcsh variable. For example:

```
set prompt2="?"
```

changes the second-level prompt to a question mark.

The third-level prompt is used when tcsh displays the corrected command line when automatic spelling correction is in effect. This prompt is set using the prompt3 variable, and it has a default value of CORRECT>%R (y¦n¦e)?. See the "Correcting Spelling Errors" section for more information on this feature.

tcsh supports special character codes in its prompt variables. These codes are similar to the codes that bash supports in its prompts. The main difference between the two is that the syntax for using them is different. Table 12.1 lists the most commonly used special character codes.

Table 12.1. tcsh prompt special character codes.

Character Code	Meaning
%/	Displays the current working directory.

Character Code	Meaning
%h, %!, !	These codes all display the current history number.
%t, %@	These codes both display the time of day.
%n	Displays the username.
%d	Displays the current day of the week.
%w	Displays the current month.
%y	Displays the current year.

The following is an example of setting the prompt variable:

```
set prompt="%h %/"
```

This command sets the prompt to display the history number of the current command, followed by the current working directory.

Job Control

Job control refers to the ability to control the execution behavior of a currently running process. Specifically, you can suspend a running process and cause it to resume running at a later time. tcsh keeps track of all the processes that it starts as a result of user input. You can suspend a running process or restart a suspended one at any time during the life of that process.

Pressing the Ctrl-Z key sequence suspends a running process. The bg command restarts a suspended process in the background, and the fg command restarts a process in the foreground.

These commands are most often used when you want to run a command in the background but by accident start it in the foreground. When a command is started in the foreground, it locks the shell from any further user interaction until the command completes execution. This is usually fine because most commands take only a few seconds to execute. If the command you're running is going to take a long time, you would typically start the command in the background so that you could continue to use tcsh to enter other commands.

For example, if you started a command that was going to take a long time in the foreground, such as

```
find / -named "test" > find.out
```

your shell will be tied up for several minutes. If you have done this and want to cause the find command to continue executing in the background, you could enter the following:

```
control-z
bg
```

This would suspend the find command and then restart it in the background. The find command would continue to execute, and you would regain control of tcsh.

Key Bindings

Like the pdksh, tcsh provides the ability to change and add key bindings. The tcsh implementation of key bindings is more powerful than the way key bindings are done in pdksh.

With tcsh you can bind to things other than the built-in editor commands. This means that you can bind a key to a UNIX command, for example. tcsh also enables you to bind vi editing commands, whereas pdksh only allows the binding of emacs editing commands.

Key bindings can be very useful, especially if you're using a favorite editor other than emacs or vi. The basic syntax for defining key bindings is

```
bindkey [option] <instring or keyname> <outstring or command>
```

The options that bindkey supports are not discussed in this book. If you want to learn about the bindkey options, refer to the tcsh man page. The basic function of the bindkey command is to bind the key sequence contained in the first argument to the command contained in the second argument.

The following list gives some of the most useful editing commands that you can bind key sequences to, along with the default key binding for that command. You can list all the bindings that are defined in tcsh by typing the bindkey command without any arguments.

- beginning-of-line (^A): Moves the cursor to the beginning of the command line.
- backward-char (^B): Moves the cursor back one character.
- end-of-line (^E): Moves the cursor to the end of the command line.
- forward-char (^F): Moves the cursor forward one character.
- backward-delete-char (^H): Deletes the character to the left of the cursor.
- kill-line (^K): Deletes all of the characters to the right of the cursor.
- clear-screen (^L): Removes all of the text from the shell window.
- down-history (^N): Moves down one command in the history list.
- up-history (^P): Moves up one command in the history list.
- kill-whole-line (^U): Deletes all of the characters on the current line.

All of these commands are the same whether you're in emacs or vi insert mode. tcsh supports many more editing commands than are listed here. To see what these commands are, refer to the tcsh man page.

The following are examples of setting key bindings:

```
bindkey ^W kill-whole-line
bindkey ^S beginning-of-line
```

Other Neat Stuff

tcsh supports a few neat features that none of the other shells discussed in this book support. This section lists a few of the most useful of these extended features.

Correcting Spelling Errors

This feature, which is not available with any of the other shells discussed in this book, is a dream come true for many people (including me). If you're plagued by recurring typos, this feature might be enough to cause you to use tcsh over any of the other shells. You can tell tcsh to correct spelling errors in a command that you typed, and you also can tell it to automatically try to correct commands that it can't figure out.

The first function isn't quite as useful, because you must know that you have made a typing mistake before you actually execute the command. This feature is invoked by pressing Esc-S on the command line before you press Enter.

For example, suppose you wanted to change to the /usr/X386/X11/bin directory, so you typed the following command on the command line:

```
cd /usr/X387/X11/bun
```

If you caught the typing errors before you executed the command (by pressing the Enter key), you could correct the errors by pressing Esc-S. tcsh will try to correct the spelling of the command. It would change the command to read

```
cd /usr/X386/X11/bin
```

You could now press the Enter key, and the command would execute just as you wanted. Obviously this command has some limitations, because the shell can't (yet) read your mind, but for simple character transpositions or capitalization errors, it works very nicely.

The second method of instructing tcsh to perform spelling corrections on your commands is to set the correct tcsh variable. This variable, depending on what options you use, will tell tcsh to try to correct spelling errors in command names or anywhere in the command. The syntax for setting the correct variable is one of the following:

```
set correct=cmd
or
set correct=all
```

After you set the correct variable, whenever you enter a command that tcsh doesn't understand, it will automatically check to see if the command has any spelling errors. If it finds possible spelling errors, it gives you the corrected command and asks you if the new command is what you intended. For example, if you had set the correct variable with the all option and then entered the following command:

```
cd /usr/gmes
```

tcsh would respond with the following prompt on the command line:

```
CORRECT>cd /usr/games (y¦n¦e)?
```

If you respond to the prompt by pressing the y (yes) key, tcsh will execute the corrected command. If you respond to the prompt by pressing the n (no) key, tcsh will execute the command that you initially entered, which will in turn will cause an error message to be displayed.

If you respond to the prompt by pressing the e (edit) key, tcsh will put the command that you entered back on the command line and enable you to edit it.

Precommands

tcsh supports a way of executing a command prior to displaying each command prompt. This is done through the use of a special variable called precmd. If the precmd variable is set, the command that it is set to will be executed before the command prompt is displayed on-screen. For example, assume that you set the precmd variable using the following command:

```
alias precmd time
```

After this alias has been declared, the time command will always be executed before the command prompt is displayed on-screen.

Change Directory Commands

tcsh also supports change directory commands. These commands are executed only when the current directory changes (usually as a result of executing the cd command). This type of command is probably more useful than the precommands just mentioned, because there are times when you might want to know something about a directory that you just entered.

This feature is supported in the same way precommands are supported, only you must provide an alias for a different variable. The variable used for this is cwdcmd. If this variable is aliased to a command, that command will be executed each time you change current working directories.

A common use for this variable is to display the current directory to the screen. This can be done by entering the command

```
alias cwdcmd 'pwd'
```

This will display the name of the new directory each time a new directory is entered.

> **WARNING**
>
> You should not put a cd command into cwdcmd. Doing so could cause an infinite loop that would cause you to lose control of tcsh.

Monitoring Logins and Logouts

tcsh provides a mechanism that enables you to watch for any user who logs on or off the system. It does this through a tcsh variable named watch.

The watch variable contains a set of user ID and terminal number pairs. These pairs can contain wildcards and also can contain the word "any," which tells tcsh to match any user or terminal. The syntax for setting the watch variable is

```
set watch=(<user> <terminal>)
```

The *user* in this command refers to a Linux user ID. *terminal* refers to a Linux terminal device number.

Most people would use this capability to watch for friends logging onto the system. For example, if you were waiting for a person with the username jules to come to work in the morning, you could set the following watch variable:

```
set watch=(jules any)
```

This command would inform you when a person with the user ID jules logged into the system on any terminal. tcsh defaults to checking the defined watches every 10 minutes. If you want to know with greater or lesser frequency, you can change this default by passing the number of minutes to wait between checks as the first parameter to the watch variable. For example, to check every five minutes to see if jules has logged in, you would use the following watch variable:

```
set watch=(5 jules any)
```

This will do the same thing as the first command, except it will check every five minutes instead of every 10 to see if jules has logged in.

Customizing *tcsh*

I've discussed many ways of customizing tcsh in this chapter. If you just enter the commands that we have discussed at the command line, the changes you make will be lost every time you log out of the system. This section describes how to store these changes in a file that will be executed each time you start tcsh.

Two initialization files are important to tcsh. The first is called the login file. The commands in this file are executed when you first log into Linux. The contents of the default login file are shown in Table 12.2.

Table 12.2. Default csh.login file.

```
if ($?prompt) then
umask 022
  set cdpath = ( /usr/spool )
  set notify
  set history = 100
    setenv OPENWINHOME /usr/openwin
    setenv MANPATH /usr/local/man:/usr/man/preformat:/usr/man:/usr/X11/man:
    ➥/usr/openwin/man
    setenv MINICOM "-c on"
    setenv HOSTNAME "`cat /etc/HOSTNAME`"
    set path = ( $path /usr/X11/bin /usr/andrew/bin
    ➥$OPENWINHOME/bin /usr/games . )
```

continues

```
endif
# I had problems with the Backspace key installed by 'tset,' but you might want
# to try it anyway, instead of the 'setenv term.....' below it.
# eval 'tset -sQ "$term"'
# setenv term  linux
#if ! $?TERM setenv TERM linux
# set to "linux" for unknown term type:
if ("$TERM" == "") setenv TERM linux
if ("$TERM" == "unknown" setenv TERM linux
set prompt = "%m:%~%# "
eval 'dircolors -t' # set up color-ls variables
alias ls 'ls -F'
if ( { tty —silent } ) then >& /dev/null
  echo "";fortune;echo ""
endif
```

This file, csh.login, can be found in the /etc directory. If you want to change any of the settings found in csh.login, you should copy it to your home directory and make the changes you want there.

The other file that tcsh makes use of is cshrc. The commands in this file are executed each time a copy of the tcsh program is run. Examples of the types of commands that usually appear in this file are aliases and variable declarations. This file, csh.cshrc, is also contained in the /etc directory. If you want to make changes to this file, you should copy it to your home directory and make your changes there.

When you first log in to Linux, tcsh executes the /etc/csh.cshrc file, followed by the /etc/csh.login file. It then checks your home directory to see if you have a personal copy of the csh.cshrc file. This file can be named either .tcshrc or .cshrc. If you have one of these files in your home directory, tcsh will execute it next.

tcsh next checks to see if you have your own copy of the csh.login file in your home directory. This file must be named .login. If you do have a .login file in your home directory, it will be executed next.

Whenever you start another copy of tcsh after you log in to the system, it will execute the commands that are in the /etc/csh.cshrc file and then check your home directory to see if there is a .tcshrc or a .cshrc file there.

tcsh Command Summary

Here are some of the most useful tcsh commands:

- alias: Used to set and display aliases, command nicknames that can be set by the user.
- bg: Background command. Forces a suspended process to continue running in the background.
- bindkey: Enables users to change the editing actions that are associated with a key sequence.
- cd: Changes the current working directory to the directory specified.

- ■ exit: Terminates the shell.
- ■ fg: Foreground command. Forces a suspended process to continue running in the foreground.
- ■ history: Enables users to display and modify the contents of the history list and the history file.
- ■ kill: Terminates another process.
- ■ logout: Terminates a login shell.
- ■ set: Used to set the value of tcsh variables.
- ■ source: Reads and executes the contents of a file. This command is discussed in more detail in Chapter 13.
- ■ unalias: Used to remove aliases that have been defined using the alias command.

tcsh Variables

Here are some of the most useful tcsh variables:

- ■ autocorrect: If this is set, tcsh will automatically try to correct command-line spelling errors.
- ■ histfile: The name of the file that is used to store the command history.
- ■ history: The size of the history list.
- ■ home: The user's home directory.
- ■ path: The search path that tcsh uses when looking for executable programs.
- ■ prompt: The first-level prompt that is displayed on the command line.
- ■ prompt2: The second-level prompt that is displayed when a for, foreach, or while loop is expecting input.
- ■ prompt3: The third-level prompt that is displayed when tcsh has attempted to correct a spelling error in a command.
- ■ savehist: This variable must be set to the number of history commands that you want to save, if you want tcsh to save the history list when you log out.
- ■ watch: Contains a list of user terminal pairs to watch for logins and logouts.

Summary

The last three chapters have presented the fundamental commands and concepts of the three most popular UNIX shells. tcsh is the most feature-rich shell of those presented, but that doesn't necessarily mean that it's the best shell for you to use. In the end, this decision will probably be based on your personal preference as opposed to what features are offered.

The next chapter looks at the programming languages that are provided by each of the shells we have discussed.

Shell Programming

13

by Rick McMullin

The last three chapters described how to use the most common Linux shell programs. I mentioned that these shell programs have powerful interpretive programming languages built into them. Now it's time to look at them in more detail.

This chapter describes the fundamentals of shell programming and compares the bash, pdksh, and tcsh programming languages. This chapter covers the following topics:

- Creating and running shell programs
- Using shell variables
- The importance of quotes
- The test command
- Conditional statements
- Iteration statements

This chapter contains several small examples of shell programs. Each new concept or command that is introduced has some example code that further helps to explain what is being presented.

Creating and Running Shell Programs

At the simplest level, shell programs are just files that contain one or more shell or Linux commands. These programs can be used to simplify repetitive tasks, to replace two or more commands that are always executed together with a single command, to automate the installation of other programs, and to write simple interactive applications.

To create a shell program, you must create a file using a text editor and put the shell or Linux commands you want to be executed into that file. For example, assume you have a CD-ROM drive mounted on your Linux system. This CD-ROM device is mounted when the system is first started. If you later change the CD in the drive, you must force Linux to read the new directory contents. One way of achieving this is to put the new CD into the drive, unmount the CD-ROM drive using the Linux umount command, and then remount the drive using the Linux mount command. This sequence of steps is shown by the following commands:

```
umount /dev/cdrom
mount -t iso9660 /dev/cdrom /cdrom
```

Instead of typing both of these commands each time you change the CD in your drive, you could create a shell program that would execute both of these commands for you. To do this, put the two commands into a file and call the file remount (or any other name you want).

Several ways of executing the commands are contained in the remount file. One way to accomplish this is to make the file executable. This is done by entering the following command:

```
chmod +x remount
```

This command changes the permissions of the file so that it is now executable. You can now run your new shell program by typing remount on the command line.

> **NOTE**
>
> The remount shell program must be in a directory that is in your search path, or the shell
> will not be able to find the program to execute. Also, if you are using tcsh to write
> programs, the first line of the shell program must start with a # for tcsh to recognize it as a
> tcsh program file.

Another way you can execute the shell program is to run the shell that the program was written for
and pass the program in as a parameter to the shell. In a tcsh program, this is done by entering the
following command:

```
tcsh remount
```

This command starts up a new shell and tells it to execute the commands that are found in the
remount file.

A third way of executing the commands in a shell program file is to use the . command (in pdksh
and bash) and the source command in tcsh. This command tells the shell to execute all the commands in the file that is passed as an argument to the command. For example, the following command can be used to tell bash or pdksh to execute the commands in the remount file:

```
. remount
```

To do the same thing in tcsh, you would type the following command:

```
source remount
```

Another situation in which a simple shell program can save a lot of time is described in the following example. Assume you were working on three different files in a directory, and at the end of
every day you wanted to back up those three files onto a floppy disk. To do this you would type a
series of commands similar to the following:

```
mount -t msdos /dev/fd0 /a
cp file1 /a
cp file2 /a
cp file3 /a
```

As stated in the example, one way of doing this would be to mount the floppy drive and then type
three copy commands, one for each file you wanted to copy. A simpler way would be to put the
four commands into a text file called backup and then execute the backup command when you
wanted to copy the three files onto the floppy drive.

> **NOTE**
>
> You will still have to ensure that the backup shell program is executable and is in a direc-
> tory that is in your path before you run the command.

Using Variables

As is the case with almost any language, the use of variables is very important in shell programs. You saw some of the ways in which shell variables can be used in the introductory shell chapters. Two of the variables that were introduced were the PATH variable and the PS1 variable. These are examples of built-in shell variables, or variables that are defined by the shell program you are using. This section describes how you can create your own variables and use them in simple shell programs.

Assigning a Value to a Variable

In all three of the shells I have discussed, you can assign a value to a variable simply by typing the variable name followed by an equal sign and the value you want to assign to the variable. For example, if you wanted to assign a value of 5 to the variable count, you would enter the following command in bash or pdksh:

```
count=5
```

With tcsh you would have to enter the following command to achieve the same results:

```
set count = 5
```

> **NOTE**
>
> With the bash and pdksh syntax for setting a variable, you must make sure that there are no spaces on either side of the equal sign. With tcsh, it doesn't matter if there are spaces or not.

Notice that you do not have to declare the variable as you would if you were programming in C or Pascal. This is because the shell language is a non-typed interpretive language. This means that you can use the same variable to store character strings that you use to store integers. You would store a character string into a variable in the same way that you stored the integer into a variable. For example:

```
name=Garry        (for pdksh and bash)
set name = Garry   (for tcsh)
```

Accessing the Value of a Variable

Once you have stored a value into a variable, how do you get the value back out? You do this in the shell by preceding the variable name with a dollar sign ($). If you wanted to print the value stored in the count variable to the screen, you would do so by entering the following command:

```
echo $count
```

> **NOTE**
>
> If you omitted the $ from the preceding command, the echo command would display the word count on-screen.

Positional Parameters and Other Built-In Shell Variables

The shell has knowledge of a special kind of variable called a positional parameter. Positional parameters are used to refer to the parameters that were passed to a shell program on the command line or a shell function by the shell script that invoked the function. When you run a shell program that requires or supports a number of command-line options, each of these options is stored into a positional parameter. The first parameter is stored into a variable named 1, the second parameter is stored into a variable named 2, and so forth. These variable names are reserved by the shell so that you can't use them as variables you define. To access the values stored in these variables, you must precede the variable name with a dollar sign ($) just as you do with variables you define.

The following shell program expects to be invoked with two parameters. The program takes the two parameters and prints the second parameter that was typed on the command line first and the first parameter that was typed on the command line second.

```
#program reverse, prints the command line parameters out in reverse #order
echo "$2" "$1"
```

If you invoked this program by entering

```
reverse hello there
```

the program would return the following output:

```
there hello
```

Several other built-in shell variables are important to know about when you are doing a lot of shell programming. Table 13.1 lists these variables and gives a brief description of what each is used for.

Table 13.1. Built-in shell variables.

Variable	Use
$#	Stores the number of command-line arguments that were passed to the shell program.
$?	Stores the exit value of the last command that was executed.
$0	Stores the first word of the entered command (the name of the shell program).
$*	Stores all the arguments that were entered on the command line ($1 $2 ...).
"$@"	Stores all the arguments that were entered on the command line, individually quoted ("$1" "$2" ...).

The Importance of Quotation Marks

The use of the different types of quotation marks is very important in shell programming. All three kinds of quotation marks and the backslash character are used by the shell to perform different functions. The double quotation marks (" "), the single quotation marks (' '), and the backslash (\) are all used to hide special characters from the shell. Each of these methods hides varying degrees of special characters from the shell.

The double quotation marks are the least powerful of the three methods. When you surround characters with double quotes, all the whitespace characters are hidden from the shell, but all other special characters are still interpreted by the shell. This type of quoting is most useful when you are assigning strings that contain more than one word to a variable. For example, if you wanted to assign the string `hello there` to the variable `greeting`, you would type the following command:

```
greeting="hello there" (for bash and pdksh)
set greeting = "hello there" (for tcsh)
```

This command would store the `hello there` string into the `greeting` variable as one word. If you typed this command without using the quotes, you would not get the results you wanted. `bash` and `pdksh` would not understand the command and would return an error message. `tcsh` would assign the value `hello` to the `greeting` variable and ignore the rest of the command line.

Single quotes are the most powerful form of quoting. They hide all special characters from the shell. This is useful if the command that you enter is intended for a program other than the shell.

Because the single quotes are the most powerful, you could have written the `hello there` variable assignment using single quotes. You might not always want to do this. If the string being assigned to the `greeting` variable contained another variable, you would have to use the double quotes. For example, if you wanted to include the name of the user in your greeting, you would type the following command:

```
greeting="hello there $LOGNAME" (for bash and pdksh)
set greeting="hello there $LOGNAME" (for tcsh)
```

NOTE

Remember that the `LOGNAME` variable is a shell variable that contains the Linux username of the person who is logged in to the system.

This would store the value `hello there root` into the `greeting` variable if you were logged in to Linux as root. If you tried to write this command using single quotes it wouldn't work, because the single quotes would hide the dollar sign from the shell and the shell wouldn't know that it was supposed to perform a variable substitution. The `greeting` variable would be assigned the value `hello there $LOGNAME` if you wrote the command using single quotes.

Using the backslash is the third way of hiding special characters from the shell. Like the single quotation mark method, the backslash hides all special characters from the shell, but it can hide only one character at a time, as opposed to groups of characters. You could rewrite the greeting example using the backslash instead of double quotation marks by using the following command:

```
greeting=hello\ there (for bash and pdksh)
set greeting=hello\ there (for tcsh)
```

In this command, the backslash hides the space character from the shell, and the string `hello there` is assigned to the `greeting` variable.

Backslash quoting is used most often when you want to hide only a single character from the shell. This is usually done when you want to include a special character in a string. For example, if you wanted to store the price of a box of computer disks into a variable named `disk_price`, you would use the following command:

```
disk_price=\$5.00 (for bash and pdksh)
set disk_price = \$5.00 (for tcsh)
```

The backslash in this example would hide the dollar sign from the shell. If the backslash were not there, the shell would try to find a variable named `5` and perform a variable substitution on that variable. Assuming that no variable named `5` were defined, the shell would assign a value of `.00` to the `disk_price` variable. This is because the shell would substitute a value of null for the `$5` variable.

> **NOTE**
>
> The `disk_price` example could also have used single quotes to hide the dollar sign from the shell.

The back quote marks (` `` `) perform a different function. They are used when you want to use the results of a command in another command. For example, if you wanted to set the value of the variable `contents` equal to the list of files in the current directory, you would type the following command:

```
contents=`ls` (for bash and pdksh)
set contents = `ls` (for tcsh)
```

This command would execute the `ls` command and store the results of the command into the `contents` variable. As you will see in the section "Iteration Statements," this feature can be very useful when you want to write a shell program that performs some action on the results of another command.

The *test* Command

In `bash` and `pdksh`, a command called `test` is used to evaluate conditional expressions. You would typically use the `test` command to evaluate a condition that is used in a conditional statement or to evaluate the entrance or exit criteria for an iteration statement. The `test` command has the following syntax:

```
test expression
```

or

```
[ expression ]
```

Several built-in operators can be used with the test command. These operators can be classified into four groups: integer operators, string operators, file operators, and logical operators.

The shell integer operators perform similar functions to the string operators except that they act on integer arguments. Table 13.2 lists the test command's integer operators.

Table 13.2. The test command's integer operators.

Operator	Meaning
int1 -eq int2	Returns True if int1 is equal to int2.
int1 -ge int2	Returns True if int1 is greater than or equal to int2.
int1 -gt int2	Returns True if int1 is greater than int2.
int1 -le int2	Returns True if int1 is less than or equal to int2.
int1 -lt int2	Returns True if int1 is less than int2.
int1 -ne int2	Returns True if int1 is not equal to int2.

The string operators are used to evaluate string expressions. Table 13.3 lists the string operators that are supported by the three shell programming languages.

Table 13.3. The test command's string operators.

Operator	Meaning
str1 = str2	Returns True if str1 is identical to str2.
str1 != str2	Returns True if str1 is not identical to str2.
str	Returns True if str is not null.
-n str	Returns True if the length of str is greater than zero.
-z str	Returns True if the length of str is equal to zero.

The test command's file operators are used to perform functions such as checking to see if a file exists and checking to see what kind of file is passed as an argument to the test command. Table 13.4 lists the test command's file operators.

Table 13.4. The `test` command's file operators.

Operator	Meaning
-d filename	Returns True if `file`, `filename` is a directory.
-f filename	Returns True if `file`, `filename` is an ordinary file.
-r filename	Returns True if `file`, `filename` can be read by the process.
-s filename	Returns True if `file`, `filename` has a nonzero length.
-w filename	Returns True if `file`, `filename` can be written by the process.
-x filename	Returns True if `file`, `filename` is executable.

The `test` command's logical operators are used to combine two or more of the integer, string, or file operators or to negate a single integer, string, or file operator. Table 13.5 lists the `test` command's logical operators.

Table 13.5. The `test` command's logical operators.

Command	Meaning
! expr	Returns True if `expr` is not true.
expr1 -a expr2	Returns True if `expr1` and `expr2` are true.
expr1 -o expr2	Returns True if `expr1` or `expr2` is true.

The *tcsh* Equivalent of the *test* Command

The tcsh does not have a `test` command, but it supports the same function using expressions. The expression operators that tcsh supports are almost identical to those supported by the C language. These expressions are used mostly in the `if` and `while` commands, which are covered later in this chapter in the "Conditional Statements" and "Iteration Statements" sections.

The tcsh expressions support the same kind of operators as the bash and pdksh `test` command. These are integer, string, file, and logical expressions. The integer operators supported by tcsh expressions are listed in Table 13.6.

Table 13.6. The `tcsh` expression integer operators.

Operator	Meaning
int1 <= int2	Returns True if `int1` is less than or equal to `int2`.
int1 >= int2	Returns True if `int1` is greater than or equal to `int2`.
int1 < int2	Returns True if `int1` is less than `int2`.
int1 > int2	Returns True if `int1` is greater than `int2`.

The string operators that `tcsh` expressions support are listed in Table 13.7.

Table 13.7. The `tcsh` expression string operators.

Operator	Meaning
str1 == str2	Returns True if str1 is equal to str2.
str1 != str2	Returns True if str1 is not equal to str2.

The file operators that `tcsh` expressions support are listed in Table 13.8.

Table 13.8. The `tcsh` expression file operators.

Operator	Meaning
-r file	Returns True if file is readable.
-w file	Returns True if file is writable.
-x file	Returns True if file is executable.
-e file	Returns True if file exists.
-o file	Returns True if file is owned by the current user.
-z file	Returns True if file is of size 0.
-f file	Returns True if file is a regular file.
-d file	Returns True if file is a directory file.

The logical operators that `tcsh` expressions support are listed in Table 13.9.

Table 13.9. The `tcsh` expression logical operators.

Operator	Meaning
exp1 ¦¦ exp2	Returns True if exp1 is true or if exp2 is true.
exp1 && exp2	Returns True if exp1 is true and exp2 is true.
! exp	Returns True if exp is not true.

Conditional Statements

The bash, pdksh, and tcsh each have two forms of conditional statements. These are the if statement and the case statement. These statements are used to execute different parts of your shell program depending on whether certain conditions are true. As with most statements, the syntax for these statements is slightly different between the different shells.

The *if* Statement

All three shells support nested if...then...else statements. These statements provide you with a way of performing complicated conditional tests in your shell programs. The syntax of the if statement is the same for bash and pdksh and is shown here:

```
if [ expression ]
then
      commands
elif [ expression2 ]
then
      commands
else
      commands
fi
```

> **NOTE**
>
> The elif and else clauses are both optional parts of the if statement. Also note that bash and pdksh use the reverse of the statement name in most of their complex statements to signal the end of the statement. In this statement the fi keyword is used to signal the end of the if statement.

The elif statement is an abbreviation of else if. This statement is executed only if none of the expressions associated with the if statement or any elif statements before it were true. The commands associated with the else statement are executed only if none of the expressions associated with the if statement or any of the elif statements were true.

In tcsh, the if statement has two different forms. The first form provides the same function as the bash and pdksh if statement. This form of if statement has the following syntax:

```
if (expression1) then
     commands
else if (expression2) then
     commands
else
     commands
endif
```

> **NOTE**
>
> Once again, the else if and else parts of the if statement are optional.

The second form of if statement provided by tcsh is a simple version of the first if statement. This form of if statement evaluates only a single expression. If the expression is true, it executes a single command; if the expression is false, nothing happens. The syntax for this form of if statement is the following:

```
if (expression) command
```

This statement could be written using the first form of if statement by writing the if without any else or else if clauses. This form just saves a little typing.

The following is an example of a bash or pdksh if statement. This statement checks to see if there is a .profile file in the current directory:

```
if [ -f .profile ]
then
     echo "There is a .profile file in the current directory."
else
     echo "Could not find the .profile file."
fi
```

The same statement written using the tcsh syntax is shown here:

```
#
if ( { -f .profile } ) then
     echo "There is a .profile file in the current directory."
else
     echo "Could not find the .profile file."
endif
```

> **NOTE**
>
> Notice that in the tcsh example the first line starts with a #. This is required for tcsh to recognize the file containing the commands as a tcsh script file.

The *case* Statement

The case statement enables you to compare a pattern with several other patterns and execute a block of code if a match is found. The shell case statement is quite a bit more powerful than the case statement in Pascal or the switch statement in C. This is because in the shell case statement you can compare strings with wildcard characters in them, whereas with the Pascal and C equivalents you can compare only enumerated types or integer values.

Once again, the syntax for the case statement is identical for bash and pdksh and different for tcsh. The syntax for bash and pdksh is the following:

```
case string1 in
     str1)
          commands;;
     str2)
          commands;;
     *)
          commands;;
esac
```

string1 is compared to str1 and str2. If one of these strings matches string1, the commands up until the double semicolon (;;) are executed. If neither str1 nor str2 matches string1, the commands associated with the asterisk are executed. This is the default case condition because the asterisk matches all strings.

The tcsh equivalent of the bash and pdksh case statement is called the switch statement. This statement's syntax closely follows the C switch statement syntax. Here it is:

```
switch (string1)
      case   str1:
            statements
      breaksw
      case   str2:
            statements
      breaksw
      default:
            statements
      breaksw
endsw
```

This behaves in the same manner as the bash and pdksh case statement. Each string following the keyword case is compared with string1. If any of these strings matches string1, the code following it up until the breaksw keyword is executed. If none of the strings matches, the code following the default keyword up until the breaksw keyword is executed.

The following code is an example of a bash or pdksh case statement. This code checks to see if the first command-line option was -i or -e. If it was -i, the program counts the number of lines in the file specified by the second command-line option that begins with the letter i. If the first option was -e, the program counts the number of lines in the file specified by the second command-line option that begins with the letter e. If the first command-line option was not -i or -e, the program prints a brief error message to the screen.

```
case $1 in
   -i)
      count=`grep ^i $2 ¦ wc -l`
      echo "The number of lines in $2 that start with an i is $count"
      ;;
   -e)
      count=`grep ^e $2 ¦ wc -l`
      echo "The number of lines in $2 that start with an e is $count"
      ;;
   * )
      echo "That option is not recognized"
      ;;
esac
```

The same example written in tcsh syntax is shown here:

```
# remember that the first line must start with a # when using tcsh
switch ( $1 )
   case -i ¦ i:
      set count = `grep ^i $2 ¦ wc -l`
      echo "The number of lines in $2 that begin with i is $count"
   breaksw
   case -e ¦ e:
      set count = `grep ^e $2 ¦ wc -l`
      echo "The number of lines in $2 that begin with e is $count"
   breaksw
   default:
      echo "That option is not recognized"
   breaksw
endsw
```

Iteration Statements

The shell languages also provide several iteration or looping statements. The most commonly used of these is the for statement.

The *for* Statement

The for statement executes the commands that are contained within it a specified number of times. bash and pdksh have two variations of the for statement.

> **NOTE**
>
> The for statement syntax is the same in both bash and pdksh.

The first form of for statement that bash and pdksh support has the following syntax:

```
for var1 in list
do
      commands
done
```

In this form, the for statement executes once for each item in the list. This list can be a variable that contains several words separated by spaces, or it can be a list of values that is typed directly into the statement. Each time through the loop, the variable var1 is assigned the current item in the list, until the last one is reached.

The second form of for statement has the following syntax:

```
for var1
do
      statements
done
```

In this form, the for statement executes once for each item in the variable var1. When this syntax of the for statement is used, the shell program assumes that the var1 variable contains all the positional parameters that were passed in to the shell program on the command line.

Typically this form of for statement is the equivalent of writing the following for statement:

```
for var1 in "$@"
do
      statements
done
```

The equivalent of the for statement in tcsh is called the foreach statement. It behaves in the same manner as the bash and pdksh for statement. The syntax of the foreach statement is the following:

```
foreach name (list)
      commands
end
```

The following is an example of the `bash` or `pdksh` style of `for` statement. This example takes as command-line options any number of text files. The program reads in each of these files, converts all the letters to uppercase, and then stores the results in a file of the same name but with a .caps extension.

```
for file
do
tr a-z A-Z < $file >$file.caps
done
```

The same example written in `tcsh` shell language is shown next:

```
#
foreach file ($*)
    tr a-z A-Z < $file >$file.caps
end
```

The *while* Statement

Another iteration statement offered by the shell programming language is the `while` statement. This statement causes a block of code to be executed while a provided conditional expression is true. The syntax for the `while` statement in `bash` and `pdksh` is the following:

```
while expression
do
      statements
done
```

The syntax for the `while` statement in `tcsh` is the following:

```
while (expression)
      statements
end
```

The following is an example of the `bash` and `pdksh` style of `while` statement. This program lists the parameters that were passed to the program, along with the parameter number.

```
count=1
while [ -n "$*" ]
do
      echo "This is parameter number $count $1"
      shift
      count=`expr $count + 1`
done
```

As you will see in the section titled "The `shift` Command," the `shift` command moves the command-line parameters over one to the left.

The same program written in the `tcsh` language is shown next:

```
#
set count = 1
while ( "$*" != "" )
      echo "This is parameter number $count $1"
      shift
      set count = `expr $count + 1`
end
```

The *until* Statement

The until statement is very similar in syntax and function to the while statement. The only real difference between the two is that the until statement executes its code block while its conditional expression is false, and the while statement executes its code block while its conditional expression is true. The syntax for the until statement in bash and pdksh is

```
until expression
do
      commands
done
```

The same example that was used for the while statement can be used for the until statement. All you have to do to make it work is negate the condition. This is shown in the following code:

```
count=1
until [ -z "$*" ]
do
      echo "This is parameter number $count $1"
      shift
      count=`expr $count + 1`
done
```

The only difference between this example and the while statement example is that the -n test command option (which means that the string has nonzero length) was removed, and the -z test option (which means that the string has zero length) was put in its place.

In practice the until statement is not very useful, because any until statement you write can also be written as a while statement.

> **NOTE**
>
> tcsh does not have an equivalent of the until statement other than rewriting it as a while loop.

The *shift* Command

bash, pdksh, and tcsh all support a command called shift. The shift command moves the current values stored in the positional parameters to the left one position. For example, if the values of the current positional parameters are

```
$1 = -r   $2 = file1   $3 = file2
```

and you executed the shift command

```
shift
```

the resulting positional parameters would be as follows:

```
$1 = file1   $2 = file2
```

You can also move the positional parameters over more than one place by specifying a number with the shift command. The following command would shift the positional parameters two places:

```
shift 2
```

This is a very useful command when you have a shell program that needs to parse command-line options. This is true because options are typically preceded by a hyphen and a letter that indicates what the option is to be used for. Because options are usually processed in a loop of some kind, you often want to skip to the next positional parameter once you have identified which option should be coming next. For example, the following shell program expects two command-line options—one that specifies an input file and one that specifies an output file. The program reads the input file, translates all the characters in the input file into uppercase, then stores the results in the specified output file.

> **NOTE**
>
> The following example was written using bash, pdksh syntax.

```
while [ "$1" ]
do
      if [ "$1" = "-i" ] then
            infile="$2"
            shift 2
      elif [ "$1" = "-o" ]
      then
            outfile="$2"
            shift 2
      else
            echo "Program $0 does not recognize option $1"
      fi
done

tr a-z A-Z <$infile >$outfile
```

The *select* Statement

pdksh offers one iteration statement that neither bash nor tcsh provides. This is the select statement. This is actually a very useful statement. It is quite a bit different from the other iteration statements because it actually does not execute a block of shell code repeatedly while a condition is true or false. What the select statement does is enable you to automatically generate simple text menus. The syntax for the select statement is

```
select menuitem [in list_of_items]
do
      commands
done
```

where square brackets are used to enclose the optional part of the statement.

When a select statement is executed, pdksh creates a numbered menu item for each element in the `list_of_items`. This `list_of_items` can be a variable that contains more than one item, such as choice1 choice2, or it can be a list of choices typed in the command. For example:

```
select menuitem in choice1 choice2 choice3
```

If the `list_of_items` is not provided, the select statement uses the positional parameters just as with the for statement.

Once the user of the program containing a select statement picks one of the menu items by typing the number associated with it, the select statement stores the value of the selected item in the menuitem variable. The statements contained in the do block can then perform actions on this menu item.

The following example illustrates a potential use for the select statement. This example displays three menu items, and when the user chooses one of them it asks whether that was the intended selection. If the user enters anything other than y or Y, the menu is redisplayed.

```
select menuitem in pick1 pick2 pick3
do
        echo "Are you sure you want to pick $menuitem"
        read res
        if [ $res = "y" -o $res = "Y" ]
        then
                break
        fi
done
```

A few new commands are introduced in this example. The read command is used to get input from the user. It stores anything that the user types into the specified variable. The break command is used to exit a while, until, repeat, select, or for statement.

The *repeat* Statement

tcsh has an iteration statement that has no equivalent in pdksh or bash. This is the repeat statement. The repeat statement executes a single command a specified number of times. The syntax for the repeat statement is the following:

```
repeat count command
```

The following is an example of the repeat statement. It takes a set of numbers as command-line options and prints that number of periods to the screen. This program acts as a very primitive graphing program.

```
#
foreach num ($*)
        repeat $num echo -n "."
        echo ""
end
```

> **NOTE**
>
> Any repeat statement can be rewritten as a while or for statement. The repeat syntax is simply more convenient.

Functions

The shell languages enable you to define your own functions. These functions behave in much the same way as functions you define in C or other programming languages. The main advantage of using functions as opposed to writing all of your shell code in line is for organizational purposes. Code written using functions tends to be much easier to read and maintain and also tends to be smaller, because you can group common code into functions instead of putting it everywhere it is needed.

The syntax for creating a function in bash and pdksh is the following:

```
fname () {
     shell commands
}
```

pdksh also allows the following syntax:

```
function fname {
     shell commands
}
```

Both of these forms behave in the exact same way.

Once you have defined your function using one of these forms, you can invoke it by entering the following command:

```
fname [parm1 parm2 parm3 ...]
```

> **NOTE**
>
> The tcsh shell does not support functions.

Notice that you can pass any number of parameters to your function. When you do pass parameters to a function, it sees those parameters as positional parameters, just as a shell program does when you pass it parameters on the command line. For example, the following shell program contains several functions, each of which is performing a task associated with one of the command-line options. This example illustrates many of the topics covered in this chapter. It reads all the files that are passed on the command line and—depending on the option that was used—writes the files out in all uppercase letters, writes the files out in all lowercase letters, or prints the files.

```
upper () {
      shift
      for i
      do
           tr a-z A-Z <$1 >$1.out
           rm  $1
           mv $1.out $1
           shift
      done; }

lower () {
      shift
      for i
      do
           tr A-Z a-z <$1 >$1.out
           rm $1
           mv $1.out $1
           shift
      done; }

print () {
      shift
      for i
      do
             lpr $1
             shift
      done; }

usage_error () {
      echo "$1 syntax is $1 <option> <input files>"
      echo ""
      echo "where option is one of the following"
      echo "p  —  to print frame files"
      echo "u  —  to save as uppercase"
      echo "l  —  to save as lowercase"; }

case $1
in
      p ¦ -p)      print $@;;
      u ¦ -u)          upper $@;;
      l ¦ -l)      lower $@;;
      *)               usage_error $0;;
esac
```

Summary

This chapter introduced you to many of the features of the bash, pdksh, and tcsh programming languages. As you become familiar with using Linux, you will find that you use shell programming languages more and more often.

Even though the shell languages are very powerful and also quite easy to learn, you might run into some situations where shell programs are not suited to the problem you are solving. In these cases you may want to investigate the possibility of using one of the other languages available under Linux. Some of your options are C and C++, which are described in Chapters 27, "Programming in C" and 28, "Programming in C++;" gawk, which is described in Chapter 26, "gawk;" and Perl, which is described in Chapter 29, "Perl."

Using Communication Tools Under Linux

14

by Uzma Husain

The communication tools discussed in this chapter include the following:

- write: For one-way communication with other users
- mesg: For controlling message reception from other users
- talk: For an interactive connection with other users
- e-mail: For sending and receiving messages
- telnet: For logging into remote sites
- ftp: For remote file transfers
- news: For reading news via nn and tin

This chapter discusses all of these communications tools in detail and gives you the basics of how to use them in Linux. With practice, you will soon begin to use these tools effectively.

Using the *write* Command

The write command is a communication tool that enables a user to interact directly with other users. If you want to ask your friend a simple question or ask her out to lunch, and you know that she is logged in, write is the tool to use. Unlike e-mail, which is discussed later, write pastes your message directly on the recipient's terminal who does not have to take any steps to receive it.

To use the write command, your terminal and that of the other user should have write permission. Having these permissions enables you to write messages on each other's terminals. To look at the terminal settings, you need to know which terminal you are on. To find your terminal number, use the tty command as shown here:

```
mpsi:~$ tty
/dev/tty2
mpsi:~$ ls -al /dev/tty2
crw--w--w-  1 calvin   users      4,   2 Jan 15 05:49 /dev/tty2
```

The preceding code sample shows that I am on /dev/tty2. Your output may be different, depending on which terminal you happen to be on. The output of the ls command shows that others have write permission available on your terminal. You can confirm this by using the mesg command as shown here:

```
mpsi:~$
mpsi:~$ mesg
Is y
```

The outcome of the mesg command shows that the terminal enables messages to be written to it. You can toggle the terminal settings on and off with the following command:

```
mpsi:~$ mesg n
mpsi:~$ mesg
Is n
```

The preceding segment turned the mesg off. Now you can't be disturbed by any other user. (You may miss out on lunch dates, though.)

A Description of the *write* Command

The write command enables you to write an actual message on the other terminal online. You have to issue the write command with the login ID of the user with whom you want to communicate. The write command informs the user at the other end that there is a message from another user. write pastes that message onto the other user's terminal if their terminal's write permissions are set. Even if they are in the middle of an edit session, write overwrites whatever is on the screen. The edit session contents are not corrupted; you can restore the original screen on most editors with Ctrl-L. write is mostly used for one-way communication, but you can have an actual conversation as well.

> **TIP**
>
> For the write command to work, mesg has to be turned on, so turn it back on.

A Sample *write* Session

Because you want your friend to be able to write to your tty as well, always begin by checking the status of the mesg command:

```
mpsi:~$
mpsi:~$ mesg
Is y
```

Let's see whether your friend Calvin is logged in. You can do this by using the who command and piping it to the grep program to search for Calvin, because you don't want the entire list of users to scroll down your terminal.

```
mpsi:~$ who | grep calvin
calvin    tty2     Jan 15 15:26
```

> **TIP**
>
> Don't forget to type /dev before the terminal name. Look at what happens when you don't type the /dev string:
>
> ```
> mpsi:~$ ls -l tty2
> ls: tty2: No such file or directory
> ```
>
> Oops! All the ttys are in /dev, so add /dev to tty2.

Now let's see whether he wants to be disturbed:

```
mpsi:~$ ls -al /dev/tty2
crw--w--w-  1 calvin   users        4,   2 Jan 15 15:28 /dev/tty2
mpsi:~$
```

This excerpt shows you that Calvin is indeed logged in. Now let's see whether he is interested in communicating with a write session:

```
mpsi:~$ write calvin
```

Calvin sees the following on his screen:

```
mpsi:~$
Message from laurel@mpsi on tty1 at 15:36 ...
```

Now you have to wait for Calvin's response to the request. He responds by typing the following on his terminal if he is interested in communicating with you:

```
mpsi:~$ write laurel
            How are you?
        Lunch tomorrow?
```

The following string appears on your terminal:

```
Message from calvin@mpsi on tty2 at 15:36 ...
            How are you?
        Lunch tomorrow?
```

You can answer Calvin by initiating another write session from your end and typing your message. You have to press Enter at the end of each line for it to be displayed at the other terminal. To simplify communications, you can type over at the logical end of your sentence. Calvin should do likewise.

write Etiquette

If you are waiting for the other party to respond to your write request, it is polite to let him reply while you wait. Only after he has accepted your invitation should the conversation begin. Also, let the called party have the first chance to reply by typing hello or any other salutation. Avoid typing until the other party stops or signals you to begin with an end-of-message word, such as over. Remember, only one person can speak at a time on this channel.

The *talk* Communication Tool

The write tool was nice for communicating one at a time. However, UNIX enables you to type simultaneously with the talk tool.

talk is an interactive communication tool that enables you to have an actual conversation in real-time mode with another user. You can actually see the conversation being typed as the other user is typing it. For talk to work, the other user has to be logged in, just as in write.

`talk` can be very annoying and disturbing if someone wants to be pesky. If you don't want to be disturbed, just turn `talk` off by entering `mesg n` at the prompt.

A Sample *talk* Session

You can talk to somebody by typing `talk` followed by the user's login ID. To see if the user is logged in, you can use the `who` command just like you did for `write`. Let's try to talk to Calvin:

```
$  talk calvin
```

The computer responds with

```
[Waiting for your party to respond]
```

The user on the other end sees the following message even if he is in the middle of an edit session. The system beeps and displays the following message on the terminal:

```
Message from Talk_Daemon@mpsi at 13:08 ...
talk: connection requested by laurel@hobbes.com.
talk: respond with:  talk laurel@hobbes.com
```

To respond to this phone call, type the command shown in the `respond with` message shown here. If your friend does not respond, the `talk` daemon persistently bothers him with the preceding message every 30 seconds.

At your terminal, you see the following messages:

```
[Ringing your party again]
[Ringing your party again]
[Ringing your party again]
[Ringing your party again]
```

Occasionally you will see the following message:

```
[Your party is refusing messages]
```

What happened? Your friend at the other end does not want to talk or be disturbed. After several of your interruptions, he has decided to turn his `mesg` off. That is why you got the message that your party is refusing messages.

Now let's look at a nicer scenario, when someone wants to talk to you. He has to respond with the following command:

```
talk laurel.
```

Then your terminal displays the following screen:

```
[Connection Established]




  — — — — — — — — — — — — — — — — — — — — — — — — — — — — — — — —



```

The screen is divided horizontally with a dotted line, and you can type your message on the top half of the screen. This appears verbatim on the other terminal at the bottom half of the screen. You can type your messages, and the other user can type his, simultaneously.

The connection can be closed by entering Ctrl-C. The following line appears on the screen:

```
[Connection closing.Exiting]
```

You should now be back at your shell's command prompt.

talk Etiquette

The same etiquette applies to `talk` as in `write`. Always use lowercase letters, because CAPS LOCK conversations are considered loud and rude. Always finish your sentence by typing `over`. If you initiated the talk session, wait for the other party to respond with the `hello` first. To prevent both of you from typing at the same time, always read your message, wait for the `over`, type your own message, and then terminate it with `over`.

Electronic Mail

Electronic mail has taken the world by storm. E-mail, short for electronic mail, is a method of sending a message from a user on one computer to one or several recipients on another computer. E-mail provides fast and efficient transportation of data and documents. This mode of communication also eliminates the need to play telephone tag or to wait for a convenient or appropriate time to call someone. For someone with Internet access, e-mail provides the means to communicate with friends around the world.

Mailboxes and Agents

E-mail is stored in a file called the system mail in the mailbox. System mail has the same name as that of the user. For example, a user named Calvin will have a mailbox under Linux in `/var/spool/mail/calvin`.

E-mail originates in the form of a file on your computer created by a Mail User Agent (MUA). E-mail is then submitted to a mail router such as sendmail, after which it is handed over to a Mail Transporter Agent (MTA). E-mail is then appended to a mailbox. The MTA delivers it to the final delivery agent by traversing one or more hosts.

The MUA is used to read and send mail. The MUA is the user interface for the mail system. Mail can be composed by using simple MUAs such as mail or mailx, or sophisticated mail user agents such as elm or pine.

Understanding the Mail Message

A mail message includes two parts: a mail header and the text body.

The mail header is generated by the mail program automatically. A typical header in a mail message looks like this:

```
Date: Fri, 6 Jan 1995 13:27:00 -0600
From: "Calvin N. Hobbes" <calvin@hobbes.com>
To: laurel@hady.com
Subject: Format for a mail header

Hi, just checking the different parts in a mail message
```

`Date` specifies the date and time the message is sent.

`From` specifies both the sender's name in quotes and the address, which includes the login ID and the address of their machine, `hobbes.com`.

`To` is the recipient's mail address.

`Subject` is a one-line description of the mail message.

The mail header is followed by the body of the mail message. Here you type the message as text. The mail message is terminated by typing a period (.) as the first character on the last line. The mail handler responds with `EOT`, for End Of Text. This is the standard procedure for Berkeley mail; other mail handlers have their own way of ending message text entry.

Types of Mail User Agents

There are several types of mail user agents, some of which are listed here. A variety of different programs can be used for reading the mail. The two most common programs are `mail` and `Mail` (also called `mailx`). Because of the similarity of their names, `Mail` is also called `capmail` or Berkeley Mail. Berkeley Mail is far superior to `mail` because it is much easier to use.

This section covers the following types of mail user agents:

- `elm`
- Pine
- `mailx` (Berkeley Mail)

Using *elm*

`elm` stands for electronic mail and provides a full-screen interface mail program with a good help feature. `elm` is a pleasure to use when compared with Berkeley Mail because of its simplicity of use and functionality.

Start the `elm` system by typing `elm` at the command prompt:

$ **elm**

The screen is cleared, and the code shown in Listing 14.1 is displayed.

Listing 14.1. `elm`'s main screen.

```
$ elm
  Mailbox is '/var/spool/mail/calvin' with 5 messages [ELM 2.4 PL24]


  N  1   Jan 12 Laurel N. Hardy     (15)    using el
  N  2   Jan 12 Laurel N. Hardy     (15)    2nd elm message
  N  3   Jan 12 Laurel N. Hardy     (16)    Using elm
  N  4   Jan 11 Laurel N. Hardy     (11)    Re: Format for a mail header
  N  5   Jan 11 Laurel N. Hardy     (11)    message # 1

    You can use any of the following commands by pressing the first character;
 d)elete or u)ndelete mail,  m)ail a message,  r)eply or f)orward mail,  q)uit
    To read a message, press <return>.  j = move down, k = move up, ? = help

Command:
```

The top line on the screen is the mailbox and the number of messages it has in it. You may also see `elm`'s version number. This is followed by a list of all the messages in the mailbox, the date the messages were sent, the sender's name, and the subject of the message.

The current message is indicated by an arrow or inverse video.

One nice feature of `elm` is that it displays the sender's name instead of the login ID as Berkeley Mail does.

The bottom part of the screen lists the options available. At this point, you can reply to the message, delete or undelete a message, or forward the mail by entering the appropriate command. You can go up and down the message list by using k and j, just as in the `vi` editor.

Some of the actions available in `elm` are listed in Table 14.1.

Table 14.1. `elm` actions.

Command	`elm` 2.4 Action
Enter, Spacebar	Displays current message.
|	Pipes current message or tagged messages to a system command.
!	Shell escape.
?	This screen of information.
=	Sets current message to first message.
*	Sets current message to last message.
<NUMBER>, Enter	Sets current message to *<NUMBER>*.
/	Searches From/Subjects for pattern.
//	Searches entire message texts for pattern.
>	Saves current message or tagged messages to a folder.
<	Scans current message for calendar entries.
C	Copies current message or tagged messages.
c	Changes to another folder.
d	Deletes current message.
Ctrl-D	Deletes messages with a specified pattern.
e	Edits current folder.
f	Forwards current message.
g	Groups (all recipients') reply to current message.
h	Headers displayed with message.
J	Increments current message by one.
j, <DOWN>	Advances to next undeleted message.
K	Decrements current message by one.
k, <UP>	Advances to previous undeleted message.
l	Limits messages by specified criteria.
Ctrl-L	Redraws screen.
m	Mails a message.
n	Next message, displaying current, then increment.
p	Prints current message or tagged messages.
q	Quits, maybe prompting for deleting, storing, and keeping messages.

Let's try to send mail using `elm`.

To send mail, press m on the main screen. The header screen appears. `elm` prompts you to enter the name(s) of the recipient(s) of the mail. Enter `calvin` and `root` as recipients. Calvin is the primary recipient, and a copy of this message is sent to root as well.

`elm` then prompts for a subject. After entering the subject heading, `elm` puts you in the `vi` editor to enter the body of the mail message. After you are finished typing, use the `vi` command `:wq` to save and quit the `vi` editor. You can now send the message by pressing s.

You can also forward mail to others on the system with the f command or reply to a message with the r command.

To quit `elm`, type q at the main screen.

If `elm` is available on your system, try to use it. `elm` is very convenient and simple and can greatly improve your electronic mail interaction.

Using Pine

Pine, a trademark of the University of Washington, stands for Program for Internet News and E-mail. Pine offers the capability to send local and remote messages using a simple user interface as well as the capability to send documents and graphics.

You invoke Pine by entering pine on the command line. The screen shown in Listing 14.2 should appear.

Listing 14.2. Pine's main screen.

```
$ pine
  PINE 3.91    MAIN MENU                        Folder: INBOX  1 Message


        ?      HELP            -  Get help using Pine

        C      COMPOSE MESSAGE -  Compose and send a message

        I      FOLDER INDEX    -  View messages in current folder

        L      FOLDER LIST     -  Select a folder to view

        A      ADDRESS BOOK    -  Update address book

        S      SETUP           -  Configure or update Pine

        Q      QUIT            -  Exit the Pine program


   Copyright 1989-1994.  PINE is a trademark of the University of Washington.
                  [Folder "INBOX" opened with 1 message]
? Help                    P PrevCmd                R RelNotes
O OTHER CMDS L [ListFldrs] N NextCmd               K KBLock
```

Pine is very easy to use, because it provides a full-screen interface with the up and down cursor controls. Simply select the item you want by using the arrow keys and press Enter at the selected line.

Let's send a message using Pine. Take the cursor to the Compose Message line and press Enter. The screen shown in Listing 14.3 appears.

Listing 14.3. Composing a message.

```
  PINE 3.91    COMPOSE MESSAGE                    Folder: INBOX  1 Message

To      : "Laurel N. Hardy" <laurel@hobbes.com>
Cc      :
Attchmnt:
Subject : using pine
---- Message Text ----
Hi, I can do everything on one screen
.




Send message? [y] :
^G Get Help  ^X Send     ^R Rich Hdr  ^Y PrvPg/Top ^K Cut Line   ^O Postpone
^C Cancel    ^D Del Char ^J Attach    ^V NxtPg/End ^U UnDel Line ^T To AddrBk
```

Pine takes you line-by-line through the mail header and the mail message. Press Ctrl-X to end the message as well as send it to the recipient. Just walk through all the options to get a feel for this mail system.

The last two lines on the screen tell you what commands are available for the current situation. Usually there are more commands than can be shown on two lines, so use the O key to see what other commands are available. The O is optional; you don't have to be able to see a command before you use it.

Pine creates a default configuration file, .pinerc, in your home directory. You can edit this file to select various options. Pine also creates a mail subdirectory for your saved-message folders. Type ? from the Main Menu for more help.

Using *mailx* (Berkeley Mail)

This section is about mailx, another common mail program for Linux. This section covers the basics of mailx. mailx has many options and features, most of which are listed in its man pages. Discussing all these features would require a book in itself.

Let's see how to receive and send mail using mailx.

Receiving Mail

Suppose someone has sent you a mail message. How would you know about it? The `Mail` system deals with this by displaying a message when you log in. A sample login session is shown in Listing 14.4.

Listing 14.4. Login notification of received mail.

```
Welcome to Linux 1.2.13.

mpsi login: laurel
Last login: Fri Jan  6 13:28:06 on tty1
Linux 1.2.13.
You have new mail.
```

To read the mail message, invoke the `Mail` handler by typing `mail` at the prompt. You will see the output shown in Listing 14.5.

Listing 14.5. Receiving mail.

```
mpɜi: $ mail
Mail version 5.5 6/1/90.  Type ? for help.
"/var/spool/mail/calvin": 1 message 1 new
>N  1 laurel@hobbes.com        Fri Jan  6 13:38  12/374    "just checking"
& 1
Message 1:
From laurel@hobbes.com Fri Jan  6 13:38:06 1995
Date: Fri, 6 Jan 1995 13:38:06 -0600
From: "Laurel N. Hardy" <laurel@hobbes.com>
To: calvin@hobbes.com
Subject: just checking

the body of the message
bye

& exit
You have mail in /var/spool/mail/calvin
```

In this example, the user Calvin has received a mail message from another user, Laurel. This message is the first message in the message queue and is declared as new, which means it has not been read yet. The message queue has an >N, indicating that it is a new message, followed by a message number (1), the sender's login ID (`laurel@hobbes.com`), the day of the week, the date and time the message was sent, and the subject of the message.

The ampersand (&) is the mail system prompt. You can now read the message by typing the message number at this prompt.

```
& 1
Message 1:
From laurel@hobbes.com Fri Jan  6 13:38:06 1995
Date: Fri, 6 Jan 1995 13:38:06 -0600
From: "Laurel N. Hardy" <laurel@hobbes.com>
To: calvin@hobbes.com
Subject: just checking

the body of the message
bye

&
```

Mail Options

All the available options in the Mail system can be listed by typing a ? after the &. The listed options are shown in Listing 14.6.

Listing 14.6. Mail options.

```
& ?

    Mail    Commands
t <message list>               type messages
n                              goto and type next message
e <message list>               edit messages
f <message list>               give head lines of messages
d <message list>               delete messages
s <message list> file          append messages to file
u <message list>               undelete messages
R <message list>               reply to message senders
r <message list>               reply to message senders and all recipients
pre <message list>             make messages go back to /usr/spool/mail
m <user list>                  mail to specific users
q                              quit, saving unresolved messages in mbox
x                              quit, do not remove system mailbox
h                              print out active message headers
!                              shell escape
cd [directory]                 chdir to directory or home if none given

A <message list> consists of integers, ranges of same, or user names separated
by spaces.  If omitted, Mail uses the last message typed.

A <user list> consists of user names or aliases separated by spaces.
Aliases are defined in .mailrc in your home directory.
&
```

Replying to a Message

Suppose you have three mail messages from different users and you want to reply to the one sent by Jeremy. Just invoke mail as before, as shown in Listing 14.7.

Listing 14.7. Three received messages.

```
mpsi:~$ mail
Mail version 5.5 6/1/90.  Type ? for help.
"/var/spool/mail/laurel": 3 messages 3 unread
>U  1 calvin@hobbes.com      Fri Jan  6 13:27  12/429   "Format for a mail hea"
 U  2 jeremy@hobbes.com      Sat Jan  7 15:25  72/23291 " Please reply soon"
 U  3 calvin@hobbes.com      Wed Jan 11 12:29  12/373   "message # 3"
```

The U in front of the second message specifies that the message is still unread. You can read the message by typing the message number.

```
& 2
Message 2:
From jeremy@hobbes.com Sat Jan  7 15:25:00 1995
Date: Sat, 7 Jan 1995 15:25:00 -0600
From: "friend22" <jeremy@hobbes.com>
To: laurel@hobbes.com
Subject: Please reply soon

What's up?
```

You can reply to the message by typing r.

```
& r
To: jeremy@hobbes.com
Subject: Re: Please reply soon
Replying to your mail message # 2
I am loo busy to reply to you now. Go away.
.
EOT
```

The Mail daemon automatically sets up the header in the reply mode, so all you have to do is type the text.

Sending and Forwarding Mail

Sending and forwarding mail can be done with the s and f commands, respectively. The procedures for creating the header and text of the message are similar to that of replying to a message.

The ~/signature file is appended to every mail message you send. You should place text in here that you want to send with every message. Some examples are your phone number or an alternative e-mail address (your recipient might not be able to reply to certain hosts). Mail etiquette requires that you keep you signature files short—four lines or less. Most recipients do not like to see pages of information about you in every mail message.

Using news

Using news is perhaps the best way of getting into what is probably the world's best online forum: the Usenet news service. There are literally thousands of giant bulletin boards for you to select topics from and post messages to. The number of subjects available can be quite overwhelming at times, since there are more than 13,000 newsgroup topics to choose from. (A newsgroup is one of the bulletin boards.) Newsgroups offer the best example of free speech and a forum for discussing just about any topic imaginable.

Topics range from the serious to the absurd. In the serious category you can talk about computer communications (`comp.dcom.telecom`), astronomy (`sci.astro`), and so forth. In the absurd corner you have `alt.tasteless`, `alt.barney.dinosaur.die.die.die`, and `alt.fan.oj-simpson.drive.faster`.

Usenet was started at Duke University in 1979 by two students, Tom Truscott and Jim Ellis, as an experiment to connect two computers between Duke and the University of North Carolina. From these two news sites in 1980, the number of news sites has grown to hundreds of thousands of sites in the 1990s, with millions of subscribers worldwide.

There are several news readers for Linux. I will cover two: `nn` and `tin`.

nn

The `nn` news reader stands for Net News. When you use `nn`, you decide which of the many news groups you are interested in. You unsubscribe those that do not interest you any more. `nn` lets you read all articles in each of the groups you subscribe to, using a menu-based article selection prior to reading the articles in the news group.

When you enter a newsgroup in `nn`, you are presented with a screen that lists the most recent unread articles. Each item on this list contains at least the sender and subject. You are now in selection mode. You can select using the A through Z and 0 through 9 keys. When you select an article, it is displayed in a highlight color. If you press the spacebar, you go into read mode.

In read mode, `nn` presents you with each article. Press the spacebar to get to the next page of each article. If you are at the end of an article, the spacebar takes you to the next article.

When you have read all the selected articles in the current group, pressing the spacebar takes you to the next group.

Here are some of the other commands in `nn`:

- `?` or help gives a one-page overview of the commands available in the current mode. This is perhaps the most used command for beginners. The best way to learn about `nn` is by using this command.
- Ctrl-L or Ctrl-R redraws the screen.
- Ctrl-P shows the previous message.
- `!` is the shell escape command. You are prompted for a command if you do not type one after the `!`.
- `Q` quits `nn`.

- ▪ V prints release and version information (for debug).
- ▪ :command executes the command by name. This is used to invoke any of nn's commands, including those that cannot be bound to a key.

The nn man pages provide about 600 lines of very detailed information about all the options and commands available to you. You do not have to use all of them—just use as many as necessary to customize your own environment.

tin

tin is a screen-oriented Net News reader. It can read news locally (/usr/spool/news) or remotely (rtin or tin -r option) via an NNTP (Network News Transport Protocol) server. tin is based on the tass newsreader, which was developed by Rich Skrenta in March 1991. tass was itself heavily influenced by NOTES, which was developed at the University of Illinois by Ray Essick and Rob Kolstad in 1982. The most relevant author to date is Iain Lea (iain.lea@erlm.siemens.de). Check the long list of contributors in the man pages.

> **TIP**
>
> Use the h (help) command to view a list of the commands available at any level.

On startup, tin shows a list of the newsgroups found in $HOME/.newsrc. An arrow (->) or high-lighted bar points to the first newsgroup. Move to a group by using the terminal arrow keys or j and k. Use Page Up and Page Down or Ctrl-U and Ctrl-D to page up and down. Select a newsgroup to read from by pressing Enter.

The Tab key advances to the next newsgroup that has unread articles and enters it.

To start and run tin, export NNTPSERVER to the address of your remote news server. Use the command

```
$ export NNTPSERVER=news.your.provider.com
```

Then run tin with the -r option to connect to this remote server.

A sample tin session is shown in Listing 14.8. It shows two newsgroups that I have subscribed to: alt.humor and tx.jobs.

When you select a message to read from and press either the right arrow or Enter key, you are shown the message itself, as shown in Listing 14.9.

Listing 14.8. A sample `tin` session.

```
                    Group Selection (news.neosoft.com  2)              h=help

      1   571   alt.humor
  u   2   398   tx.jobs

         <n>=set current to n, TAB=next unread, /=search pattern, c)atchup,
      g)oto, j=line down, k=line up, h)elp, m)ove, q)uit, r=toggle all/unread,
         s)ubscribe, S)ub pattern, u)nsubscribe, U)nsub pattern, y)ank in/out

  Group tx.jobs ('q' to quit)...
```

Listing 14.9. Another sample `tin` session.

```
                        tx.jobs (368T 401A 0K 0H R)                    h=help

      171  +    US-TX-Dallas    MicroFocus Cobol Contract      Mark Allen
      172  +    CA-CLARIS HR, WINDOWS DEVELOPMENT POSITIONS A   CLARIS HR
      173  +    CA-CLARIS HR, DIRECTOR OF WORLDWIDE PRODUCT D   CLARIS HR
      174  +    CA-CLARIS HR, INTERNATIONAL WINDOWS ENGINEER    CLARIS HR
      175  +    CA, CLARIS CORP - TELECOMMUNICATIONS ANALYST    CLARIS HR
      176  +    CA- CLARIS HR, SYBASE PROGRAMMER/ANALYST AT C   CLARIS HR
      177  +    CA-CLARIS HR, DOCUMENTATION CONTROL SPECIALIST  CLARIS HR
      178  +    CA-CLARIS, SUPERVISOR, DIRECT ACCOUNT SERVICE   CLARIS HR
      179  +    CA-DEVELOPERS & TEST ENGINEERS - JAPANESE PRO   CLARIS HR
      180  +    CA-CLARIS HR, DATABASE INTERNALS ENGINEER POS   CLARIS HR
      181  +    CA, CLARIS CORPORATION - PRICING ANALYST        CLARIS HR
      182  +    WA-CLARIS HR, MAC & WINDOWS DEV'RS/ INTERFACE   CLARIS HR
      183  +    USA-TX-DALLAS -    Informix 4GL/ESQL            imi
      184  +    USA-TX-DALLAS - SONET Telephany Engineers       imi
      185  +    USA-TX-DALLAS - PowerBuilder                    imi
      186  +    USA-TX-DALLAS - Oracle DBAs                     imi
      187  +    USA-TX-DALLAS - CICS, Cobol, JCL, VSAM (ALC +   imi

     <n>=set current to n, TAB=next unread, /=search pattern, ^K)ill/select,
  a)uthor search, c)atchup, j=line down, k-linc up, K=mark read, l)isl thread,
     ¦=pipe, m)ail, o=print, q)uit, r=toggle all/unread, s)ave, t)ag, w=post
```

In Listing 14.9, you see a list of subject headers and their index numbers. The + sign indicates that you have not read this message. For example, the SONET job for Dallas, Texas, has an index of 184 and is unread. To read this message, use the arrow keys to move to it, and then press Enter.

Command-Line Options

`tin` has several command-line options, some of which are listed in Table 14.2.

Table 14.2. `tin`'s command-line options.

Option	Description
-c	Creates or updates index files for every group in $HOME/.newsrc or every file specified by the -f option and marks all articles as read.
-f file	Uses the specified file of subscribed newsgroups instead of $HOME/.newsrc.
-h	A help listing of all command-line options.
-m dir	The mailbox directory to use. The default is $HOME/Mail.
-n	Loads only groups from the active file that are also subscribed to in the user's .newsrc. This enables a noticeable speedup when connecting via a slow line.
-p program	Prints program with options.
-q quick	Starts without checking for new newsgroups.
-r read	News specified in the environment variable NNTPSERVER or contained in the file /etc/nntpserver.
-R read	News saved by -S option (not yet implemented remotely from the default NNTP server).
-s dir	Saves articles to a directory. The default is $HOME/News.
-v	Verbose mode for the -c, -M, -S, -u, and -Z options.

To add a new group, type g*groupname*. For example, gmisc.invest adds the newsgroup misc.invest.

`tin` offers an emacs-style editing facility for entering messages. The command strings include a history of commands to enable reuse of previous commands. The man pages for `tin` list all the commands available to you for editing, deleting, and removing messages.

`tin` uses the following important environment variables:

NNTPSERVER	The default NNTP server to remotely read news from. This variable needs to be set only if the -r command-line option is specified and the file /etc/nntpserver does not exist.
VISUAL	This variable overrides the default editor that is used in all editing operations within `tin`.

tin can pretty much be navigated by using the four arrow keys. The left arrow key goes up a level; the right arrow key goes down a level; the up arrow key goes up a line or page; and the down arrow key goes down a line or page. Most prompts within tin can be aborted by pressing Esc.

Using FTP

File transfer protocol (FTP) is a method of transferring files from one computer to another. FTP provides the capability of transferring files to and from a remote network site as well as means for sharing public files. In this section you go through a sample FTP session and follow the steps for finding and getting software from a remote site.

ftp is the user interface to the ARPANET standard FTP. The ftp service is the interface to the file transfer protocol. It lets a user connect to another site and send and receive files.

In this section you will try to get a file from the address tsx-11.mit.edu by logging in as anonymous. This anonymous use of FTP is very convenient and provides access to innumerable servers, providing a wealth of information. Publicly accessible FTP servers are called anonymous FTP servers.

Anonymous FTP

Anonymous FTP enables users to access remote sites without having an authorized user ID and password. Generally the login ID is anonymous and the password is guest. Most current systems require your e-mail address as the password instead of guest.

> **TIP**
>
> FTP stands for File Transfer Protocol; ftp is the program you run on Linux.

The client host with which ftp is to communicate may be specified on the command line. If this is done, ftp immediately attempts to establish a connection to an FTP server on that host. Otherwise, ftp enters its command interpreter and awaits instructions from the user. When ftp is awaiting commands from the user, the prompt ftp> is provided to the user. Enter ftp at the prompt, along with the site address:

```
$ ftp hostname
```

A hostname can be either a hostname or an Internet address. For example, you can use the following Internet address:

```
mpsi$ ftp tsx-11.mit.edu
```

If your system connects to the MIT server, the text shown in Listing 14.10 appears.

Listing 14.10. An `ftp` session.

```
220 tsx-11 FTP server (Version wu-2.4(3) Mon Jun 5 16:40:22 EDT 1995) ready.
Name (tsx-11.mit.edu:uzma): anonymous
331 Guest login ok, send your complete e-mail address as password.
Password:
230-Welcome, archive user!  This is an experimental FTP server.  If have any
230-unusual problems, please report them via e-mail to ftp-bugs@tsx-11.mit.edu.
230-If you do have problems, please try using a dash (-) as the first character
230-of your password -- this will turn off the continuation messages that may
230-be confusing your ftp client.
230-
230-The Linux archives are in /pub/linux/
230-
230-In most places, 'get <directory>.tar' will retrieve a tar file containing
230-that directory.  'get <file>.gz' gets a gzipped version of a files, and
230-'get <file>.Z' gets a compressed version of the file.  'get <dir>.tar.gz'
230-is possible, but not recommended.  'get <dir>.zip' will get a zip archive
230-with *NO* compression of the directory <dir>.
230-
230-If you find something on TSX-11 which doesn't work, or which you
230-believe is obselete, please send mail to ftp-linux@TSX-11.MIT.EDU.
230-INCLUDE THE FULL PATHNAME OF THE FILE AND WHY YOU THINK IT IS OBSOLETE.
230-
230-                                    - Ted and Michael
230-
230 Guest login ok, access restrictions apply.
Remote system type is UNIX.
Using binary mode to transfer files.
ftp>
```

The first line confirms that the connection is established. Line 220 indicates that the FTP server is ready. The system then prompts for a name, which is anonymous in this case, and a password. The password is not echoed, so any typing mistakes you make are not apparent. You are then connected to the remote FTP server, which awaits your commands.

ftp Commands

The `ftp` service enables the user to execute several commands. Some of the local commands are listed in Table 14.3.

Table 14.3. Some `ftp` commands.

Command	Description
[account [*passwd*]]	Supplies a supplemental password required by a remote system for access to resources once a login has been successfully completed. If no argument is included, the user is prompted for an account password in a non-echoing input mode.
ascii	Sets the file transfer type to network ASCII. This is the default type.

Command	Description
bell	Sounds a bell after each file transfer.
binary	Sets the file transfer type to binary mode.
bye	Terminates the FTP session with the remote server and then exits.
cd *remote-directory*	Changes the working directory on the remote machine to the remote directory.
cdup	Goes to the parent of the current remote machine's working directory.
chmod *mode file-name*	Changes the permission modes of the file.
close	Terminates the FTP session with the remote server.
delete *remote-file*	Deletes the remote file on the remote machine.
dir [*remote-directory*]	Prints a listing of the remote directory to the terminal.
disconnect	Same as close.
get *remote-file* [*local-file*]	Retrieves the remote file and stores it on the local machine. If the local filename is not specified, it is given the same name it has on the remote machine.
hash	While a file is being transferred, the hash sign (#) is printed for each data block transferred.
help [*command*]	Prints an informative message about the meaning of the command. If no argument is given, ftp prints a list of the known commands.
lcd [*directory*]	Changes the working directory on the local machine. If no directory is specified, the user's home directory is used.
ls [*remote-directory*]	Lists the contents of the remote directory.
mdelete [*remote-files*]	Deletes the remote files on the remote machine.
mdir *remote-files*	Like dir, except multiple remote files may be specified.
mget *remote-files*	Expands the remote files on the remote machine and does a getfiles based on regular expressions. For example, mget f*.tar will get all the files starting with the letter f.
open *host* [*port*]	Establishes a connection to the specified host FTP server on the optional port number.
put *local-file*	Stores a local file on the remote machine.
pwd	Prints the name of the current working directory on the remote machine.
quit	Same as bye.

continues

Table 14.3. continued

Command	Description
remotehelp [*command-name*]	Requests help from the remote FTP server. If a command name is specified, it is supplied to the server as well.
reset	Resets the communications connection.
rmdir *directory-name*	Deletes a directory on the remote machine.
size *file-name*	Returns the size of the file on the remote machine.
status	Shows the current status of ftp.
verbose	Displays all responses to the user.
? [*command*]	Same as help.

Some of the options that may be specified at the command line are listed as follows:

- -v   The verbose option. Gives a report on the transfer statistics and forces ftp to show all responses from the remote server.
- -n   Restrains ftp from attempting auto-login upon initial connection. In auto-login, ftp checks for the user's account on the remote machine.
- I   Turns off interactive prompting during multiple file transfers.
- -d   Enables debugging.

Some ftp commands share the same name as Linux commands but perform a different function. For example, the ls command in ftp behaves like the ls-al command in Linux. To illustrate how this works, let's look at the directory listing command on a remote server:

> **NOTE**
>
> On some systems, ls at the ftp prompt will behave like the ls-F command.

```
ftp>
ftp> ls
200 PORT command successful.
150 Opening ASCII mode data connection for /bin/ls.
total 6
drwxrwxr-x  2 root      ftp-linu      512 Feb  8 1995  bin
drwxrwxr-x  2 root      wheel         512 Nov  5 1994  dev
drwxrwxr-x  3 root      wheel         512 Nov  9 17:22  etc
lrwxr-xr-x  1 tytso     wheel           1 Nov  5 02:17  ftp -> .
drwxrwx-wx  4 tytso     ftp-linu      512 Dec  8 07:44  incoming
drwxrwxr-x  9 tytso     ftp           512 Dec  1 22:35  pub
226 Transfer complete.
ftp>
```

As you can see, you did not have to type -al. You get the long listing from the ls command.

To abort a file transfer, use the terminal interrupt key (usually Ctrl-C). Sending transfers are immediately halted. Receiving transfers are halted by sending an `ftp ABOR` command to the remote server and discarding any further data received.

The ftp specification specifies many parameters that may affect a file transfer. The type may be `ascii`, `image` (binary), or `ebcdic`.

telnet

The `telnet` command is used to communicate with another host using the TELNET protocol. If `telnet` is invoked without the host argument, it enters command mode, indicated by its prompt, `telnet>`. Normally you would use

```
$ telnet hostname [port]
```

where *hostname* is the host you want to connect to and *port* indicates a port number (an application's address). If a number is not specified, the default telnet port is used.

telnet can log you in either one of two modes: character-by-character or line-by-line. In character-by-character mode, most text typed is immediately sent to the remote host for processing. In line-by-line mode, all text is echoed locally, and only completed lines are sent to the remote host.

While connected to a remote host, you can enter the `telnet` command mode by typing the telnet escape character, Ctrl-]. When in command mode, the normal terminal editing conventions are available.

The following commands are available under the command mode:

`close`	Closes a `telnet` session and returns to command mode.
`open host` `[[-l] user][-port]`	Opens a connection to the named host. If no port number is specified, `telnet` attempts to use the default port. The `[-l]` option may be used to specify the user name.
`quit`	Closes any open `telnet` session and exits `telnet`. An end-of-file (in command mode) will also close a session and exit.

Check the man pages for a list of long, detailed options for telnet.

Let's use `telnet` to do an Archie session. An Archie server is helpful for searching for files by giving a keyword in a title. See Listing 14.11.

Listing 14.11. Logging in via `telnet`.

```
$ telnet archie.internic.net
.
.
.
SunOS UNIX 4.1 (ds) (ttypa)
```

continues

bootutils/	indent/	popclient/	util-linux-2.2/
clisp/	ispell/	portmap/	vim/
cnews/	jpeg/	rcs/	x3270/
cpio-2.3/	keytables/	rdist/	xboard-3.0.pl9/
deliver/	ldso/	sasteroids/	xfm-1.3/
dialog/	less/	sendmail/	xlock/
diffutils/	lilo@	seyon/	xpaint/
dip/	lrzsz/	splitvt/	xpm-3.4c/
f2c/	m4/	strace/	xspread/
faq/	mc/	svgalib/	xv/
file/	minicom/	sysklogd/	yp-clients-1.6/
flex/	modules/	sysvinit/	ypserv-0.13.1/
ftape/	mt-st/	tar/	zip/
gawk/	mtools/	term/	zsh/

Each subdirectory in the preceding list contains more specific information about each tool. For example, if you want more specific information about the tape tool, look in the /usr/doc/mt-st directory for a README file for a listing of the contents.

HOWTO Documents

Let's face it. This one chapter (or text for that matter) cannot possibly hope to cover all the scenarios that you will encounter as you work with Linux. The number of combinations of hardware devices, software interfaces, and versions of Linux make it impossible to list them all here. That one specific CD-ROM or Ethernet card in your PC may not be listed here in this book, but may very well be supported under Linux. To get more specific information about specific topics, you have to read the HOWTO files for that topic.

Basically, a HOWTO file is compiled by someone who has tracked problems related to a specific issue. Topics include booting, printing, tape support, and so on. There are a number of HOWTO files included with the CD-ROM (and installed to the hard drive with most installations of Linux). If your mount point is /cdrom, the HOWTO files are found in /cdrom/docs. The files are in text format in that directory, so you can use any text editor to view them. A complete listing of the /cdrom/docs/00_index.txt file is shown here to help you get an idea of where to look for more information:

Bootdisk-HOWTO	This is the file you would read to get more information about creating boot and root disks for your machine.
Busmouse-HOWTO	This file contains information on installing and using a bus mouse with your Linux system.
CDROM-HOWTO	Linux supports a variety of CD-ROM drives. Unfortunately, not all the CD-ROM drives on the market are supported. Look in this file for more information about CD-ROM drive devices and Linux drivers.
COPYRIGHT	This file contains the copyright restrictions and information about Linux.
Commercial-HOWTO	Looking for commercial software available for Linux? Check out this file, which contains lists of companies and products for Linux.

DOSEMU-HOWTO	Linux has a DOS emulator called DOSemu. This HOWTO contains information about the Linux MS-DOS emulator.
Danish-HOWTO	How to configure Linux for use with the Danish character set.
Distribution-HOWTO	A general list of mail order distributions and other commercial services.
ELF-HOWTO	In the future, Linux binaries will be distributed in the Information on ELF binaries for Linux.
Ethernet-HOWTO	Information on Ethernet hardware compatibility for Linux.
Firewall-HOWTO	How to set up a firewall using Linux.
Ftape-HOWTO	Information on ftape drive compatibility with Linux.
German-HOWTO	Information on using Linux with German-specific features.
HAM-HOWTO	How to configure amateur radio software for Linux.
HOWTO-INDEX	Index of HOWTO documents about Linux.
Hardware-HOWTO	A list of hardware known to work with Linux.
INFO-SHEET	Generic introduction to the Linux operating system.
Installation-HOWTO	How to obtain and install the Linux software.
JE-HOWTO	Information on JE, a set of Japanese language extensions for Linux.
Kernel-HOWTO	Upgrading and compiling the Linux kernel.
META-FAQ	A listing of Linux sources of information.
MGR-HOWTO	Information on the MGR graphics interface for Linux.
Mail-HOWTO	Information on Linux-based mail servers and clients.
NET-2-HOWTO	How to configure TCP/IP networking, SLIP, PLIP, and PPP under Linux.
NIS-HOWTO	Linux NIS (Network Information Service) and YP (Yellow Pages).
News-HOWTO	Information on Usenet news server and client software for Linux.
PCI-HOWTO	Information on PCI-architecture compatibility with Linux.
PCMCIA-HOWTO	How to install and use PCMCIA Card Services.
PPP-HOWTO	Information on using PPP networking with Linux.
Printing-HOWTO	Information on how to set up printing under Linux.
Printing-Usage-HOWTO	How to use the printing system for a variety of file types and options.
SCSI-HOWTO	Linux SCSI drive tape CD-ROM HOWTO.
SCSI-Programming-HOWTO	Information on programming the generic Linux SCSI interface.

It's time to look at editors. This chapter will show you

- What editors are and why you need one
- The basic editing functions
- The vi editor in more detail
- The emacs editor in more detail

What Are Editors and Why Do I Need One?

A *text editor* is one of the most essential tools provided with the Linux (or virtually any) operating system. With an editor, you can create and modify text files that have a wide variety of applications:

- User files such as .login and .cshrc
- System files
- Shell programs
- Documents
- Mail messages

These are but a few of the many different types of text files that you will use when working with Linux. Basically, editors enable you to insert, delete, move, and search text ranging from individual characters to thousands of lines.

Two of the most popular editors for the Linux system are emacs and vi. These editors are both full-screen text editors: Put simply, they use every row and column of your terminal screen to display the textual contents of a file. Both of these editors feature a rich set of commands. The essential commands for manipulating text can be learned reasonably quickly; the more sophisticated commands may take a little longer to master. However, you will likely appreciate this investment as you see how much time these powerful tools can save you.

Choosing one editor over another can be a matter of taste. Both emacs and vi are efficient and can handle virtually any size of file. The emacs editor is better suited to complex editing tasks and comes with an online help facility, but, for simple editing jobs, either editor is equally good. It really just comes down to whichever one you feel more comfortable using.

The Editing Functions

Although there are a variety of text editors for Linux that have different interfaces, they all basically do the same things. Any useful text editor should support the following features at a minimum.

Inserting and Deleting Text

The most intrinsic function of a text editor is to enable you to enter and erase characters as you see fit. This also implies that you have complete control over the movement of the cursor and its placement in the text.

Reading and Writing Files

Because you will want to save the text files that you create for future use and reuse, an editor can write your text to an external file. Whenever you need to make changes to your file, an editor can read the file from disk. A nice feature is that text editors are designed to accommodate ASCII formatted files, so an editor (such as emacs) can read any file written by another editor (such as vi), and vice versa.

Searching Text

Personally scanning line after line of a large file for instances of a particular word is either a great way to improve your powers of concentration or an exercise in self-torture. That is why text editors provide sophisticated search capabilities. These include the use of regular expressions as well as fixed strings. Remember that regular expressions include metacharacters (such as ., ?, and *) that replace and expand unknown text patterns.

Editors also support search-and-replace functions that enable you to change multiple instances of a string pattern with a single command.

Copying and Moving Text

Because there is no guarantee that the way text is initially typed into a file is the way it should forever remain, editors provide you with the means to copy, cut, and move (or paste) blocks of text. These blocks can range in size from several pages to a single character. The distinction between copying and cutting text is that cutting deletes the selected block of text after it has been copied to a buffer, whereas copying does not.

> **NOTE**
>
> Imagine having to retype Dickens's *A Tale of Two Cities* after realizing that you have somehow placed "It was the best of times, it was the worst of times" at the end of the file and not the start!

Editing Buffers

What is a buffer, you ask? *Buffers* are places in the memory of the editing program where text can reside as you make changes to a file. For example, the first time you edit a file, the text you have entered actually exists in a buffer that is written to an external file when you do a save. Buffers can also be used at other times in editing, particularly when it is necessary to temporarily move a block of text to memory as you make changes (in other words, cutting and pasting). Many editors enable you to manage multiple buffers simultaneously.

These editors have many commands that will not be fully detailed in this chapter. Before engaging in any long and arduous editing task, consult the man page for the editor you are using. There may be an easier way of doing whatever it is that you want to do. As you gain experience with an editor, you will discover convenient shortcuts and functions to perform your most tedious editing chores.

The *vi* Editor

The vi editor is installed with virtually every UNIX system in existence. Because of this, vi is considered by many to be the default text editor of the UNIX system (upon which Linux is based). vi has two modes of operation and terse commands, both of which make it a somewhat more difficult editor to learn than emacs. However, it is a useful editor to learn if emacs has not been installed on your Linux system.

Starting *vi*

You invoke vi from the command line by typing

```
vi
```

The screen will clear and a column of tildes (~) will appear in the leftmost column. You are now editing an empty, unnamed file. Whatever text you place in this file will exist in a buffer until you write the contents of the buffer to some named file. The tilde is vi's way of telling you that the line where the tilde appears is empty of text.

vi can also be started with a file or a list of files to edit:

```
vi filename1 filename2 filename3 ...
```

Typically, you will probably edit only one file per vi session. If you are editing a list of files, vi will edit each one in the sequence that they appear on the command line.

Alternatively, vi can be invoked from the command line as

```
vi +n filename
```

where *n* represents the line number where vi will place its cursor in *filename*. This is useful for programmers debugging large source code files who need to quickly jump to a known line containing an error.

Another example will be of use in illustrating the vi editor. If you still have a vi session on your screen, exit it by pushing Esc, and then typing :q!. To start a new vi session, enter

```
vi asong
```

at the command line.

vi modes

At the bottom of the screen in the left corner, you will see

```
"asong" [NEW FILE] 1 line, 1 char
```

The messages displayed on this status line tell you what vi is doing or has just done. In this case, vi is telling you that it has opened an empty buffer whose contents will be saved (whenever you do a save) to the file asong.

At this moment, you are in the command mode of vi. This is the major conceptual leap required in working with this editor. When editing text, you must remember if you are in command mode or text mode. In *command mode,* any character sequences that you enter are interpreted as vi commands. In *text mode,* every character typed is placed in the buffer and displayed as text on-screen.

Four commands are echoed at the bottom of the screen on the status line:

/	Searches forward.
?	Searches backward.
:	An ex command (ex is a standalone line-based editor used within vi).
!	Invokes a shell command.

Each of these types of status-line commands must be entered by pressing Return. This is not true for other types of vi commands, such as the ones that do insertions.

> **TIP**
>
> To find out whether you are in command mode, use the set showmode preference described in the section entitled "Setting Preferences" later in this chapter.

Inserting Text

So, knowing that you are in command mode, let's insert some text. Basically, there are two commands for entering text on the current line: the letters i and a. These letters in lowercase insert (i) text to the left of the cursor or append (a) text to the right of the cursor. As with many vi commands, the uppercase versions of these letters have similar effects with subtle differences: uppercase I and A insert and append at the beginning and end of the current line, respectively.

After you type either of these letters, you will be placed in input mode. Any text entered after this point will be displayed on-screen.

Type an i and then type the following:

```
Down I walk<Enter>
by the bay,<Enter>
Where I can<Enter>
hear the water.<Enter>
Down we walk<Enter>
by the bay,<Enter>
My hand held<Enter>
by my daughter.<Enter>
```

To exit from input mode, press Esc. Notice that you did not see the letter i displayed before you entered the text, meaning that the i was correctly interpreted as a command. Also, it is important to note that it was not necessary to press Return after pressing i for input mode.

Quitting vi

Now that you have some text for your file, let's quit the editor to see the results. The commands used for saving the file and exiting vi are slightly different from the i and d commands used in editing text: you must precede the command with a colon (:).

In this case, you want to do a save and exit, which are actually combined in one command. Type a :. At the bottom left of your screen, you will notice that a colon has appeared. vi has recognized that you are about to enter an ex command, and it will echo the remaining characters of the command after the colon. Type wq and press Return. vi quickly informs you that it has written the file to disk and tells you how many lines it contains. If the file is small and you have a fast system, this message may appear and be erased so quickly you won't catch it. Don't worry—the file has been saved if you issued the command properly. vi exits and you find yourself back at the shell prompt. Another way to save and exit is to type ZZ. The difference between this method and using wq is that ZZ will write the file only if it has been modified since the last save.

You can quit vi by typing :q if no changes have been made to the file you opened. This will not work if the file has been modified. If you are sure that you don't want to save what you have done, enter :q!. This command forces vi to quit, regardless of any edits.

To make sure that vi saved the file asong correctly, use the cat command to quickly view the file's contents:

```
$ cat asong
Down I walk
by the bay,
Where I can
hear the water.
Down we walk
by the bay,
My hand held
by my daughter.
$
```

Everything is exactly as you typed it in the file, so no surprises here.

Moving the Cursor

Moving the cursor around in vi essentially involves the following four keys:

    h   Moves the cursor one space to the left.

    j   Moves the cursor down one line.

    k   Moves the cursor up one line.

    l   Moves the cursor one space to the right.

These keys can perform their operations only when vi is in command mode. For convenience, most implementations of vi map these keys to their directional counterparts on the keyboard arrow keys.

vi enables you to move through a file in bigger "leaps" as well. Following are some commands for scrolling more than one line at a time:

Ctrl-U	Scrolls up a half-screen.
Ctrl-D	Scrolls down a half-screen.
Ctrl-F	Scrolls down one full screen.
Ctrl-B	Scrolls up one full screen.

The size of these movements largely depends on the terminal settings.

It is also possible to move the cursor to a specific line in a file. If you want to move to the tenth line, type 10G or :10 in command mode. G by itself will move the cursor to the end of the file. The cursor will not move if the number given is not applicable (for example, typing :10 in a eight-line file will have no effect).

vi will also enable you to move the cursor a word at a time. A word is defined as any sequence of non-whitespace characters. To move to the beginning of the next word or punctuation mark on the current line, type w. Type b to move the cursor to the beginning of the current or previous word or punctuation mark.

Deleting Text

vi has commands for deleting characters, lines, and words. *Deletion* means that the selected text is removed from the screen but is copied into an unnamed text buffer from which it can be retrieved.

To delete a word, use the dw command. If you want to delete the word to the right of the cursor, type dw. If you are in the middle of a word, it will delete from the cursor position to the end. You can also delete several words at a time. For example, the command 4dw will delete the next four words on the current line.

Lines can be deleted individually or by specifying a range of lines to delete. To delete the current line, type dd. The command 4dd deletes four lines (the current line and three below it). dG will delete all lines from the current one to the end of the file.

On the current line, you can delete in either direction: d^ will delete backward to the beginning of the line; d$ (or D) will delete forward to the end of the line.

To delete individual characters, x deletes the character underneath the cursor, and X deletes the character to the left of the cursor. Both of these commands will accept a number modifier: For example, 4x deletes the current character and the four characters to the right.

Unwanted changes such as deletions can be immediately undone by the u command. This "rolls back" the last edit made.

TIP

Not sure what command you just typed? When in doubt, press Esc and then enter the command again.

Copying and Moving Text

Moving sections of text around in a file basically requires three steps:

1. Yank the text into a buffer.
2. Move the cursor to where you want to insert the text.
3. Place the text from the buffer at the new location.

Yanking text means to copy it into either a named or unnamed buffer. The *unnamed buffer* is a temporary storage space in memory that is continually overwritten by successive yanks. vi has 26 named buffers that correspond to each letter of the alphabet.

To yank the current line into the unnamed buffer, the command is yy or Y. These commands can be modified by a number indicating how many lines beneath the cursor are to be yanked. For example, the command

```
3yy
```

in your file asong (with the cursor on the top line) yanks the following text into the temporary buffer:

```
Down I walk
by the bay,
Where I can
```

This text could also be yanked into the named buffer a by the following command:

```
"a3yy
```

The double quote (") tells the yank command to overwrite the contents of the named buffer a. If you had typed a capital A instead of a lowercase a, the three lines would have been appended to the end of the a buffer. This overwrite-versus-append concept works the same for all of the named buffers.

If you move the cursor to the end of the file using the :$ command, you can then paste the contents of the unnamed buffer to the end of the file. This is done using the p command, which pastes the contents of a buffer to the right of the cursor (P pastes to the left of the cursor). The paste command can also specify a named buffer in the same way as the yank command:

```
"ap
```

Yanks can also be performed on words using the command yw. This command can also use named buffers and accepts numeric modifiers.

Searching and Replacing Text

Text searches in vi can be performed in either direction: forward or backward. Searches are always started from the current cursor location and continue from the top or bottom of the file depending on which direction you use. In other words, searches "wrap around" the file.

You can use your file asong to illustrate searches. To search forward through asong for the word "bay," you would type

```
/bay
```

and press Return. Notice that this is a status-line command. The command /bay is echoed on the status line and the cursor is moved to the first occurrence it finds in the forward direction of the string "bay." Interested in finding another instance of "bay"? Enter a / character. This command continues the search for "bay" in the forward direction and places the cursor at the next instance of "bay." Each time you enter the / key, vi will try to find an instance of the previous string pattern. When it reaches the end of the file, vi will loop back and continue its search at the start of the file.

You can also search backward for strings in vi by using the ? command. It works in exactly the same manner as the / command, but in the opposite direction. Try it out by typing

?I

in asong, instructing vi to search back for instances of "I." This search can be repeated by typing ?, as you may have suspected. You can continue a search by pressing n, which always continues a search in the same direction as the previous search. However, typing N will use the same search string but in the opposite direction.

As I mentioned earlier, searches can be made very powerful through the use of regular expressions. The search command is supplied in the same fashion as described before (/ or ?), but square brackets are added to instruct vi to do a regular expression expansion of the enclosed characters. For example, search forward through asong from the first line for all strings containing the substring "er". Type

/er

vi's first matching string arrives at "Where." If you type n, vi will move the cursor to "where," and so on. You can also specify collections of characters or ranges of characters to match. Try typing the following:

/[a-z]y

This command used in asong will find the strings "by" and "my," as well as any word with these strings inside them (such as "bay"). This works because the range of characters given are treated as an enumerated range of ASCII values. Thus, you could also include a range of numbers (for example, 0-9). Now try the following command:

/[Mm]y

This will locate the strings "My" and "my."

In vi, searches without regular expressions will find only exact matches of the supplied pattern (including the case of the letters in the pattern). Clearly, regular expressions can be used to enhance many types of searches in which you may not know exactly how a pattern appears in a file.

One of the more common applications of a search is to replace instances of one word (or pattern) with another. This is done with an ex command that starts with a colon. To search the entire asong file for the string "Down" and replace it with the string "Up," type

:%s/Down/Up/g

The s indicates that this is a search operation, the % means that the entire file is to be searched, "Down" is the pattern to be found, "Up" is the new pattern, and the g tells vi that the search should continue until there are no more pattern matches. Without the g, vi would perform the replacement on only the first match it finds. This command also works with regular expressions appearing in the search pattern and the replacement pattern.

Setting Preferences

vi is *configurable,* which means that you can set options to control your editing environment. These options are initialized with default values that you can modify in vi at any time. vi is configured using the set command. The set command must be preceded by a colon and entered by pressing Return. For example, to display line numbers in the editor, you would issue

`:set number`

The following table describes a few of the more common set commands.

all	Displays a list of all available set options and their current status.
errorbells	Sounds the terminal bell when an error occurs.
ignorecase	Searches are case-insensitive.
number	Displays line numbers in the leftmost column of the screen (these are not written to the file).
showmode	An indication appears at the bottom right of the screen if you are in input mode, change mode, replace mode, and so on.

set commands that do not take a value can be switched off by inserting a "no" as a prefix to the set parameter. For example, the command

`:set nonumber`

switches line numbering off. The command

`:set`

shows only the options that you have changed.

The settings that you use in a vi session are (unfortunately) lost each time you exit vi. If you do not like the idea of resetting these options each time you use vi, there is an easier way to perform this initialization. Use the vi initialization file called .exrc. vi searches for this file in your home directory each time it is invoked. If it can't find this file, it uses the defaults set within the vi program. As you will see in the following example, the .exrc file can also be used to define vi macros.

A sample .exrc file would look something like this:

```
set number
set errorbells
set showmode
```

Note that the colon is not required before a set command in a .exrc file.

A Summary of Commands

The following is a summary of the more essential commands described in this chapter. You should consult the vi man page for more details on the many other vi commands.

i	Starts inserting text at the cursor.
h	Moves the cursor one character to the left.
j	Moves the cursor down one line.
k	Moves the cursor up one line.
l	Moves the cursor one character to the right.
C-f	Scrolls forward one screen.
C-b	Scrolls backward one screen.
*n*dd	Deletes the next *n* lines.
*n*yy	Yanks the next *n* lines into the unnamed buffer.
p	Puts the contents of the unnamed buffer to the right of the cursor.
u	Undoes the last change.
:wq	Writes changes and exits vi.
:q!	Exits vi without saving changes.
:set all	Shows all set parameters and their values.
/*string*	Searches forward for *string*.

The *emacs* Editor

emacs has become the editor of choice for many users because of its online help facility and its extensive collection of editing commands. For programmers, emacs is especially attractive because it can be configured to format source code for a variety of languages such as C, C++, and Lisp. emacs is somewhat easier to learn than vi, but it also features a much larger set of commands.

Starting *emacs*

emacs is invoked from the command line by entering

```
emacs
```

To start emacs with a file to be edited, enter

```
emacs filename
```

If you start emacs with a file, the screen will display the contents starting from the first line. Note the two lines at the bottom of the screen. The first of these lines, known as the *mode line,* displays the name of the file being edited and which part of the file that you are looking at (for example, TOP, 20%, BOT). The last line on the screen is the echo line, which emacs uses to display system messages and as a prompt for more input.

Control and Meta Keys

You are quite free at this point to start entering text into the edit buffer at the cursor location. However, you're probably wondering, "How do I move the cursor around?" Before I fill you in on this little detail, there are two keys that you should know about: the Control key (which I will refer to as C) and the Meta key (denoted by M). The Control key is used in most of the commands for emacs, but some use the Meta key instead. Commands in emacs consist of combinations of the Control or Meta key followed by some other character. It is necessary to hold down the Control key when pressing the next character, whereas the Meta key can be pressed and released before you enter the next character. For the PC, the Meta key is usually the Alt key.

> **NOTE**
>
> You may see the Control key abbreviated as C and the Meta key denoted by M.
> On the PC, you should use the Alt key for the Meta key.

Moving the Cursor

Now that you know about the Control key, we can talk about the cursor-movement commands. The basic ones that you need to remember are:

C-f	Moves the cursor forward one character.
C-b	Moves the cursor back one character.
C-p	Moves the cursor to the previous line.
C-n	Moves the cursor to the next line.
C-a	Moves the cursor to the beginning of the line.
C-e	Moves the cursor to the end of the line.

> **NOTE**
>
> When I refer to a command such as C-b, I mean press and hold the Control key while you press the letter b. The same is true for Meta commands such as M-v.

Most implementations of emacs conveniently map the first four movement commands to the arrow keys on the keyboard. Let's edit a new file called asong2. (If you are in the middle of a previous file, exit the editor by typing Ctrl-X, Ctrl-C.) Start up a new copy of emacs by entering the following command from the shell:

```
emacs asong2<Enter>
```

Now enter the following text into the buffer:

```
This is a file for edit
And you have to give emacs some credit
It's really quite swell
And all you have to do is spell
emacs works, if you let it!
```

Now use the C-b command to move back through this horrendous piece of poetry. Notice how the cursor jumps up to the end of each line after the reaching the beginning of the previous line. This works the same way in the opposite direction using the C-f command.

Another useful way of moving around is by scrolling through a file one screen at a time. The command C-v moves the cursor forward one screen at a time. The command M-v moves the cursor in the opposite direction.

Like vi, emacs treats a sequence of non-whitespace characters as a word. You can move the cursor forward one word at a time with the M-f command. The M-b command moves back one word.

Quitting emacs

At this time, you can stop editing to save the contents of the buffer to your file asong2. To do this, issue the command sequence C-x C-s. As you enter this command, notice how the command is displayed on the echo line as you type it. To quit emacs and return to the shell, enter the command C-x C-c. If you have made changes that haven't been saved using C-x C-s, emacs will ask for confirmation before quitting.

Deleting Text

You can delete text in several ways. The Backspace (or Delete) key is used to erase the character immediately preceding the cursor. The command C-d deletes the character underneath the cursor, and C-k deletes or "kills" all characters from the cursor to the end of the line. Words can be deleted also: M-d deletes the word the cursor is currently located over and M-Del (the Delete key) deletes the word previous to the current word.

If you ever find that you have committed an edit that you didn't really want, just type C-x u to undo the previous editing changes. You can repeat the undo command as many times as you want, rolling over all the changes you made. This is an advantage over vi, which can only undo the last change.

TIP

Change your mind about a command? Type C-g to abort the current command operation.

Working with Multiple Files

emacs enables you to edit several files in one session, each contained within its own buffer. To copy an external file into a new buffer, use the C-x C-f command. After entering this command, you will see the following prompt on the echo line:

```
Find file: ~/
```

emacs is smart when it looks for files. It supports *filename completion,* which means that you can simply type a few characters of a filename and emacs will attempt to match a file (or files) to what you have typed so far. To do this, type in the letters ".log" and press the Tab key. emacs expands this to ~/.login (or any other filename that matches). If two or more files match the pattern supplied, pressing the Tab key will cycle through them.

After you have loaded a new file into emacs, you can switch between buffers by using the C-x b command followed by the name of the buffer that you want. The buffer's name is that of the file that was loaded into it. The C-x b command also uses filename completion, so you can use the Tab key to cycle through your edit buffers after supplying a few relevant characters.

When you have finished editing a buffer, instead of saving the contents using the C-x C-s command, you may decide that you do not really want to keep the edits you have made. You can "kill" the current buffer by entering the command C-x k. emacs will prompt you for the name of the buffer to kill, but you can kill the current buffer by simply pressing Return. emacs will ask for confirmation, to which you can respond by typing yes (if you're sure) and press Return.

> **TIP**
>
> Whenever you are working with just two buffers, you can simply press Return after entering the C-x b command to switch to the other buffer.

Copying and Moving Text

In order to copy and move blocks of text in emacs, you must define the region of text by marking the beginning and end points of the text block. This is done by moving the cursor to where you want the block to begin and marking it using the C-Space command (in this case, Space means literally the spacebar). The end of the block is defined by wherever you place the cursor after that. To make a copy of the block, enter the command M-w. The text within the block is copied to emacs's internal clipboard, from which it can be pasted at another location using the C-y command. Alternatively, you can cut the block into the clipboard using C-w instead of M-w. Cutting, of course, deletes the text from its current location.

Let's try out some of these techniques on your buffer asong2. Use the M-< command to jump to the beginning of the buffer. Enter a C-Space to mark the start of the block and then use C-n to move down a line. Cut the block to the clipboard using C-w, move the cursor to the end of the buffer using M->, and paste it using C-y. The result should look like this:

```
It's really quite swell
And all you have to do is spell
emacs works, if you let it!
This is a file for edit
And you have to give emacs some credit
```

Searching and Replacing Text

You can search forward and backward through text using the C-s and C-r commands, respectively. These commands, like many in emacs, use *command completion*. This is the same concept as filename completion: you supply a few characters and emacs tries to fill in the rest. In this case, however, emacs moves the cursor to each instance it finds of the string supplied.

As you enter more characters, emacs narrows its search further. When you have found a correct match, press Return or use any of the cursor-movement commands to halt the search.

As with vi, searching in either direction wraps around the beginning or end of the file, depending on in which direction you are searching. However, when emacs reaches the top or bottom of the file, it will tell you that the search failed. You can keep searching by pressing C-s or C-r accordingly and emacs will continue using the current string.

To illustrate how searching in emacs works, let's search backward through your file asong2. Enter C-r and type an s. emacs moves the cursor to the "s" in "works". Now type a w. emacs now tries to find a pattern that matches the string sw. The cursor ends up on the "w" in "swell". You can edit the search string using the Backspace or Delete key. Delete the w and type a p. What happens?

Search-and-replaces are done by entering the query-replace command. This is qualified by the M-x command, which tells emacs that the text to follow is a full command and not a key combination. After you have entered the query-replace command, you will be prompted for the string to be found. Enter the string and press Return. emacs will then prompt you for the replacement string. Once you have entered the replacement string, emacs will search for every instance of the first string and, if it finds one, asks you if it should be replaced with the second string.

> **NOTE**
>
> emacs is actually composed of a set of explicit command names that are bound to key combinations. The query-replace command is bound to M-% in some implementations of emacs.

Using Modes with Buffers

emacs is versatile enough to handle many different types of editing chores. It enables you to associate modes to buffers so that you can have text formatting specific to your editing application. If you enter the command C-x m, emacs enters mail mode, which formats a buffer with To: and Subject: fields as well as a space for the body of the mail message. emacs can even send the mail message for you (by entering C-c C-c) after you have finished editing it.

```
.LI
thing 1
.LI
thing 2
.LE
thing 3
```

creates a bulleted list of the three bits of text. You can create a list with dashes instead of bullets using the `.DL` (dash list) command. The mark list command, `.ML`, creates a list with the character of your choice.

If you want a numbered list, use the `.AL` (automatic list) command. Lists with no arguments are created with Arabic numbers. To create an alphabetical list (A, B, C, and so on), use the macro command `.AL A`. Roman numerals (i, ii, iii, iv, v, and so on) can be used with the `.AL I` command.

You can nest list types as necessary. For example, the command

```
.AL I
.LI
groff
.AL
.LI
macros
.LI
mm
.LE
.LI
gtbl
.LI
geqn
.LE
```

will create output that looks like this:

```
I.   groff
        1. macros
        2. mm
II.   gtbl
III.  geqn
```

You have to be careful when terminating each list with an `.LE` command to ensure that you terminate the proper one. Experimentation and practice help you get the hang of this. You may have noticed that it takes a lot of commands to make a little list!

Font Changes

Changing fonts with mm is quite simple. When working from a period command, the command `.B` (bold) creates bold text until an `.R` (restore) command, while `.I` (italics) does the same until an `.R` command. If you want to bold or italicize only one word, you can do it after the period command, as this example shows:

```
This is normal text
.B
This is bold.
So is this.
```

```
.R
This is normal.
This is a single
.Bbold
word, though.
```

When you change only one word, you don't need a .R command.

Changes can be performed within text in the same manner as with groff:

```
This is an \fIitalics set of words\fR until here.
```

Footnotes

To create a footnote, use the .FS (footnote start) and .FE (footnote end) commands. Every foot-note on a single page will be collected and printed at the bottom. Footnotes are automatically num-bered unless you specify another character:

```
This is normal text.
.FS
This is a footnote with its proper number in front of it.
.FE
This is more normal text.
.FS *
But this is a footnote marked with an asterisk.
.FE
This is even more normal text.  At the bottom of the page
will be a numbered footnote and an asterisked footnote.
```

You can use any valid character for the optional footnote mark, including special characters sup-ported by groff.

Summary

As you might expect, there is a lot to both groff and mm that we haven't looked at. Because groff is seldom used these days, we covered only the most important aspects. As I said earlier, if you want to learn more about groff or mm, find a good reference book on the subject.

geqn and *gtbl*

18

by Tim Parker

IN THIS CHAPTER

You can subscript subscripts, and superscript superscripts, simply by combining the formats:

```
y sub x sub 3
```

You can also produce both subscript and superscript on the same character using the two commands together:

```
x sub y sup 3
```

Because a space is used to indicate the end of a subscript or superscript, this can cause a problem when you want spaces either as part of the equation, or to separate words to be converted. To get around this problem, use braces to enclose the subscript or superscript:

```
w sup {x alpha y}
```

This shows that the Greek letters are also available, as they are within groff. You can have braces within braces, as well:

```
omega sub { 2 pi r sup { 2 + rho }}
```

Try these commands for yourself, and experiment to see the output.

Fractions

To create a proper-looking fraction, use the keyword over. The geqn preprocessor automatically adjusts the length of the line separating the parts. For example, the command

```
a = 2b over {3c alpha}
```

produces an equation with a horizontal line separating the two components, just as if you were writing the equation out on paper.

You can, of course, combine all the other elements of geqn to create more complex-looking equations:

```
{alpha + beta * gamma sup 3} over {3 sub {4 + alpha}}
```

When you are combining sup and sub with over, geqn processes sup and sub first, and then it does over, much as you would when writing the equation.

Square Roots

To draw a square root symbol, use the keyword sqrt, and geqn ensures that the square root symbol is properly drawn to enclose all parts of the equation that are indicated as belonging to the square root. Very large square root signs that cover a lot of material on many lines, for example, do not look particularly good when printed. You should consider using the superscript 0.5 instead.

You can use sqrt quite easily. For example, the command

```
sqrt a+c - 1 over sqrt {alpha + beta}
```

has the first square root sign over a+c, and the second over the part in braces.

Summations, Set Theory, and Integrals

To produce a summation, use the keyword sum and the keywords from and to to show the upper and lower parts of the command. For example, use the command

```
sum from x=1 to x=100 x sup 2
```

to create the formula for summing x squared over the range 1 to 100. If you want to use a special word, use braces:

```
sum from x=1 to {x= inf} x sup 2
```

This is the same command, except summing from 1 to infinity. The braces ensure that the to component is properly interpreted. If no from or to component is specified, they are not printed.

To use integrals, the keyword int is used, and can again take a from argument:

```
lim from n=1 xy sup 3 = 9
```

Other reserved words for geqn are used with set theory. You can use the keywords union and inter for the union and intersect of sets.

Brackets, Bars, and Piles

As equations get more complicated, you need to use more brackets and braces. You can generate brackets ([]), braces ({}), and parentheses (()) as needed using the left and right commands:

```
left { b over d+1} = left ( alpha over {beta + gamma} )
```

This produces large braces, and parentheses are required to surround the terms. You can nest these, of course, with geqn adjusting the sizes properly. Braces are usually bigger than brackets and parentheses.

For floor and ceiling characters, use the left floor, right floor, left ceiling, and right ceiling commands. For example:

```
left ceiling x over alpha right ceiling > left floor beta over 2 right floor
```

draws the equation with the proper vertical bars and ceiling and floor markers.

To create a pile of elements, use the reserved word pile. The following example shows the usage best:

```
X = left [ pile { a above b above c } right ]
```

This produces output with the three elements a, b, and c stacked vertically within big braces.

Matrices

To make a matrix requires a little more work. You could probably make a matrix using the pile command, but if the elements are not of equal height, they will not line up. For that reason, use the keyword matrix. The general format is

```
matrix {
 ccol { elements }
 ccol { elements }
```

in which `ccol` produces centered columns. For left-adjusted columns, use `lcol`; `rcol` produces right-adjusted columns. The elements are specified individually. For example, the command

```
matrix {
 ccol { x sub 1 above y sub 1 }
 ccol { x sub 2 above y sub 2 }
```

produces the matrix

$x_1\ x_2$
$y_1\ y_2$

All matrices must have the same number of elements in each column or geqn can't process the matrix properly.

Quoted Text

Any characters placed within quotation marks are not interpreted by geqn. This is useful for text strings that may contain reserved words, such as the following:

```
italics "beta" = beta + gamma
```

Here, the word `beta` will appear in italics without being converted to the beta character.

Character Changes

You can change font and point size with geqn in much the same way as with groff. The default setting is usually Roman 10 point. If you want to set bold characters, use the keyword `bold`; `italic` sets italic font.

```
x=y bold alpha
```

You can also use the keyword `fat`, which widens the character (useful for things such as grad characters). These reserved words affect only what immediately follows, so you must use braces if the area to be changed is more than a single block of characters.

```
x=y*2 bold {alpha + gamma}
```

To change the size of characters, use the `size` keyword:

```
size 16 {alpha + beta}
```

This sets the enclosed text in 16 point size. Incremental changes are acceptable.

To affect the entire equation, you can use the `gsize` (global size) and `gfont` (global font) commands at the start of the geqn block:

```
.EQ
gsize 14
```

```
gfont H
....
```

This makes it easy to format the equations however you wish.

Using *geqn*

As you have seen, geqn is quite friendly and easy to use, especially if you are used to writing out equations longhand. You should play around with the system and learn the different features. There are more commands available within geqn, but the main ones have been shown to you. For more information, check the man pages or a good troff book that includes eqn.

gtbl

The gtbl routine is designed to help in the preparation of charts, multicolumn lists, and any other material presented in a tabular format. The gtbl commands are not difficult to work with, but can be awkward to learn, so studying examples is the best method.

To use gtbl, two special commands are used to indicate to groff that the area between the two commands is to be processed as gtbl instructions. These two key commands are .TS (table start) and .TE (table end). Commands between these two are processed by gtbl first, which converts the gtbl commands to groff commands; then, the source is passed to groff.

Tables are independent of each other with gtbl, meaning that each must contain all the information for formatting the data within the table and can't rely on a previous format. Tables contain three types of information: text for the table itself, options that control the behavior of gtbl, and formatting commands to lay out the table itself. The general format of a gtbl source code section is as follows:

```
.TS
options;
format.
data
.TE
```

Let's look at the important parts of the gtbl layout first, and then see how they are combined to produce finished tables.

Executing *gtbl*

Because gtbl is a preprocessor, it is invoked on the source file, and then the results are passed to groff. The simplest way to do this is with the command

```
gtbl filename | groff
```

in which the gtbl preprocessor runs against the source in *filename* and then sends the output to groff. If you are processing more than one file at a time, or you need to send the output of gtbl to another preprocessor, such as geqn, you use piping slightly differently. The command

```
gtbl filename ¦ geqn ¦ groff
```

sends the output to geqn and then to groff.

Options

There can be a single line of options after a .TS command that affects the entire table. Any options must follow the .TS command. If more than one option is specified, they must be separated by spaces, commas, or tabs, and terminate in a semicolon. gtbl accepts the following options:

center	Centers the table (default is left-justified).
expand	Makes tables as wide as current line length.
box	Encloses the table in a box.
allbox	Encloses each element of the table in a box.
doublebox	Encloses the table in two boxes.
tab (*n*)	Uses *n* instead of a tab to separate data.
linesize (*n*)	Uses point size *n* for lines or rules.
delim (*mn*)	Uses *m* and *n* as equation delimiters.

When gtbl tries to lay out a table, it tries to keep the entire table on one page if possible, even if it has to eject the previous page only partially completed. This can sometimes cause problems because gtbl can make mistakes estimating the size of the table prior to generating it, especially if there are embedded line commands that affect spacing or point size. To avoid this problem, some users surround the entire table with the display macros .DS (display start) and .DE (display end). You can ignore this for most tables, unless you start embedding commands within the data.

Format

The format section of the table structure indicates how the columns are to be laid out. Each line in the format section corresponds to one line of data in the finished table. If not enough format lines are specified to match all the lines of data, the last format line specified is used for the remainder of the table. This lets you use a specific format for headers and a single format line for the rest of the table. The format section ends with a period.

Each line in the format section contains a keyletter for each column in the table. Keyletters should be separated by spaces or tabs for each column to enhance readability. Keyletters are case-independent (so you can use upper- or lowercase for the keyletters, or a mixture of the two, without affecting the layout). Supported gtbl keyletters are as follows:

l	Left-justified entry
r	Right-justified entry
c	Centered entry
n	Numeric entries lined up by units

a   Aligned on left so that widest entry is centered

s   Previous column format applies across rest of column

A sample format section consists of a letter for each column, unless the entry is repeated across the page. A sample format section looks like this:

```
c    s    s
1    n    n .
```

In this sample, the first line of the table is formatted with the first, second, and third columns centered (the s repeats the previous entry). The second and subsequent lines have the first entry left-justified, and the next two lined up as numbers. The period ends the format section. If you like, you can put all these format keyletters on a single line, using a comma to separate the lines:

```
c s s, 1 n n .
```

A table formatted by this set of commands looks like this (with random numbers inserted to show the lineup):

```
        Centered_Title
Entry1  12.23  231.23
Entry2   3.23   45.2
Entry3  45     123.2344
Entry4   3.2     2.3
```

Numeric data is usually aligned so that the decimal places are in a vertical column. However, sometimes you want to override this format by forcing a movement. The special character \& is used to move the decimal point. The special characters disappear when the table is printed. To show the effect of this special character, the following sample shows normal formatting and entries with the special character embedded (the first column is the source input, and the second is the generated output):

```
14.5          14.5
13            13
1.253          1.253
3\&1.21        31.21
53.2          53.2
6\&2.23        62.23
```

You can see that the numbers usually line up with the decimal point in a vertical row, except where moved over by the \& characters. Even if a number has no decimal point specified (as in the second line of the example), it is lined up as though one were present after the last digit.

The following are a few additional keyletters that can be used to create special formats and make the tables more attractive:

_   Horizontal line in place of column entry.

=   Double horizontal line in place of column entry.

¦   Between column entries, draws a vertical line between columns. Before the first keyletters, draws a line to the left of the table. After the last keyletters, draws a line to the right of the table.

¦¦	Between column entries, draws a double vertical line.
e/E	Sets equal width columns. All columns that have a keyletter followed by e or E are set to the same width.
f/F	Followed by a font name or number, changes the entry to the font specified.
n	Any number following a keyletter. Indicates the amount of separation between columns.
p/P	Followed by a number, changes the point size of the entry to the specified number. Increments acceptable.
t/T	Vertically spanned items begin at the top line. Normally, vertically spanning items (more than one line in the table) are centered in the vertical range.
v/V	Followed by a number, gives vertical line spacing.
w/W	Followed by a number, sets the width.

The order of these characters on the format line is not important, although the spacing between each format identifier must still be respected. Multiple letters can be used. The entry

```
np14w(2.5i)fi
```

sets the numeric entry (n) in italics (fi), with a point size of 14 (p14) and a minimum column width of 2.5 inches (w(2.5i)).

You may need to change the format of a table midway through—for example, to present summaries. If you must change the format, use the .T& (table continue) command.

Data

Data for the table is entered after all the format specifications have been completed. Data for columns is separated by tabs or any other character indicated in the tabs option. Each line of data is one line of the table. Long lines of data can be broken over several lines of source by using the backslash character as the last character in a line.

Any line starting with a period and followed by anything other than a number is assumed to be a groff command and is ignored by the preprocessor. If a single line of the data consists of only underscore or equal sign characters (single and double lines), it is treated as extending the entire width of the table.

You can embed a block of text within a table by using the text commands of T{ (start of text) and }T (end of text). This lets you enter something that can't be easily entered as a string separated by tabs.

Examples

The best way to understand how to use gtbl is to look at some simple examples. Here's a basic table command:

```
.TS
doublebox;
c c c, l l n.
Name          Dept          Phone
Joe           8A            7263
Mike          9F            2635
Peter         2R            2152
Yvonne        2B            2524
.TE
```

All of the entries in the data section are separated by tabs. This produces a table with three columns, the first line of which is centered text. The rest of the table has the first and second column left-justified, and the last column aligned by decimal point (there are none in this case). The entire table is surrounded by two boxes.

A slightly more complex example uses a table title, followed by a row of column headings, and then the data. Separate each element in the table by a box in this case:

```
.TS
allbox;
c s s
c c c
n n n .
Division Results
East          West          North
15            12            14
12            12            18
36            15            24
.TE
```

Try typing in these examples, or create your own, to see what effect the different commands have. When you've started using gtbl, it isn't that difficult.

Summary

Although word processors have made utilities such as geqn and gtbl less popular than they used to be, some diehard UNIX people still like to use them. There are times when you might not be able to produce an equation the way you want with your favorite word processor, so you might have to return to the basics. Also, because word processors capable of fancy formulas tend to be expensive, utilities such as geqn and gtbl are ideal for the occasional user who doesn't want to spend a lot of money on a seldom-used tool.

TeX

19

by Peter MacKinnon

IN THIS CHAPTER

Mathematical Symbols

One of the most powerful features of TeX is its capability to generate correct mathematical notation for formulas with convenient commands. This is one of the key reasons behind TeX's popularity among engineers and scientists.

TeX distinguishes between formulas that must appear within regular text (inline formulas) and those that must appear on their own line (displayed formulas). You must use the $ symbol to denote inline formulas, as in

```
The equation $2+3=x$ must evaluate to $x=5$.
```

which is generated as the following:

```
The equation 2+3=x must evaluate to x=5.
```

However, displayed formulas are denoted using two consecutive $ symbols, as in

```
The equation $$2+3=x$$ must evaluate to $$x=5$$.
```

which produces the following:

```
        The equation

          2+3=x
```

```
must evaluate to
```

```
          x=5.
```

Table 19.1 shows some of the math symbols that TeX can generate, their associated commands, and their meaning.

Table 19.1. Some of the math symbols that TeX can generate.

Symbol	TeX *Command*	*Meaning*
Π	\pi	Pi
Σ	\sum	Sum
{	\{	Open bracket
}	\}	Close bracket
f	\int	Integral
≤	\leq	Less than or equal to
≥	\geq	Greater than or equal to
≠	\neq	Not equal to
•	\bullet	Bullet
...	\ldots	Horizontal ellipses
◆	\diamond	Diamond
Δ	\Delta	Delta

TeX uses particular fonts for the formulas it produces. These can be overridden in the usual fashion, but the changes are applicable only to letters and digits.

Using Figures in Your Document

Figures that are drawn outside of TeX can be inserted into their own space. This space "floats." In other words, TeX knows that it must keep track of the figure space as the text around it is added or deleted. This flexibility means that you, the writer, need not worry about exactly where in the document your figures will appear.

To insert a figure that must appear at the top of a page, use the following command:

```
\topinsert figure \endinsert
```

Here, *figure* can be an external reference or an internal definition. TeX tries to place the figure at the top of the next page with sufficient space.

You can also tell TeX that you want a figure to appear on its own page by using this command:

```
\pageinsert figure \endinsert
```

Macros

Macros have made TeX a highly extendible system. They essentially enable you to create new commands by associating existing commands and text sequences to a macro name. After they are defined, these macros can be used in other parts of your document to replace repetitive pieces of text, or to encapsulate abstract operations.

A macro is defined once, using the following format:

```
\def macroname {new text}
```

In this case, *macroname* is a name or TeX command preceded by a backslash character. Any reference to this macro name is replaced by the new text throughout the document. For example, the macro definition

```
\def\brg{burger}
Ham\brg, cheese\brg, lim\brg.
```

is output as follows:

```
Hamburger, cheeseburger, limburger.
```

Macros can refer to other macros, as in

```
\def\tig{a tigger }
\def\wond{a wonderful thing }
\def\pooh{\wond is \tig cause \tig is \wond}
\pooh\par
```

which produces the following:

```
a wonderful thing is a tigger cause a tigger is a wonderful thing
```

> **WARNING**
>
> You must be careful of recursive macro definitions: macros that refer to their own names within their definition. Such macro definitions cause TeX to continuously (and vainly) evaluate the macro, leading to an infinite loop. The following is an example of this:
>
> ```
> \def\itself{\itself}
> \itself
> ```

TeX macros have the added feature of being able to accept parameters when expanded, if a list of formal parameters has been specified in the macro definition. To create a macro using parameters, you would use this format:

```
\def macroname (list of formal parameters) {new text}
```

Here, the list of parameters is specified as #1, #1#2, #1#2#3, and so on. This is a powerful aspect of macros because it can change the output of an expanded macro based on the parameter in use. For example, the code

```
\def\parm#1{This is the #1 time I'll say this.}
\parm{first}
\parm{second}
\parm{last}
```

produces the following:

```
This is the first time I'll say this.
This is the second time I'll say this.
This is the last time I'll say this.
```

Each parameter that is used must be passed separately by enclosing it in braces, as in

```
\def\family#1#2{My #1 is #2.}
\family{wife}{Cindy}
\family{sister}{Sheila}
\family{father}{Myles}
```

which makes the following output:

```
My wife is Cindy.
My sister is Sheila.
My father is Myles.
```

You must specify an appropriate match of parameters in your macro definition. The macro definition

```
\def\mistake#1{This is wrong because of #2.}
```

is incorrect because it refers to a second parameter that is not specified in the formal parameter list.

Macros can be redefined in your document, but you should be aware that only the most recent definition will be applied. Also, macros defined within groups are only valid within the scope of the group.

Macro definitions can be nested within each other, as in the following:

```
\def\hey{Hey\def\hey{hey}}
\hey, \hey, \hey.
```

This has the following output:

```
Hey, hey, hey.
```

As with many topics within this book, we have examined only some of the highlights of TeX. There is much more to learn but, having covered the basics regarding macros, you can now look at the most popular extension of TeX, which uses macros to enhance the creation of documents. This extension is LaTeX.

LaTeX: An Enhancement of *TeX*

LaTeX is a collection of macros that build on the capabilities of TeX and provide a higher level of abstraction for the creation of documents. It is essentially a style library that encourages uniform formatting and typesetting across documents. LaTeX macros shift the emphasis away from the details of things such as "set text to 8-point slanted" to concepts that writers identify more readily with, such as the emphasis of a word or phrase. Thus, LaTeX macros have names that are more representative of the way writers *think* when they are writing.

Because LaTeX is an extension of TeX, you'll find it easy to become quickly productive in LaTeX, assuming that you have some experience in TeX. White space and spacing between paragraphs are handled in the same manner as in TeX. The special characters in TeX are the same in LaTeX, and comments are denoted using the % character.

The key differences between TeX and LaTeX become apparent as you learn more about the macros that define the layout of your document in a convenient fashion.

Defining a *LaTeX* Document

Every LaTeX document begins with the \documentclass command. The parameter passed to this command specifies what kind of document you want to write. The basic document classes are described in Table 19.2.

Table 19.2. Document classes.

Document Class	Description
article	Used for short reports, reference cards, presentations, scientific journals, and so on.
book	Used for complete books.
report	Used for reports having several chapters, theses, and so on.

The Infamous *lpr, lpd,* and *lpc* Commands

The lpr, lpd, and lpc commands are perhaps the programs hated the most by novices in the Linux community. If everything falls in place with these programs, you are set. If something is wrong, you have to know how these commands work together to get printing up and running.

You can always print directly to the printer by using the following command:

```
ls > /dev/lp0
```

Unfortunately, this command can interfere with other users trying to print. Also, this command may not even work if the computer is not able to time the sending of characters to the lineprinter correctly. On a slow printer, or a printer which is deselected or disconnected, this could cause your shell to hang.

What Linux does is spool the data. *Spooling* means collecting data into a file, and then starting up a background process to send the data to the printer. There is a spool area for each printer connected to your machine. Data designated for the printer is collected in the spool area at the rate of one file per print job. A background process—called the *printer daemon*—constantly scans the spool areas for new files to print. When one appears, the data is removed from the spool area and sent to the appropriate printer. When more than one file is waiting to be printed, they will be printed in the order they were completed. The spool area is really a queue.

The printer daemon needs the following information to do its job: the physical device to use, the spool area to look in, and if printing on a remote machine, the name of the remote machine and printer for remote printing. All this information is stored in a file called /etc/printcap.

There are five programs that use this information. These programs are in the /usr/bin and /usr/ sbin directories: lpr, lpq, lpc, lprm, and lpd. The first four are used to submit, cancel, and inspect print jobs. The /etc/lpd program is the printer daemon. There are man pages for all these commands, which you should consult for more information.

The thing to remember is that by default lpr, lprm, lpc, and lpq operate on a printer called lp. You can define an environment variable called PRINTER to specify the printer name. For example, to print to the hplj printer, use lp -Phplj to override any setting of the PRINTER variable. Here is a quick introduction to some of the key commands related to printing under Linux:

■ The lpr command submits a job to the printer.

■ The lpq command shows you the contents of the spool directory for a given printer. Each file is specified by an ID and its location in the queue.

■ The lprm command removes a job from the printer queue. You have to specify the ID returned for that job specified by lpq.

■ The lpc command is the printer control command. This command lets you check the status of each printer and set its state. You can enable or disable printers and their queues. If no parameters are specified, lpc is in interactive mode, and you can type in your commands at a prompt. Replies to your commands are printed immediately. Type a ? for a list of commands you can use.

All these programs work off one directory, usually the /usr/spool/lpd. Each printer has its own area under this directory to spool data in. For my ps printer, I have a /usr/lpd/spool/lpd/ps directory.

The printer spool directories should belong to the *daemon* group and are both user and group read/writable, and world *-readable*. That is, the directory has to have permissions of -rwxrwxr-x (0775).

Each spool directory should contain four files: .seq, errs. lock, and status. These files should have the permissions -rw-rw-r-. The .seq file contains the job number counter for lpr to assign a job. The status file contains the message to be reported by lpc stat. The lock file is used by lpd to prevent itself trying to print two jobs to the same printer at once. The errs file is a log of printer failures and is not required. The status file has a text description of what the lpd program is doing with that file, for example printing, waiting, and so on.

The */etc/printcap* File

The file /etc/printcap is a text file and is owned by root. The contents of /etc/printcap are not the easiest things to read. Each entry in this file contains a description for a printer and how data is to be handled for that printer. For example, a printcap entry will define what physical device is to be used, what spool directory data for that device should be stored in, what preprocessing should be performed on the data, where errors on the physical device should be logged, and so forth. You can limit the amount of data that may be sent in a single job, or limit access to a printer to certain types of users.

You can have multiple printcap entries defining several different ways to handle data destined for the same physical printer. For example, a physical printer may support both PostScript and HP LaserJet data formats, depending on some setup sequence being sent to the physical printer before each job. It would make sense to define two printers, one of which preprocesses the data by prepending the HP LaserJet sequence, while the other prepends the PostScript sequence. Programs that generate HP data would send it to the HP printer, while programs generating PostScript would print to the PostScript printer.

Programs that change the data before it is sent to the physical printer are called *filters*. It is possible for a filter to send no data at all to a physical printer. An example of such a filter entry in a printcap file is shown in the following lines:

```
# Sample printcap entry with two aliases
myprinter¦laserwriter:\
# lp is the device to print to - here the first parallel printer.
    :lp=/dev/lp0: \
    # sd means 'spool directory' - where print data is collected
    :sd=/usr/spool/lpd/myprinter:
```

Here's a brief summary of some of the entries in /etc/printcap. All fields in each entry are enclosed between a pair of colons and are denoted by a two-letter code. The two-letter code is followed by a value that depends on the type of field. There are three types of fields—string, boolean, and numeric. See Table 20.2 for a listing of some /etc/printcap fields.

Table 20.2. Some fields for /etc/printcap.

Code	type	Description
lp	string	Specifies the device to print to, such as /dev/lp0
sd	string	Specifies the name of the spool directory for this printer
lf	string	Specifies the file to which errors on this printer are to be logged
if	string	Specifies the input filter name
rm	string	Specifies the name of a remote printing host
rp	string	Specifies the name of a remote printer
sh	boolean	Specifies this to suppress headers (banner pages)
sf	boolean	Specifies this to suppress end-of-job form feeds
mx	numeric	Specifies the maximum allowable print job size (in blocks)

Input filters are programs that take print data on their standard input and generate output on their standard output. A typical use of an input filter is to detect plain text and convert it into PostScript. That is, raw text is its input, and PostScript is its output.

When you specify an input filter, the printer daemon does not send the spooled print data to the specified device. Instead, it runs the input filter with the spooled data as standard input and the print device as standard output.

Sending your print data to a printer attached to another machine is done via the remote machine rm field and the remote printer rp field. Make sure that the print device field lp is empty. Note that data will still be spooled locally before being transferred to the remote machine, and any input filters you specify will also be run.

Suppressing form feeds (sf) is most useful if your printer is typically used for output from word-processing packages. Most WP packages create complete pages of data, so if the printer daemon is adding a form feed to the end of each job, you get a blank page after each job. If the printer is usually used for program or directory listings, however, having that form feed ensures that the final page is completely ejected, so each listing starts at the top of a new page.

The mx field enables you to limit the size of the print data to be spooled. The number you specify is in BUFSIZE blocks (1KB under Linux). If you specify zero, the limit is removed, enabling print jobs to be limited only by available disk space. Note that the limit is on the size of the spooled data, *not* the amount of data sent to the physical printer. If a user tries to exceed this limit, the file is truncated. The user will see a message saying lpr: *<filename>*: copy file is too large. This is useful if you have users or programs that may deliberately or accidentally create excessively large output. For PostScript physical printers, the limit is not useful at all because a very small amount of spooled PostScript data can generate a large number of output pages.

In order for any other machines to print using your printers, their names have to be registered in either the file /etc/hosts.equiv or /etc/hosts.lpd. Both files are simple text files with one host name per line. For security, add hosts to /etc/hosts.lpd only. Do not use /etc/hosts.equiv because that gives more access rights to tasks other than simply sending print jobs out to the printer.

How It All Fits

Let's go through the steps of setting up printer support on /dev/lp1. Make sure you do this as root.

1. Create the spool directory for your printer, which we will call foobar for now. Make the permission -rwxrwxr-x.

```
mkdir /usr/spool/lpd /usr/spool/lpd/foobar
chown root.daemon /usr/spool/lpd /usr/spool/lpd/foobar
chmod ug=rwx,o=rx /usr/spool/lpd /usr/spool/lpd/foobar
```

2. In the directory /usr/spool/lpd/foobar, create the necessary files and give them the correct permissions and owner:

```
cd /usr/spool/lpd/foobar
touch .seq errs status lock
chown root.daemon .seq errs status lock
chmod ug=rw,o=r .seq errs status lock
```

3. Create the shell script input_filter in the directory /usr/spool/lpd/foobar. You can have this as an empty file, too. Just be sure that the file is owned by root, group daemon, and is executable by anyone.

```
cd /usr/spool/lpd/foobar
chmod ug=rwx,o=rx input_filter
```

4. Create the file /etc/printcap if it doesn't already exist. Remove all entries in it and add the test printcap entry given in Listing 20.1. Make sure the file is owned by root, and read-only to everyone else (-rw-r-r-).

Listing 20.1. A sample /etc/printcap file.

```
#
# Copyright (c) 1983 Regents of the University of California.
# All rights reserved.
#
# Redistribution and use in source and binary forms are permitted
# provided that this notice is preserved and that due credit is given
# to the University of California at Berkeley. The name of the University
# may not be used to endorse or promote products derived from this
# software without specific prior written permission. This software
# is provided "as is" without express or implied warranty.
#
# @(#)etc.printcap    5.2 (Berkeley) 5/5/88
#
# DecWriter over a tty line.
#lp¦ap¦arpa¦ucbarpa¦LA-180 DecWriter III:\
# :br#1200:fs#06320:tr=\f:of=/usr/lib/lpf:lf=/usr/adm/lpd-errs:
#lp:lp=/dev/lp0:sd=/usr/spool/lp0:of=/usr/lib/lpf: lf=/usr/adm/lpd-errs
#
# Generic printer:
lp:lp=/dev/lp1:sd=/usr/spool/lp1:sh
#
# typical remote printer entry
#ucbvax¦vax¦vx¦ucbvax line printer:\
# :lp=:rm=ucbvax:sd=/usr/spool/vaxlpd:lf=/usr/adm/lpd-errs:
#varian¦va¦Benson Varian:\
```

continues

356

Listing 20.1. continued

```
# :lp=/dev/va0:sd=/usr/spool/vad:mx#2000:pl#58:px#2112:py#1700:tr=\f:\
# :of=/usr/lib/vpf:if=/usr/lib/vpf:tf=/usr/lib/rvcat:cf=/usr/lib/vdmp:\
# :gf=/usr/lib/vplotf:df=/usr/local/dvif:\
# :vf=/usr/lib/vpltdmp:lf=/usr/adm/lpd-errs:
#versatec¦vp¦Versatec plotter:\
# :lp=/dev/vp0:sd=/usr/spool/vpd:sb:sf:mx#0:pw#106:pl#86:px#7040:py#2400:\
# :of=/usr/lib/vpfW:if=/usr/lib/vpsf:tf=/usr/lib/vcat:cf=/usr/lib/vdmp:\
# :gf=/usr/lib/vplotf:vf=/usr/lib/vpltdmp:lf=/usr/adm/lpd-errs:\
# :tr=\n\n\n\n\n\n\n\n\n\n\n\n\n\n\n\n\n\n\n\n\n\n\n\n\n\n\n\n\n\n\n\
#\n\n\n\n\n\n\n\n\n\n\n\n\n\n\n\n\n\n\n\n\n\n\n\n\n\n\n\n\n\n\n\
#\n\n\n\n\n\n\n\n\n\n\n\n\n\n\n\n\n\n\n\n\n\n\n\n\n\n\n\n\n\n\n:
#
#lp¦panasonic:lp=/dev/lp1:sd=/usr/spool/lp/panasonic:lf=/usr/bin/mail:mc#1:\
#            ft=$$c$$p$$r$$f:hl#2:fl#3:ht=$$c$$n$$r$$t:sh:
#
# HP Laser jet plus
#lp¦hpj:\
#        :lp=/dev/lp1:\
#        :sd=/usr/spool/lp1:\
#        :mx#0:\
#        :of=/usr/spool/lp1/hpjlp:\
#        :lf=/usr/spool/lp1/hp-log:
#
#lp¦Generic dot-matrix printer entry:\
#        :lp=/dev/lp1:\
#        :sd-/var/spool/lp1/lp:sh:\
#        :if=/usr/bin/lpf:\
#        :df=/var/spool/lp1/filter.ps:\
#        :tf=/var/spool/lp1/filter.ps:\
#        :af=/var/spool/lp1/lp-acct:\
#        :lf=/var/spool/lp1/lp-err:
```

5. Start the lp daemon with the lpd command.

6. Do a test print using the command:

   ```
   ls -l ¦ lpr -Pmyprinter
   ```

You can restrict remote users by group name by specifying the groups permitted, using one or more rg fields; for example, /etc/printcap - :rg=admin: restricts access to a printer to those users belonging to the group admin. You can also restrict access to those users with accounts on your system, by specifying the boolean flag :rs: in your /etc/printcap.

The Staircase Effect

The staircase effect results in lines printed one after another, with each line beginning where that last one ended. Usually, the output results in a few lines on the first page followed by many blank pages. An example of such an output is as follows:

one

two

three

four

Linux terminates each line of a file with a linefeed but not a carriage return. Therefore, the physical printing device should start each line below the end of the previous line. Some printers can be set to treat "linefeed" as "carriage return, linefeed," others cannot be set this way. If your printer can be set to treat "linefeed" as "carriage return, linefeed," then do that. If the printer cannot be modified, you should create a shell script filter that reads:

```
#!/bin/sh
if [ "$1" = -c ]; then
  cat
else
  sed -e s/$/^M/
fi
# the "echo -ne" assumes that /bin/sh is really bash
echo -ne \\f
```

Install this filter as the `if` filter by putting `:if=/usr/lib/lpf:` (or whatever) in your `/etc/printcap` entry for the printer.

Magic filters deduce their input files types from "magic numbers," which is a distinctive byte pattern at particular offsets. Magic filters are usually Perl scripts, Shell scripts, or C programs that simply identify the file type and then call the appropriate non-magic filter. A magic filter usage example is the "file" command which tries to interpret the type of file by reading the first few bytes.

PostScript Support

The Linux and UNIX community is completely PostScript dependent when it comes to documentation. If you don't have PostScript printing capability in your printer, there are times when you cannot even read documentation for software packages.

If you have access to a PostScript printer, no problem. Print all you want. On the other hand, if you want to save paper or do not have access to a PostScript printer, consider using Ghostscript. See Chapter 25, "Ghostscript," for more information about installing and using Ghostscript. In a nutshell, Ghostscript, which comes from the GNU project, is a PostScript interpreter that accepts PostScript input and generates output appropriate for X displays, printers, and some specialized display hardware and fax software.

There are a number of utilities that enable text to be printed to a PostScript device.

- a2ps. This utility takes text and turns it into a PostScript document with headers and footers and page numbers. You can even print two pages on one sheet of paper.

- ◼ nenscript. The nenscript program is a clone of commercial enscript program. The functionality is the same as that of a2ps.
- ◼ gslp. This is a PostScript program that comes with Ghostscript and is used to print a preamble to text files to convert the text files into PostScript. Check the man pages for gslp.ps.

Printing DVI Files

A DVI file is the processed output from a LaTeX or TeX input file. To print a DVI file to a Postscript printer, you can use dvips or eps. The dvips program converts DVI into PostScript. The output can be piped into Ghostscript or sent directly via lpr to a PostScript printer. eps is a program which converts DVI files directly into the standard Epson printer language. It is a DVI driver for Epson printers.

Summary

This chapter has given you a quick tour of the printing system under Linux. Armed with the information in this chapter, you should be able to get printing to work on your Linux machine.

IN THIS PART

IV

PART

GUI

> **NOTE**
>
> If you have a grayscale display, you have to run the color server because grayscale behaves just like color, not like monochrome.

The monochrome server also supports generic VGA cards (using 64KB of the video memory as a single bank), the Hercules card, and the Hyundai HGC-1280. These drivers are not part of the XF86_Mono server by default. If you want to use these, you have to reconfigure your XF86_Mono server using the LinkKit, or of course, the source distribution—but the LinkKit needs less disk space and a shorter compile time.

XFree86 supports at least the following accelerated chip sets with separate servers:

- S3 86C911, 86C924, 86C801, 86C805, and 86C928 supported by the XF86_S3 server
- ATI mach8 supported by the XF86_Mach8 server
- ATI mach32 supported by the XF86_Mach32 server
- IBM 8514/a and true clones supported by the XF86_8514 server
- S3 Vision864 and Vision964.
- Weitek P9000.

The hardware that is not currently supported is:

- TIGA. TIGA will never be supported because it requires licensing materials from TI and may disallow source distributions.
- Microfield boards. Microfield boards will never be supported because they use proprietary and undocumented custom microcode interfaces.
- MGA chip sets (Matrox cards).

For some of these chip sets there are specific README files to be found in /usr/X386/lib/X11/doc. If there is one for the chip set you use, read it! In these READMEs, the specific options that can be used to configure the server are explained. Currently, there are special READMEs for ATI, Trident, Tseng, Western Digital, Cirrus, and manufacturer-specific chip sets.

More information on the servers can be found in their man pages. Another place to check is the XFree86-HOWTO file in the sunsite and tsx-11 archives. The HOWTO document will generally be more up-to-date than any printed matter.

Summary

This section covered one of the hardest things you will have to do when installing a package on Linux—installing XFree86. Naturally, all of the possible problems you will face while installing this are too long to list here. After reading this chapter, though, you should have an idea of what you are getting yourself into and the general steps you have to take.

Do not despair if things don't work out just as the instructions say they will. You should be able to look at the configuration files to determine where the problem is and what might be done to fix it. If nothing works despite your best efforts, you have the recourse of knowing where to look for answers in FAQs, newsgroups, and FTP sites on the Internet for HOWTO and other documents on Linux.

Configuring X Window on Linux

22

by Kamran Husain

IN THIS CHAPTER

This chapter details the way to configure the X Window System for Linux. This version of X Window for Linux is called XFree86 Version 3.1.1.

This chapter covers the following topics with regard to configuring your X Window System:

- How to configure XFree86 on your system
- Working with ConfigXF86 and the XF86Config file
- What the .xinitrc file is
- Your personal X resource file
- Using xdm
- Configuration of the window manager

Setting Up Your XFree86 System

This section covers another one of the most difficult, time-consuming, and frustrating parts of installing XFree86: setting up an XF86Config file.

If you have XFree86 3.1.1 and your graphic card is listed in the Hardware-HOWTO file (see Chapter 1, "Introduction to Linux"), you should use the ConfigXF86 program to do your configuration. This ConfigXF86 program is a comfortable and safe way to set up your system. If your graphics card is not listed, you have some work ahead of you.

The *XF86Config* File

To be able to set up an XF86Config file, you need to read from /usr/X386/lib/X11/etc these files: README, README.Config, VideoModes.doc, and README.Linux. You also need to read the man pages on the following topics: XF86Config, XFree86, XFree86kbd, and the server you are using.

The XF86Config file can be located in several places in this order:

- /usr/X386/lib/X11. This is the standard location for the sample XF86Config file, but in some cases you cannot use it (for example, a read-only /usr partition).
- /etc.
- In your home directory.
- As XF86Config.eg in /usr/X386/lib/X11.

The Linux file system standard places the XF86Config file in /etc/X11. The XFree86 servers will not "expect" an XF86Config file at this location, so there must be a link from one of the places in the preceding list to /usr/X386/lib/X11. Find this link first and use it to access the file. This way, you can be sure your changes take effect.

To give you some hints, here is a list of what you need to set up the XF86Config file correctly:

- The server suitable for your system. To get a hint as to which is the correct one, run the SuperProbe program that comes with XFree86. It will identify your chip set, and you can look at the XFree86HOWTO file on the CD at the back of this book to see which server supports this chip set. Note that SuperProbe can detect far more hardware than XFree86 supports.

■ Your monitor's specifications, most importantly the maximum horizontal and vertical scan frequency ranges and the bandwidth. This information can be obtained from your monitor's datasheet.

■ The name of the chip set for your video card. For example, Tseng Labs, ET3000, ET4000, and so on.

■ The available dot clocks for your card or (if supported) the name of the programmable dot clock generator. Learn how to obtain these by reading the file /etc/RE/usr/X386/lib/ X11/README.Config. Running XF86Config sets your system's dot clocks.

■ "Mouse type" refers to the protocol the mouse is using, not to the manufacturer. For example, a serial Microsoft mouse connected to the PS/2 port uses the PS/2 protocol, not the Microsoft protocol.

■ The type of device your mouse is connected to: serial or bus. (Usually you can use /dev/ mouse.)

■ Whether you want to use a national keyboard map or if you want to run the generic U.S. key table.

CAUTION

Do not share XF86Config files with people who do not have the same configuration (graphics card and monitor). By sharing, you could fry your monitor.

It isn't so hard to figure out modes for multisync monitors. Don't ever use a mode that you haven't verified as being within your monitor's specs. Even if you have exactly the same setup as the computer you're sharing the file with, check all modes before trying them. There are many people who run their computers from specs that may not damage their hardware but could damage yours.

Using *XF86Config*

ConfigXF86 is a configuration tool written by Stephen Zwaska, (e-mail address stz@netcom.com). XF86Config is located in /usr/X386/lib/XF86Config.

This utility provides an easy interface to the database of tested graphics cards and monitors. It also has some tools for correctly configuring your XF86Config file. The documentation for XF86ConfigX is located in /usr/X11R6/lib/doc. This documentation is provided in several formats. You can read a text version (XF86Configtxt) online, and you can print a PostScript version (XF86Config.PS) if a PostScript printer is available.

Start `ConfigXF86` as `root`. The program cannot be loaded while an X server is running on the system, so run `ConfigXF86` only from the console. The program probes your system and attempts to recognize your PC's setup. If both your graphics card and monitor are supported, pat yourself on the back for a lucky purchase. Now you shouldn't have any problems. The only thing you should do now is test the video modes and make changes to them to suit your monitor better.

> **TIP**
>
> The XFree86 servers parse the `XF86Config` file in case-insensitive mode, so do not worry about capitalization.

Examining the *XF86Config* File

The `XF86Config` file contains all the configuration parameters for your X Window installation. Space does not permit me to print the whole file. You will have to look in the directory `/usr/lib/X11` for the `XF86Config.eq` file. Copy this `XF86Config.eg` file to `XF86Config`. Then edit the `XF86Config` file. The format of the `XF86Config` file consists of different sets that are listed in the following sections:

- Pathnames
- Font paths
- Keyboard type
- Mouse type
- Server type
- Video modes

Each of these sections describes your hardware configuration, location of files, or both, to the X server. Each section is enclosed by the words:

```
Section "SectionName"
< information for the section >
EndSection
```

The Pathnames

There is no reason to fiddle with the standard paths as provided in the sample `XF86Config` file. In fact, any distribution that provides a different path structure should have edited this section of the `XF86Config.sample` or the template `XF86Config` file for `ConfigXF86`. You do have to know where these paths are pointing to in case of difficulties.

Your `XF86Config` file should look similar to the lines from my `XF86Config` file, as shown in Listing 22.1.

Listing 22.1. Font paths.

```
#
# Multiple FontPath entries are allowed (which are concatenated together),
# as well as specifying multiple comma-separated entries in one FontPath
# command (or a combination of both methods)
#
FontPath        "/usr/X11R6/lib/X11/fonts/misc/"
FontPath        "/usr/X11R6/lib/X11/fonts/Type1/"
FontPath        "/usr/X11R6/lib/X11/fonts/Speedo/"
FontPath        "/usr/X11R6/lib/X11/fonts/75dpi/"
# FontPath      "/usr/X11R6/lib/X11/fonts/100dpi/"
```

To see whether these lines are correct, please look into each of the directories mentioned in Listing 22.1 to see whether they have files in them. If these directories are empty, you do not have the fonts installed, or they may be at another location.

The Keyboard Section

You should specify the `ServerNumlock` option. This is an easy way to specify your keyboard for XFree86. Otherwise, only those keyboard modifications needed for international keyboard support have to be set manually. In a typical `XConfig` file, this section looks like the one shown in Listing 22.2.

Listing 22.2. Keyboard selection.

```
#
# Keyboard and various keyboard-related parameters
#
Section "Keyboard"
  AutoRepeat 500 5
  ServerNumLock
#  Xleds      1 2 3
#  DontZap
#
# To set the LeftAlt to Meta, RightAlt key to ModeShift,
# RightCtl key to Compose, and ScrollLock key to ModeLock:
#
#  LeftAlt     Meta
#  RightCtl    Compose
#  ScrollLock  ModeLock

# EndSection
```

The Pointer Section

The pointer section keyword is the name for the protocol the mouse uses. The available protocol names are listed in the XF86Config man page.

The Logitech serial mouse uses several keywords. The MouseMan uses the MouseMan keyword. The more recent Logitech serial mouse uses the Microsoft keyword. The older Logitech serial mouse uses the Logitech keyword.

Any mouse connected to the PS/2 port uses the PS/2 keyword even if it is in fact a serial mouse.

TIP

If you are not sure which kind of bus mouse you have, look at the kernel's startup messages. It identifies the bus mouse type.

CAUTION

Ensure that the kernel bus mouse driver is using the same IRQ as the bus mouse. If not, you have to change the IRQ and rebuild the kernel. The IRQ for bus mouse devices is given in /usr/src/linux/include/linux/busmouse.h. The macro MOUSE_IRQ contains this IRQ and is set to 5 by default.

The following is a list of device names for the mouse selection:

- /dev/inportbm   Use for the Microsoft bus mouse. Note that this uses the bus mouse protocol, not the Microsoft protocol.
- /dev/logibm   Use this for the Logitech bus mouse. Note that this uses the bus mouse protocol, not the Logitech protocol.
- /dev/psaux   Select for a PS/2 or quick port mouse. This uses the PS/2 protocol.
- /dev/atibm   For the ATI XL bus mouse. Note that the ATI GU bus mouse is a Logitech or Microsoft bus mouse, depending on the version you have.
- Other supported mice are serial mice; therefore, the device names are the same as the serial devices (/dev/ttyS? or /dev/ttyS?? for Linux).

TIP

If you have a two-button mouse, you might want to emulate the third button by setting Emulate3Buttons in the mouse section. Emulation is accomplished by pressing both buttons simultaneously. There are quite a number of other settings available, but they usually are not needed. Look at the XF86Config man page for a list of available settings.

You have to select one type of mouse and its baud rate if it's serial. Note in Listing 22.3 that I have "uncommented" the Microsoft mouse selection for my mouse and the 1200-baud rate line, and you will have to uncomment the line that matches your mouse selection. The 1200-baud rate seems to work fine with older mice and using the 9600 rate did not result in a speed difference for newer mice. Your results may vary.

Listing 22.3. Mouse selection.

```
#
Section "Pointer"
# Mouse definition and related parameters
#
#MouseSystems  "/dev/mouse"
Microsoft      "/dev/mouse"
#MMSeries      "/dev/mouse"
#Logitech      "/dev/mouse"
#MouseMan       "/dev/mouse"
#Busmouse       "/dev/mouse"
  BaudRate     1200
#  BaudRate    9600
#  SampleRate 150
#  Emulate3Buttons
... <deleted some stuff here > ..
EndSection
```

The Server Section

If you want to identify the chip set your graphics card uses, run `SuperProbe`, a program that comes with XFree86 and is capable of identifying a wide range of graphics hardware. Note that `SuperProbe` can probe far more hardware than XFree86 supports.

Listing 22.4 shows a plain setting for a 640×480 monitor for X with a virtual space of 800×600. A virtual space is an area where the display portion of your monitor is mapped onto. Your monitor is a window into this space.

Listing 22.4. Server selection.

```
#
# First the 8-bit color SVGA driver
#
vga256

#
# To disable SpeedUp, use NoSpeedUp
#
#  NoSpeedUp
#  Virtual     1152 900

  # Virtual     800 600
  Virtual       640 480
```

continues

Listing 22.4. continued

```
   ViewPort       0 0
   # Modes                "640x480" "800x600" "1024x768"
   # Modes                "640x480" "800x600"
   Modes                  "640x480"

#
# Next the 1-bit mono SVGA driver
#
vga2

   Virtual        800 600
   ViewPort       0 0
   Modes                  "640x480"
   # Modes              "800x600" "640x480"
```

Setting Up Video Modes

This is the hardest part. Please read VideoModes.doc before beginning. If you are using ConfigXF86 (which I strongly recommend), and your monitor is not in the database, choose the generic modes and start making your own modes from there. If you do not have ConfigXF86, read the tutorial on building modes in the README.Config file.

> **NOTE**
>
> I know this entire chapter is full of warnings. Please do not be alarmed. Just be careful and read the instructions for each step before taking it.

ConfigXF86 includes a neat utility to tune video modes. Because there is no check on the usability of a mode, you have to check the mode data against your monitor's specifications before testing the mode. The first line of the tuning modes screen gives you information on the specifications of the mode. You have to continuously check that these values are within your monitor's capabilities before testing that mode.

See Listing 22.5 for the common video modes for XFree86.

Listing 22.5. Video modes.

```
Section "Device"
    Identifier "Generic VGA"
    VendorName "Unknown"
    BoardName "Unknown"
    ChipSet "generic"
#   VideoRam 256
#   Clocks 25.2 28.3
EndSection
```

```
# ***********************************************************************
# Screen sections
# ***********************************************************************

# The color SVGA server

Section "Screen"
    Driver      "svga"
    Device      "Generic SVGA"
    Monitor     "Generic Monitor"
    Subsection     "Display"
        Depth      8
        Modes      "640x480"
        ViewPort   0 0
        Virtual    800 600
    EndSubsection
EndSection

# The 16-color VGA server

Section "Screen"
    Driver      "vga16"
    Device      "Generic VGA"
    Monitor     "Generic Monitor"
    Subsection "Display"
        Modes      "640x480"
        ViewPort   0 0
        Virtual    800 600
    EndSubsection
EndSection

# The Mono server

Section "Screen"
    Driver      "vga2"
    Device      "Generic VGA"
    Monitor     "Generic Monitor"
    Subsection "Display"
        Modes      "640x480"
        ViewPort   0 0
        Virtual    800 600
    EndSubsection
EndSection
```

The Mode line in a video section can have up to 10 values. Be very careful when modifying these values because a wrong setting may wind up destroying your monitor! It does not matter if these are not present because defaults can be used. A typical line to override defaults for a monitor would be:

```
"640x400" 28 640 480 728 776 480 480 482 494
```

The 10 values in order from left to right are shown in the following section. These values only make sense to video engineers or those folks who have to work with a monitor not defined in the default modes. Check your monitor's hardware specifications and get the values from there to fill in these ten parameters. The following are the fields to set:

- Label for screen resolution; for example, 640×480 or 1024×768.
- The clock frequency in mHz.
- The Horizontal Display End in number of visible dots per line on the screen.
- The Start Horizontal Retrace value. This specifies the number of pulses before the video sync pulse starts.
- The End Horizontal Retrace value defines the end of the sync pulse.
- The Horizontal Total value. This is the total number of dots per line invisible and visible.
- The Vertical Display End value. The number of visible lines on the screen.
- The Start Vertical Retrace value. The number of lines before the sync pulse starts.
- The End Vertical Retrace value is the number of lines at the end of the sync pulse.
- The Vertical Total value. The total number of lines, invisible plus visible, on the screen.

Multiscan monitors handle frequencies of 15 to 40 mHz. Some monitors work at 72 mHz vertical scan to prevent the flicker. You have to be able to calculate the frequency from the monitor's specification and come up with these numbers. A good place to start would be the XFree86-HOWTO document on how to get these values. Keep in mind that your video monitor is just a glorified television. You give it wrong values and you can fry it.

International Keyboard Layout for XFree86

XFree86 servers are able to read the key table from the Linux kernel, so you need to set up only one keyboard layout file (for the kernel). There are some restrictions, though; the kernel can support more keyboard functions than X11. X11 can only modify one of the four key tables. This modifier is called ModeShift.

Configurable keys for the ModeShift modifier are LeftAlt, RightAlt (=AltGr), RightCtl, and ScrollLock.

Usually the AltGr key is used for international keyboard modifications. To enable the XFree86 server to read the AltGr key table from the kernel, you should put the following line in the .olvwmrc file:

```
RightAlt "ModeShift"
```

Besides supporting only one additional key map, X11 cannot use *dead* keys. A key is called *dead* if when it is typed, it does not print a character until a second character is typed. A typical example is an accent key. Such keys are not supported by X11, so you need to replace all dead-key symbols with non-dead equivalents. Table 22.1 lists what you have to change:

Table 22.1. Key symbols.

Dead	Non-Dead
dead_tilde	ASCII tilde
dead_grave	grave
dead_circumflex	ASCII circum
dead_acute	apostrophe
dead_diaeresis	diaeresis

Instead of supporting dead keys, XFree86 supports a Compose key. This feature is described in the XFree86kbd man page and can be modified by assigning the Compose function to one of the keys. By default the ScrollLock key has the Compose function.

If you still want to have the dead keys on the console, you will have to use an xmodmap file to map the keys to the correct symbols under X. This is also the method that must be used with earlier versions of XFree86. On sunsite in the directory /pub/Linux/X11/misc, you can find sample xmodmap files for several languages. Note that you have to set the ModeShift modifier to get the right key table working.

Please read the kbd.FAQ that comes with the kbd package for Linux. You will find many hints for modifying your keyboard layout on the console, as well as for X.

The *.xinitrc* File

To use X, you need a startup file that calls the local modifications, the window manager, and an application you want to use right after X has started. If you are using startx (or runx) to start X, this startup file is called xinitrc. There is a standard xinitrc file, /usr/lib/X11/xinit/xinitrc, which is the traditional location for this file. The Linux file system standard places this file in /etc/X11/xinit/xinitrc in order to allow a read-only mounted /usr partition, so look in that location first.

If you are not content with what this file does (for instance, if you want to use a different window manager), you should copy it to the file .xinitrc in your home directory. After copying the file, you can edit it. Look at the man pages for startx and xinit for more information.

Note that both the .xinitrc and the .Xresources files must be readable and executable, so run the following commands on these files after editing them. You only have to run the chmod command once on the application.

```
$ chmod u+rx .xinitrc .Xresources
```

This command makes these files executable.

See the Listing 22.6 for a sample `.xinitrc` file.

Listing 22.6. Sample `.xinitrc` file.

```
 1 #!/bin/sh
 2 # $XConsortium: xinitrc.cpp,v 1.4 91/08/22 11:41:34 rws Exp $
 3 # modified by obz

 4 userresources=$HOME/.Xresources
 5 usermodmap=$HOME/.Xmodmap
 6 sysresources=/usr/lib/X11/xinit/.Xresources
 7 sysmodmap=/usr/lib/X11/xinit/.Xmodmap

 8 # merge in defaults and keymaps

 9 if [ -f $sysresources ]; then
10     xrdb -merge $sysresources
11 fi

12 if [ -f $sysmodmap ]; then
13     xmodmap $sysmodmap
14 fi

15 if [ -f $userresources ]; then
16     xrdb -merge $userresources
17 fi

18 if [ -f $usermodmap ]; then
19     xmodmap $usermodmap
20 fi

21 # Set the background to a dull gray
22 if [ -f /usr/bin/X11/xsetroot ]; then
23 xsetroot -solid gray32
24 fi

25 if [ -f /usr/bin/X11/xclock ]; then
26       xclock -geometry 80x80 &
27 fi

28 olvwm &
29 # fvwm &

30 xterm  -e /bin/bash
```

The line numbers in this listing have been added for your benefit. Let's look at these lines in greater detail.

Lines 4 to 7 set the resource environment variables for the X Window installation for your system. Change these to the path of your system's X Window system distribution.

Lines 9 through 20 check for the existence of these resources and then run the appropriate program, xmodmap or xrdb, with these resources as parameters. I will cover xmodmap and xrdb in Chapter 23, "Using Motif." For now you can use this the way it stands.

Lines 22 to 24 check for the xsetroot program, and if present, execute it to set the background to a solid color, gray32.

The olvwm & command in line 28 starts the OPEN LOOK window manager for you. If you want to use fvwm instead of olvwm, uncomment line 29 and comment line 28 instead. The window manager must be run in the background if you have more commands following this one.

Line 30 starts a terminal to work with. Because this is the last line in the .xinitrc file, exiting this terminal causes your X session to stop. If you want to start more xterms, you can start them from within this xterm.

A simpler .xinitrc file to start with would be the following:

```
xterm -name Console &
olvwm
```

You can then enhance this .xinitrc file with what you want.

The Personal X Resource File

Sometimes you won't be content with default settings for applications that don't have a configuration file of their own. You can change some of these defaults by setting X resources in the .Xresources file in your home directory.

> **NOTE**
>
> You should know what effects setting the resources will have on the programs you use. Read the man pages for the program and for xrdb before editing the Xresources file. See Chapter 2, "Types of Linux Available," and Chapter 25, "Ghostscript," for more information about X resources.

A resource file looks like an application default file. The difference is that in the resource file, resources for several applications are set. You should use the full names (*Progname.Resourcename*) instead of abbreviating the program name with an asterisk. Examples of application default files can be found in the /usr/X386/lib/X11/app-defaults directory. The resources available for a single application are usually shown in the man pages for that application.

If you are running a color server, you might want to put the following lines into your .Xresources file if some programs start in black and white:

```
#ifdef COLOR
*customization: -color
#endif
```

If this change is made, the program *foo* will read both the *Foo* and the *Foo-color* application default file from /usr/X386/lib/X11/app-defaults. The usual behavior is for *Foo* only to be read.

> **NOTE**
>
> If you *are* running a color server, the preceding code definitely should be added to the system Xresources file. You might mention that to the person or entity who maintains the program you are running.

Note that the black-and-white color scheme of a program may be caused by the program rather than its resources.

The -xrm can be used with most X programs to override the parameters set in your .Xresources file. The usage is

```
-xrm "resource"
```

Alternatively, you can use xrdb <*filename*> command to enforce any changes you have made in <*filename*> apply to your current session.

Using xdm

If you want to run X on your system all the time, you could run xdm from the system startup. xdm is preconfigured on most systems, so you should not have to edit any of the xdm configuration files. Usually a run level is attached to an X-only system (look at /etc/inittab). All you have to do to get it working is change the default run level. On systems that use an init without run levels (run man init to see whether your system uses an init), you should look into the /etc/rc and /etc/rc.d/rc.local files; you usually only have to remove comment signs at the beginning of a line that calls xdm. If no such line is present, you probably have a system that has no preconfigured xdm. In any event, xdm by default runs your .xinitrc file for you.

Configuration of the Window Manager

Window managers are a user- and site-specific issue. Several window managers are available for Linux. The configuration of one window manager is quite different from that of another. The window manager used in the configuration is usually explained in your .xinitrc file, so look there. The most commonly used window managers for Linux are

- olwm or olvwm for the OPEN LOOK Window manager. (It is on the CD at the back of this book.)
- mwm for the Motif window manager, possibly the most common commercial window manager. You have to buy it along with Motif.
- twm. (It is part of the XFree86 distribution on the CD at the back of this book.)

■ fvwm. (This seems to be the most popular shareware window manager and is on the CD at the back of this book.)

I discuss some window managers in greater detail in the next few chapters on OPEN LOOK and Motif.

Compiling Programs That Use X

Before compiling any programs for X, please read the GCC-FAQ file. This file can be found in the pub/Linux/docs/faqs directories of sunsite. Many questions on compiling programs with Linux are answered in this FAQ. Many Linux distributions include the most relevant FAQs in the directory /usr/doc, so you might look there first.

If you have the source code for a program that uses X11, it is usually shipped with an Imakefile instead of a Makefile.

Imakefiles are files that create Makefiles for your system. Discussing Imakefiles is beyond the scope of this book; however, you will have to work with Imakefiles if you work at all with X sources. Just remember the shell script xmkmf, and you should be okay.

TIP

xmkmf is an abbreviation for X Make Makefile.

CAUTION

The xmkmf shell script actually runs the imake command with a set of arguments. The most common argument is the -DUseInstalled argument. If you examine xmkmf, (look in /usr/X11/bin/); you will see that the xmkmf script is a basic wrapper around a call to imake. It's very tempting to use imake on a command line by itself. Do not do so. Run the imake command with the -DUseInstalled argument if you must run imake on the command line. If you do not use this argument, imake will behave as if it were re-creating the X Window system on your current directory.

Of course, before ever running xmkmf, you should read the documentation that usually comes with such packages.

Run xmkmf in the directory that contains the Imakefile. If there is a hierarchy of directories with Imakefiles, you usually only have to run xmkmf in the root directory of that hierarchy.

The `xmkmf` command builds the `Makefiles` in all directories in the hierarchy.

Then you should run the `make` command with an argument to let `make` resolve its dependencies, using the following command:

```
$ make depend
```

> **TIP**
>
> Don't be afraid if `include` files, such as `stddef.h`, `varargs.h`, and so on, are not found. They are `gcc` proprietary header files, and therefore not in the standard `include` directories.

After that, you can make the program by running `make`, and you can install your new utility (usually in `/usr/X386/bin`) by running this line:

```
$ make install
```

The installation of the man pages is accomplished by running

```
$ make install.man
```

Some Common Problems

Some of the problems you might see when you work with Xfree86 are outlined in the following list.

- No Windows—all you get is a gray background and no windows. This is due to running without a window manager. Running X only starts the X server, not the window manager. You should use a script shown earlier in `startx` in Chapter 21, "Installing X Window on Linux."

- Your Logitech serial mouse does not work. The keyword `Logitech` is reserved for older Logitech serial mice. Use the keyword `MouseMan` (or `Microsoft`) for newer mice. Logitech serial mice plugged into a PS/2 port require the keyword `PS/2`.

- You get errors about not finding any font files. First check the `XF86Config` file to see whether the directories in the font path are named correctly and contain fonts. If they are correct, run `mkfontdir` in each of those directories to set them up for use with X.

- After leaving X, your screen fonts are not restored. This is a known bug with some servers. There are utilities called `runx` or `restoretext` included with `svgalib` that can help you in most cases. You can get them from sunsite.unc.edu in the file `/pub/Linux/libs/graphics/svgalib-1.2.8.tar.gz`.

- You will have some problems on uncommon, extremely new, or extremely old cards. This is what you have to live with when you are dealing with freeware.

- The server dies with the message `Cannot find a free VT`. XFree86 needs a free virtual terminal (VT) on which to run. So if you have put a `getty` process on every virtual console in your /etc/inittab, XFree86 is not able to start. The common practice is to leave /dev/ tty8 (for kernel messages) and /dev/tty7 (for XFree86) free of a getty process.

This is not an exhaustive list. Please read the HOWTO documents in /usr/docs on the CD-ROM for more information about other video card problems that are too specific to list here.

Compiling Sources for XFree86

You do not typically want to compile sources for XFree86 unless you really want to make changes to the sources because something is not working. You will need a lot of disk space and CPU time to do a complete build of the XFree86 system. Anything you need to know for compiling XFree86, you can find in the following files (in /usr/X386/lib/X11/etc): INSTALL, README, and README.Linux.

Note that you should not compile XFree86 to get rid of hardcoded restrictions (on the maximal pixel clock, for example) because without these restrictions, your hardware will probably break down.

To build a server that includes only those drivers you need, you should use the LinkKit instead of compiling the complete system. This is a little easier than trying to build it from scratch. The LinkKit package is specific and complicated and is therefore beyond the scope of this chapter.

Read /usr/X386/lib/Server/README for a description of how to use LinkKit. This file is not included in the standard XFree86 tar files but is part of the file that includes the LinkKit.

For adding drivers to the SVGA servers, you need the LinkKit only.

The documentation on how to build servers can be found in the /usr/X386/lib/Server/ VGADriverDoc directory after installing the LinkKit package.

Summary

This chapter covered the topic of configuring the XFree86 system. After reading this chapter, you should have an idea of how to set up your XF86Config file to generate your X environment. Just remember to start with the basic configuration settings for VGA cards and then make enhancements. Keep backups of your work and do not change the video settings unless you know what you are doing. If nothing works despite your best efforts, you have the recourse of knowing where to look for answers in FAQs, newsgroups, and FTP sites on the Internet for HOWTO and other documents on Linux.

Using Motif

23

by Kamran Husain

In this chapter, you will cover the following topics:

- Installing Motif on your Linux machine.
- Some of the basic concepts required for using X Window. Displays, windows, screens, and the Client Server Architecture in X are introduced.
- An introduction to Window Managers, specifically the Motif Window Manager (mwm) because this is a chapter on Motif!
- Navigating in mwm windows with the keyboard and mouse.
- Widgets and their characteristics.
- Customizing your desktop with resource files and client applications, and how to set your environment to your liking.
- Using some standard X tools available in Linux.

The following assumptions are made about you, the reader, as we go further into this chapter:

- You have completely read Chapter 21, "Installing X Window on Linux," and successfully installed X Window on your system.
- You have played at least a little with Linux or UNIX, and know the syntax of using some basic UNIX commands such as find, cpio, tar, and ln.
- You have the X11R6 version of X Window, called XFree86, installed on your machine.

CAUTION

As you did with XFree86, please read this entire chapter thoroughly before proceeding with the installation.

A Brief Introduction to Window Managers and Motif

How the windows in an X session are arranged is a function of a special program called the *window manager*. The window manager controls the look and feel of all the windows on a particular display. The window manager enables the user to move, restack, resize, and iconify windows (that is, reduce windows to an icon).

X Window comes with three window managers by default. These managers are called the Freeware Window Manager (fvwm), the Tab Window Manager (twm) and the Open Look Window Manager (olwm). The twm is also referred to as Tom's Window Manager, after its author, Tom LaStrange. Earlier versions of X also offered the Universal Window Manager (uwm); however, this is no longer offered because it does not conform to the X Consortium's *Inter-Client Communications Conventions Manual* (ICCCM) standards. Please see Chapter 24, "OPEN LOOK and OpenWindows."

Window managers in X are different from other windowing system managers because you are allowed to choose whichever manager you like. As long as a manager follows the ICCCM standard, it can serve as your window manager.

The most prevalent commercial Linux (or UNIX-based) window manager today is the Motif Window Manager (mwm) from the OSF/Motif distribution. In fact, if you use fvwm, you see the similarities between fvwm and mwm. The Motif Window Manager is more important now than ever before, because it has been adopted by Common Open Software Environment (COSE) as the standard interface for future UNIX GUIs. It's most famous for its borders around all the windows it displays.

Motif applications look more like a Mayan temple than a menu system. Almost every item on the screen is rectangular. A rectangular button rests on a rectangular menu bar, which may rest on another rectangular form, which sits on a square window. We will discuss Motif in great detail in this chapter.

NOTE

The latest version at the time of writing was Motif 2.0. There are several updates to Motif (1.2.3, 1.2.4, and so on), but Motif 2.0 is a major release from their last major release 1.2.4. The 2.0 release includes a lot of bug fixes, and adds Widgets to its list of convenience functions. Get an upgrade if you are running an older version, and you may be surprised to see some of your existing bugs disappear!

Getting Motif for Linux

Unlike most of the software for Linux, Motif is not free and is not shareware. You have to pay for a Motif license. The cost is approximately $150. I have listed three vendors here that can sell you Motif for Linux. Due to lack of time before going to press, there was no time to research other vendors; you can check the Internet resources listed in Appendix A, "Linux FTP Sites and Newsgroups," for more information.

Metrolink Incorporated
4711 North PowerLine Rd.
Fort Lauderdale, FL 33309
(305) 938-0283
sales@metrolink.com

SWiM $149.95 (US)
ACC Bookstore
136 Riverside
Westport, CT 06880
800 546-7274
orders@acc.corp.com

MOO-TIFF
InfoMagic
11950 N. Highway 89
Flagstaff, AZ 86004
(520) 526-9565
orders@infomagic.com

General Installation Procedures

Each Motif distribution has its own distinct installation procedure. The documentation provided by each vendor should give you enough to get started. By reading about one vendor's installation procedure, you can get an idea of how other distributions are installed. For this description, I use the MetroLink installation guidelines. Other distributions may follow a different installation procedure, but you will know what to look for when you are done with the installation.

General software requirements for Motif include the following:

- XFree86 2.1 or later
- C library version of libc 4.4.4 or later
- ld.so runtime linker/loader

The version on the CD-ROM at the back of the book satisfies these requirements for you. However, if you have installed from another source, you should confirm that you meet these requirements before installing Motif.

You must do all the installation as root. Be sure that you are root before proceeding.

Motif requires the following directories to exist in the X11 installation on your machine.

```
/usr/lib/X11
/usr/bin/X11
/usr/include/X11
```

If these directories do not exist, you must create links to them from where equivalent XFree86 directories are kept. The XFree86 distributions are kept in the following directories:

```
/usr/X11R6/lib/X11
/usr/X11R6/bin/X11
/usr/X11R6/include/X11
```

In some cases, the installation program creates the required links to these directories for you. However, if you do not see these directories, you can create them with the following steps:

```
# ln -s /usr/X11R6/lib/X11 /usr/lib/X11
# ln -s /usr/X11R6/bin/X11 /usr/bin/X11
# ln -s /usr/X11R6/include/X11 /usr/include/X11
```

> **NOTE**
>
> Check to see whether you have /lib/libXm.so.1 or /lib/libXm.so.1.2.2 installed on your machine. Remove these files before proceeding.
>
> Also check and remove, if present, the directory (and its contents) /usr/lib/X11/Motif before you start the installation process. This way you will avoid keeping old files around.

The MetroLink distribution consists of five 3.5-inch, high-density disks. They are labeled as follows:

- Runtime 1 and 2
- Developers Disk 1, 2 and 3.

> **TIP**
>
> The floppy disks on Linux are addressed by a syntax that describes how to read and write them. For example, a 3.5-inch, high-density floppy disk in drive A is addressed as /dev/fd0H1440. For a 5.25-inch, high-density drive in drive B, you have to use /dev/fd1H1200. (The fd0 implies the fast floppy disk as a high-density, 3.5-inch, 1.44MB floppy disk drive. For a 5.25-inch, high-density drive as the second drive you would use /dev/fd1H1200.)
>
> Most Motif distributions come on 3.5-inch, high-density floppy drives, so you should use /dev/fd0H1440 or /dev/fd1H1440 for drive A and B, respectively.

Now insert the first Runtime disk into your floppy drive, and issue the following commands if you are using drive A.

```
# cd /tmp
# cpio — extract — verbose — block-size=32 -I /dev/fd0H1440
```

The cpio program prompts you for the second disk. Replace the disk and press the Enter key to continue.

After cpio is finished with the extraction, you have a large file in the tmp directory. This file is called run.tar.z. Now, you have to extract all the files from file into your directory tree. Issue the following commands:

```
# cd /
# gzip -dc /tmp/run.tar.z ¦ tar -xvf -
```

The gzip -dc command extracts all files in the compressed archive and passes the resulting tar file to the tar program. This tar program extracts (x) all the files it receives on its standard input (-), and lets you know what it's doing by being verbose (v) while extracting each file.

Now, remove the temporary file with the following command:

```
# rm /tmp/run.tar.z
```

Do the same procedure for the developers disks. Use cpio to copy the dev.tar.z file into the tmp directory. The use the gzip command as before for the runtime libraries, except use the name dev.tar.z instead of run.tar.z.

Getting Started with X Window

On some systems, you may have to start X from the command line after you log in. On other systems, you may have to interface through the xdm client. Let's start with the easy case of the xdm manager already running on your system.

> **CAUTION**
>
> The first thing to remember is that X is very flexible. You can customize almost anything in X. Therefore, be warned that even though I attempt to describe the most common features of X, they may not work exactly as described. This is the price of flexibility. *This is especially true for all the different versions of X and window managers offered in X.*

Starting X and *mwm*

If you do not see any windows at all, and you do not see a cursor, you do not have the X server running. In this case, you have to start X yourself.

There are several steps to take before you start X.

1. Confirm that startx exists in your PATH. Use the echo $PATH command to see whether /usr/X11R6/bin is in your path.

   A sample startx is shown in Listing 23.1.

2. Look for a file called XF86Config in /usr/X11R6/lib/X11. This file contains very hardware-specific information about your system. Read Chapters 21 and 22 to ensure that you have installed X correctly.

> **TIP**
>
> Always make a copy of XF86Config and save it away before you modify it. Do not edit this file while you are already in X.

3. Type the command startx at your prompt.

4. Wait a few seconds (or minutes, depending on your hardware). You should see several messages whisk by, and the screen should change to that of a session without a window manager.

5. At this point, you can run a crippled windowing system without a window manager, or you can start a window manager. For example, to get the Motif Window Manager, use the following command in an xterm. (Of course, you can use fvwm, or whatever manager you fancy and have installed.)

```
mwm &
```

Listing 23.1. A sample startx file.

```
$ less /usr/X11R6/bin/startx
#!/bin/sh

# $Xconsortium: startx.cpp,v 1.4 91/108/22 11:41:29 rws Exp $
# $Xfree86: xc/programs/xinit/startx.cpp,v 3.0 1994/05/22 00:02:28 dawes Exp $
#
# This is just a sample implementation of a slightly less primitive
# interface than xinit.  It looks for user .xinitrc and .xserverrc
# files, then system xinitrc should probably do things like check
# for .Xresources file and merge them in, startup in a window manager,
# and pop a clock and serveral xterms.
#
# Site administrators are STRONGLY urged to write nicer versions.
#

userclientrc=$HOME/.xinitrc
userserverrc=$HOME/.xserverrc
sysclientrc=/usr/X11R6/lib/X11/xinit/xinitrc
sysserverrc=/usr/X11R6/lib/X11/xinit/xserverrc
clientargs=""
serverargs=""

if [ -f $userclientrc ]; then
    clientargs=$userclientrc
else if [ -f $sysclientrc]; then
    clientargs=$sysclientc
fi
fi

if [ -f $userserverrc ]; then
    serverargs=$userserverrc
else if [ if $sysserverrc ]; then
    serverargs=$sysserverrc
fi
fi

whoseargs="client"
while [ "x$1" != "x" ]; do
    case "$1" in
        /''*¦\.*)        if [ "$whoseargs" = "client" ]; then
                    clientargs="$1"
            else
                    serverargs="$1"
            fi ;;
        --)    whoseargs="server" ;;
        *)     if [ "$whoseargs" = "client" ]; then
                clientargs="$clientargs $1"
            else
```

continues

Listing 23.1. continued

```
                serverargs="$serverargs $1"
            fi ;;
    esac
    shift
done

xinit $clientargs -- $serverargs
```

By the way, you can run any ol' manager you have, `fvwm`, `twnm`, `olwm`, and so on. I am simply using `mwm` as an example. Also note that you are running the `mwm` in the background. If you do not do this, you can't issue any commands to the `xterm`. See Figure 23.1 for what your display might now look like. Keep in mind that your display may look quite different from the picture in Figure 23.1 because your startup code has different applications.

FIGURE 23.1.

A typical Motif session.

> **TIP**
>
> If you are in the `bash`, KORN, C, or any other common shell at this point, and you forgot the &, type Ctrl-Z to put the job in the background. If you are not running the Korn or C shells, you can kill `mwm` with Ctrl-C, and then restart it with the ampersand.

Congratulations! You are now running Motif.

Note that a lot of things can go wrong while getting to this point. Here are a few of the most common problems:

■ You cannot find the correct files. Ensure that the path includes /usr/X11/bin or the like.

■ You moved the cursor into the window, but now you have to click to be able to type commands to your xterm. By itself, X Window gives the focus to a window when a cursor is moved on to it. mwm, on the other hand, requires that you actually click the left mouse button (Button1) for that window to get focus. *Focus* means that all user input (keyboard and pointer) is now be sent to that window. mwm changes the color of the window border to show that it has received focus.

■ There is not enough memory to run the system. This is especially true if you are on a PC-based platform. Typically, you can get away with 4MB of dynamic RAM for a simple X Window system, but you almost certainly need 8MB or more to be able to get a reasonable response time on a PC. The memory upgrade to 8MB is well worth it, given the performance on a 4MB machine. Only the patient can live with 4MB.

■ The configuration does not look right. You have to modify the default startup parameters. See the "Customizing Motif" section.

■ Exiting the last command in your .xinitrc file terminates your entire X session. If your last command was an xterm and you logged off that xterm, your entire session is terminated. Generally, the last command in your .xinitrc file would be the window manager so that terminating the window manager will also terminate your session.

Working with Motif Windows in *mwm*

Look at the typical xterm window in Motif, shown in Figure 23.2.

FIGURE 23.2.

A typical xterm *window.*

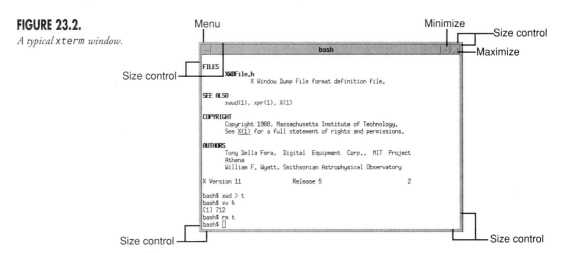

The Title bar is the wide horizontal band on the top of the window. This contains the title for the application itself. In this case, this is the application itself, xterm. You can modify it to your needs. Try the following:

```
xterm -name "I am here" &
```

The minimize button is used to iconify this xterm. The maximize button can be used to resize the window to occupy the entire display area. All corners can be used to resize the window by using the mouse. Note the pseudo-three-dimensional appearance of the borders.

Using the Pointer

You will now work with some of the Motif windows that you have on the screen. Typically, you work with a mouse for the pointer, so the text refers to mice at times. However, you can always substitute your device name for the word *mouse* or *pointer*, and not lose any meaning of the discussion.

Pointers in the mwm environment typically use three buttons, called Button1, Button2, and Button3. As an affront to left-handed individuals, Button1 is usually referred to as the *left button* because it is the most used button of the three. The left button on a mouse is the one that is pressed with your right index finger. When you take the pointer to an item and press a button, you are *clicking* the button.

If you are left handed, you can map your mouse or pointer buttons differently. See the section entitled, "Help for Left-Handed Users," later in this chapter.

Icons and Windows

The minimize button enables you to iconify an application. An icon is a small symbol that represents an inactive window. The contents of that window are not visible, although they may be updated internally by its process. Icons can be moved around on a screen, but they cannot be resized. Inactive windows that become active may hide icons. Icons save valuable screen space when you're using applications that do not require your constant attention.

Iconifying a Window

Move the cursor to the minimize button, and press the left button on the mouse. The window is removed from the screen, and a smaller icon is seen somewhere on the left of the screen. The minimize button is the one with the smaller square near the right side of the frame. The maximize button is the one with the bigger square and can be found on the right side of the frame.

To restore an icon to a screen, move the cursor to the icon and click on Button1 twice in quick succession. This is known as *double-clicking* the mouse. Some Motif icons are shown in the bottom left side of Figure 23.3.

FIGURE 23.3.

Typical Motif icons.

Motif icons

Maximizing a Window

Move the cursor to the maximize button, and press Button1. This enlarges the window to the size of the root window. This way, you can have a huge clock on your screen. Some applications, such as older versions of calc, do not adjust their internal graphic areas when their frame is resized. This leads to annoying blank space on a screen.

Use the maximize button as a toggle. Clicking on an already maximized window causes it to revert to its size and position (also known as geometry) before it was maximized. Clicking on it again remaximizes it.

> **TIP**
>
> Avoid resizing a window when running a vi session under an xterm. This leads to unpredictable results and may cause vi to behave very strangely.

Sizing a Window

The entire frame on a Motif window is a control that enables you to resize the window. See Figure 23.2 for the size controls. The four corners enable you to stretch the window by each corner. The four long bars let you move the edges of the window with the mouse.

To stretch the window using a corner, move the mouse to that corner. Press Button1 and, while keeping it pressed, move the mouse. You should see the cursor change its shape to a double-headed arrow, and a thin border will appear, indicating the size and orientation of the current stretch operation. Size the window by moving the mouse with Button1 pressed. Release the button when you have achieved the desired size.

Note that some applications do not have these sizing controls enabled. An example is the cute, but not very useful, pointer tracking program called xeyes, or the clock program called oclock. (See Figure 23.4.)

FIGURE 23.4.

The oclock *program has a window without resize borders.*

To move the edges of the window, move the mouse to that edge. You should see your cursor change shape to a vertical double-headed arrow if you are on a horizontal edge (top or bottom of window). As you move the pointer, a thin border will appear indicating the size and orientation of the current stretch operation. If you are on a vertical edge, the double-headed arrow is horizontal. Press Button1 and, while keeping it pressed, move the pointer around. This moves the edge along with your pointer. Release the button when you have the edge where you want it.

While you are resizing this window, you see a small box come up in the center of the display. This box contains the size of the window in pixels if it's a graphics image, or in rows and columns (in number of characters) if it's an xterm. On some systems, you can use the arrow keys on your keyboard to achieve precision when resizing your windows. Remember to keep the button pressed while you use the arrow keys on your keyboard to do the precise adjustment.

Focus and Selecting a Window

You can select a window or icon to get *focus* by moving the pointer to that item and pressing the left button. This moves the window or icon to the top of the stack. This way, the window or icon isn't obscured by any other screen item.

When a window has focus, it collects all the user input from the pointer and the keyboard. There are two types of focus for a window: click to type and explicit. The click to type focus requires a user to click a pointer button in a window for it to get focus. The explicit focus requires only that the cursor be in the window for the window to get focus. Explicit focus is sometimes referred to as *real estate driven* focus.

In some cases, you want to have the focus where the mouse is, without having to click the pointer button. Sometimes this is not useful for touch typists, because a single movement of the pointer can have the keystroke sent to wrong window.

> **TIP**
>
> Sometimes it's a good idea to click on the frame to get focus to a window because clicking in the window might accidentally press a button or other control in the window.

After you give the focus to a client, it collects all typed or graphics information until the user clicks elsewhere. It has the focus.

Getting focus also raises the window to the top of the stack. The window frame color changes at this point. You can set the focus to an icon too by selecting it with a mouse. The name of the icon expands at that point, and you see the window menu for that icon. You can move the mouse away from the menu, but the icon retains the focus until you click elsewhere.

The color change scheme depends on your site's default colors. In some cases, you may not see any color change at all if the focused and out-of-focus colors are the same.

Moving a Window or Icon

In order to move a window's location on the screen, complete the following steps:

- Move the cursor on top of the title bar.
- Press and hold down pointer Button1.
- Move the pointer to the desired location. You should see an outline of the window border move with your pointer.
- Place the outline at the part of the screen where you want your window to be. This is referred to as *dragging* the window.
- Release Button1. The window now appears at the new location. It is also the window with the focus by default.

This procedure can be duplicated for an icon. In the case of an icon, you click and drag with the cursor in the icon itself.

While you are moving the window, you see a small box in the center of the screen with two numbers in it. These are positive X and Y offsets of the top left corner of the window from the top left corner of the screen. This is very useful information when trying to precisely place a window on the screen.

You can achieve some fine precision by pressing the arrow keys on the numeric keypad to move the window one step at a time. You must keep the pointer button pressed while you use the arrow keys.

Adding a New Window

Say you want to add a calculator to your screen. Type in

```
$ xcalc &
```

at the prompt in an xterm window. The calculator should appear on the screen. To get another xterm, type the following command:

```
$ xterm &
```

Depending on your site, this can appear anywhere on the screen. Typically, the new window is placed in the upper-left corner (x=0,y=0) of the root window, or in the center of the root window.

The size and location of a window is referred to as the window's *geometry*.

NOTE

The reason why you launch applications with an ampersand (&) at the end of the command is to run the application in the background and free up the xterm from which the application is being run. If you do not type the ampersand, the xterm will not accept input until that application is either suspended or killed. Also, the use of the ampersand allows the application to run even after the xterm from which it was run is killed.

Window Geometry

Almost all clients accept the -geometry command line option. This option tells the window manager where to locate the window on the screen. If you do not specify any geometry, the window manager uses its defaults.

The coordinate system for the root window is as follows:

- The origin is top left (0,0).
- The number of display units is in pixels for graphics.
- The number of display units are in character sizes for xterms.

A pixel is the smallest unit available on a screen. Usually, screens are displayed in 1024×768 pixels, 2048×2048 pixels, or something similar. The size of a pixel on screen is very much hardware-dependent. A 200×200 window appears as different sizes on monitors with different resolutions.

The geometry parameter is of the following form:

```
widthxheight[{+-}xoff{-+}yoff]
```

The height and width are usually given in pixels. In the case of xterms, height is given in lines, and width is given in characters per line. It is common to have a 24×80 xterm.

The xoff and yoff are offsets from the start of left and top edges of the screen respectively. These represent the location of the window on the root window. The curly braces represent either the - or the + character, but not both.

+xoff	A positive offset from the left edge of the screen to the left edge of the window.

-xoff	A negative offset from the right edge of the screen to the right edge of the window.
+yoff	A positive offset from the top edge of the screen to the top edge of the window.
-yoff	A negative offset from the bottom edge of the screen to the bottom edge of the window.

A visual representation of the geometry is shown in Figure 23.5. For example, the line

```
xterm -geometry -50+50 &
```

places the xterm on the top right corner, 50 pixels from the right edge of screen and 50 pixels from the top of the screen.

FIGURE 23.5.

Window geometry.

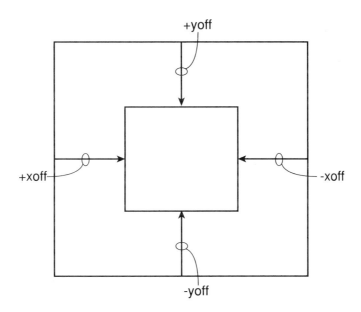

The following parameters specify the edges of the screen:

-0-0	Lower right corner
-0+0	Upper right corner
+0-0	Lower left corner
+0+0	Upper left corner

Using the Window Menu

Using the window menu requires you to have the focus on a window. Let's look at a typical window menu. This also may be different on your screen, but the basic functionality listed here should exist for all later versions of Motif. Take the cursor to the window menu button, and press the left button. The following menu (or something close to it) should appear:

```
Restore       alt-F5
Move          alt-F7
Size          alt-F8
Minimize      alt-F9
Maximize      alt-F10
Lower         alt-F3
Close         alt-F4
```

Using the Keyboard in X and the Meta Key

It's important to bring this point up about the keyboard and its special keys under X. Keyboards come in different types, and the most important key for using keystrokes in X can be radically different from one keyboard to another. On PC-based keyboards, it is usually the Alt key; on Macintoshes, it is the fan-shaped key; on Suns, it is Left, Alternate; and other keyboards use other keys. The list goes on.

In short, the *Meta key* is the special key for your special keyboard. For a PC-based keyboard, this is the Alt key. So, do not look for a key called Meta on your keyboard. Where it says Meta, use Alt, fan, or whatever key your special keyboard is mapped to.

Now you can invoke any item on this window menu in one of two ways:

■ Use the pointer. This way, you click on the window menu and press Button1. Now, move the cursor to the item you want, and release Button1; or, press the Meta key and the character that is underlined in the menu. For moving a window, you press Meta-M. Note that this does not work on some Motif distributions.

NOTE

Alt-key combinations may not always work. In Metro's version of Motif 1.2, the Meta-F7 key allows moving a window, but the Meta-M key does not work at all. You may have a completely different experience with *your* keyboard.

■ While the window has focus, press the Meta-function key combination. Then use the arrow keys on your keyboard to simulate the movement of the cursor, or just use the pointer.

Note that some of these functions may not be available for a menu shown for an icon. You might not be able to size or minimize an icon, but you can move, maximize, or close it.

Using the Root Menu

Click Button3 while the cursor is in the root window. You see a menu pop up on top of all the windows. This is known as the root menu. Keep in mind that this menu is very customizable, and may look radically different on your machine. You will learn all about creating your own menu later in this chapter in the "Customizing mwm" section.

A typical root menu may list the following items. (Your system may have a different list depending on the type of Motif you purchased.)

```
"Root Menu"
New Window
Shuffle Up
Shuffle Down
Refresh
Utils >
Restart
Exit
```

While holding down Button1, move the cursor down the list to the item you want to select. When you get to the menu item you want, release the button. If you do not want to select any items, move the cursor off the menu and release the button.

In the previous list, the functionality can be set to the following:

- New Window starts a new xterm and sets focus to it.

- Refresh redraws the entire screen and all windows.

- Restart kills mwm and restarts it.

- Exit kills mwm and leaves you without a window manager. If this is the last command in your startup script, your windowing session terminates.

- Shuffle Up and Shuffle Down shuffles the stacking order of the windows up or down. The current window with focus is moved down to the bottom when shuffling down, and the next highest window is given the focus. The last window in the stack is brought to the top and given the focus when shuffling up.

- The Utils item brings up another submenu with more choices to select from. See the "Customizing Motif" section, later in this chapter, for details on how to set your menu items.

Now, let's work with Motif clients.

Working with Motif Clients

Most programmers find the X Window system libraries too basic to work with, so they use the next building block called Toolkits. The most common interface toolkit is the XtIntrinsics toolkit from MIT. This is called Xt. On top of Xt, you can have other toolkits such as Motif or the Open Look Interface Toolkit (OLIT). When you are working with Motif, you are working with a Motif toolkit. In Motif, you are working with Motif Widgets.

Widgets help developers program consistent user interfaces in Motif. By using Widgets, programmers can quickly put together interfaces that have the same look and feel of all Motif applications.

Some Widgets display information. Some Widgets collect user input (mouse or keyboard) information. Some Widgets react to user input by changing their appearance or performing some programmed function. Some Widgets are simply containers for other Wigdets. All Widgets can be customized in one form or another, whether it is appearance, font size or style, colors, or whatever other parameter is required.

All Widgets of the same type have two data structures with information that describes their attributes: class and instance. The instance data structure contains information for a specific Widget on the screen. The class information contains information required for all Widgets of the class.

Widgets are grouped into several classes. Each class depends on the type of functionality offered by the Widget. Normally, the internal functions of a Widget are hidden from the applications programmer (encapsulation). A Widget class shares a set of functions and data structures for all Widgets in that class. A new Widget class can be derived from an existing Widget class. The newly derived class can inherit all the data structures and functions of the parent class. A Widget is created and destroyed during a Motif program execution.

> **NOTE**
>
> The destruction of a Widget is a bit more complicated, and will be discussed in detail in the next chapter.

> **NOTE**
>
> This should sound familiar to C++ programmers. True polymorphism is somewhat harder to find in Widgets. This is all done in C. For C++ programmers, the class data structure is to the class for an object, as the instance data structure is to the instance of an object.

A Widget is really a pointer to a data structure when viewed in a debugger. This data structure is allocated on the creation of a Widget, and is destroyed when a Widget is destroyed.

Let's look at a typical application screen to see some Widgets in action. You will work with a demo application called xmdialogs, shown in Figure 23.6. The Widgets shown here will be described later in this chapter. The xmdialogs application can be found in the /usr/bin/X11 directory. If you do not have this application, you can still learn about working with Widgets by applying these concepts to different applications.

> **NOTE**
>
> Don't worry if you cannot find this application on your machine. There are plenty of other applications just like this one. If you have the Motif 1.2.3 release or later from Metro Link, you will have this application in your /usr/bin/X11 directory.

FIGURE 23.6.

The xmdialogs *demo application.*

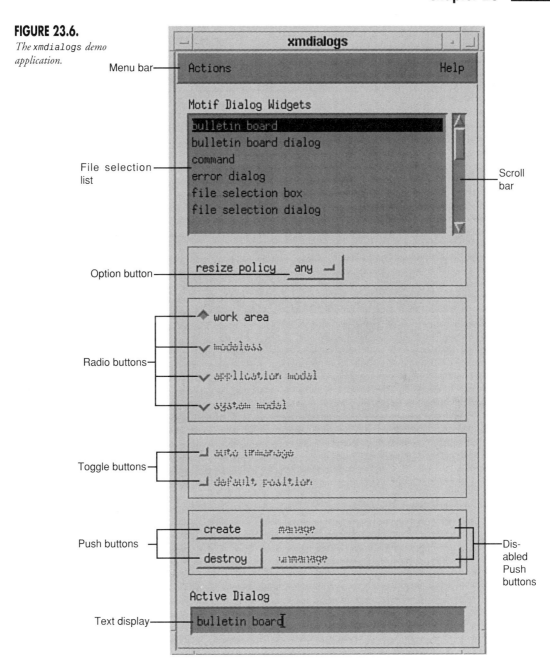

Figure 23.6 shows a Menu Bar, a File Selection List with Scrollbars, an Option Button, some Radio and Toggle buttons, some Push buttons, some Labels, and a Text Display dialog box.

The Actions and Help items are shown on a menu bar. By moving the pointer to either of these items and pressing Button1, you are presented with a menu of options very similar in operation to the window and root menu.

Underneath this menu bar is a list of items in a scrollable list. This widget is of the type XmList. The XmList lets you keep a selection of items in a visible list. It has scroll bars to enable the user to scroll the list if the entire list isn't visible. A programmer can set the number of items that are visible at one time. If you resize the window, and if the list box sizes itself proportionately with the window, the number of visible items in a list may change.

To select an item, move the pointer to the item of your choice and press Button1 once. The item is highlighted in a darker color. Some lists enable you to select more than one item, and others, just one item. In this application, you only select one type of dialog box. (Figure 23.6 shows the bulletin board item to be the selected item.)

The scroll bars on the side of the list Widget are of the class XmScrollbar. A scroll bar is either a horizontal or vertical rectangle. There is a raised box in the rectangle called the slider box. This slider moves within the larger rectangle. The movable space for the slider bar is called the scroll region. The ratio of the size of the slider bar to the scroll region is proportional to the size of the work area to the total area being viewed.

The XmSrollBar rectangle has two arrows at each end. The arrows point outward relative to the rectangle, and in opposite directions. The arrow keys can be used to move the slider bar within the scroll region.

1. Move the mouse to the slider bar arrow.
2. Click on Button1.
3. The slider bar should move closer to the arrow. The slider moves as close as possible to the arrow being clicked in the scroll area.
4. Release Button1.

Users can also move the slider bar by dragging it with the mouse:

1. Move the pointer on to the slider bar.
2. Press the Button1.
3. Move the pointer up or down for a vertical scroll bar.
4. Move the pointer left or right for a horizontal scroll bar.

   The contents of the work area, as well as the slider bar, scroll with the movement of the pointer. The viewable portion is the work area.
5. Release Button1 when the list area contains the desired viewing data.

Now move your cursor to the selection item of the resize policy button. When you click on this button, you are presented with a pop-up menu of the types of resize policies for the dialog box you want to create. When you press the button, a menu pops out and presents you with a list of options. You make the selection with your pointer by moving the pointer to that button and releasing it. The menu disappears, and your selection is displayed in the box. In Figure 23.6, shown previously, the resize policy is set to *any*. This is known as an *option button*.

Note the diamond-shaped buttons and selections below this current menu. This is a list of one of four possible selections for the dialog box. One of the items is shown in a lighter gray color. This is known as *grayed out*, meaning that the option is a not a valid option at the time. The option for the Work Area is *disabled*. You can select one of the three options. These items are grouped together with a rectangular frame drawn around them. Usually, buttons are grouped together this way in Motif when their functionality falls in the same group of actions. The actions are similar to the buttons on a radio: push one button and the rest of the buttons in the row all come up. This is why these are referred to as *radio buttons*.

Look at the two buttons: *auto manage* and *default position*. These are *toggle buttons* for this application. When you select one button, the other is not influenced at all. The functionality provided by each button is completely independent of the other. Do you see the difference between radio buttons and toggle buttons?

Sometimes a scrollbar is used on each side of a drawing area. This is called a Scrolled Window, and belongs to the XmScrolledWindow class. This Widget can hold graphics instead of a list of items. The XmScrolledWindow is used primarily to view large graphic items in a small window, whereas XmList is used to show items for the user to select from.

Under the toggle buttons, you see four *push buttons*. When a push button is pressed, the colors on the border of the button reverse. Also, the color of the pressed rectangle changes to show the user action. Push buttons are used to invoke some sort of action. When you select the file selection dialog from the list and press the push button to manage it, the display shown in Figure 23.7 appears. This is the standard file selection box under Motif, and you should see it for most applications.

FIGURE 23.7.

A typical File Selection dialog box.

To see a more detailed picture of what types of Widgets are available within Motif, run /usr/bin/ X11/periodic. (See Figure 23.8.) Note that the menu item for this application can be removed to become a separate application, by dragging on the dashed line. The menu is shown as torn off in Figure 23.9.

FIGURE 23.8.
The Periodic Table of Widgets.

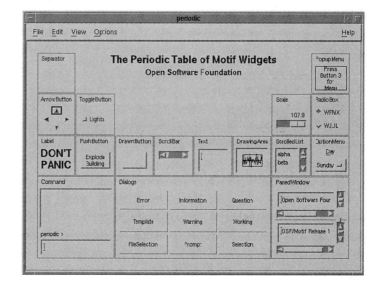

FIGURE 23.9.
A tear-off menu torn off.

Other Types of Widgets

The Motif toolkit also supplies the following Widgets. Please refer to the items in the periodic table in Figure 23.8 to see what each Widget should like on screen.

XmArrowButton   This is a directional arrow with a border around it. A programmer can modify the arrow's direction, thickness, and border color by setting the Widget's parameters. Look at the ends of a scrollbar to see two examples of such a Widget.

XmDrawnButton   A drawn button provides a rectangular area with a border for the programmer. The programmer can size, redraw, or reposition text or graphics within this window. This Widget provides hooks to set parameters for its border appearance, as well as to attach functions for accepting user input.

XmLabel   This is a rectangular box consisting of either text or graphics. It is instantiated, but is also used as a base class for all button Widgets. A label's text can be multiline, multifont, or even multidirectional. In the xmdialogs example, this would be the labels Active Dialog and the Motif Dialog Widgets strings.

Many features of the labels can be modified. This includes the fonts, foreground and background colors, and alignment (left, center, or right justification); in fact, this can even store a pixmap graphic image.

XmPushButton   This is a text label or pixmap with a border around it. This Widget accepts keystrokes or mouse button presses. In the smdialogs example, these are the *create*, *destroy*, *manage*, and *unmanage* buttons. When a button has focus, it draws a heavy border around itself.

When you press the enter key or a pointer on a button, the button has focus. Move the cursor to the button. Press a key or button and hold it down. You have armed the button. The color on the button should change, and the border colors should reverse. This gives the impression that the button has been pressed inwards. When you release the button, the button reverts to its original state. When a mouse button is pressed in this Widget the foreground and background colors of the Widget usually also invert.

XmSeparator   This is used to create a line between functional sections of a screen. There is really not much that users can do with this Widget except position it on the screen.

XmText   This is used to create a fully functional multiline text editor on a screen. The user can select text by dragging the mouse from one location to another while Button1 is pressed. Users can also click anywhere on the Widget to mark the insertion point. If the text Widget is enabled for user input, the user can type at the insertion point and insert the text into the text Widget.

Pull-down menus   These are rectangular areas in the window that enable users to select from a number of items. The items are generally laid out in push buttons. Users can select a push button either by moving the mouse to that selection, or by pressing Alt-K, in which K is the letter of the alphabet that is underlined in the menu button. In the xmdialogs function, the Meta-F key selected the file item, and Meta-h selected the Help item.

Pop-up menus   The Motif root window menu is a good example of a pop-up menu. When you press the mouse button, a menu is displayed. You can select an item in the menu by moving the cursor onto the item and pressing Button1.

Scale Widgets   The scale Widget is used to display the value of a data item between two extremes. It can also be used to accept user input. A scale Widget has a scroll region that is very similar to the scroll bar. However, it does not have the arrow buttons at each end.

XmScrolledWindow   This is a combination of a horizontal scroll bar, a vertical scroll bar, and a drawing area. If the size of the drawing area fits within the window, you can't see the scrollbars. If the size of the drawing area is greater than the visible area of the scrolled window, you see the horizontal or vertical scrollbars, or both. You can then use the scrollbars to move the visible portion on top of the drawing area. This is known as panning the window.

XmFrame   This is a simple Widget used to put a consistent border around one single Widget. Frames can only hold one Widget at a time.

`XmRowColumn`   This is a general-purpose Widget organizer. The Widget can layout its Widget collection in a variety of ways, including the following:

Row major   In this case, all Widgets on this Row Column Widget are stored until one row fills up, and a new row is created when another Widget is added that doesn't fit on this Widget. The creation of a new row is sometimes called *wrap-around*.

Column major   This is the same as a row major, but it wraps around in a columnar fashion.

In conjunction with this, you can specify the width of each column to be that of the widest Widget; you can also specify the number of fixed columns, the packing (whether all Widgets should be packed as closely as possible), or that the individual Widgets specify their own positions.

There are several other Widgets available in the Motif Widget set. You can see the complete listing and their options in *The Programmers Reference Manual* from the Open Software Foundation.

Gadgets

Motif Widgets create a window in X Window. A complex Motif application can create several X windows very quickly. Each window uses X resources in the server, and many windows can slow your overall system performance.

Gadgets are windowless versions of a Widget. Most Gadgets have the same names as Widgets, but have the string `Gadget` appended to their name. So, `XmLabel` has a `XmLabelGadget` counterpart.

Gadgets do not have all the features of Widgets. For example, Gadgets share the foreground and background colors of their parent. Also, some Gadgets actually turn out to be slower than the Widgets they are trying to replace. Given the troubles that you can get into by using Gadgets, you may be better off not using them.

Customizing with Resources

Now that you are familiar with Widgets, let's talk about the parameters that affect them—resources.

What Are Resources?

As you saw in the previous sections, you can customize some aspects of an application from the command line prompt. X enables you to modify the aspects of an existing application every time a client runs that application. X does this by setting control variables for that client. These control variables are called *resources* and have a value associated with them.

For example, consider the case of an `xterm`. An `xterm`'s resources are its font size, its pointer shape, the foreground color for all displayed text, its background color, and so on. These are only a few of the resources for an `xterm`. Most of these resources exist as predefined defaults for all the common clients in a system.

You can specify resources on an application-specific basis, or for all applications on your system. These resources are normally stored in an ASCII file called `.Xresources`, in your home directory.

This file affects only those applications that you run. This file normally contains only those options that you would like to customize over those values that are set in system files.

You can always override the defaults specified in the system-wide file with defaults in your `.Xresources` file. In turn, your command line options for a single client override those in the `.Xresources` file. Keep in mind, however, that the command line default applies only to a specific client. The `.Xresources` default setting becomes the default for all your clients.

Also, remember that the command line operations override any default resources set in a file. Normally, you set how you want your application to look under normal circumstances, and then override the changes via command line options.

> **TIP**
>
> In some systems, the `.Xdefaults` file can also be called `.Xresources`.

To make your resource specifications available to all clients, use the X resource database manager program, `xrdb`. This stores the resources directly on the server and makes the resource available to all clients on the system. This step takes some care because your change will affect all your clients, regardless of what platform they are running on.

Defining Resources

A resource definition file is basically a line-by-line list of all the resources in the file. Each line consists of two entries: one for the resource type, and the other for the value for the resource. The two entries are colon-separated.

The simplest syntax for a resource definition is as follows:

```
client*variable:  value
```

`client` is the name of the client. The `variable` for that client is set to the `value`. Note that the colon follows the `variable` without any spaces.

Let's look at the resource declaration for an `xterm` client.

```
XTerm*foreground: white
XTerm*background: blue
XTerm*font: 10x20
...
```

If you do not already have an `.Xdefaults` file, you can create one yourself with a text editor.

The values can be Boolean, numeric, or string. Values can be specified for Widgets in an application as well. For example, if you want to set the background color for all `PushButtons` in an application, `myWorld`, you set the following resource:

```
myWorld*PushButton.background: red
myWorld*background: blue
```

Note that the asterisk represents the Widgets in between the actual `myWorld` application and all `PushButtons` in that application. If you specify

```
myWorld.mainForm.PushButton: blue
```

only the buttons on the Widget `mainForm`, which in turn must exist on `myWorld`, are affected. This is *tight binding*. Using the asterisk (`*`) is *loose binding* because it allows for multiple levels of Widget hierarchy between the objects on either side of the asterisk. If this has a hierarchy of

```
myWorld.mainForm.subForm.PushButton
```

the first two of the following declarations affects the `PushButtons` on the `subForm`, and the last does not:

```
myWorld*PushButton.background: red
myWorld*background: blue
myWorld.mainForm.PushButton: blue
```

Another example is the settings for an `xterm`. If you attempt to set the scrollbars using

```
xterm.scrollbar: true
```

it probably won't work. Most likely, there is a Widget hierarchy between the top-level application and the scrollbar Widgets. In this case, it works if you use the following:

```
xterm*scrollbar: true
```

> **TIP**
>
> When you use a very general setting for a Widget in your resource files, say `*labelString`, you affect all such occurrences of `labelString` in all files. Be careful!

After you have modified the `.Xresources` file, you probably expect to see the changes occur immediately. Not so. You now have to inform the server of your defaults by using the `xrdb` command. Use the following command:

```
xrdb -load .Xresources
```

This reflects the changes for all subsequent executions of your client. These remain in effect until overridden, or until your session terminates. If you save your `.Xresources` file in your login directory, these changes are loaded whenever you start X with the following command:

```
xrdb -load .Xresources
```

This command is useful when creating `.Xresources` for the first time in a session. That is why, in most cases, this command is run when the windowing system is first created. If you want to keep the previous settings, use the `-merge` command option instead of `-load`, like so:

```
xrdb -merge .myOwnResources
```

So, how do yo
for the descri

Looking at th
Some of the r
at some of th
front of them

    XmNac
    ➡ N
    ➡
    ➡
    XmNde
    XmCde
    ....

Note the lett

    *
    *
    *
    *

So, in the ca
at the time it
to a pointer

The other v
because it d
read from a

Using E

Motif uses

The XENVIR
file. This m
in .Xresou

The XUSERF
delimited s
of the mos

    %C
    %l
    %L
    %N
    %S

The RESOU
at startup.

Also, you can use the exclamation point as the comment character at any point in the input line before text begins. So, the following lines are comments:

```
! This is a comment
! another one
! commented*labelString: This resource is not used.
```

You can also use the cpp preprocessor's directives #if, #ifdef, #else, and #endif. This is running through xrdb only. The cpp preprocessor is not run when the .Xresources file is parsed. You can override the run through cpp by using the -nocpp parameter on the command line. No other parameters are required. If you want to remove a resource, use the -remove operation.

```
xrdb -remove .myOldResources
```

User and Class Resource Files

There are two types of resource files: user and class. User files apply to each instance of all applications. These are the resources you set in the .Xresources file. Class files pertain to all the instances of a particular class. These exist in files usually in your home directory or your path. The name of this file is the name of the class. The class name is the name of the application class with the first letter capitalized.

For example, all xterms belong to the class XTerm. Note that the class name is the name of a type of application with the first letter capitalized. XTerm is an exception in this regard because it has XT capitalized instead of only X.

Let's look at setting the resources for a particular class of an application:

```
*labelString:  Hello World
```

This command sets the labelString resource to Hello World for all Widgets in every application in your session. This may not be exactly what you want.

```
Xapp*labelString:  Hello World
```

This command sets the labelString resource to Hello World for all Widgets in every Xapp application in your session. This doesn't affect Widgets within other applications. This effect may be desirable if you are trying to set only one type of application resource.

You can also specify your own class for setting resources. This is done by setting the -name option on a client. For example, you can define all the resources for an xterm with 10×20 font to be of class hugeterm. Then, whenever you run

```
xterm -name hugeterm &
```

it uses the resources in the class hugeterm. Now you can set the foreground color to whatever you want for xterms with a name of hugeterm.

Note that the name resource cannot contain the * or . characters. These values cause your resource setting to be ignored. The mwm environment simply ignores bad syntax, instead of informing the user about these errors.

Cus

Custor
set of
changi
applica
tions t
some

■

■

■

Har

You c
"Mot

Hard

■

■

■

■

Us

This
resou
man

Use
is as

xcli

Not

xcli

The XFILESEARCH environment variable holds a colon-delimited list of directories for the app-defaults file. Usually, these defaults are in the /usr/lib/X11/app-defaults directory.

Note that some of the classes in the directory have the first two letters of their names capitalized, instead of just one (XTerm, XDbx, XMdemos). So, if your class resource settings do not work as expected, look in this directory for some hints on what the resource class name might look like. Again, the contents of this directory depend your installation of Motif and X.

The search for the missing .Xresources occurs in the following order:

```
Check in XUSERFILESEARCHPATH,
  if not successful or XFILEUSERSEARCHPATH not set,
       Check in XFILESEARCHPATH,
  if not successful or XFILESEARCHPATH not set,
       Check user HOME directory
```

Now that you have all this information, keep this advice in mind: In all but the most unavoidable cases, you should *not* rely on environments to set your application resources.

The methods are too complicated to learn, especially for the end user. However, they can be a very powerful customization tool. Editing resource files is hard enough on the programmer; it's even worse on the user. However, in order to be a good Motif user, you should know about the environment variables that affect applications that come from other vendors.

Listing an Application's Resources

There are two Motif applications that can assist you in determining an application's resources: appres and editres. Here is the appres program's syntax:

appres Class [instance]

This lists all the resources in a given class for the named instance of an application. Listing 23.2 shows the manual options of the command appres XTerm for advanced users.

Listing 23.2. Manual options for advanced users.

```
$ appres XTerm
*VT100*font5:
*VT100*font5:       9x15
*VT100*font3:       6x10
*VT100*font4:       7x13
*VT100*font2:       5x7
*VT100*font1:       nil2
*VT100*font6:       10x20
*tekMenu*vtshow*Label:      Show VT Window
*tekMenu*tektextsmall*Label:     Small Characters
*tekMenu*vtmode*Label:      Switch to VT Mode
*tekMenu*tektextlarge*Label:      Large Characters
```

```
*tekMenu*tekpage*Label:        PAGE
*tekMenu*tekreset*Label:       RESET
*tekMenu*tektext2*Label:       #2 Size Characters
*tekMenu*tekhide*Label:        Hide Tek Window
*tekMenu*tekcopy*Label:        COPY
*tekMenu*tektext3*Label:       #3 Size Characters
*tekMenu.Label:        Tek Options
*fontMenu*font5*Label:        Large
*fontMenu*font6*Label:        Huge
*fontMenu*font2*Label:        Tiny
*fontMenu*fontescape*Label:        Escape Sequence
*fontMenu*fontdefault*Label:        Default
*fontMenu*font3*Label:        Small
*fontMenu*fontsel*Label:        Selection
*fontMenu*font1*Label:        Unreadable
*fontMenu*font4*Label:        Medium
*fontMenu.Label:        VT Fonts
*SimpleMenu*menuLabel.font:        -adobe-helvetica-bold-r-normal--*-120-*-*-*-*-
➥iso8859-*
*SimpleMenu*menuLabel.vertSpace:        100
*SimpleMenu*Sme.height:        16
*SimpleMenu*BackingStore:        NotUseful
*SimpleMenu*HorizontalMargins:        16
*SimpleMenu*Cursor:        left_ptr
*mainMenu*terminate*Label:        Send TERM Signal
*mainMenu*securekbd*Label:        Secure Keyboard
*mainMenu*suspend*Label:        Send STOP Signal
*mainMenu*continue*Label:        Send CONT Signal
*mainMenu*allowsends*Label:        Allow SendEvents
*mainMenu*kill*Label:        Send KILL Signal
*mainMenu*interrupt*Label:        Send INT Signal
*mainMenu*logging*Label:        Log to File
*mainMenu*quit*Label:        Quit
*mainMenu*hangup*Label:        Send HUP Signal
*mainMenu*redraw*Label:        Redraw Window
*mainMenu.Label:        Main Options
*vtMenu*hardreset*Label:        Do Full Reset
*vtMenu*scrollbar*Label:        Enable Scrollbar
*vtMenu*scrollkey*Label:        Scroll to Bottom on Key Press
*vtMenu*scrollttyoutput*Label:        Scroll to Bottom on Tty Output
*vtMenu*jumpscroll*Label:        Enable Jump Scroll
*vtMenu*clearsavedlines*Label:        Reset and Clear Saved Lines
*vtMenu*allow132*Label:        Allow 80/132 Column Switching
*vtMenu*reversevideo*Label:        Enable Reverse Video
*vtMenu*tekshow*Label:        Show Tek Window
*vtMenu*cursesemul*Label:        Enable Curses Emulation
*vtMenu*autowrap*Label:        Enable Auto Wraparound
*vtMenu*tekmode*Label:        Switch to Tek Mode
*vtMenu*visualbell*Label:        Enable Visual Bell
*vtMenu*reversewrap*Label:        Enable Reverse Wraparound
*vtMenu*vthide*Label:        Hide VT Window
*vtMenu*marginbell*Label:        Enable Margin Bell
*vtMenu*autolinefeed*Label:        Enable Auto Linefeed
*vtMenu*altscreen*Label:        Show Alternate Screen
```

continues

Listing 23.2. continued

```
*vtMenu*appcursor*Label:      Enable Application Cursor Keys
*vtMenu*softreset*Label:      Do Soft Reset
*vtMenu*appkeypad*Label:      Enable Application Keypad
*vtMenu.Label:      VT Options
*tek4014*fontLarge:      9x15
*tek4014*font2:      8x13
*tek4014*font3:      6x13
*tek4014*fontSmall:      6x10
XTerm.JoinSession:      False
```

> **NOTE**
>
> The appres application sometimes does not run under Motif, use twm.

The second command is a menu-driven GUI program, editres, which enables you to edit the given resources for an application. This is available for X11R5 and later. The program displays a tree-like representation of all the Widget classes in a program, and enables the user to move through the tree node by node. Search your release for this file. If you do not have this file, don't despair; use the find command. See Figure 23.10 for an editres session.

FIGURE 23.10.

The editres *application.*

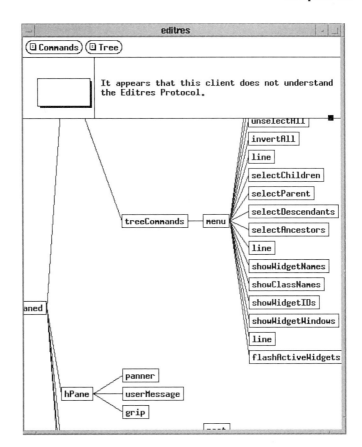

Using the *.mwmrc* File

Create this file from the `system.mwmrc` file by copying it into your `$HOME` directory as `.mwmrc`, and then edit it. (Look in the `/var/X11R6/lib` directory, and search for the `system.mwmrc` file using the `find` command.)

Listing 23.3 shows a sample `.mwmrc` file. As I stated earlier when working with `.Xresources`, comments are started with a ! character on a line. Note that, depending on your version of Motif, your listing may look very different than the one shown here. However, you will be able to see the general information presented here.

Listing 23.3. A sample `.mwmrc` file.

```
!!
!!              $HOME/.mwmrc
!!      Modified system.mwmrc for personal changes. kh.
!!
!!
!! Root Menu Description
!!

Menu DefaultRootMenu
{
        "Root Menu"             f.title
        "New Window"            f.exec "xterm &"
        "Shuffle Up"            f.circle_up
        "Shuffle Down"          f.circle_down
        "Refresh"               f.refresh
        "Pack Icons"            f.pack_icons
!       "Toggle Behavior..."    f.set_behavior
        no-label                f.separator
        "Restart..."            f.restart
!       "Quit..."               f.quit_mwm

}

Menu RootMenu_1.1
{
        "Root Menu"             f.title
        "New Window"            f.exec "xterm &"
        "Shuffle Up"            f.circle_up
        "Shuffle Down"          f.circle_down
        "Refresh"               f.refresh
!       "Pack Icons"            f.pack_icons
!       "Toggle Behavior"       f.set_behavior
        no-label                f.separator
        "Restart..."            f.restart
}

!!
!! Default Window Menu Description
!!

Menu DefaultWindowMenu
{
```

```
        Restore          _R    Alt<Key>F5   f.restore
        Move             _M    Alt<Key>F7   f.move
        Size             _S    Alt<Key>F8   f.resize
        Minimize         _n    Alt<Key>F9   f.minimize
        Maximize         _x    Alt<Key>F10  f.maximize
        Lower            _L    Alt<Key>F3   f.lower
        no-label                            f.separator
        Close            _C    Alt<Key>F4   f.kill
}


!!
!! Key Binding Description
!!8

Keys DefaultKeyBindings
{
        Shift<Key>Escape   window¦icon       f.post_wmenu
        Alt<Key>space      window¦icon       f.post_wmenu
        Alt<Key>Tab        root¦icon¦window  f.next_key
        Alt Shift<Key>Tab       root¦icon¦window    f.prev_key
        Alt<Key>Escape          root¦icon¦window    f.circle_down
        Alt Shift<Key>Escape    root¦icon¦window    f.circle_up
        Alt Shift Ctrl<Key>exclam root¦icon¦window  f.set_behavior
        Alt<Key>F6         window                f.next_key transient
        Alt Shift<Key>F6   window                f.prev_key transient
        Shift<Key>F10              icon           f.post_wmenu
!       Alt Shift<Key>Delete    root¦icon¦window  f.restart
}


!!
!! Button Binding Description(s)
!!

Buttons DefaultButtonBindings
{
        <Btn1Down>   icon¦frame   f.raise
        <Btn3Down>   icon¦frame   f.post_wmenu
        <Btn3Down>   root        f.menu        DefaultRootMenu
}

Buttons ExplicitButtonBindings
{
        <Btn1Down>   frame¦icon   f.raise
        <Btn3Down>   frame¦icon   f.post_wmenu
        <Btn3Down>   root        f.menu        DefaultRootMenu
!       <Btn1Up>     icon        f.restore
        Alt<Btn1Down>       window¦icon f.lower
!       Alt<Btn2Down>       window¦icon f.resize
!       Alt<Btn3Down>       window¦icon f.move

}

Buttons PointerButtonBindings
{
        <Btn1Down>   frame¦icon   f.raise
        <Btn3Down>   frame¦icon   f.post_wmenu
```

continues

Listing 23.3. continued

```
      <Btn3Down>   root        f.menu       DefaultRootMenu
      <Btn1Down>   window      f.raise
 !    <Btn1Up>     icon        f.restore
      Alt<Btn1Down>      window¦icon f.lower
 !    Alt<Btn2Down>      window¦icon f.resize
 !    Alt<Btn3Down>      window¦icon f.move
 }

 !!
 !!  END OF mwm RESOURCE DESCRIPTION FILE
 !!
```

There are several key features here:

- Key bindings
- Button bindings
- Menu items

A *binding* is a mapping between a user action and a function. The key bindings map keystrokes to actions, and the button bindings map button presses and releases to actions. Menus display the menu items for the user, and let you organize action items into sections.

The format for all the items is as follows:

```
Section_type Section_Title
{
      .. definitions..
      .. definitions..
}
```

In this format, Section_type can be Menu, Keys, or Buttons. The Section_Title is a string defining the variable name. It's a name that can be used to refer to this section in other portions of the file.

The functions shown in the sample file begin with an f. keyword. Some actions are fairly obvious: f.move, f.resize, f.maximize, f.minimize, f.title, f.lower and so on. Some actions are not so obvious: f.separator (displays a line on the menu item), f.circle_up (shuffles window stacking order up), f.circle_down (shuffles window stacking order down).

See Table 23.1 for all the features available for you to work with.

Table 23.1. Motif menu item descriptions.

Function	Description
f.circle_down[icon¦window]	Shuffles window stacking order down.
f.circle_up[icon¦window]	Shuffles window stacking order up.
f.exec or ! [command]	Executes command.

Function	*Description*
f.focus_color	Sets colormap focus of a client window.
f.focus_key	Sets keyboard input focus to a window or icon.
f.goto [*x*¦*y*]	Hops to a different location on the virtual desktop.
f.kill	Terminates a client window.
f.lower [-*client*¦*within*¦*freeFamily*]	Lowers a window to the bottom of the stack.
f.maximize	Maximizes a window.
f.menu	Associates a pull-right menu with the menu pane.
f.minimize	Minimizes a window to an icon.
f.move	Enables the interactive movement of a window.
f.move_constrained	Similar to f.move but restricts movement of the window to within the boundary of the screen.
f.next_cmap	Changes the colormap of the current window to the next colormap in the list.
f.next_key[*icon*¦*window*¦*transient*]	Sets keyboard focus to the next window/icon.
f.nop	No operation. It's a filler only.
f.normalize	Restores a window to original size.
f.normalize_and_raise	Restores a window to original size and brings to top of stack.
f.pack_icons	Rearranges the icons on a desktop.
f.pan[*dx*¦*dy*]	Pans the view of the virtual canvas.
f.pass_keys	Enables/disables (toggles) key bindings.
f.post_wmenu	Posts the window menu.
f.prev_cmap	Changes the colormap of the current window to the previous colormap in the list.
f.prev_key[*icon*¦*window*¦*transient*]	Sets keyboard focus to the previous window or icon.
f.quit_mwm	Terminates Motif.
f.raise[-*client*¦*within*¦*freeFamily*]	Raises a window to the top of the stack.
f.raise_lower[*within*¦*freeFamily*]	Raises a window to the top of the stack if it is partially obscured, or lowers it if not at all obscured.
f.refresh	Redraws all windows.
f.refresh_win	Redraws only a specific window.
f.resize	Enables the interactive sizing of a window.

Table 23.2. continued

Function	*Description*
f.restore	Restores the state of an icon/window to its normal state.
f.restore_and_raise	Restores and raises a window to the top of the stack.
f.restart	Restarts mwm.
f.screen [*next¦prev¦backscreen_number*]	Jumps cursor to a specific screen, or to the next, previous, or last visited screen.
f.send_msg *message_number*	Sends a client message
f.separator	Draws a line.
f.set_behavior	Restarts Motif, toggling between default or custom behaviors.
f.title	Names the menu.
f.track_pan	Moves the canvas interactively.

You can get more information from the *OSF/Motif Reference* book. In my humble opinion, it's dry but informative; the book will supply you with all the information you could possibly want about these commands.

Adding Your Own Menu Items

Let's see about defining your own menu items. The following could be a sample menu item:

```
Menu MyGames
{
"Kamran Games"  f.title
no-label        f.separator
"Tetris"        f.exec "xtetris &"
"Mahhjong"      f.exec "xmahjongg &"
"Chess"         f.exec "xchess &"
}
```

The f.title action specifies a heading for the submenu. The f.separator draws a line under the title. The f.exec fires up the command shown in double quotes.

TIP

Note the ampersand in f.exec for starting these tasks in the background. Do not start a task that may never return and thus hang up your mwm session.

Now, you can add this new menu to the root menu by adding the following line in your `DefaultRootMenu` definitions:

```
"Utils"          f.menu       MyGames
```

More on Button and Key Bindings

The key and button bindings work in the same way as menus. The first obvious difference is the extra column with the words `icon`, `frame`, `window`, and `root` in it. These words force the bindings on the context. The `root` applies to any location of the pointer on the root window, the `frame` or `window` keywords apply binding only when the pointer is in a window or its frame. The `icon` bindings apply to icons.

In your `.Xdefaults` file, refer to these key bindings for the class `Mwm`:

`Mwm*keyBindings: DefaultKeyBindings`

Here are some of the descriptions in the key bindings:

```
Shift<Key>Escape  window¦icon      f.post_wmenu
Alt<Key>space     window¦icon      f.post_wmenu
Alt<Key>Tab       root     f.menu  DefaultRootMenu
```

The syntax for a keystroke binding is

```
modifier<Key>key
```

in which *modifier* is `Alt`, `Control`, or `Shift`. The key can be a keystroke, function key, and so on. The first two declarations describe the same action: show the window menu, but with different keystrokes. The third key binding shows a method for displaying the root menu.

The button bindings are the bindings for your buttons. The three important bindings to remember are as follows:

```
Buttons DefaultButtonBindings
Buttons ExplicitButtonBindings
Buttons PointerButtonBindings
```

In your `.Xresource` or `.Xresources` file, refer to one of these button bindings for the class `Mwm` as

`Mwm*buttonBindings: DefaultButtonBindings`

or

`Mwm*buttonBindings: ExplicitButtonBindings`

or

`Mwm*buttonBindings: PointerButtonBindings`

Customizing Your Desktop with Clients

This is done by using some of the client software that comes with your X11R6 distribution. We will cover the following applications:

* xsetroot
* xset
* xdpyinfo
* xmodmap

There are several more utilities in the /usr/bin/X11 directory for you to play with: bitmap, xmag, xcalc, and so on. Check each one out to customize your desktop. The ones described here are not so intuitively obvious.

xsetroot

This client customizes the root window characteristics. Here are some of the options available:

-cursor cursorfile maskfile   This option changes the cursor to a displayed mask value. See the sidebar for creating your own cursor using bitmap.

-cursor_name name   This is the name of the standard cursors in the X11 protocol.

-bitmap filename   This option creates a tiled surface on the root window with a bitmap. Check the /usr/lib/X11/bitmaps directory for a list of the standard bitmaps.

-fg color foreground   This option sets the color for the bitmap on the root display.

-bg color background   This option sets the color for the bitmap on the root display.

-gray or -grey   This option sets the background to a pleasant (for some) gray background.

-rv   This option reverses the foreground and background colors.

-solid *color*   This option sets the root window to a solid color; for example, -solid red will set a red background.

Look in the /usr/lib/X11 directory of the file called rgb.txt for a list of colors, and look at the later section on colors in this chapter for more information.

See the man pages for additional features for xsetroot.

NOTE

The cursorfile is an ASCII file with arrays of characters. You create a bitmap using the bitmap utility. Then, run this bitmap through bmtoa to convert a bitmap to arrays. There is a reverse utility called atobm to convert existing arrays to bitmaps, for use with the bitmap editor.

Using *xset*

This command sets up some of the basic options on your environment. Some of these options may not work on your particular system. It's worth it to check these out.

Set your bell volume with this command:

```
xset b volume frequency durationInMilliseconds.
```

For example, the command

```
xset b 70 4000 60
```

sets the keyboard bell to about 70 percent of maximum, a frequency of 4000 Hz, and on for 60 milliseconds.

To turn on the speaker, use the following command:

```
xset b on
```

To turn it off, type this:

```
xset b off
```

Turning the speaker back on will return the volume to its default.

Use xset c *volume* to set the keyclick volume in percentages. A volume setting of 0 turns it off. Any other number (1 through 100) turns it on for that percentage. Of course, for this command to work, you must have your speaker turned on.

To set the mouse speed, use the following command at the prompt:

```
xset m acceleration threshold
```

The acceleration is the number of times faster than the threshold that each mouse movement travels. This way, you can zip across the screen with a twitch. Use care in setting this feature unless you are very dexterous.

Invoking the Screen Saver

Use xset s *seconds* to enable the screen saver. You can turn off the screen saver with the off option. The default option reverts to system default time for blanking the screen.

For more options type in xset.

Using Fonts

For example, to load your own fonts, use the following command:

```
$     xset fp /user/home/myfont,/usr/lib/X11/fontsdir
$     xset fp rehash
```

The rehash command forces the server to reread its systems files for your command to take effect.

To restore to normal, use the following command:

```
$       xset fp default
$       xset fp rehash
```

See the section, "Fonts," later in this chapter.

Getting More Information about Your Display: *xdpyinfo*

The xdpyinfo utility gives you more information about your X server. It is used to list the capabilities of your server and all predefined parameters for it. Some of these include the following:

- Name of display
- Version number
- Vendor name
- Extensions

The list is too exhaustive to included here, and will be different for your installation. Pipe its output to a file, and review it for information about the server. Your output may look different. (See Listing 23.4.)

Listing 23.4. Output from `xdpyinfo`.

```
$ xdpyinfo
name of display:      :0.0
version number:     11.0
vendor string:      XFree86
vendor release number:     2110
maximum request size:  262140 bytes
motion buffer size:  0
bitmap unit, bit order, padding:    32, LSBFirst, 32
image byte order:     LSBFirst
number of supported pixmap formats:    2
supported pixmap formats:
    depth 1, bits_per_pixel 1, scanline_pad 32
    depth 8, bits_per_pixel 8, scanline_pad 32
keycode range:     minimum 8, maximum 134
focus:  window 0x200000d, revert to Parent
number of extensions:     6
    XTestExtension1
    SHAPE
    MIT-SHM
    Multi-Buffering
    XTEST
    MIT-SUNDRY-NONSTANDARD
default screen number:     0
number of screens:     1

screen #0:
  dimensions:     800x600 pixels (270x203 millimeters)
8  resolution:     75x75 dots per inch
```

```
depths (2):    1, 8
root window id:    0x29
depth of root window:    8 planes
number of colormaps:    minimum 1, maximum 1
default colormap:    0x27
default number of colormap cells:    256
preallocated pixels:    black 1, white 0
options:    backing-store YES, save-unders YES
current input event mask:    0x30003c
  ButtonPressMask           ButtonReleaseMask        EnterWindowMask
  LeaveWindowMask           SubstructureRedirectMask FocusChangeMask
number of visuals:    6
default visual id:  0x20
visual:
  visual id:    0x20
  class:    PseudoColor
  depth:    8 planes
  size of colormap:    256 entries
  red, green, blue masks:    0x0, 0x0, 0x0
  significant bits in color specification:    6 bits
visual:
  visual id:    0x21
  class:    DirectColor
  depth:    8 planes
  size of colormap:    8 entries
  red, green, blue masks:    0x7, 0x38, 0xc0
  significant bits in color specification:    6 bits
(... this is a very long listing ... )
***END LISTING
```

Help for Left-Handed Users: *xmodmap*

If you are a left-handed user, it might a bit uncomfortable to use the "left" button with your third or second finger. The X designers kept you in mind. If you want to swap the functionality of the pointers on your mouse or pointer, use the xmodmap command. First, display the current mappings like so:

```
xmodmap -pp
```

You see the following display:

```
Physical    Button
Button      Code
1           1
2           2
3           3
```

This shows you that button code 1 is mapped to physical button 1, button code 2 is mapped to physical button 2, and button code 3 is mapped to physical button 3.

Now issue this command:

```
xmodmap -e 'pointer =  3 2 1'
```

This reverses the mappings on the buttons. Now, physical button 1 is mapped to button code 3, and so forth. To confirm this, retype the xmodmap -pp command.

```
Physical    Button
Button      Code
1           3
2           2
3           1
```

You can always revert to the default with xmodmap -e 'pointer = default'.

Useful Command-Line Options

Some other standard input parameters that can be used to change the behavior of a window from the command line are as follows:

-borderwidth or -bw	Border width of pixels in the frame. This may not be available for all clients.
-foreground or -fg	The foreground color. For example, this can be the text color for an xterm.
-background or -bg	The background color. For example, this can be the text color for an xterm.
-display	Display on which the client runs.
-font or -fn	The font to use for a particular text display.
-geometry	Specifies the geometry.
-iconic	Starts the application in an iconic form.
-rv or -reverse	Swaps foreground and background colors.
-title	The title for the title bar.
-name	The name for the application.

Of course, the man pages on an application can give you more detailed information than one chapter in a book. Explore a little. For example, you can call one terminal name editor, and set your resources in the .Xresources file for name editor.

```
-display nodename:displayname.ScreenName
```

This starts up a remote session on another node. The *displayname* and *ScreenName* are optional and default to zero if not entered.

Logging into Remote Machines

You can log into remote machines by using the xterm -display option, provided you have set your Linux machine up for networks. The remote system must allow you to open a display on its machine. This is done with the xhost + command on its machine. The xhost + command is dangerous because it allows anyone to access your machine, so use it cautiously.

When you want to open an xterm on the remote machine, alma, run this command:

```
xterm -display alma:0.0 &
```

The format for the option into the display parameter is as follows:

```
[host]:[server][:screen]
```

If you are given permission to open a display, you are logged into the remote machine. You can verify this with the uname command. Check the DISPLAY with the echo $DISPLAY command.

When you log out with the exit command, the remote session and the xterm are terminated.

> **TIP**
>
> One of the most common reasons for not being able to open a remote terminal is that the remote host does not allow you to open windows there. Ask the remote users to use the xhost command at the remote machine as a part of their login.

Colors

All the colors in the X Window system are located in the /usr/lib/X11/rgb.txt file. This file consists of four columns: The first three columns specify red, green, and blue values; the last entry specifies the name that you can use in your parameters.

A partial listing of the rgb.txt file is shown in Listing 23.5.

Listing 23.5. Excerpt from rgb.txt file.

```
255 250 250      snow
248 248 255      ghost white
248 248 255      GhostWhite
245 245 245      white smoke
245 245 245      WhiteSmoke
220 220 220      gainsboro
255 250 240      floral white
255 250 240      FloralWhite
253 245 230      old lace
253 245 230      OldLace
250 240 230      linen
250 235 215      antique white
255 239 213      PapayaWhip
255 235 205      blanched almond
255 235 205      BlanchedAlmond
255 218 185      peach puff
255 218 185      PeachPuff
255 222 173      navajo white
255 228 181      moccasin
255 248 220      cornsilk
255 255 240      ivory
```

Listing 23.5. continued

```
255 250 205        lemon chiffon
255 250 205        LemonChiffon
255 245 238        seashell
240 255 240        honeydew
245 255 250        mint cream
255 240 245        LavenderBlush
255 228 225        misty rose
255 228 225        MistyRose
255 255 255        white
  0   0   0        black
 47  79  79        dark slate grey
 47  79  79        DarkSlateGrey
105 105 105        dim gray
105 105 105        DimGray
105 105 105        dim grey
105 105 105        DimGrey
112 128 144        slate gray
112 128 144        SlateGray
112 128 144        slate grey
112 128 144        SlateGrey
119 136 153        light slate gray
119 136 153        LightSlateGray
119 136 153        light slate grey
119 136 153        LightSlateGrey
190 190 190        gray
190 190 190        grey
211 211 211        light grey
```

Because red, green, and blue have 256 values each, the number of possible colors is 16,777,216. Not many workstations can display that many colors at one time. So, X uses a facility to map these colors onto the display, called a *colormap*. A color display uses several bits for displaying entries from this map. The xdpyinfo program gives you the number of bits for the display. This is a frame buffer. A 1-bit frame signifies a black and white display. An 8-bit frame buffer signifies 2 to the power of 8 entries, or 256 possible colors.

Unfortunately, due to different phosphors on different screens, your color specification on one monitor may be completely different on another monitor. Tektronix provides a tool called *xtici*, an API, and docs to counter such problems by using the international CIEXYZ standard for color specifications. This is called the Color Management System (CMS), which uses a model called HVC (Hue-Value-Chroma). In the X11R5 (or later) release, look for *Xcms* for more details, or contact Tektronix.

Fonts

Fonts in the X Window system are designed for maximum flexibility. The following are two good utilities to help you sift through some of the 400 or so font types on a basic system:

xlsfonts   Lists the fonts in your system.

xfontsel   Enables you to interactively see what fonts are available on your system and what they look like on the screen.

Using *xlsfonts*

First, let's examine the font names themselves. Use the xlsfonts command to list the fonts on your system. Type the command on an xterm, and because the listing from xlsfonts is very long, be sure to pipe to a text file for review. You should see a listing in which each line is of this form:

```
-foundry-family-wt-sl-wd-p-pts-hr-vr-sp-ave-charset-style
```

The *foundry* is the company that first developed the font. The most common ones are misc, Adobe, Bitstream, and B&H. You may see more on your system from the results of your xlsfonts command. A *foundry* of misc implies a font with fixed width and height per character; the rest were donated by their respective manufacturers.

The *family* is the general type of font: Courier, Helvetica, New Century Schoolbook, Lucida, and so on. Some families are monospaced, meaning that all their characters have the same width. The other families are proportionally spaced, meaning that each character has a separate width. Courier and Lucida are monospaced fonts. New Century Schoolbook is proportionally spaced.

Use monospaced information for tabular information or running text. This makes your text line up cleanly in running displays. Proportionally spaced fonts are helpful for text in buttons or menu items.

The wt and sl parameters stand for weights and slants, respectively. The common weights are bold and medium. Bold text is drawn with a thicker pen than the normal pen. The common slants are (r) roman, (o) oblique, and (i) italic. The roman text is drawn upright, and oblique text has characters sheared to the right. The italic text is similar to oblique text, but the characters are touched up to show a smoother effect. You may also have reverse oblique (ro) and reverse italic (ri), which make the text lean to the left instead of the right.

The p stands for the point size, which traditionally is 1/72 of an inch. Most monitors support only 75 or 100 dots per inch (dpi) resolution. Because X fonts are bitmaps, it seems logical that the most common fonts within X are of two types: 75dpi and 100dpi.

This number is found in the two fields hr and vr, which stand for the horizontal and vertical resolution, respectively. In almost all cases, you specify either 75 or 100 in each of these fields.

The sp refers to the spacing between two characters on the screen. This can be m for monospaced, p for proportional, or c for fixed fonts that have each character occupy a fixed box.

The ave is 1/10 of the average width of all the characters in the set.

The character set and style is usually set to ISO8859-1. This refers to the ISO Latin-1 character set, which includes characters found in ASCII and other European character sets.

Now that you've seen the large number of options that can define a font, you can rely on using wildcards to specify most of the options for a font. The server matches the first font name that matches your specification with a wildcard. In other words, you only have to specify the parameters you want to change, and use the asterisk for the rest.

For example, `*courier-roman` gets the first specification for the roman-weighted Courier font. However, `*courier` gets the bold Courier font. This is because the bold specification exists before the roman specification in the fonts file.

TIP

Use the `xset fp=fontpath` command to set the directory (75 or 100 dpi) you want searched first in the front of the font path. This guarantees that the correct dpi size directory is searched first.

The font search path is the path used by the server to search for the fonts in your system. This path is usually set to the following value:

```
/usr/lib/X11/fonts/misc,/usr/lib/X11/fonts/75dpi,/usr/lib/X11/fonts/100dpi
```

In each of these directories is a file called `fonts.dir`. This is a list of all the fonts in the directory, and has two entries per line. The first entry gives a font filename; the second entry gives the complete font description. The first line in the file gives the number of entries in the file.

TIP

Font names are not case-sensitive. `New Century Schoolbook` is the same as `new century schoolbook`.

You can create another file in the font path to alias your own font names by using the file called `fonts.alias`. The server uses only the first one it finds in its path, so just keep one such file in the first directory in your font path. The `fonts.alias` format is very similar to the `fonts.dir` file, except that the first entry is not a filename; it is an alias for a font name. So, if you want to specify a special font type for all your editor `xterms`, you need the following line:

```
editterm    *lucida-medium-r-*-100*
```

Then, you can invoke your `xterm` with this command:

```
xterm -fn editterm &
```

This gets an `xterm` window with the desired font, and is a lot better than typing in the full font specification. Also, by changing the alias once, you can change it for all scripts that use this alias, rather than modifying each script individually.

A good place to start is the `/usr/lib/X11/fonts/misc` directory, where a `fonts.alias` exists from your initial X installation. This file has the fixed and variable aliases defined for you to work with.

Using *xfontsel*

The xfontsel program helps you get a better feel for some of the parameters of a particular font. (See Figure 23.11.)

FIGURE 23.11.

Using xfontsel.

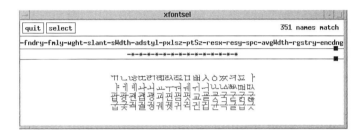

You can move your pointer to any one of the parameters in the first line and click Button1. As you move the pointer on a field, it draws a box around itself to show that it has focus.

If any fonts options exist for your selection, you are presented with a pop-up menu to select from. Move the mouse to a selection, and click on the selection. You see your selection displayed in the font specification string, as well as a sample of what the font will look like on the fonts display screen below that.

Where To Go from Here

In Chapter 32, "Motif for Programmers," you will learn how to program your application.

If you want more information about specific vendors, you can get a wealth of information from the Internet about the latest releases and sources to shareware utilities. Listed in Table 23.3 are some of the newsgroups that can provide you with more information about vendors.

Table 23.2. Some newsgroups with more information.

Newsgroup	Focus
comp.sources.x	Sources for X Window system
comp.windows.x.apps	X Window applications
comp.windows.x.motif	Motif programming issues
comp.os.windows.x.i386	XF86 discussions.

A good starting point for progammers is the site at arachnid.cs.cf.ac.uk/Dave/X_lecture/ X_lecture.

Summary

In this chapter, you have learned the following:

- How to install Motif on Linux.
- How to start an X Window session from the prompt.
- The basics of the Motif Window Manager, mwm.
- How to move about in mwm and control windows with the keyboard and mouse.
- How to customize your desktop with resource files and client applications.
- How to set your environment to your liking with resources.
- How to use some standard tools available in X to further set up your desktop.
- Where to look next for more information.
- How to use Widgets and the characteristics of these Widgets. This provides the basis for learning how to program your own applications in the Motif environment.

OPEN LOOK and OpenWindows

24

by Kamran Husain

This chapter introduces you to OPEN LOOK on Linux. Ideally, this chapter could be expanded into a book of its own. That being impossible however, we will cover some of the basics of OPEN LOOK in this chapter, including

- What is OPEN LOOK?
- What to install on Linux.
- How to work with a look and feel that's different from Motif.
- How to work with the virtual desktop.
- How to customize your desktop.
- Troubleshooting tips.
- Where to get more information about OPEN LOOK.

If you have not already done so, please read Chapter 23, "Using Motif." This chapter will build on that chapter, so there won't be duplicate information for you to weed through. The information you require from the Motif chapter is the discussion on X Window, working with pointers, and the Motif environment. You will definitely need to know how to use resources in the .Xdefaults files and starting X Window via shell scripts like startx.

What Is OPEN LOOK?

OPEN LOOK is a specification of a *Graphical User Interface* (GUI). A GUI determines the look and feel of a system—the shape of windows, buttons, and scrollbars; how you resize things; how you edit files; and so on. The OPEN LOOK GUI is specified, developed, and maintained primarily by Sun Microsystems Inc. XView is simply the port on Linux. When I talk about OpenWindows, I will refer to XView for Linux in this chapter.

OpenWindows is a windowing environment that conforms to the OPEN LOOK Graphical User Interface Specifications. It's compatible with the X11 window system from MIT as well as (currently) Sun's NeWS and SunView, so you can intermix programs written for any of these systems. It comes from Sun and also with UNIX System V Release 4 from certain vendors.

> **TIP**
>
> OpenWindows should not be called "Windows" or "OPEN LOOK" or "OpenLook," because these terms are either wrong or apply to something else. OpenWindows is sometimes also called openwin or xnews, after the program used to start it and the main executable itself, respectively.

Several toolkits exist for programmers to use in developing programs that conform to the OPEN LOOK specifications:

- OPEN LOOK Intrinsics Toolkit (OLIT)
- XView (This is what you have for Linux.)
- The NeWS Toolkit (TNT)
- C++ User Interface Toolkit

OLIT was AT&T's OPEN LOOK Intrinsics Toolkit for the X Window system. OLIT used a widget set and was therefore easy to learn for people who were already X11/Xt programmers. You could buy the source from AT&T, although you didn't get the same version that Sun would ship.

Sun includes the OLIT library in OpenWindows. OLIT is also often included in UNIX System V Release 4. OLIT was written in C. The last release of OLIT in OpenWindows 3.0 was OLIT 3.0. OLIT support passed to USL (UNIX System Laboratories), who replaced it with MoOLIT (see the following Tip).

> **TIP**
>
> You need an OLIT source in order to develop a large application or anything else that uses subclasses.

XView is Sun's toolkit for X11, written in C. It is similar in programmer interface to SunView. There's even a shell script to help migrate source code from SunView to XView. XView is often said to be the easiest toolkit to learn if you are not familiar with X Window.

The XView toolkit is included in OpenWindows, and full source is available by anonymous FTP from export.lcs.mit.edu (and elsewhere). The current version of XView from Sun is 3.2p1.

The NeWS Toolkit (TNT) is an object-oriented programming system based on the PostScript language and NeWS. TNT implements many of the OPEN LOOK interface components required to build the user interface of an application. It's currently included in OpenWindows.

The current version of TNT from Sun is 3.1. Release 3 contains some incompatibilities with TNT 1.0 and TNT 2.0, but Sun is committed to supporting the API, at least until it stops NeWS support some time later this year and replaces it with Display PostScript. Wait. You might ask what "is committed to" means in this context; the answer seems to be that it means absolutely nothing.

Sun currently asserts that it is committed to OLIT, however.

The C++ User Interface Toolkit (UIT) consists of an object-oriented C++ class library layered on top of XView and a tool to generate code from files written in a graphical interface language called DevGuide 2 GIL. The UIT also includes features that simplify event management and the use of PostScript and color. It is said to be compatible with OpenWindows Versions 2 and 3, and presumably Version 3.0.1, as the release mentions that it works on Solaris 2.

UIT is not an official Sun-supported product but an ongoing project of various people within Sun. It can be found on export.lcs.mit.edu in the MIT /R5contrib directory as UITV3.tar.Z (use binary mode!).

> **TIP**
>
> If you cannot decide which GUI to use, consider the MoOLIT interface. MoOLIT is a version of OLIT from AT&T/USL that lets users choose between a Motif- and an OPEN LOOK–type feel at runtime.

olwm and *olvwm*

There are two window managers for OpenWindows: olwm and olvwm. A *window manager* is responsible for deciding how to lay out windows on the screen, and for managing the user's interaction with the windows.

olwm is the standard OPEN LOOK window manager. It is included with all of the OpenWindows implementations, and you can also get the source via FTP because Sun donated it to the freeware domain.

The olvwm program is a version of olwm that manages a virtual desktop (hence the v in its name). It shows a little map on the screen, with the currently displayed area represented by a small rectangle. You can move around by dragging the rectangle or with the arrow keys. This enables you to run several clients (applications) that occupy the full screen and move the display around from one to the other. Olvwm was derived from the OpenWindows 3.0 olwm by Scott Oaks. You need to have XView 3.0 to compile it.

The olvewm and olwm packages are included on the CD at the back of the book.

Getting Started with OpenWindows

First, confirm that you have installed the XView system on your Linux system. You need the xv disk set, which consists of two disks: xv1 and xv2. The files in this disk set are detailed in Listing 24.1.

Listing 24.1. XView **package contents.**

```
xv32_a.tgz   Static Libraries for developing Xview 3.2
applications.
xv32_sa.tgz  Static Libraries for debugging Xview 3.2
applications.
xv32_so.tgz  Shared Libraries for Xview 3.2.
xv32exmp.tgz Sample programs for Xview 3.2.
xvinc32.tgz  Include files for Xview 3.2 programming.
xvmenus.tgz  Menus and help files for the OpenLook Window
Manager.
xvol32.tgz   Xview 3.2 Configuration files, programs, and
documentation.
```

Install the packages shown in Listing 24.1 for your XView system using the setup program as shown in Chapter 3, "Installing Linux." If you have already done this installation, you should have at least some files in /usr/openwin/bin.

Starting OpenWindows

You need one of two files to get started with OpenWindows: either .xinitrc or .xsessionrc.

The first time you run OpenWindows, a .xinitrc file is created in your login directory ($HOME). If it already exists, you might have to edit it somewhat. It's best to move all old X11 files you have to another directory, and then merge the old and new files.

> **TIP**
>
> If you use xdm, you should use .xsessionrc instead of .xinitrc, because xdm doesn't look at your .xinitrc file.

Please refer to Chapter 23 for a detailed discussion on .xinitrc and installing X on your Linux system.

You should take the following steps to convert this .xinitrc file into one for using OpenWindows:

- Change the reference to your window manager to either olwm or olvwm depending on which window manager you want to use.
- Ensure that the /usr/openwin/bin directory is in your path.
- You need an environment variable, OPENWINHOME, to be set to the directory where the files for your openwin system will reside. This variable is usually set to /usr/openwin when you log in.
- Copy the .xinitrc file into .xsessionrc file if you are going to use xdm.

There are other optional files you can create in your $HOME directory, depending on which version of olwm or olvwm you use:

- .openwin-init

This file is used to initialize your desktop when you start OpenWindows with olwm or olvwm. A sample .openwin-init file is shown in Listing 24.2. This sample file shows how two xterms and one clock application are started every time you start a session. OpenWindows looks at a file called .openwin-init in your home directory. If .openwin-init is not found in the home directory, OpenWindows looks in the $OPENWINHOME/lib directory. The .openwin-init file contains a list of applications to start by default.

Listing 24.2. A sample `.openwin-init` file.

```
#!/bin/sh
#
# Created by 'xtoolplaces' on Fri Dec  9 23:10:23 1994
#

/usr/bin/X11/xterm -sb -sl 500 -j -ls -fn 7x14 -geom 82x24+45+52 &
clock -Wp 4 5 -Ws 172 52 -WP 224 533 +Wi &
xterm -e /bin/bash -geom 80x24+103+89 &
```

■ `.openwin-menu*`

Look in `$OPENWINHOME/lib` (normally `/usr/openwin/lib`) for this and other similarly named (`openwin-menu-s`, `openwin-menu-d`, and so on) files without the leading period (.). We will discuss these files in the "Environment Variables" section later in this chapter.

■ `.Xdefaults`

The `.Xdefaults` file applies to OpenWindows as well. You can put X Window resource specifications in here. In particular, it is a good idea to include at least

```
OpenWindows.FocusLenience:    true
*Input: TRUE
```

These enable non-ICCCM-compliant programs to receive input even if they forget to ask for it.

TIP

`props`, the program that runs when you select Properties from the default root menu under `olwm` or `olvwm`, writes your choices into `.Xdefaults`.

Don't put comments in `.Xdefaults`, because `props` deletes them.

NOTE

Note that the mouse speed for OpenWindows is best set in your `.xinitrc` with `xset m`. See the man page for `xset` (`man xset` and `xset -help`) for more information. Do not use the `.startup.ps` file for setting the mouse speed as suggested by some texts. This is because the `.startup.ps` method can cause more problems if not used correctly.

Start your program up with the `startx` support. See Figure 24.1 for what you should see when you start OpenWindows.

FIGURE 24.1.

The Xterm *in OpenWindows.*

SELECT and MENU

In OpenWindows (and Sun Workstations, for that matter), the left and right buttons on a mouse are referred to as SELECT and MENU, respectively. Clicking the SELECT button in a window selects a window. Clicking the MENU button in a window displays any menu for that application.

> **TIP**
>
> If you have a three-button mouse, the middle button is called the ADJUST button. You can simulate an ADJUST button on a two-button mouse by clicking both buttons together.

> **TIP**
>
> The Shift-Button1 combination is also ADJUST, and Ctrl-Button1 is also MENU. These two combinations are useful if you have a one-button mouse.

Working Within OpenWindows and *olwm*

Let's examine the borders on an Xterm in OpenWindows in greater detail. (See Figure 24.2.) These borders are drawn by olwm and have special functionality.

FIGURE 24.2.

OpenWindows borders.

The resize handles (buttons) are the indentations on each window. You can resize a window by pressing and holding SELECT over any of the resize corners and then dragging the mouse to the new location.

Releasing the mouse button sets the new size of the window. If you hold down the Ctrl key while you are dragging, the resize operation is constrained to resize vertically or horizontally, depending on which direction you move first.

The window button is the small box with a downward-pointing triangle near the left end of the title bar. Clicking MENU over the window button brings up the window menu. Clicking SELECT over the left mouse button on the window button executes the window menu's default action. This usually closes the window into an icon. You can change the window menu's default action by holding down the Ctrl key while manipulating the window menu.

An icon represents a closed window. You can still do most of the same operations as with an open window. Moving and selecting icons with SELECT and ADJUST is exactly the same as for open windows. A similar version of the Window menu is available on an icon by pressing MENU. Double-clicking SELECT opens the icon. Icons cannot be resized.

You can select a group of windows and icons by using the left or middle mouse buttons over the *workspace* (the area of the screen outside of all windows and icons, commonly known as the "root window"). Pressing either SELECT or ADJUST and dragging the mouse defines a rubber band rectangle.

When you release the mouse button, you will be operating on the set of windows and icons enclosed by this rectangle. If you created the rectangle using SELECT, the windows and icons within will be selected, and all other objects will be deselected. If you used ADJUST, the objects within will have their selected state toggled, and any other windows and icons already selected will remain selected.

TIP

Some OPEN LOOK pop-up windows have a pushpin instead of a Window button. The pin is either in or out, and you can click SELECT on the pin to change it to the other state. If the pin is out, pressing a command button inside the window executes the command and then dismisses (takes down) the window. If the pin is in, the window is "pinned" to the workspace, and it remains on the screen even after you have pressed a command button in the window. This enables you to press several command buttons in the same window. Pulling the pin out (by clicking SELECT over it) dismisses the window immediately.

Menus

XView supports menus of the form shown in Figure 24.3. This is a sample menu containing options for you to choose. These menus are called *pop-up menus*.

Pop-up menus are operated using the MENU mouse button. There are two methods of operating with an OPEN LOOK menu: the click-move-click method and the press-drag-release method. You choose either method by clicking the MENU button (pressing and releasing it quickly) or by pressing it down and holding it.

If you click the MENU button, a menu pops up and will stay up indefinitely. To continue operating the menu, click the MENU button over a menu item. To dismiss the menu, click the MENU button on an area of the screen outside the menu. To operate menus in press-drag-release mode, press the MENU button and hold it down while you move the mouse. The menu remains on the screen as long as you hold down the MENU button. To execute an action, move the pointer over a menu item and release the mouse button. To dismiss the menu, move the pointer outside the menu and release the MENU button. Some menu items have a submenu. This is indicated by a right-pointing triangle at the right edge of the item. To activate a submenu, click on the item (in click-move-click mode) or move the pointer to the item and then move toward the right edge of the menu (in press-drag-release mode).

Some menus have pushpins. If a menu has a pushpin, it will initially be in the "out" state. If you click on the pin (in click-move-click mode) or move over it and release (in press-drag-release mode), you will pin the menu to the workspace. The menu will remain on the screen indefinitely, and you can execute commands from it by clicking on its items. To remove the menu, move over the pin and click SELECT on it.

The Workspace Menu

Pressing MENU over the workspace brings up the Workspace menu. This menu is customizable, but it typically contains at least the following items. The arrows to the right of any item indicate a submenu for the displayed item. (See Figure 24.3.)

FIGURE 24.3.

The pinnable Workspace menu.

- Shells   This item opens up another submenu with shells to choose from, including color terminals, X Terminals, VT100 emulator, and other assorted shells. (See Figure 24.4.) You can also pin this menu to your desktop. Clicking the MENU button on the menu brings up another submenu enabling you to resize this menu.

FIGURE 24.4.

The Shell selections from the main menu.

Shells

Xterm (7x14 font)
Rxvt (VT100 emulator)
Color Xterm (7x14 font)
Large Xterm (10x20 font)
Large Rxvt (10x20 font)
Large Color Xterm (10x20 font)
Cmdtool (OpenWindows Command Tool)
Cmdtool —C (OpenWindows Console)
Shelltool (OpenWindows Shell Tool)

■ Editors   This item lets you select many types of editors, including Textedit, the standard OpenWindows text editor. See Figure 24.5 for a view of the Textedit.

FIGURE 24.5.

The Textedit utility.

Window button   Title bar   Resize button

Text Editor – (NONE), dir; /home/kamran

File ▽   View ▽   Edit ▽   Find ▽

Resize button

Resize button

Resize button

The Cut utility can be used to cut and paste sections between files. You can access any of the menu items by using the SELECT button on any of the menu items.

■ Tools   This opens up the File Manager, manual reader, calculator, spreadsheet, and other assorted items. (See Figure 24.6.)

FIGURE 24.6.

The File Manager utility.

- ■ **Games**   This item has a submenu that enables you to invoke games. Check it out.
- ■ **Utilities**   This item has a submenu that contains several utility functions for the workspace, including Refresh (redisplay all windows on the screen), Lock Screen, and Save Workspace.
- ■ **Properties**   This item brings up the Workspace Properties window, which enables you to view and customize settings of the OpenWindows environment.
- ■ **X11 programs**   This items brings up a very long menu of all the X11 programs in `/usr/bin/X11`.
- ■ **XView programs**   This item brings up a very long menu of all the X11 programs in `/usr/bin/openwin`.
- ■ **XV 3.00**   This brings up the program that I used to capture all the screens for this book.
- ■ **The Window menu**   This lets you choose any window on your desktop as your active window.
- ■ **Screen saver option**   This item lets you select a screen saver for your session. The Lock screen item is similar to screen saver except that it requires your password to restore the desktop.
- ■ **Exit**   This selection shuts down all applications and exits the windowing system. A confirmation notice appears first to give you a chance to cancel the operation.

NOTE

In the menu for a window, you will see two selections: Close and Quit. The Close selection closes the window into an icon, but the application for that window is not terminated. The Quit selection actually terminates the program and gets rid of the window.

Configuring Menus for OpenWindows

Look in $OPENWINHOME/lib (normally /usr/openwin/lib) for the file openwin-menu and other files of the form openwin-menu-*. Copy these files into your home directory with a period in front of them. For example, copy openwin-menu as .openwin-menu.

The .openwin-menu file is used to set up your workspace menu. Look at Listing 24.3 for this file.

Listing 24.3. The default .openwin-menu file.

```
#
# @(#)openwin-menu      23.15 91/09/14 openwin-menu
#
#     OpenWindows default root menu file - top level menu
#

"Workspace" TITLE

"Shells " MENU              $OPENWINHOME/lib/openwin-menu-s

"Editors " MENU             $OPENWINHOME/lib/openwin-menu-e

"Tools " MENU               $OPENWINHOME/lib/openwin-menu-t

"Games " MENU               $OPENWINHOME/lib/openwin-menu-g

"Utilities " MENU           $OPENWINHOME/lib/openwin-menu-u

#"Slingshot Examples " MENU     $OPENWINHOME/lib/openwin-ss-ex
#
#"UIT Examples " MENU     $OPENWINHOME/lib/openwin-uit

"Properties "               PROPERTIES

SEPARATOR
"X11 Programs "             DIRMENU      /usr/X386/bin

"XView Programs " DIRMENU       $OPENWINHOME/bin
"XV 3.00"           exec /usr/X386/bin/xv

"Window Menu "     WINMENU

SEPARATOR

"Screensaver " MENU         $OPENWINHOME/lib/openwin-menu-screensave

"Lock Screen " MENU         $OPENWINHOME/lib/openwin-menu-xlock

"Exit"              EXIT
```

Let's look at some of the entries in this .openwin-menu file.

- The # signs mark lines as comments.
- The line "Workspace" TITLE defines the name of the menu.

- The next line defines `"Shells "` as a menu located in a file `$OPENWINHOME/lib /openwin-menu-s`.

- The `"XV 3.00"` entry executes the command `/usr/X386/bin/xv` via the `exec` command.

- The `"Window Menu "` entry invokes a special entry for selecting windows via a `WINMENU` type of window.

- The `"XView Programs "` entry uses a type `DIRMENU` to list all the files in `$OPENWINHOME/bin`.

- The `SEPARATOR` type draws an empty box at its position.

You can now use different files for customizing your menus differently by adding or deleting items to this file.

The menu specification language has a number of keywords, all of which are in all-uppercase letters.

The syntax for this file is straightforward. Each line typically specifies one menu button. There are three fields per each uncommented line. The first field defines a label, an optional keyword, and an action to take if the item is selected.

The label is either a single word or a string enclosed in double quotes. This string appears in the menu button. If the optional keyword `DEFAULT` appears next, this menu item becomes the default item for this menu. The rest of the line (excluding leading whitespace) is considered to be a command. It is executed by sending it to `bash`. Any shell metacharacters are passed through to the shell unchanged.

The command field can be extended onto the next line by placing a backslash (\) at the end of the line. The newline will not be embedded in the command.

A submenu is specified using the special keyword `MENU` in place of a command. A button is added to the current menu, and clicking or pulling right on this button brings up the submenu. Subsequent lines in the menu file define buttons for the submenu, until a line that has the special keyword `END` in the command field is encountered. The label of the `MENU` line must match the label on the `END` line; otherwise an error is signaled.

Submenus can be nested arbitrarily, bracketed by `MENU` and `END` lines with matching labels.

Submenus can be defined in a different file using either the `MENU` or the `INCLUDE` keyword. To include a submenu from another file, use a line with a label, either the `MENU` or the `INCLUDE` keyword, and then the filename. The file so named is assumed to contain lines that specify menu buttons. The submenu file need not have any `MENU` or `END` lines (unless it has submenus itself). The current file need not have a matching `END` line if the submenu is read from another file. Submenu files included with the `MENU` keyword are considered to be an integral part of the menu tree, and any error encountered during the reading of the file will cause the entire menu to be considered invalid. A submenu file included with the `INCLUDE` keyword is considered optional, and any error encountered during reading of the file is not considered fatal. If an error occurs during `INCLUDE` processing, a disabled (grayed-out) item is inserted in place of the submenu and processing of the current menu file continues.

NOTE

"The Virtual Desktop" section was authored by Scott Oaks, scott.oaks@sun.com, who is also responsible for its maintenance. This olwm and olvwm code is not supported by Sun Microsystems in any way. The staff at Sun Microsystems, and especially Stuart Marks, deserve credit as original author(s) of olwm for most of the work contained in XView.

By default, the VDM (and hence the desktop) is divided into a grid. Each square of the grid represents a screen size. The dividing lines between each logical screen are represented by dashed lines in the VDM. This division into logical screens is purely informational. If you like, windows can straddle these boundaries, the current view into the desktop can straddle them also, and windows can be moved at will between them. However, by default, most actions in the VDM keep the current view along these boundary lines.

You can use the resize corners on the VDM to resize the virtual desktop. If you make the virtual desktop smaller, windows that might be off the new virtual desktop are NOT moved (though they are not lost, either, because you can get them back by resizing the desktop again). Space added or subtracted is always done so from the right and bottom of the desktop (regardless of which resize corner you used).

Working with Virtual Windows

Events that occur in a particular virtual window behave just as if they were delivered to the corresponding application's frame. Thus, pressing the MENU button over a virtual window brings up the Frame menu and enables the real (and virtual) windows to be opened, closed, resized, and so on.

Pressing the SELECT button selects that real (and virtual) window. Pressing the ADJUST button adds (or subtracts) that window from the selection list.

SELECTing and dragging one or more virtual windows moves the real and virtual windows (just as in olwm). Note that if you drag the mouse outside of the VDM, the window can be moved onto to the screen. Conversely, when dragging a window on the screen, if the mouse moves into the VDM the window's icon moves to another location within the VDM. However, if part of the VDM is obscured, you cannot move a window into that part of the VDM.

NOTE

Note that events are delivered **only** to the real application's frame. Thus, typing characters or using the COPY/CUT/PASTE keys has no effect.

It is possible to drop something onto a virtual window as if it were dropped onto the corresponding application. This enables you to drag a file in one window on the screen to another application on another part of the desktop.

Double-clicking the SELECT button on an area in the VDM background moves the current view to the logical screen containing the point where the mouse was double-clicked.

The MENU button brings up a (pinnable) menu that enables movement based on full screen sizes in the direction indicated. See Figure 24.8.

FIGURE 24.8.

A pinnable menu.

Sticky Windows

You'll notice that the Virtual Desktop Manager never moves on your screen if you change views into the desktop. That's because the VDM is permanently sticky.

Windows that are *sticky* never move position on the screen when you change your view into the desktop. To set a particular window as sticky, simply select Stick in its Frame menu. You may similarly unstick the window via its menu.

Menus for base windows include the Stick and Unstick commands.

> **NOTE**
>
> Only base frames—those that can be iconified, as opposed to those that have a pushpin— are eligible to become sticky. Some frames inherit the stickiness of their base frames. Thus, for most applications, either all windows are sticky or none of them are. The exception to this is applications that create two or more base frames: All base frames are originally created as unsticky (but see the following discussion on the `VirtualSticky` resource).

Windows that are sticky always appear in the same place on the screen no matter which part of the virtual desktop you're viewing. Windows that are not sticky (by default, all windows except the VDM) move when you change the current view on the virtual desktop.

Like `olwm`, `olvwm` uses key bindings for certain actions. All actions are specified in `olwm` as well as an additional set of actions to control the view into the desktop. You can use the Function keys F1 through F9 with the Alt key to switch virtual screens.

> **NOTE**
>
> The X Window system is a trademark of the Massachusetts Institute of Technology. OPEN LOOK is a trademark of AT&T. OpenWindows is a trademark of Sun Microsystems, Inc.

Resources in OpenWindows

You can customize OpenWindows using resources. Resources affect the behavior of applications in olwm. Global resources in olwm consist of two resource components:

- The resource name is taken from the trailing pathname component of argv[0]. This value is typically olwm.
- The second resource component names the global attribute being set.

Thus, to set the AutoColorFocus attribute, one would use olwm.AutoColorFocus as the resource specification in .Xdefaults. olvwm will read a resource file ($HOME/.olvwmrc) for your resources.

olwm automatically picks up changes to many of these resources if the resource database changes at runtime. You can modify olwm's behavior by changing the resource database with xrdb or with Workspace Properties.

If a resource value is specified on olwm's command line, it overrides the value in the resource database. Therefore, changing the resource's value in the database has no effect on this resource setting.

Some customizations include the following:

Hot Keys	You can specify that when a certain key (or, more likely, key in combination with modifiers) is pressed, certain actions are performed. You can warp to a particular application, and open, raise, close, execute, and quit applications.
Screen Bindings	You can specify that certain applications will always start on a particular logical screen.
Menu Options	You can alter the behavior of WINMENU selections on a particular window.

More resources are listed in the man pages for olwm, olvwmrc, and olvwm.

Using Text-Editing Features

In general, the editing/moving commands go in the opposite direction when shifted—that is, Ctrl-W deletes a word, and Ctrl-Shift-W deletes the word to the right of the insertion point.

```
Alt-i - include file      Alt-f - find selection (forward/backward)

Ctrl-a - start of line    Ctrl-< - back word
Ctrl-e - end of line      Ctrl-> - forward word
Ctrl-w - delete word      Ctrl-u - delete to start/END of line
Ctrl-Return - move to end/START of document
```

See the olwm and olvwm man pages for a list of some of the default keys.

You can and paste between XTerm and other OpenWindows programs. I will use textedit as a sample program.

To go from XTerm to textedit (for this example):

1. Select the text you want to copy by dragging the SELECT mouse button in xterm.
2. Press COPY in the XTerm (this key is Alt-C).
3. Move to the textedit window, and press PASTE (Alt-V).

To go the other way, from textedit to XTerm:

1. Select the text in textedit. No need to use COPY.
2. Move to the XTerm window and press the middle mouse button.

(If you have a two-button mouse, press both left and right buttons together.)

> **NOTE**
>
> You can also use the COPY/CUT and PASTE buttons.

For Quick Copy within textedit, mailtool, and similar programs:

1. Click SELECT to get a text caret where you want the copied text to go.
2. Press and **hold down** the PASTE (or CUT) button.
3. Select the text you want to copy/move. You'll see that it's underlined or crossed out—or even a different color.
4. Let go of the PASTE (or CUT) button. The text you underlined or crossed out appears at the insert caret.

To drag-and-drop to move a selection, follow these steps:

1. Select the text you want to copy or move by dragging or multiple-clicking the SELECT or ADJUST mouse button.
2. Put the mouse pointer anywhere within the selection.
3. Press and **hold down** the SELECT mouse button and move the mouse pointer a little to the right. You'll see the cursor change into the first three letters of the text (or some other icon).

4. Still holding down the SELECT button, move the mouse over the point where you want to drop the text.

5. You may see the mouse pointer change to a rifle sight or target, to show that it's OK to drop things there.

6. Release SELECT and the text is moved. This works in text fields of dialog boxes as well as in text subwindows.

TIP

To drag-and-drop to copy a selection, you must hold the Ctrl key down as well as the SELECT mouse button.

Support for Left-Handed Users

You can configure OPEN LOOK for a left-handed mouse and keyboard. Use xmodmap to change the mouse buttons. Type man 7 xview for a list of key bindings you can change, at least for XView programs.

CAUTION

Unlike the Motif release, the xmodmap for mouse-key reversal sometimes does not work right. In fact, it may actually reverse some keys on your keyboard or have some other surprising results. You have been warned.

With OpenWindows 2.0, you can use defaultsedit to set the mouse mappings and then let SunView handle them. The status returned by svenv should tell you whether your server is running under SunView or not; put this in your .xinitrc:

```
if eval 'svenv -env'
then
      xmodmap -e "pointer = 1 2 3"
      input_from_defaults
else
      xmodmap -e "pointer = 3 2 1"
fi
```

Troubleshooting

Here are some solutions to problems you might have:

- If man doesn't seem to find OpenWindows commands, even though you are running OpenWindows, try setting the MANPATH environment variable:

```
MANPATH=$OPENWINHOME/share/man:/usr/man; export MANPATH
```

or

```
setenv MANPATH $OPENWINHOME/share/man:/usr/man
```

for csh users. $OPENWINHOME should be /usr/openwin on most systems. Set your path so that $OPENWINHOME/bin (and $OPENWIN/bin/xview for OpenWindows 2) come before /bin (or /usr/bin, they're the same), or you'll get the SunView versions of mailtool, cmdtool, shelltool, and so on.

■ Dropped characters when you type into applications.

In this case, include the following lines in your .Xdefaults file, as these enable non-ICCCM-compliant programs to receive input even if they forget to ask for it.

```
OpenWindows.FocusLenience:    true
*Input: TRUE
```

■ CUT and PASTE just do not work. Add the following either to your $HOME/.Xdefaults file or to $OPENWINHOME/lib/app-defaults/XTerm instead:

```
XTerm*VT100.Translations: #override \
<Key>L6:select-set(CLIPBOARD)\n\
<Key>L8:insert-selection(CLIPBOARD)
```

If this text is already in the app-defaults file, so if it isn't working, check that XFILESEARCHPATH is set to

```
/usr/openwin/lib/%T/%N%S
```

If it isn't, either set it or copy/merge these lines from $OPENWINHOME/lib/app-defaults/XTerm into /usr/lib/X11/app-defaults/XTerm.

This version automatically puts each xterm selection onto the Clipboard:

```
XTerm*VT100.translations: #override\n\
~Ctrl ~Meta<Btn2Up>: insert-selection(PRIMARY,CUT_BUFFER0)\n\
~Ctrl ~Meta<BtnUp>: select-end(PRIMARY,CUT_BUFFER0,CLIPBOARD)\n\
<KeyPress>L8: insert-selection(CLIPBOARD)
```

TIP

Be sure that the \n\ is at the very end of all lines in the middle.

■ If you get error messages that look like the following lines,

```
Xlib:  connection to ":0.0" refused by server
Xlib:  Internal error during connection authorization check
Error: Can't Open display
```

try the command xhost-machine, where machine is the computer on which you ran the command that failed.

If you want to let other users run programs on the same machine as you, using your display, you have to type the command xhost +'hostname', which lets any user on 'hostname' access your display.

■ Your screen flashes between applications. This is because most hardware can only display a few colors at a time. Try the following steps:

1. Start all the applications with colors that you wish to reserve.

2. Run cmap_compact save to create the .owcolors file.

3. Put the line cmap_compact init near the start of your I start-up file (.xinitrc).

4. Exit and then restart the window system.

5. cmap_compact init pushes those .owcolors colors to the end of the colormap and reserves them.

Also note that Ctrl-L2 locks the colors of the current window, and Ctrl-L4 unlocks them—this is described in the olwm man page.

See the X*.faq in the /usr/docs/faq directory for detailed information on problems specific to different platforms. The FAQ file can be give you a lot of information about Linux and what problems to expect.

Environment Variables

XView for Linux uses the following environment variables:

■ DISPLAY   The name of the X Window display to use :0.0 (on the local machine, the one actually running X11 or xnews) :0.1 (on some machines for a second, monochrome screen) machine-running-unix:0.0 (on other machines). (You may need to do xhost +other-machine to let programs on other machines use your display.)

■ HELPPATH   Where XView looks when you press the Help key (or F1): /usr/openwin/lib/ locale:/usr/openwin/lib/help.

■ LD_LIBRARY_PATH is set to find shared C libraries. It is usually defaulted to this value:

   /usr/lib:/usr/5lib:/usr/openwin/lib:/usr/CC/'arch'

■ OPENWINHOME   Where OpenWindows lives (/usr/openwin).

■ PATH   Where the shell searches for programs to run.

■ Include this line in it:

   $(OPENWINHOME)/bin:$(OPENWINHOME)/bin/xview

■ XFILESEARCHPATH   Where programs look for app-defaults files (/usr/openwin/lib/%T/ %N%S). This is usually set to: $OPENWINHOME/lib/%T/%N%S:/usr/lib/X11/%T/%N%S.

Special Help for Sun Workstation Users

If you work with Sun Microsystems Sun Workstations, then the olwm and olvwm managers should make life easier for you. If you want to make life even easier, you can map the function keys to reflect that of Sun workstations. To do this, you have to modify the .Xmodmap file in your home directory. If you do not have a .Xmodmap file, you can create one with a text editor.

The best place to look is in the man pages for xmodmap. The man pages are full of examples, some of which I will describe briefly here. For issues specific to your setting, read the man pages.

A typical .Xmodmap file will look like this:

```
keysym F1 = xman
keysym F2 = F19
keysym F3 = F20
keysym F4 = F16
keysym F5 = F18
```

The undo button is ominously absent from the .Xmodmap entries. To get this entry, add the following line. (The text after the ! is a comment and ignored by X.)

```
keysym F6 = F14   ! The undo button.
```

For example, if you hate the location of the shift and control keys on your PC, you can swap the location. Simply put these lines in your .Xmodmap file:

```
remove Lock = Caps_Lock
remove Control = Control_L
keysym Control_L = Caps_Lock
keysym Caps_Lock = Control_L
add Lock = Caps_Lock
add Control = Control_L
```

You can also assign the meta key to a function key using this line:

```
keysym F9 = Meta_L
```

Finally, when you have made your changes, you have to tell the server to use them. It's too cumbersome to shut down the window manager and restart it. Instead, you can use the rdb command:

```
$ xrdb .Xdefaults.
```

You can also invoke specific settings from the command line using xmodmap. For example, type the following line:

```
$ xmodmap -e "keysym F9=Meta_L"
```

Modifying the .Xmodmap file is better in that the changes are preserved for future sessions.

Internet Sites for XView

XView 3.0 is available by anonymous FTP from export.lcs.mit.edu if you want to upgrade the CD-ROM version.

OpenWindows can also be obtained from Sun, or you can get the source from Interactive Systems Inc. It is also included in some vendors' System V Release 4 implementations, although that's not always the latest version.

> **NOTE**
>
> The current release of OpenWindows from Sun for supported architectures is 3.0; for the Sun 3 series it is frozen at OpenWindows 2.0.

Sun includes OpenWindows with SunOS, and it is also included as the windowing system for Solaris.

There are said (by Sun) to be more than 35 ports of OpenWindows either available now or in progress. Unfortunately, none of them seem to be available from anywhere.

Douglas N. Arnold (`dna@math.psu.edu`) keeps an up-to-date FAQ on `ftp.math.psu.edu` (currently `146.186.131.129`) in the file `/pub/FAQ/open-look`.

MoOLIT can be bought from AT&T in source form.

Where To Go for More Information

Nabajyoti Barkakati gives an excellent introduction to X and to OLIT programming, as well as setting up and using X and OpenWindows, in

> *UNIX® Desktop Guide to OPEN LOOK,*
> Sams, 1992, ISBN 0-672-30023-0

The OPEN LOOK Graphical Interface is documented in two books:

> Sun Microsystems Inc., *OPEN LOOK Graphical User Interface Application Style Guidelines,* Addison Wesley, 1989.
>
> Sun Microsystems Inc., *OPEN LOOK Graphical User Interface Functional Specification,* Addison Wesley, 1989.

David Miller describes programming with OLIT in his book, *An OPEN LOOK At UNIX* (M&T Press).

You could also try *The X Window System: Programming and Applications with Xt, OPEN LOOK Edition,* by Doug Young and John Pew (Prentice Hall, 1992, ISBN 0-13-982992-X).

Sun Microsystems supplies a large amount of documentation with OpenWindows, although you may have to order it separately. The following list shows what I have; they are each 8.5×11 and vary from about 1 to 2 inches thick. They say "User's Guide" or "Programmer's Guide" on the front cover. The user manuals have a red stripe on the bottom, and the programmer versions have a green stripe:

800-6006-10	*OpenWindows Version 3 Release Manual*
800-6029-10	*OpenWindows Version 3 Installation and Start-Up Guide*
800-6231-10	*OpenWindows Version 3 DeskSet Reference Guide*

800-6618-10	*OpenWindows Version 3 User's Guide*
800-6323-10	*Desktop Integration Guid*
800-6027-10	*Programmer's Guide*
800-6005-10	*OpenWindows Version 3 Reference Manual* (the man pages)
800-6319-10	*The NeWS Toolkit 3.0 Reference Manual*
800-6736-10	*NeWS 3.0 Programming Guide*
800-6055-10	*OLIT 3.0 Widget Set Reference Manual*
800-6198-10	*XView 3.0 Reference Manual: Converting SunView Applications*
800-6854-10	*F3 Font Format Specification* (order separately)

Sun's AnswerBook CD-ROM contains much of this documentation and can prove to be a valuable source of information if you intend to port applications to Sun Workstations.

Summary

Here is what you should remember from this chapter on OPEN LOOK:

- XView is the OPEN LOOK GUI interface for Linux and is also referred to as OpenWindows. All three terms (XView, OPEN LOOK, and OpenWindows) are used interchangeably, but really refer to the same windowing interface.

- OPEN LOOK is not Motif. Not only are the window decorations different—the terminology used to convey actions is also different. (For example, Close in Motif generally kills an application and its window, whereas Close in OPEN LOOK iconifies a window.)

- You can use two types of OPEN LOOK window managers: olwm and olvwm. The olwm is the base OPEN LOOK window manager and the olvwm extends olwm by providing many virtual screens for your desktop.

- You can use the .Xdefaults files with the olwm keyword to set resources for your applications under olwm. See the man pages for olwm and olvwm for details on all resources for your distribution.

- You can get more information from Sun Microsystems about OPEN LOOK.

- Most OPEN LOOK menus offer a feature that enables you to pin a menu onto your desktop. You must either unpin this menu, or kill its underlying application, to get rid of it.

- On the Virtual Desktop Manager (VDM), you can stick windows on your screen regardless of your virtual desktop by using the Stick/Unstick selection on the Applications menu. All dialog boxes with that menu will stick with it too.

- XView applications enable you to have drag-and-drop capabilities. For example, with the File Manager application you can manage files and directories by dragging them around with the mouse.

- Standard Motif applications should run under XView. XView applications should also run under Motif if you have the shared libraries in your path.
- You can customize dialog box menus to include all executables files in a directory. Check the openwin-menu file for examples.

Ghostscript

25

by Kamran Husain

IN THIS CHAPTER

This chapter covers installation and use of Ghostscript, a PostScript interpreter. Almost everything related to Linux is in PostScript. If you have a PostScript printer, you simply send the file to the printer for a hardcopy.

What is Ghostscript?

Ghostscript is actually a set of programs. Collectively, these programs provide two important features:

- An interpreter for the PostScript language.
- A library of C functions for implementing primitive PostScript constructs.

> **NOTE**
>
> PostScript is a trademark of Adobe Systems, Incorporated.

Ghostscript has been ported to several platforms from PCs, OS/2, Apple Macintoshes, Ataris, to various flavors of UNIX, for example, Sun workstations, IBM AIX machines, and so on. Since Ghostscript is written in C, chances are that it will be portable to your platform. If you support X11, you will probably be able to run Ghostscript.

Several executable files come with Ghostscript. Some of the executables are also used by other packages under Linux. For example, HylaFAX (Chapter 59, "Using HylaFAX, `sendfax`, and `mgetty`") uses the main Ghostscript program, `gs`. In short, if you use Linux, you will find a need for Ghostscript.

Ghostscript Information

The primary contact for getting information about Ghostscript is:

Aladdin Enterprises
P.O. Box 60264
Palo Alto, CA 94306
voice (415) 322-0103
fax (415) 322-1734
`ghost@aladdin.com`

In fact, the Ghostscript package that you get with Linux is from Aladdin Enterprises. The information about Ghostscript is best summarized in its README file:

"L. Peter Deutsch, president of Aladdin Enterprises, was the original creator, and is the primary developer and maintainer, of Ghostscript. Aladdin Enterprises owns the copyright on Ghostscript; Ghostscript is distributed with the GNU General Public License, and is also available for commercial licensing."

Installation

To run Ghostscript, you need the executable program and some external initialization files:

```
/usr/lib/ghostscript/bdftops.ps
/usr/lib/ghostscript/decrypt.ps
/usr/lib/ghostscript/font2c.ps
/usr/lib/ghostscript/gs_dbt_e.ps
/usr/lib/ghostscript/gs_dps1.ps
/usr/lib/ghostscript/gs_fonts.ps
/usr/lib/ghostscript/gs_init.ps
/usr/lib/ghostscript/gs_lev2.ps
/usr/lib/ghostscript/gs_statd.ps
/usr/lib/ghostscript/gs_sym_e.ps
/usr/lib/ghostscript/gs_type0.ps
/usr/lib/ghostscript/gslp.ps
/usr/lib/ghostscript/impath.ps
/usr/lib/ghostscript/landscap.ps
/usr/lib/ghostscript/level1.ps
/usr/lib/ghostscript/prfont.ps
/usr/lib/ghostscript/ps2ascii.ps
/usr/lib/ghostscript/ps2epsi.ps
/usr/lib/ghostscript/ps2image.ps
/usr/lib/ghostscript/pstoppm.ps
/usr/lib/ghostscript/quit.ps
/usr/lib/ghostscript/showpage.ps
/usr/lib/ghostscript/type1ops.ps
/usr/lib/ghostscript/wrfont.ps
/usr/lib/ghostscript/uglyr.gsf
/usr/lib/ghostscript/Fontmap
```

The Ghostscript file set includes a set of fonts (.gsf files). You should have them online as well.

Installing Ghostscript on a Linux system simply requires getting it from the CD-ROM or Internet. The name of the executable is gs.

You can build Ghostscript on your machine if you want to. The makefiles that come with the sources will install all the files and directories under your /usr/local directory.

The fonts for Ghostscript are stored in /usr/lib/ghostscript/fonts.

The Ghostscript Interpreter

The Ghostscript interpreter is the gs command in /usr/bin/gs. This is an interactive interpreter that also reads in files for its input. To invoke the gs interpreter, use the command

```
gs [filename1] ... [filenameN]
```

The interpreter will read in the files in sequence and interpret them. After doing this, it reads further input from the primary input stream (normally the keyboard). Each line (that is, characters up to a <return>) is interpreted separately. To exit from the interpreter, type quit and press the Return key. The interpreter also exits gracefully if it encounters end-of-file. Typing the interrupt character (Ctrl-C), is also safe.

See Figure 25.1 for the input to the interpreter. (Your version number may be different than that shown in the figure.) The output is shown in a separate window as shown in Figure 25.2 (which shows the FlexFAX FAQ). The file in this example is the FAQ for the `HylaFAX` program (see Chapter 59) and is called `fax-112894.ps`. You can get this file via Mosaic (see Chapter 56, "Using Mosaic and Netscape") from `www.vix.com` from the `HylaFAX` directory.

FIGURE 25.1.

The gs *interpreter.*

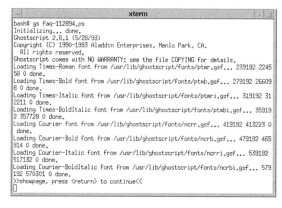

FIGURE 25.2.

The output from gs
interpreter.

Getting Help While in *gs*

The gs interpreter recognizes several arguments. We will cover most of the important ones in this chapter. However, you can get help from gs too. Either the -h or -? option tells gs to print out a help screen. The help screen also lists all available devices for gs on your system.

Choosing the Output Device

Ghostscript may be built with multiple output devices. Ghostscript normally opens the first one and directs output to it. To use device Laserjet as the initial output device, include the following argument in the command line:

```
-sDEVICE=laserjet
```

> **NOTE**
>
> Command line arguments to gs can appear anywhere on the command line. Once specified, these arguments apply to all subsequent files listed in the command line. These arguments will not apply to any files specified before the argument. So if you have important arguments like sDEVICE, specify these arguments before you specify the PostScript file.

> **TIP**
>
> PostScript files are usually specified with the .ps extension.

For example, for printer output in a normal configuration that includes a Laserjet printer driver, you might use the shell command

```
gs -sDEVICE=laserjet showme.ps
```

Alternatively, in the interpreter you can type

```
(laserjet) selectdevice
(showme.ps) run
```

All output then goes to the printer instead of the display until changed. You can switch devices at any time by using the selectdevice function, for example,

```
(vga) selectdevice  # for VGA screen
```

or

```
(nec) selectdevice    #for NEC printer
```

As yet a third alternative, you can define an environment variable `GS_DEVICE` as the desired default device name. The order of precedence for these alternatives, highest to lowest, is this:

```
selectdevice
(command line)
GS_DEVICE
(first device in build list)
```

To select the density on a printer, use the command

```
gs -sDEVICE=<device> -r<xres>x<yres>
```

For example, on a nine-pin, Epson-compatible printer, you can get the lowest-density (fastest) mode with the command

```
gs -sDEVICE=epson -r60x72
```

For the highest-density mode with Epson printers, use

```
gs -sDEVICE=epson -r240x72.
```

If you select a printer as the output device, Ghostscript also enables you to control where the device sends its output.

```
-sOutputFile=print%d.xyz
```

For compatibility with older versions of Ghostscript, `-sOUTPUTFILE=` also works.

The `%d` is a `printf` format specification. You can use other formats like `%02d`. Each file will receive one page of output. Alternatively, to send the output to a single file `bigfile.xyz`, with all the pages concatenated, use the command line argument: `-sOutputFile=foo.xyz`

On UNIX-like systems, you can send the output directly to a pipe. For example, to pipe the output to the command `lpr` (which, on many UNIX systems, is the command that spools output for a printer), use the switch

```
-sOutputFile=\¦lpr
```

Don't forget to escape the pipe symbol (¦). You can also send output to `stdout` for piping with the dash as the output file. That is, use the option `-sOutputFile=-`. In this case you must also use the `-q` switch to prevent Ghostscript from writing messages to `stdout`.

To find out what devices are available, type `"devicenames =="` after starting up Ghostscript.

Paper Size Configuration

Ghostscript is normally configured to expect U.S. letter size paper. To select a different paper size as the default, use the argument `-sPAPERSIZE=known_paper_size`. (You can create your own paper sizes with the `devs.mak` file.) Generally, you have a large selection available. The entire list can be found in the file

```
/usr/lib/ghostscript/gs_statd.ps
```

Print this file out if you can, to keep it handy. Some examples of setting the paper size are

```
-sPAPERSIZE=a4
-sPAPERSIZE=legal
-sPAPERSIZE=11x17
-sPAPERSIZE=ledger
```

TIP

A PostScript file may explicitly specify the paper size. In this case, the file's specification will override any command line argument specification.

Environment Variables

Ghostscript uses these environment variables: GS_LIB, GS_LIB_DEFAULT, and GS_FONTPATH.

When looking for the initialization files (gs_*.ps), the files related to fonts, or the file for the run operator, Ghostscript first tries opening the file with the name as given (that is, using the current working directory if none is specified). If this fails, and the filename doesn't specify an explicit directory or drive (that is, doesn't begin with / on UNIX), Ghostscript will try directories in the following order:

- The GS_LIB variable specifies several directories for gs to look in for files if a full path name of an input file is not specified. The directory names are separated by colons (like the PATH command).

- The GS_LIB_DEFAULT variable is similar to the GS_LIB variable and is searched if GS_LIB's directories showed nothing. Both of these variables (GS_LIB and GS_LIB_DEFAULT) can be overridden by the -I argument.

- The GS_FONTPATH environment variable is a list of directories for PostScript fonts. All those files and fonts listed in this directory are added to gs's internal copy of the Fontmap. A Fontmap is a catalog of fonts and the files that contain them.

CAUTION

Ghostscript will create temporary files by using the TEMP environment variable as the location of the /tmp directory. These files are named gs_*XXXXX*, where *XXXXX* is replaced by a number or a string of jumbled characters. Ghostscript doesn't do a very good job of deleting temporary files when it exits. If you see your /tmp space being used by these files you may have to delete them using the rm /tmp/gs_* command.

Configuring for X Window

Ghostscript looks for the resources under the program name ghostscript and class name Ghostscript in the .Xdefaults file. To set a resource, put the resource in .Xdefaults in the following form:

```
Ghostscript*geometry:      -0+0
Ghostscript*xResolution:   72
Ghostscript*yResolution:   72
```

Then load the defaults into the X server:

```
% xrdb -merge ~/.Xdefaults
```

Table 25.1 lists the options available to you.

Table 25.1. Ghostscript resources.

Name	Class	Default
background	Background	white
foreground	Foreground	black
borderColor	BorderColor	black
borderWidth	BorderWidth	1
geometry	Geometry	NULL
xResolution	Resolution	calculated
yResolution	Resolution	calculated
useExternalFonts	UseExternalFonts	true
useScalableFonts	UseScalableFonts	true
logExternalFonts	LogExternalFonts	false
externalFontTolerance	ExternalFontTolerance	10.0
palette	Palette	Color
maxGrayRamp	MaxGrayRamp	128
maxRGBRamp	MaxRGBRamp	5
useBackingPixmap	UseBackingPixmap	true
useXPutImage	UseXPutImage	true
useXSetTile	UseXSetTile	true
regularFonts	RegularFonts	see next page
symbolFonts	SymbolFonts	see next page
dingbatFonts	DingbatFonts	see next page

Here are a few points on these resources:

- The geometry resource only affects window placement. This does not affect the position of the image on the display in the window.
- All resolution numbers are given in pixels per inch.
- The font tolerance gives the largest acceptable difference in the height of the screen font. The tolerance is expressed as a percentage of the height of the desired font.
- The palette resource can be used to restrict Ghostscript to using a grayscale or monochrome palette.
- The maxRGBRamp and maxGrayRamp control the maximum number of colors that Ghostscript allocates ahead of time for dithering. Ghostscript will never pre-allocate more than half of the cells in a color map.

To use native X11 fonts, Ghostscript must map PostScript font names to the XLFD font names. The regularFonts, symbolFonts, and dingbatFonts resources give the name mapping for different encodings. The XLFD font name in the mapping must contain seven dashes. The X driver adds the additional size and encoding fields to bring the total number of dashes in the font name to 14. The default font mappings are found in the FontMap file in /usr/lib/ghostscript or check the man pages.

Command-Line Arguments

Ghostscript takes a lot of command-line arguments. Generally you would want to put these in a shell script file instead of having to type them in all the time. Some of the most often used arguments are listed here. For a comprehensive list check out the documents in /usr/lib/ghostscript/ doc. Let's look at the most commonly used arguments:

- @filename   The filename specified here will contain a list of all the input file names. This beats typing in long names on every execution of gs with lots of input files.
- -Idirectories   Adds the list of directories at the head of the library files' search path.
- -ffilename   Executes the given file, even if its name begins with a -.
- -Dname=token or -dname=token   Defines a name with the given token. The token must not contain any whitespace. You must specify each token with its own -Dname option. -Dname or -dname without the = will set the value to null.
- -Sname=string or -sname=string   Defines a string.

NOTE

The differences between -d and -s are these:

-dfoo=hello is equivalent to /foo hello def

-sfoo=hello is equivalent to /foo (hello) def

- ■ `-q` Suppresses normal startup messages.

- ■ `-gnumber1xnumber2` `Number1` is the width, `Number2` is the height of the display device. This is for devices that enable width and height to be specified. This is equivalent to `-dDEVICEWIDTH=number1` and `-dDEVICEHEIGHT=number2`.

- ■ `-rnumber` or `-rnumber1xnumber2` This is for the benefit of devices (such as printers) that support multiple X and Y resolutions. You can also use `-dDEVICEXRESOLUTION=number1` and `-dDEVICEYRESOLUTION=number2`.

- ■ `-` Uses standard input instead of the file. Ghostscript will read from `stdin` until reaching `end-of-file`, and execute it as another file. After the end of file, `gs` will process any other items as arguments but will not go into interactive mode.

- ■ `-dDISKFONTS` This argument causes individual character outlines to be loaded from the disk the first time they are encountered. Normally Ghostscript loads all the character outlines when it loads a font. This may enable loading more fonts into RAM at the expense of slower rendering.

- ■ `-dNODISPLAY` Suppresses the normal initialization of the output device. This may be useful when debugging.

- ■ `-dNOPAUSE` Disables the prompt and pause at the end of each page. This is useful for applications where another program is "driving" Ghostscript.

- ■ `-dNOPLATFONTS` Disables the use of fonts supplied by your machine. It is needed if the platform fonts look bad when compared to scaleable fonts.

- ■ `-dSAFER` Disables the `deletefile` and `renamefile` operators and the ability to open files in any mode other than read-only.

- ■ `-sDEVICE=device` Selects an alternate initial output device.

- ■ `-sOutputFile=filename` Selects an alternate output file instead of the default destination.

PostScript Viewer: Ghostview

Ghostview is used to display encoded PostScript files. Ghostview is free. It was written and copyrighted by Tim Theisen. The `ghostview` command shows PostScript documents using Ghostscript.

Use the command line below to view a text file.

```
$ ghostview [filename]
```

The `ghostview` program will create an X window, open the file, and display it. If the filename is `'-'`, `ghostview` will read from `stdin`. The `ghostview` program provides an X11 user interface for the Ghostscript interpreter. `ghostview` and Ghostscript function as two cooperating programs. `ghostview` creates the viewing window and Ghostscript draws in it.

NOTE

Please use Ghostscript to view files, especially those that require typesetting before sending them to the printer. You can save a lot of trees this way and get a quicker response about what to expect on the output. There are many programmers who still print out files to see what the output would look like instead of previewing on the screen.

In fact you may not even have to print out a document if you intend to send it to a remote site. If you have to FAX it, use HylaFAX (Chapter 59) with your FAX/modem to send it directly. If you have to e-mail it, uuencode it and then send it out.

Ghostview has a bewildering number of options. You do not have to use any of these options at all. Most of the options are there to override any Xresources that you set in .Xdefaults. Let's look at the main window, which consists of a main viewer and control menus (of HylaFAX). (See Figure 25.3.)

FIGURE 25.3.

Ghostscript main window.

The main viewport is on the right side of the main window. If the page is larger than the viewport, there will be scroll bars along the bottom and right edges of the viewport. To the left of the viewport is the table of contents. If the PostScript file has document structuring convention (DSC) comments, the table of contents will display the page labels (these are usually page numbers). To the left of the table of contents is a menu box. Each push button brings up a pop-up menu.

Above the menu box and table of contents there are three optional labels that contain the title, date, and locator.

The title label contains the document title found in the DSC comments. If no title can be found, the filename is used in its place. The date label contains the document date found in the DSC comments. If no date can be found, the last modified date of the file is used in its place. Since the title and date labels may be clipped by the main viewport, the date and title labels are pushbuttons that bring up a pop-up window with the title or date. These pop-up windows also show the document icon when the displayed string comes from the DSC comments.

The locator shows the location of the cursor in the viewport. The location is expressed in the default user coordinate system. The locator is useful for measuring bounding boxes. Within the main viewport, the mouse cursor is a "target" when Ghostscript is doing work. The cursor is a crosshair when Ghostscript is idle.

TIP

When moving to another page in a document, it is generally best to wait for Ghostscript to become idle. Ghostscript does not handle a series of mouse clicks very well while it's working and can hang. You then have to use the kill command to get rid of it, and start over.

Ghostview will always check to see if the file has been modified just before it displays a page or when the application is de-iconified. If the file has changed, it will re-open the file. This causes a bit of an overhead, but is helpful when you are trying to edit a file from another program and need to see your progress.

Clicking anywhere within the viewport will pop up a zoom window. The window is centered on the location that was clicked. Clicking with the left mouse button pops up a low-resolution zoom window. Clicking with the center mouse button pops up a medium-resolution zoom window. Clicking with the right mouse button pops up a high-resolution zoom window.

In the table of contents, the left mouse button selects text and the right mouse button extends selections. However, clicking on a page label with the center mouse button will display that page. The page being displayed is marked with a greater than symbol (>) in the right margin of the table of contents.

There are five buttons in the menu box. These are listed below:

- **File**   This menu enables you to open, reopen, print, show a copyright message, and quit the application. A Select File dialog box will appear when you click the open button. The Select File dialog widget enables you to select a file by typing the path or by browsing in directory listings and selecting entries with the mouse. The Select File dialog box is system modal; that is, no other controls in ghostview will be active during this time.

- **Page**   This pop-up menu controls which page you display. Next shows the next page, Redisplay redraws the current page, Previous shows the previous page, Mark and Unmark set a page in the table of contents as marked and unmarked.

- **Magstep**   This menu controls the magnification of the display. Zero implies no magnification (what you see is what you get). The multiplication factor is 1.2, so with a magstep of -1, the document is reduced by -1.2, a magstep of 1 zooms in by 1.2.

- ▪ Orientation   This enables you to select either a landscape or portrait orientation of the display. You can also flip the image with the Upsidedown to see FAXed documents. The Seascape option rotates the image 90 degrees counterclockwise.

- ▪ Media   The entries on the Media menu set the page media. The standard sizes you can select are: Letter, Tabloid, Letter, Tabloid, Ledger, Legal, Statement, Executive, A3, A4, A5, B4, B5, Folio, Quarto, and 10×14.

Keyboard Accelerators

Some of the pop-up menu commands can be executed with the keyboard. The pop-up menu has to be active (in other words, selected by the user for input) for the action to have effect. Some of the bindings are listed in Table 25.2.

Table 25.2. Keyboard shortcuts.

Key	Action
Q	The Quit menu button
O	The Open... menu button on the File menu
R	The Reopen... menu button on the File menu
S	The Save marked pages on the File menu
P	The Print marked pages on the File menu
Shift-P	The Print all pages on the File menu
BackSpace, B	The Previous menu button on the Page menu
space, Return, F	The Next menu button on the Page menu
period, Ctrl-L	The Redisplay menu button on the Page menu
M	The Mark menu button on the Page menu
N	The Unmark menu button on the Page menu
0-5	Selecting the 0 through 5 menu button on the Magstep menu
+	Increases the magstep by 1
-	Decreases the magstep by 1
U	Scrolls Up
D	Scrolls Down
H	Scrolls Left
L	Scrolls Right

X Resources

You can set the following resources for Ghostview. Only the most frequently used resources are listed. Please check the lengthy man page for Ghostview script for its long list of resources.

- showTitle (class Labels)   Displays the Title comment. The default is true.

- showDate (class Labels)   Displays the % %% %Data comment. The default is true.

- showLocator (class Labels)   Displays the locator. The default is true.

- autoCenter (class AutoCenter)   Centers the page in the viewport whenever the page size changes. The default is true.

- horizonalMargin (class Margin)   Shows how many pixels ghostview should reserve for horizontal window decorations. The default value is 20.

- verticalMargin (class Margin)   Shows how many pixels ghostview should reserve for vertical window decorations. The default value is 44.

- minimumMagstep (class Magstep)   Sets the smallest magstep to display. The default is -5.

- maximumMagstep (class Magstep)   Sets the largest magstep to display. The default is 5.

- magstep (class Magstep)   Sets the default magstep. The default is 0.

- orientation (class Orientation)   Sets the default orientation. The default is Portrait.

- page (class Page)   Gives the initial page to display.

- pageMedia (class PageMedia)   Sets the default page media. The default is Letter.

- forceOrientation (class Force)   Forces the orientation on the document. The default is false.

- forcePageMedia (class Force)   Forces the page media on the document. The default is false.

- swapLandscape (class SwapLandscape)   Swaps the meaning of Landscape and Seascape. The default is false.

- printCommand (class PrintCommand)   Sets the command used for printing.

- printerVariable (class PrinterVariable)   Gives the name of the printer environment variable. The default value is PRINTER.

- busyCursor (class Cursor)   The cursor shown when Ghostscript is drawing to the window. This is defaulted to a target icon.

- cursor (class Cursor)   The cursor shown when Ghostscript is idle. The default cursor is the crosshair.

- safer (class Safer)   Tells Ghostscript whether to run in safer mode. The default value is true.

Remember that almost all of these resources can be set with the command line argument. For example, the -title argument is equivalent to setting Ghostview.showTitle resource to True, whereas the -notitle argument is equivalent to setting the Title resource to False. Similarly, you can turn the date on or off with the -date and -nodate arguments, respectively.

Using Other Fonts

The versions of Ghostscript come with a set of default fonts that you can use with any program capable of reading PostScript Type 1 and Type 3 fonts. If you have created your own Type 1 or Type 3 fonts, or have purchased some fonts from another source, you can use these with Ghostscript. Place your fonts in the lib/ghostscript/fonts directory. Then edit the lib/ghostscript/FontMap file to add a line telling Ghostscript where to find the font. For example,

```
/Helvetica (hlv_xyz.pfb);
```

where hlv_xyz.pfb is the name of the font file you have just added. You do not have to reset any X resources for this to work. Simply place the file in the directory, edit the FontMap and restart gs.

Getting More Help

Aladdin Enterprises, the inventors of Ghostscript, do not have the resources to respond to questions from general users of Ghostscript. There are plenty of other places where you can get very detailed information about Ghostscript.

If you have access to newsgroups, post your questions to gnu.ghostscript.bug. There are literally hundreds of Ghostscript users all over the world who are very willing to help you. After all, we all started learning on our own. Using this newsgroup is perhaps the quickest way to get more information on gs.

If you have access to Internet mail, but not news, send e-mail to bug-ghostscript@prep.ai.mit.edu. If you are having trouble with a specific device driver, look in the file devs.mak and see if it is a user-maintained driver. If so, please contact directly the person listed.

There are several files in the /usr/lib/ghostscript/doc directory which can provide more information. Some of these files are:

- readme.doc   Information about problems, major changes, and new features in the current release.
- NEWS   A detailed history of changes in the most recent Ghostscript releases.
- use.doc   Information about how to install and use Ghostscript.
- devices.doc   Detailed information about specific devices that Ghostscript supports.
- make.doc   How to install, compile, and link Ghostscript.
- gs.1   The man page for Ghostscript.
- fonts.doc   Information about the fonts distributed with Ghostscript, including how to add or replace fonts.

- `language.doc`   A description of the Ghostscript language and its differences from the documented PostScript language.
- `psfiles.doc`   Information about the `.ps` files distributed with Ghostscript other than fonts.
- `drivers.doc`   The interface between Ghostscript and device drivers.
- `ps2epsi.doc`   Documentation for the PostScript to EPSI conversion utility. Most commercial word processing packages can import EPSI documents for typesetting.
- `hershey.doc`   Information about the Hershey fonts, which are the basis of some of the Ghostscript fonts.
- `history.doc`   A history of changes in older Ghostscript releases.
- `lib.doc`   Information about the Ghostscript library.

Summary

This chapter scratched the surface of a very important PostScript processing program called Ghostscript. The executable file for Ghostscript is called `gs`. You can use `gs` to decode PostScript files for displaying or printing hard copies.

Ghostscript is also used by other programs as a filter for working with PostScript printers that cannot switch from PostScript to text and back just by looking at a document. In this case, the `gs` command is used to convert text to PostScript with an output filter for `lp` before sending the text to a PostScript printer. As another example, `HylaFAX` uses `gs` as its primary PostScript output filter program.

Ghostview is an X Window–based program that provides a canvas for `ghostscript` to write its output to. Ghostview enables you to scroll through a multi-page document, zoom in and out, and save marked pages. The ability to view EPSI or PostScript via Ghostscript saves time and paper when typesetting documents.

V

PART

Linux for Programmers

gawk

26

by Tim Parker

The awk programming language was created by the three people who gave their last-name initials to the language: Alfred Aho, Peter Weinberger, and Brian Kernighan. The gawk program included with Linux is the GNU implementation of that programming language.

The awk language is more than just a programming language; it is an almost indispensable tool for many system administrators and UNIX programmers. The language itself is easy to learn, easy to master, and amazingly flexible. Once you get the hang of using awk, you'll be surprised how often you can use it for routine tasks on your system.

To help you understand gawk, I will follow a simple order of introducing the elements of the programming language, as well as showing good examples. You are encouraged, or course, to experiment as the chapter progresses.

I can't cover all the different aspects and features of gawk in this chapter, but we will look at the basics of the language and show you enough, hopefully, to get your curiosity working.

What Is the *awk* Language?

awk is designed to be an easy-to-use programming language that lets you work with information either stored in files or piped to it. The main strengths of awk are its abilities to do the following:

- Display some or all the contents of a file, selecting rows, columns, or fields as necessary.
- Analyze text for frequency of words, occurrences, and so on.
- Prepare formatted output reports based on information in a file.
- Filter text in a very powerful manner.
- Perform calculations with numeric information from a file.

awk isn't difficult to learn. In many ways, awk is the ideal first programming language because of its simple rules, basic formatting, and standard usage. Experienced programmers will find awk refreshingly easy to use.

Files, Records, and Fields

Usually, gawk works with data stored in files. Often this is numeric data, but gawk can work with character information, too. If data is not stored in a file, it is supplied to gawk through a pipe or other form of redirection. Only ASCII files (text files) can be properly handled with gawk. Although it does have the ability to work with binary files, the results are often unpredictable. Since most information on a Linux system is stored in ASCII, this isn't a problem.

As a simple example of a file that gawk works with, consider a telephone directory. It is composed of many entries, all with the same format: last name, first name, address, telephone number. The entire telephone directory is a database of sorts, although without a sophisticated search routine. Indeed, the telephone directory relies on a pure alphabetical order to enable users to search for the data they need.

Each line in the telephone directory is a complete set of data on its own and is called a *record*. For example, the entry in the telephone directory for "Smith, John," which includes his address and telephone number, is a record.

Each piece of information in the record—the last name, the first name, the address, and the telephone number—is called a *field*. For the gawk language, the field is a single piece of information. A record, then, is a number of fields that pertain to a single item. A set of records makes up a *file*.

In most cases, fields are separated by a character that is used only to separate fields, such as a space, a tab, a colon, or some other special symbol. This character is called a *field separator*. A good example is the file /etc/passwd, which looks like this:

```
tparker:t36s62hsh:501:101:Tim Parker:/home/tparker:/bin/bash
etreijs:2ys639dj3h:502:101:Ed Treijs:/home/etreijs:/bin/tcsh
ychow:1h27sj:503:101:Yvonne Chow:/home/ychow:/bin/bash
```

If you look carefully at the file, you will see that it uses a colon as the field separator. Each line in the /etc/passwd file has seven fields: the user name, the password, the user ID, the group ID, a comment field, the home directory, and the startup shell. Each field is separated by a colon. Colons exist only to separate fields. A program looking for the sixth field in any line needs only count five colons across (because the first field doesn't have a colon before it).

That's where we find a problem with the gawk definition of fields as they pertain to the telephone directory example. Consider the following lines from a telephone directory:

```
Smith, John    13 Wilson St.              555-1283
Smith, John    2736 Artside Dr, Apt 123   555-2736
Smith, John    125 Westmount Cr           555-1726
```

We "know" there are four fields here: the last name, the first name, the address, and the telephone number. But gawk doesn't see it that way. The telephone book uses the space character as a field separator, so on the first line it sees "Smith" as the first field, "John" as the second, "13" as the third, "Wilson" as the fourth, and so on. As far as gawk is concerned, the first line when using a space character as a field separator has six fields. The second line has eight fields.

NOTE

When working with a programming language, you must consider data the way the language will see it. Remember that programming languages take things literally.

To make sense of the telephone directory the way we want to handle it, we have to find another way of structuring the data so that there is a field separator between the sections. For example, the following uses the slash character as the field separator:

```
Smith/John/13 Wilson St./555-1283
Smith/John/2736 Artside Dr, Apt 123/555-2736
Smith/John/125 Westmount Cr/555-1726
```

By default, gawk uses blank characters (spaces or tabs) as field separators unless instructed to use another character. If gawk is using spaces, it doesn't matter how many are in a row; they are treated as a single block for purposes of finding fields. Naturally, there is a way to override this behavior, too.

Pattern-Action Pairs

The gawk language has a particular format for almost all instructions. Each command is composed of two parts: a pattern and a corresponding action. Whenever the pattern is matched, gawk executes the action that matches that pattern.

Pattern-action pairs can be thought of in more common terms to show how they work. Consider instructing someone how to get to the post office. You might say, "Go to the end of the street and turn right. At the stop sign, turn left. At the end of the street, go right." You have created three pattern-action pairs with these instructions:

```
end of street: turn right
stop sign: turn left
end of street: turn right
```

When these patterns are met, the corresponding action is taken. You wouldn't turn right before you reached the end of the street, and you don't turn right until you get to the end of the street, so the pattern must be matched precisely for the action to be performed. This is a bit simplistic, but it gives you the basic idea.

With gawk, the patterns to be matched are enclosed in a pair of slashes, and the actions are in a pair of curly braces:

```
/pattern1/{action1}
/pattern2/{action2}
/pattern3/{action3}
```

This format makes it quite easy to tell where the pattern starts and ends, and when the action starts and ends. All gawk programs are sets of these pattern-action pairs, one after the other. Remember these pattern-action pairs are working on text files, so a typical set of patterns might be matching a set of strings, and the actions might be to print out parts of the line that matched.

Suppose there isn't a pattern? In that case, the pattern matches every time and the action is executed every time. If there is no action, gawk copies the entire line that matched without change.

Here are some simple examples. The gawk command

```
gawk '/tparker/' /etc/passwd
```

will look for each line in the /etc/passwd file that contains the pattern tparker and display it (there is no action, only a pattern). The output from the command will be the one line in the /etc/passwd file that contains the string tparker. If there is more than one line in the file with that pattern, they all will be displayed. In this case, gawk is acting exactly like the grep utility!

This example shows you two important things about gawk: It can be invoked from the command line by giving it the pattern-action pair to work with and a filename, and it likes to have single quotes around the pattern-action pair in order to differentiate them from the filename.

The gawk language is literal in its matching. The string cat will match any lines with cat in them, whether the word "cat" by itself or part of another word such as "concatenate." To be exact, put spaces on either side of the word. Also, case is important. We'll see how to expand the matching in the section "Metacharacters" a little later in the chapter.

Jumping ahead slightly, we can introduce a gawk command. The command

```
gawk '{print $3}' file2.data
```

has only an action, so it performs that action on every line in the file file2.data. The action is print $3, which tells gawk to print the third field of every line. The default field separator, a space, is used to tell where fields begin and end. If we had tried the same command on the /etc/passwd file, nothing would have been displayed because the field separator used in that file is the colon.

We can combine the two commands to show a complete pattern-action pair:

```
gawk '/UNIX/{print $2}' file2.data
```

This command will search file2.data line by line, looking for the string UNIX. If it finds UNIX, it prints the second column of that line (record).

> **NOTE**
>
> The quotes around the entire pattern-action pair are very important and should not be left off. Without them, the command might not execute properly. Make sure the quotes match (don't use a single quote at the beginning and a double quote at the end).

You can combine more than one pattern-action pair in a command. For example, the command

```
gawk '/scandal/{print $1} /rumor/{print $2}' gossip_file
```

scans gossip_file for all occurrences of the pattern "scandal" and prints the first column, and then starts at the top again and searches for the pattern "rumor" and prints the second column. The scan starts at the top of the file each time there is a new pattern-action pair.

Simple Patterns

As you might have figured out, gawk numbers all of the fields in a record. The first field is $1, the second is $2, and so on. The entire record is called $0. As a short form, gawk allows you to ignore the $0 in simple commands, so the instructions matching. If you only want to match the word "cat" but not "concatenate," you should put spaces on either side of the pattern:

```
/ cat / {print}
```

What about matching different cases? That's where the or instruction, represented by a vertical bar, comes in. For example

```
/ cat ¦ CAT / {print}
```

will match "cat" or "CAT" on a line. However, what about "Cat?" That's where we also need to specify options within a pattern. With gawk, we use square brackets for this. To match any combination of "cat" in upper- or lowercase, we must write the pattern like this:

```
/ [Cc][Aa][Tt] / {print}
```

This can get pretty awkward, but it's seldom necessary. To match just "Cat" and "cat," for example, we would use the pattern

```
/ [Cc]at / {print}
```

A useful matching operator is the tilde (~). This is used when you want to look for a match in a particular field in a record. For example, the pattern

```
$5 ~ /tparker/
```

will match any records where the fifth field is tparker. It is similar to the == operator. The matching operator can be negated, so

```
$5 !~ /tparker/
```

will find any record where the fifth field is not equal to tparker.

A few characters (called *metacharacters*) have special meaning to gawk. Many of these metacharacters will be familiar to shell users, because they are carried over from UNIX shells. The metacharacters shown in Table 26.6 can be used in gawk patterns.

Table 26.6. Metacharacters.

Metacharacter	Meaning	Example	Meaning of Example
~	The beginning of the field	`$3 ~ /^b/`	Matches if the third field starts with b
$	The end of the field	`$3 ~ /b$/`	Matches if the third field ends with b
.	Matches any single character	`$3 ~ /i.m/`	Matches any record that has a third field value of i, another character, and then m
¦	Or	`/cat¦CAT/`	Matches cat or CAT

Metacharacter	Meaning	Example	Meaning of Example
*	Zero or more repetitions of a character	`/UNI*X/`	Matches UNX, UNIX, UNIIX, UNIIIX, and so on
+	One of more repetitions of a character	`/UNI+X/`	Matches UNIX, UNIIX, and so on, but not UNX
`\{a,b\}`	The number of repetitions between a and b (both integers)	`/UNI\{1,3\}X`	Matches only UNIX, UNIIX, and UNIIIX
?	Zero or one repetitions of a string	`/UNI?X/`	Matches UNX and UNIX only
[]	Range of characters	`/I[BDG]M/`	Matches IBM, IDM, and IGM
[^]	Not in the set	`/I[^DE]M/`	Matches all three character sets starting with I and ending in M, except IDM and IEM

Some of these metacharacters are used frequently. You will see some examples later in this chapter.

Calling *gawk* Programs

Running pattern-action pairs one or two at a time from the command line would be pretty difficult (and time consuming), so gawk allows you to store pattern-action pairs in a file. A gawk program (called a *script*) is a set of pattern-action pairs stored in an ASCII file. For example, this could be the contents of a valid gawk script:

```
/tparker/{print $6}
$2 != "foo" {print}
```

The first line would look for tparker and print the sixth column, and the second line would start at the top of the file again and look for second columns that don't match the string "foo", then display the entire line. When you are writing a script, you don't need to worry about the quotation marks around the pattern-action pairs as you did on the command line, because the new command to execute this script makes it obvious where the pattern-action pairs start and end.

After you have saved all of the pattern-action pairs in a program, they are called by gawk with the -f option on the command line:

```
gawk -f script filename
```

This command causes gawk to read all of the pattern-action pairs from the file *script* and process them against the file called *filename*. This is how most gawk programs are written. Don't confuse the -f and -F options!

If you want to specify a different field separator on the command line (they can be specified in the script, but use a special format you'll see later), the -F option must follow the -f option:

```
gawk -f script -F":" filename
```

If you want to process more than one file using the script, just append the names of the files:

```
gawk -f script filename1 filename2 filename3 ...
```

By default, all output from the gawk command is displayed on the screen. You could redirect it to a file with the usual Linux redirection commands:

```
gawk -f script filename > save_file
```

There is another way of specifying the output file from within the script, but we'll come back to that in a moment.

BEGIN and END

Two special patterns supported by gawk are useful when writing scripts. The BEGIN pattern is used to indicate any actions that should take place before gawk starts processing a file. This is usually used to initialize values, set parameters such as field separators, and so on. The END pattern is used to execute any instructions after the file has been completely processed. Typically, this can be for summaries or completion notices.

Any instructions following the BEGIN and END patterns are enclosed in curly braces to identify which instructions are part of both patterns. Both BEGIN and END must appear in capitals. Here's a simple example of a gawk script that uses BEGIN and END, albeit only for sending a message to the terminal:

```
BEGIN { print "Starting the process the file" }
$1 == "UNIX" {print}
$2 > 10 {printf "This line has a value of %d", $2}
END { print "Finished processing the file.  Bye!"}
```

In this script, a message is initially printed out, and each line that has the word UNIX in the first column is echoed to the screen. Next, the file is processed again to look for any line with the second column greater than 10, and the message is generated with its current value. Finally, the END pattern prints out a message that the program is finished.

Variables

If you have used any programming language before, you know that a *variable* is a storage location for a value. Each variable has a name and an associated value, which may change.

With gawk, you assign a variable a value using the assignment operator, =:

```
var1 = 10
```

This assigns the value 10 (numeric, not string) to the variable var1. With gawk, you don't have to declare variable types before you use them as you must with most other languages. This makes it easy to work with variables in gawk.

should help, as ga

programs of your

Incidentally, gawk

starts with a # sig

immediately obvi

The *if* State

The if statemen

commands. The

if (expression

The expression i

expression. Here

```
# a simple if
(if ($1 == 0){
      print "T
      }
else {
      printf "
      })
```

You will notice t

this could all ha

nicely formattec

gram becomes n

In this simple s

effect is printed.

The flow of the

as long as the cu

be left out entir

```
(if ($1 == 0).
      print "1
      })
```

The gawk langu

the if statemen

is harder to read

here's the if sta

```
# a nicely fo
(if ($1 > $2)
      print "
      }
else {
      print "
      })
```

> **NOTE**
>
> Don't confuse the assignment operator, =, which assigns a value, with the comparison operator, ==, which compares two values. This is a common error that takes a little practice to overcome.

The gawk language lets you use variables within actions, so the pattern-action pair

```
$1 == "Plastic" { count = count + 1 }
```

checks to see if the first column is equal to the string "Plastic", and if it is, increments the value of count by one. Somewhere above this line we should set a preliminary value for the variable count (usually in the BEGIN section), or we will be adding one to something that isn't a recognizable number.

> **NOTE**
>
> Actually, gawk assigns all variables a value of zero when they are first used, so you don't really have to define the value before you use it. It is, however, good programming practice to initialize the variable anyway.

Here's a more complete example:

```
BEGIN { count = 0 }
$5 == "UNIX" { count = count + 1 }
END { printf "%d occurrences of UNIX were found", count }
```

In the BEGIN section, the variable count is set to zero. Then, the gawk pattern-action pair is processed, with every occurrence of "UNIX" adding one to the value of count. After the entire file has been processed, the END statement displays the total number.

Variables can be used in combination with columns and values, so all of the following statements are legal:

```
count = count + $6
count = $5 - 8
count = $5 + var1
```

Variables can also be part of a pattern. The following are all valid as pattern-action pairs:

```
$2 > max_value {print "Max value exceeded by ", $2 - max_value}
$4 - var1 < min_value {print "Illegal value of ", $4}
```

Two special operators are used with variables to increment and decrement by one, because these are common operations. Both of these special operators are borrowed from the C language:

count++	increments count by one
count--	decrements count by one

Built-In

The gawk
number of
important

Table 26

Variab

NR

FNR

FILENA

FS

RS

OFMT

OFS

ORS

NF

The NR ar
than one

The FS va
/etc/pas

FS=":"

in the scr

You can

NF <= 5

gives you
message i

Cont

Enough
Althoug
importar

If you h;
these cor

```
END {var=NR                # output lines in reverse order
     while (var > 0){
     print line[var]
     var—
     }
}
```

In this simple program (try and do the same task in any other programming language to see how efficient gawk is!), we used the NR (number of records) built-in variable. After reading each line into the array line[ ], we simply start at the last record and print them again, stepping down through the array each time. We don't have to declare the array or do anything special with it, which is one of the powerful features of gawk.

Summary

We've only scratched the surface of gawk's abilities, but you might have noticed that it is a relatively easy language to work with and places no special demands on the programmer. That's one of the reasons gawk is so often used for quick programs. It is ideal, for example, for writing a quick script to count the total size of all the files in a directory. In the C language, this would take many lines, but it can be done in less than a dozen lines in gawk.

If you are a system administrator or simply a power user, you will find that gawk is a great complement to all the other tools you have available, especially because it can accept input from a pipe or redirection. For more information on gawk, check the man pages or one of the few awk books that are available.

Programming in C

27

by
Rick McMullin

IN THIS CHAPTER

Linux is distributed with a wide range of software-development tools. Many of these tools support the development of C and C++ applications. This chapter describes the tools that can be used to develop and debug C applications under Linux. It is not intended to be a tutorial on the C programming language, but rather to describe how to use the C compiler and some of the other C programming tools that are included with Linux. In this chapter you will learn about the following:

- What C is
- The GNU C compiler
- Debugging GCC applications with `gdb`

You also will look at some of the useful C tools that are included with the Linux distribution. These tools include pretty print programs, additional debugging tools, and automatic function prototypers.

> **NOTE**
>
> *Pretty print* programs are programs that automatically reformat code so that it has consistent indenting.

What Is C?

C is a general-purpose programming language that has been around since the early days of the UNIX operating system. It was originally created by Dennis Ritchie at Bell Laboratories to aid in the development of UNIX. The first versions of UNIX were written using assembly language and a language called B. C was developed to overcome some of the shortcomings of B. Since that time, C has become one of the most widely used computer languages in the world.

Why did C gain so much support in the programming world? Some of the reasons that C is so commonly used include the following:

- It is a very portable language. Almost any computer that you can think of has at least one C compiler available for it, and the language syntax and function libraries are standardized across platforms. This is a very attractive feature for developers.
- Executable programs written in C are fast.
- C is the system language with all versions of UNIX.

C has evolved quite a bit over the last 20 years. In the late 1980s, the American National Standards Institute published a standard for the C language known as ANSI C. This further helped to secure C's future by making it even more consistent between platforms. The 1980s also saw an object-oriented extension to C called C++. C++ will be described in the next chapter, "Programming in C++."

The C compiler that is available for Linux is the GNU C compiler, abbreviated GCC. This compiler was created under the Free Software Foundation's programming license and is therefore freely distributable. You will find it on the book's companion CD-ROM.

The GNU C Compiler

The GNU C Compiler (GCC) that is packaged with the Slackware Linux distribution is a fully functional, ANSI C compatible compiler. If you are familiar with a C compiler on a different operating system or hardware platform, you will be able to learn GCC very quickly. This section describes how to invoke GCC and introduces many of the commonly used GCC compiler options.

Invoking GCC

The GCC compiler is invoked by passing it a number of options and a number of filenames. The basic syntax for invoking gcc is this:

```
gcc [options] [filenames]
```

The operations specified by the command-line options will be performed on each of the files that are specified on the command line. The next section describes the options that you will use most often.

GCC Options

There are more than 100 compiler options that can be passed to GCC. You will probably never use many of these options, but you will use some of them on a regular basis. Many of the GCC options consist of more than one character. For this reason you must specify each option with its own hyphen, and you cannot group options after a single hyphen as you can with most Linux commands. For example, the following two commands are not the same:

```
gcc -p -g test.c
gcc -pg test.c
```

The first command tells GCC to compile test.c with profile information for the prof command and also to store debugging information within the executable. The second command just tells GCC to compile test.c with profile information for the gprof command.

When you compile a program using gcc without any command-line options, it will create an executable file (assuming that the compile was successful) and call it a.out. For example, the following command would create a file named a.out in the current directory.

```
gcc test.c
```

To specify a name other than a.out for the executable file, you can use the -o compiler option. For example, to compile a C program file named count.c into an executable file named count, you would type the following command.

```
gcc -o count count.c
```

> **NOTE**
>
> When you are using the -o option, the executable filename must occur directly after the -o on the command line.

There are also compiler options that allow you to specify how far you want the compile to proceed. The -c option tells GCC to compile the code into object code and to skip the assembly and linking stages of the compile. This option is used quite often because it makes the compilation of multifile C programs faster and easier to manage. Object code files that are created by GCC have a .o extension by default.

The -s compiler option tells GCC to stop the compile after it has generated the assembler files for the C code. Assembler files that are generated by GCC have a .s extension by default. The -E option instructs the compiler to perform only the preprocessing compiler stage on the input files. When this option is used, the output from the preprocessor is sent to the standard output rather than being stored in a file.

Optimization Options

When you compile C code with GCC, it tries to compile the code in the least amount of time and also tries to create compiled code that is easy to debug. Making the code easy to debug means that the sequence of the compiled code is the same as the sequence of the source code, and no code gets optimized out of the compile. There are many options that you can use to tell GCC to create smaller, faster executable programs at the cost of compile time and ease of debugging. Of these options the two that you will typically use are the -0 and the -02 options.

The -0 option tells GCC to perform basic optimizations on the source code. These optimizations will in most cases make the code run faster. The -02 option tells GCC to make the code as fast and small as it can. The -02 option will cause the compilation speed to be slower than it is when using the -0 option, but will typically result in code that executes more quickly.

In addition to the -0 and -02 optimization options, there are a number of lower-level options that can be used to make the code faster. These options are very specific and should only be used if you fully understand the consequences that using these options will have on the compiled code. For a detailed description of these options, refer to the GCC manual page by typing man gcc on the command line.

Debugging and Profiling Options

GCC supports several debugging and profiling options. Of these options, the two that you are most likely to use are the -g option and the -pg option.

The -g option tells GCC to produce debugging information that the GNU debugger (gdb) can use to help you to debug your program. GCC provides a feature that many other C compilers do not have. With GCC you can use the -g option in conjunction with the -0 option (which generates optimized code). This can be very useful if you are trying to debug code that is as close as possible to what will exist in the final product. When you are using these two options together you should be aware that some of the code that you have written will probably be changed by GCC when it optimizes it. For more information on debugging your C programs, refer to the "Debugging GCC Programs with gdb" section in this chapter.

The -pg option tells GCC to add extra code to your program that will, when executed, generate profile information that can be used by the gprof program to display timing information about your program. For more information on gprof, refer to the "gprof" section in this chapter.

Debugging GCC Programs with *gdb*

Linux includes the GNU debugging program called gdb. gdb is a very powerful debugger that can be used to debug C and C++ programs. It enables you to see the internal structure or the memory that is being used by a program while it is executing. Some of the functions that gdb provides for you are these:

- It enables you to monitor the value of variables that are contained in your program.
- It enables you to set breakpoints that will stop the program at a specific line of code.
- It enables you to step through the code, line by line.

You can run gdb by typing gdb on the command line and pressing Enter. If your system is configured properly, gdb should start and you will see a screen that resembles the following:

```
GDB is free software and you are welcome to distribute copies of it
under certain conditions; type "show copying" to see the conditions.
There is absolutely no warranty for GDB; type "show warranty" for details.
GDB 4.14 (i486-slakware-linux), Copyright 1995 Free Software Foundation, Inc.
(gdb)
```

When you start gdb, there are a number of options that you can specify on the command line. You will probably run gdb in the following way:

```
gdb <fname>
```

When you invoke gdb in this way, you are specifying the executable file that you want to debug. This tells gdb to load the executable file with the name fname. There are also ways of starting gdb that tell it to inspect a core file that was created by the executable file being examined, or to attach gdb to a currently running process. To get a listing and brief description of each of these other options, you can refer to the gdb man page or type gdb -h at the command line.

Compiling Code for Debugging

To get gdb to work properly, you must compile your programs so that debugging information will be generated by the compiler. The debugging information that is generated contains the types for each of the variables in your program as well as the mapping between the addresses in the executable program and the line numbers in the source code. gdb uses this information to relate the executable code to the source code.

To compile a program with the debugging information turned on, use the -g compiler option.

gdb Basic Commands

The gdb supports many commands that enable you to perform different debugging operations. These commands range in complexity from very simple file-loading commands to complicated commands that allow you to examine the contents of the call stack. Table 27.1 describes the commands that you will need to get up and debugging with gdb. To get a description of all of the gdb commands, refer to the gdb manual page.

Table 27.1. Basic gdb commands.

Command	Description
file	Loads the executable file that is to be debugged
kill	Terminates the program that you are currently debugging
list	Lists sections of the source code that was used to generate the executable file
next	Advances one line of source code in the current function, without stepping into other functions
step	Advances one line of source code in the current function, and does step into other functions
run	Executes the program that is currently being debugged
quit	Terminates gdb
watch	Enables you to examine the value of a program variable whenever the value changes
break	Sets a breakpoint in the code; this causes the execution of the program to be suspended whenever this point is reached
make	Enables you to remake the executable program without quitting out of gdb or using another window
shell	Enables you to execute UNIX shell commands without leaving gdb

The gdb environment supports many of the same command-editing features as do the UNIX shell programs. You can tell gdb to complete unique commands by pressing the Tab key just as you do when you are using bash or tcsh. If what you have typed in is not unique, you can make gdb print a list of all the commands that match what you have typed in so far by pressing the Tab key again. You can also scroll up and down through the commands that you have entered previously by pressing the up and down arrow keys.

Sample *gdb* Session

This section takes you step by step through a sample gdb session. The sample program that is being debugged is quite simple, but it is sufficient to illustrate how gdb is typically used.

We will start by showing a listing of the program that is to be debugged. The program is called greeting and is supposed to display a simple greeting followed by the greeting printed in reverse order.

```c
#include  <stdio.h>

main ()
{
  char my_string[] = "hello there";

  my_print (my_string);
  my_print2 (my_string);
}

void my_print (char *string)
{
  printf ("The string is %s\n", string);
}

void my_print2 (char *string)
{
  char *string2;
  int size, i;

  size = strlen (string);
  string2 = (char *) malloc (size + 1);
  for (i = 0; i < size; i++)
    string2[size - i] = string[i];
  string2[size+1] = '\0';
  printf ("The string printed backward is %s\n", string2);
}
```

You can compile the preceding program using the gcc command followed by the filename. If you want to rename the generated binary (instead of using the default a.out filename), use the -o option followed by the binary name, such as:

```
gcc -o test test.c
```

The program, when executed, displays the following output:

```
The string is hello there
The string printed backward is
```

The first line of output comes out correctly, but the second line prints something that was unexpected. We intended the second line of output to be

```
The string printed backward is ereht olleh
```

For some reason the `my_print2` function is not working properly. Let's take a look at the problem using `gdb`. First you need to start `gdb`, specifying the greeting program as the one to debug. You do this by typing the following command:

```
gdb greeting
```

NOTE

Remember that you must compile the greeting program with the compiler debug options turned on.

If you forget to pass the program to debug as a parameter to `gdb`, you can load it in after `gdb` is started by using the file command at the `gdb` prompt:

```
(gdb) file greeting
```

This command will load the greeting executable just as if you had told `gdb` to load it on the command line.

You can now run `greeting` by entering the `gdb` run command. When the program is executed from within `gdb`, the result should resemble the following:

```
(gdb) run
Starting program: /root/greeting
The string is hello there
The string printed backward is
Program exited with code 041
```

The output of the greeting program is the same as when we executed the program outside of `gdb`. The question is, why is the backward print not working? To find the problem we can set a breakpoint at the line after the `for` statement in the `my_print2` function. To do this, list the source file by entering the `list` command three times at the `gdb` prompt:

```
(gdb) list
(gdb) list
(gdb) list
```

TIP

Pressing Enter by itself at the `gdb` prompt will repeat the last command that was entered.

The first time you enter the `list` command, you get output that resembles the following:

```
1       #include  <stdio.h>
2
3       main ()
4       {
5         char my_string[] = "hello there";
6
```

```
7          my_print (my_string);
8          my_print2 (my_string);
9      }
10
```

If you press Enter, gdb will execute the list command again, giving you the following output:

```
11     my_print (char *string)
12     {
13        printf ("The string is %s\n", string);
14     }
15
16     my_print2 (char *string)
17     {
18        char *string2;
19        int size, i;
20
```

Pressing Enter one more time will list the rest of the greeting program:

```
21        size = strlen (string);
22        string2 = (char *) malloc (size + 1);
23        for (i = 0; i < size; i++)
24           string2[size - i] = string[i];
25        string2[size+1] = '\0';
26        printf ("The string printed backward is %s\n", string2);
27     }
```

By listing the file you can see that the place where you want to set the breakpoint is line 24. Now, to set the breakpoint, type the following command at the gdb command prompt:

```
(gdb) break 24
```

gdb should now print a response resembling the following:

```
Breakpoint 1 at 0x139: file greeting.c, line 24
(gdb)
```

Now you can run the program again by typing the run command. This command will generate the following output:

```
Starting program: /root/greeting
The string is hello there

Breakpoint 1, my_print2 (string = 0xbfffdc4 "hello there") at greeting.c :24
24    string2[size-i]=string[i]
```

You can see what is actually going wrong with your program by setting a watch to tell you the value of the string2[size - i] variable expression.

To do this, type

```
(gdb) watch string2[size - i]
```

gdb will return the following acknowledgment:

```
Watchpoint 2: string2[size - i]
```

The version of gdb included on the CD-ROM accompanying this book changes the prompt to Hardware Watchpoint, but this is simply a change in the naming convention used by gdb. Now you can step through the execution of the for loop using the next command:

```
(gdb) next
```

After the first time through the loop, gdb tells us that string2[size - i] is 'h'. gdb informs you of this by writing the following message on the screen:

```
Watchpoint 2, string2[size - i]
Old value = 0 '\000'
New value = 104 'h'
my_print2(string = 0xbffffdc4 "hello there") at greeting.c:23
23 for (i=0; i<size; i++)
```

> **NOTE**
>
> The version of gcc on the CD-ROM accompanying this book appears to have some bugs in the include files. Some tasks, including checking the next watchpoint, cause error messages. You should check the FTP sites for updates or previous versions which do not have this fault if this presents a problem for your C compiler usage.

This is the value that you expected. Stepping through the loop several more times reveals similar results. Everything appears to be functioning normally. When you get to the point where i=10, the value of the string2[size - i] expression is equal to 'e', the value of the size - i expression is equal to 1, and the program is at the last character that is to be copied over into the new string.

If you step through the loop one more time, you see that there was not a value assigned to string2[0], which is the first character of the string. Because the malloc function initializes the memory it assigns to null, the first character in string2 is the null character. This explains why nothing was being printed when you tried to print string2.

Now that you have found the problem, it should be quite easy to fix. You must write the code so that the first character going into string2 is being put into string2 at offset size - 1 instead of string2 at offset size. This is because the size of string2 is 12, but it starts numbering at offset zero. The characters in the string should start at offset 0 and go to offset 10, with offset 11 being reserved for the null character.

There are many ways to modify this code so that it will work. One way is to keep a separate size variable that is one smaller than the real size of the original string. This solution is shown in the following code:

```
#include  <stdio.h>

main ()
{
  char my_string[] = "hello there";

  my_print (my_string);
  my_print2 (my_string);
```

```
}

my_print (char *string)
{
  printf ("The string is %s\n", string);
}

my_print2 (char *string)
{
  char *string2;
  int size, size2, i;

  size = strlen (string);
  size2 = size -1;
  string2 = (char *) malloc (size + 1);
  for (i = 0; i < size; i++)
    string2[size2 - i] = string[i];
  string2[size] = '\0';
  printf ("The string printed backward is %s\n", string2);
}
```

Additional C Programming Tools

The Slackware Linux distribution includes a number of C development tools that have not yet been described. This section describes many of these additional tools and their typical uses.

xxgdb

xxgdb is an X Window system–based graphical user interface to gdb. All of the features that exist in the command-line version of gdb are present in xxgdb. xxgdb enables you to perform many of the most commonly used gdb commands by pressing buttons instead of typing in commands. It also graphically represents where you have placed breakpoints.

You can start xxgdb by typing the following into an Xterm window.

xxgdb

When you initiate xxgdb you can specify any of the command-line options that were available with gdb. xxgdb also has some of its own command-line options. These are described in Table 27.2.

Table 27.2. The xxgdb command-line options.

Option	Description
db_name	Specifies the name of the debugger to be used. The default is gdb.
db_prompt	Specifies the debugger prompt. The default is gdb.
gdbinit	Specifies the filename of the initial gdb command file. The default is .gdbinit.
nx	Tells xxgdb not to execute the .gdbinit file.
bigicon	Uses a large icon size for the xxgdb icon.

When you start xxgdb, a window opens on your screen. This window is shown in Figure 27.1.

FIGURE 27.1.

The xxgdb *main window.*

The xxgdb main window contains a message that is similar to the one displayed on the screen when you start the command-line version of gdb. Near the bottom of the xxgdb main window there are four buttons. The Source Listing, Command Buttons, and Display Window buttons each bring up an additional window when they are activated. The Quit button terminates the xxgdb program.

The Source Listing button brings up a window that will display the source code for the program that is being debugged. This window is shown in Figure 27.2.

FIGURE 27.2.

The xxgdb *source listing window.*

```
#include <stdio.h>

main()
{
        char my_string[] = "hello there";

        my_print(my_string);
        my_print2(my_string);
}

my_print (char *string)
{
        printf("The string is %s\n", string);
}

my_print2 (char *string)
```

The Command Buttons button brings up a window that contains 26 other buttons. These buttons each execute a gdb command. The gdb command-button window is illustrated in Figure 27.3.

The Display Window button brings up a window that is used to display the results of any display command. You can tell xxgdb what variable or expression to display by selecting it from the source listing and then clicking on the Display button in the command-button window. The display window is illustrated in Figure 27.4.

For more information on using xxgdb, refer to the xxgdb manual page and the gdb manual page.

#### Chapter 27

FIGURE 27.3.

The xxgdb *command-button window.*

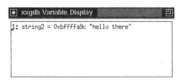

run	cont
next	step
finish	break
tbreak	delete
up	down
print	print *
display	undisplay
show display	args
locals	stack
edit	search
interrupt	file
show brkpts	yes
no	quit

FIGURE 27.4.

The xxgdb *display window.*

> xxgdb Variable Display
>
> 1: string2 = 0xbffffa9c "hello there"

calls

calls is a program that is not included on the Linux CD-ROM accompanying this book, but you can obtain a copy from the sunsite FTP site under the directory /pub/Linux/devel/lang/c/ calls.tar.Z. Some older CD-ROM distributions of Linux include this file. Because it is a useful tool, we will cover it here. If you think it will be of use to you, obtain a copy from an FTP or BBS site or another CD-ROM. calls runs the GCC preprocessor on the files that are passed to it on the command line, and displays a function call tree for the functions that are in those files.

NOTE

To install calls on your system, perform the following steps while you are logged in as root:

1. Uncompress and untar the file.
2. cd into the calls subdirectory that was created by untarring the file.
3. Move the file named calls to the /usr/bin directory.
4. Move the file named calls.1 to the /usr/man/man1 directory.
5. Remove the /tmp/calls directory.

This will install the calls program and man page on your system.

When `calls` prints out the call trace, it includes the filename in which the function was found in brackets after the function name.

```
main [test.c]
```

If the function was not in one of the files that was passed to `calls`, it does not know where that function lives and prints only the function name.

```
printf
```

`calls` also makes note of recursive and static functions in its output. Recursive functions are represented in the following way:

```
fact <<< recursive in factorial.c >>>
```

Static functions are represented as follows:

```
total [static in calculate.c]
```

As an example, assume that you executed calls with the following program as input:

```
##include <stdio.h>

main ()
{
char my_string[] = "hello there";
my_print (my_string);
my_print2(my_string);
}

my_print (char *string)
{
printf ("The string is %s\n", string);
}

my_print2 (char *string)
{
  char *string2;
  int size, size2, i;

  size = strlen (string);
  size2 = size -1;
  string2 = (char *) malloc (size + 1);
  for (i = 0; i < size; i++)
    string2[size2 - i] = string[i];
  string2[size] = '\0';
  printf ("The string printed backward is %s\n", string2);
}
```

This would generate the following output:

```
1 main [test.c]
2        my_print [test.c]
3              printf
4        my_print2 [test.c]
5              strlen
6              malloc
7              printf
```

> **WARNING**
>
> The version of gcc included with this book's CD-ROM may generate error messages
> running this code. Again, you may want to check FTP sites for a more recent version or
> bug fixes, or revert to an older compiler version.

calls recognizes a number of command-line options that enable you to specify the appearance of
the output and what function calls get displayed. For more information on these command-line
options, refer to the calls manual page or type calls -h at the command line.

cproto

cproto is another program that is not included on this Linux CD-ROM but is readily available
from FTP and BBS sites. cproto reads in C source files and automatically generates function prototypes for all of the functions. Using cproto saves you from having to type in a function definition
for all of the functions that you have written in your programs.

> **NOTE**
>
> To install cproto on your system, perform the following steps while you are logged in as
> root:
>
> 1. Uncompress and untar the file.
> 2. cd into the cproto subdirectory that was created by untarring the file.
> 3. Move the file named cproto to the /usr/bin directory.
> 4. Move the file named cproto.1 to the /usr/man/man1 directory.
> 5. Remove the /tmp/cproto directory.
>
> This will install the cproto program and man page on your system.

If you ran the following code through the cproto program

```c
#include  <stdio.h>

main ()
{
  char my_string[] = "hello there";
  my_print (my_string);
  my_print2(my_string);
}

my_print (char *string)
{
  printf ("The string is %s\n", *string);
}

my_print2 (char *string)
```

```
{
  char *string2;
  int size, size2, i;

  size = strlen (string);
  size2 = size -1;
  string2 = (char *) malloc (size + 1);
  for (i = 0; i < size; i++)
    string2[size2 - i] = string[i];
  string2[size] = '\0';
  printf ("The string printed backward is %s\n", string2);
}
```

you would get the following output:

```
/* test.c */
int main(void);
int my_print(char *string);
int my_print2(char *string);
```

WARNING

As with the calls program, discussed earlier, the version of gcc included on this book's CD-ROM may cause errors when compiling this program. You should obtain a bug fix (if one is available) or revert to an earlier version of the compiler to avoid these problems.

This output could be redirected to an include file and used to define the prototypes for all of the functions.

indent

The indent utility is another programming utility that is included with Linux. This program, in its simplest form, reformats or pretty prints your C code so that it is consistently indented and all opening and closing braces are represented consistently. There are numerous options that enable you to specify how you want indent to format your code. For information on these options, refer to the indent manual page or type indent -h at the command line.

The following example shows the default output of the indent program.

C code before running indent:

```
#include  <stdio.h>

main () {
     char my_string[] = "hello there";
  my_print (my_string);
     my_print2(my_string); }

my_print (char *string)
{
  printf    ("The string is %s\n", *string);
}
```

```
my_print2              (char *string) {
    char *string2;
      int size, size2, i;

      size = strlen (string);
      size2 = size -1;
      string2 = (char *) malloc (size + 1);
  for (i = 0; i < size; i++)
            string2[size2 - i] = string[i];
      string2[size] = '\0';
      printf ("The string printed backward is %s\n", string2);
}
```

C code after running indent:

```
#include   <stdio.h>

main ()
{
  char my_string[] = "hello there";
  my_print (my_string);
  my_print2 (my_string);
}

my_print (char *string)
{
  printf ("The string is %s\n", *string);
}

my_print2 (char *string)
{
  char *string2;
  int size, size2, i;

  size = strlen (string);
  size2 = size -1;
  string2 = (char *) malloc (size + 1);
  for (i = 0; i < size; i++)
    string2[size2 - i] = string[i];
  string2[size] = '\0';
  printf ("The string printed backward is %s\n", string2);
}
```

Indent does not change how the code compiles; it just changes how the source code looks. It makes the code more readable, which is always a good thing.

gprof

gprof is a program that is installed in the /usr/bin directory on your Linux system. It allows you to profile programs that you write to determine where most of the execution time is being spent.

gprof will tell you how many times each function that your program uses is called, and also the percentage of the total execution time the program spent in each function. This information can be very useful if you are trying to improve the performance of a program.

To use gprof on one of your programs, you must compile the program using the -pg gcc option. This causes the program to create a file called gmon.out each time it is executed. gprof uses the gmon.out file to generate the profile information.

After you run your program and it has created the gmon.out file, you can get its profile by entering the following command:

```
gprof <program_name>
```

The program_name parameter is the name of the program that created the gmon.out file.

> **TIP**
>
> The profile data that gprof displays to the screen is quite large. If you want to examine this data, you should redirect gprof's output to a file.

f2c and p2c

f2c and p2c are two source code conversion programs. f2c converts FORTRAN code into C code, and p2c converts Pascal code into C code. Both are included in the Linux installation when you install GCC.

If you have some code that has been written using either FORTRAN or Pascal that you want to rewrite in C, f2c and p2c can prove to be very useful programs. Both programs produce C code that can typically be compiled directly by GCC without any human intervention.

If you are converting small, straightforward FORTRAN or Pascal programs, you should be able to get away with using f2c or p2c without any options. If you are converting very large programs consisting of many files, you will probably have to use some of the command-line options that are provided by the conversion program that you are using.

To invoke f2c on a FORTRAN program, enter the following command:

```
f2c my_fortranprog.f
```

> **NOTE**
>
> f2c requires that the program being converted has either a .f or a .F extension.

To convert a Pascal program to C, enter the following command:

```
p2c my_pascalprogram.pas
```

Both of these commands create C source code files that have the same name as the original file, except with a .c extension instead of .f or .pas.

For more information on the specific conversion options that are available with f2c or p2c, refer to their respective man pages.

Summary

This chapter introduced the GNU C compiler and many of the options that you will typically use when you compile C code. It also introduced the concepts behind debugging code with the GNU debugger, and illustrated the usefulness of some of the other C utility programs that are included on the Linux CD-ROM.

TIP

> If you will be writing C code, the time that you spend learning how to use gdb and some of the other tools mentioned in this chapter will be more than worth the eventual time-saving that you will gain.

The next chapter will discuss many of the same topics, but with a focus on C++ development rather than C development.

Programming in C++

28

by
Rick McMullin

IN THIS CHAPTER

Chapter 27, "Programming in C," introduced you to the C programming environment and C programming tools that come with Linux. This chapter describes the same kinds of information for C++. This chapter covers the following topics:

- What C++ is
- Why to use C++
- The GNU C++ compiler
- Debugging C++ applications

In addition to these topics, this chapter also looks at some of the C++ programming tools and class libraries that are included on the Linux CD.

What Is C++?

C++ is an object-oriented extension to the C programming language. It was developed at Bell Labs in the early 1980s and is quickly becoming the language of choice in the computer industry. Dozens of C++ compilers are available on the market today. The most common of these for PC-based systems are Borland C++, Microsoft's Visual C++, Zortech C++, and Watcom C++. These compilers compile MS DOS and MS Windows applications, and some of them compile code to run on OS/2 and Windows NT as well. In addition to the number of C++ compilers that are available on DOS-based machines, a great number are also based on other hardware architectures.

Most UNIX systems have C++ compilers available from the system vendor. Linux also comes with a C++ compiler. This is the GNU C++ compiler. The GNU C++ compiler is very closely related to the GNU C compiler (GCC). In fact, since Release 2.0 of GCC, the GNU C++ compiler has been integrated with GCC. Previous to Release 2.0 of GCC, the GNU C++ compiler was a separate program known as g++. One of the major enhancements in Release 2.0 of GCC was merging these two compilers.

GCC now incorporates a C compiler, a C++ compiler, and an Objective C compiler. You will still find the g++ executable on your system, but it is now a script file that calls GCC with all the standard C++ options.

Why C++?

C++ and object-oriented programming (OOP) did not just happen. There were many fundamental reasons for the shift from structured programming to OOP. In the early days of computer programming, back when PDP-8s still roamed the earth in great numbers, there was a shift from machine language coding to assembler language coding. This was done because the computers of the day were a little more powerful than their predecessors. Programmers wanted to make their lives easier by moving some of the burden of programming onto the computer.

As the years went by and computers got even more powerful, new, higher-level languages started to appear. Examples of these languages are FORTRAN, COBOL, Pascal, and C. With these languages came a programming methodology known as structured programming. Structured programming helped to simplify the systems being designed by enabling programmers to break the problem into small pieces and then implement these pieces as functions or procedures in whatever language was being used.

The structured programming approach worked well for small to medium-sized software applications, but it started to fall apart as systems reached a certain size. OOP tried to solve some of the problems that structured programming was causing. It did this by extending some of the structured programming concepts and by introducing some of its own.

The main concepts that OOP focuses on are the following:

- Data encapsulation
- Inheritance
- Polymorphism

Data Encapsulation

In structured programming, problems often arose where there was a data structure that was common to several different pieces of code. One piece of code could access that data without the other piece of code being aware that anything was happening.

Data encapsulation is a process of grouping common data together, storing it into a data type, and providing a consistent interface to that data. This ensures that no one can access that data without going through the user interface that has been defined for that data.

The biggest benefit that this kind of mechanism provides is that it protects code outside the code that is directly managing this data from being affected if the structure of the data changes. This greatly reduces the complexity of large software systems.

C++ implements data encapsulation through the use of classes.

Inheritance

Inheritance is a form of code reuse in which you can inherit or use the data and behavior of other pieces of code. Inheritance is typically used only when a piece of software logically has many of the same characteristics as another piece of software, such as when one object is a specialization of another object.

Inheritance is implemented in C++ by allowing objects to be subclassed by other objects.

Polymorphism

Polymorphism occurs when a language allows you to define functions that perform different operations on objects depending on their type. The true power of this lies in the fact that you can send a message to a base class and that message can be passed down to each of its subclasses and mean different things to each of them.

Polymorphism is implemented in C++ using virtual functions.

Classes of Objects and Methods

In C++, classes can be thought of as C structures that contain not only the data fields but also operations that can be performed on those data fields. A simple example of this concept is a geometric shape. A geometric shape can be many things, such as a rectangle, a triangle, or a circle. All geometric shapes have certain attributes in common, including area and volume. You could define a structure in C called shape in the following way:

```
struct shape{
        float area;
        float volume;
}
```

If you added some common behavior to this structure, you would have the equivalent of a C++ class. This would be written as follows:

```
class shape {
public:
                float area;
                float volume;
                float calc_area();
                float calc_volume():
};
```

You have now defined a C++ class. The calc_area and calc_volume items are known as methods of the class (instead of functions, as in C). If you were to define a variable that was of type shape as

```
shape circle;
```

you would have created a circle object. An object is an instance of a class, or a variable that is defined to be of the type of a class.

GCC Options

This section describes some of the GCC options that are most commonly used. I will first talk about some of the options that can be used both with C and C++ and then talk about C++ specific options. Any of the compiler options that you use with C you can use with C++ as well, but some of them may not make any sense in the context of a C++ compile. If you specify options that don't make sense, the compiler just ignores them.

> **NOTE**
>
> When you are compiling C++ programs, it is easiest to use the g++ script. This sets all the default C++ options so you don't have to.

A great number of compiler options can be passed to GCC. Many of these options are specific to a certain hardware platform or are for making fine-tuning adjustments to the code that is produced. You will probably never use any of these kinds of options. The options covered in this chapter are those that you will use on a regular basis.

Many of the GCC options consist of more than one character. For this reason, you must specify each option with its own hyphen and not group options after a single hyphen as you can with most Linux commands.

When you compile a program using GCC without any command-line options, it creates an executable file (assuming that the compile was successful) and calls it a.out. For example, the following command would create a file named a.out in the current directory:

```
gcc test.C
```

To specify a name other than a.out for the executable file, you can use the -o compiler option. For example, to compile a C++ program file named count.C (the capital C is used to show C++ code, as opposed to a small c for C code) into an executable file named count, you would type the following command:

```
gcc -o count count.C
```

> **NOTE**
>
> When you are using the -o option, the executable filename must occur directly after the -o on the command line.

Other compiler options allow you to specify how far you want the compile to proceed. The -c option tells GCC to compile the code into object code and skip the assembly and linking stages of the compile. This option is used quite often because it makes the compilation of multifile C++ programs faster and easier to manage. Object code files created by GCC have an .o extension by default.

The -S compiler option tells GCC to stop the compile after it has generated the assembler files for the C code. Assembler files generated by GCC have an .s extension by default. The -E option instructs the compiler to perform only the preprocessing compiler stage on the input files. When this option is used, the output from the preprocessor is sent to the standard output rather than being stored in a file.

Debugging and Profiling Options

GCC supports several debugging and profiling options. Of these options, the two that you are most likely to use for C++ programs are the -gstabs+ option and the -pg option.

The -gstabs+ option tells GCC to produce stabs format debugging information that the GNU debugger (gdb) can use to help you debug your program. For more information on debugging your C++ programs, refer to the "Debugging C++ Applications" section later in this chapter.

The -pg option tells GCC to add extra code to your program that will, when executed, generate profile information that can be used by the gprof program to display timing information about your program. For more information on gprof, refer to the "gprof" section in Chapter 27.

GCC C++ Specific Options

The GCC options that control how a C++ program is compiled are listed in Table 28.1.

Table 28.1. GCC options.

Option	Meaning
-fall-virtual	Treats all possible member functions as virtual. This applies to all functions except for constructor functions and new or deleted member functions.
-fdollars-in-identifiers	Accepts $ in identifiers. You can also prohibit the use of $ in identifiers by using the -fno-dollars-in-identifiers option.
-felide-constructors	Tells the compiler to leave out constructors whenever possible.
-fenum-int-equiv	Permits implicit conversion of int to enumeration types.
-fexternal-templates	Produces smaller code for template declarations. This is done by having the compiler generate only a single copy of each template function where it is defined.
-fmemorize-lookups	Uses heuristics to compile faster. These heuristics are not enabled by default because they are effective only for certain input files.
-fno-strict-prototype	Treats a function declaration with no arguments the same way that C would treat it. This means that the compiler treats a function prototype that has no arguments as a function that will accept an unknown number of arguments.
-fno-null-objects	Assumes that objects reached through references are not null.
-fsave-memorized	Same as -fmemorize-lookups.
-fthis-is-variable	Permits assignment to "this."
-nostdinc++	Does not search for header files in the standard directories specific to C++.
-traditional	This option has the same effect as -fthis-is-variable.
-fno-default-inline	Does not assume that functions defined within a class scope are inline functions.
-wenum-clash	Warns about conversion between different enumeration types.
-woverloaded-virtual	Warns when derived class function declaration may be an error in defining a virtual function. When you define a virtual function in a derived class, it must have the same signature as the function in the base class. This option tells

Option	Meaning
	the compiler to warn you if you have defined a function that has the same name and a different signature as a function that is defined in one of the base classes.
-wtemplate-debugging	If you are using templates, this option warns you if debugging is not yet available.
+eN	Controls how virtual function definitions are used.
-gstabs+	Tells the compiler to generate debugging information in stabs format, using GNU extensions understood only by the GNU debugger. The extra information produced by this option is necessary to ensure that gdb handles C++ programs properly.

Debugging C++ Applications

A very important part of developing C++ programs is being able to debug them efficiently. The GNU debug application that was introduced in Chapter 27 can also be used to debug C++ applications. This section describes some of the differences between debugging C applications and debugging C++ applications.

The basic gdb commands that were introduced in Chapter 27 are listed again for your convenience in Table 28.2.

Table 28.2. Basic gdb commands.

Command	Description
file	Loads the executable file that is to be debugged.
kill	Terminates the program you are currently debugging.
list	Lists sections of the source code used to generate the executable file.
next	Advances one line of source code in the current function, without stepping into other functions.
step	Advances one line of source code in the current function, and does step into other functions.
run	Executes the program that is currently being debugged.
quit	Terminates gdb.
watch	Enables you to examine the value of a program variable whenever the value changes.

continues

Table 28.2. continued

Command	Description
break	Sets a breakpoint in the code; this causes the execution of the program to be suspended whenever this point is reached.
make	This command enables you to remake the executable program without quitting gdb or using another window.
shell	Enables you to execute UNIX shell commands without leaving gdb.

From the programmer's perspective, you have more details to be aware of when debugging C++ code than when you are debugging C code. This is because of the C++ features such as virtual functions and exception handling. gdb has added features to support debugging both of these C++ specific features.

Debugging Virtual Functions

As described in the "Polymorphism" section of this chapter, virtual functions are C++'s way of implementing polymorphism. This means that there may be more than one function in a program with the same name. The only way to tell these functions apart is by their signatures. The signature of a function is composed of the types of all the arguments to the function. For example, a function with the prototype

```
void func(int, real);
```

has a signature of int, real.

You can see how this could cause the gdb a few problems. For example, if you had defined a class that had a virtual function called calculate, and two objects with different definitions for this function were created, how would you set a breakpoint to trigger on this function? You set breakpoints in C by specifying the function name as an argument to the gdb break command, as follows:

```
(gdb) break calculate
```

This does not work in the case of a virtual function because the debugger would not be able to tell which calculate you wanted the breakpoint to be set on. gdb was extended in a few ways so that it could handle virtual functions. The first way to solve the problem is to enter the function name by specifying its prototype as well. This would be done in the following way:

```
break 'calculate (float)'
```

This would give gdb enough information to determine which function the breakpoint was meant for. A second solution that gdb supports is using a breakpoint menu. Breakpoint menus allow you to specify the function name of a function. If there is more than one function definition for that function, it gives you a menu of choices. The first choice in the menu is to abort the break command. The second choice is to set a breakpoint on all the functions that the break command matches.

Strings

The GNU string class exte
tially replaces the characte
along with the character a

The string class adds UNI
ber of additional operator
class.

Table 28.4. String cla

Operator
str1 == str2
str1 != str2
str1 < str2
str1 <= str2
str1 > str2
str1 >= str2
compare(str1,str2)
str3 = str1 + str2

A number of other operat
comparisons, concatenati

Random Numbe

Classes are provided in th
of random numbers. The
class.

Data Collection

The class library provide:
The two classes are Samp.
a way of collecting sampl
lations on the collected
standard deviation, mini

The SampleHistogram cl
and display of samples ir

The remaining choices correspond to each function that matches the break command. The following code shows an example of a breakpoint menu:

```
 (gdb) break shape::calculate
[0] cancel
[1] all
[2] file: shapes.C: line number: 153
[3] file: shapes.C: line number: 207
[4] file: shapes.C: line number: 247
> 2 3
Breakpoint 1 at 0xb234: file shapes.C, line 153
Breakpoint 2 at 0xa435: file shapes.C, line 207
Multiple breakpoints were set
Use the "delete" command to delete unwanted breakpoints
(gdb)
```

Debugging Exception Handlers

Exceptions are errors that occur within your program. Exception handlers are pieces of code that are written to handle errors and potential errors. For example, if you were writing a C program and calling the malloc function to get a block of memory, you would typically check malloc's return code to make sure the memory allocation was successful. If C supported exception handling, you could specify a function that would receive or catch exceptions, and the malloc function would send or throw an exception to your function if one occurred.

The gdb added two new commands to support C++ exception handling: the catch command and the catch info command. The catch command is used to set a breakpoint in active exception handlers. The syntax of this command is as follows:

```
catch exceptions
```

exceptions is a list of the exceptions to catch.

The catch info command is used to display all the active exception handlers.

Summary of *gdb* C++ Specific Commands

In addition to the gdb commands that have been added to support some of the new language features contained in C++, there are also some new set and show options. These options are listed in Table 28.3.

Table 28.3. gdb's C++ set and show options.

Command	Description
set print demangle	Prints C++ names in their source form rather than in the encoded or mangled form that is passed to the assembler.
show print demangle	Shows whether print demangle is on or off.

continues

Table 28.3. contir

Command
set demangle-st
show demangle-s
set print objec
show print obje
set print vtbl
show print vtb:

GNU C++

GNU C++ comes p
that can be used to
class libraries that h
gramming, and clas

Examples of graphi
Borland's Object W
Windows applicatic

This section introd

Streams

The GNU iostrean
cilities. This library
main parts of the io
standard input, out
respectively. The st
>> operator for inp

The following prog

```
#include <iostre
int maim ()
{
        char nam
        cout <<
        cin >> n
        cout <<
}
```

Table 28.10. continued

Operator	Description
i = s.seek(z)	Sets i to the index of z if z is in s, and 0 otherwise
set1 == set2	Returns TRUE if set1 contains all the same elements as set2
set1 != set2	Returns TRUE if set1 does not contain all the same elements as set2
set1 <= set2	Returns TRUE if set1 is a subset of set2
set1 ¦= set2	Adds all elements of set2 to set1
set1 -= set2	Deletes all the elements that are contained in set2 from set1
set1 &= set2	Deletes all elements from set1 that occur in set1 and not in set2

The class library contains another class that is similar to sets. This class is known as the bag. A bag is a group of elements that can be in any order (just as is the case with sets) but in which there can also be duplicates. Bags use all the operators that sets use except for the ==, !=, ¦=, <=, ¦=, -=, and &= operators. In addition, bags add two new operators for dealing with elements that are in the bag more than once. These new operators are shown in Table 28.11.

Table 28.11. Additional operators for bags.

Operator	Description
b.remove(z)	Deletes all occurrences of z from b
b.nof(z)	Returns the number of occurrences of z that are in b

Many other classes available in the GNU C++ class library provide functions other than those listed here. In addition to what comes with the compiler, many other freely available class libraries can be useful as well.

Summary

C++ offers many advantages over C. Some of these advantages come from the concepts of object-oriented programming, and others come from the highly flexible class libraries that are available to C++ programmers. This chapter gave a brief introduction to object-oriented programming and also talked about the C++ features that exist in the GNU C compiler and the GNU debugger.

One problem that has existed with C++ for quite some time is the lack of freely available C++ development tools. You may notice that the number of free tools available for C++ programming is much smaller than the number available for C, but the tide is turning. As more and more people choose C++ over C, the number of tools and class libraries available keeps increasing. The tool support has reached the stage where learning C++ in the Linux environment is something that you can enjoy rather than avoid.

Perl

29

by
Rick McMullin

Perl, which stands for Practical Extraction and Report Language, is an interpreted programming language that was developed by Larry Wall. Perl was initially designed to make scanning and manipulating text files easier than it is in languages such as awk. This chapter includes the following topics:

- What Perl is
- Creating and executing Perl programs
- Data, variables, and arrays
- Perl programming constructs
- Perl functions

After reading this chapter, you should be familiar with some of the advantages that Perl offers over other programming languages. You should also be able to write simple Perl programs to help you in your day-to-day interactions with Linux.

What Is Perl?

As stated, Perl was originally created to make scanning and manipulating text files easier. People who are familiar with the awk programming language (refer to Chapter 26, "gawk") will not be surprised to learn that Perl borrowed many of its features from awk. Perl also includes some of the best features of C, sed, and the UNIX shell languages such as bash and tcsh.

Perl is very similar to the shell programming languages both in syntax and in function. There are, however, a few differences worth mentioning. One of the biggest differences between how Perl works and how shell programs work is that Perl is not purely an interpreted language. Perl programs are actually read in full and stored in an intermediate form before they are executed. Shell programs are read and executed one command at a time. This offers two advantages for Perl over shell programs. First, Perl programs execute much faster than shell programs. This is because the Perl interpreter does all the syntax checking and stripping of comments before the code execution is started. Second, you don't have to worry about a large shell program stopping halfway through its execution as a result of a syntax error, because all the code is parsed before it starts executing.

The fact that Perl is not a pure interpreted language also has one disadvantage. For small programs whose execution time is not that large, the extra compile time involved in using Perl actually makes it slower than using a shell language. This is a relatively small problem and one that few people actually notice.

Creating and Executing Perl Programs

The steps you take to create and execute a Perl program are very similar to those used in creating and executing a Linux shell program. Perl programs consist of one or more Perl commands that are placed into a text file. The first thing you must do to create a Perl program is create a file in which to put Perl commands. You can do this using your text editor of choice. I will start by showing a very simple example of a Perl program. The following Perl program, called `hello`, prints a greeting on the screen.

```
#!/usr/bin/perl
print "Hi there!\n";
```

There are several things worth mentioning about this example. The first is the strange-looking first line of the program. This line tells the shell program what program to run to execute the code contained in the file.

The second line of the program prints `Hi there!`, followed by a new line on the screen. C programmers will notice how much this line looks like C code.

You have one more step to take before the program will actually work. This is to change the permissions on the file so that it is executable. This is done by entering the following command:

```
chmod +x hello
```

You can now run the program by typing the following on the command line:

```
hello
```

Running this program causes the Perl interpreter to be invoked. The Perl interpreter parses the whole program and then executes the compiled code.

This is the standard way of running a Perl program. You could also run the `hello` program by invoking Perl on the command line and passing the `hello` code to it as a command-line parameter. This is done by typing the following command:

```
perl hello
```

Handling Data in Perl

At the simplest level, Perl deals with two different kinds of data: numbers and strings. This section describes how Perl handles these two forms of data and also how each can be used in Perl programs. I will start things off with a description of how variables are used in Perl programs.

Variables

Variables in Perl are similar in function and syntax to variables found in the shell programming languages. The biggest difference is that in the shell languages you get the value of a variable by preceding it with a dollar sign, and you assign a value to a variable by using the variable name without a dollar sign in front of it.

In Perl you always use a dollar sign in front of the variable name no matter whether you are assigning a value to the variable or getting the value of the variable. The following command assigns the value `hello` to the variable named `greeting`.

```
$greeting="hello";
```

In the shell languages this command would be written as follows:

```
greeting="hello"
or set greeting = "hello" (when using tcsh)
```

Another difference is that you can perform integer operations on a variable directly without using another command like `expr`. For example the command

```
$a = 1 + 2;
```

would assign the value of 3 to the variable $a. If you entered the following two commands

```
$a = 1 + 2;
$b = 3 * $a;
```

the $b variable would be assigned a value of 9.

This is the expected result, but how does Perl know that $a is a numeric value and not a string? The answer is that it does not know. Whenever a variable or literal is used as an argument to a numeric operator, it is converted to a number. In this case there is no problem because the value stored in $a is a number. There would be a problem if the value stored in $a had been a string that contained a character such as b, because this type of string could not be converted to a numeric value. Perl handles this situation in a not so elegant way. If the value is not convertible to a number, it just makes it equal to 0. By default, Perl does not even warn you about this conversion.

> **TIP**
>
> If you invoke Perl with a -w command-line option, it warns you when this type of conversion takes place.

Numbers

Perl stores all numeric data as floating-point values. You can use integers in your Perl programs, but Perl treats them all as floating-point numbers.

Perl provides a set of operators that can be used to perform comparisons between two numeric values and for performing the standard mathematical operations on numbers. Table 29.1 lists some of the operators that Perl provides for numeric data.

Table 29.1. Numeric operators.

Operator	Description
$a = op1 + op2	Stores the value of op1 plus op2 into $a
$a = op1 - op2	Stores the value of op1 minus op2 into $a
$a = op1 * op2	Stores the value of op1 times op2 into $a
$a = op1 / op2	Stores the value of op1 divided by op2 into $a

Operator	Description
$a = op1 ** op2	Stores the value of op1 to the power of op2 into $a
$a = op1 % op2	Stores the value of op1 modulus op2 into $a
op1 == op2	Returns True if op1 is equal to op2
op1 != op2	Returns True if op1 is not equal to op2
op1 < op2	Returns True if op1 is less than op2
op1 > op2	Returns True if op1 is greater than op2
op1 <= op2	Returns True if op1 is less than or equal to op2
op1 >= op2	Returns True if op1 is greater than or equal to op2

Strings

Strings are sequences of one or more characters. Usually strings contain alphanumeric characters, such as the numbers from 0 to 9, the upper- and lowercase alphabet, and a handful of punctuation characters. Perl does not distinguish between these characters and nonprintable characters. This means that you can actually use Perl to scan binary files.

Strings are represented in a Perl program in one of two ways: you can enclose a string in double quotations marks, or you can enclose a string in single quotation marks. When a string is enclosed in double quotation marks, it behaves in a similar way to strings that are in double quotation marks in C. A backslash can be used in a double quoted string to represent special control characters. A list of the backslash special control characters is shown in Table 29.2.

Table 29.2. Perl's special control characters.

Character	Description
\a	Causes an audible beep
\b	Inserts a backspace
\cD	Allows you to put control characters in a string (in this case Ctrl-D)
\f	Inserts a formfeed
\e	Inserts an escape character
\E	Terminates a \L or \U special control character
\l	Causes the next letter to be lowercase
\L	Causes all characters following it to be lowercase until the next \E
\n	Inserts a newline character
\r	Inserts a return character

continues

Table 29.2. continued

Character	Description
\t	Inserts a tab character
\\	Inserts a backslash character
\"	Inserts a double quote character
\u	Causes the next letter to be uppercase
\U	Causes all characters following it to be uppercase until the next \E

Variable substitution can occur within a string that is enclosed in double quotation marks as well. For example, if you defined a variable as

```
$name="Doreen";
```

that variable could be substituted into a greeting displayed on the screen by typing the following Perl command:

```
print "Hello $name, how are you?\n";
```

This command would result in the following output being displayed on the screen:

```
Hello Doreen, how are you?
```

Strings enclosed in single quotation marks differ from strings enclosed in double quotation marks because the single quotation marks hide most special characters from the Perl interpreter. The only special characters that single quotes do not hide completely are the single quote character (') and the backslash character (\). When Perl encounters a single quote character within a string that is enclosed in single quotation marks, it assumes that it is the end of the string. This means that if you want to put a single quote in a string that is enclosed in single quotes, you must precede it with a backslash. The same rule applies if you want to put a backslash into a string enclosed in single quotes.

For example, if you wanted to print the string Don't do that! to the screen by enclosing it in single quotes, you would enter the following command:

```
print 'Don\'t do that!',"\n";
```

> **NOTE**
>
> Remember that if you put a newline character into a single quoted string, it just prints \n and doesn't insert a newline character.

Just as is the case with numbers, Perl provides several operators that can be used to manipulate and compare strings. Table 29.3 lists Perl's string operators.

Table 29.3. Perl's string operators.

Operator	Description
op1 . op2	Concatenates op1 and op2
op1 x op2	Repeats op1, op2 times
op1 eq op2	Returns True if op1 equals op2
op1 ge op2	Returns True if op1 is greater than or equal to op2
op1 gt op2	Returns True if op1 is greater than op2
op1 le op2	Returns True if op1 is less than or equal to op2
op1 lt op2	Returns True if op1 is less than op2
op1 ne op2	Returns True if op1 is not equal to op2

File Operators

Just like the shell programming languages, Perl has a number of operators that exist only to test for certain conditions that exist with directories and files. The most useful of these operators are listed in Table 29.4.

Table 29.4. Perl file operators.

Operator	Description
-B	File is a binary file
-d	File is a directory
-e	File exists
-f	File is an ordinary file
-r	File is readable
-s	File has a non-zero size
-T	File is a text file
-w	File is writeable
-x	File is executable
-z	File has zero size

These file operators can be used in any Perl expression. For example, the following code uses an `if` statement to decide if the `.profile` file exists in the current directory.

```
if (-e ".profile") {
        print ".profile is there\n";
}
```

Perl `if` statements are discussed in the "Perl Programming Constructs" section of this chapter.

Arrays

An array is an indexed list of data elements. Perl provides two different kinds of arrays. The first kind of array is similar to the arrays that are available in most high-level languages. This kind of array stores single data elements (numbers or strings) into a variable that can store any number of elements. You can get at the elements you store in this variable by using the offset value of the element you are trying to find. This means that you can assign a number or a string value to an offset in an array and later use that offset to retrieve that value. For example, the following Perl statement assigns the strings January, 1st, 1995 to the array named `date`.

```
@date = ("January", "1st", "1995");
```

Actually, the number of elements you can have in the array is limited by the amount of memory you have on your system.

If you later want to retrieve one of the values you have placed into the `date` array, you can do so by stating the array name and the offset of the element you want. When you are retrieving the value of an array element, you must precede the name of the array with a `$` instead of the `@` that you used to define the array. This is because you are now referring to a single array element, which is really the same as a regular variable. For example, to assign the value of January, which is the first element in the array, to a variable called `month`, you would write the following command:

```
$month=$date[0];
```

Perl starts its array indexes at offset 0. This means that an array of length 5 would have the elements [0], [1], [2], [3], and [4].

The second kind of array that is available in Perl is called an associative array. Associative arrays are like normal arrays—they store data elements and have an index. Unlike normal arrays, the index or key is defined by the user and can be a number or a string.

Because you can define the key values for associative arrays as well as the data associated with each of these key values, assigning and accessing data from an associative array is somewhat different than it is with normal arrays. To assign a value to an associative array, you must also provide the key that you want that value to be associated with. Just as with normal arrays, associative arrays have a special symbol that is used whenever you are performing operations on the entire associative array. You usually assign variables only to elements of an associative array, as opposed to dealing with the entire array all at once. The following command assigns the value `hello` to the associative array named `words`, with a key value of `greeting`:

```
$words{"greeting"} = "hello";
```

An operation that applies to the entire associative array would look like the following:

```
%words2 = %words;
```

This command would assign the entire contents of the `words` associative array to the `words2` associative array.

To retrieve a value from the `words` associative array, you would use the following command:

```
$value=$words{"greeting"};
```

This would assign the string `hello` to the `value` variable.

In addition to the assignment operations that could be performed on normal arrays, associative arrays have four more operations: `keys`, `values`, `delete`, and `each`.

The `keys` operator returns a list of all the keys that have been defined in the specified associative array. The following commands would result in `keyarray` being equal to `("greeting", "greeting2")`.

```
$words("greeting") = "hello";
$words("greeting2") = "good-bye";
@keyarray = keys(%words);
```

The first two commands assign values to individual elements in the associative array `words`. The first command assigns `hello` with a key value of `greeting` to the array, and the second command assigns `good-bye` with a key value of `greeting2` to the array.

The last command assigns all the key values contained in the `words` associative array to the normal array called `keyarray`. Notice the `%` in front of the `words` variable in the `keys` operator. This means that the operation being performed applies to the entire associative array and not just one element of the array.

NOTE

The value of `keyarray` that is returned by the preceding commands could actually be `("greeting2", "greeting")`, because values in associative arrays are not stored in any particular order.

foreach Statements

Another iteration statement available in Perl is the foreach statement. This statement is very similar to the for statement in the bash and pdksh languages and the foreach statement in the tcsh language. It executes its statement block for each element in the list that is specified as its second argument. The syntax for the foreach statement is

```
foreach $i (@list) {
     statements;
}
```

The @list variable can be passed to the foreach statement either as a variable or as a list of elements that you type directly as the second argument to the foreach statement. The following is an example of the foreach statement:

```
@myarray = (5,10,15,20,25);
foreach $i (@myarray) {
        print $i * 3, " ";
}
print "\n";
```

This program iterates through each element in @myarray and prints the result of three times that array element on the screen. The output generated by running this program is as follows:

```
15 30 45 60 75
```

Another interesting use of the foreach statement is to use it to change all the values in an array. This can be done by assigning a value to the variable that is being used by the foreach statement. For example, the following code multiplies each array element in the array by three and actually stores the result of this back into the array.

```
@myarray = (5,10,15,20,25);
foreach $i (@myarray) {
        $i = $i * 3;
}
```

After this code executes, @myarray is equal to (15,30,45,60,75).

while Statements

The while statement is another form of iteration statement that Perl provides. The while statement executes its statement block while a conditional expression is True. The syntax for the while statement is

```
while (expression) {
        statements;
}
```

When the while statement is executed, it evaluates its expression. If the result is True, the statements that are contained in the statement block are executed. If the result of the expression is False, Perl goes to the first line after the while statement's statement block and continues there. Here is an example of the while statement:

```
$i = 0;
@temparray = (1,2,3,4,5,6,7);
while ($temparray[$i]) {
        print $temparray[$i];
        $i = $i + 1;
}
```

This example simply prints each of the array elements that are contained in @temparray to the screen. Notice that you do not need to know how many elements are in the array. The while statement continues executing until the value of $temparray[$i] is undefined, which occurs when it tries to access an element that is outside the bounds of the array.

until Statements

The until statement is very similar to the while statement. The only difference is that the until statement executes its statement block until its conditional expression becomes True, and the while statement executes its statement block while its conditional expression is True. The following program contains an example of the until statement:

```
$i = 0;
until ($i > 10) {
        print "$i ";
        $i = $i + 1;
}
```

This statement continues to execute and print the value of $i until $i is larger than 10. The output from this command is

```
0 1 2 3 4 5 6 7 8 9 10
```

Any until statement can also be written as a while statement. For this reason, the until statement is not used very often. The example shown for the until statement can be rewritten as a while statement, as shown by the following code:

```
$i = 0;
while ($i <= 10 ) {
        print "$i ";
        $i = $i + 1;
}
```

Functions

You have already seen some of the built-in Perl functions, such as print, but you have not seen how to create your own functions. Perl refers to functions that you create as subroutines. The syntax for creating a subroutine is

```
sub subroutine_name {
        statements;
}
```

The subroutine_name is a name you provide and is the name you use when calling the subroutine from your Perl code. The statements in the statement block are the statements that are executed every time you make a call to your subroutine.

To run the s2p program, enter the following command:

```
s2p sed_program >perl_program
```

sed_program is the name of the sed program you want to convert to Perl, and perl_program is the name you want to give to your new Perl program.

Summary

This chapter introduced what is arguably the most powerful language available on Linux. Perl is a vast language. It contains operators that provide you with almost any function you could possibly want to perform in the Linux environment. The size of the language makes becoming an expert Perl programmer difficult, but at the same time it isn't that hard to learn to use Perl for simpler tasks.

Although this chapter presented a fairly complete overview of the Perl language, it barely scratched the surface of the features that are available in Perl. If you want to learn more about Perl, refer to the Perl man page.

Introduction to Tcl and Tk

30

by
Rick McMullin

IN THIS CHAPTER

This chapter introduces the Tcl programming language and its most popular extension, Tk. This chapter covers the following topics:

- What Tcl is
- What Tk is
- The Tcl language
- The Tk language extensions

By the end of this chapter, you should understand what Tcl and Tk are, and also how to write simple applications using Tcl and Tk.

What Is Tcl?

Tcl stands for Tool Command Language. (It is pronounced "tickle.") It is a scripting language similar to the shell scripting languages introduced in Chapter 13, "Shell Programming." Tcl can be used to quickly write text-based application programs.

Tcl was developed by John Ousterhout, then of the University of California at Berkeley. Tcl is an interpreted language and therefore has the usual advantages and disadvantages of all interpreted languages. The key disadvantage of interpreted languages is that they execute much slower than compiled languages. The biggest advantage of interpreted languages is that developing applications using them is usually much faster than using compiled languages. This is because you don't have to wait for code to compile and can see any changes you make to the code almost instantly.

Tcl has a core set of built-in functions that provide the basic features of its programming language. The true power of Tcl, however, is that it is easily extendible. Application programmers can add functions to Tcl and can even imbed the Tcl function library directly into their applications. This gives programmers the power to include an interpretive scripting language directly in their own application without having to do any of the work of developing the language. This means that you can provide users of your application with all the commands that exist within Tcl and also any that you create and add to the Tcl library.

Invoking Tcl commands is done by starting up the Tcl shell, called `tclsh` (or on some systems, `tcl`). Once you have started `tclsh`, you can type Tcl commands directly into it. Straying slightly from the "hello world" example that you find in almost every introductory language text, the following example shows you how to write `Hello there` instead to the screen:

```
puts stdout "Hello there"
```

This command contains three separate words. The first word in the command is the actual command name, `puts`. The `puts` command is an abbreviation for put string; it simply writes something to the device that is specified in the second word of the command. In this case the second word tells `puts` to write to the standard output device, which is typically the screen. The third word in the `puts` command is `"Hello there"`. The quotation marks tell Tcl to interpret everything contained within them as a single word.

> **NOTE**
>
> The default output device is `stdout` (standard output, usually the screen), so if you intend to write something to `stdout` using the `puts` command, the second argument is optional.

Even though this is a very simple example, it illustrates the basic command syntax of the Tcl language. There are obviously many more commands contained within Tcl, but the basic syntax of all Tcl commands is the same:

```
command parameter1 parameter2 ...
```

The command can be any of the built-in Tcl commands, or it can be a user-defined extension to the Tcl command set in the form of a Tcl procedure. In either case, the fundamental syntax remains unchanged.

What Is Tk?

Tk, which was also developed by Ousterhout, is a graphical user interface extension to Tcl. Tk is based on the X Window system and allows application developers to develop X Window-based applications much faster than they could using other X Window toolkits, such as Motif or OPEN LOOK.

Like Tcl, Tk also has a shell that enables you to enter commands to be interpreted. The Tk shell is a superset of the Tcl command shell. This means that anything you can do in the Tcl command shell you can also do in the Tk command shell. The big difference between the two is that the Tk command shell was designed to enable you to build X Window front ends to your applications.

The Tk command shell is called `wish`, which stands for windowing shell. You must be running X Window when you invoke `wish`. This is because when `wish` is invoked, it brings up a window to display the results of any of the graphical commands it interprets. When you invoke `wish`, a window should appear on your screen.

Now that you have seen what the Tk environment looks like, let's try enhancing the earlier "Hello there" example by displaying `Hello there` in a button in the `wish` window. To accomplish this, you must first ensure that `wish` has been started. This is easily done by typing the following command into an Xterm window:

```
wish
```

This command brings up the `wish` window and also executes the Tk interpreter in the Xterm window. You can now type Tcl or Tk commands directly in the Xterm window. The commands necessary to print `Hello there` in a button in the `wish` window are as follows:

```
button .b -text "Hello there." -command exit
pack .b
```

Notice how the syntax of the command on the first line is essentially the same as the syntax of the puts command. It contains the command name followed by a number of arguments. The first argument is the name you are giving to the new button. The rest of the arguments passed to the button command are slightly different from the arguments you saw in the Tcl version of the "Hello there" example. These arguments each consist of two parts. The first part tells Tk what the argument name is, and the second part tells Tk the value of the argument.

The second argument has the name text, and the value of the argument is the string you want to display in the button. The third argument has the name command and is used to specify the command that you want to execute when that button is pushed. In this example, you do not really want anything to happen if the button is pushed, so you just tell wish to exit from the current script.

The button command created a button widget that you called .b. To get the button to show up in the wish window, you must tell Tk to display the button. This is done by the pack command.

In this example, the pack command has only one argument: the name of the button that you created in the first command. When the pack command is executed, a button with the string Hello there displayed in it appears in the wish window.

Two things about this example are worth discussing in more detail. The first is why you called the button .b instead of b, bob, or button1. The significance is not the actual text in the button name (this in fact could be bob or button1), but the period (.) preceding the name of the button.

The period notation is used to represent the widget hierarchy. Each widget is contained in another widget. The root widget, or the highest level widget, is contained in the wish window and is called . (this is analogous to the Linux directory structure, in which each directory has an owner or a parent directory and the root or highest level directory is named /). Each time you create a new widget, you must tell Tk which widget the new widget should be contained in. In the "Hello there" example, the container specified for the button widget was ., the root widget.

The second item of interest is the resizing of the wish window that occurs after you enter the pack command. The wish window shrinks down to a size that is just large enough to hold the button you created. Tk causes the wish window to default to a size just large enough to hold whatever it has in it. Many commands can be used to change this behavior and customize how things are displayed on the screen. You will see some of these commands later in this chapter.

The Tcl Language

Now that you have seen examples of both Tcl and Tk in action, it is appropriate to take a step back and look at the underlying Tcl language in more detail. Tcl contains a rich set of programming commands that support all the features found in most high-level languages. This section discusses many of these features and gives examples that explain how to use them.

Tcl Variables and Variable Substitution

Like the UNIX shell programming languages, Tcl supports the concept of variables. Variables are temporary storage places used to hold information that will be needed by a program at some later point in time. In Tcl, variable names can consist of any combination of printable characters.

Typically, variable names are meaningful names that describe the information being stored in them. For example, a variable that is being used to hold the monthly sales of a product might have one of the following names:

```
Monthly_sales
"Monthly sales"
```

> **NOTE**
>
> Quotation marks cause Tcl to ignore the whitespace characters (spaces and tabs) in the variable name and treat it as one word. This is discussed in the "Quotes" section of this chapter.

The value that is placed into a variable can also be any combination of printable characters. Possible values for the `Monthly_sales` variable are

```
"40,000"
40000
"refer to table 3"
```

The Tcl `set` command is used to assign values to variables. The `set` command can pass either one or two arguments. When two arguments are passed to the `set` command, the first one is treated as the variable name and the second is the value to assign to that variable.

When the `set` command is used with only one argument, Tcl expects the argument to be the name of a variable, and the `set` command returns the value of that variable. The following command assigns the value of 40000 to the variable `Monthlysales` and then echoes the value to the screen:

```
set Monthlysales 40000
```

To print the value of the `Monthlysales` variable to the screen, you would type

```
set Monthlysales
```

All values that are assigned to variables are stored as character strings. If you defined a variable to be equal to the integer 40, as in the following command

```
set num 40
```

the value 40 would be represented as the character string `40`, not as an integer.

So far you have seen how to set variables and how to display their values to the screen, but you have not seen how they are used with commands other than the `set` command. To use the value of a variable in another command, you must precede the variable name with an unquoted dollar sign ($). This tells Tcl to expect a variable name and to substitute the value of that variable for the variable name. The following example shows a simple use of variable substitution:

```
set Monthlysales 40000
expr $Monthlysales * 12
```

The first command assigns the value of 40000 to the variable `Monthlysales`. The `expr` command is used to perform mathematical evaluations of expressions. In this case it takes the value of the variable `Monthlysales` and multiplies it by 12.

Tcl Command Substitution

Command substitution provides a way of substituting the result of a Tcl command (or commands) into an argument of another command. The syntax for command substitution is to include the commands that are being substituted in square brackets, as follows:

```
set Monthlysales 40000
set Yearlyforecast [ expr Monthlysales * 12 ]
```

The first command once again sets the variable `Monthlysales` to the value of 40000. The second command makes use of command substitution to set the value of `Yearlyforecast` equal to the result of the command in the square braces.

In this example the substitute consisted of only one command. Tcl allows the substitute to consist of any valid Tcl script, meaning that it can contain any number of Tcl commands.

Quotes

Often you want to use commands containing special characters that you don't want Tcl to interpret. By quoting these characters, you hide the special characters from the Tcl interpreter.

Three kinds of quoting can be used in Tcl scripts. The first is quoting with double quotation marks (""). This kind of quoting is used to hide whitespace characters and command separators from the Tcl interpreter.

Whenever you have two or more words that you want Tcl to treat as a single word, you can do so by surrounding the words with quotation marks. A good example of this type of quoting is when you want to create variable names that contain more than one word, or you want to assign a value that contains more than one word to a variable, as follows:

```
set "Monthly sales" 40000

set Heading1 "Description of item"
```

The second kind of quoting uses the backslash character (\). This type of quoting can hide any single character from the interpreter. This form of quoting is most commonly used to hide special characters, such as $, from the Tcl interpreter. The following example illustrates the need for backslash quoting:

```
set Header1 "The cost is \$3.50"
```

In this example the Header1 variable is being assigned the value The cost is $3.50. The quotation marks are necessary to hide the fact that there are four separate words contained in the character string. The backslash in this command tells the Tcl interpreter to treat the $ as a regular character instead of the variable substitution character. If the backslash was not used in the command, the interpreter would attempt to substitute the variable named 3.50 into the command. This would result in an error, because there is no variable with that name defined.

The third type of quoting available in Tcl uses curly braces ({}). This quoting is more powerful than quoting using quotation marks or backslashes. Quoting using braces hides not only whitespace and command separators from the Tcl interpreter but also any other kind of special character. This type of quoting can be used to eliminate the need for backslash quoting in character strings. The example used for backslash quoting could be written using brace quotation as follows:

```
set Header1 {The cost is $3.50}
```

The most important use of curly brace quoting is to defer the evaluation of special characters. This means that special characters are not processed immediately by the Tcl interpreter but are instead passed to a command that processes the special characters on its own. An example of when deferred evaluation is used is in the while command:

```
set count 0
while {$count < 3} {
        puts "count equals $count"
        set count [expr $count + 1]
}
```

The while command has to evaluate both of its arguments each time it iterates through the loop. It is therefore necessary for the interpreter to ignore the special characters in both of these arguments and leave the evaluation of these characters up to the while command.

Now that you have all the language basics out of the way, you can move on to some of the more advanced Tcl commands.

The *if* Command

The if command, just like in other languages, evaluates an expression and, based on the results of the expression, executes a set of commands. The syntax of the if command is the following:

```
if {expr} {commands}
```

The if command expects two arguments. The first argument is an expression that is used to determine whether to execute the commands contained in the second argument. The expression argument is typically an expression that evaluates to either True or False. For example:

```
$i < 10
$num = 2
```

Expressions such as the following, although valid, do not make much sense in the context of an `if` command:

```
$i + $b
10 * 3
```

The second argument to the `if` command is a Tcl script, which can contain any number of Tcl commands. This script is executed if the expression contained in the first argument evaluates to True.

The `if` commands can have one or more `elseif` commands and one `else` command associated with them. The syntax for these commands is shown here:

```
if {expr} {
     commands }
elseif {expr} {
     commands }
elseif {expr} {
     commands }
else {
     commands }
```

The commands associated with the first `if` or `elseif` whose expression evaluates to True are executed. If none of these expressions evaluate to True, the commands associated with the `else` command are executed.

The *for* Command

The `for` command in Tcl provides a way of implementing `for` loops. Tcl `for` loops are very similar to `for` loops in other languages, such as C. The `for` command expects four arguments. The first argument is a script that is used to initialize the counter. The second argument is an expression that is evaluated each time through the loop to determine whether to continue. The third argument is used to define the increment to be used on the counter. The fourth argument is the set of commands to be executed each time through the loop.

```
for { set i 0} {$i < 10} {incr I 1} {
     puts [expr 2 * $i]
}
```

The preceding loop executes ten times. The counter i is initially set to 0. The for loop executes while i is less than 10, and the value of i is increased by 1 each time through the loop. The command that is executed each time through the loop is the puts command. This evaluates 2 × i each time through the loop and prints the result to the screen. The output that results from running this command is listed here:

```
0
2
4
6
8
10
12
14
16
18
```

The *while* Command

The while command is used to implement while loops in Tcl. while loops are very similar to for loops. The only real difference between them is that the for loop provides more enhanced features for controlling entrance and exit criteria for the loop. The syntax for the while loop is shown in the following example:

```
set I 0
while {$i < 10} {
     puts [expr 2 * $i]
     set i [expr $i + 1]
}
```

This while loop performs the same function as the example that was presented in the section describing the for loop. It calculates 2 × i each time through the loop and prints the result to the screen. Notice that in this example you have to handle incrementing the counter yourself. With the for loop, the counter incrementing was taken care of by the for command.

The *switch* Command

The switch command provides the same function as an if statement that has multiple elseif clauses associated with it. The switch command compares a value (this value is usually stored in a variable) with any number of patterns, and if it finds a match it executes the Tcl code associated with the matching pattern.

```
switch $thing {
     car {puts "thing is a car"}
     truck {puts "thing is a truck"}
     default {puts "I don't know what this thing is"}
}
```

> **NOTE**
>
> The Tcl `switch` command is equivalent to the `case` statement found in Pascal and some other languages.

This `switch` command compares the value that is stored in the `thing` variable (which must be set prior to these statements, of course) with the string `car` and the string `truck` to see if it matches either of them. If the value of the `thing` variable is equal to `car`, then `thing is a car` is displayed on the screen. If the value of the `thing` variable is equal to `truck`, then `thing is a truck` is displayed on the screen. If neither of these cases are true, the default clause is executed and `I don't know what this thing is` displays on the screen.

> **TIP**
>
> Whenever you need to check to see if a variable is equal to one of a number of values, you should use a `switch` command instead of an `if` command with multiple `elseif` clauses. This makes your code much easier to read and understand.

Comments

It is always a good idea to include comments in any Tcl code you write—or code you write in any other language, for that matter. This becomes especially important if any of the following situations are possible:

- Someone else needs to look at or maintain your code.
- Your programs get large.
- You won't be looking at code that you have written for long periods of time after you write it.

Chances are that at least one of these situations will come up with Tcl code you have written.

Comments cannot be placed in the middle of a command. They must occur between commands. The pound sign (#) is used to inform Tcl to expect a comment.

```
# This is a valid comment

set a 1 ;   # This is a valid comment

set a 1         # This is an invalid comment
```

The third comment shown here is invalid because it occurs in the middle of a command.

> **NOTE**
>
> Recall that Tcl interprets everything up to a newline character or a semicolon to be part of the command.

The Tk Language Extensions

Earlier in this chapter, a simple example of Tk displayed Hello there in a button in the wish window. Tk is much more powerful than that example showed. Along with the button widget are many other widgets provided by Tk. These include menus, scrollbars, and list boxes. This section gives you an overview of some of the other Tk widgets and gives short examples explaining how these widgets can be used.

Frames

Frame widgets are containers for other widgets. They do not have any interesting behavior like the other Tk widgets. The only visible properties of frame widgets that you can set are their color and their border appearance. You can give three different border appearances to a frame widget: flat, raised, and sunken. You can experiment with the different frame widgets to see how they look.

The flat border frame widget is not too exciting. It looks exactly the same as the default wish window (because the default border appearance is flat).

Buttons

Button widgets are used to get specific input from a user. A button can be turned on or activated by the user of a Tk program by moving the mouse pointer over the button and then pressing the left mouse button. Tk provides the following three kinds of button widgets:

- Button
- Check button
- Radio button

The button widget is used to initiate some specific actions. The button usually has a name such as "Load file" that describes the action that results if you press the button.

Check button widgets are used to allow users of a program to turn program options on or off. When the check button is shaded the program option is on, and when the check button is not shaded the program option is off.

Radio buttons are similar to check buttons except that they are defined in groups, where only one member of a group of radio buttons is allowed to be on at one time. This means that if one radio button in a group of radio buttons is on, none of the other radio buttons in that group can be turned on. When the radio button is shaded it is on, and when the radio button is not shaded it is off.

Menus and Menu Buttons

Menu widgets are used to implement pull-down menus, cascading menus, and pop-up menus. A menu is a top-level widget that contains a set of menu entries that have values or commands associated with them. Five kinds of entries can be used in menus:

- Cascade entries display a submenu when the mouse pointer passes over them. The cascade entry is similar in function to the menu button widget.

- Command entries invoke a Tcl script when activated. The command entry is similar to the button widget in function.

- Check button entries toggle a program option between on and off. When the check button is shaded the option is on, and when the check button is not shaded it is off. The check button entry is similar in function to the check button widget.

- Radio button entries toggle a program option. The difference between the radio button entry and the check button entry is that radio buttons are typically defined in groups, with the restriction that only one of the radio buttons in the group can be active at once. The radio button entry is similar in function to the radio button widget.

- Separator entries display a horizontal line in the menu. This is used for appearance purposes only. There is no behavior associated with a separator entry.

The main difference between the menu entries and the button widgets is that the button widgets can exist by themselves, but the menu entries must exist within the context of a menu widget.

Menu button widgets are similar to button widgets. The only real difference between the two is that when menu buttons are invoked they bring up menus instead of executing Tcl scripts as button widgets would. The menu button name usually describes the types of menu entries contained in the menu that the menu button activates. This means that you should find menu entries that perform some kind of file operations contained within the File menu.

You can activate a menu by moving the mouse pointer to the menu button widget and pressing the left mouse button. This activates the menu associated with the menu button and displays the menu entries that are contained in that menu to the screen. You can now move the mouse pointer down through the list of menu entries and select the one you want.

The File menu contains two command entries (the Open entry and Quit entry), one cascade entry (the Save As entry), and one separator entry. The menu that comes up as a result of clicking the mouse pointer on the Save As cascade entry contains three command entries: the Text entry, the Ver 1 file entry, and the Ver 2 file entry.

List Boxes

The list box widget enables users of a Tk application to select items from a list of one or more items. If the number of items to be displayed in the list box is larger than the number of lines in the list box, you can attach scrollbars to make the extra items accessible.

Scrollbars

Scrollbar widgets are used to control what is displayed in other widgets. Scrollbar widgets are attached to other widgets to allow users to scroll up and down through the information contained in the widget. You typically put scrollbars on any widget that is designed to contain an arbitrary number of lines of information (such as a list box) or on widgets that contain more lines of information than the widget can display, given its size.

Summary

This chapter started off by introducing Tcl and the Tk tool kit and describing the uses of both. Although this chapter contained a lot of information, it barely scratched the surface of the programming tools provided by Tcl and the Tk tool kit.

Tcl has many more programming features than were described in this book. Some of the most notable are arrays, lists, and procedures.

Not all of the Tk widgets were described here, either. Some of the widgets that were not described are canvasses, scales, labels, messages, and `textedit` widgets.

Tk is just one example of an extension to Tcl. There are many other extensions available that extend the behavior of Tcl in different ways. Some of these extensions are as follows:

- Ak: An audio extension for Tcl, Ak provides numerous commands for sound recording and playback.
- XF: This is an interactive graphical user interface developer for Tk.
- Tcl-DP: This is a Tcl extension that helps programmers develop distributed applications using Tcl.

If you would like to learn more about Tcl and Tk, a good place to start is the manual pages for Tcl, Tk, and any of the specific commands you want information about. There are also a few books available that are devoted to Tcl and Tk programming.

Other Compilers and Languages Ported to Linux

31

by Kamran Husain

This chapter gives you a brief introduction to some languages other than those that have been assigned whole chapters in this book. You will learn details about the following languages and how to get packages for them:

- Ada
- FORTRAN
- Digital Signal Processing
- Modula-3
- OGI
- Eiffel
- COBOL
- LISP
- Scheme
- REXX

All the packages here have accompanying documentation and "how-to-use" instructions for them.

The list of programming languages covered here is not complete. As Linux becomes more and more acceptable in the programming community, you will see more languages being ported to Linux.

Ada

The Ada programming language was named after Ms. Ada Lovelace, a member of the original Ada software development team. Ada is the choice of many real-time system software developers and has been enhanced significantly for this purpose. Needless to say, some greatly enthused individuals have ported this language over to Linux. The Ada package is referred to as the GNAT (for GNu Ada Translator). The authors therefore appropriately belong to the GNAT project at New York University.

The latest update at the time of this writing was in September 1994. The Ada83 and Ada90 standards of the Ada language are covered in this release. The Ada for Linux package comes in the following files:

- gcc-drv-2.4.5.tar.gz
- gnat-1.83-bin-disk1.tar.gz
- gnat-1.83-bin-disk2.tar.gz
- gnat-2.0-linux-1.tar.gz
- gnat-2.0-linux-2.tar.gz
- gnat-2.0-linux-bin.tgz
- gnat-2.0-linux-lib.tgz
- gnat-2.0-linux.lsm
- gnat-1.83.lsm

For more information, you can contact the support folks via e-mail at gnat-request@cs.nyu.edu. The FTP site at tsx-11.mit.edu has the latest information and release of this software in the directory /pub/linux/packages/Ada.

To compile the source files you need gcc 2.6.0 or higher. The compiler can be found in the gnat-2.0.tar file. Altogether, this package chews up about 5MB of your hard disk space.

FORTRAN

The FORTRAN programming language is also ported to Linux. Only versions up to FORTRAN 77 have been ported over. There are only commercial ports of FORTRAN 90 as of this publication. The package in the tsx-11.mit.edu archives under the /pub/linux/packages/fortran directory contains the following files:

- ftnchek-2.7.lsm
- ftnchek-2.7.tgz
- libf2c-0.9.lsm
- libf2c-0.9.tar.gz
- mpfun-1.0.lsm
- mpfun-1.0.tar.gz
- toolpack-1.2.lsm
- toolpack-1.2.tar.gz

For a more up-to-date description of the files, check the INDEX file in the same directory as the above files. The libf2c-0.9.tar.gz contains the functions for converting FORTRAN code to C. Actually, the program f2c does a pretty decent job on all my class assignments at the university. The output is not idiot = proof, but it does the major portion of the job of translation.

The toolpack files are tools for FORTRAN programmers. Functions include printing aids for clean output listings and some sort of lint checker. Tools in this package include those for portability testing and dynamic programming analysis. All the script files in the toolpack are written for the C shell, so you will need to have the tcsh program installed on your system.

You will use at least 5 – 10MB of your disk space depending on which package you install.

The mpfun package is a multiple precision (FORTRAN MP) library and translator. This package performs multiprecision floating-point arithmetic with up to 16 million decimal digits, using advanced, recent algorithms and automatic translation from FORTRAN 77 code to FORTRAN multiprocessor code. The translation is done via directives within comment fields.

Digital Signal Processing

The ObjectProDSP package is an X Window system, object-oriented tool for Digital Signal Processing design development and implementation. The package contains the basics for building interactive scientific and engineering applications. The package was developed by Paul P. Budnik, Jr.

(mtnmath@mtnmath.com). The amount of disk space required is about 5MB. You can get it from `tsx-11.mit.edu` archives in the `/pub/linux/packages/dsp` directory.

Modula-3

The Modula-3 language is available from Digital Equipment Corporation's research center SRC. Modula-3 is an object-oriented language designed for multiprocess, distributed application development. Modula-3 resembles PASCAL in many ways but is more suited for building large applications.

The key features of the Modula-3 package include a full-blown GUI interface, runtime typing, support for multithreaded applications, garbage collection, and exception handling. The garbage collection and storage reallocation features of the language are of keen interest to object-oriented programmers. After all, who frees an object—the portion of the code that created it, or the portion to which the object was passed? The garbage collector for removing a large number of these problems is built into the language.

Modula-3 uses threads to process its incoming messages. Unlike other X-based applications, where one event queue has to be managed between several listening applications, Modula-3 allows the invocation of threads to perform message handling. A good example of the usage of this feature is the Trestle package—the interface package to X. With Trestle you can create threads to run in the background while you're doing other processing.

You can get Modula-3 from the Internet from the FTP site at: `gatekeeper.dec.com: /pub/DEC/ Modula-3/release-3.5.3`. Prebuilt binaries exist in `ftp.vlsi.polymtl.ca:/pub/m3/binaries/LINUX/ m3-3.4`. There is a home page on the Web at `http://www.research.digital.com/SRC/`.

OGI

The OGI Speech Tools version 1.0.1 for Linux are speech data manipulation research tools. These tools are primarily used for signal manipulation, phonetic, phonemic, and word analysis. This package has the capability to build audio databases that can be used to train neural networks, with a neural network trainer (NN) also in the package. The OGI speech tools were developed at the Center for Spoken Language Understanding (CSLU-OGI). You can get more information about them from `tools@cse.ogi.edu`.

The FTP site for this package is `sunsite.unc.edu` in the file `/pub/Linux/apps/sound/ogi- speech.tar.gz` or in `tsx-11.mit.edu` in the directory `/pub/linux/packages/ogi`.

You need some sort of sound card that is capable of digitizing sound under Linux. A good package for digitizing sound would be the Sox package.

In order to compile the package, you need the following X libraries (or later versions): `libXaw.so.3.1`, `libXt.so.3.1`, `libX11.so.3.1`, `libc.so.4.4.4`, `libm.so.4.4.4`.

If you are into computational linguistics, or are interested in speech compression, recognition, or applications of neural networks, this is one great research package to check out. The documentation in this package consists of man pages, and TeX source. Check `ogi-doc-PS.tar.gz` for TeX documentation in Postscript format. For the document in DVI format, try using the file `ogi-doc-dvi.tar.gz`.

Eiffel

Eiffel is a nonproprietary object-oriented language developed by Dr. Bertrand Meyer and his colleagues. An excellent reference book for Eiffel is Dr. Meyer's Book *Object-Oriented Software Construction*, Prentice Hall, 1988. In 1994, Dr. Meyer's company ported Eiffel to Linux.

The most advertised feature of Eiffel is its capability to reuse code without modifications. In conventional C++ and some other object-oriented languages, code reuse is still in its infancy. Eiffel is a new language primarily written with reuse in mind. Polymorphism, garbage collection, dynamic binding, multiple inheritance, and templates are built into the language. Even so, Eiffel code is interoperable with C and C++.

The design of Eiffel has been placed in the public domain. The Eiffel trademark is owned by the Nonprofit International Consortium for Eiffel (NICE). You should really have no fear using this trademark because NICE is quite nice about using the Eiffel trademark. The official language description is *Eiffel: The Language*, by Dr. Meyers, Prentice Hall, 1992. The formal syntax is included in the 600-plus page book along with examples, source code, and application guidelines.

Tower Technologies Corporation is promoting its commercial release of Eiffel, called TowerEiffel. Visit the web site at `http://www.cm.cf.ac.uk/Tower`. This site is a bit slow to get access to at times.

COBOL

Though not the preferred choice of "real" systems programmers, COBOL is a very widely used language in the business community. Naturally, there are ports to Linux in this database-oriented language. A good commercial port worth looking into is the ACUCOBOL-85 port by the Acucobol, Inc., company. Check the Web site at `www.acucobol.com` for more information about Cobol.

The ACUCOBOL-85 version of Cobol offers programmable hot keys, advanced windows capabilities (not X), its own file system, and a source = level debugger. Acucobol, Inc., also offers more than 600 tools to work with the Linux compiler. The COBOL code on Linux is portable to other platforms running COBOL-85.

LISP

LISP stands for LISt Processing. LISP was developed around 1958 and has been used in all areas of computer science research (for example, in artificial intelligence), as well as being the basis for products, such as `emacs` and AutoCAD. (Actually, AutoCAD uses AutoLISP, an enhanced version of LISP.)

The Common LISP language interpreter and compiler (`clisp`) package is in the Slackware Linux distribution. As the name suggests, the package contains both an interpreter and a compiler for generating machine-executable code. Invoked without arguments, `clisp` executes a `read-eval-print` loop, in which expressions are read from standard input, evaluated by the LISP interpreter, and their results output to standard output. When invoked with the `-c` option, the specified LISP files are compiled to a machine-readable code that can be executed more efficiently.

To get more information about the `clisp` package, type `clisp -h` at the prompt. If you are short of RAM on your machine, specify the amount of memory that clisp will use with the `-m` *XXX*K option, where *XXX* is the amount of memory to use in kilobytes. The `clisp` package has support for three languages: English, German, and French.

If you are an `emacs` user, you will want to use the `-I` option to make `clisp` ILISP compatible. ILISP is the LISP interface for the `emacs` editor.

The language implemented conforms to the book by Guy L. Steele Jr., *Common LISP—The Language*, Digital Press, First edition, 1984.

Scheme

Another language closely related to LISP is the Scheme language. A Scheme programmer has at his or her disposal the power of C and LISP. Scheme allows free data-typing of variables by offering lists, arrays of lists, associative lists, and arrays, in addition to the numeric and string data types.

Scheme, like `clisp`, is available in compiled or interpreted form. You can create output files from Scheme using two of three types of options: fast, cheap, and algorithmically correct. The fast option produces a large executable, the "correct" version has more error checking, and the cheap version produces a smaller, though (maybe) slower version of the program.

The interpreted environment produces a rapid development front end because there is no edit-compile-run cycle. You simply edit what you have changed and reexecute, just like in LISP.

Several versions of Scheme are available on various sites on the Internet:

■ `bigloo-bin.tar.gz`:	The Bigloo version, which is the de facto standard for Scheme
■ `bigloo-ELF-bin.tar.gz`:	The ELF version of the Bigloo version
■ `scheme2c-bin.tar.gz`:	The Scheme to C converter libraries for converting Scheme code to C code
■ `scm-bin.tar.gz` and `slib.tar.gz`:	The SCM package by Aubrey Jaffer (`jaffer@ai.mit.edu`) contains sockets, I/O, POSIX interfaces, and a `curses` screen-management library
■ `stk-bin.tar.gz`:	The `Tk` compatible library

REXX

As this book goes to print, IBM will have released a port of its version of the object-oriented language REXX. The REXX language is a scripting language available on most IBM platforms and is now ported to Windows. Object REXX extends the standard REXX language with classes, objects and methods. It also supports messaging, polymorphism, and multiple inheritance. Object REXX is a trademark of IBM.

Check out the IBM web site at `http://www.ibm.com` for more information.

Summary

The number of languages and software packages available for Linux continues to grow with Linux's popularity. This chapter has given you a snapshot of some of the languages available for Linux. Time and space have limited us to introducing in detail only a few of the more common languages, such as C, C++, Smalltalk, and so on. There are, however, many more languages which may be ideal for your project. It might be worth your while to check out some of these languages and get that ideal fit.

Motif for Programmers

32

by Kamran Husain

This chapter will cover the following topics:

- The basics of writing Motif applications for Linux
- Special naming conventions in Motif and X
- Writing and compiling your first Motif application
- Revisiting the widget hierarchy
- Using labels and strings in Motif
- Using various common widgets
- Designing layout
- Using menus
- Dialog boxes
- Event handling and other sources of input
- Colors in X
- Drawing lines, points, arcs, and polygons

A question you might be asking is "Why include a topic on a development system that you have to pay for when just about everything for Linux is free?" Well, if you want to develop any applications for the Common Desktop Environment (CDE), you should know how to program Motif applications. Linux is a mature enough system to enable you this luxury of building portable applications. (Plus, the $150 or so (U.S.) you pay for the Motif license will well pay for itself if you can do the work at home on your Linux system rather than commuting!)

Writing Motif Applications

This chapter introduces you to writing Motif applications. The information here will not be limited to writing applications for Linux alone, because the concepts in this chapter can be applied to other UNIX systems as well.

In programming Motif applications, you have to get used to programming in an event-driven environment. A typical C application runs from start to finish at its own pace. When it needs information, the application looks for this information from a source such as a file or the keyboard and (almost always) gets the information as soon as it asks for it. If the information is not available when the application asks for it, the application either waits for it or displays an error message. Also, the order of the incoming data is important for such applications; pieces of data that are out of sequence may cause the application to behave strangely.

In the case of event-driven programming, an application must wait for events on an input queue. The queue orders all incoming events in the order they are received. The first message to come in from one end of a queue is the first one to leave the queue. (Such queues are often called *FIFO*s, for First In, First Out.) An *event* can be anything from a mouse click, key button, or other event such as a timeout notification.

Because events can come in at any time, and in no predefined order, they are referred to as asynchronous events. That is, the order and time of arrival of each event is not deterministic. The application must wait for an event to occur and then proceed based on that event. Thus the term *event-driven programming*.

In the case of X Window, each X Window application has one input queue for all of its incoming events. The application must wait for events on this input queue. Similarly, a server waits for an event from a client and then responds based on the type of event received. This event handling and other aspects of X programming are handled by a toolkit called XtIntrinsics, or Xt for short.

In Xt, an application will typically run in a loop forever. This loop is called an *event loop*. An application enters the loop by calling a function XtAppMainLoop(). While in this event loop, an application will always wait for an event, When the application receives an event, the application handles the event itself or almost always "dispatches" the event to a window or *Widget*.

A Widget registers functions that it wants called when a type of event is received. This function is called a *callback* function. In most cases, a callback function is independent of the entire application. For example, some Widgets will redraw themselves when a pointer button is clicked in their display area. In this case, they would register a redraw callback function on a button click.

Xt also supports *actions*, which enable applications to register a function with Xt. An action is called when one or more sequences of specific event types are received. For example, pressing Ctrl-X would call the exit function. The mapping of the action to an event is handled via a translation table within Xt. Functions that handle specific events are referred to as *event handlers*.

Look at Figure 32.1 to see how the toolkit exists with Motif. As you can see from the connections in the figure, an application can get to the core Xlib functions through three means: via Motif, via the Xt library, or directly. This flexible hierarchy gives you many options when developing Motif applications because you are at liberty to take full advantage of all functions in all three libraries.

FIGURE 32.1.

The toolkit hierarchy for X, Xt, Motif.

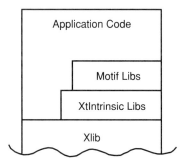

Naming Conventions

By default, most Xlib functions begin with the letter X, but you should not always rely on this being true for all functions. Several macros and functions in the X Window system do not begin with X. For example, the name BlackColor, WhiteColor are not macros. In general, though, if a name in Xlib begins with X, it's probably a function. If a name begins with a capital letter (A through Z), it's a macro.

With Xt, the naming conventions get better, but only slightly. In Xt, macros are not differentiated from functions in any way.

TIP

Do not rely on the name of a toolkit function to give you information about whether it's a macro. Read the manual to be absolutely sure.

In Motif, almost all declarations begin with Xm. Therefore, XmC refers to a class, XmR refers to a resource, XmN refers to a name, and XtN refers to Xt resources used by Motif. Declarations ending with the words WidgetClass define the base class for a type of Widget. A few conventions to remember about parameters for most Xlib functions are

- Width always to the left of height
- X always to the left of y
- Source always to the left of destination
- Display usually is the first parameter

With practice, you will be able to identify the type of parameters to pass and which toolkit a function belongs to, and be able to make some educated guesses as to what parameters an unknown function might expect.

Writing Your First Motif Application

Let's look at the basic format for a Motif application, shown in Listing 32.1. (I added line numbers for your benefit.) I will discuss this application in detail. You will build other Motif applications based on the structure in this particular application as you progress through this chapter.

NOTE

The line numbers are for reference only.

Listing 32.1. A sample Motif application.

```
1      /*
2      ** This is a typical Motif application with one button that
3      ** exits it.
4      */

5      #include <X11/Intrinsic.h>
```

```
 6      #include <Xm/Xm.h>
 7      #include <Xm/Form.h>
 8      #include <Xm/PushB.h>
 9      void  bye(Widget w, XtPointer clientdata, XtPointer calldata);
10      int main(int  argc, char **argv)
11      {
12      Widget top;
13      XtAppContext app;
14      Widget aForm;
15      Widget aButton;
16      Arg    args[5];

17      /**
18      *** Initialize the toolkit.
19      **/
20      top = XtAppInitialize(&app, "KBH", NULL, 0, (Cardinal *)&argc,
21                 argv, NULL, args, 0);

22      /**
23      *** Create a Form on this top level Widget. This is a nice Widget
24      *** to place other Widgets on top of.
25      **/
26      aForm = XtVaCreateManagedWidget("Form1",
27           xmFormWidgetClass, top,
28           XmNheight,90,
29           XmNwidth,200,
30           NULL);

31      /**
32      *** Add a button on the form you just created. Note how this Button
33      *** Widget is connected to the form that it resides on. Only
34      *** left, right, and bottom edges are attached to the form. The
35      *** top edge of the button is not connected to the form.
36      **/
37      aButton = XtVaCreateManagedWidget("Push to Exit",
38           xmPushButtonWidgetClass, aForm,
39           XmNheight,20,
40           XmNleftAttachment,XmATTACH_FORM,
41           XmNrightAttachment,XmATTACH_FORM,
42           XmNbottomAttachment,XmATTACH_FORM,
43           NULL);

44      /**
45      *** Call the function "bye" when the PushButton receives
46      *** an activate message; i.e. when the pointer is moved to
47      *** the button and Button1 is pressed and released.
48      **/
49      XtAddCallback( aButton, XmNactivateCallback,
50         ➥bye, (XtPointer) NULL);
51      XtRealizeWidget(top);
52      XtAppMainLoop(app);
53      return(0);
54      }

55      void  bye(Widget w, XtPointer clientdata, XtPointer calldata)
56      {
57      exit(0);
58      }
```

The listing shows an application in which a button attaches itself to the bottom of a form. See Figure 32.2.

FIGURE 32.2.
The output of
`l32_1.c`.

No matter how you resize the window, the button will always be on the bottom. The application does the following things in the order listed:

1. Initializes the toolkit to get a shell Widget.
2. Makes a Form Widget.
3. Manages all Widgets as they are created.
4. Makes the Button Widget on top of the Form Widget.
5. Attaches a callback function to the button.
6. Realizes the Widget (that is, makes the hierarchy visible).
7. Goes into its event loop.

Let's look at the application in more detail. The `include` files in the beginning of the listing are required for most applications. Notably, the two files shown in lines 5 and 6 are required for just about any Motif application you'll ever write.

```
#include <X11/Intrinsic.h>
#include <Xm/Xm.h>
```

These two lines declare the definitions for `XtIntrinsics` and Motif, respectively. In some systems, you may not require the first inclusion, but it's harmless to put it in there because multiple inclusions of `Intrinsic.h` are permitted. In addition, each Motif Widget requires its own header file. In Listing 32.1, the Widgets Form and PushButton are included via statements in lines 7 and 8:

```
#include <Xm/Form.h>
#include <Xm/PushB.h>
```

The variables in the program are declared in lines 12 through 16:

```
Widget top;
XtAppContext app;
Widget aForm;
Widget aButton;
int    n;
```

The `top`, `aForm`, and `aButton` represent Widgets. Even though their functions are different, they can all be referred to as Widgets.

The `XtAppContext` type is an *opaque* type, which means that a Motif programmer does not have to be concerned about how the type is set up. Widgets are opaque types as well; only the items that are required for the programmer are visible.

The first executable line of the program calls the `XtAppInitialize()` function (in line 20) to initialize the Xt toolkit and create an application shell and context for the rest of the application. This value is returned to the Widget *top* (for top-level shell). This Widget will provide the interface between the window manager and the rest of the Widgets in this application.

The application then creates a Form Widget on this top-level Widget. A *form widget* is used to place other Widgets on top of itself. It is a *manager widget* because it "manages" other Widgets.

There are two steps required for displaying a Widget: First you have to *manage* (with `XtVaCreateManagedWidget`) it and then you have to *realize* (with `RealizeWidget`) it.

Managing a Widget enables it to be visible. If a Widget is unmanaged, it will never be visible. By managing a Widget, the program gives the viewing control over to the windowing system to enable it to display it. Any child Widgets remain invisible, even if they are managed, if the parent Widget is unmanaged.

Realizing a Widget actually creates all the subwindows under an application and displays them. Normally only the top-level Widget is realized after all the Widgets are managed. This call will realize all the children of this Widget.

Note that realizing a Widget takes time. A typical program will manage all the Widgets except the topmost one. This way the application will only have to realize the topmost Widget when the entire tree has to display only the topmost parent. You have to realize a Widget at least once, but you can manage and "unmanage" Widgets as you want to display or hide them.

You can always create and manage a Widget to call `XtCreate` and `XtManageChild` in two separate calls. However, the samples in this chapter will use a single call to create and manage a Widget: `XtVaCreateManagedWidget`.

Note the parameters in this call to create the Form Widget shown in lines 26 through 30:

```
aForm = XtVaCreateManagedWidget("Form1",
          xmFormWidgetClass, top,
          XmNheight,90,
          XmNwidth,200,
          NULL);
```

The first parameter is the name of the new Widget. The second parameter describes the class of the Widget being created. Recall that this is simply the Widget name sandwiched between xm and `WidgetClass`. So, in this case, it is `xmFormWidgetClass`. Note the lowercase x for the class pointer. This class pointer is declared in the header files included at the beginning of the file, `Form.h`.

The next argument is the parent Widget of this new Widget. In this case, `top` is the parent of `Form1`. The `top` Widget is returned from the call to `XtAppInitialize`.

The remaining arguments specify the parameters of this Widget. In this case you are setting the width and height of the Widget. This list is terminated by a `NULL` parameter.

After the form is created, a button is placed on top of it. A Form Widget facilitates placement of other Widgets on top of it. In this application you will cause the button to "attach" itself to the bottom of the form. The following three lines (40–42) attach themselves to the form:

```
XmNleftAttachment,XmATTACH_FORM,
XmNrightAttachment,XmATTACH_FORM,
XmNbottomAttachment,XmATTACH_FORM,
```

The class of this button is included in the `PushB.h` file and is called `xmPushButtonWidgetClass`. The name of this Widget is also the string that is displayed on the face of the button. Note that the parent of this button is the `aForm` Widget. The hierarchy is as follows:

```
top -> is the parent of aForm -> is the parent of -> aButton.
```

The next step is to add a callback function when the button is pressed. This is done with the call to `XtAddCallback`, as shown in the following:

```
XtAddCallback( aButton, XmNactivateCallback, bye, (XtPointer) NULL);
```

Here are the parameters for this call:

- `aButton` is the PushButton Widget.
- `XmNactivateCallback` is the action that will trigger a call to this function.
- `bye` is the name of the function that will be called when the action is triggered. (You should declare this function before making this function call, or you will get a compiler error.)
- `NULL` is a pointer. This pointer could point to some structure meaningful to function `bye`.

This will register the callback function `bye` for the Widget. Now the topmost Widget, `top`, is realized. This causes all managed Widgets below `top` to be realized. The application then goes into a loop that processes all incoming events.

The `bye` function of this program simply exits the application.

Compiling This Application

Now comes the tough part of compiling this application into a working application. You will use the gcc compiler that comes with Linux for this purpose.

First, check the location of the libraries in your system. Check the /usr/lib/X11 directory for the following libraries: libXm.a, libXt.a, and libX11.a. If possible, use the shared library versions of these libraries with .so extensions followed by some numbers. The advantage of using shared libraries is a smaller Motif application; a typical application like the one you've been working on can be up to 1MB in size because of Motif's overhead.

The disadvantage of shared libraries is that your end user may not have the correct version of the library in his path. This does annoy some end users, especially if no fast method of acquiring this resource is available. Also, shipping a shared library with your application may cause you to pay some licensing fees to the original library vendor. From a programmer's perspective, shared libraries are sometimes impossible to use with your debugger. Of course, if your debugger supports them, use it. Check your compiler documentation. In most cases, if you intend to use shared libraries, use the static versions to do your debugging and testing, and then compile the shared version. Always check your vendor's licensing agreement for details on how to ship shared libraries.

The application can be compiled with this command:

```
gcc l32_1.c -o list1 -lXm -lXt -lX11
```

The program can be run from a command line if you create a script file:

```
$ cat mk
gcc $1.c -o $1 -lXm -lXt -lX11
```

and pass it just the filename without the extension. The best way is to create a makefile, but this script file will work with the examples in this text. So, to compile l32_1.c, you would use the script as follows:

```
$ mk l32_1
```

You should see the output in Figure 32.2 on your screen. Your application is the one with l32_1 in its frame.

The Widget Hierarchy

The Motif Widget set is a hierarchy of Widget types. (See Figure 32.3.) Any resources provided by a Widget are inherited by all its derived classes. Consider the three most important base classes: Core, XmPrimitive, and XmManager.

FIGURE 32.3.

The partial Motif hierarchy.

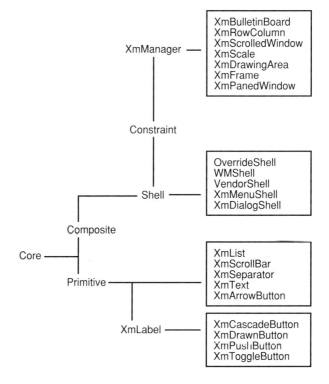

Core

The Core Widget class provides the basis for all classes. It provides at least the following resources for all Widgets:

XmNx, XmNy: A Widget's position on the display.

XmNheight, XmNwidth: A Widget's size.

XmNborderWidth: Set to 1 by default.

XmNsensitive: A Boolean resource that specifies whether this Widget can receive input.

XmNcolorMap: The default color map.

XmNbackground: The background color.

Check the Motif Programmer's reference manual for a complete listing.

XmPrimitive

The XmPrimitive Widget class inherits all the resources from Core and adds more functionality.

XmNforeground: The foreground color.

XmNhighlightOnEnter: Changes color when the pointer is within a displayed area of Widget.

XmNhighlightThickness: If XmNhighlightOnEnter is TRUE, changes the border to this thickness.

XmNhighlightColor: The color it changes to when highlighted.

XmNshadowThickness: This is the thickness to show the pseudo-three-dimensional look for which Motif is famous. The default value is 2.

XmNtopShadowColor and XmNbottomShadowColor: Sets the color for top and bottom lines around a Widget.

XmNuserData: A pointer available for the programmer's use.

The XmPrimitive Widget also provides the XmNdestroyCallback resource. This can be set to a function that would do clean-up when a Widget is destroyed. In Motif 1.2.*x* or later, the XmPrimitive class also provides a XmNhelpCallback that is called when the F1 key is pressed in the Widget's window. This is to allow specific help information for a button, for example.

XmManager

The XmManager class provides support for all Motif Widgets that contain other Widgets. This is never used directly in an application, and it works in a manner similar to the XmPrimitive class. It provides the following resources:

XmNforeground: The color of the pixels in the foreground.

XmNshadowThickness: For the three-dimensional effect.

XmNtopShadowColor: For the three-dimensional effect. This is automatically defaulted to a color derived from the background color. This color is used on the left and top borders of a Widget.

XmNbottomShadowColor: For the three-dimensional effect. This is automatically defaulted to a color derived from the background color. This color is used on the right and bottom borders of a Widget.

XmNuserData: For storing user data. Could be used as a void pointer.

The Label Widget

The Label Widget is used to display strings or pixmaps. Include the Xm/Label.h file in your source file before using this Widget. Some of the resources for this Widget include the following:

XmNalignment: Determines the alignment of the text in this Widget. The acceptable values are XmALIGNNMENT_END, XmALIGNMENT_CENTER, and XmALIGNEMENT_BEGIN for right, center, and left justification, respectively.

XmNrecomputeSize: A Boolean resource. If set to TRUE, the Widget will resize should the size of the string or pixmap change dynamically. This is the default. If set to FALSE, the Widget will not attempt to resize itself.

XmNlabelType: The default value of this type is XmSTRING to show strings. However, it can also be set to XmPIXMAP when displaying a pixmap specified in the XmNpixmap resource.

XmNlabelPixmap: This is used to specify which pixmap to use when the XmNlabelType is set to XmPIXMAP.

XmNlabelString: This is used to specify which XmString compound string to use for the label. This defaults to the name of the label. See the section, "Strings in Motif: Compound Strings."

To get acquainted with left and right justification on a label, see Listing 32.2. The listing also shows how the resources can be set to change Widget parameters programmatically and via the .Xresource files.

Listing 32.2. How to use a Label Widget.

```
/*
** This application shows how to use a Label Widget.
*/

#include <X11/Intrinsic.h>
#include <Xm/Xm.h>
#include <Xm/Form.h>
#include <Xm/PushB.h>
#include <Xm/Label.h>    /** <---- for the label **/


void   bye(Widget w, XtPointer clientdata, XtPointer calldata);

int main(int   argc, char **argv)
{
Widget top;
XtAppContext app;
Widget aForm;
Widget aLabel;            /** <---- for the label ***/
Widget aButton;
Arg    args[5];

/**
*** Initialize the toolkit.
**/
top = XtAppInitialize(&app, "KBH", NULL, 0, (Cardinal *)&argc,
          argv, NULL, args, 0);

/**
*** Create a Form on this top-level Widget. This is a nice Widget
*** to place other Widgets on top of.
**/
aForm = XtVaCreateManagedWidget("Form1",
      xmFormWidgetClass, top,
      XmNheight,90,
      XmNwidth,200,
      NULL);

/**
*** Add a button on the form you just created. Note how this Button
*** Widget is connected to the form that it resides on. Only
```

```
*** left, right, and bottom edges are attached to the form. The
*** top edge of the button is not connected to the form.
**/
aButton = XtVaCreateManagedWidget("Push to Exit",
    xmPushButtonWidgetClass, aForm,
    XmNheight,20,
    XmNleftAttachment,XmATTACH_FORM,
    XmNrightAttachment,XmATTACH_FORM,
    XmNbottomAttachment,XmATTACH_FORM,
    NULL);

/**
*** Now let's create the label for us.
*** The alignment is set to right-justify the label.
*** Note how the label is attached to the parent form.
**/

aLabel = XtVaCreateManagedWidget("This is a right justified Label",
    xmLabelWidgetClass, aForm,
    XmNalignment, XmALIGNMENT_END,
    XmNleftAttachment,XmATTACH_FORM,
    XmNrightAttachment,XmATTACH_FORM,
    XmNtopAttachment,XmATTACH_FORM,
    NULL);

/**
*** Call the function "bye" when the PushButton receives
*** an activate message; i.e. when the pointer is moved to
*** the button and Button1 is pressed and released.
**/
XtAddCallback( aButton, XmNactivateCallback, bye, (XtPointer) NULL);
XtRealizeWidget(top);
XtAppMainLoop(app);
return(0);
}

void  bye(Widget w, XtPointer clientdata, XtPointer calldata)
{
exit(0);
}
```

Output is shown in Figure 32.4.

FIGURE 32.4.

Using the Label Widget.

Avoid using the \n in the label name. If you have to create a multistring Widget, use the XmStringCreate calls to create a compound string (see the next section). Another way to set the string is by specifying it in the resource file and then merging the resources.

XmNfillColor: The color to show when set.

XmNset: A Boolean resource indicating whether the button is set or not. If this resource is set from a program, the button will automatically reflect the change.

It's easier to use the convenience functions:

```
XmToggleButtonGetState(Widget w)
```

to get the Boolean state for a Widget, and to use

```
XmToggleButtonSetState(Widget w, Boolean b)
```

to set the value for a ToggleButton Widget.

Similar to the PushButton class, the ToggleButton class has three callbacks:

XmNarmCallback: Called when the ToggleButton is armed.

XmNvalueChangedCallback: Called when a button is released in the Widgets area while the Widget is armed. This is not invoked if the pointer is outside the Widget when the button is released.

XmNdisarmCallback: Called when a button is released with the pointer outside the Widget area while the Widget was armed.

For the callbacks, the data passed into the Callback function is a structure of type:

```
typedef struct {
    int     reason;
    Xevent      *event;
    int     set;
} XmToggleButtonCallbackStruct;
```

The reason for the callback is one of the following events: XmCR_ARM, XmCR_DISARM, or XmCR_ACTIVATE. The event is a pointer to XEvent, which caused this callback. The set value is 0 if the item is not set, or nonzero if set. Look at Listing 32.3, which shows the use of ToggleButton. The ToggleButtons are arranged in one column via the RowColumn Widget, discussed later in this chapter.

Listing 32.3. Using ToggleButton in Motif.

```
/*
** This is a typical Motif application that demonstrates the use of
** a ToggleButton Widget(s) stored on a RowColumn Widget.
*/

#include <X11/Intrinsic.h>
#include <Xm/Xm.h>
#include <Xm/Form.h>
#include <Xm/ToggleB.h>
#include <Xm/RowColumn.h>
```

```
#include <Xm/PushB.h>


void  bye(Widget w, XtPointer clientdata, XtPointer calldata);

#define MAX_BTNS 4

int main(int  argc, char **argv)
{
Widget top;
XtAppContext app;
Widget aForm;
Widget aButton;
Widget aRowCol;
char  str[32];
Widget      aToggle[MAX_BTNS];
Arg         args[5];
int   i;

/**
*** Initialize the toolkit.
**/
top = XtAppInitialize(&app, "KBH", NULL, 0, (Cardinal *)&argc,
          argv, NULL, args, 0);

/**
*** Create a Form on this top-level Widget. This is a nice Widget
*** to place other Widgets on top of.
**/
aForm = XtVaCreateManagedWidget("Form1",
      xmFormWidgetClass, top,
      XmNheight,150,
      XmNwidth,100,
      NULL);


/**
*** Add a button on the form you just created. Note how this Button
*** Widget is connected to the form that it resides on. Only
*** left, right, and bottom edges are attached to the form. The
*** top edge of the button is not connected to the form.
**/
aButton = XtVaCreateManagedWidget("Push to Exit",
      xmPushButtonWidgetClass, aForm,
      XmNheight,20,
      XmNleftAttachment,XmATTACH_FORM,
      XmNrightAttachment,XmATTACH_FORM,
      XmNbottomAttachment,XmATTACH_FORM,
      NULL);

#define DO_RADIO
/**
*** A quick intro to the hierarchy in Motif.
*** Let's create a RowColumn Widget to place all ToggleButtons.
```

continues

Listing 32.3. continued

```
*** Note how the RowColumn button attaches itself to
*** the top of the button.
**/
aRowCol = XtVaCreateManagedWidget("rowcol",
      xmRowColumnWidgetClass, aForm,
#ifdef DO_RADIO
      XmNradioBehavior, TRUE,
      XmNradioAlwaysOne, TRUE,
#endif
      XmNleftAttachment,XmATTACH_FORM,
      XmNrightAttachment,XmATTACH_FORM,
      XmNtopAttachment,XmATTACH_FORM,
      XmNbottomAttachment,XmATTACH_WIDGET,
      NULL);
/**
*** Make ToggleButtons on this form called RowCol. Attach them all to the
*** RowColumn Widget on top of the form.
***
*** Note the radioBehavior setting
**/

for (i=0; i< MAX_BTNS; i++)
      {
      sprintf(str,"Button %d",i);
      aToggle[i] = XtVaCreateManagedWidget(str,
            xmToggleButtonWidgetClass, aRowCol,
            XmNradioBehavior, TRUE,
            NULL);
      }

XmToggleButtonSetState(aToggle[0],TRUE, FALSE);
/**
*** Call the function "bye" when the PushButton receives
*** an activate message; i.e. when the pointer is moved to
*** the button and Button1 is pressed and released.
**/
XtAddCallback( aButton, XmNactivateCallback, bye, (XtPointer) NULL);
XtRealizeWidget(top);
XtAppMainLoop(app);
return(0);
}

void  bye(Widget w, XtPointer clientdata, XtPointer calldata)
{
exit(0);
}
```

See Figure 32.6, shown previously, for the output of this listing with the #define DO_RADIO line commented out. By defining the DO_RADIO label, you can make this into a Radio Button application. That is, only one of the buttons can be selected at one time. See Figure 32.5, shown previously, for the radio behavior of these buttons.

Convenience Functions

Usually the way to set resources for a Widget is at the time of the Widget's creation. This is done either with the XtVaCreateManagedWidget call or with the XmCreateYYY call, where YYY is the name of the Widget you are creating.

This test uses the variable argument call to create and manage Widgets. I do it simply because it's easier for me to see what resources I am setting and create them all in one function call. You might have a personal preference to do it in two steps. Either way is fine. Keep in mind, though, that if you do use the XmCreateYYY call, you have to set the resource settings in a list of resource sets. Listing 32.4 is an example of creating a Label Widget. This is a function that creates a Label Widget on a Widget given the string x.

Listing 32.4. Sample convenience function for creating a Label on a form.

```
/**
*** This is a sample convenience function to create a label
*** Widget on a parent. The string must be a compound string.
**/
Widget makeLabel( Widget onThis, XmString x)
{
Widget   lbl;
Cardinal n;
Arg    arg[5];

n = 0;
XtSetArg(arg[n], XmNalignment, XmALIGNMENT_BEGIN); n++;
XtSetArg(arg[n], XmNlabelString, x); n++;
lbl = XmCreateLabel("A Label", onThis, arg, n);
XtManageChild(lbl);
return(lbl);
}
```

Or you could use the variable argument lists in creating this Label, as shown in Listing 32.5.

Listing 32.5. Creating a label.

```
/**
*** Another way of making a label on a parent.
**/
Widget makeLabel( Widget onThis, XmString x)
{
Widget   lbl;
lbl = XmCreateManagedWidget("A Label",
     xmLabelWidgetClass, onThis,
     XmNalignment, XmALIGNMENT_BEGIN,
     XmNlabelString, x,
     NULL);

return(lbl);
}
```

Listing 32.6. continued

```
XtSetArg(args[i], XmNbottomWidget,aButton); i++;
aList =  XmCreateScrolledList(aForm,"groceryList",args,i);
XtManageChild(aList);
#endif

/**
*** Call the function "bye" when the PushButton receives
*** an activate message; i.e. when the pointer is moved to
*** the button and Button1 is pressed and released.
**/
XtAddCallback( aButton, XmNactivateCallback, bye, (XtPointer) NULL);
XtRealizeWidget(top);
XtAppMainLoop(app);
return(0);
}

void  bye(Widget w, XtPointer clientdata, XtPointer calldata)
{
exit(0);
}
```

The output is shown in Figure 32.7.

FIGURE 32.7.

Using the List Widget.

XmScrollBar

The ScrollBar Widget enables the user to select a value from a range. Its resources include the following:

> XmNvalue: The value representing the location of the slider.
>
> XmNminimum and XmNmaximum: The range of values for the slider.
>
> XmNshowArrows: Boolean value if set shows arrows at either end.
>
> XmNorientation: Set to XmHORIZONTAL for a horizontal bar or XmVERTICAL (default) for a vertical bar.
>
> XmNprocessingDirection: Set to either XmMAX_ON_LEFT or XmMAX_ON_RIGHT for XmHORIZONTAL orientation, or XmMAX_ON_TOP or XmMAX_ON_BOTTOM for XmVERTICAL orientation.

XmNincrement: The increment per move.

XmNpageIncrement: The increment if a button is pressed in the arrows or the box. This is defaulted to 10.

XmNdecimalPoint: Shows the decimal point from the right.

Note that all values in the ScrollBar Widget's values are given as integers. Look at the radio station selection example in Listing 32.7. A point to note in this listing is that the exit button for the application is offset on the left and right by 20 pixels. This is done via the XmATTACH_FORM value for each side (left or right) being offset by the value in XmNleftOffset and XmNrightOffset, respectively. See Listing 32.3 on how to attach items to a Form.

Listing 32.7. Using the Scale Widget.

```
/*
** An application to show the radio station selection via a scale.
*/

#include <X11/Intrinsic.h>
#include <Xm/Xm.h>
#include <Xm/Form.h>
#include <Xm/PushB.h>
#include <Xm/Scale.h>


#define MAX_SCALE 1080
#define MIN_SCALE 800
void  bye(Widget w, XtPointer clientdata, XtPointer calldata);
void myfunction(Widget w, XtPointer dclient,  XmScaleCallbackStruct *p);

int main(int  argc, char **argv)
{
Widget top;
XtAppContext app;
Widget aForm;
Widget aScale;
Widget aButton;
XmString xstr; /* for the scale title */
Arg   args[5];

/**
*** Initialize the toolkit.
**/
top = XtAppInitialize(&app, "ScaleMe", NULL, 0, (Cardinal *)&argc,
          argv, NULL, args, 0);

/**
*** Create a Form on this top-level Widget. This is a nice Widget
*** to place other Widgets on top of.
**/
aForm = XtVaCreateManagedWidget("Form1",
     xmFormWidgetClass, top,
```

continues

Listing 32.7. continued

```
        XmNheight,90,
        XmNwidth,240,
        NULL);

/**
*** Add a button on the form you just created. Note how this Button
*** Widget is connected to the form that it resides on. Only
*** left, right, and bottom edges are attached to the form. The
*** top edge of the button is not connected to the form.
**/
aButton = XtVaCreateManagedWidget("Push to Exit",
        xmPushButtonWidgetClass, aForm,
        XmNheight,20,
        XmNleftAttachment,XmATTACH_FORM,
        XmNleftOffset,20,
        XmNrightAttachment,XmATTACH_FORM,
        XmNrightOffset,20,
        XmNbottomAttachment,XmATTACH_FORM,
        NULL);
/**
***    Create the radio FM selection scale here.
***    Note that since we have to work with integers,
***    we have to set the frequency scale to 10x actual
***    value and then set the decimal point explicitly
***    for the display. No provision is made for selecting
***    odd frequencies.
**/

xstr = XmStringCreateLtoR("Radio Stations", XmSTRING_DEFAULT_CHARSET);
aScale =  XtVaCreateManagedWidget("sample it",
        xmScaleWidgetClass, aForm,
        XmNheight,40,
        XmNminimum, 800,
        XmNvalue, 1011,
        XmNmaximum, 1080,
        XmNdecimalPoints,1,
        XmNtitleString,xstr,
        XmNshowValue,TRUE,
        XmNorientation,XmHORIZONTAL,
        XmNprocessingDirection,XmMAX_ON_RIGHT,
        XmNleftAttachment,XmATTACH_FORM,
        XmNrightAttachment,XmATTACH_FORM,
        XmNtopAttachment,XmATTACH_FORM,
        XmNbottomAttachment,XmATTACH_WIDGET,
        XmNbottomAttachment,aButton,
        NULL);
XmStringFree(xstr);


/**
*** Call the function "bye" when the PushButton receives
*** an activate message; i.e. when the pointer is moved to
*** the button and Button1 is pressed and released.
**/
XtAddCallback( aButton, XmNactivateCallback, bye, (XtPointer) NULL);
XtAddCallback( aScale, XmNvalueChangedCallback, myfunction, (XtPointer) NULL);
```

```
XtRealizeWidget(top);
XtAppMainLoop(app);
return(0);
}

void  bye(Widget w, XtPointer clientdata, XtPointer calldata)
{
exit(0);
}

void myfunction(Widget w, XtPointer dclient,  XmScaleCallbackStruct *p)
{
int k;

k = p->value;
if ((k & 0x1) == 0)   /** % 2  is zero ** check limits and increase **/
      {
      k++;
      if (k >= MAX_SCALE) k = MIN_SCALE + 1;
      if (k <= MIN_SCALE) k = MAX_SCALE - 1;
      XmScaleSetValue(w,k);  /** this will redisplay it too **/
      }
}
```

In the case of FM selections, you would want the bar to show odd numbers. A good exercise for you would be to allow only odd numbers in the selection. Hint: Use XmNvalueChangedCallback as follows:

```
XtAddCallback(aScale, XmNvalueChangedCallback, myfunction);
```

Output is shown in Figure 32.8.

FIGURE 32.8.

Using the Scale Widget.

The callback sends a pointer to the structure of type XmScaleCallbackStruct to a function called myfunction. A sample function, myfunction(), follows:

```
/**
*** Partial listing for not allowing even numbers for FM selection.
**/
#define MAX_SCALE 1080
#define MIN_SCALE 800
static void myfunction(Widget w, XtPointer dclient,  XmScaleCallbackStruct *p)
{
int k;

k = p->value;
```

Listing 32.9. continued

```
/**
*** Create a Form on this top-level Widget. This is a nice Widget
*** to place other Widgets on top of.
**/
masterForm = XtVaCreateManagedWidget("MasterForm",
     xmFormWidgetClass, top,
     XmNheight,150,
     XmNwidth,200,
     NULL);

buttonForm = XtVaCreateManagedWidget("ButtonForm",
     xmFormWidgetClass, masterForm,
     XmNtopAttachment,XmATTACH_POSITION,
     XmNtopPosition, 75,
     XmNheight,30,
     XmNbottomAttachment,XmATTACH_FORM,
     XmNleftAttachment,XmATTACH_FORM,
     XmNrightAttachment,XmATTACH_FORM,
     NULL);

labelForm = XtVaCreateManagedWidget("LabelForm",
     xmFormWidgetClass, masterForm,
     XmNtopAttachment,XmATTACH_FORM,
     XmNbottomAttachment,XmATTACH_POSITION,
     XmNbottomPosition, 75,
     XmNleftAttachment,XmATTACH_FORM,
     XmNrightAttachment,XmATTACH_POSITION,
     XmNrightPosition,50,
     NULL);

inputForm = XtVaCreateManagedWidget("InputForm",
     xmFormWidgetClass, masterForm,
     XmNtopAttachment,XmATTACH_FORM,
     XmNbottomAttachment,XmATTACH_POSITION,
     XmNbottomPosition, 75,
     XmNrightAttachment,XmATTACH_FORM,
     XmNleftAttachment,XmATTACH_POSITION,
     XmNleftPosition,50,
     NULL);

/**
*** Now create the RowColumn manager Widgets
**/

buttonRC = XtVaCreateManagedWidget("buttonRC",
     xmRowColumnWidgetClass, buttonForm,
     XmNbottomAttachment,XmATTACH_FORM,
     XmNtopAttachment,XmATTACH_FORM,
     XmNleftAttachment,XmATTACH_FORM,
     XmNrightAttachment,XmATTACH_FORM,
     XmNorientation, XmHORIZONTAL,
     NULL);
```

```
labelRC = XtVaCreateManagedWidget("buttonRC",
     xmRowColumnWidgetClass, labelForm,
     XmNbottomAttachment,XmATTACH_FORM,
     XmNtopAttachment,XmATTACH_FORM,
     XmNleftAttachment,XmATTACH_FORM,
     XmNrightAttachment,XmATTACH_FORM,
     XmNorientation, XmVERTICAL,
     NULL);

textRC = XtVaCreateManagedWidget("buttonRC",
     xmRowColumnWidgetClass, inputForm,
     XmNbottomAttachment,XmATTACH_FORM,
     XmNtopAttachment,XmATTACH_FORM,
     XmNleftAttachment,XmATTACH_FORM,
     XmNrightAttachment,XmATTACH_FORM,
     XmNorientation, XmVERTICAL,
     NULL);

for (i = 0; i < NUMITEMS; i++)
     {
     inputLabel[i] = XtVaCreateManagedWidget(thisLabel[i],
          xmLabelWidgetClass, labelRC,  NULL);
     inputText[i] = XtVaCreateManagedWidget(thisLabel[i],
          xmTextWidgetClass, textRC,  NULL);
     }

searchBtn = XtVaCreateManagedWidget("Search",
          xmPushButtonWidgetClass, buttonRC,  NULL);
cancelBtn = XtVaCreateManagedWidget("Cancel",
          xmPushButtonWidgetClass, buttonRC,  NULL);

XtAddCallback( cancelBtn, XmNactivateCallback, bye, (XtPointer) NULL);

/** Add the handler to search here. **/
XtRealizeWidget(top);
XtAppMainLoop(app);
return(0);
}

void  bye(Widget w, XtPointer clientdata, XtPointer calldata)
{
exit(0);
}
```

The output of this application is shown in Figure 32.10. Notice how the labels do not line up with the Text Widget. There is a problem in the hierarchy of the setup. See the hierarchy of the application in Figure 32.11.

FIGURE 32.10.

The output of Listing 32.9.

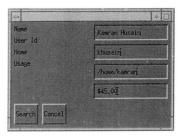

FIGURE 32.11.

The hierarchy of Listing 32.9.

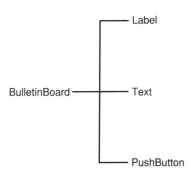

The Form Widgets are created to maintain the relative placements of all of the Widgets that correspond to a type of functionality. The RowColumn Widgets allow the placement of items on themselves. The best route to take in this example would be to lay one text and one label on one RowColumn Widget and have three RowColumn Widgets in all, one for each instance up to NUM_ITEMS. This will ensure that each label lines up with its corresponding text Widget.

Here are a few points to note about laying out applications:

- Think about what the form or dialog is trying to achieve. Draw it on paper if you have to. Coding is the easy part; determining what to do is much harder.

- Be consistent. Users will love you for it. If Alt-X is a shortcut for Exit in one screen, do not make it a Cut operator in another. Keep controls on the same side of all dialogs and forms. Use separators to separate different functions on the same window.

- Choose a color scheme for your end users. What may be cool to you may be grotesque to the end user. They may not even be using a color monitor in some rare cases. A combination of white, gray, and black may be your best bet in this case if you do not want to deal with different color schemes in your code.

- Colors on your monitor may not be the same on the end user's monitor.

- Do not assume that the user has the same resolution monitor as yourself. Keep fonts clean, and buttons big enough for a large cursor. Allow windows to be resized as much as possible to enable users to customize their desktops.

- Assume nothing. If the user can size your window to an unworkable size, either limit the size in the resize callback to the lowest size or do not allow sizing at all.

■ Offer some help for the user. In the future, Help will be required as a standard option on menu bars, so plan ahead.

■ Avoid clutter. Too many options and entries on one huge form tend to confuse and baffle the user. Consider a two-or-more-tiered approach via dialogs. Default everything as much as possible.

■ Allow the program to be more forgiving. Sometimes an "Are you sure?" dialog with an option to change a list of parameters can be endearing to the user. On the other hand, some users hate this type of checking.

Menus

Designing a Widget hierarchy is especially important when working with Motif menus. Motif menus are a collection of Widgets, so there is no "menu" Widget for a menu. You create menus using a hierarchy of different types of Widgets: `RowColumn`, `PushButton`, `CascadeButton`, `ToggleButton`, `Label`, and `Separator`.

There are three kinds of menus in Motif:

■ Pop-up: This appears as a list of items when a pointer button is pressed on a Widget.

■ Pull-down: This appears when a button on an existing menu is pressed.

■ Option: This enables the user to select from a list of options with the current selection visible at all times.

The procedure to create a menu is different for each type of menu.

Pop-Up Menus

To create a pop-up menu, follow these steps:

1. Include the correct header files. You will need the header files for the menu:

   ```
   Label.h
   RowColumn.h
   PushB.h
   Separator.h
   BulletinB.h
   CascadeB.h
   ```

2. Create the menu pane with a call to `XmCreatePopupMenu`. This is a convenience call to create `RowColumn` and `MenuShell` Widgets with the proper settings.

3. Create the buttons on the menu pane. Use `XmPushbuttons`, `XmToggleButtons`, `XmSeparator`, and `XmCascadeButtons`.

4. Attach callback functions to the Widgets.

Listing 32.10 shows how to set up a simple pop-up menu.

Listing 32.10. continued

```
        XtManageChild(menu);
        }
}

/**
*** This echos the selection on the controlling terminal
**/
void  showSelection(Widget w, XtPointer clientdata, XtPointer calldata)
{
printf("\n %s ",  XtName(w));
}

void  bye(Widget w, XtPointer clientdata, XtPointer calldata)
{
exit(0);
}
```

Note three important items about this listing:

- ■ You can use printf functions within Motif applications. The output goes to the controlling terminal by default. This is invaluable in debugging.

- ■ The menu is not visible by itself. An event handler on the menu's parent is registered before the menu can be displayed. This enables the menu to be displayed whenever a button is pressed.

- ■ The XmMenuPosition call sets the position of the pop-up menu. It is then managed (that is, after placement).

The Menu Bar

A menu bar is a horizontal bar that is always available to the user. Motif uses the RowColumn Widget as a bar with cascading buttons on it for each option.

The procedure for creating a menu bar is as follows:

1. Include the correct header files. You will need the header files for the menu:

   ```
   Label.h
   RowColumn.h
   PushB.h
   Separator.h
   BulletinB.h
   CascadeB.h
   ```

2. Create the menu bar with a call to XmCreateMenuBar().

3. Create the pull-down menu panes with a call to XmCreatePulldownMenu().

4. For each pull-down pane, create a cascade button on the menu bar. Use the menu bar as the parent. A cascade button is used to link the items in a menu with the menu bar itself.

5. Attach the menu pane to its corresponding cascade button. Use the XmNsubMenuId resource of the cascade button to the appropriate menu pane.

6. Create the menu entries in the menu panes.

Listing 32.11 shows you how to set up a simple menu application.

Listing 32.11 Creating a menu bar.

```
/*
** This listing shows how to set up a menu bar and pulldown menus
*/

#include <X11/Intrinsic.h>
#include <Xm/Xm.h>
#include <Xm/Form.h>
#include <Xm/PushB.h>
#include <Xm/Label.h>
#include <Xm/Text.h>
#include <Xm/RowColumn.h>
#include <Xm/CascadeB.h>
#include <Xm/Separator.h>

void doBackup(Widget w, XtPointer x, XtPointer c)
{
printf("\n Start backup ");
}
void doRestore(Widget w, XtPointer x, XtPointer c)
{
printf("\n Start restore ");
}
void bye(Widget w, XtPointer x, XtPointer c)
{
exit(0);
}
void selectTape(Widget w, XtPointer x, XtPointer c)
{
printf("\n Select tape drive...");
}
void selectDisk(Widget w, XtPointer x, XtPointer c)
{
printf("\n Select Floppy disks...");
}

void helpBtn(Widget w, XtPointer x, XtPointer c)
{
printf("\n ... No help available ");
}

int main (int argc, char*argv[])
{
Widget top;
XtAppContext app;
Widget masterForm;
Widget menu;      /* for the menu bar */
```

continues

Listing 32.11 continued

```
Widget submenu; /* for pulldown menus */
Widget cascade; /* for cascade button on the menu bar */
Widget filler;
Arg    args[10];
int    n;
/**
*** Initialize the toolkit.
**/
top = XtAppInitialize(&app, "KBH", NULL, 0, (Cardinal *)&argc,
          argv, NULL, args, 0);


/**
*** Create a Form on this top-level Widget. This is a nice Widget
*** to place other Widgets on top of.
**/
masterForm = XtVaCreateManagedWidget("Form1",
       xmFormWidgetClass, top,
       XmNheight,150,
       XmNwidth,200,
       NULL);


n = 0;
XtSetArg(args[n],XmNheight, 50); n++;
menu = XmCreateMenuBar(masterForm,"mastermenu",
       args, n);
submenu = XmCreatePulldownMenu(menu,"submenupane1", NULL, 0);
cascade = XtVaCreateManagedWidget("File",
       xmCascadeButtonWidgetClass, menu,
       XmNsubMenuId, submenu,
       NULL);

filler = XtVaCreateManagedWidget("Backup",
       xmPushButtonWidgetClass, submenu,   NULL);
XtAddCallback( filler, XmNactivateCallback, doBackup, (XtPointer) NULL);

filler = XtVaCreateManagedWidget("Restore",
       xmPushButtonWidgetClass, submenu,   NULL);
XtAddCallback( filler, XmNactivateCallback, doRestore, (XtPointer) NULL);

filler = XtVaCreateManagedWidget("Quit",
       xmPushButtonWidgetClass, submenu,   NULL);
XtAddCallback( filler, XmNactivateCallback, bye, (XtPointer) NULL);


submenu = XmCreatePulldownMenu(menu,"submenupane2", NULL, 0);

cascade = XtVaCreateManagedWidget("Options",
       xmCascadeButtonWidgetClass, menu,
       XmNsubMenuId, submenu,
       NULL);

filler = XtVaCreateManagedWidget("Tape",
       xmPushButtonWidgetClass, submenu,   NULL);
XtAddCallback( filler, XmNactivateCallback, selectTape, (XtPointer) NULL);
```

```
filler = XtVaCreateManagedWidget("Floppy",
     xmPushButtonWidgetClass, submenu,  NULL);
XtAddCallback( filler, XmNactivateCallback, selectDisk, (XtPointer) NULL);

submenu = XmCreatePulldownMenu(menu,"submenupane3", NULL, 0);

cascade = XtVaCreateManagedWidget("Help",
     xmCascadeButtonWidgetClass, menu,
     XmNsubMenuId, submenu,
     NULL);
filler = XtVaCreateManagedWidget("Floppy",
     xmPushButtonWidgetClass, submenu,  NULL);
XtAddCallback( filler, XmNactivateCallback, selectDisk, (XtPointer) NULL);


XtVaSetValues( menu,
     XmNmenuHelpWidget, cascade,
     NULL);
XtAddCallback( cascade, XmNactivateCallback, helpBtn ,NULL);


XtManageChild(menu);
/** Add the handler to search here. **/
XtRealizeWidget(top);
XtAppMainLoop(app);
return(0);

}
```

Note that the Motif programming style requires you to provide the Help button (if you have any) to be right-justified on the menu bar. This Help Cascade button should then be set to the XmNmenuHelpWidget of a menu bar. The menu bar will automatically position this Widget to the right-hand side of the visible bar. See Listing 32.12 on how to create pull-down menu items on a menu items on a menu bar.

Listing 32.12. Creating menu bars with pull-down menu items.

```
/*
** This listing shows how to set up a menu bar and pull-down menus
*/

#include <X11/Intrinsic.h>
#include <Xm/Xm.h>
#include <Xm/Form.h>
#include <Xm/PushB.h>
#include <Xm/Label.h>
#include <Xm/Text.h>
#include <Xm/RowColumn.h>
#include <Xm/CascadeB.h>
#include <Xm/Separator.h>

void doBackup(Widget w, XtPointer x, XtPointer c)
```

continues

Listing 32.12. continued

```
{
printf("\n Start backup ");
}
void doRestore(Widget w, XtPointer x, XtPointer c)
{
printf("\n Start restore ");
}
void bye(Widget w, XtPointer x, XtPointer c)
{
exit(0);
}
void selectTape(Widget w, XtPointer x, XtPointer c)
{
printf("\n Select tape drive...");
}
void selectDisk(Widget w, XtPointer x, XtPointer c)
{
printf("\n Select Floppy disks...");
}

void helpBtn(Widget w, XtPointer x, XtPointer c)
{
printf("\n ... No help available ");
}

int main (int argc, char*argv[])
{
Widget top;
XtAppContext app;
Widget masterForm;
Widget menu;     /* for the menu bar */
Widget submenu; /* for pull-down menus */
Widget cascade; /* for CascadeButton on the menu bar */
Widget filler;
Arg    args[10];
int    n;
/**
*** Intialize the toolkit.
**/
top = XtAppInitialize(&app, "KBH", NULL, 0, (Cardinal *)&argc,
          argv, NULL, args, 0);

/**
*** Create a Form on this top-level Widget. This is a nice Widget
*** to place other Widgets on top of.
**/
masterForm = XtVaCreateManagedWidget("Form1",
      xmFormWidgetClass, top,
      XmNheight,150,
      XmNwidth,200,
      NULL),

n = 0;
XtSetArg(args[n],XmNheight, 50); n++;
```

```
menu = XmCreateMenuBar(masterForm,"mastermenu",
      args, n);

/********************* The change is here ******************/
n = 0;
XtSetArg(args[n],XmNtearOffModel, XmTEAR_OFF_ENABLED); n++;
submenu = XmCreatePulldownMenu(menu,"submenupane1", args, n);
/********************* The change is here ******************/
cascade = XtVaCreateManagedWidget("File",
      xmCascadeButtonWidgetClass, menu,
      XmNsubMenuId, submenu,
      NULL);

filler = XtVaCreateManagedWidget("Backup",
      xmPushButtonWidgetClass, submenu,  NULL);
XtAddCallback( filler, XmNactivateCallback, doBackup, (XtPointer) NULL);

filler = XtVaCreateManagedWidget("Restore",
      xmPushButtonWidgetClass, submenu,  NULL);
XtAddCallback( filler, XmNactivateCallback, doRestore, (XtPointer) NULL);

filler = XtVaCreateManagedWidget("Quit",
      xmPushButtonWidgetClass, submenu,  NULL);
XtAddCallback( filler, XmNactivateCallback, bye, (XtPointer) NULL);


submenu = XmCreatePulldownMenu(menu,"submenupane2", NULL, 0);

cascade = XtVaCreateManagedWidget("Options",
      xmCascadeButtonWidgetClass, menu,
      XmNsubMenuId, submenu,
      NULL);

filler = XtVaCreateManagedWidget("Tape",
      xmPushButtonWidgetClass, submenu,  NULL);
XtAddCallback( filler, XmNactivateCallback, selectTape, (XtPointer) NULL);

filler = XtVaCreateManagedWidget("Floppy",
      xmPushButtonWidgetClass, submenu,  NULL);
XtAddCallback( filler, XmNactivateCallback, selectDisk, (XtPointer) NULL);

submenu = XmCreatePulldownMenu(menu,"submenupane3", NULL, 0);

cascade = XtVaCreateManagedWidget("Help",
      xmCascadeButtonWidgetClass, menu,
      XmNsubMenuId, submenu,
      NULL);
filler = XtVaCreateManagedWidget("Floppy",
      xmPushButtonWidgetClass, submenu,  NULL);
XtAddCallback( filler, XmNactivateCallback, selectDisk, (XtPointer) NULL);


XtVaSetValues( menu,
      XmNmenuHelpWidget, cascade,
      NULL);
```

continues

Listing 32.12. continued

```
XtAddCallback( cascade, XmNactivateCallback, helpBtn ,NULL);


XtManageChild(menu);
/** Add the handler to search here. **/
XtRealizeWidget(top);
XtAppMainLoop(app);
return(0);

}
```

The Options Menu

An Options menu enables the user to select from a list of items while displaying the most recently selected item. The procedure for creating an Options menu is similar to creating menu bars:

1. Include the correct header files. You will need the header files for the menu:

   ```
   Label.h
   RowColumn.h
   PushB.h
   Separator.h
   BulletinB.h
   CascadeB.h
   ```

2. Create the menu bar with a call to XmCreateOptionMenu().
3. Create the pull-down menu panes with a call to XmCreatePulldownMenu().
4. For each pull-down pane, create a CascadeButton on the menu bar.
5. Attach the menu pane to its corresponding CascadeButton. Use the XmNsubMenuId resource of the CascadeButton to the appropriate menu pane.
6. Create the menu entries in the menu panes.

Accelerators and Mnemonics

An accelerator for a command is the keystroke that invokes the callback for that particular menu item. For example, for opening a file, you could use Ctrl-O. The resource for this accelerator could be set in the resource file as

```
*Open*accelerator: Ctrl<Key>O
```

The corresponding menu item should read "Open Ctrl+O" to let the user know about this short-cut. Note the + instead of -. You can also set this resource via the command in the .Xresources file:

```
*Open*acceleratorText: "Ctrl+O"
```

Using the .Xresource file is the preferred way of setting these resources.

Mnemonics are a short form for letting the user select menu items without using the mouse. For example, the user could press <meta>F to invoke the File menu. These are also usually set in the .Xresource file. The syntax for the File menu to use the <meta>F key would be:

```
*File*mnemonic:F
```

TIP

With Linux on your PC, *meta* means the Alt key.

Dialog Boxes

A *dialog box* is used to convey information about something to the user and requests a canned response in return. For example, a dialog box might say "Go ahead and Print" and present three buttons—OK, Cancel, and Help. The user must then select one of the three buttons to process the command.

A typical dialog box displays an icon, a message string, and usually three buttons (OK, Cancel, and Help). Motif provides predefined dialog boxes for the following categories:

- Errors
- Information
- Warnings
- Working
- Questions

Each of these dialog box types displays a different icon: a question mark for the Question dialog box, an exclamation mark for an Information dialog box, and so on. Convenience functions ease the creation of dialog boxes. These are

- `XmCreateErrorsDialog`
- `XmCreateInformationDialog`
- `XmCreateWarningDialog`
- `XmCreateWorkingDialog`
- `XmCreateQuestionDialog`

The infamous "OK to quit?" dialog box can be implemented as shown in Listing 32.13. There is another example in Listing 32.17.

Listing 32.13. Code fragment to confirm quit command.

```
/*
** Confirm quit one last time
*/
void reallyQuit(Widget w, XtPointer clientdata, XtPointer calldata)
{
exit(0);
}
void confirmQuit(Widget w, XtPointer clientdata, XtPointer calldata)
{
static Widget quitDlg = NULL;
static char *msgstr = "Really Quit?"

if (quitDlg != NULL)
    {
    /* first time called */
    quitDlg = XmCreateQuestionDialog(w,"R U Sure",NULL,0);
    XtVaSetValues(quitDlg, XtVaTypedArg,
        XmNmessageString,
        XmRString,
        msgstr,
        strlen(msgstr),
        NULL);

    XtAddCallback(quitDlg, reallyQuit, NULL);
    }
XtManageChild(quitDlg);
]
```

Append this code fragment to the end of any sample listings in this chapter to get instant checking before you actually quit the application. Note that the `quitDlg` dialog box is set to NULL when the function is first called. It does not have to be re-created on every call after the first one; it is only managed for all subsequent calls to this function.

Modes of a Dialog Box

A dialog box can have four modes of operation, called *modality*. The mode is set in the XmNdialogStyle resource. The possible values are

- Nonmodal: The user can ignore the dialog box and work with any other window on the screen. Resource value is XmDIALOG_MODELESS.

- Primary Application Modal: All input to the window that invoked the dialog box is locked out. The user can use the rest of the windows in the application. Resource value is XmDIALOG_PRIMARY_APPLICATION_MODAL.

- Full Application Modal: All input to all the windows in the application that invoked the dialog box is locked out. The user cannot use the rest of the windows in the application. Resource value is XmDIALOG_FULL_APPLICATION_MODAL.

- System Modal: All input is directed to the dialog box. The user cannot interact with any other window in the system. Resource value is XmDIALOG_SYSTEM_MODAL.

The dialog boxes provided by Motif are based on the `XmMessageBox` Widget. Sometimes it is necessary to get to the Widgets in a dialog box. This is done with a call to `XmMessageBox GetChild( Widget dialog, typeOfWidget);` where `typeOfWidget` can be one of the following:

> `XmDIALOG_HELP_BUTTON`   `XmDIALOG_CANCEL_BUTTON`
>
> `XmDIALOG_SEPARATOR XmDIALOG_MESSAGE_LABEL`
>
> `XmDIALOG_OK_BUTTON XmDIALOG_SYMBOL_LABEL`

The dialog box may have more Widgets that can be addressed. Check the man pages for the descriptions of these Widgets. For example, to hide the Help button on a dialog box, use the call

`XtUnmanageChild(XmMessageBoxGetChild(dlg, XmDIALOG_HELP_BUTTON));`

or, in the case of adding a callback, use

```
XtAddCallback(XmMessageBoxGetChild(dlg, XmDIALOG_OK_BUTTON),
         XmNactivateCallback, yourFunction);
```

A typical method of creating custom dialog boxes is to use existing ones. Then, using the `XmMessageBoxGetChild` function, you can add or remove any function you want. For example, by replacing the message string Widget with a Form Widget, you have a place for laying out Widgets however you need to.

Events

An *event* is a message sent from the X server to the application that some condition in the system has changed. This could be a button press, a keystroke, requested information from the server, or a timeout. An event is always relative to a window and starts from the bottom up. It propagates up the window hierarchy until it gets to the root window, where the root window application makes the decision to either use or discard it. If an application in the hierarchy does use the event or does not allow upward propagation of events, the message is used at the window itself. Only device events are propagated upward (such as keyboard or mouse)—not configuration events.

An application must request an event of a particular type before it can begin receiving events. Each Motif application calls `XtAppInitialize` to create this connection automatically.

Events contain at least the following information :

- The type of event
- The display where it happened
- The window of the event, called the *event window*
- The serial number of the last event processed by the server

Look in the file `<X11/Xlib.h>` for a description of the union called `XEvent`, which enables access to these values. The file `<X11/X.h>` contains the descriptions of constants for the types of events. All event types share the header:

```
typedef struct {
      int type;
      unsigned long serial;   /* # of last request processed by server */
      Bool send_event;  /* true if this came from a SendEvent request */
      Display *display;/* display the event was read from */
      Window window;    /* window on which event was requested in event mask */
} XAnyEvent;
```

Expose Events

The server generates an Expose when a window that was covered by another is brought to the top of the stack, or even partially exposed. The structure for this event type is

```
typedef struct {
      int type;            /* type of event */
      unsigned long serial;   /* # of last request processed by server */
      Bool send_event;  /* true if this came from a SendEvent request */
      Display *display; /* display the event was read from */
      Window window;
      int x, y;
      int width, height;
      int count;           /* if nonzero, at least this many more */
} XExposeEvent;
```

Note how the first five fields are shared between this event and `XAnyEvent`. Expose events are guaranteed to be in sequence. An application may get several Expose events from one condition. The count field keeps a count of the number of Expose events still in the queue when the application receives this one. Thus, it can be up to the application to wait to redraw until the last Expose event is received (that is, `count == 0`).

Pointer Events

A Pointer event is generated by a mouse press, release, or movement. The type of event is called `XButtonEvent`. Recall that the leftmost button is Button1, but it can be changed. (See the section on left-handed users in the previous chapter.) The structure returned by this button press and release is

```
typedef struct {
      int type;          /* of event */
      unsigned long serial;   /* # of last request processed by server */
      Bool send_event;  /* true if this came from a SendEvent request */
      Display *display; /* display the event was read from */
      Window window;              /* "event" window it is reported relative to */
      Window root;                /* root window that the event occured on */
      Window subwindow; /* child window */
      Time time;        /* milliseconds */
      int x, y;         /* pointer x, y coordinates in event window */
```

```
        int x_root, y_root;     /* coordinates relative to root */
        unsigned int state;     /* key or button mask */
        unsigned int button;    /* detail */
        Bool same_screen;       /* same screen flag */
} XButtonEvent;

typedef XButtonEvent XButtonPressedEvent;
typedef XButtonEvent XButtonReleasedEvent;
```

The event for a movement is called XMotionEvent, with the type field set to MotionNotify.

```
typedef struct {
        int type;            /* MotionNotify */
        unsigned long serial;   /* # of last request processed by server */
        Bool send_event;   /* true if this came from a SendEvent request */
        Display *display; /* display the event was read from */
        Window window;              /* "event" window reported relative to */
        Window root;                /* root window that the event occured on */
        Window subwindow; /* child window */
        Time time;          /* milliseconds */
        int x, y;            /* pointer x, y coordinates in event window */
        int x_root, y_root;     /* coordinates relative to root */
        unsigned int state;     /* key or button mask */
        char is_hint;           /* detail */
        Bool same_screen; /* same screen flag */
} XMotionEvent;

typedef XMotionEvent XPointerMovedEvent;
```

Keyboard Events

A keyboard event is generated when the user presses or releases a key. Both types of events, KeyPress and KeyRelease, are returned in a XKeyEvent structure.

```
typedef struct {
        int type;               /* of event */
        unsigned long serial;   /* # of last request processed by server */
        Bool send_event;   /* true if this came from a SendEvent request */
        Display *display; /* display the event was read from */
        Window window;              /* "event" window it is reported relative to */
        Window root;                /* root window that the event occured on */
        Window subwindow; /* child window */
        Time time;          /* milliseconds */
        int x, y;            /* pointer x, y coordinates in event window */
        int x_root, y_root;     /* coordinates relative to root */
        unsigned int state;     /* key or button mask */
        unsigned int keycode;   /* detail */
        Bool same_screen; /* same screen flag */
} XKeyEvent;

typedef XKeyEvent XKeyPressedEvent;
typedef XKeyEvent XKeyReleasedEvent;
```

The keycode field gives information on whether the key was pressed or released. These constants are defined in <X11/keysymdef.h> and are vendor-specific. These are called KeySym and are generic across all X servers. For example, the F1 key could be described as XK_F1. The function XLookupString converts a KeyPress event into a string and a KeySym (a portable key symbol). The call is

```
int XLookupString(XKeyEvent *event,
            char *returnString,
            int max_length,
            KeySym *keysym,
            XComposeStatus *compose);
```

The returned ASCII string is placed in returnString for up to max_length characters. The keysym contains the key symbol. Generally, the compose parameter is ignored.

Window Crossing Events

The server generates crossing EnterNotify events when a pointer enters a window and LeaveNotify events when a pointer leaves a window. These are used to create special effects for notifying the user that the window has focus. The XCrossingEvent structure looks like the following:

```
typedef struct {
        int type;           /* of event */
        unsigned long serial;   /* # of last request processed by server */
        Bool send_event;  /* true if this came from a SendEvent request */
        Display *display; /* display the event was read from */
        Window window;              /* "event" window reported relative to */
        Window root;                /* root window that the event occured on */
        Window subwindow; /* child window */
        Time time;          /* milliseconds */
        int x, y;           /* pointer x, y coordinates in event window */
        int x_root, y_root;     /* coordinates relative to root */
        int mode;               /* NotifyNormal, NotifyGrab, NotifyUngrab */
        int detail;
        /*
         * NotifyAncestor, NotifyVirtual, NotifyInferior,
         * NotifyNonlinear, NotifyNonlinearVirtual
         */
        Bool same_screen; /* same screen flag */
        Bool focus;         /* boolean focus */
        unsigned int state;     /* key or button mask */
} XCrossingEvent;
typedef XCrossingEvent XEnterWindowEvent;
typedef XCrossingEvent XLeaveWindowEvent;
```

These are generally used to color a window on entry and exit to provide feedback to the user as he moves the pointer around.

Event Masks

An application requests events of a particular type by calling a function named XAddEventHandler(). The prototype for this function is

```
XAddEventHandler( Widget ,
            EventMask ,
            Boolean maskable,
            XtEventHandler handlerfunction,
            XtPointer clientData);
```

The handler function is of the form

```
void handlerFunction( Widget w, XtPointer clientData,
                XEvent *ev, Boolean *continueToDispatch);
```

The first two arguments are the `clientdata` and `Widget` passed in `XtAddEventHandler`. The `ev` argument is the event that triggered this call. The last argument enables this message to be passed to other message handlers for this type of event. This should be defaulted to TRUE.

You would use the following call on a `Widget` `w` to be notified of all pointer events of the type `ButtonMotion` and `PointerMotion` on this Widget.

```
extern void handlerFunction( Widget w, XtPointer clientData,
                XEvent *ev, Boolean *continueToDispatch);

XAddEventHandler( w, ButtonMotionMask ¦ PointerMotionMask, FALSE,
        handlerFunction, NULL );
```

The possible event masks are

- NoEventMask
- KeyPressMask
- KeyReleaseMask
- ButtonPressMask
- ButtonReleaseMask
- EnterWindowMask
- LeaveWindowMask
- PointerMotionMask
- PointerMotionHintMask
- Button1MotionMask
- Button2MotionMask
- Button3MotionMask
- Button4MotionMask
- Button5MotionMask
- ButtonMotionMask
- KeymapStateMask
- ExposureMask
- VisibilityChangeMask
- StructureNotifyMask
- ResizeRedirectMask
- SubstructureNotifyMask
- SubstructureRedirectMask

- FocusChangeMask
- PropertyChangeMask
- ColormapChangeMask
- OwnerGrabButtonMask

Listing 32.14 is a sample application that shows how to track the mouse position.

Listing 32.14. Tracking a pointer.

```
/*
** This application shows how to track a pointer
*/

#include <X11/Intrinsic.h>
#include <Xm/Xm.h>
#include <Xm/Form.h>
#include <Xm/PushB.h>
#include <Xm/Label.h>

static int track;

void  upMouse(Widget w, XtPointer clientdata, XEvent *x, Boolean *f)
{
track = 0;
}
void  moveMouse(Widget w, XtPointer clientdata, XEvent *x, Boolean *f)
{
if (track == 1)
    {
    printf("\n x: %d, y: %d", x->xmotion.x, x->xmotion.y);
    }
}
void  downMouse(Widget w, XtPointer clientdata, XEvent *x, Boolean *f)
{
track = 1;
}

void  bye(Widget w, XtPointer clientdata, XtPointer calldata);

int main(int  argc, char **argv)
{
Widget top;
XtAppContext app;
Widget aForm;
Widget aLabel;
Widget aButton;
Arg    args[5];

/**
*** Initialize the toolkit.
**/
top = XtAppInitialize(&app, "KBH", NULL, 0, (Cardinal *)&argc,
          argv, NULL, args, 0);

/**
```

```
*** Create a Form on this top-level Widget. This is a nice Widget
*** to place other Widgets on top of.
**/
aForm = XtVaCreateManagedWidget("Form1",
     xmFormWidgetClass, top,
     XmNheight,90,
     XmNwidth,200,
     NULL);

/**
*** Add a button on the form you just created. Note how this Button
*** Widget is connected to the form that it resides on. Only
*** left, right, and bottom edges are attached to the form. The
*** top edge of the button is not connected to the form.
**/
aButton = XtVaCreateManagedWidget("Push to Exit",
     xmPushButtonWidgetClass, aForm,
     XmNheight,20,
     XmNleftAttachment,XmATTACH_FORM,
     XmNleftOffset,20,
     XmNrightAttachment,XmATTACH_FORM,
     XmNrightOffset,20,
     XmNbottomAttachment,XmATTACH_FORM,
     NULL);

/**
*** Now let's create the label for us.
*** The alignment is set to right-justify the label.
*** Note how the label is attached to the parent form.
**/

aLabel = XtVaCreateManagedWidget("This is a Label",
     xmLabelWidgetClass, aForm,
     XmNalignment, XmALIGNMENT_END,
     XmNleftAttachment,XmATTACH_FORM,
     XmNrightAttachment,XmATTACH_FORM,
     XmNtopAttachment,XmATTACH_FORM,
     XmNbottomAttachment,XmATTACH_WIDGET,
     XmNbottomWidget,aButton,
     NULL);

/**
*** Now add the event handlers for tracking the mouse on the
*** label. Note that the LeaveWindowMask is set to release
*** the pointer for you should you keep the button pressed
*** and leave the window.
**/
XtAddEventHandler( aLabel, ButtonPressMask, FALSE, downMouse, NULL);
XtAddEventHandler( aLabel, ButtonMotionMask, FALSE, moveMouse, NULL);
XtAddEventHandler( aLabel, ButtonReleaseMask | LeaveWindowMask,
            FALSE, upMouse, NULL);
/**
*** Call the function "bye" when the PushButton receives
*** an activate message; i.e. when the pointer is moved to
*** the button and Button1 is pressed and released.
**/
```

continues

Listing 32.14. continued

```
XtAddCallback( aButton, XmNactivateCallback, bye, (XtPointer) NULL);
XtRealizeWidget(top);
XtAppMainLoop(app);
return(0);
}

void  bye(Widget w, XtPointer clientdata, XtPointer calldata)
{
exit(0);
}
```

Managing the Queue

Managing the X server is critical if you have to handle lots of incoming events. The XtAppMainLoop() function handles all the incoming events via the following functions:

- XtAppPending checks the queue to see if any events are pending.
- XtAppNextEvent removes the next event from the queue.
- XtDispatchEvent passes the message to the appropriate window.

The loop can do something else between checking and removing messages via the replacement code segment:

```
while (!done)
     {
     while (XtAppPending( applicationContext))
          {
          XtAppNextEvent( applicationContext, &ev));
          XtDispacthEvent( &ev));
          }
     done = interEventFunction();
     }
```

There are some caveats with this scheme:

- This is a nonblocking function. It must be fed at all times with events, or it will take over all other applications' time.
- There is no guarantee when your inter-event function will be run if the queue is flooded with events.
- Note the while loop for checking messages. It's more efficient to flush the queue first and then call your function rather than calling it once every time you check for messages.
- The inter-event function must be fast or you will see the user interface slow down. If you want to give some response back to your user about what's going on while in a long inter-event function, you can make a call to XmUpdateDisplay(Display *). This will handle only the Expose events in the queue so that you can update some status display.

> **TIP**
>
> Consider using the select call to handle incoming events of file descriptors. This is a call that enables an application to wait for events from various file descriptors on read-ready, write-ready, or both. The file descriptors can be sockets, too!
>
> See the man page for more information on the select call.
>
> *Open all the files with an open call.*
>
> *Get the file descriptor for the event queue.*
>
> *Use the Select macros to set up the parameters for select call ret = return from the select function:*
>
> *switch (ret)*
>
>   *case 0:*
>
>   *process the event queue*
>
>   *case 1: ...*
>
>   *process the file descriptor*

Work Procedures

These are functions called by the event-handler loop whenever no events are pending in the queue. The function is expected to return a Boolean value indicating whether it has to be removed from the loop after it is called. If TRUE, it wants to be removed; if FALSE, it wants to be called again. For example, you could set up a disk file transfer to run in the background, which will keep returning FALSE until it is done, at which time it will return TRUE.

The work procedures are defined as

```
Boolean yourFunction(XtPointer clientdata);
```

The way to register a work procedure is to call

```
XtWorkProcId    XtAppAddWorkProc ( XtAppContext app,
                    XtWorkProc    functionPointer,
                    XtPointer     clientData);
```

The return ID from this call is the handle to the work procedure. It is used to remove the work procedure with a call to the function XtRemoveWorkProc(XtWorkProcId id);

Using Timeouts

A *timeout* is used to perform some task at (almost) regular intervals. Applications set up a timer callback function that is called when a requested time interval has passed. This function is defined as

```
void thyTimerCallback( XtPointer clientdata, XtInterval *tid);
```

where `clientdata` is a pointer to client-specific data. The `setup` function for the timeout returns the timer ID and is defined as

```
XtIntervalId XtAddTimeOut ( XtAppContext app,
                    int milliseconds,
                    XtTimerCallback TimerProcedure,
                    XtPointer clientdata);
```

This call sets up a timer to call the `TimerProcedure` function when the requested milliseconds have passed. It will do this only once. If you want cyclic timeouts—for example, in a clock application— you have to explicitly set up the next function call in the timer handler function itself. So generally, the last line in a timer handler is a call to set a timeout for the next time the function wants to be called.

Linux is not designed for real-time applications, and you can't expect a deterministic time interval between successive timer calls. Some heavy graphics updates can cause delays in the timer loop. For user-interface applications, the delays are probably not a big drawback; however, consult your vendor before you attempt to write a time-critical control application. Depending on your application, your mileage may vary. See Listing 32.15 for an example of setting up cyclic timers.

Listing 32.15. Setting up cyclic timers.

```
/*
** This application shows how to set a cyclic timer
*/

#include <X11/Intrinsic.h>
#include <Xm/Xm.h>
#include <Xm/Form.h>
#include <Xm/PushB.h>
#include <Xm/Text.h>

int counter;
char buf[32];
#define ONE_SECOND 1000L   /* **APPROXIMATELY** 1000 milliseconds..*/

/* Timing is *not* precise in Motif... so do not rely on this time
** for a time-critical application. Use interrupt handlers instead.
*/
void makeTimer(Widget w, XtIntervalId id);

void  bye(Widget w, XtPointer clientdata, XtPointer calldata);

int main(int  argc, char **argv)
{
Widget top;
XtAppContext app;
Widget aForm;
Widget aText;
Widget aButton;
Arg    args[5];

/**
*** Initialize the toolkit.
**/
```

```
top = XtAppInitialize(&app, "KBH", NULL, 0, (Cardinal *)&argc,
         argv, NULL, args, 0);

/**
*** Create a Form on this top-level Widget. This is a nice Widget
*** to place other Widgets on top of.
**/
aForm = XtVaCreateManagedWidget("Form1",
    xmFormWidgetClass, top,
    XmNheight,90,
    XmNwidth,200,
    NULL);

/**
*** Add a button on the form you just created. Note how this Button
*** Widget is connected to the form that it resides on. Only
*** left, right, and bottom edges are attached to the form. The
*** top edge of the button is not connected to the form.
**/
aButton = XtVaCreateManagedWidget("Push to Exit",
    xmPushButtonWidgetClass, aForm,
    XmNheight,20,
    XmNleftAttachment,XmATTACH_FORM,
    XmNleftOffset,20,
    XmNrightAttachment,XmATTACH_FORM,
    XmNrightOffset,20,
    XmNbottomAttachment,XmATTACH_FORM,
    NULL);

/**
*** Now let's create the label for us.
*** The alignment is set to right-justify the label.
*** Note how the label is attached to the parent form.
**/

aText = XtVaCreateManagedWidget("This is a Label",
    xmTextWidgetClass, aForm,
    XmNalignment, XmALIGNMENT_CENTER,
    XmNleftAttachment,XmATTACH_FORM,
    XmNrightAttachment,XmATTACH_FORM,
    XmNtopAttachment,XmATTACH_FORM,
    XmNbottomAttachment,XmATTACH_WIDGET,
    XmNbottomWidget,aButton,
    NULL);

/**
*** Now add the timer handler
**/

counter = 0;
makeTimer(aText, (XtIntervalId )NULL);
/**
*** Call the function "bye" when the PushButton receives
*** an activate message; i.e. when the pointer is moved to
*** the button and Button1 is pressed and released.
**/
```

continues

Listing 32.15. continued

```
XtAddCallback( aButton, XmNactivateCallback, bye, (XtPointer) NULL);
XtRealizeWidget(top);
XtAppMainLoop(app);
return(0);
}

void  bye(Widget w, XtPointer clientdata, XtPointer calldata)
{
exit(0);
}

/** This function creates the timer code. **/
void makeTimer(Widget w, XtIntervalId id)
{
Widget tmp;
extern int counter;

sprintf(buf,"%4d",counter++);
XmTextSetString(w,buf);

if (counter < 10) /** reinvoke yourself if < 10 times **/
XtAppAddTimeOut( XtWidgetToApplicationContext(w), ONE_SECOND,
          (XtTimerCallbackProc)makeTimer, (XtPointer)w);

}
```

Handling Other Sources

The XtAddInput function is used to handle inputs from sources other than the event queue. The definition is

```
XtInputId XtAddInput( XtAppContext  app,
                  int           LinuxfileDescriptor,
                  XtPointer     condition,
                  XtInputCallback   inputHandler,
                  XtPointer     clientdata);
```

The return value from this call is the handle to the inputHandler function. This is used to remove the call via the call

```
XtRemoveInput( XtInput Id);
```

The inputHandler function itself is defined as

```
void InputHandler(XtPointer clientdata, int *fd, XtInputId *id);
```

Unlike timers, you have to register this function only once. Note that a pointer to a file descriptor is passed in to the function. The file descriptor must be a Linux file descriptor. You do not have support for Linux IPC message queues or semaphores through this scheme. The IPC mechanism is considered dated and is limited to one machine. Consider using sockets instead.

NOTE

AIX enables pending on message queues via the select call. Look at the AIX man pages for this call.

The Graphics Context

Each Widget draws itself on the screen using its set of drawing parameters called the *graphics context* (GC). For drawing on a Widget, you can use the X primitive functions if you have its window and its graphics context. It's easier to limit your artwork to the DrawingArea Widget, which is designed for this purpose. You can think of the GC as your paintbrush and the Widget as the canvas. The color and thickness of the paintbrush are just some of the factors that determine how the paint is transferred to the canvas.

The function call to create a GC is to use

```
GC XCreateGC (Display dp, Drawable d, unsigned long mask, XGCValue *values);
```

For use with a Widget w, this call would look like this:

```
GC gc;
XGCVvalue gcv;
unsigned long mask;

gc = XCreate(XtDisplay(w), DefaultRootWindow(XtDisplay(w)),
             mask, gcv);
```

Also, you can create a GC for a Widget directly with a call to XtGetGC(). The prototype for this function is

```
gc = XtGetGC (Widget w, unsigned long mask, XGCValue *values);
```

The values for the mask parameter are defined as an ORed value of the following definitions:

- GCFunction
- GCPlaneMask
- GCForeground
- GCBackground
- GCLineWidth
- GCLineStyle
- GCCapStyle
- GCJoinStyle
- GCFillStyle
- GCFillRule

Listing 32.16. continued

```
void  bye(Widget w, XtPointer clientdata, XtPointer calldata);

int main(int  argc, char **argv)
{
Widget top;
XtAppContext app;
Arg    args[5];

/**
*** Initialize the toolkit.
**/
top = XtAppInitialize(&app, "KBH", NULL, 0, (Cardinal *)&argc,
          argv, NULL, args, 0);

/**
*** Create a Form on this top-level Widget. This is a nice Widget
*** to place other Widgets on top of.
**/
aForm = XtVaCreateManagedWidget("Form1",
     xmFormWidgetClass, top,
     XmNheight,200,
     XmNwidth,200,
     NULL);

/**
*** Add a button on the form you just created. Note how this Button
*** Widget is connected to the form that it resides on. Only
*** left, right, and bottom edges are attached to the form. The
*** top edge of the button is not connected to the form.
**/
aButton = XtVaCreateManagedWidget("Push to Exit",
     xmPushButtonWidgetClass, aForm,
     XmNheight,20,
     XmNleftAttachment,XmATTACH_FORM,
     XmNleftOffset,20,
     XmNrightAttachment,XmATTACH_FORM,
     XmNrightOffset,20,
     XmNbottomAttachment,XmATTACH_FORM,
     NULL);

/**
*** Now let's create the label for us.
*** The alignment is set to right-justify the label.
*** Note how the label is attached to the parent form.
**/

aDraw = XtVaCreateManagedWidget("paperusitto",
     xmDrawingAreaWidgetClass, aForm,
     XmNalignment, XmALIGNMENT_END,
     XmNleftAttachment,XmATTACH_FORM,
     XmNrightAttachment,XmATTACH_FORM,
     XmNtopAttachment,XmATTACH_FORM,
     XmNbottomAttachment,XmATTACH_WIDGET,
     XmNbottomWidget,aButton,
     NULL);
```

```
gcv.foreground = BlackPixel(XtDisplay(aDraw), DefaultScreen(XtDisplay(aDraw)));
gcv.background = WhitePixel(XtDisplay(aDraw), DefaultScreen(XtDisplay(aDraw)));
gcv.line_width = 2;
thisGC = XtGetGC( aDraw,
 GCForeground | GCBackground | GCLineWidth,
            (XGCValues *) &gcv);
/**
*** Now add the event handlers for tracking the mouse on the
*** label. Note that the LeaveWindowMask is set to release
*** the pointer for you should you keep the button pressed
*** and leave the window and disables tracking.
**/
XtAddEventHandler( aDraw, ButtonPressMask, FALSE, downMouse, NULL);
XtAddEventHandler( aDraw, ButtonMotionMask, FALSE, moveMouse, NULL);
XtAddEventHandler( aDraw, ButtonReleaseMask,FALSE, upMouse, NULL);
XtAddEventHandler( aDraw, LeaveWindowMask, FALSE, lostMouse, NULL);
/**
*** Call the function "bye" when the PushButton receives
*** an activate message; i.e. when the pointer is moved to
*** the button and Button1 is pressed and released.
**/
XtAddCallback( aButton, XmNactivateCallback, bye, (XtPointer) NULL);

XtRealizeWidget(top);
XtAppMainLoop(app);
return(0);
}

void reallyQuit(Widget w, XtPointer clientdata, XtPointer calldata)
{
exit(0);
}

/**
*** pesky quit routine
**/
void  bye(Widget w, XtPointer clientdata, XtPointer calldata)
{
static Widget quitDlg = NULL;
static char *msgstr = "Are you sure you want to Quit?";

if (quitDlg != (Widget )NULL)
      {
      /* first time called */
      quitDlg = XmCreateQuestionDialog(w,"R U Sure", (XtPointer *)NULL,0);
      XtVaSetValues(quitDlg,
                  XmNdialogStyle, XmDIALOG_FULL_APPLICATION_MODAL,
            XtVaTypedArg, XmNmessageString, XmRString,
            msgstr,
 strlen(msgstr),
            NULL);

      XtAddCallback(quitDlg, XmNokCallback, reallyQuit, NULL);
      }
XtManageChild(quitDlg);
}
```

The output from Listing 32.16 is shown in Figure 32.12.

FIGURE 32.12.

Drawing points and lines.

This is an example of the primitives required to draw one line on the Widget. Note the number of GCValues that have to be set to achieve this purpose. The XDrawLine function definition is as follows:

```
XDrawLine( Display *dpy,
      Drawable d,
      GC gc,
      int x1,
      int y1,
      int x2,
      int y2);
```

It's more efficient to draw multiple lines in one call. Use the XDrawLines function with a pointer to an array of points and its size.

The mode parameter can be set to

- CoorModeOrigin to use the values relative to the drawables' origin.
- CoorModePrevious to use the values as deltas from the previous point. A *delta* is the change in x and y coordinates between this coordinate and the previous one.

The first point is always relative to the drawables' origin. To draw boxes, use the XDrawRectangle function:

```
XDrawRectangle( Display *display, Drawable dwindow,
            GC    gc,int    x,int      y,
            unsigned int width, unsigned int height);
```

will draw a rectangle at (x,y) of geometry (width, height). To draw more than one box at a time, use the XDrawRectangles() function. This function is declared as

```
XDrawRectangles( Display *display, Window dwindow,
            GC    gc, XRectangle *xp, int number);
```

where xp is a pointer to an array of number rectangle definition structures.

For filled rectangles, use the XFillRectangle and XFillRectangles calls, respectively.

Drawing a Point

To draw a point on-screen, use the XDrawPoint or XDrawPoints function call. This is similar to line-drawing functions. (Refer back to Listing 32.16.)

Drawing an Arc

To draw circles, arcs, and similar shapes, use the XDrawArc function:

```
XDrawArc(Display *display, Window dwindow,
        GC   gc, int x, int y,
        unsigned int width, unsigned int height,
        int        a1, int a2);
```

This function is very flexible. It draws an arc from an angle a1 starting from the 3 o'clock position to angle a2. The units for angles are in one sixty-fourths (1/64) of a degree. The arc is drawn counterclockwise. The largest value is (64×360) units because the angle arguments are truncated. The width and height define the bounding rectangle for the arc. The XDrawArcs() function is used to draw multiple arcs, given pointers to the array. The prototype for this function is

```
XDrawArcs (Display *display, Window dwindow,
        GC gc, XArc *arcptr, int number);
```

To draw polygons, use the call

```
XDrawSegments( Display *display, Window dwindow, GC gc,
        XSegment *segments, int number);
```

The XSegment structure includes four short members—x1,y1,x2, and y2—which define the starting and ending points of all segments. For connected lines, use the XDrawLines function shown earlier. For filled polygons, use the XFillPolygon() function call.

Using Fonts and FontLists

Fonts are perhaps the trickiest aspect of Motif to master. See the section on fonts in Chapter 23, "Using Motif," before reading this section to familiarize yourself with font definitions.

The function XLoadQueryFont(Display *dp, char *name) returns an XFontStruct structure. This structure defines the extents for the character set. This is used to set the values of the Font field in a GC.

To draw a string on the screen, use

```
XDrawString ( Display *dp, Drawable dw, GC gc,
        int x, int y, char *str, int len);
```

which uses only the foreground color. To draw with the background and foreground colors, use

```
XDrawImageString ( Display *dp, Drawable dw, GC gc,
        int x, int y, char *str, int len);
```

The X Color Model

The X Color Model is based on an array of colors called a *colormap*. Applications refer to a color by its index into this colormap. The indices are placed in the application's frame buffer, which contains an entry for each pixel of the display. The number of bits in the index defines the number of bitplanes. The number of bitplanes defines the number of colors that can be displayed on-screen at one time. For example, one bit per pixel gives two colors, four bits per pixel gives 16 colors, and eight bits per pixel gives 256 colors.

Applications generally inherit the colormap of their parent. They can also create their own colormap using the XCreateColormap call. The call is defined as

```
Colormap XCreateColormap( Display *display, Window   dwindow,
                 Visual   *vp, int requested);
```

This allocates the number of requested color entries in the colormap for a window. Generally, the visual parameter is derived from the macro

```
DefaultVisual (Display *display, int screenNumber);
```

where screenNumber = 0 in almost all cases. (See the previous chapter on Screens, Displays, and Windows for a definition of screens.) Colormaps are a valuable resource in X and must be freed after use. This is done via the call XFreeColormap(Display *display, Colormap c);

Applications can get the standard colormap from the X server by using the XGetStandardColormap() call, and set it via the XSetStandardColormap() call. These are defined as

```
XGetStandardColormap( Display *display, Window   dwindow,
         XStandardColormap *c, Atom property);
```

and

```
XSetStandardColormap( Display *display, Window   dwindow,
XStandardColormap *c, Atom property);
```

Once applications have a Colormap to work with, they have to follow two steps:

1. Define the colormap entries.

   The property atom can take the values of RGB_BEST_MAP, RGB_GRAY_MAP, or 2RGB_DEFAULT_MAP. These are names of colormaps stored in the server. They are not colormaps in themselves.

2. Set the colormap for a window via the call

   ```
   XSetWindowColormap ( Display *display, Window   dwindow,   Colormap c );
   ```

For setting or allocating a color in the Colormap, use the XColor structure defined in <X/Xlib.h>.

To see a bright blue color, use the segment

```
XColor color;
color.red = 0;
color.blue = 0xffff;
color.green = 0;
```

Then add the color to the Colormap using the call to the function:

```
XAllocColor(Display *display,
            Window dwindow,
            XColor *color );
```

See Listing 32.17 for a sample function to set the color of a Widget.

Listing 32.17. Convenience function for getting colors.

```
/**
*** Convenience function to get colors
**/
Pixel GetPixel( Widget w, int r, int g, int b)
{
Display *dpy;
int     scr;
Colormap cmp;
XColor        clr;

dpy = XtDisplay(w);
scr = DefaultScreen(dpy);
cmp = DefaultColormap(dpy);

clr.red = (short)r;
clr.green = (short)g;
clr.blue = (short)b;
clr.flags = DoRed ¦ DoGreen ¦ DoBlue;

/**
*** Note that the default black pixel of the display and screen
*** is returned if the color could not be allocated.
**/
return(XAllocColor(dpy,cmp,&clr) ? clr.pixel : BlackPixel(dpy,scr));
}
```

The default white and black pixels are defined as

```
Pixel BlackPixel( Display *dpy, int screen);
Pixel WhitePixel( Display *dpy, int screen);
```

and will work with any screen as a fallback.

The index (Pixel) returned by this function is not guaranteed to be the same every time the application runs. This is because the colormap could be shared between applications requesting colors in different orders. Each entry is allocated on a next-available-entry basis. Sometimes, if you overwrite an existing entry in a cell, you might actually see a change in a completely different application. So be careful.

Applications can query the RGB components of a color by calling the function

```
XQueryColor( Display *display, Colormap *cmp, Xcolor  *clr);
```

For many colors at one time, use

```
XQueryColors( Display *display, Colormap *cmp,
        Xcolor     *clr,      int number);
```

At this time the application can modify the RGB components. Then you can store them in the colormap with the call

```
XStoreColor( Display *display, Colormap *cmp,XColor *clr);
```

Recall that X11 has some strange names for colors in the /usr/lib/rgb.txt file. Applications can get the RGB components of these names with a call to

```
XLookupColor( Display *display, Colormap cmp,
        char  *name,XColor *clr, XColor  *exact);
```

The name is the string to search for in the rgb.txt file. The returned value clr contains the next closest existing entry in the colormap. The exact color entry contains the exact RGB definition in the entry in rgb.txt. This function does not allocate the color in the colormap. To do that, use the call

```
XAllocNamedColor( Display *display, Colormap cmp,
        char  *name, Xcolor    *clr, XColor  *exact);
```

Pixmaps, Bitmaps, and Images

A Pixmap is like a window, but is off-screen and therefore invisible to the user. This is usually the same depth of the screen. You create a Pixmap with the call

```
XCreatePixmap (Display *dp,
        Drawable dw,
        unsigned int width,
        unsigned int height,
        unsigned int depth);
```

A drawable can be either a Window (on-screen) or a Pixmap (off-screen). *Bitmaps* are Pixmaps of a depth of one pixel. Look in

```
/usr/include/X11/bitmaps
```

for a listing of some of the standard bitmaps.

The way to copy Pixmaps from memory to the screen is via the call to XCopyArea. The prototype for this call is

```
XCopyArea( Display dp,
    Drawable Src, Drawable Dst,
    GC gc, int src_x, int src_y,
    unsigned int width, unsigned int height,
    int dot_x, int dsl_y);
```

The caveat with this XCopyArea is that the depth of the Src and Dst drawables have to be of the same depth. To show a bitmap on a screen with depth greater than 1 pixel, you have to copy the bitmap one plane at a time. This is done via the call

```
XCopyPlane( Display dp,
    Drawable Src, Drawable Dst,
    GC gc, int src_x, int src_y,
    unsigned int width, unsigned int height,
    int dst_x, int dst_y, unsigned long plane);
```

where the plane specifies the bit plane to which this one-bit-deep bitmap must be copied. The actual operation is largely dependent on the modes set in the GC.

For example, to show the files in the /usr/include/bitmaps directory that have three defined values for a sample file called gumby.h:

- gumby_bits = pointer to an array of character bits.
- gumby_height and gumby_width = integer height and width.

First, create the bitmap from the data using the XCreateBitmapFromData() call. To display this one-plane-thick image, copy the image from this plane to plane 1 of the display. You can actually copy to any plane in the window. A sample call could be set for copying from your Pixmap to the Widget's plane 1 in the following manner:

```
XCopyPlane( XtDisplay(w), yourPixmap, XtWindow(w), gc,
    0,0, your_height, your_width, 0,0,1);
```

where it copies from the origin of the pixmap to the origin of plane 1 of the window.

There are other functions for working with images in X. These include the capability to store device-dependent images on disk and the Xpm format.

Summary

This chapter covered the following topics:

- The basics of writing Motif applications
- The special naming conventions in Motif and X
- Writing and compiling your first Motif application
- An overview of the Motif Widget hierarchy
- Working with various common Widgets
- Designing layouts
- Creating pop-up menus and menu bars
- Creating simple dialog boxes
- How to use the mouse in event handling
- How to use colors in X
- How to draw lines and points.

This chapter could easily expand into a book. (Please do not tempt me!) I have only covered the basics of writing Motif applications. However, given the vast number of tools in Linux, you can see how you can port any existing Motif application code to and from a Linux machine. Similarly, a Linux machine can also prove to be a good development platform for developing Motif applications.

Programming XView Applications

33

by
Kamran Husain

IN THIS CHAPTER

In this chapter you will learn how to program in an older, but still widely found, OPEN LOOK–based user interface manager called XView. You will find this distribution helpful when you work with older code or when you port code from the OPEN LOOK style to Motif.

A Note About CDE

In March 1993, the Common Open Software Environment (COSE) committees adopted the Common Desktop Environment (CDE). CDE is based on the Motif interface. Sun Microsystems Inc., the primary developer of OPEN LOOK applications, agreed to conform to CDE as well. In short, this means that OPEN LOOK interface–based applications will soon be out of style. However, applications with an OPEN LOOK interface still exist and have to be ported to Motif eventually. A good knowledge of how OPEN LOOK applications work will be very beneficial to you if you ever have to port old existing code to conform to CDE.

Overview

To a programmer, the XView toolkit is an object-oriented toolkit. Think of XView objects as building blocks from which the user can create complicated applications, and think of each block as part of a package. Each package provides properties that you can modify to configure the object.

The XView toolkit consists of the objects shown in Figure 33.1. The subclasses are derived from the classes to their left. For example, Icon is a subclass of Window. Each class is also referred to as a package.

FIGURE 33.1.

XView class hierarchy.

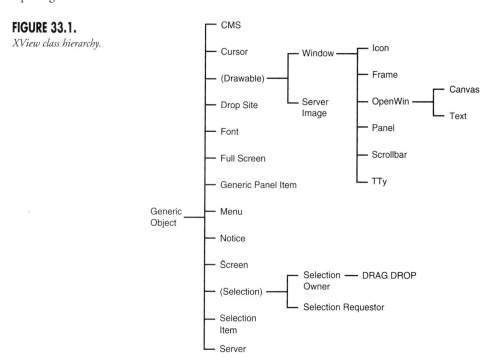

Some objects are visible and some are not. The visible objects provide the windows, scrollbars, and so on. The invisible objects, such as the font, display, or server, provide frameworks that aid in the display or layout of visible objects.

When you create an object, you get a handle to the object back from the XView libraries. Handles are opaque pointers to structures. This means that you can pass information via functions to these objects via their handles but you cannot see their structures directly.

The following functions enable you to manipulate all XView objects:

- `xv_init()`   Establishes the connection to the server, initializes the notifier (message handler), and loads the resource databases
- `xv_create()`   Creates an object
- `xv_destroy()`   Destroys an object
- `xv_find()`   Finds an object with given criteria; if not found, creates the object
- `xv_get()`   Gets an attribute value
- `xv_set()`   Sets an attribute value

There are three categories of attributes: generic attributes apply to all objects; common attributes are shared by some, but not all, objects; and specific attributes belong to one class of objects only. Attributes that are specific to a type of object are prefixed with the name of the object; for example, `FRAME_*`, `ICON_*`, `MENU_*`, and so on. Common and generic attributes are prefixed by `XV_`. For example, `XV_HEIGHT` applies to all objects, but `FRAME_HEIGHT` applies only to frame objects.

Each attribute may have different types of values. For example, the following code sets a `panel_item`.

```
panel_item = (Panel_item) xv_create( masterpanel, PANEL_CYCLE,
    XV_HEIGHT,        100,
    XV_WIDTH,         50,
    PANEL_LABEL_X,       100,
    PANEL_LABEL_Y,       100,
    PANEL_LABEL_STRING, "Help",
    PANEL_CHOICE_STRINGS, "About ... ",
              "How to use Help",
              "Search Index",
           NULL,

    NULL);
```

Note how the types of values are mixed in this function call. All attributes except `PANEL_CHOICE_STRINGS` take a single argument. The `PANEL_CHOICE_STRINGS` attribute takes a list of arguments. The list is terminated with a `NULL` value.

We will go over the details of each object in this chapter.

Requirements

To create an XView program you must link in the XView and OPEN LOOK graphics library, which include all the toolkit functions for you. You will also need the X11 library. The command line to use the gcc compiler for a simple XView application is

```
$ gcc sample.c -lxview -lolgx -lX11 -o sample
```

This compile command relies on the fact that your libraries are located in /usr/lib or you have links to this location. The libraries are located in the /usr/openwin directories.

See the sample makefile in Listing 33.1 that you can use with the applications in this chapter. Please note that this is not a fully functional makefile; you will have to modify it for your applications. The excerpt shown in Listing 33.1 is for the LIST33_1.c sample file in this chapter.

Listing 33.1. Sample `makefile` for creating XView applications.

```
CC= gcc
LIBPATH=/usr/openwin/lib
INCPATH=/usr/openwin/include
LIBS= -lxview -lolgx -lX11


LIST33_1: LIST33_1.c
    $(CC) $< -I$(INCPATH) -L$(LIBPATH) $(LIBS) -o $@

LIST33_2: LIST33_2.c
    $(CC) $< -I$(INCPATH) -L$(LIBPATH) $(LIBS) -o $@

LIST33_3: LIST33_3.c
    $(CC) $< -I$(INCPATH) -L$(LIBPATH) $(LIBS) -o $@

LIST33_4: LIST33_4.c
    $(CC) $< -I$(INCPATH) -L$(LIBPATH) $(LIBS) -o $@
```

The -lxview in LIBS refers to the libxview.a library. The libxview.a library contains the code for all the windows manipulation and libolgx.a contains the OPENLOOK graphics library. The libX11.a is required by the libxview.a library, and libolgx.a is required by the libxview.a library.

Header Files

The basic definitions you must use for XView are located in two files: xview/generic.h and xview/xview.h in the /usr/openwin/include directory tree. The header files required by other packages, such as FONT or FRAME, are declared in files of the same name as the package. For example, for the FONT package you must use the xview/font.h header file. You can include these files more than once.

NOTE

In some source distributions, the file generic.h is not explicitly called out in the source files. In order to compile source files under Linux, you will need the generic.h file.

Sample Application

Take a look at the simple application shown in Listing 33.2, which places a window with a Quit button on it.

Listing 33.2. A simple application.

```
/*
** A sample program to show you how to present items for
** selection to the user.
**
*/
#include <xview/generic.h>
#include <xview/xview.h>
#include <xview/frame.h>
#include <xview/panel.h>
#include <xview/cms.h>

Frame frame;

#define FORE 0
#define BACK 2

int main(int argc, char *argv[])
{
Cms    cms;
Panel panel;
void quit();

printf("\n 0\n");
xv_init(XV_INIT_ARGC_PTR_ARGV, &argc, argv, NULL);


cms = (Cms ) xv_create((int)NULL,CMS, /* NULL -> use the default Frame*/
    CMS_SIZE, CMS_CONTROL_COLORS + 4,
    CMS_CONTROL_CMS, True,
    CMS_NAMED_COLORS, "LightBlue", "Blue", "Red", "Green", NULL,
    NULL);

frame = (Frame)xv_create((int)NULL, FRAME,
    FRAME_LABEL, argv[0],
    XV_WIDTH, 200,
    XV_HEIGHT, 100,
    NULL);

xv_set(frame,
    WIN_CMS, cms,
    WIN_FOREGROUND_COLOR, CMS_CONTROL_COLORS + FORE,
    WIN_BACKGROUND_COLOR, CMS_CONTROL_COLORS + BACK,
    NULL);

panel = (Panel)xv_create(frame, PANEL,NULL);
```

continues

```
PANEL_NOTIFY_PROC,  show_greeting,
NULL);

(void) xv_create(fpanel, PANEL_BUTTON,
PANEL_LABEL_STRING, "Push Me",
PANEL_NOTIFY_PROC,  push_it,
NULL);
```

At this point you are ready to create the main application frame, show it, and go into the main loop. The important call that does this is shown next. The function show_popup() is assigned to be called when the Hello button is pressed.

```
(void) xv_create(panel, PANEL_BUTTON,
   PANEL_LABEL_STRING, "Hello",
   PANEL_NOTIFY_PROC,  show_popup,
   NULL);
```

Now look at the functions that are called when each button is pressed. The show_greeting function simply prints out a string. (You can use your imagination here for the contents of the string for your own application.) The show_popup() function will use the call to the xv_set() function to actually make the pop-up frame visible.

```
xv_set(popup, XV_SHOW, TRUE, NULL);
```

Now for the function that will emulate the behavior of pushing in the pin. This is the push_it() function. The FRAME_CMD_PIN_STATE parameter requests the state of the pushpin on the dialog box. The state for the pin is defined as FRAME_CMD_PIN_IN if the pushpin is already pushed in. This is the state for which you check. If the pushpin is not in this state, it is pushed in with the xv_set(popup, FRAME_CMD_PIN_STATE, FRAME_CMD_PIN_IN, NULL); function call.

> **TIP**
>
> A command frame has no resize corners by default. To turn these corners on, set FRAME_SHOW_RESIZE_CORNERS to TRUE.

Setting Colors on Frames

The colors on an XView frame object are defaulted to the OpenWindows.WindowColor resource. This resource is inherited by all subframes as well. You can override these colors with the CMS package. The CMS package is created by a call to xv_create():

```
cms = (Cms *) xv_create(parent, CMS, attrs, NULL);
```

A CMS can contain as many colors as are allowed in the largest color map you can create. You can have several color maps referencing the same color; in fact, the system can share the location of colors between two independent applications. For this reason, you should allocate all your colors once, at cms creation, to allocate all the colors in your color map to prevent another application from changing the colors you absolutely need.

For example, to create a cms with four named colors, you would use the following function call:

```
cms = (Cms  *)xv_create(parent, CMS,
    CMS_SIZE, 4,
    CMS_NAMED_COLORS, "Violet", "Yellow", "Blue", "Orange",
    NULL);
```

The CMS_SIZE value asks for a four-entry color table that is indexed from 0 to 3, with the values of the named colors "Violet", "Yellow", "Blue", and "Orange". The foreground color for a frame is the first indexed color in a Cms and the background color for a frame is the last indexed (n-1) color in a Cms. Setting a CMS_SIZE will give you either an error or a monochromatic display. Of course, to avoid runtime errors you must know that the colors you just specified by name do exist in the /usr/lib/rgb.txt file.

Listing 33.5 is an example of an application that sets the colors. This will let you set the foreground and background colors of a frame and all its children.

Listing 33.5. Using CMS.

```
#include <xview/generic.h>
#include <xview/xview.h>
#include <xview/frame.h>
#include <xview/panel.h>
#include <xview/cms.h>

Frame frame;

#define FORE 3
#define BACK 0

int main(int argc, char *argv[])
{
Cms    cms;
Panel panel;
void quit();

printf("\n 0\n");
xv_init(XV_INIT_ARGC_PTR_ARGV, &argc, argv, NULL);


cms = (Cms ) xv_create((int)NULL,CMS, /* NULL -> use the default Frame*/
    CMS_SIZE, CMS_CONTROL_COLORS + 4,
    CMS_CONTROL_CMS, True,
    CMS_NAMED_COLORS, "LightBlue", "Blue", "Red", "Green", NULL,
    NULL);

frame = (Frame)xv_create((int)NULL, FRAME,
    FRAME_LABEL, argv[0],
    XV_WIDTH, 200,
    XV_HEIGHT, 100,
    NULL);

xv_set(frame,
    WIN_CMS, cms,
```

continues

678

Listing 33.5. continued

```
        WIN_FOREGROUND_COLOR, CMS_CONTROL_COLORS + FORE,
        WIN_BACKGROUND_COLOR, CMS_CONTROL_COLORS + BACK,
        NULL);

panel = (Panel)xv_create(frame, PANEL,NULL);

(void) xv_create(panel, PANEL_BUTTON,
    PANEL_LABEL_STRING, "Quit",
    PANEL_NOTIFY_PROC, quit,
    NULL);

xv_main_loop(frame);
exit(0);
}

void quit()
{
xv_destroy_safe(frame);
}
```

> **TIP**
>
> You cannot use xv_get with the CMS_NAMED_COLORS attribute.

> **CAUTION**
>
> Use xv_set() to override the colors on a frame. Any color requests on a frame at the time of creation are overridden by values of the .Xdefaults resources values.

Canvases

A *canvas* is an XView object that is used to display items that are too large to fit on a window. The viewable portion of the image is seen through a viewport or view window of the object. You can have multiple views of the same data that is stored on a canvas by splitting each scrollable portion into two or more views. The split views must all reside on the same canvas because you cannot have multiple views of canvas data that are not on the same frame.

There are three components of a canvas object:

- The Paint window, which contains the actual painted data
- The View window, which has the scrollbars but no painted data
- The canvas subwindow, which contains the union of the View window and Paint window

Look at a simple example in Listing 33.6 of how to use scrollbars and how to paint on a paint window. (I have added line numbers for readability.)

Listing 33.6. Using canvases and scrollbars.

```
1    /*
2    ** An example of a scrolled window
3    */

4    #include <X11/Xlib.h>
5    #include <xview/generic.h>
6    #include <xview/xview.h>
7    #include <xview/frame.h>
8    #include <xview/panel.h>
9    #include <xview/canvas.h>
10   #include <xview/scrollbar.h>
11   #include <xview/xv_xrect.h>

12   /*
13   ** Declare our callback functions for this application.
14   */
15   Frame frame;
16   void redraw(Canvas c, Xv_Window pw, Display *dp, Window xwin,
17           Xv_xrectlist *rp) ;

18   int main(int argc, char *argv[])
19   {
20   Canvas canvas;
21   Panel panel;
22   Scrollbar h_s, h_v;
23   void quit();

24       xv_init(XV_INIT_ARGC_PTR_ARGV, &argc, argv, NULL);

25   frame = (Frame)xv_create(NULL, FRAME,
26       FRAME_LABEL, argv[0],
27       XV_WIDTH, 400,
28       XV_HEIGHT, 200,
29       (int)NULL);

30   /*
31   ** Create the canvas.
32   */
33   canvas = (Canvas) xv_create(frame, CANVAS,
34       CANVAS_REPAINT_PROC, redraw,
35       CANVAS_X_PAINT_WINDOW, TRUE,
36       CANVAS_AUTO_SHRINK, FALSE,
37       CANVAS_AUTO_EXPAND, TRUE,
38       CANVAS_WIDTH, 500,
39       CANVAS_HEIGHT, 500,
40       XV_WIDTH, 400,
41       XV_HEIGHT, 200,
42       NULL);

43   /*
```

continues

Listing 33.6. continued

```
44      ** Create the splittable scrollbars
45      */
46          h_s = (Scrollbar)xv_create(canvas, SCROLLBAR,
47          SCROLLBAR_DIRECTION, SCROLLBAR_HORIZONTAL,
48          SCROLLBAR_SPLITTABLE, TRUE,
49          NULL);

50          h_v = (Scrollbar)xv_create(canvas, SCROLLBAR,
51          SCROLLBAR_DIRECTION, SCROLLBAR_VERTICAL,
52          SCROLLBAR_SPLITTABLE, TRUE,
53          NULL);

54      xv_main_loop(frame);
55      exit(0);
56      }

57      void redraw(Canvas c, Xv_Window pw, Display *dp, Window xwin,
58              Xv_xrectlist *rp)
59      {
60          GC gc;
61          int wd, ht;
62          int i;
63          int j;
64          int dx;
65          int dy;

66          gc = DefaultGC(dp, DefaultScreen(dp));
67          wd = (int)xv_get(pw, XV_WIDTH);
68          ht = (int)xv_get(pw, XV_HEIGHT);

69          dx = ht / 10;
70          for (i = 0; i < ht; i += dx)
71              XDrawLine(dp,xwin,gc, i,0,i,ht);

72
73          dx = wd / 10;
74          for (i = 0; i < wd; i += dx)
75              XDrawLine(dp,xwin,gc, 0,i,wd,i);
76      /* XDrawLine(dp,xwin,gc, 0,0,wd,ht);   */

77      }
78      void quit()
79      {
80      xv_destroy_safe(frame);
81      }
```

Lines 33 through 42 create the canvas. The CANVAS_AUTO_EXPAND and CANVAS_AUTO_SHRINK parameters maintain the relation of the canvas subwindow and the paint subwindow. These values default to TRUE. When both values are TRUE, the canvas and paint subwindows will expand or shrink based on the size of the window on which they are being displayed.

Setting the CANVAS_AUTO_EXPAND value to TRUE enables the paint subwindow to expand larger than the canvas subwindow. If the canvas subwindow expands to a bigger size than the paint subwindow, the paint subwindow is expanded to at least that size as well. If the canvas subwindow size shrinks, the paint subwindow does not shrink because it is already at the same size or bigger than canvas subwindows at that time.

Setting the CANVAS_AUTO_SHRINK value to TRUE forces the canvas object to always confirm that the paint subwindow's height and width are never greater than the canvas subwindow. In other words, the size of the paint subwindow is always changed to be at least the same or less than the size of the canvas subwindow.

You can explicitly set the size of the canvas window with the CANVAS_WIDTH and CANVAS_HEIGHT parameters. (See lines 38 and 39.) These canvas dimensions can be greater than the viewing window dimensions set with XV_WIDTH and XV_HEIGHT (lines 40 and 41).

We have to add the include file <xview/scrollbar.h> to get the definitions for the scrollbar package. These are created in lines 46 through 53. Note how we have to create two separate scrollbars, one vertical and one horizontal.

The scrollbars in this example show how they can split to provide multiple, tiled views of the data in the canvas window. To split a view, press the right mouse button on a scrollbar and you will be presented with a pop-up menu. Choose the Split View option to split the view or the Join View option to join two views together. You will not see a Join View option if a scrollbar does not dissect a view.

You can programmatically split a canvas view even if scrollbars are not present. Use the OPENWIN_SPLIT attribute in an xv_set() function call. For example:

```
xv_window xv;
xv = (xv_window)xv_get(canvas,OPENWIN_NTH_VIEW,0);

xv_set(canvas,
    OPENWIN_SPLIT,
    OPENWIN_SPLIT_VIEW, xv,
    OPENWIN_SPLIT_DIRECTION,
    OPENWIN_SPLIT_HORIZONTAL,
    NULL);
```

TIP

You may want to group your xv_set() function calls into distinct logical calls to set each type of parameter instead of one long convoluted list of parameters to one xv_set() function. Splitting the code into these groups makes the code easier to read and debug.

Note that only OPENWIN_* type of attributes are allowed in the xv_set() call with the OPENWIN_SPLIT parameter. Do not mix other types of attributes. To get the first view you can use a value of 0 to the OPENWIN_NTH_VIEW parameter. For the next view, use 1, and so on. To get an idea of how many views there are for this canvas use the call

```
int number;
number = (int)xv_get(canvas, OPENWIN_NVIEWS);
```

To get the paint window to do your own drawing, perhaps in response to other user input, you can use the xv_get() function to get the paint window. For example,

```
xv_window xv_paint;
xv_paint = (xv_window)xv_get(canvas, CANVAS_VIEW_PAINT, null);
```

Listing 33.6 shows how to use the standard Xlib function calls to draw on the canvas. (See Figure 33.5.) You must use the include file <X/Xlib.h> for all the definitions and declarations. The XDrawLine function used in this example is somewhat simple. However, this example shows you how to set up your Graphics Context and use the standard XDrawLine function to draw a grid. You can use other X drawing functions just as easily.

FIGURE 33.5.

The scrolled window example.

Scrollbar

Paint windows

Buttons

A *button* item enables a user to select an action. Several types of buttons are available to you as a programmer. Figure 33.6 shows how various buttons are used. There are four distinct examples shown in Figure 33.6:

- The Menu Item is shown as "Y/N/Q".
- The 1 of N choice items from four items.
- The M of N choice of items from three items to match others.
- Choosing via four checkboxes.

The listing for generating Figure 33.6 is shown in Listing 33.7. We will go over this listing in detail.

#### Chapter 33

FIGURE 33.6.

Using buttons.

Listing 33.7. Using menus, buttons, and choices.

```
/*
** A sampler of some of the choices to present to a user
*/
#include <xview/generic.h>
#include <xview/xview.h>
#include <xview/frame.h>
#include <xview/panel.h>
#include <xview/openmenu.h>

Frame frame;
int menuHandler( Menu item, Menu_item selection);
int selected( Panel_item item, Event *ev);
void quit();

int main(int argc, char *argv[])
{
Rect   *rt;
Rect   *qrt;
Panel panel;
Panel quitbtn;
Panel oneN;
Panel manyN;
Panel chooser;
Menu   menu1;

    xv_init(XV_INIT_ARGC_PTR_ARGV, &argc, argv, NULL);

frame = (Frame)xv_create(NULL, FRAME,
    FRAME_LABEL, argv[0],
    XV_WIDTH, 400,
    XV_HEIGHT, 200,
    NULL);

panel = (Panel)xv_create(frame, PANEL,NULL);

quitbtn =   (Panel)xv_create(panel, PANEL_BUTTON,
    PANEL_LABEL_STRING, "Quit",
    PANEL_NOTIFY_PROC, quit,
    XV_X, 20,
    NULL);
```

continues

Listing 33.7. continued

```c
menu1 = (Menu) xv_create(NULL, MENU,
    MENU_STRINGS, "Yes", "No", "Maybe", "Bye", NULL,
    MENU_NOTIFY_PROC, menuHandler,
    NULL);

xv_create (panel, PANEL_BUTTON,
    PANEL_LABEL_STRING, "Y/N/Q",
    PANEL_ITEM_MENU, menu1,
    PANEL_NOTIFY_PROC, .selected,
    NULL);

qrt = (Rect *) xv_get(quitbtn, XV_RECT);

oneN =  (Panel) xv_create(panel, PANEL_CHOICE,
    PANEL_LABEL_STRING, "1 of N",
    PANEL_CHOICE_STRINGS,
        "extra", "large", "medium", "small", NULL,
    XV_X, 20,
    XV_Y, rect_bottom(qrt) + 20,
    NULL);

rt = (Rect *) xv_get(oneN, XV_RECT);

manyN = (Panel) xv_create(panel, PANEL_CHOICE,
    PANFL_LABEL_STRING, "M of N",
    PANEL_CHOICE_STRINGS,
        "tomato", "celery", "carrot" , NULL,
    PANEL_CHOOSE_ONE, FALSE,
    XV_X, 20,
    XV_Y, rect_bottom(rt) + 20,
    NULL);

rt = (Rect *) xv_get(manyN, XV_RECT);

chooser = (Panel) xv_create(panel, PANEL_CHECK_BOX,
    PANEL_LAYOUT, PANEL_HORIZONTAL,
    PANEL_LABEL_STRING, "Extras",
    PANEL_CHOICE_STRINGS,
        "fries", "potato", "Q. potato", "salad" , NULL,
    PANEL_CHOOSE_ONE, FALSE, /* Let 'em have it all */
    XV_X, 20,
    XV_Y, rect_bottom(rt) + 20,
    NULL);

xv_main_loop(frame);
exit(0);
}

/*
** This function is called when you select an item
*/
int selected( Panel_item item, Event *ev)
{
printf(" %s .. \n ", xv_get(item, PANEL_LABEL_STRING));
}

/*
```

```
** This function handles the menu selection item.
** Shows you how to exit via menu item too.
*/
int menuHandler(Menu item, Menu_item thing)
{
printf("%s .. \n", xv_get(thing, MENU_STRING));
if (!strcmp((char *)xv_get(thing,MENU_STRING), "Bye")) quit();
}

/*
** Make a clean exit.
*/
void quit()
{
xv_destroy_safe(frame);
}
```

Take a look at the part where the "Y/N/Q" menu button was created. First we created the menu items on the menu as menu1. Note that we did not display all of the choices in the menu, just its header.

```
menu1 = (Menu) xv_create(NULL, MENU,
    MENU_STRINGS, "Yes", "No", "Maybe", "Bye", NULL,
    MENU_NOTIFY_PROC, menuHandler,
    NULL);
```

Then we created the panel button that will house this menu with the following lines:

```
xv_create (panel, PANEL_BUTTON,
    PANEL_LABEL_STRING, "Y/N/Q",
    PANEL_ITEM_MENU, menu1,
    PANEL_NOTIFY_PROC, selected,
    NULL);
```

That was it. Now you can click the right button on the "Y/N/Q" button to get the selection items as a pull-down menu. If you click the left button, the first item in the menu item will be displayed momentarily and selected. Two functions are assigned as callbacks in the previous code segments:

- menuHandler(): This function will show on your terminal the menu item selected.
- selected(): This function merely displays the menu item string. You could just as easily display another menu or other items instead of this simple example.

Now look at the example for the "1 of N" selection. As the name of this item suggests, you can choose only one of a given number of items. This is called an *exclusive selection*.

The following lines are used to create this exclusive selection item:

```
oneN =  (Panel) xv_create(panel, PANEL_CHOICE,
    PANEL_LABEL_STRING, "1 of N",
    PANEL_CHOICE_STRINGS,
        "extra", "large", "medium", "small", NULL,
    XV_X, 20,
    XV_Y, rect_bottom(qrt) + 20,
    NULL);
```

Note how we used the core class's XV_X and XV_Y attributes to position this box below the Quit button. We got the position as a rectangle (typedef Rect) of the Quit button via the xv_get call given the XV_RECT attribute:

```
qrt = (Rect *) xv_get(quitbtn, XV_RECT);
```

The position given by XV_X and XV_Y was relative to the top-left position of the panel. This given position is known as absolute positioning because we are using hard-coded numbers to position items.

NOTE

To position items generally we can use two functions: xv_row() and xv_col(). These functions use the WIN_ROW_GAP and WIN_COLUMN_GAP to set the spaces between the items. The following example shows you how to position twelve items on a panel:

```
#define ROW 3
#define COL 4
extern char *name[ROW][COL];
int i, j;
for (i = 0; i < ROW; i++)
        for (j = 0; j < COL; j++)
        {
        xv_create(panel, PANEL_BUTTON,
              XV_X, xv_col(panel,j),
              XV_Y, xv_row(panel,i),
              PANEL_LABEL_STRING, name[i][j],
              NULL);
        }
```

All items presented in this list are shown with the NULL-terminated list passed in with the PANEL_CHOICE_STRINGS attribute. The default function of PANEL_CHOICE is to enable only one selection. To get more than one selection if you have a list of choices, you can follow the same procedure you used for the exclusive selection panel. The difference between 1 of M and M of N lies in setting the value of the PANEL_CHOOSE_ONE to FALSE. This usage creates the M of N items shown in the following lines:

```
manyN = (Panel) xv_create(panel, PANEL_CHOICE,
    PANEL_LABEL_STRING, "M of N",
    PANEL_CHOICE_STRINGS,
        "tomato", "celery", "carrot" , NULL,
    PANEL_CHOOSE_ONE, FALSE,
    XV_X, 20,
    XV_Y, rect_bottom(rt) + 20,
    NULL);
```

With 1 of M, we use the XV_RECT call to position this choice of many item's button on the screen.

Finally, this example showed you how to use check boxes to create the input items shown for our (United States) ex-president's choices of a side order. Checkboxes are always non-exclusive. The text to do this is shown in the following lines:

```
chooser = (Panel) xv_create(panel, PANEL_CHECK_BOX,
    PANEL_LAYOUT, PANEL_HORIZONTAL,
    PANEL_LABEL_STRING, "Extras",
    PANEL_CHOICE_STRINGS,
        "fries", "potato", "Q. potato", "salad" , NULL,
    XV_X, 20,
    XV_Y, rect_bottom(rt) + 20,
    NULL);
```

This set of checkboxes was also positioned to align with the qv_get and rect_bottom() calls.

List Items

Use the PANEL_LIST attribute to show lists of items. An example is shown in Figure 33.7. The corresponding listing is shown in Listing 33.8. Lists enable you to insert text (and graphics as glyphs) in them. You can have duplicates in a list. If you do not want to allow duplicates, set the PANEL_LIST_INSERT_DUPLICATE to FALSE.

FIGURE 33.7.

Using lists to display data.

Listing 33.8. Using lists to display data.

```
/*
** Using Lists
*/
#include <xview/generic.h>
#include <xview/xview.h>
#include <xview/frame.h>
#include <xview/panel.h>

Frame frame;
```

continues

Listing 33.8. continued

```
int main(int argc, char *argv[])
{

Panel panel;
void quit();

    xv_init(XV_INIT_ARGC_PTR_ARGV, &argc, argv, NULL);

frame = (Frame)xv_create(NULL, FRAME,
    FRAME_LABEL, argv[0],
    XV_WIDTH, 200,
    XV_HEIGHT, 100,
    NULL);

panel = (Panel)xv_create(frame, PANEL,NULL);

(void) xv_create(panel, PANEL_BUTTON,
    PANEL_LABEL_STRING, "Quit",
    PANEL_NOTIFY_PROC, quit,
    NULL);

(void) xv_create(panel, PANEL_LIST,
    PANEL_LIST_STRINGS,
        "Business", "Economics", "History",
"Literature", "TomFoolery", "Math",
        "Computer Sci.", "Engineering", NULL,
    NULL);



xv_main_loop(frame);
exit(0);
}

void quit()
{
xv_destroy_safe(frame);
}
```

Lists are ordered from 0 and up, so the first row is 0, the second row is 1, and so on. To delete the rows 7 through 9 from a long list, use the xv_set function:

```
xv_set(list_item,
    PANEL_LIST_DELETE_ROWS, 6, 3
    NULL);
```

In the preceding example you are requesting that 3 rows be deleted starting from row index number 6 (which is the seventh row). All other rows are adjusted upward after these rows are deleted.

To insert items into this list you can use PANEL_LIST_INSERT and PANEL_LIST_STRING calls. If you wanted to replace the third row with a string pointed to by a pointer called buffer, you would use the following function call:

```
xv_set(list_item,
    PANEL_LIST_DELETE, 2,
    PANEL_LIST_INSERT, 2,
    PANEL_LIST_STRING, buffer,
    NULL);
```

The PANEL_NOTIFY_PROC function for a list is called when an item is selected, deselected, added, or deleted. The prototype for this function call is

```
listCallBack(
    Panel_item      item,
    char            *string,
    Xv_opaque       client_data,
    Panel_list_op   op,
    Event           *event,
    int             row);
```

The item is the panel list itself in this function call. The string is the label for the row, or NULL if no item is defined in the list for the row. The opaque client_data is a user-specified value specified at list creation time with the PANEL_LIST_CLIENT_DATA parameter. For example, the line

```
PANEL_LIST_CLIENT_DATA, 2, "Hello",
```

will assign the value of client_data to 2 for the row with the string "Hello" in it. Each client_data value must be assigned one line at a time.

The op parameter can be one of the following values:

- PANEL_LIST_OP_SELECT when the row is selected
- PANEL_LIST_OP_DESELECT when the row is deselected
- PANEL_LIST_OP_VALIDATE when a new row is added
- PANEL_LIST_OP_DELETE when the row has been deleted

You can take action based on the value of the op parameter in one handy function or have this function call other functions. For example, the following pseudocode illustrates how you could handle the op parameter:

```
switch (op)
    {
    case    PANEL_LIST_OP_SELECT: selectHandler();
    break;
    case    PANEL_LIST_OP_DESELECT: unSelectHandler();
    break;
    case    PANEL_LIST_OP_VALIDATE: addRowHandler();
    break;
    case    PANEL_LIST_OP_DELETE: deleteRowHandler();
    break;
    }
```

Scale Bars

Now look at how you create slider bars so the user can set the value of a variable. An example of this application is shown in Figure 33.8 and a corresponding listing is given in Listing 33.9.

FIGURE 33.9.

Using text items.

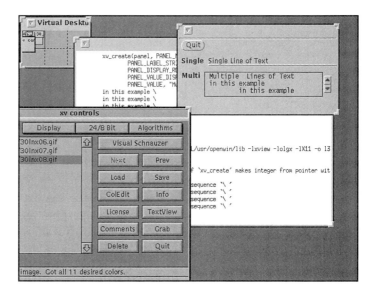

If you want the user to enter private data such as password information, you can set the PANEL_MASK_CHAR value to something like an asterisk. This setting displays an asterisk for each character that the user types in. The value of the text remains what the user typed in.

You can have notification procedures for four types of input for a text item with the PANEL_NOTIFY_LEVEL. (See Table 33.1.)

Table 33.1. Notification procedures.

Notification	Action to take on input
PANEL_NONE	Never inform this package.
PANEL_NON_PRINTABLE	On each non-printable character.
PANEL_SPECIFIED	If the input character is found in a string specified by the attribute PANEL_NOTIFY_STRING.
PANEL_ALL	On all characters input.

You can also have multiple lines of text on a display. A sample of this is shown in Listing 33.10. Look at the following excerpted lines:

```
xv_create(panel, PANEL MULTILINE_TEXT,
    PANEL_LABEL_STRING, "Multi",
    PANEL_DISPLAY_ROWS, 3,
    PANEL_VALUE_DISPLAY_LENGTH, 30,
    PANEL_VALUE, "Multiple  Lines of Text \
in this example\
This is a line 1\
```

```
This is a line 2\
This is a line 3\
of some long string",
        NULL);
```

The PANEL_MULTILINE_TEXT package can have the following attributes set for it: PANEL_DISPLAY_ROWS sets the number of lines that the viewing window will display, and PANEL_VALUE_DISPLAY_LENGTH is the number of characters wide you want the display to be.

Where To Go from Here

This chapter is a very brief introduction to the XView packages available under Linux. In this section you have learned a little about putting user interface items together on a panel. You should now have enough knowledge to start creating your own interfaces in XView. There are several other locations for getting more information about XView under Linux.

The following are XView packages for Linux:

- xv32exmp. Perhaps the most important example for the newbie. This package contains the examples for XView that demonstrate the Slingshot and UIT extensions, which are libraries that make it much easier to program a user interface under X.

- xv32_a. This package contains static libraries for developing XView applications (Version 3.2). This is required if compiling XView apps with the -g or -static flags for debugging.

- xv32_sa and xv32_so. These are shared libraries for your compiled programs.

- xvinc. The include files you use when you are compiling XView programs.

- xvol32. Configuration files, programs, and other documentation for the OPEN LOOK Window Manager, olwm.

- xvmenus. Menus and help files for olwm.

Some cool binaries to look for in the /usr/openwin/bin directory are workman, which enables you to play music CDs on your CD player; props, for setting window parameters; and perfmeter for performance metering.

Look in the /usr/openwin/man directory for all the man pages for the XView package. The /usr/openwin/include file contains valuable information about some of the structures used by XView.

Summary

You use objects to build XView applications. Each object is a class and is referred to as a package. Each package has attributes that can have values. Attributes can be shared among other objects, be common to a few objects only, or be specific to one object.

You can retrieve an attribute's values by calling xv_get() and set a value by calling xv_set. An attribute may be assigned more than one value. Each attribute can have a different type of value attached to it.

FIGURE 34.5.

The Class List pop-up menu.

Table 34.3. Class List pop-up menu functions.

Function	Description
fileOut	Saves the source code of the currently selected class in a file named className.st.
printOut	Sends the source code of the currently selected class to the printer.
printOut protocol	Sends a protocol description of the currently selected class to the printer. The output will contain the class description, class comment, and the classes protocol and method comments.
spawn	Starts a class browser on the currently selected class.
spawn hierarchy	Starts a browser on all subclasses of the currently selected class.
hierarchy	Shows the hierarchy of the currently selected class in the code view.
definition	Shows the class definition in the code view and allows you to change the class definition.
comment	Shows the class comment in the code view and allows you to edit it.
class instvars	Shows the class-instance-variables for the selected class and allows you to edit them.
variable search	Provides a search facility to find different variable references and all methods referencing the searched-for variable.
new class	Allows you to create a new class using as a template the currently selected class.
new subclass	Same as new class but it will create a subclass of the currently selected class.
rename	Changes the name of the currently selected class.
remove	Removes the currently selected class and all of its subclasses.

The method category pop-up menu appears when you press the menu mouse button while the pointer is in the method category view. The functions available from this menu are shown in Figure 34.6 and explained in Table 34.4.

FIGURE 34.6.

The Method Category pop-up menu.

Table 34.4. Method Category pop-up menu functions.

Function	Description
fileOut	Saves the source code of the currently selected method category in a file named className-category.st
printOut	Sends the source code of the currently selected method category to the printer
spawn	Starts a method category browser on the currently selected method category of the currently selected class
spawn category	Starts a browser on all methods of the class which have the same category as the currently selected one
find method here	Searches for the method that implements a specified selector
find method	Searches in the class hierarchy for the first class implementing the selector you specify in the dialog box
new category	Enables you to add a new category to the list
copy category	Enables you to copy all methods in a class category to the currently selected class
create access methods	Creates methods to access instance variables
rename	Renames the currently selected method category
remove	Removes all methods in the currently selected class that are members of the currently selected method category

The method list pop-up menu appears when you press the menu mouse button while the pointer is in the method list view. The functions available from this menu are shown in Figure 34.7 and explained in Table 34.5.

FIGURE 34.14.

The File List pop-up menu.

Table 34.9. The File List pop-up menu functions.

Function	Purpose
spawn	Starts another file browser on the current directory or the directory selected in the file list.
get contents	Shows the contents of the currently selected file in the contents view.
show info	Displays a view with type, size, access, and owner information for the currently selected file or directory.
show full info	Displays the same as above with more details such as the last access, last modification date, and time.
fileIn	Loads the selected file into the system by reading and evaluating Smalltalk expressions from it.
update	Rereads the directory and updates the file list.
execute UNIX command	Allows execution of any UNIX command through a pop-up box.
remove	Removes the selected file(s) or directory(s).
rename	Renames the selected file.
display long list	Shows file information in the file list. This option toggles with display short list which is the default.
show all files	Displays all the files including hidden files. This option toggles with hide hidden files which is the default.
create directory	Creates a new directory.
create file	Creates a new file.

The pop-up menu for the contents view is the same edit menu as the other text editors and is discussed in the "Editing in Browsers" section of this chapter.

The Projects Option

The Projects option of the Launcher menu enables you to create a new project or select a previously created project. When the new project function is selected, a new project is automatically created for you and the new project object appears on your screen. If you select the select project function, a dialog box appears with a list of existing projects from which to choose. Simply select a project and it will be loaded in to the environment.

The Utilities Option

The Utilities option provides thirteen tools that assist you in programming in the ST/X environment. Table 34.10 gives you a brief description of each tool.

Table 34.10. The Utilities option.

Utility	Description
Transcript	Opens the Transcript view.
Window tree	Displays a graphical tree representation of the window hierarchy of all windows that are active or in wait state at the time it was requested.
Class tree	Displays a graphical tree representation of the class hierarchy of the system.
Event monitor	Displays a view that monitors events.
Process monitor	Displays a view that gives information about all currently active or waiting processes. This information changes as the state of the processes change.
Memory monitor	Displays a graph that tells you the present memory usage and changes as the memory usage changes.
Memory usage	Displays a table of the classes and the number of instances of each, average size, bytes, and percentage of memory used by each.
Collect Garbage	Runs a Generation Scavenge algorithm to collect short term objects and destroy them. If an object survives long enough, it is moved to an area of memory where it remains until the user requests its collection.
Collect Garbage & compress	Same as Collect Garbage but also compresses to recover space.
Fullscreen hardcopy	Takes a picture of the screen and asks you for a name of a file with a `.tiff` extension in which to save the image.

continues

Table 34.10. continued

Utility	Description
Screen area hardcopy	Same as Fullscreen hardcopy but for only a specific area of the screen.
View hardcopy	Same as Fullscreen hardcopy but for one specific view only.
ScreenSaver	Enables you to choose from one of three different screen savers to use in the ST/X environment.

The Goodies Option

The Goodies option of the Launcher menu provides a pull-right menu of six different tools that are useful at any time, not just when you program in Smalltalk. The Goodies are described in Table 34.11.

Table 34.11. The Goodies.

Tool	Description
Clock	Displays an analog clock in a square with a toggle for the second hand.
Round Clock	Same as the clock but it's round and remains visible when it is minimized.
Directory View	Displays a pictorial representation of files and directories. A folder represents a directory and a document is a file.
Mail Tool	A tool for managing electronic mail.
News Tool	A repository for news, information and documents.
Draw Tool	A fairly comprehensive tool for drawing diagrams, charts, pictures, and so on.

The Games & Demo Option

Contained in the pull-right menu of this option are games for your enjoyment and example applications that may be useful. The Games & Demos option menu is shown in Figure 34.15.

FIGURE 34.15.

*The Games & Demos
option menu.*

Editing in Browsers

All views that show text allow the usual editing functions of that text through a pop-up menu. The functions available in this menu are described in Table 34.12.

Table 34.12. Editing functions.

Function	Description
again	Repeats the last edit.
copy	Copies the selected text.
cut	Cuts the selected text out of the file.
paste	Pastes the text that was copied or cut prior to choosing the paste option to the current position of the pointer.
accept	Once you have completed editing, you must use this option to save the changes to the file; otherwise, the changes will not be written to the file.
doIt	Evaluates the highlighted text.
printIt	Prints a representation of the result of the evaluation at the current cursor position.
inspectIt	Invokes the Inspector view on the result.
search...	Enables you to search for a specific string.
goto...	Enables you to move to a specific location in the file.
font...	Enables you to change the font of the file.
indent...	Enables you to change the indenting of the file.
save as...	Enables you to save the file under a different name.
print	Prints the file.

To select or highlight text, press the left mouse button over the first character and move the mouse (while pressing the mouse button) to the end of the text you wish to select and then release the mouse button. If you press the left mouse button again, the highlighting is removed and you can select something else.

To scroll through the text, use the scroll bars on the left of the view. By clicking the mouse below or above the thumb, the text scrolls one page for every click. If you press the Shift key at the same time as you click, the text scrolls to the position of the pointer in the scroll bar. This is useful for scrolling rapidly through long documents.

Using the Inspector

The Inspector enables you to inspect an object. It consists of two subviews, one showing the names of the object's instance variables and the other showing the value of the selected instance variable. You can start an inspector by using the `inspectIt` function on the edit menu or by sending one of the following messages to an object:

```
anObject inspect
```

or

```
anObject basicInspect
```

The `basicInspect` command will open a general inspector that shows instance variables as they are physically present in the object. The `inspect` command is redefined in some classes to open an inspector showing the logical contents of the object.

Using the Debugger

The Debugger is displayed whenever an error occurs in your Smalltalk code. It shows you where the error occurred and how the system got there. The Debugger runs in one of three modes: `normal`, `modal`, and `inspecting`.

When in normal mode and an error occurs in a process, which is not the event handler process, the debugger will start up on top of the erroneous process. This blocks all interaction with the affected process and its views. Other views are still active and respond as usual.

When an error occurs in the Smalltalk event handler process, the debugger starts in modal mode. While a modal debugger is active you cannot interact with any other view.

The inspecting mode can be entered from the ProcessMonitor by the pop-up menu and allows inspection of the state of other processes. But since the debugged process may continue to run, it is only possible to inspect a snapshot of the affected process.

The Debugger contains four subviews:

- The Context Walkback List shows the context chain that led to the error
- The Method Source View shows the method that caused the error

- The Receiver Inspector allows inspection of the receiver of the selected message
- The Context Inspector provides information about the arguments and local variables of this context.

The Debugger is shown in Figure 34.16.

FIGURE 34.16.

The Debugger.

The functions that are common to each view appear as a set of buttons below the context walkback list. These functions are described in Table 34.13.

Table 34.13. The Debugger function buttons.

Button	Description
continue	Continues execution
terminate	Terminates the erroneous process
abort	Aborts the current activity if possible
step (single step)	Lets the process continue execution until the next send is executed in the currently selected context
send (single send)	Lets the process continue execution for one message send
return	Continues execution as if the selected context returned
restart	Continues execution by restarting the selected context

The walkback subview has a pop-up menu with the functions described in Table 34.14.

Table 34.14. Walkback Subview pop-up menu function.

Function	Description
exit smalltalk	Leaves ST/X without saving an image
show more	Shows 50 more contexts of the walk-back

continues

Table 34.14. continued

Function	Description
breakpoints	Not yet available
trace on/off	Not yet available
trace step	Not yet available

A miniDebugger is entered if an error occurs within the Debugger itself. This is a line-by-line debugger that allows limited debugging without the use of a graphical user interface. It is controlled by entering commands in the Xterm window where ST/X was started. If you type ? at the miniDebugger prompt, you will get a list of commands that are available for use in this stripped down debugger.

Summary

This chapter introduced you to the Smalltalk environment that is provided by the Smalltalk/X application. If you are interested in learning how to program using Smalltalk and do not have access to one of the commercial versions of Smalltalk, then Smalltalk/X is perfect for you. Not only does Smalltalk/X come with all the tools and programming aids that were talked about in this chapter, but it also comes with many examples and some fairly complete documentation that will make learning Smalltalk easier for you.

Mathematics on Linux

35

by Kamran Husain

IN THIS CHAPTER

FIGURE 35.3.

Sample of using EIGEN-VALUES.

```
┌─────────────────────────────  Console  ─────────────────────────────┐
│ ▽                                                                    │
│ MULTIPLE-VALUE-PROG1                                                 │
│ MULTIPLE-VALUE-LIST                                                  │
│ MULTIPLE-VALUE-BIND                                                  │
│ > (apropos 'eigen)                                                   │
│ EIGENVALUES                                                          │
│ EIGENVECTORS                                                         │
│ EIGEN                                                                │
│ > (help 'EIGENVALUES)                                                │
│ EIGENVALUES                                            [function-doc] │
│ Args: (a)                                                            │
│ Returns list of eigenvalues of square, symmetric matrix A           │
│ NIL                                                                  │
│ > (def a (matrix '(4 4) '(12 -11 0 0 -11 24 -12 0 0 -12 36 -25 00 -25 48))) │
│ Error: list not divisible by this length                            │
│ Happened in: #<Byte-Code-Closure: #16b128>                          │
│ > (def a (matrix '(4 4) '(12 -11 0 0 -11 24 -12 0 0 -12 36 -25 0 0 -25 48))) │
│ A                                                                    │
│ > eigenvalues(a)                                                     │
│ Error: The variable EIGENVALUES is unbound.                         │
│ > (eigenvalues(a))                                                   │
│ Error: The function A is unbound.                                   │
│ > (eigenvalues a)                                                    │
│ #(69.04822731759916 33.29833131480792 14.646576347252257 3.0068650203406837) │
│ > []                                                                 │
└──────────────────────────────────────────────────────────────────────┘
```

A Last Note

For simple math operations involving spreadsheets, you can always use the xspread program provided with the X package. (The CD-ROM at the back of the book has version 2.1.) For more powerful spreadsheet functions, you might want to resort to a commercial spreadsheet package and take advantage of its support, too. The XESS spreadsheet is available for Linux from Applied Information systems, (919) 842-7801 or info@ais.com. You can share data between spreadsheets, or use the API to develop and have access to a full suite of math functions available on spreadsheets that run under DOS or UNIX.

Wolfram Research has released its Mathematica program for Linux. The Mathematica package has extensive numeric and symbolic capabilities, 2-D and 3-D graphics, and a very large library of application programs. With an additional feature called MathLink, you can exchange information between other applications on a network. You can get more information about Mathematica from info@wri.com or http://www.wri.com.

Summary

You have several options when it comes to performing mathematical operations or writing such applications under Linux. You can either write the code yourself using C, FORTRAN, or other available languages—or you can use a package. If you are familiar with MATLAB, consider using Scilab. For regular expressions and polynomials, try using Pari. If you are a LISP user or want to do vector operations or statistics, consider using the LISP-STAT package.

Database Products for Linux

36

by
Kamran Husain

IN THIS CHAPTER

System Administration Basics

37

by Tim Parker

Compressing Files with *gzip* and *compress*

Files abound on a UNIX system, adding up to a large chunk of disk real estate. Instead of deleting files, an alternative is to compress them so that they take up less space. Several compression utilities are available for UNIX and Linux systems. The most commonly used are compress and the newer GNU gzip.

When run on a file, compress creates a smaller file with the extension .Z, which immediately identifies the file as being compressed. To compress a file, use the following command:

```
compress filename
```

You can also use wildcards to compress several files at once. compress supports a number of options, but most aren't used often. By default, when a file is compressed, the uncompressed original is deleted, although this can be changed with a command-line option.

To uncompress a compressed file, run the uncompress program:

```
uncompress filename
```

Alternatively, you can use a wildcard such as *.Z to uncompress all the compressed files. Remember to include the .Z suffix when specifying the filename.

The gzip utility is a new compression tool that uses different algorithms than compress. The gzip program has a few extra features that were added since compress was released, such as adjustable compression (the more compression required, the longer it takes to compress). To use gzip, specify the filename to be compressed and the compression type:

```
gzip -9 filename
```

The -9 option, which tells gzip to use the highest compression factor, will probably be the option you use the most. Alternatively, leave this option off and let gzip work with its default settings. A gzip compressed file has the extension .gz appended, and the original file is deleted. To uncompress a gzipped file, use the gunzip utility.

Using *tar*

The tar (tape archiver) utility has been used with UNIX systems for many years. Unfortunately, it's not very friendly and can be quite temperamental at times, especially when you're unfamiliar with the syntax required to make tar do something useful.

The tar program is designed to create a single archive file, much as the ZIP utilities do for DOS. With tar, you can combine many files into a single larger file, which makes it easier to move the collection or back it up to tape. The general syntax used by tar is as follows:

```
tar [options] [file]
```

The options available are lengthy and sometimes obtuse. Files can be specified with or without wildcards. A simple example of creating a tar archive file is

```
tar cvf archive1.tar /usr/tparker
```

which combines all the files in /usr/tparker into a tar archive called archive1.tar. The c option tells tar to create the archive; the v tells it to be verbose, displaying messages as it goes; and the f tells it to use the filename archive1.tar as the output file.

The extension .tar is not automatically appended by tar, but is a user convention that helps identify the file as an archive. This convention isn't widely used, though, although it should be as it helps identify the file.

The c option creates new archives. (If the file existed before, it is deleted.) The u (update) option is used to append new files to an existing archive, or to create the archive if it doesn't exist. This is useful if you keep adding files. The x option is used to extract files from the archive. To extract with the tar command all the files in the archive in the earlier example, you would use the command

```
tar xvf archive1.tar
```

There's no need to specify a filename, because the filenames and paths will be retained as the archive is unpacked. It's important to remember that the path is saved with the file. So if you archived /usr/tparker and then moved into /usr/tparker and issued the extract command, the files would be extracted relevant to the current directory, which would place them in /usr/tparker/usr/tparker. You must be very careful to extract files properly. If you want to force a new directory path on extracted files, a command-line option allows this.

The tar system does not remove the original files as they are packed into the archive, nor does it remove the archive file when files are extracted. These steps must be performed manually.

You can use tar to copy files to tapes or floppies by specifying a device name and the f option as a device name. To archive files in /usr/tparker to a floppy disk in the first drive, you could use the following command:

```
tar cvf /dev/fd0 /usr/tparker
```

This can cause a problem if the floppy doesn't have enough capacity, however, so tar lets you specify the capacity with the k option. In this case, the command for a 1.44MB floppy is as follows:

```
tar cvfk /dev/fd0 1440 /usr/tparker
```

If the floppy is full before the entire archive has been copied, tar prompts you for another one. It's important to keep the arguments in the right order. You see that the f is before the k, so the device name must be before the capacity. All the argument keyletters are gathered together instead of issued one at a time followed by their value, which is one aspect of tar that can be very confusing.

As a last issue for backing up to floppy, it is sometimes necessary to tell the tar program about the blocking used (blocking identifies how many blocks are used for each chunk of information on the device). A floppy usually has a blocking factor of 4, so the command becomes the following:

```
tar cvfkb /dev/fd0 1440 4 /usr/tparker
```

A final problem with tar is that it can't always handle a generic device such as /dev/fd0, and must be specifically told the disk type.

This chapter is devoted to devices that might be attached to your Linux system, such as terminals, modems, and printers. It shows you how to add and manage the different devices, and it also looks at many of the Linux commands you will need to properly administer your system.

In this chapter, you will learn the following:

- What a device driver is
- The difference between block mode and character mode devices
- Major and minor device numbers
- The mknod command
- How to manage printers and the print spooler
- How to add a printer
- How to add a terminal and modem
- The configuration files used by terminals
- The startup sequence used to permit logins

All of this information is necessary if you are to have a smoothly running system. Even if you don't intend to add terminals or modems, you should know about the startup process and how the configuration files are handled.

Character and Block Mode Devices

Everything attached to the computer you are using to run Linux is treated as a device by the operating system. It doesn't matter whether the device is a terminal, a hard disk, a printer, a CD-ROM drive, or a modem. Everything that accepts or sends data to the operating system is a device.

The concept of treating everything on the system as a device is one of the benefits of the UNIX architecture. Each device has a special section in the kernel, called a device driver, which includes all the instructions necessary for Linux to communicate with the device. When a new device is developed, it can be used with Linux by writing a device driver, which is usually a set of instructions that explains how to send and receive data.

Device drivers allow the Linux kernel to include only the operating system and support software. By having the instructions for talking to devices within a set of files, they can be loaded as needed (in the case of rarely used devices), or kept in memory all the time when the operating system boots. As refinements are made to a peripheral, small changes to the device driver file can be linked into the kernel to keep the operating system informed of the new features and capabilities.

When an application instructs a device to perform an action, the Linux kernel doesn't have to worry about the mechanism. It simply passes the request to the device driver and lets it handle the communications. Similarly, when you're typing at the keyboard, your terminal's device driver accepts the keystrokes and passes them to the shell or application, filtering out any special codes that the kernel doesn't know how to handle by translating them into something the kernel can perform.

Linux keeps device files in the /dev directory by default and convention. It is permissible to keep device files anywhere on the file system, but keeping them all in /dev makes it obvious that they are device files.

Every type of device on the Linux system communicates in one of two ways: character by character or as a set of data in a predefined chunk or block. Terminals, printers, and asynchronous modems are character devices, using characters sent one at a time and echoed by the other end. Hard drives and most tape drives, on the other hand, use blocks of data, because this is the fastest way to send large chunks of information. These peripherals are called either character mode or block mode devices, based on the way they communicate.

> **NOTE**
>
> Another way to differentiate between character and block mode devices is by how the buffering to the device is handled. Character mode devices want to do their own buffering. Block mode devices, which usually communicate in chunks of 512 or 1,024 bytes, have the kernel perform the buffering.
>
> Some devices can be both character and block mode devices. Some tape drives, for example, can handle both character and block modes, and therefore have two different device drivers. The device driver that is used depends on how the user wants to write data to the device.

The device file has all the details about whether the device is a character mode or block mode device. There is an easy way to tell which type of device a peripheral is: Look at the output of the listing command that shows file permissions (such as ls -l). If the first character is a b, the device is a block mode device; a c indicates a character mode device.

Device files are usually named to indicate the type of device they are. Most terminals, for example, have a device driver with the name tty followed by two or more letters or numbers, such as tty1, tty1A, or tty04. The letters tty identify the file as a terminal (tty stands for teletype), and the numbers or letters identify the specific terminal referred to. When coupled with the directory name /dev, the full device driver name becomes /dev/tty01.

Major and Minor Device Numbers

There might be more than one device of the same type on a system. For example, your Linux system might have a multiport card (multiple serial ports) with 10 Wyse 60 terminals hanging off it. Linux can use the same device driver for each of the terminals because they are all the same type of device.

However, there must be a method for the operating system to differentiate which one of the 10 terminals you want to address. That's where device numbers are used. Each device is identified by two device numbers: The major number identifies the device driver to be used, and the minor number identifies the device number. For example, the 10 Wyse 60 terminals on the multiport card can all use a device file with the same major number, but each will have a different minor number, thereby uniquely identifying it to the operating system.

As part of its spooling task, lpr also checks for instructions on how to print the file. It can get the information from three sources: the command line (supplied as arguments), environment variables (set by the shell or the user), or the system's default values.

The lpr program knows which spool to put the print request in because of the destination printer designation. The printer destination can be specified on the lpr command line, or through an environment variable. When the destination printer name has been determined, lpr checks the file /etc/printcap to look up the printer's information, including the spool directory. The spool directory is usually of the form /usr/spool/printer_name, such as /usr/spool/lp1.

Within the spool directory, lpr creates two files. The first has the letters cf (control file) followed by a print ID number. The cf file contains information about the print job, including the owner's name. The second file starts with df (data file) and has the actual contents of the file to be printed with it. When lpr has finished creating the df file, it sends a signal to lpd that informs the daemon that a print job is waiting in the spool directory.

When lpd gets the signal from lpr, it checks the file /etc/printcap to see whether the printer is for a local or remote printer. If the print job is for a remote printer (one attached to another machine on the network), lpd opens a connection to the remote machine, transfers both the control and data files, and deletes the local copies.

If the print job is for a local printer, lpd checks to make sure the printer exists and is active, and then sends the print request to the printing daemon running that queue.

The /etc/printcap File and Spooling Directories

The /etc/printcap file is consulted by both the user's print command lpr and the lpd print daemon. It contains information about every printer that is accessible from the Linux machine.

The format of /etc/printcap is straightforward (and similar to the /etc/termcap file for terminal descriptions). The following is an extract from /etc/printcap:

```
# HP Laserjet
lp¦hplj¦laserjet-acctng¦HP LaserJet 4M in Room 425:\
      :lp=/dev/lp0:\
      :sd=/usr/spool/lp0:\
      :lf=/usr/spool/errorlog:\
      :mx#0:\
      :of=/usr/spool/lp0/hpjlp:\
```

The first field in each entry is a list of all the allowable names for the printer. These can be used with the environment variables set by a user's shell or by the system, as well as with options on the lpr command line with a destination printer specified. Valid names are separated by a vertical bar.

Usually, each entry includes at least three names: a short name that is four characters or less (such as hplj); a more complete name with an owner, if necessary (such as laserjet-acctng); and a full, descriptive name with any other information necessary to identify the printer (such as HP LaserJet 4M in Room 425).

NOTE

If a print job is submitted without a destination name, and one can't be determined from environment variable values, it is routed to the printer lp. Therefore, one of the printers (usually the system default printer) should also have the name lp as part of its identifier.

A comment in the file is shown with a pound symbol (sometimes called a hash mark) as the first character. Following the printer name is a set of two-character parameters and values used by the printer. The format of these entries is always one of the following:

NN	A Boolean value
NN=string	Set equal to string
NN#number	Set not equal to number

When a Boolean value is used (no assignment follows the two-character identifier), the value is set to True by default. If the value of False was required, the two-character identifier would not be included in the description.

Most assignments are shown with colons beginning and ending each definition to enhance readability and make the file easier for the print utilities to parse. Null values are valid assignments employed by putting two colons together.

A few of the parameters in the /etc/printcap file are worth highlighting because they are useful for administration purposes. Not all of these parameters might be present in every printer definition in the /etc/printcap file, but most appear:

sd	The spool directory
lf	The log directory for error messages
af	Accounting log file
mx	Determines the type of files that can be printed
of	Output filter program to be used when printing

All printers should have their own spool directories, usually under the printer name in /usr/spool, such as /usr/spool/hplj. Spool directories are necessary for both remote and local printers. When a new printer is added to the system, the spool directory might have to be created manually (using mkdir). The permissions for the spool directory should be set to 775. The directory must be owned by root or daemon. The group ID should be set to root or daemon, too. In both cases, daemon theoretically is the better ID for user and group, although root will work also.

The error log file can be located anywhere on the system. It can be shared by all printers, if desired, because each log entry includes the name of the printer.

The accounting log file is used to record printouts for systems in which users are charged. If accounting records are not to be used on the system, ignore the entry entirely in the /etc/printcap

> **WARNING**
>
> Be warned that lpc is one of the most unpredictable and unreliable programs included with the Linux operating system! It can hang up for no obvious reason, and it can also display erroneous status messages. In some cases, the only way to fix a severely screwed-up printer system is to reset the machine completely!

When used without any arguments, lpc prompts you for a command. The following are several valid lpc commands and their arguments (a vertical bar indicates a choice of arguments):

abort *printer_name* ¦ all   Is similar to the stop command, except it doesn't allow any print job that is currently being printed to finish before stopping the printer. When used with the all argument, all printers are stopped. Any job that is abnormally terminated by the abort command is requeued when the printer is started again. See the stop command for more details about the printer daemon and lock files.

clean *printer_name* ¦ all   Removes all print jobs that are queued, including any active print jobs. In many cases, the currently printing job proceeds normally because it has been passed to the printer daemon or the printer's buffer. All other jobs are removed, though. If the all argument is used, all printers have their print queues cleaned.

disable *printer_name* ¦ all   Disables the spooling of print requests to the printer (or all printers, depending on the argument). Any jobs that are already queued are unaffected. Any user trying to send a print job to the disabled printer receives a message indicating that the printer is disabled, and the print job is refused. Printers are enabled and disabled through changes in the lock file in the spool directory.

down *printer_name message*   Is used to take a printer completely offline, usually for an extended period. If a message is included, it can be as long as you want. It is placed in the status file in the spool directory and displayed to users trying to queue to the printer. The down command is usually used when a printer has serious problems and must be removed from the system for more than a day.

enable *printer_name* ¦ all   Enables the spooling of print requests to the printer or all printers.

exit   Exits from lpc (the same as quit).

help or ?   Shows a short list of all lpc commands. If an argument is supplied, it displays a one-line description of that command (such as help abort).

quit   Exits from lpc (the same as exit).

restart *printer_name* ¦ all   Restarts the printer daemon, and is usually used after it has died for an inexplicable reason (which the BSD printer daemons tend to do). If the argument all is supplied, all printer daemons are restarted.

`start` *printer_name*   Starts the printer, allowing it to print requests. This command starts the printer queue daemon for that printer.

`status` *printer_name*   Displays the printer name, whether it has the spool queue enabled, whether printing is enabled, the number of entries in the print queue, and the status of the daemon for that printer. If there are no entries in the queue, no printer daemon will be active. However, if there are entries in the queue and the printer daemon shows as `no daemon present`, the daemon has died and must be started again with the `restart` command.

`stop` *printer_name*   Stops the printer. Print requests can still be spooled, but they are not printed until the printer is started. If a job is being printed when the `stop` command is issued, the job completes the print process and then stops printing. The `start` and `stop` commands alter the contents of the lock file in the print spool directories. The `stop` command also kills the daemon for spooling to that printer.

`topq` *printer_name print_ID*   Moves the print request with *print_ID* to the top of the print queue.

`topq` *printer_name username*   Moves all print requests owned by *username* to the top of the queue. (This is very handy for system administrators who don't want to wait!)

`up` *printer_name*   Is used to reactivate a printer that was taken down. See the `down` command for more information.

The `lpc` utility isn't very user-friendly, but it's the only way to handle printers and their queues in Linux. Several front-end menu-driven utilities are beginning to appear that simplify this task.

Managing the Printer Queue with *lpq* and *lprm*

Several commands help you administer the printer queue specifically, instead of relying on the `lpc` command. Two tasks are commonly required by a system administrator: displaying the current queue and removing print jobs in a queue.

To display the current print queue for any printer, use the `lpq` command. It has the following syntax:

```
lpq [-l] [-Pprinter_name] [job_ID ...] [username ...]
```

With no arguments at all, `lpq` displays information about the current printer queues. The `lpq` command normally displays information about who queued the print job, where it is in the queue, the files being printed, and the total size of the files. The `-l` option displays more information about each entry in the printer queue. Usually, only one line of information is displayed.

A specific printer can be displayed with the `-P` option, followed by the printer's name. If no name is supplied, the default system printer is displayed. If one or more *job_IDs* or *usernames* are provided, only information about the job or jobs queued by the user is shown.

communications parameters based on information in the file /etc/gettydefs (getty definitions). The getty process then generates the login prompt on the remote terminal.

Many special handling and command options are available with the getty process, but most of them are of little interest to users and casual system administrators. If you want complete information on the getty command, consult the man pages that accompany Linux.

The /etc/gettydefs file is used to supply the settings getty uses for communications. The format of each line in the gettydefs file is as follows:

```
label:initial flags: final flags: login prompt: next label
```

The *label* is used to identify each line, so that when /sbin/getty is started with an argument (as it usually is, transparent to the user), the argument is used to match the *label* and provide the configuration information. The *initial* and *final* flags are used to set any behavior for the connection before and after the login program has executed.

The *login* prompt is the prompt to be displayed on the terminal. Usually it is just login:, but it can be any string. Finally, the *next label* is used to send getty to another line, in case it can't use the current one. This is typically used with modem lines, which start at a high speed (such as 9600 baud) and go to 4800, 2400, and 1200 in sequence, trying to connect at each step. For terminals, the *next label* is usually a pointer back to the line's first *label*.

An extract from a sample /etc/gettydefs file looks like this:

```
console# B19200 OPOST ONLCR TAB3 BRKINT IGNPAR ISTRIP IXON IXANY PARENB ECHO
ECHOE ECHOK ICANON ISIG CS8 CREAD # B19200 OPOST ONLCR TAB3 BRKINT IGNPAR ISTRIP
IXON IXANY PARENB ECHO ECHOE ECHOK ICANON ISIG CS8 CREAD #Console Login: #console

9600H# B9600 # B9600 SANE IXANY PARENB TAB3 HUPCL #login: #4800H

4800H# B4800 # B4800 SANE IXANY PARENB TAB3 HUPCL #login: #2400H

2400H# B2400 # B2400 SANE IXANY PARENB TAB3 HUPCL #login: #1200H

1200H# B1200 # B1200 SANE IXANY PARENB TAB3 HUPCL #login: #300H

300H# B300 # B300 SANE IXANY PARENB TAB3 HUPCL #login: #9600H
```

If you look at the file that accompanies your Linux system, you see that there are many more lines, but they all have the same format as the preceding samples. The easiest lines to look at are the shorter ones (the last five lines in the preceding extract), but they all have the same format as the preceding samples.

These lines are for a modem, starting at 9600 baud. The initial flag is set to B9600, which sets the baud rate at 9600 baud. The final flags, used when a connection has been established, set the characteristics of the line (such as a TAB meaning three spaces). Finally, the field at the end points to the next lower speed to provide checks for slower modems or poor lines that prevent fast logins.

The first line in the preceding extract is typical for a terminal. It sets many initial and final flags that control how the terminal behaves. The reference at the end of the line is back to the same definition, because the terminal is hardwired to the system.

NOTE

You shouldn't have to change the entries in the `gettydefs` file, because the default file contains many different configurations. You should examine the file carefully to find an entry that will work with the terminal you are using. If you do make changes to the `gettydefs` file, you should run the command `getty -c gettydefs` to make the changes effective.

Terminal Files: /etc/ttys and /etc/inittab

Terminal configuration information is stored in the files `/etc/ttys` and `/etc/inittab`. These files can be modified by any editor. Some menu-driven programs are now appearing that perform changes to the files for you.

WARNING

Before making any changes to the terminal configuration files, make a safe copy in case the changes aren't effective and the file can't be returned to its original state easily. Simply copy the two files to new names such as `/etc/tty.original` and `/etc/inittab.original`.

The `/etc/ttys` file has two columns. The first shows the type of terminal, and the second shows the device name. A typical `/etc/ttys` file from a new installation of Linux looks like this:

```
console tty1
console tty2
console tty3
console tty4
console tty5
console tty6
vt100 ttyp0
vt100 ttyp1
vt100 ttyp2
vt100 ttyp3
```

The terminal type in the first column is used to set the TERM environment variable when you log in, unless you override the value.

The `/etc/inittab` file is used to set the behavior of each terminal. The format of the `/etc/inittab` file follows this pattern:

ID:runlevel:action:process

The *ID* is a one- or two-character string that uniquely identifies the entry. In most cases, this corresponds to the device name, such as 1 for `tty1`.

The *runlevel* decides the capabilities of the terminal with the various states that the Linux operating system can be in (run levels vary from 0 to 6, and A, B, and C). If no entry is provided, all *runlevels* are supported. Multiple *runlevels* may be mentioned in the field.

If the terminal isn't behaving at this point, try typing reset and pressing Enter or Ctrl-J. If this doesn't work, the terminal has hung and should be reset manually.

Adding a Modem

The process for adding a modem is very similar to that for adding a terminal. In most cases, the procedure outlined earlier in "Adding a Terminal" can be followed.

Modems are used for several purposes on a Linux system, such as networking, connecting to remote systems, and accepting incoming calls. If the modem is to act as a conduit into the Linux system for remote terminals to connect, the procedure given in "Adding a Terminal" is followed, except for the entries that will be selected in the /etc/inittab file. In the case of a modem, find a set of lines that move through the different baud rates the modem supports.

Modems that are to be used for networking through the UUCP utility are dealt with in Chapter 42, "Networking," and Chapter 43, "UUCP." It includes information on setting the different configuration files properly.

For modems used to call out of the system, Linux has a menu-driven configuration utility as part of the setup command, which can set the proper configuration information automatically.

Summary

This chapter has shown you the basics of devices, device management, and how to add new devices to your Linux system. The information presented applies to most distributions of Linux, although there might be some slight changes in options and arguments as the different utilities are enhanced or streamlined. If you want more information about any of the commands, refer to the man pages that came with Linux, or consult a comprehensive system administration book.

Users and Logins

39

by Tim Parker

Listing 39.1. continued

```
lp:*:4:7:lp:/var/spool/lpd:
sync:*:5:0:sync:/sbin:/bin/sync
shutdown:*:6:0:shutdown:/sbin:/sbin/shutdown
halt:*:7:0:halt:/sbin:/sbin/halt
mail:*:8:12:mail:/var/spool/mail:
news:*:9:13:news:/usr/lib/news:
uucp:*:10:14:uucp:/var/spool/uucppublic:
operator:*:11:0:operator:/root:/bin/bash
games:*:12:100:games:/usr/games:
man:*:13:15:man:/usr/man:
postmaster:*:14:12:postmaster:/var/spool/mail:/bin/bash
nobody:*:-1:100:nobody:/dev/null:
ftp:*:404:1::/home/ftp:/bin/bash
```

Each line in the /etc/passwd file is composed of seven fields, separated by a full colon. If there is nothing to be entered in a field, the field is left blank, but the colons are retained to make sure each line has seven fields (which also means each line will have six colons). The seven fields (from left to right on each line) are:

user name	A unique identifier for the user.
password	The user's password (encrypted).
user ID (UID)	A unique number that identifies the user to the operating system
group ID (GID)	A unique number that identifies the user's group (for file permissions).
comment	Usually the user's real name, but sometimes phone numbers, departments, and so on.
home directory	The directory in which users are placed when they log in.
login command	The command executed when the user logs in, normally a shell.

We can look at each field in a little more detail. You should know what each field does and how it is used by other programs on your Linux system. Note that this type of user file is used with almost every UNIX system in the world, so once you know it for Linux, you know it for most UNIX versions.

User Names

The user name is a single string, usually eight characters or less, that uniquely identifies each user. Since the user name is the basis of most communications between users and other machines, the user name you use (or assign to others) should be simple and obvious. Usually, this means a permutation of the user's real name. A typical user name may be a combination of the user's first and last names, such as tparker or timp. The former example, composed of the first initial and last name, is fairly common in large networks.

Note that the characters in these examples are all lowercase. Case is important in Linux (as with all UNIX versions), so tparker and Tparker are two different logins. Since most Linux commands are lowercase, convention is to also keep user names lowercase. Underscores, periods, numbers, and some special characters are allowed, but should be avoided.

Small systems, such as on a single machine, may use more familiar names, such as the user's first name only. A small system may have users with the names tim, bill, yvonne, and so on. If two users have the same name, then there must be some method found to differentiate between the two (such as bill and billy).

A few users like to create cryptic user names that reflect their hobbies, nicknames, pets, lifestyle, or personality. You may find user names such as vader, grumpy, wizard, and hoops. This type of naming is fine on small systems that are used by one or two users, but quickly becomes awkward on larger systems where other users may not know their coworkers' user names. On the whole, if your system is used by more than a couple of friends, discourage this type of user name.

Passwords

The system stores the user's encrypted password in this field. (Actually, the password is encoded, not encrypted, although the convention has always been to use the term encrypted.) This field is very sensitive to changes, and any modification whatsoever can render the login useless until the system administrator performs a password change. A user's password can only be changed by the system administrator by using the passwd command when logged in as root (or by the users themselves).

> **NOTE**
>
> Some versions of UNIX do not keep the passwords in the /etc/passwd file because of potential security problems. If the password fields on your system are all set to x, then another file (called a *shadow password* file) is in use. However, all versions of Linux currently available do use this field normally.
>
> Systems running either Yellow Pages or NIS (Network Information Service), both of which rely on a central file of user names and passwords, do not use this field. However, few Linux systems will use either YP or NIS, so this distinction can be ignored for the moment.

When a user logs in, the login program logically compares the password the user typed to a block of zeros, and then compares that result to the entry in the password field. If they match, the user is granted access. Any deviation causes login to refuse access.

This field can be used to restrict access to the system. If you want a login to never be used for access, such as a system login like lp or sync, place an asterisk between the two colons for this field. This restricts all access. In the example /etc/passwd file shown earlier, you can see that many system logins have an asterisk as their password, effectively blocking access.

This field can also be used to allow unrestricted access by leaving it blank. If there is no password, anyone using the user name is granted access immediately, with no password requested. This is a very bad habit to get into! Do not leave passwords open unless you are using your Linux system for your own pleasure and have nothing of value on the file system.

Don't attempt to put a password in the password field—you cannot recreate the encryption method, and you'll end up locking the user out. Then, only the system administrator is able to change the password and allow access.

User ID

Every user name has an associated, unique user ID. The user ID, also called the UID, is used by Linux to identify everything associated with the user. The user ID is preferable to the user name because numbers are easier to work with than the characters in a name, and they take up much less space. Linux tracks all processes started by a user, for example, by the user ID and not the user name. A translation can take place in some utilities to display the user name, but the utility generally examines the /etc/passwd file to match the UID to the name.

The user ID numbers are usually assigned in specific ranges. Most UNIX systems, for example, allocate the numbers from zero to 99 for machine-specific logins, and the user ID numbers from 100 and up for users. This is a good working model and makes your system consistent with others. In the example /etc/passwd file shown earlier, you can see that root has a UID of 0, while the other system-created logins have numbers ranging upward. The login nobody is a special login used for NFS (Network File System) and has a UID of -1, an invalid number. When you assign user ID numbers, it is a good idea to assign them sequentially, so the first user is 100, the second 101, and so on.

Group ID

The group ID (GID) is used to track the users' startup group (in other words, the ID of the group the users belongs to when they log in). A group, as you will see later, is used for organization purposes to set file permissions, although many organizations don't bother with them. Group ID numbers range from zero and upwards. Linux systems assign a group called users with the group number 100 for this purpose.

The GID is used by the system when tracking file permissions, access, and file creation and modification specifications. If your system has only a single user group, then you need not worry about the GID. If you work with several groups (as might be implemented on a large system), then you need to examine the /etc/group file.

Comments

This field is used for the system administrator to add any information necessary to make the entry more self-explanatory. Typically, this area is used to enter the user's full name, although some system administrators like to add department or extension numbers for convenience. (This field is sometimes called the GECOS field, after the operating system that first used it.)

The comment field is used by some utilities to display information about users, so make sure you don't place any sensitive information there. Electronic mail systems, for example, can access this field to show who is sending mail. While you don't have to use the field, on larger systems it can make things much easier for administrators and other users when they can discover the real name of the person the user name belongs to.

Home Directory

The home directory field indicates to the login process where to place users when they log in. This is usually their home directory. Each user on the system should have her own dedicated home directory, and then the startup files will initialize the environment variable HOME to this value. The directory indicated in this field is the user's initial working directory only, and places no restrictions on the user (unless file permissions have been set to restrict movement).

For the most part, user home directories are located in a common area. Linux tends to use the /home directory, so you will find home directories such as /home/tparker, /home/ychow, and so on. Other versions use /usr, /user, or /u as user home directories. In some cases where the system administrator has experience with another type of UNIX that uses an alternate directory structure, you may find the home directories changed to make life easier (and more familiar) for that administrator. As far as Linux is concerned, it doesn't care what the name of the home directory is, as long as it can be entered.

Login Command

The login command is the command to be executed when login terminates. In most cases this is a shell command that is started, such as the C Shell or Bourne Shell, to provide the user with a shell environment. In some cases, it may be a single application or front-end system that restricts what the user can do. For example, the uucp login (used for e-mail and other simple networking tasks) executes the uucp command only. If the login command field is left empty, the operating system usually defaults to the Bourne shell (although this may change depending on the manner in which the operating system is set up).

Many versions of Linux enable users to change their login shell with the command chsh or passwd -s. When either command is used, the file /etc/shells is searched for a match. Only those commands in the /etc/shells file are allowed as valid entries when the user tries to change his startup shell. (You can add or remove lines in the /etc/shells file using any editor.) This helps you keep tighter security on the system. The superuser account has no restrictions on the entry in this field (or any other user's field). If your system uses the /etc/shells file, make sure it has the same file permissions and ownership as the /etc/passwd file, or a user can sneak through the system security by modifying the startup command for her login.

Default System User Names

The extract from the /etc/passwd file shown in the preceding section lists over a dozen system-dependent user names. These all serve special purposes on the Linux system. A few of these logins are worth noting because they have specific uses for the operating system and for system administrators:

root	The superuser account (UID 0) with unrestricted access and owns many system files.
daemon	Used for system processes. This login is used only to own the processes and set their permissions properly.

`bin`	Owns executables.
`sys`	Owns executables.
`adm`	Owns accounting and log files.
`uucp`	Used for UUCP communication access and files.

The other system logins are used for specific purposes (`postmaster` for mail, and so on) that are usually self-explanatory. You should not change any of the system logins. In most cases, they have an asterisk in the password field preventing their use for entry purposes.

Adding Users

There are two ways to add users to your system: manually edit the /etc/passwd file, or use an automated script that prompts you for the new user's details and writes a new line to the /etc/passwd file for you. The automated approach is handy for new system administrators who are uneasy about editing a file as important as /etc/passwd, or for those occasions when you have to add several users and the risk of error is thus increased. You must modify the /etc/passwd file when you are logged in as root.

> **CAUTION**
>
> Before making changes to your /etc/passwd file, make a copy of it! If you corrupt the /etc/passwd file you will not be able to log in, even as root, and your system is effectively useless except in system administration mode. Keep a copy of the /etc/passwd file on your emergency floppy or boot floppy in case of problems.

To add an entry to the /etc/passwd file, use any editor that saves information in ASCII. Add the new users to the end of the file, using a new line for each user. Make sure you use a unique user name and user ID (UID) for each user. For example, to add a new user called `bill` to the system with a UID of 103 (remember to keep UIDs sequential for convenience) and a GID of 100 (the default group), a home directory of /home/bill, and a startup shell of the Bourne shell, add the following line to the /etc/passwd file:

```
bill::103:100:Bill Smallwood:/home/bill:/bin/sh
```

Note that we have left the password blank because you can't type in an encrypted password yourself. As soon as you have saved the changes to /etc/passwd, set a password for this account by running the command:

```
passwd bill
```

This command prompts you for an initial password. Set the password to something that Bill will be able to use, and ask him to change the password the first time he works on the system. Many system administrators set the initial password to a generic string (such as "password" or the login name) and then force the new user to change the password the first time they log in. Using generic strings is usually acceptable if the user logs in quickly, but don't leave accounts with generic login strings sitting around too long—someone else may use the account.

After you have added the necessary line to the /etc/passwd file, you should create the user's home directory. Once created, you must set the ownership to have that user own the directory. For the preceding example, you would issue the following commands:

```
mkdir /home/bill
chown bill /home/bill
```

All users must belong to a group. If your system has only one group defined, then add the user's user name to the line in the /etc/group file that represents that group. If the new user should belong to several groups, add the user name to each group in the /etc/group file. The /etc/group file and groups in general are discussed in the "Groups" section later in the chapter.

Finally, the configuration files for the users' shells should be copied into their home directory and set to allow them access for customization. For example, if you copy the Bourne shell's .profile file from another user called yvonne, you would issue the following commands:

```
cp /home/yvonne/.profile /home/bill/.profile
chown bill /home/bill/.profile
```

You should also manually check the configuration file to ensure there are no environment variables that will be incorrectly set when the user logs in. For example, there may be a line defining the HOME environment variable or the spool directories for printer and mail. Use any ASCII editor to check the configuration file. If you are using the Korn or C shell, there are other configuration files that need to be copied over and edited. Bourne shell compatibles need only a .profile, while the C shell and compatibles need .login and .cshrc. The Korn shell and compatibles need a .profile and usually another file with environment variables embedded in it.

In general, the process for manually adding a new user to your system is:

1. Add an entry for the user in the /etc/passwd file.

2. Create the user's home directory and set the ownership.

3. Copy the shell startup files and edit their settings and ownerships.

Some distributions of the Linux system have a hold-over command from the Berkeley BSD UNIX version. The command vipw invokes the vi editor (or whatever the default system editor has been set to) and edits a temporary copy of the /etc/passwd file. The use of a temporary file and file lock acts as a lock mechanism to prevent two different users from editing the file at the same time. When the file is saved, vipw does a simple consistency check on the changed file, and if all appears proper, the /etc/passwd file is updated.

The automated scripts for Linux tend to have the names useradd or adduser. When run, they prompt you for all the information that is necessary in the /etc/passwd file. Both versions let you exit at any time to avoid changing the /etc/passwd file. The automated scripts also tend to ask for an initial password, which you can set to anything you want or leave blank. One advantage of the automated scripts is that they copy all the configuration files for the supported shells automatically, and in some cases, make environment variable changes for you. This can significantly simplify the process of adding users.

A quick note on passwords—they are vitally important to the security of your system. Unless you are on a standalone Linux machine with no dial-in modems, every account should have a secure password. Passwords are assigned and changed with the passwd command. The superuser can change any password on the system, but a user can only change his own password.

Deleting Users

Just like adding new users, deleting users can be done with an automated script or manually. The automated scripts deluser or userdel asks which user you want to delete, and then removes the entry from the /etc/passwd file. Some scripts also clean out the spool and home directory files, if you want. You must make any deletions to the /etc/passwd file when logged in as root.

If you delete users manually, simply remove their entries from the /etc/passwd file. Then you can clean up their directories to clear disk space. You can completely delete all their files and their home directory with the command:

```
rm -r /home/userdir
```

where /home/userdir is the full pathname of the user's home directory. Make sure there are no files you want to keep in that directory before you blow them all away!

Next, you should remove the user's mail spool file, which is usually kept in /usr/spool/mail/ username. For example, to remove the user walter's mail file, issue the command:

```
rm /usr/spool/mail/walter
```

The spool file is a single file, so this command cleans up the entries properly. To finish off the mail clean-up, check that the user has no entries in the mail alias files (usually /etc/aliases) or you can force all mail for that user to another login (such as root). To make any changes to the /etc/aliases file effective, you must run the newaliases command.

Finally, clean up the user's cron and at jobs. You can display the user's crontab file using the crontab command.

If you need to retain the user for some reason (such as file ownerships, a general access account, or accounting purposes), you can disable the login completely by placing an asterisk in the password field of the /etc/passwd file. That login can never be used once an asterisk is in the password field. If you need to reactivate the account, simply run the passwd command.

The process for manually deleting a user (or using an automated script that doesn't clean up directories and files) is:

1. Remove the user's entry from /etc/passwd and /etc/group.
2. Remove the user's mail file and any mail aliases.
3. Remove any cron or at jobs.
4. Remove the home directory if you don't want any files it holds.

Occasionally, you may want to temporarily disable a user's account, such as when he or she goes on extended leave, vacation, or because you are mad at them! If you want to temporarily disable the login but be able to recover it at any time in the future, add an asterisk as the first character of the encrypted password. Don't alter any characters in the existing password, but just add the asterisk to the front. When you want to reactivate the account, remove the asterisk and the password is back to whatever it was set at before you made the changes.

Groups

Every user on a UNIX and Linux system belongs to a group. A group is a collection of individuals lumped together for some reason. The users in a group may all work in the same department, may need access to a particular programming utility, or they may all have access to use a special device, such as a scanner or color laser printer. Groups can be set up for any reason, and users can belong to any number of groups. However, a user can only be a member of one group at a time, because groups are used for determining file permissions and Linux only allows one group ID per user at any point in time.

Groups can have their permissions set so that members of that group have access to devices, files, file systems, or entire machines that other users who do not belong to that group may be restricted from. For example, this can be useful when you have an accounting department, all members of which need access to the company's accounts. However, you wouldn't want non-accounting people to go snooping through financial statements, so creating a special group that has access to the accounting system makes sense.

Many small Linux systems have only one group, the default group, because that is the simplest way to manage a system. Then, each user's access to devices and files is controlled by the devices' or files' permissions, not the group. When you start to get several different users in logical groupings, though, groups start to make more sense. You can even use groups to control your friends' or children's access to areas on your home Linux system.

Group information is maintained in the file /etc/group, which is similar in layout to the /etc/passwd file. The default /etc/group file from a newly installed Linux system is shown in Listing 39.2.

Listing 39.2. The default /etc/group file.

```
root::0:root
bin::1:root,bin,daemon
daemon::2:root,bin,daemon
sys::3:root,bin,adm
adm::4:root,adm,daemon
tty::5:
disk::6:root,adm
lp::7:lp
mem::8:
kmem::9:
wheel::10:root
floppy::11:root
mail::12:mail
news::13:news
uucp::14:uucp
```

continues

Listing 39.2. continued

```
man::15:man
users::100:games
nogroup::-1:
```

Each line in the file has four fields separated by colons. Two colons together mean that the field is empty and has no value specified. Each line in the file follows this format:

`group name:group password:group ID:users`

Each group has a line of its own in the file. The fields in the /etc/group file (from left to right) are listed as follows:

- group name—A unique name usually of eight characters or less (usually standard alphanumeric characters only).
- password—Usually left as an asterisk or blank, but a password can be assigned that a user must enter to join the group. Not all versions of Linux or UNIX use this field, and it is left in the file for backward compatibility reasons.
- group ID (GID)—A unique number for each group, used by the operating system.
- users—A list of all user IDs that belong to that group.

Every Linux system has a number of default groups which belong to the operating system, usually called bin, mail, uucp, sys, and so on. You can see the system-dependent groups in the default /etc/group file as shown in Listing 39.2. In that file, all but the last two entries are system groups. You should never allow users to belong to one of these groups because it gives them access permissions that can be the same as root's. Only system logins should have access to these operating system groups.

Default System Groups

You may have noticed in the startup /etc/group file shown in Listing 39.2 that there are several groups defined. These groups are used to set file permissions and access rights for many utilities. It's worth taking a quick look at some of the most important groups and their functions:

root/wheel/system	Usually used to enable a user to employ the su command to gain root access, it owns most system files.
daemon	Used to own spooling directories (mail, printer, and so on).
kmem	Used for programs that need to access kernel memory directly (including ps).
sys	Owns some system files; on some systems this group behaves the same as kmem.
tty	Owns all special files dealing with terminals.

The default group for the Slackware Linux version /etc/group file, shown previously, is called users, and has a GID of 100. (Many UNIX systems have the default group called group with a group ID of 50 which is the convention.)

Adding a Group

You can edit the information in the /etc/group file manually, using any ASCII editor, or you can use a shell utility such as addgroup or groupadd which go through the process for you. As a system administrator, you may find it easier to do the changes manually because you can see the entire group file at the time you are editing it. Not all versions of Linux have an addgroup or groupadd utility.

To manually add a group to the /etc/group file, first make a backup copy of the file. Use any ASCII editor and add one line to the file for each new group you want to create. Make sure you follow the syntax of the file carefully because incorrect entries prevent users from belonging to that group. In the following lines, two new groups have been created:

```
accounts::101:bill
scanner::102:yvonne
```

The two groups have GIDs of 101 and 102, and like user IDs, the GIDs should be assigned sequentially for convenience. The users that are in the group are appended. In these cases, only one user is in each group. You'll see how to assign multiple users to a group in the next section. The groups do not have to be in order of the GID or group name, although for convenience you usually have the file ordered by GID. You could add new lines anywhere in the file.

The /etc/group file should be checked for file permissions and ownership after you have made changes to it. The file should be owned by root and have a group owner of root (or system, depending on the group with GID 0). The file permissions should prevent anyone but root from writing the file.

Adding a User to New Groups

Users can belong to many groups, in which case their user IDs should be on each group line that they belong to in the file /etc/group. Each user name on a line in the /etc/group file is separated by a comma. There is no limit to the number of users that can belong to a group, in theory, but in practice, the line length of the Linux system (255 characters) acts as an effective limiter. There are ways around this limit, but few systems will require it.

The following excerpt from a /etc/group file shows several groups with multiple members:

```
accounts::52:bill,yvonne,tim,roy,root
prgming::53:bill,tim,walter,gita,phyliss,john,root
cad::54:john,doreen,root
scanner::55:john,root,tim
```

The user names on each line do not have to be in any particular order. Linux searches along each line to find the user names it wants.

A user can be a member of only one group at a time while logged in, so they must use the command newgrp to change between groups they are members of. The starting group a user belongs to when they log in is given by the GID field in the /etc/passwd file.

Deleting a Group

If you decide you don't want a particular group to exist anymore, you can simply remove the group name from the /etc/group file. You should also check the /etc/passwd file to see if any users have that group ID as their startup GID, and change it to another group of which they are members. If you don't change the GIDs, those users will not be able to log in because they have no valid group membership. You should also scan the entire file system for files and directories that are owned by that group and change them to another group. Failure to make this change may prevent access to the file or directory.

Some Linux versions have shell scripts that remove group lines from the /etc/group file for you. The utility is generally called delgroup or groupdel. However, most versions of Linux don't bother with this utility.

The *su* Command

Sometimes you want to execute a command as another user. If you are logged in as superuser and want to create files with bill's permissions and ownership set, it is easier to log in as bill than work as root and then reset all the parameters. Similarly, if you are logged in as a user and need to be superuser for a little while, you would have to log out and back in to make the change. An alternative is the su command.

The su command changes your effective user name and grants you the permissions that user name has. The su command takes the user name you want to change to as an argument. For example, if you are logged in as a typical user and want to be root, you can issue the command:

```
su root
```

and the Linux system prompts you for the root password. If you supply it correctly, you will be root until you issue a Ctrl-D to log out of that account and back to where you started. Similarly, if you are logged in as root and want to be a user, you can issue the command with the user name, such as:

```
su tparker
```

You won't be prompted for a password when changing from root to another user because you have superuser powers. When you Ctrl-D out of the login, you are back as root. If you are logged in as a normal user and want to switch to another non-root login, you have to supply the password, though.

Summary

In this chapter we've looked at the basics of the /etc/passwd and /etc/group files, the two files intimately connected with user access to Linux. As you have seen, these are simple files and can easily be modified by a system administrator to add users and groups at any time. Always bear in mind that these are vital files, and they should be copied to a backup filename, then edited carefully and their permissions checked after each edit.

Processes

40

by Tim Parker

Everything that runs on a Linux system is a process—every user task, every system daemon—*everything* is a process. Knowing how to manage the processes running on your Linux system is an important (indeed even critical) aspect of system administration. This chapter looks processes in some detail. In this chapter you will see:

- How to find out what processes are running
- Determine when a process is hogging the system
- How to find out which processes are locked up
- How to terminate a process
- How to properly manage processes

In the course of discussing processes, we don't bother with the mechanics behind how processes are allocated, or how the Linux kernel manages to time-slice all the processes to run a multitasking operating system. Instead, we'll look at the nitty-gritty aspects of process control that you need in order to keep your system running smoothly.

You may come across the terms *process* and *job* used when dealing with multitasking operating systems. For most purposes, both terms are correct. However, a *job* is usually a process started by a shell (and may involve many processes), while a *process* is a single entity that is executing. To be correct, we'll use the term process throughout.

Processes

A formal definition of a process is that it is a single program running in its own virtual address space. This means that everything running under Linux is a process. This is compared to a job, which may involve several commands executing in series. Alternatively, a single command line issued at the shell prompt may involve more than one process, especially when pipes or redirection are involved. For example, the command

```
nroff -man ps.1 ¦ grep kill ¦ more
```

will start three processes, one for each command.

Types of Processes

There are several types of processes involved with the Linux operating system. Each has its own special features and attributes. The processes involved with Linux are:

- Interactive processes: A process initiated from (and controlled by) a shell. Interactive processes may be in foreground or background.
- Batch processes: Processes that are not associated with a terminal but are submitted to a queue to be executed sequentially.
- Daemon processes: Processes usually initiated when Linux boots and that run in the background until required.

Using the *ps* command

The easiest method of finding out what processes are running on your system is to use the ps (process status) command. The ps command has a number of options and arguments, although most system administrators use only a couple of common command-line formats. We can start by looking at the basic usage of the ps command, and then examine some of the useful options.

The ps command is available to all system users, as well as root, although the output changes a little depending on whether you are logged in as root when you issue the command.

When you are logged in as a normal system user (in other words, any login but root) and issue the ps command on the command line by itself, it displays information about every process you are running. For example, you might see the following output when you issue the command:

```
$ ps
  PID TTY STAT   TIME COMMAND
   41 v01 S     0:00 -bash
  134 v01 R     0:00 ps
```

ps Command Output

The output of the ps command is always organized in columns. Every process on the system has to have a unique identifier so Linux can tell which processes it is working with. Linux handles processes by assigning a unique number to each process, called the "Process ID" number (or PID). PIDs start at zero when the system is booted and increment by one for each process run, up to some system-determined number (such as 65,564) at which point it starts numbering from zero again, ignoring those that are still active. Usually, the lowest-number processes are the system kernel and daemons, which start when Linux boots and remain active as long as Linux is running. When you are working with processes (such as terminating them), you must use the PID.

The TTY column in the ps command output shows you which terminal the process was started from. If you are logged in as a user, this will usually be your terminal or console window. If you are running on multiple console windows, you will see all the processes you started in every window displayed.

The STAT column in the ps command output shows you the current status of the process. The two most common entries in the status column are S for sleeping and R for running. A running process is one that is currently executing on the CPU. A sleeping process is one which isn't currently active. Processes may switch between sleeping and running many times every second.

The TIME column shows the total amount of system (CPU) time used by the process so far. These numbers tend to be very small for most processes because they require only a short time to complete. The numbers under the TIME column are a total of the CPU time, not the amount of time the process has been alive.

Finally, the COMMAND column contains the name of the command line you are running. This is usually the command line you used, although some commands start up other processes. These are called "child" processes, and they show up in the ps output as if you had entered them as commands.

If the process doesn't terminate properly with the `kill` command, you need to use sterner measures. The `kill` command actually has several levels of operation. When issued with no arguments other than the PID, `kill` tries to gracefully terminate the process (which means any open files are closed, and generally, `kill` is polite to the process). If this doesn't work, you should use the `-9` option, which is a little more forceful in its attempt to terminate the process. For example, to forcefully terminate the process with PID 726, issue the following command:

```
kill -9 726
```

If that doesn't work, then the process may be unkillable. This does happen occasionally with Linux, and the only solution is to shut down and reboot the machine.

killing Rights

To help prevent a user from killing another user's processes, `ps` checks for the process owner. If a user tries to `kill` another user's process, a message like this one is displayed:

```
kill: - Not owner
```

The superuser doesn't get this message because the superuser login can `kill` anything.

Summary

This chapter has shown you how to obtain listings of the processes currently executing on your Linux system and how to terminate them when they require it. Although you may not have to use this knowledge often, every operating system has occasions where something gets out of hand and you need to control it. The problems multiply as the number of users increases. Instead of rebooting the Linux system, process commands enable you to correct the problem without terminating the operating system.

SCSI Device Support

41

by Tim Parker

The tape drive is not recognized at boot time Try booting with a tape in the drive.

A networking kernel does not work with new SCSI devices The autoprobe routines for many network drivers are not passive and can interfere with some SCSI drivers. Try to disable the network portions to identify the guilty program, and then reconfigure it.

A SCSI device is detected, but the system is unable to access it You probably don't have a device file for the device. Device drivers should be in /dev and configured with the proper type (block or character) and unique major and minor device numbers. Run mkdev for the device.

The SCSI controller card fails when it uses memory-mapped I/O This problem is common with Trantor T128 and Seagate boards and is caused when the memory-mapped I/O ports are incorrectly cached. You should have the board's address space marked as uncacheable in the XCMOS settings. If you can't mark them as such, disable the cache and see if the board functions properly.

Your system fails to find the SCSI devices and you get messages when the system boots, such as scsi : 0 hosts *or* scsi%d : type: The autoprobe routines on the controller cards rely on the system BIOS autoprobe and can't boot properly. This is particularly prevalent with these SCSI adapters: Adaptec 152x, Adaptec 151x, Adaptec AIC-6260, Adaptec AIC-6360, Future Domain 1680, Future Domain TMC-950, Future Domain TMC-8xx, Trantor T128, Trantor T128F, Trantor T228F, Seagate ST01, Seagate ST02, and Western Digital 7000. Check that your BIOS is enabled and not conflicting with any other peripheral BIOSes (such as on some adapter cards). If the BIOS is properly enabled, find the board's "signature" by running DOS's DEBUG command to check if the board is responding. For example, use the DEBUG command d=c800:0 to see if the board replies with an acknowledgment (assuming you have set the controller card to use address 0xc8000; if not, replace the DEBUG command with the proper address). If the card doesn't respond, check the address settings.

Sometimes the SCSI system locks up completely There are many possible solutions, including a problem with the host adapter. Check the host adapter with any diagnostics that came with the board. Try a different SCSI cable to see if that is the problem. If the lockups seem to occur when multiple devices are in use at the same time, there is probably a firmware problem. Contact the manufacturer to see if upgrades are available that would correct the problem. Finally, check the disk drives to ensure that there are no bad blocks that could affect the device files, buffers, or swap space.

Summary

SCSI has a reputation for being difficult to work with, but in fact it is one of the easiest and most versatile systems available. Once you get used to the nomenclature, SCSI offers many useful features to the Linux user. Indeed, most veteran UNIX people prefer working with SCSI because it is easy to use with the UNIX kernel, and the same applies to Linux.

Networking

by Tim Parker

Most Ethernet ca
fully check the d
work properly.

If you plan to do
need a network ca
to use. For examp
porting at least V

Configur

Let's assume you
run TCP/IP over
because there are
and unique softw

If, after following
fully scan all the c
about the Linux l
Linux from which

To configure the
you haven't instal
ing. Your kernel r
is usually done d
recompilation ma

First we'll deal wi
handle SLIP over

What You N

Before you start r
pieces of informat
handy when you r
causing major pro

IP Address

First you need an
has to be identifie
to uniquely ident
are called *Interne*

The 32 bits of the
numbers ranging

IP (Interne
ICMP (Int
and networ
RIP (Routi
routing me
OSPF (Op

Network Address
and a more comn

ARP (Addi
chines on t
DNS (Dor
RARP (Re
network, b
BOOTP (I
tion from a

User Services: T
FTP (File
excessive o
TFTP (Tri
transport.
TELNET:
machine ar

Gateway Protoc
as well as handle
EGP (Exte
GGP (Gat
gateways.
IGP (Inter

Others: These ar
portant services c
NFS (Netw
another, th
NIS (Netw
logins and
RPC (Rem
other usin

In this chap...

- Wha...
- How...
- Wha...
- How...
- Wha...

Linux offe...
Protocol), ...
networks ii...
machine to...
Linux syste...

Whether yo...
machine to...

What

TCP/IP is...
aspects of t...
hardware a...
TCP/IP arc...
has helped...
TCP/IP for...
erating syst...

TCP/IP is...
TCP/IP far...
mary comp...

Transmissi...
TCP/IP far...
according t...

Transport:

TCP...
send...
UDI...
don'...

Routing: T...
destination...
nation.

SMT...
betw(...
SNM...
TCP...
opera...

If you want...
Ethernet, a...
is *packet*, w...
Ethernet to...
properly at...

All the TCI...
organizatio...
methods o...
backward-c...

Hardv

You can ac...
work at all, ...
of TCP/IP...
between a s...
figurations, ...
you are cre...
assembled ...
Protocol), v...
attached to...

Linux requ...
list:

3Con...
3Con...
Nove...
Nove...
West...
West...
Hew...
Hew...
Hew...

The /etc/ppp/chap-secrets file consists of four columns for the client name, the server name, the secret password string, and an optional list of IP addresses. The behavior of the system is different depending on whether the local machine is being challenged to authenticate itself or is issuing a challenge to the remote. When the local machine has to authenticate itself, pppd examines the /etc/ppp/chap-secrets file for an entry in the client field that matches the local host name and the server field equal to the remote hostname, and then uses the string to build the authentication message. Such an entry in the /etc/ppp/chap-secrets file looks like this:

```
#   client            server            string          addresses
merlin.tpci.com    big_guy.big_net.com  "I hate DOS"
```

This entry uses the string I hate DOS to build an authentication message back to big_guy .big_net.com. The quotations are necessary to surround the string in the file. (We will look at the addresses column in a moment.) If you are setting up your system to connect to three different PPP remotes, you will want an entry for each server, so your file may look like this:

```
#   client            server            string          addresses
merlin.tpci.com    big_guy.big_net.com "I hate DOS"
merlin.tpci.com    chatton.cats.com      "Meow, Meow, Meow"
merlin.tpci.com    roy.sailing.ca        "Hoist the spinnaker"
```

When your machine is sending the challenge, the process is reversed. The pppd daemon looks for the remote hostname in the client field, the local hostname in the server field, and uses the string to compare the encryption results with the string sent back by the remote. Entries in the /etc/ppp/ chap-secrets file for this purpose look like this:

```
#   client            server            string          addresses
big_guy.big_net.com    merlin.tpci.com    "Size isn't everything"
```

Again, you need an entry for each remote machine you may need to authenticate. You can see that you will end up having mirror image entries for the client and server fields for each machine you connect to (because either end may require authentication at any time). A simple /etc/ppp /chap-secrets file really looks like this:

```
#   client            server            string          addresses
merlin.tpci.com    big_guy.big_net.com  "I hate DOS"
big_guy.big_net.com merlin.tpci.com      "Size isn't everything"
merlin.tpci.com    chatton.cats.com      "Meow, Meow, Meow"
chatton.cats.com    merlin.tpci.com      "Here, Kitty, Kitty"
merlin.tpci.com    roy.sailing.ca        "Hoist the spinnaker"
roy.sailing.ca      merlin.tpci.com      "Man overboard"
```

The size of the file could get quite large, so CHAP enables you to use a wildcard match, usually only for your local machine. For example, in the following /etc/ppp/chap-secrets file, the last entry allows any other machine connecting to the localhost and requiring authentication to use the same string:

```
#   client            server            string          addresses
merlin.tpci.com    big_guy.big_net.com  "I hate DOS"
big_guy.big_net.com merlin.tpci.com      "Size isn't everything"
merlin.tpci.com    chatton.cats.com      "Meow, Meow, Meow"
chatton.cats.com    merlin.tpci.com      "Here, Kitty, Kitty"
merlin.tpci.com    roy.sailing.ca        "Hoist the spinnaker"
*                   merlin.tpci.com      "Man overboard"
```

Of course, the remote must have the same string in it's chap-secrets file. This is a little less secure than a dedicated string for each remote, but can be a handy time-saver when using a number of machines only rarely.

The addresses field, which wasn't used in the preceding samples, lets you list either symbolic names or IP addresses for the clients. This is necessary if the remote wants to use another IP address than its normal one, which would normally cause the authentication to fail. If the address field is empty (as they all are in the samples), any IP address is allowed. A hyphen in the field disallows all IP addresses with that client.

The /etc/ppp/pap-secrets file is much the same as the chap-secrets file. The fields in the pap-secrets file are the client (called a user in the pap-secrets format) and server names, a secret string, and valid address aliases. However, the look of the file is different because the client and server names are not full domain names, and the secret string is a single block of text. A sample pap-secrets file looks like this:

```
# /etc/ppp/pap-secrets
#   user        server          string          addresses
merlin          darkstar        yG55Sj29        darkstar.big_net.com
darkstar        merlin          5Srg7S          merlin.tpci.com
merlin          chatton         MeowMeow        chatton.cats.com
chatton         merlin          73wrh6s         merlin.tpci.com
```

In this example, the first two lines show a connection to the machine darkstar. The first line is how you authenticate a request from darkstar, and the second is how you authenticate a request from us to them. The user name in the first column is the name you send to the remote, while the server field is their identification to you. This poses a problem: The pppd daemon has no way of knowing the remote host's name because all it gets is an IP address. You can put the IP address in the addresses column of the file, or you can specify the remote host name at the end of the pppd command line like this:

```
pppd ..... remotename chatton user merlin
```

This shows that the remote is called chatton, and your local host is merlin. The last portion giving the local host name will override any default values.

Summary

In this chapter you've seen how to install, configure, and test Ethernet connections to your Linux machine. You've also seen how to set up a SLIP or PPP connection. The only other networking process usually found on a Linux box uses UUCP (UNIX-to-UNIX Copy), which is described in Chapter 43.

If you want to install a network to connect several of your machines (assuming you have more than one), you will find it quite easy and useful. If you have two machines, it is fast and efficient to connect a Linux machine and a DOS machine, as long as the DOS machine is running TCP/IP. There are shareware versions of TCP/IP for Windows and many commercial implementations for both DOS and Windows.

UUCP

43

by Tim Parker

UUCP (UNIX to UNIX CoPy) was developed to provide a simple dial-up networking protocol for UNIX systems. It is most often used today as an e-mail transfer system, allowing non-networked machines to transfer e-mail easily over a modem connection. It can also be used for Usenet news and access to similar services that do not require a dedicated connection. UUCP is a two-machine connection, between your Linux machine and another machine running UUCP. UUCP cannot be used as a remote system access system (like FTP or Telnet), nor can it be used as a standard login because the protocols do not support this type of interactive behavior. UUCP does have security features that are adequate for most purposes, but UUCP is the primary source of break-ins for many systems because most system administrators don't bother to set the security system up properly.

Linux can run any of several different versions of UUCP, most of which are compatible with each other to a reasonable extent, except when it comes to configuration and installation procedures. Many Linux versions offer you a choice between the Taylor UUCP version and the HDB (HoneyDanBer) UUCP. You can use whichever single version came with your Linux software, or if you have both, you can choose between the two (or use both versions as the mood strikes you). Many Linux users prefer the Taylor UUCP implementation, while users who have worked on other UNIX systems prefer HDB because it is more recent. We'll look at both versions in this chapter. (There are even more UUCP versions, but we will ignore them because they are seldom used under Linux.) The first part of the chapter deals with configuring UUCP, while the rest covers using it.

UUCP Configuration

Most of the configuration required for UUCP takes place under the /usr/lib/uucp directory. There are several files used by UUCP, most of which need direct administrator modification to set up properly. While the configuration process can seem awfully complex to someone who has never done it before, there are really only a few files that need changing, and only one or two entries in each file.

The configuration process for Taylor UUCP and HDB UUCP are completely different, so we will look at them separately. However, you don't have to worry which version of UUCP is being run at the remote end of the connection because both can talk to each other (at least that's usually the case), as long as the configuration files are set up properly.

Some versions of Linux have semiautomated UUCP configuration scripts. These are more common with HDB UUCP than Taylor UUCP, but a few helpful scripts are also available for the latter. If you have one of these scripts, by all means use it, but do check the files manually afterwards.

For the configuration processes discussed in the following section, we will assume that our host machine's name is merlin, and we want to connect via UUCP to another Linux system called arthur. As you go through the process, take care to enter the information in the same format as the examples, but don't mix Taylor and HDB UUCP information.

Taylor UUCP Configuration

We can begin with a quick look at the configuration files involved in the Taylor UUCP system. These are the filenames and their primary purposes:

- `/usr/lib/uucp/config`—Defines the local machine name.

- `/usr/lib/uucp/sys`—Defines the remote systems and how to call them.

- `/usr/lib/uucp/port`—Describes each port for calling out and its parameters.

- `/usr/lib/uucp/dial`—Describes the dialers for calling out.

- `/usr/lib/uucp/dialcodes`—Used to contain expansions for symbolic dialcodes, but is rarely used when a straight-out telephone connection exists.

- `/usr/lib/uucp/call`—Can contain the login name and password for remote systems, but it is rarely used now.

- `/usr/lib/uucp/passwd`—Contains the login names and passwords used when remote systems connect to your local machine. Used only when uucico is password checking instead of using the login process.

To make the configuration process easier, we will ignore all the theory and background information and proceed with a sample configuration. You need only modify the entries to suit your own names, telephone numbers, device files, and so on, and the configuration process will be the same. It can then be repeated for as many systems as you want to connect to.

The first file to modify holds your system name and other general parameters. The file `/usr/lib/uucp/config` needs a single line entry for your system name such as this one:

```
nodename    merlin
```

The keyword `nodename` must be first on the line followed by whitespace (spaces or tabs), then your machine name. The information in this file may have been completed when you installed Linux, but you should manually check the contents to make sure. If your system's name isn't set correctly, the connection to the remote system won't work properly.

> **NOTE**
>
> To use UUCP, you must have a system name. For compatibility with most versions of UUCP, keep the name to seven characters or less. Ideally, the UUCP name is the same name you assigned to your host during configuration. The name doesn't have to follow a convention (such as the system name used by TCP/IP for Internet access), but if you use other network protocols, keep a consistent name. If you have a domain name (for TCP/IP access) use the first component of the machine's full TCP/IP name as the UUCP name. For example, if your full domain name is `merlin.wizards.com`, use the UUCP name `merlin`.

Linux for System Administrators

Part VI

You also need information about the remote system you want to connect to. The /usr/lib/uucp/ sys file holds all the information about remote systems. This file usually has a few sample entries in it, which you can copy or modify. Make sure you don't leave comment marks (pound or hash marks) in the first column or the entries will be ignored. A /usr/lib/uucp/sys entry for the remote machine merlin looks like this:

```
# system: arthur (Bill Smallwood's Linux system)
system     arthur
time       Any
phone      555-1212
port       com1
speed        9600
chat       login: merlin password: secret1
```

The first line in the preceding extract is a comment line. Most system administrators like to put a comment line in to identify each system. The next lines identify the different aspects of the remote system, including its name (arthur), times at which it can be called (Any in this case, meaning no restrictions), the telephone number (including any area code or special digits that have to be dialed), the serial port to be used for the connection (in this case, com1), the speed at which to connect (9600 baud), and the chat script or login process. In this case, the chat script tells UUCP to wait until it sees the string login: then to send merlin, then wait for the prompt password: and then to send secret1.

Most login scripts will require a login and password, and they must be placed in the configuration file because UUCP doesn't allow interactive sessions. This can be a bit of a problem because it allows other users on your system to see the login password for the remote machine, but since it can only be used by UUCP, this is not a major concern. Also, the file permissions on the UUCP configuration files can be set to prevent any system users (other than root) from looking into the file.

NOTE

Not all remote sites need a password for entry through UUCP. For example, some public archives let you log in and retrieve files using the uucp login with no password. Some sites use readily available passwords, such as uucp.

The port name used in the /usr/lib/uucp/sys entry does not have to match a device name on the Linux system, because another file is used to match the entry to a physical device. This file is /usr/ lib/uucp/port, and it requires an entry similar to this for a 9600 baud modem:

```
# com1 device port
port       com1
type       modem
device     /dev/cua0
speed      9600
dialer     Hayes
```

In the /usr/lib/uucp/port file, the name of the port used in the /usr/lib/uucp/sys file is identified on the first line. The type of connection to be used (usually modem) is on the next. The actual Linux device that corresponds to the port name is specified as a device driver (for many Linux systems this can be /dev/modem, which is linked to the serial port device driver).

The modem connection speed comes next, and shows the maximum speed the modem can be used at. Finally, the name of a dialer is entered. This is a throwback to the days when modems couldn't dial themselves, but used another device (called a dialer) to make the connection.

The dialer entry in the /usr/lib/uucp/port file is then matched to an entry in the file /usr/lib/uucp/dial, which tells the modem how to dial the phone. Here's a simple entry:

```
# Hayes modem
dialer      Hayes
chat        "" ATZ OK ATDT\T CONNECT
```

This shows the script that the system uses to communicate to the Hayes modem. In this case, the \T in the command line is replaced with the telephone number to be called. Some Linux systems simplify the use of the /usr/lib/uucp/port and /usr/lib/uucp/dial files into one single entry in the /usr/lib/uucp/sys file, which names the modem file directly.

The remote end of the connection (in this case, the system arthur) must have corresponding entries for merlin. The files will be similar with only name, telephone number, and (possibly) device name and chat script changes. Until both ends are configured properly, you can't get a connection between the two machines.

Some Linux systems with Taylor UUCP have a utility called uuchck that verifies the syntax in the UUCP configuration files and prints out summary information. If you don't have the uuchck utility, it can be downloaded from many FTP and BBS sites. Check Appendix A for some of the possible sites.

By default, Taylor UUCP allows a remote system to execute only a limited number of commands when they log into your system. Typically, the remote is only allowed to execute rmail and rnews, to transfer mail and news, respectively. If you want to allow extra programs to be executed, add a line to the /usr/lib/uucp/sys file that includes all the commands the remote system can execute. For example, the entry:

```
system      chatton
....
commands    rmail rnews rsmtp rdataupdate
```

specifies that the system chatton can execute any of the four commands given after the commands keyword. Note that all four commands must be in the usual search path used by the UUCP utilities (actually by uuxqt).

If you intend to transfer files between two machines, you must also modify the configuration files. When a remote system sends a file to your machine, the files usually should be stored in the directory /usr/spool/uucppublic (some systems use /var/spool/uucppublic) as a safety precaution. You don't want to allow a remote system to write files anywhere on your file system, or they could overwrite critical system files. The convention for most UUCP systems is to use either /usr/spool/uucppublic or /usr/spool/uucp/*system* (where *system* is the remote system's name) as the transfer directories.

If a modem program is not available to handle the modem, an entry in the file /usr/lib/uucp/ Dialers can be used. The format of the Dialers entries is:

```
dialer translation  expect  send  ...
```

where *dialer* is the name of the dialer (matching the Devices file), *translation* is the translation table to use for the phone number (converting characters where needed to pauses, beeps, and so on), and the *expect/send* entries are the chat script to set up the modem. A sample line in the Dialers file looks like this:

```
hayes1200 =,-,    " " AT\r\c OK\r \EATDT\T\r\c CONNECT
```

This is the entry for a Hayes 1200 Smartmodem, identified by the name hayes1200, with translations for the = and - characters, followed by the AT commands used to set up the modem. Since these entries are usually supplied in the Dialers file for most popular modems, we won't bother going into detail about them.

Permissions for file transfers are a little more convoluted with HDB UUCP than Taylor UUCP, because HDB UUCP adds many features for special handling. Instead of looking at all the file transfer permissions, you are better advised to consult a specialty book on UUCP, because the subject can easily consume 100 pages by itself! For this reason, we'll look at the fundamentals—just enough to get you set up properly.

Permissions for remote system access and file transfers are handled by the file /usr/lib/uucp/ Permissions. The general format of the entries in this file is:

```
MACHINE=remotename LOGNAME=uucp \
    COMMANDS=rmail:rnews:uucp \
    READ=/usr/spool/uucppublic:/usr/tmp \
    WRITE=/usr/spool/uucppublic:/usr/tmp \
    SENDFILES=yes REQUEST=no
```

where MACHINE identifies the remote machine's name, LOGNAME is the name they use to log in (or you use to log in to their system), COMMANDS are the commands they can execute on your local system, READ is the list of directories they can read files from, WRITE is the list of directories where they can write files, SENDFILES means they can send files (yes or no), and REQUEST means they can request files from your system (yes or no). Notice the use of slashes at the end of the first four lines, to indicate this is really a single long line broken up for readability. This is a typical UNIX convention.

A complete entry for the remote system wizard shows that it is allowed to both send and receive files, but only from the /usr/spool/uucppublic directory, and it can only execute mail and uucp commands (the later transfers files):

```
MACHINE=wizard LOGNAME=uucp1 \
    COMMANDS=rmail: uucp \
    READ=/usr/spool/uucppublic: \
    WRITE=/usr/spool/uucppublic: \
    SENDFILES=yes REQUEST=yes
```

To prevent the remote system from sending files, change SENDFILES to no. To prevent the remote system from requesting files, change REQUEST to no.

A UUCP Connection

When UUCP connects to a remote machine, it follows a particular series of steps. You can better understand the configuration files used by UUCP, and the processes that are involved, by following through a typical session. UUCP uses a process called uucico (UUCP Call In/Call Out) to handle the process of connecting and sending information. A UUCP connection can be started with the uucico command followed by the remote system name, such as:

```
uucico -s arthur
```

When uucico starts, it examines the /usr/lib/uucp/sys file (Taylor UUCP) or /usr/lib/uucp/ Systems (HDB UUCP) to see if the remote system name exists there. When it finds the proper remote system name, uucico reads the rest of the entries for that system, including the port to be used. From there, uucico uses /usr/lib/uucp/port and /usr/lib/uucp/dial (Taylor UUCP) or /usr/lib/uucp/Devices and /usr/lib/uucp/Dialers (HDB UUCP) to start the modem connection (assuming it is a modem used to establish the session, of course). When the modem is in use, uucico creates a lock on the device so no other application can use it (the lock is a file starting with LCK.. and followed by the device name, such as LCK..cua0).

Once the chat scripts for setting up and dialing the modem have been executed and the remote system is connected, uucico uses the chat script in the /usr/lib/uucp/sys or /usr/lib/uucp/Systems file to log into the remote. Once logged in, the remote machine starts up its copy of uucico, and the two uucico processes establish handshaking between themselves. Finally, after the handshaking has been established, uucico goes ahead and handles any transfers that are queued.

When completed with the session, the local machine checks to make sure that the remote has nothing further to send and then breaks the connection. Finally, uucico terminates.

Direct Connections

If your two machines are directly connected through a serial port, for example (no modems involved in the connection), you can use UUCP as a simple network protocol for file transfer. The only changes to the configuration files mentioned earlier are in the port specification. Instead of using a modem device, you specify a direct connection. For example, in the /usr/lib/uucp/sys file (Taylor UUCP), you would have an entry like this:

```
port      direct1
```

with a matching entry in the /usr/lib/uucp/port file that looks like this:

```
port      direct1
type      direct
speed     38400
device     /dev/cua1
```

with the speed of the direct connection and the port which uses it specified. The entries in the HDB UUCP version are similar, using the /usr/lib/uucp/Systems and /usr/lib/uucp/Devices files.

Login Scripts

The login scripts that form part of the /usr/lib/uucp/sys or /usr/lib/uucp/Systems file can be the most difficult part of a UUCP connection to get correct. If the machine you are logging into is a typical UNIX system, there should be only the usual login and password prompts to worry about. Other systems may require some special handling to gain access. For this reason, the login script is worth a quick look.

Generally, the layout of the login script is in a pattern-action pair, with the pattern coming from the remote machine and the action from the local. A simple login is:

```
login: merlin password: secret1
```

In this case, the local system waits until it sees the string login: coming from the remote, sends merlin, waits for password:, then sends secret1. You can simplify the script a little by cutting out extra letters from the remote, because all you really need are the last couple of characters and the colon. The script could have been written like this:

```
gin: merlin word: secret1
```

This type of script has a good use. Suppose the remote system sends Login: instead of login:; then the shortened form will work and the longer match won't.

One useful feature of the uucico login script is the ability to wait for the remote machine to reset itself (or start a getty process, more likely). This is implemented by using a hyphen and the word BREAK in the script, which tells uucico to send a break sequence if the remote site hasn't responded in a timely manner. For example, the script would be similar to this:

```
ogin:-BREAK-ogin: merlin sword: secret1
```

In this case, if the remote machine doesn't respond with a ogin: prompt after a short period of time, the local machine sends a break sequence and waits for the prompt again.

A few special characters can be used in the login script. The most important ones for most UUCP purposes are the following:

\c	Suppresses sending carriage return (send only)
\d	Delays one second (send only)
\p	Pauses for a fraction of a second (send only)
\t	Sends a tab (send and receive)
\r	Sends a carriage return (send and receive)
\s	Sends a space (send and receive)
\n	Sends a newline (send and receive)
\\	Sends a backslash (send and receive)

Sometimes you need to use one or more of the characters to get the remote machine to respond to a modem login. For example, the following script

```
\n\r\p ogin: merlin word: secret1
```

sends a carriage return-line feed pair before starting to match characters. This is usually enough to get the remote machine to start a getty on the port.

Changing Access Times

Both Taylor and HDB UUCP versions let you specify a time to call the remote systems. While the examples so far show Any (meaning the system can be called at any time, day or night), you may want to restrict calls to local-cost times, or on certain days of the week. The reason for limiting calls may be at your end (costs, for example), or at the remote (limited access times during the day, for example).

To specify particular days of the week to allow calls, use a two digit abbreviation of the day (Mo, Tu, We, Th, Fr, Sa, Su), or Wk for weekdays (Monday through Friday), Any (for any time), or Never (for not allowed to connect). Any combination of the days may be used, as you will see in a moment. The times for connecting are specified as a range, in 24-hour format, when a time span is required. If no time is given, it is assumed that any time during the day is allowed.

Dates and times are run together without spaces, while subsequent entries are separated by commas. Examples of restricted access times are as follows:

```
Wk1800-0730
MoWeFi
Wk2300-2400, SaSu
```

The first example allows connection only on weekdays between 6 p.m. and 7:30 a.m. The second allows connection any time on Monday, Wednesday, or Friday. The last example allows connections only between 11 p.m. and midnight on weekdays, and any time on weekends. You can build up any time and date specifications you want. These apply to both Taylor and HDB UUCP versions.

UUCP Security

The permissions of the UUCP configuration files must be carefully set to allow UUCP to function properly, as well as to allow better security for the system. Simply stated, the files should all be owned by uucp, and the group should be uucp on most systems that have that group in the /etc/group file. The ownerships can be set either by making all the file changes while logged in as uucp, or by setting the changes as root and then issuing the following commands when you are in the /usr/lib/uucp directory:

```
chown uucp *
chgrp uucp *
```

As a security precaution, you should set a strong password for the uucp login if there is one on your system. Some versions of Linux do not supply a password by default, leaving the system wide open for anyone who can type uucp at the login prompt!

The file permissions should be set very tightly, preferably to read-write (and execute for directories) only for the owner (uucp). The group and other permissions should be blanked because a read access can give valuable login information, as well as passwords to someone.

When UUCP logs into a remote system it requires a password and login. This information is contained in the /usr/lib/uucp/sys or /usr/lib/uucp/Systems files, and should be protected to prevent unauthorized snooping by setting file ownerships and permissions as mentioned.

If you have several systems connecting into yours, they can all use the same uucp login and password, or you can assign new logins and passwords as you need them. All you need to do is create a new /etc/passwd entry for each login (with a different login name from uucp, such as uucp1, uucp_arthur, and so forth) and a unique passwd. The remote system can then use that login to access your system. When you create new UUCP users in the /etc/passwd, force them to use uucico only to prevent access to other areas of your system. For example, the login uucp1, shown here, forces uucico as the startup command:

```
uucp1::123:52:UUCP Login for Arthur:/usr/spool/uucppublic:/usr/lib/uucp/uucico
```

The home directory is set to the uucppublic directory, and uucico is the only startup program that can be run. Using different logins for remote machines also allows you to grant different access permissions for each system, preventing unwanted access.

You should also carefully control the commands that remote systems can execute on your local machine. This is done through the permissions fields of the local access file and should be monitored carefully to prevent abuse and unauthorized access. In a similar manner, if you are allowing forwarding of files through your system, you should control who is allowed to forward, and where they are forwarded to.

Most important of all is to ensure that whoever accesses your system on a regular basis is someone you want access to be granted to. Don't leave your system wide open for anyone to enter because you are guaranteeing yourself disaster. Carefully watch logins and make sure file permissions and ownerships are properly set at all times.

Using UUCP

Once you have configured UUCP, you can use it to transfer files and e-mail. In order to use UUCP, you have to know the addressing syntax, which is different than what you may know from the Internet. The UUCP address syntax is:

```
machine!target
```

where *machine* is the remote machine name and *target* is the name of the user or file that you are trying to get to. For example, to send mail to the user yvonne on machine arthur, you would use the mail command with the destination user name:

```
mail arthur!yvonne
```

UUCP lets you move through several machines to get to a target. This can help save on telephone bills, or make a much wider network available to you from a small number of connections. Suppose you want to send mail to a user called `bill` on a system called `warlock`, which isn't in your configuration files but can be connected to through `arthur`. If you have permission to send mail through the system `arthur` (called a "hop"), you could send the mail with this command:

```
mail arthur!warlock!bill
```

When UUCP decodes this address, it reads the first system name (`arthur`) and sends it to that system. The UUCP processes on `arthur` then examines the rest of the address and realizes the mail is to be sent on to `warlock`. If you have permission to forward through `arthur`, UUCP on `arthur` sends the mail through to `warlock` for you. You can have many hops in an address, as long as each system you are connecting to allows the pass-through and can connect to the next machine on the list. For example, the address:

```
arthur!warlock!chatton!vader!alex
```

would send data through `arthur`, `warlock`, `chatton`, and `vader` in order, and then to the user `alex`. The addresses must be specified in the proper hop order or the address will fail. This multihop addressing can be very useful if a number of friends have local connections to other machines, allowing you to easily set up a complex network. The hard part is usually tracking the names of the systems involved. (The exclamation mark in the address is called a *bang*, so the address above is spoken as "arthur-bang-warlock-bang-chatton-bang-vader-bang-alex.")

> **NOTE**
>
> Some shells don't like the bang character because they are interpreted as a special shell command. Shells, such as the C Shell, use the exclamation mark to recall previous commands, so you must escape the bang with a slash to prevent the shell's interpretation. Addresses then become `arthur\!chatton\!yvonne`. This looks funny, but you get used to it.

Depending on how you have your UUCP system set, it may call out to the other systems in an address whenever something is submitted to it, or if callout times are limited, the data may be spooled until a call is allowed. You have already seen how to set callout times in the `/usr/lib/uucp/sys` and `/usr/lib/uucp/Systems` files.

A quick caution about relying on UUCP for delivery of information. If the systems that are being used are not set to call immediately when there is something queued, your data can take a long time to get to its destination. For example, if one of the hops in your address calls the next machine in the address only once a day, you may have a 24-hour delay in delivery. This can be exacerbated by each machine in the network.

> **CAUTION**
>
> Don't rely on the contents of your data sent through UUCP to be kept confidential. Once on a remote system, any user with access privileges to the queue could snoop into your data. Ideally, the file permission prevents anyone but the superuser accessing the data, but not all systems keep tight security. If you must send sensitive data, encrypt it and let the recipient know the decryption key through another format (not in a mail message!).

UUCP deals with all transfers as *jobs*, a term you'll encounter often when working with UUCP and its documentation. A job is a command that is to be executed on the remote system, a file that is to be transferred to or from the remote, or any other task that you want performed between the two systems.

Sending E-Mail with UUCP

Most utilities like mail packages understand the UUCP addresses, so that you don't have to worry about e-mail not reaching the proper destination. You don't usually have to make any changes at all to applications running under Linux to get them to understand this UUCP address format. In the last section you saw how the mail package can be used with UUCP addresses.

You can use any of the usual `mail` command options to modify the behavior of the package. For example, to send the contents of the file data_1 to yvonne on system chatton through the system arthur, and tag the mail with a subject heading, you would issue the command:

```
mail -s "Data file" arthur\!chatton\!yvonne < data_1
```

Most mail packages available for Linux, including X-based mailers, work perfectly well with UUCP addresses, as well as the more common Internet addresses, but you may want to check before adopting a new mail package.

Transferring Files with UUCP

UUCP's most common use is to transfer files from one machine to another. To transfer files using UUCP, you use the uucp command. The syntax of the uucp command is:

```
uucp [options] source destination
```

The options supported by UUCP vary a little depending on the version and type of UUCP implementation, but most versions support the following useful options:

-c   Do not copy the file to a spool directory before sending. The default action is to copy to a spool directory, and using the -c option explicitly specifies it.

-f   Don't create directories on the remote system if needed. The default action is to create directories as needed and can be explicitly specified with the -d option.

-m   Sends mail to the person who issued the uucp command when the copy is complete.

-n   user   Sends mail to user on the remote system when the copy is complete.

The default behaviors are usually sufficient for most users, although you may want the mail options when you need confirmation of an action.

Both source and destination are the names of files or directories as appropriate, much like the cp command. However, when you are dealing with a remote system for the source or destination, you need to format the file or directory in valid UUCP address formats. For example, to send the file data_1 from your local machine's current directory to the directory /usr/spool/uucppublic on the machine arthur, you would use the command:

```
uucp data_1 arthur\!/usr/spool/uucppublic
```

Notice that the remote machine name was prepended to the full target directory name. In most cases, when transferring files to remote systems you will want to use the uucppublic directories as you likely will not have permission to transfer files anywhere else in the file system. Once on the remote system in the /usr/spool/uucppublic directory, it is up to the remote system's users to find the file and copy it to its intended destination directory.

If you want to send the same file to the user bill on the remote machine, and store it in a subdirectory called /usr/spool/uucppublic/bill and send mail to both yourself and bill when the copy is completed, you would issue the command:

```
uucp -m -nbill data_1 arthur\!/usr/spool/uucppublic/bill/
```

To copy a file from a remote machine to yours, you need to specify the location of the remote. Remember, you must have access to the directory that the files reside in (as well as read permission on the file), or have the sender copy them to uucppublic. The command

```
uucp chatton\!/usr/tmp/bigfile /usr/tparker/
```

would transfer the bigfile file from the directory /usr/tmp on the machine chatton to your /usr/tparker directory.

UUCP allows wildcards to be used, although you must escape them in quotation marks to prevent the shell from interpreting them. For example, to copy all the files starting with chap on the remote machine warlock's /usr/bill/book directory (assuming you have permission) to your own /usr/bigbook directory, you would issue the command

```
uucp "warlock!/usr/bill/book/chap*" /usr/bigbook/
```

You can also specify hops in the machine transfers by adding the extra machine names to the command. This requires permissions to be set on all the machines that the hop will pass through, and is seldom done. Although you probably don't want to do this either, you could transfer files from one remote system to another by specifying their names on the command line like this:

```
uucp arthur\!/usr/lib/uucppublic/bigfile warlock\!/usr/lib/uucppublic/
```

This sends the file from the `arthur` system to the `warlock` system. In most cases, the users on either of the two remote systems would issue the commands, relieving some of the file permission problems.

Checking on Transfers

You can check on the status of transfers that are scheduled but haven't taken place yet using the `uustat` command. When you issue the `uustat` command, all the UUCP transfers that are queued are listed. The format of the list is:

```
jobID system user date command size
```

where *jobID* is the ID of the UUCP job, *system* is the name of the system to transfer to (the first system in an address when multiple hops are taking place), *user* is the user name who queued the job, *date* is when the job was queued, *command* is the exact command to be executed, and *size* is the size of the transfer in bytes.

If you issue the command as a user (not superuser), only your jobs are listed. The superuser lists all jobs that are queued. If you are logged in as a regular user and want to see all jobs, use the `-a` option:

```
uustat -a
```

To cancel a queued job, use the `-k` option of the `uustat` command along with the job ID. For example, to cancel jobID 17, issue the command:

```
uustat -k 17
```

You can only cancel your own jobs, unless you are logged in as superuser, in which case you can cancel any jobs.

Summary

UUCP is quite easy to set up, as long as you follow the rules. Once the configuration files are properly set, UUCP offers an easy way to transfer e-mail, news, and files to other systems. UUCP is also one of the easiest methods to establish a low-volume network because all you need is a modem or a direct connection. Using UUCP to transfer mail and files is as easy as using the usual `mail` and `cp` commands.

Although UUCP is less popular nowadays because of the LAN craze, it does provide a simple, very low-cost network for those who need to connect only a couple of machines. It's also great for connecting your machine to those of your friends, allowing e-mail back and forth, and really making your Linux system feel like a well-connected workstation.

Installing Mail and News

44

by Tim Parker

If you have access to other machines through a local area network or through the Internet, you will probably want to install the mail and news software. Both offer a lot of interaction with other users and add a whole new dimension to your Linux system.

To handle electronic mail, most systems rely on *UUCP* (UNIX-to-UNIX Copy). Setting up UUCP is covered in many different online guides and documents, as well as in most UNIX books. You can exchange e-mail with other users, or with the world at large, by connecting to an Internet service provider such as UUNET Technologies.

Reading Usenet newsgroups is a little more complicated, because you have to download the news yourself (100MB per day!) or connect to a site that offers news—a *news server.* Linux includes the software to connect you, although most users will find it easier to use an online service such as CompuServe or Delphi for news access.

In this chapter we look at the following:

- The types of mail software you can use
- Simple UUCP-based configuration of e-mail systems
- Setting your machine to access Usenet newsgroups

Mail

If you installed Linux from a CD-ROM (such as the Slackware distribution included with this book), one of the installation options was to install the e-mail systems. Some Linux distributions give you a choice of mail packages, whereas others default to one particular type.

During the installation, most Linux setup procedures will install the software properly except for some configuration information about the network. With this kind of installation, there is little you have to do with the mail system except add your host name and configure UUCP (if you are using it to connect to other systems to transfer Mail).

If you didn't get Mail with your Linux system, you will have to pick up one of the archive libraries from an FTP site, or from a user group or CD-ROM utility disk. In this case, installation procedures are included as part of the archive.

Mail software for most UNIX systems (including Linux) has two components: a transport and a mailer. The *transport* is the low-level software that takes care of delivering the mail, both locally and across other machines. Users never work with the transport, although system administrators must configure it and understand the basic principles. The *mailer* is the user interface that presents mail to the user and accepts new mail. Many mailers are available.

Mail Transport Agents

Transport agents are the underlying software that connects your local machine to remote systems. Several transport agents are available with Linux, but the most commonly used are called *smail* (for send mail) and *sendmail.* You can find both on the CD that accompanies this book. The program you use probably will be determined by the Linux software supplied to you.

The smail and sendmail programs are ideally suited for sites that rely on UUCP for mail (either between other machines or to an Internet service provider), and they can be used with some *SMTP* (Simple Mail Transfer Protocol) sites. smail and sendmail are usually provided as an executable binary form with most Linux distributions, although only one of the transport agents is usually supplied.

The configuration changes needed to set up smail or sendmail on your Linux system depend on the type of connection you have to the outside world.

smail

If you are running a UUCP-based mail system and you use a remote system for all processing to other sites (usually used with local area networks that employ a communications server), the changes to your system configuration files are minimal.

The changes occur in the files /usr/local/lib/smail/config and /usr/local/lib/smail/paths. Look for the lines that have to do with hostname and subdomain names and perform the following changes:

- Replace subdomain.domain with your machine's domain name.
- Replace myhostname with your "undomainized" hostname.
- Replace my_uucp_neighbor with the UUCP name of your upstream site.

For example, the following extract shows the settings for a machine called vader that attached to the machine deathstar in the domain starwars.com, first for the file /usr/local/lib/smail/config:

```
#/usr/local/lib/smail/config
# domains we belong to
visible_domain=deathstar.starwars:uucp
# who we're known as (fully-qualified-site-name)
visible_name=vader.starwars
# who we go through
smart_path=deathstar
```

The changes for /usr/local/lib/smail/paths are the machine name only:

```
#/usr/local/lib/smail/paths
# we're a domainized site, make sure we accept mail to both names
vader          %s
vader.starwars.com      %s
```

If you want to run the smail program as an SMTP daemon, you must add the following line to the file /etc/inetd.conf (or whatever the equivalent file is called in your distribution):

```
  smtp stream tcp nowait  root  /usr/bin/smtpd smtpd
```

When this is added, any outgoing mail gets sent automatically when using a mailer like elm.

sendmail

The sendmail program is quite popular with small Linux installations. It is included with the Slackware distribution of Linux.

If you are running a UUCP-only site and you want to use sendmail instead of smail when you have both on your system, you should make sure that all files from smail are removed to prevent conflicts (you can use whereis and find to locate smail files).

To configure sendmail, change to the /etc directory and edit the sendmail.cf file. This file has enough information to help you determine which lines to replace with your system values. Usually you will edit the hostname, aliases, and smarthost settings.

Local Delivery Agents

Unlike most UNIX versions, Linux does not have a mail-delivery package built in. Mail-delivery packages send the received mail to the proper user. One of the most widely used is called deliver.

In most cases, you don't have to do anything to install and configure deliver. When you installed the mail software using the Linux installation routine, the necessary software was installed and configured properly.

Mail User Agents

Mail user agents are the mailreaders you use to see your e-mail. Many newsreaders are available. Your choice of mailreader is more a personal preference than a feature-based decision.

Elm is probably the most widely used mailreader with Linux. It uses the configuration file /usr/lib/elm.rc to provide basic information about the machine name and its connections. You should edit the elm.rc file to replace the names with proper values.

Another popular mailreader is Mailx, which has been available for UNIX systems for many years. Versions of Mailx are available for Linux on many archive sites. Make sure you get version 5.3b or higher because there are security problems in version 5.3a.

Other interesting and popular mailreaders are Pine and Metamail, both of which are freely available from Linux archive sites and user groups.

News

Usenet is a service provided over the Internet. It's composed of more than 9,000 newsgroups on every subject imaginable. If you want to set your system to download the entire day's news, you must dedicate a lot of money to hardware and telephone lines. Such a connection is beyond the scope of most users.

However, accessing newsgroups from another machine that downloads them is quite easy, using software provided with Linux.

There are two parts to the News software: the server and the client. The *server* is the software that controls the newsgroups and handles delivering articles to other machines. The *client* or newsreader software is the user interface.

You do not have to hook up to the Internet to use News. You can run News locally (on your own machine for all the users) or across a small network. In this case, you don't have to worry about connecting to the Internet's Usenet newsfeed, which generally is expensive and very time-consuming.

News Transport Software

News transport software, as its name implies, carries the news to your system and its newsreaders and helps your users post news to Usenet. Two main news transport software packages are used with Linux: Cnews and INN. The two should not be mixed. Use one or the other, or major hassles will result!

If you plan to use News locally only, much of the configuration required for connecting to the Internet or other newsfeed can be ignored. News normally is stored in the directory /usr/spool/news, so all the news transport and client software should be set to point to this location.

The most popular news transport software is Cnews, which has been available for almost a decade. Cnews runs on many different machines, and many people understand it very well, providing technical resources should you need them. Cnews is designed primarily for capturing news over a UUCP connection and a standard telephone modem, so it requires additional software to provide access to the Internet. This additional software is called *NNTP* (Network News Transfer Protocol). NNTP isn't necessary for local news support.

Installing Cnews is straightforward, as long as you follow the directions in the accompanying documentation files. Configuration involves editing several files, which usually reside in /usr/lib/news. The files of primary interest are as follows:

- active: The active file
- batchparms: Batch parameters
- explist: Article expiration
- mailname: Header names for mailed replies
- mailpaths: Path to mail moderated postings
- organization: Your company name
- sys: Controls what you take and feed
- whoami: Your hostname

Most of Cnews is configured with shell scripts or utility programs (such as addgroup to change the active file and addfeed to change newsfeed information). Again, check the documentation for complete information.

To download news automatically, cron makes an excellent choice. A sample cron entry for the Cnews newsfeed is

```
20 * * * * /usenet/sw/news/bin/input/newsrun
0 * * * * /usenet/sw/news/bin/batch/sendbatches feedsite
59 0 * * * /usenet/sw/news/bin/expire/doexpire
10 5 * * * /usenet/sw/news/bin/newsdaily
00 5 * * * /usenet/sw/new/bin/newswatch
```

This sample does things every hour, which is fine for a large site but considerable overkill for a small network or single machine where you might want to connect only once a day. Modify the files as necessary to meet your requirement.

InterNetNews (*INN*)

INN is newer than Cnews but is faster and has NNTP built in, making it easier to use for direct newsfeeds. Unfortunately, it is a little harder to install and configure than Cnews. INN uses a daemon (sometimes two) that runs continually, whereas Cnews is invoked by the user (or cron). Novices to Linux should probably stick with Cnews at the beginning until they gain more experience.

Installation is a little more complex than with Cnews, but following the documentation helps. INN is very particular about its file permissions, so make sure you set them properly. Configuration is a matter of making sure all of the site information is correct. Once correctly installed and configured, though, INN requires virtually no maintenance.

Newsreaders

Many newsreaders are available for Linux. A newsreader presents the messages in a newsgroup and lets you step through them or reply to them, as well as create new messages. Some of the most popular newsreaders are tin, trn, and nn.

Choosing a newsreader is essentially a personal choice. Experiment with several and stay with the one you find easiest to work with and that offers the features you need. They all have some slight twist that gives you different methods of looking at news or moving through newsgroups.

Summary

Both e-mail and news extend the Linux system to be a full-featured UNIX implementation, and make your machine part of a much larger network. Even if you are using your Linux machine only for yourself and have no interest in connecting to the outside world, e-mail is simple and easy to install, configure, and use. Once you've used e-mail, you'll probably never go back to the paper-based kind!

If you have several users on your Linux system or plan to connect to a network, News is a great way to get discussions and information flowing amongst the users. On top of that, News is just plain fun!

Network Security

45

by Tim Parker

Setting Up an Internet Site

46

by Tim Parker

system's directories and have found a file you want to transfer back to your local system, use the get command. This is followed by the filename. For example:

```
get "soundcard_driver"
```

This will transfer the file soundcard_driver from the remote machine to the current directory on your local machine. When you issue a get command, the remote system will transfer data to your local machine and display a status message when it is completed. There is no indication of progress when a large file is being transferred, so be patient. (Most versions of FTP allow you to use the hash option, which displays pound signs every time a kilobyte of information has been transferred. This can be used to show that the transfer is underway, but it doesn't offer a time to completion.)

```
FTP> get "file1.txt"
200 PORT command successful.
150 BINARY data connection for FILE1.TXT (27534 bytes)
226 BINARY Transfer complete.
27534 bytes received in 2.35 seconds (12 Kbytes/s).
```

If you want to transfer a file the other way (from your machine to the remote, assuming you are allowed to write to the remote machine's file system), use the put command in the same way. The command:

```
put "comments"
```

will transfer the file comments from your current directory on the local machine (you can specify full pathnames) to the current directory on the remote machine (unless you change the path).

The commands get (download) and put (upload) are always relative to your home machine. You are telling your system to get a file from the remote and put it on your local machine, or to put a file from your local machine onto the remote machine. (This is the exact opposite of telnet, which has everything relative to the remote machine. It is important to remember which command moves in which direction, or you could overwrite files accidentally.)

The quotation marks around the filenames in the preceding examples are optional for most versions of FTP, but they do prevent shell expansion of characters, so it's best to use them. For most files, the quotation marks are not needed, but using them is a good habit to get into.

Some FTP versions provide a wildcard capability using the commands mget and mput. Both the FTP get and put commands usually transfer only one file at a time, which must be completely specified (no wildcards). The mget and mput commands enable you to use wildcards. For example, to transfer all the files with a .doc extension, you could issue the command:

```
mget *.doc
```

You will have to try the mget and mput commands to see if they work on your FTP version. (Some FTP get and put commands allow wildcards, too, so you can try wildcards in a command line to see if they work, instead.)

FTP allows file transfers in several formats, which are usually system dependent. The majority of systems (including Linux systems) have only two modes: ASCII and binary. Some mainframe installations add support for EBCDIC, while many sites have a local type that is designed for fast transfers between local network machines (the local type may use 32- or 64-bit words).

The difference between the binary and ASCII modes is simple. Text transfers use ASCII characters separated by carriage return and new-line characters. Binary mode allows transfer of characters with no conversion or formatting. Binary mode is faster than text and also allows for the transfer of all ASCII values (necessary for non-text files). FTP cannot transfer file permissions because these are not specified as part of the protocol.

Linux' FTP provides two modes of file transfer: ASCII and Binary. Some systems automatically switch between the two when they recognize a file is binary format, but you shouldn't count on the switching unless you've tested it before and know it works. To be sure, it is a good idea to manually set the mode. By default, most FTP versions start up in ASCII mode, although a few start in Binary.

To set FTP in binary transfer mode (for any executable file or file with special characters embedded for spreadsheets, word processors, graphics, and so on), type the command

```
binary
```

You can toggle back to ASCII mode with the command ascii. Since you will most likely be checking remote sites for new binaries or libraries of source code, it is a good idea to use binary mode for most transfers. If you transfer a binary file in ASCII mode, it will not be usable on your system.

ASCII mode includes only the valid ASCII characters and not the 8-bit values stored in binaries. Transferring an ASCII file in Binary mode does not affect the contents except in very rare instances.

To quit FTP, type the command quit or exit. Both will close your session on the remote machine, and then terminate FTP on your local machine. Users have a number of commands available within most versions of FTP. The following list outlines the ones most frequently used:

ascii	Switches to ASCII transfer mode
binary	Switches to binary transfer mode
cd	Changes directory on the server
close	Terminates the connection
del	Deletes a file on the server
dir	Displays the server directory
get	Fetches a file from the server
hash	Displays a pound character for each block transmitted
help	Displays help
lcd	Changes directory on the client
mget	Fetches several files from the server
mput	Sends several files to the server
open	Connects to a server
put	Sends a file to the server
pwd	Displays the current server directory
quote	Supplies an FTP command directly
quit	Terminates the FTP session

Summary

The information in this chapter enables you to set up your system as a full anonymous FTP site or just a site for the users you want to gain access. Although the process is simple, you have to take care to ensure the file permissions are properly set. Once your FTP site is up, you can let others on the Internet or your local area network know that you are running, as well as the type of material you store on your system. Then sit back and share!

Checklist: Protecting an Anonymous FTP System

Anonymous FTP is fast, relatively easy to use, and a huge security problem if you don't carefully set up your system. The following list summarizes a few simple steps to setting up a better anonymous FTP site:

1. Create a user account called `ftp`. Edit the `/etc/passwd` file manually and replace the password with an asterisk in the second field. This prevents anyone from gaining access through the `ftp` account.

2. If a home directory wasn't created for the `ftp` user when you created the account, set up a home directory for the `ftp` user's sole use (such as `/home/ftp`).

3. Set the `ftp` home directory so that the `root` user is the owner:

   ```
   chown root /usr/ftp
   ```

4. Make the `ftp` home directory unwritable to anyone with the command:

   ```
   chmod ugo-w /usr/ftp
   ```

5. Create a `bin` directory under the `ftp` home directory:

   ```
   mkdir ~ftp/bin
   ```

6. Make the `~ftp/bin` directory owned by `root` and unwritable to anyone else:

   ```
   chown root ~ftp/bin
   chmod ugo-w ~ftp/bin
   ```

7. Place a copy of the listing commands (and any others that you want anonymous FTP users to use) in the `bin` directory:

   ```
   cp /bin/ls ~ftp/bin
   ```

8. Create an `etc` directory under the `ftp` home directory and make it owned by `root` and unwritable:

   ```
   mkdir ~ftp/etc
   chown root ~ftp/etc
   chmod ugo-w ~ftp/etc
   ```

9. Copy the `/etc/passwd` and `/etc/group` files into the `~ftp/etc` directory. Edit both files to remove all user accounts except `ftp` (and `ftp`'s group). (At the very least, remove all passwords for other accounts by placing asterisks in the password field.)

10. Create the directory `~ftp/pub/incoming`, and make it owned by `root`. Then, make the directory writable by anyone:

    ```
    mkdir ~ftp/pub/incoming
    chown root ~ftp/pub/incoming
    ```

```
chmod ugo+w ~ftp/pub/incoming
```

11. Place any files you want accessible by anonymous FTP into the `~ftp/pub` directory. Users logging in through anonymous FTP will be able to transfer the files out. Allowing users to write files into the directory may not be desirable, so change the permissions or check the files frequently.

By following these steps (modified for your own particular needs), you can create a secure site that lets you breathe a little easier.

Configuring a WAIS Site

48

by Tim Parker

IN THIS CHAPTER

■ GIF	GIF images, one image per file. The filename is used as the headline.
■ mail_or_rmail	Indexes the mbox mailbox contents as individual items.
■ mail_digest	Standard e-mail, indexed as individual messages. The subject field is the headline.
■ netnews	Standard Usenet news, each article a separate item. The subject field is the headline.
■ one_line	Indexes each sentence in a document separately.
■ PICT	PICT image, one image per file. The filename is used as the headline.
■ ps	A PostScript file with one document per file.
■ text	Indexes the file as one document, the pathname as the heading.
■ TIFF	TIFF image, one image per file. The filename is used as the headline.

To tell waisindex the type of file to be examined, use the -t option followed by the proper type. For example, to index standard ASCII text, you could use the command:

```
waisindex -t text -r /usr/waisdata/*
```

This command indexes all the files in /usr/waisdata recursively, assuming they are all ASCII files.

> **NOTE**
>
> When a document has been indexed, any changes in the document will not be reflected in the WAIS index unless a complete reindex is performed. Using the -a option does not update existing index entries. Instead, start the index process again. You should do this at periodic intervals as a matter of course.

Getting Fancy

You can provide some extra features for users of your freeWAIS service in a number of ways. Although this section is not exhaustive by any means, it shows you two of the easily implementable features that make a WAIS site more attractive.

To begin, suppose you want to make video, graphics, or audio available on a particular subject. Suppose, for example, your site deals with musical instruments, and you have several documents on violins. You may want to provide an audio clip of a violin being played, a video of the making of a violin body, or a graphic image of a Stradivarius violin. To make these extra files available, you should have all the files with the same filename but different extensions. For example, if your primary document on violins is called violins.txt, you may have the following files in the WAIS directories:

■ `violins.TEXT` Document describing violins

■ `violins.TIFF` Image of a Stradivarius

■ `violins.MPEG` Video of the making of a violin body

■ `violins.MIDI` MIDI file of a violin being played

All these files should have the same root name (`violins`) but different types (recognized by `waisindex`). Then, you have to associate the multimedia files with the document file. You can do this with the following command:

```
waisindex -d violin -M TEXT,TIFF,MPEG,MIDI -export /usr/waisdata/violin/*
```

This tells `waisindex` that all four types of files are to be handled. When a user searches for the keyword "violin," all four types of files will be matched, and options on the browser may let them play, view, or hear the non-text components.

Another common feature is the use of synonyms to account for different methods of specifying a subject. For example, a scientist may use the keyword "feline" when a non-scientist may use "cat." You want to be able to match these two words to the same thing. This is done through a file called `SOURCE.syn`, which is automatically read by the search engine when it is working. The `SOURCE.syn` file has the following format:

```
word    synonym [synonym ...]
```

where *word* is the word to be used to search the databases, and *synonym* is the word(s) that should match it. For example, if you are dealing with domestic pets in your WAIS site, you may have the following entries in the `SOURCE.syn` file:

```
cat     feline
dog     canine hound pooch
bird    parrot budgie
```

The synonym file can be very useful when people use different terms to refer to the same thing. An easy way to check for the need for synonyms is to set the logging option for `waisindex` to 10 for a while, and see what words people are using on your site. Don't keep it on too long, though, because the logfiles can become enormous with a little traffic.

Summary

Now that WAIS is up and running on your server, you can go about the process of building your index files and letting others access your server. WAIS is quite easy to manage, and offers a good way of letting other users access your system's documents. The alternative approach, for text-based systems, is Gopher, which we examine in the next chapter.

Setting Up a Gopher Service

49

by Tim Parker

Gopher is one of the most useful Internet services available, because it is widely used by beginners and veterans alike. Gopher is a text-based file location system that leads you through a series of hierarchical menus to find specific files you want. Setting up a Gopher site is really just a matter of configuring the Gopher server software and creating a number of logical directory structures with files indexed in a Gopher format.

Gopher works by having a client program (started by a user) connect to a Gopher server and retrieve information about files available on the Internet (or local area network, if the Gopher server is limited to that area). At the end of 1995, there were more than 6,000 Gopher servers on the Internet, all accessible by anyone with a Gopher client. Those servers contain information about more than 10 million items, ranging from text files to movies, sounds, images, and many types of application binaries. Gopher enables you to display and manipulate lists of files, looking for items of interest to you.

If you or the users of your Linux system want to connect to another Gopher server, you need a Gopher client. There are several clients available with Linux distributions, on FTP and BBS sites, and through several other sources. If you don't want to allow users (or yourself) to start a Gopher client, you can use telnet to connect to sites known as public Gopher clients. These sites allow you to log in as an anonymous user and access the Gopher system. Most Gopher client packages offer more than just Gopher programs. Typical Gopher clients enable you to access WAIS indexes, use FTP, and to some extent, interwork with the World Wide Web.

This chapter looks at how you can set up a Gopher server, allowing others to access your machine's Gopher listings. Although we won't go into detail about how you should structure your Gopher service, you will see how to configure your software.

Gopher and Linux

There are currently two versions of Gopher available for Linux systems: Gopher and Gopher+ (Gopher Plus). Gopher is freely available, but Gopher+ is a commercial product. The difference between the two is functionality. If the additional capabilities of Gopher+ are important to you and your Gopher site, you may want to consider purchasing the product. Essentially, Gopher+ adds the following features:

- Makes extended file information available
- Offers a description of a file
- Can retrieve multiple versions of a file at one time (such as ASCII and PostScript simultaneously)
- Allows file retrieval based on search criteria determined by the user

Gopher+ works with Gopher, but Gopher cannot use the advanced features of Gopher+. Gopher+ and Gopher both work with WWW browsers. Gopher+ licenses tend to cost about $100 or $500, depending on the site's conditions.

The versions of Gopher usually offered with Linux come from one of two sources: University of Minnesota Gopher and Gopher+, or GN Public License Gopher. The most recent public version of UM Gopher is version 1.3 (version 2.13 is free only to educational institutions), but the university is no longer working on the freeware Gopher product, instead concentrating on the commercial Gopher+ product. The GN Public License Gopher includes a WWW service but does not provide full functionality at present.

Gopher uses a TCP/IP family protocol known, surprisingly enough, as the Gopher protocol. This is a fairly simple request-answer protocol that is implemented for speed. When Gopher transfers information about a file it knows about (called a Gopher menu file), it follows a set format. The format used by Gopher is:

```
<type><display_name><selector string><hostname><port>
```

The fields in the Gopher menu file have the following meanings:

- `type`—A one character description of the item (see the following bulleted list for valid codes).
- `display_name`—The menu or display name, followed by a tab character.
- `selector_string`—A unique identifier for a document on each server (usually based on the filename). The selector string is followed by a tab character.
- `hostname`—The host where the file resides, followed by a tab character.
- `port`—The port to access the host, followed by a carriage return/line feed pair (usually port 70).

The Gopher+ version of the system adds a few new attributes to each line, including the name of the system administrator responsible for the service, a simple description of the document type (text, for example), the language the file is written in, the last date the file was updated, and the size in bytes.

When a user wants to retrieve a file through the Gopher system, the hostname and port are used to create the connection to the remote server, while the selector string can be used to identify the file to be downloaded.

There are several types of files supported by Gopher, all given a unique one-character type code. The following is a list of valid codes:

- 0   Plain text file
- 1   Directory
- 2   CSO phonebook server (the hostname is the machine to connect to, the selector string is blank)
- 3   Error
- 4   BinHex Macintosh file
- 5   Binary DOS archive file
- 6   UNIX uuencoded file

- 7   Index-search server
- 8   Pointer to text-based telnet session (hostname is the machine name to connect to and selector string is the name to log in as)
- 9   Binary file
- g   GIF file
- h   HTML document
- I   Graphic image
- i   Unselectable inline text
- M   MIME-encapsulated mail document
- P   Adobe PDF file
- s   Sound
- T   Pointer to 3270 telnet session (hostname is machine to connect to and selector string is login name)

The Gopher system uses a number of other files on a Linux system, all of which must exist. The files necessary for Gopher are as follows:

- `tn3270` or similar 3270 emulator—Used for telnet 3270 connections.
- `kermit` or `zmodem` communications programs—Used for downloading files. The binaries are usually called `kermit`, `sz`, `sb`, and `sx`.
- graphics utility—If you allow the display of graphics, you need a graphics utility such as `xv`.

You can modify these requirements if you have a private site (such as for your local area network), but if you are offering open access you should have all the components.

Configuring Gopher

Installing and configuring Gopher (and Gopher+) is a matter of setting a number of configuration options prior to compiling the system software (it is usually not precompiled for you) and configuring some standard files. Gopher+ is done in the same manner, although with some extra parameters. Since Gopher is more likely to be on a Linux site than Gopher+, we'll concentrate on that.

Throughout this section, we will use filenames without full path extensions because it really doesn't matter where you install the Gopher software, as long as the directory paths are set correctly. There is no real standard configuration for directory locations, so feel free to choose whatever works best for you.

The *gopherd.conf* File

The configuration parameters for Gopher (and Gopher+) are in a file called `gopherd.conf`, which is read by the Gopher daemon `gopherd`. The default settings generally need a little modification, although many changes are simply changing commented lines to uncommented, and vice versa.

The first step is to create an alias for the Gopher service on your machine. Perform this step with the line that defines the `hostalias`. There should be a line in the file that looks like this:

```
hostalias: tpci
```

The alias is used to find the Gopher server on your system and should not be directly tied to a real machine, so you can make changes whenever you wish. The best approach is to create an alias and tie it to a physical machine with DNS. If you are running a stand-alone machine, you can either use an alias tied to your machine name or use your machine name directly.

You can also control the number of Gopher connections allowed at one time. This is sometimes necessary to prevent a system from bogging down due to excessive user load. The maximum number of connections Gopher allows is given in a file, usually in the directory `PIDS_Directory`. A line in the `gopherd.conf` file usually has this variable commented out because early versions didn't implement it properly, or it was unstable. If you want to allow this feature, remove the comment symbol and make sure the directory it points to has the necessary files for your version of Gopher. The line usually looks like this:

```
#PIDS_Directory: /pids
```

A better way to handle the load on your system is to use the `MaxConnections` keyword, which sets the number of clients you support concurrently. You have to experiment to determine the best balance between system load and user service. A good starting point for a fast Linux system (80486 or Pentium CPU) is 15 to 25 users. This variable is set like this:

```
MaxConnections: 15
```

If the number of users is exceeded, an error message is generated when the connection is attempted. You can set a number of file decoders for your system. This is used when a user requests a file from Gopher and adds an extension (such as `.Z`, `.gz`, or `.zip`) for a compression or archive utility. The decoders recognize the extension the user supplies and invoke the proper utility to send the file properly decoded. Most `gopherd.conf` files have the following decoder lines already in the setup:

```
decoder: .Z /usr/ucb/zcat
decoder: .gz /usr/gnu/bin/zcat
#decoder: .adpcm /usr/openwin/bin/adpcm_dec
#decoder: .z /usr/gnu/bin/zcat
```

The last two decoders are commented out and can be uncommented if you want to offer files in these formats through Gopher. You can also add other extensions by adding new lines with the binary name (and its full path).

In addition, the amount of time a cache file stays valid should be set. This is controlled by the line using the keyword `Cachetime`. Set this value to a reasonable value, such as 180 seconds. You should have a line that looks like this in the `gopherd.conf` file:

```
Cachetime: 180
```

You can use the `gopherd.conf` file to restrict access to some files on your system by using the `ignore` keyword. Usually the `gopherd.conf` file will have a number of defined `ignore`s, such as these:

```
ignore: lib
ignore: bin
ignore: etc
ignore: dev
```

Any file with this type of extension is ignored. If you have a particular file extension you want to protect, add it to the list. For example, if your accounting system uses the extension `.acct`, you could have the Gopher clients ignore all these files by adding this line:

```
ignore: acct
```

Note that these `ignore` statements only work with file extensions. To be more broad, you can use wildcards and the keyword `ignore_patt` (for ignore pattern). For example, the line:

```
ignore_patt: ^usr$
```

ignores any file with the letters `usr` at the beginning of the name.

The *gopherdlocal.conf* File

In the file `gopherdlocal.conf`, you have to make two small changes to identify the system administrator, otherwise your system generates many annoying notes. The lines in the `gopherdlocal.conf` file look like this by default:

```
Admin: blank
AdminEmail: blank
```

If you do not change these entries to actual values, Gopher can generate all kinds of weird error messages. The `Admin` field usually has the administrator's name and sometimes a telephone number. For example, the file could be filled out as follows:

```
Admin: Yvonne Chow, 555-1212
AdminEmail: ychow@chatton.com
```

Another setting you should provide in the `gopherdlocal.conf` file is the `Abstract`, a short description of what your particular Gopher service provides. If you don't change the default setting, users get a message prompting them to request the Abstract, so you may as well do it right away. Multiple lines in an abstract value are followed by a backslash to show the continuation. A sample Abstract setting looks like this:

```
Abstract: This server provides sound and graphics files \
collected by the administrator on a recent trip to Outer \
Mongolia.
```

General information about your site is provided with a number of general settings for the site name, the organization that runs the site, your machine's geographic location, the latitude and longitude of your site, and a time zone setting. You can leave these blank if you want, but providing the information leads to a more complete Gopher site. The settings in a sample `gopherdlocal.conf` file look like this:

```
Site: Explore_Mongolia
Org: Mongolia Tourist Bureau
Loc: North Bay, Ontario, Canada
Geog: blank
TZ: EDT
```

The setting of `blank` for `Geog` leaves the setting with no value. Obviously, the system administrator didn't know the latitude and longitude settings.

You can set a language option used by Gopher clients to show what language most of the documents available on your site are written in. This is done like this:

```
Language: En_US
```

which refers to American English.

The setting `BummerMsg` is used to display a brief text string to a user who exceeds your maximum number of concurrent users or causes an error when accessing the system. The default value is this:

```
BummerMsg: Sorry, we have exceeded the number of permissible users
```

You can change this to whatever message you want. Try not to be rude or obnoxious because you never know who will get this message.

The last step in modifying the `gopherdlocal.conf` file is to set access procedures for users who log in to your Gopher server. Limiting the users who can get to your server is done through entries with the keyword access. The general format of the access line is:

```
access: hostname permissions num_users
```

where `hostname` is either the name or IP address of the host that is connecting to your server, `permissions` is the permission set for those users, and `num_users` is the maximum number of users that can be connected to the service concurrently.

The permissions are set using any combination of the following four words, either as they are or preceded by an exclamation mark to mean "not allowed." The permission keywords are as follows:

- `browse`—Can examine directory contents. If this is forbidden, users can access entries, but they can't get directory contents.
- `ftp`—Allows server to act as gateway to FTP services.
- `read`—Can access a file. If forbidden, the users get the `BummerMsg` when they ask for the file.
- `search`—Can access indexes (type 7 items). If forbidden, access to the indexes is not allowed. This is used primarily with Gopher+.

For example, to set access permissions to allow up to 10 users from the network `chatton.com` to access your Gopher server with full rights, you would add a line like this:

```
access: chatton.com     browse ftp read search 10
```

There is at least one space between each entry, even between permissions. This access entry:

```
access: bignet.org !browse !ftp read search 3
```

allows three concurrent users from `bignet.org` to access the Gopher server and read and search, but not use FTP gateways or browse the directory listings.

If you are using IP addresses, you can use a subset of the IP address to indicate the entire network. For example, if `bignet.com`'s network address is 147.12, you can indicate the entire network with a line like this:

```
access: 147.12. !browse !ftp read search 3
```

You must follow the last quad of numbers specified in the IP address with a period, otherwise 147.120 through 147.129 will also have the same permissions (because they match the digits specified).

If you want to enable access from a particular machine, you can do that, too. For example, to allow your friend's `darkstar` machine to access your Gopher server with full permissions, you would add a line like this:

```
access: darkstar.domain.name browse ftp read search 1
```

Most general Gopher servers tend to allow anyone to connect, so they use a default entry to refer to anyone not explicitly defined by another access entry. The default setting is usually like this:

```
access: default !browse !ftp read search 15
```

which allows anyone to read and search Gopher directories, but not move through them or use your machine as an FTP gateway.

Setting Up the *Makefile*

Two files need modification for the compilation process to proceed properly. These two files are `Makefile.config` and `conf.h`. With many versions of Gopher available on Linux systems, the configuration parameters these files need have already been set, but you should check the values carefully to prevent problems.

The `Makefile.config` file (used by `Makefile` to build the executables) is a lengthy file, so you should be careful while moving through it to avoid accidental changes. The important areas to examine are the directory definitions and server and client settings. These are dealt with individually in the following sections.

One setting you may wish to alter is the debugging utility, which is enabled by default in most systems. This can help you get the system running properly, but when the operation is correct, you should recompile the source with the debugging features removed to make the process faster and smaller, as well as to reduce debug information overhead. To remove debugging features, comment out the DEBUGGING line so it looks like this:

```
#DEBUGGING = -DDEBUGGING
```

By default this line is probably not commented out.

The directory definitions are usually in a block with five to seven entries, depending on the number of entries for the man pages. A typical directory definition block looks like this:

```
PREFIX = /usr/local
CLIENTDIR = $(PREFIX)/bin
CLIENTLIB = $(PREFIX)/lib
SERVERDIR = $(PREFIX)/etc

MAN1DIR = $(PREFIX)/man/man1
MAN5DIR = $(PREFIX)/man/man5
MAN8DIR = $(PREFIX)/man/man8
```

The primary change to most Makefile.config files will be the PREFIX, which is used to set the basic directory for Gopher. The default value is usually /usr/local, although you can change it to anything you want (such as /usr/gopher). The rest of the variables define subdirectories under the primary Gopher directory and are usually acceptable as they are. Each of the subdirectories can be left the way it is, or you can change it to suit your own needs. You can place all the files in one directory, if you want. The meaning of each variable appears in the following list:

CLIENTDIR	Gopher client software
CLIENTLIB	Client help file (gopher.hlp)
MAN1DIR	Man pages for gopher client
MAN8DIR	Man pages for gopherd
SERVERDIR	Gopher server (gopherd) and configuration file (gopherd.conf)

For a Gopher client to run properly on your system, you must modify the CLIENTOPTS line in the Makefile.config file. The two options for the CLIENTOPTS line to control its behavior are as follows:

-DNOMAIL	Forbids remote users from mailing files.
-DAUTOEXITONU	Allows the Gopher client to be exited with the u command as well as q command.

To use either or both or these options, add them to the CLIENTOPS line like this:

```
CLIENTOPTS = -DNOMAIL -DAUTOEXITONU
```

Four variables relating to the Gopher server must also be set. These specify the host domain name, the port Gopher should use to listen for connections, the location of the data files, and option flags.

The domain name is set with the DOMAIN variable. It should have a leading period in the name, such as:

```
DOMAIN = .tpci.com
```

You do not need to set this variable if the hostname command returns the fully qualified domain name of the server. In this case, leave the value blank.

The SERVERPORT variable defines the port Gopher uses to wait for services and is usually set for TCP port 70. This line usually looks like this:

```
SERVERPORT = 70
```

If you are not allowing general access to your Gopher site by Internet users, you can change this value. However, if you want to allow Internet users (even a very small subset) to gain access, you should leave this as port 70. If you are setting up your Gopher site for a small network only, then choose any port number you want (between 1024 and 9999) and make sure all the Gopher clients use that number, too.

The SERVERDATA variable defines the location of the data your Gopher server offers. It's default setting is usually as follows:

```
SERVERDATA = /gopher-data
```

Set the variable to point to the file location you use for your Gopher items.

The SERVEROPTS variable accepts a number of keywords that change the behavior of the Gopher service. A typical entry looks like this:

```
SERVEROPTS = -DSETPROCTITLE -DCAPFILES # -DBIO -DDL
```

Any keywords after the pound sign are ignored when Makefile runs, so you can adjust its location to set the options you want if the order of the variables allows such a simple approach. The following lists the meaning of the different keywords allowed in the SERVEROPTS entry:

-DADD_DATE_AND_TIME	Adds dates and times to titles.
-DBIO	Used only with the WAIS versions developed by Don Gilbert (wais8b5).
-DDL	Provides support for the dl database utility (requires the dl system in a directory variable called DLPATH and the DLOBJS line uncommented out to show the files getdesc.o and enddesc.o locations).
-DCAPFILES	Offers backwards compatibility with the cap directory.
-DLOADRESTRICT	Restricts user access based on the number of concurrent users (see the following section).

-DSETPROCTITLE   Sets the name displayed by ps command
                          (BSD UNIX-based systems only).

The conf.h file is used during the compilation to set other parameters about the Gopher service. The important settings, at least when setting up a Gopher service, are those that relate to the number of queries and timeout variables. These tend to occur at the end of the conf.h file.

The WAISMAXHITS variable defines the maximum number of hits a query to a WAIS database can offer, usually set to around 40. This variable is defined like this:

```
#define WAISMAXHITS 40
```

Note that the pound sign is not a comment symbol because this is written in C. The pound sign is an important part of the processor directive and should be left in place. There is no equal sign in the definition, either.

The MAXLOAD variable is used if the -DLOADRESTRICT keyword was used in the SERVEROPTS variable of Makefile.config. The MAXLOAD defines the maximum load average the Gopher service will respond to requests under (this value can be overridden on the command line). The usual definition is like this:

```
#define MAXLOAD 10.0
```

The READTIMEOUT and WRITETIMEOUT variables set the amount of time a service waits for a network read or write operation before timing out. The default settings are usually adequate. These lines look like the following:

```
#define READTIMEOUT (1*60)
#define WRITETIMEOUT (3*60)
```

The Gopher clients configuration is straight-forward. Begin by defining the Gopher servers the local machine connects to with the CLIENT1_HOST and CLIENT2_HOST entries. The Gopher client chooses one of the two (if both are defined) when it is started. The entries look like this:

```
#define CLIENT1_HOST "gopher_serv.tpci.com"
#define CLIENT2_HOST "other_gopher_serv.tpci.com"
```

The ports to be used to connect to the hosts are defined with these options:

```
#define CLIENT1_PORT 70
#define CLIENT2_PORT 70
```

If you have a local service and don't want to use port 70 (to prevent access from the Internet, for example), set the proper port values. If only one Gopher server is used, set the second value to 0.

Define the language the Gopher client will use by choosing one value out of a number of options. The default is American English, set by this command:

```
#define DEFAULT_LANG "En_US"
```

Other language defines are commented out below this one. If you want to change the default language, comment the American English setting and uncomment the one you want.

When all the configuration changes have been made, you can invoke the compilation process for the client and server with these commands:

```
make client
make server
```

Or you can do both client and server systems at once by using the make command with no argument. The programs and data files must be installed, too, using the command:

```
make install
```

WAIS and Gopher

Gopher clients have the ability to use WAIS indexes to search for documents, but the system must be configured to allow this. We looked at WAIS in Chapter 48, "Configuring a WAIS Site," so for the sake of providing WAIS index access to Gopher, we will assume you have installed WAIS properly and have WAIS indexes ready for Gopher.

To provide WAIS services through Gopher, you may have to make a change in the WAIS source code. Examine the WAIS source code for a line that looks like this:

```
if (gLastAnd) printf("search_word: boolean 'and' scored/n:);
```

This line should be commented out to provide Gopher services, so if it is not, add C comment symbols before and after the line, like this:

```
/* if (gLastAnd) printf("search_word: boolean 'and' scored/n:); */
```

If the line was already commented out (or didn't exist) then you need not make any change. If you changed the line, though, you have to recompile WAIS by changing into the WAIS top directory and running the makefile (type the command make).

Next, examine the Gopher Makefile.config file and look for the WAISTYPE variable. It should be defined on a line like this:

```
WAISTYPE = #-DFREEWAIS_0_4
```

Then, you have to link the Gopher and WAIS services. Suppose your Gopher source directory is /usr/gopher/source and the WAIS source directory is /usr/wais/source. You can link these services by entering the following commands:

```
cd /usr/gopher/source
ln -s /usr/wais/source/include ./ir
ln -s /usr/wais/source/client/ui .
ln -s /usr/wais/source/bin .
```

When Gopher is recompiled, it will make the links between Gopher and freeWAIS and allow the two services to interwork.

Setting Up Your Gopher Directories

Gopher directories and files are quite simple to set up and follow standard naming conventions for the most part. Before you begin, though, you should know which documents and files are to be provided through Gopher to other users, and you should be able to write a short description of each. (If you don't know the contents of a file, either read it or get the author to summarize the file for you.) To begin, we'll assume you will use only a single directory for all your Gopher documents.

Begin by changing to the top directory you use for your Gopher directories (which you may have to create if you haven't already done so). This directory should not be where the Gopher source and configuration files are located, for convenience. Simply choose a useful name and create the directory. For example, to create the Gopher home directory /usr/gopher/data, you would issue a standard mkdir command:

```
mkdir /usr/gopher/data
```

Change into your Gopher directory and copy the files you want to make available into it. When you have done that, you can create a descriptive filename for each file (instead of the more obtuse filenames usually used) up to 80 characters long. For example, if you have a filename called q1.sales you may want to rename it to Company_Sales_1887_Q1 to help users identify the contents a little more easily.

The process for providing better filenames is to first create a .cap directory under your Gopher main directory (such as /usr/gopher/data/.cap). For each file in the main directory, you want to create a file in the .cap directory with the same name, but with a name and number. For example, suppose you have a file called q1.sales in /usr/gopher/data. In /usr/gopher/data/.cap you would create a file with the same name, q1.sales, which has the following contents:

```
Name=Company Sales for the First Quarter, 1887
Numb=1
```

The Name entry can have spaces or other special symbols in it, because it is echoed as a complete string. The Numb entry is for the location of the entry on your Gopher menu. For example, suppose you had the preceding entry and two other files, shown by using cat to display their contents:

```
$ cat q1.sales
Name=Company Sales for the First Quarter, 1887
Numb=1

$ cat q2.sales
Name=Company Sales for the Second Quarter, 1887
Numb=2

$cat q3.sales
Name=Company Sales for the Third Quarter, 1887
Numb=3
```

Configuring a
WWW Site

50

by Tim Parker

The next configuration file to check is `srm.conf`, which is used to handle the server resources. The variables that have to be checked or set in the `srm.conf` file are as follows:

`AccessFileName`	The file that gives access permissions (default is `.htaccess`).
`AddDescription`	Provides a description of a type of file. For example, an entry could be `AddDescription PostScript file *.ps`. Multiple entries are allowed.
`AddEncoding`	Indicates that files with a particular extension are encoded somehow, such as `AddEncoding compress Z`. Multiple entries are allowed.
`AddIcon`	Gives the name of the icon to display for each type of file.
`AddIconType`	Uses `MIME` type to determine the icon to use.
`AddType`	Overrides `MIME` definitions for extensions.
`Alias`	Substitutes one pathname for another, such as `Alias data /usr/www /data`.
`DefaultType`	The default `MIME` type, usually `text/plain`.
`DefaultIcon`	The default icon to use when `FancyIndexing` is on (default is `/icons/unknown.xbm`).
`DirectoryIndex`	Filename to return when the URL is for your service only. Default value is `index.html`.
`DocumentRoot`	Absolute path to the HTML document directory. Default is `/usr/local/etc/httpd/htdocs`.
`FancyIndexing`	Adds icons and filename information to the file list for indexing. Default is on. (This option is for backward compatibility with the first release of HTTP.)
`HeaderName`	The filename used at the top of a list of files being indexed. Default is `Header`.
`IndexOptions`	Indexing parameters (including `FancyIndexing`, `IconsAreLinks`, `ScanHTMLTitles`, `SuppressLastModified`, `SuppressSize`, and `SuppressDescription`).
`ReadmeName`	The footer file is displayed with directory indexes. Default is `README`.
`Redirect`	Maps a path to another URL.
`ScriptAlias`	Similar to `Alias` but for scripts.
`UserDir`	Directory users can use for `httpd` access. Default is `public_html`. Usually set to a user's home page directory. Can be set to `DISABLED`.

The third file to examine and modify is `access.conf-dist`, which defines the services available to WWW browsers. Usually, everything is accessible to a browser, but you may want to modify the file to tighten security or disable some services not supported on your Web site. The format of the `conf-dist` file is different than the two preceding configuration files. It uses a set of "sectioning directives" delineated by angle brackets. The general format of an entry is

```
<Directory Dir_Name>
...
</Directory>
```

and anything between the beginning and ending delimiters (<Directory> and </Directory>, respectively) are directives. It's not quite that easy, because there are several variations that can exist in the file. The best way to customize the access.conf-dist file is to follow these steps for a typical Web server installation:

1. Locate the Options directive and remove the Indexes option. This prevents users from browsing the httpd directory. Valid Options entries are discussed shortly.

2. Locate the first Directory directive and check the path to the cgi-bin directory. The default path is /usr/local/etc/httpd/cgi-bin.

3. Find the AllowOverride variable and set it to None (this prevents others from changing the settings). The default is All. Valid values for the AllowOverride variable are discussed shortly.

4. Find the Limit directive and set to whichever value you want.

The Limit directive controls access to your server. The following are valid values for the Limit directive:

allow	Allows specific host names following the allow keyword to access the service.
deny	Denies specific host names following the deny keyword from accessing the service.
order	Specifies the order in which allow and deny directives are evaluated (usually set to deny,allow but can also be allow,deny).
require	Requires authentication through a user file specified in the AuthUserFile entry.

The Options directive can have several entries, all of which have a different purpose. The default entry for Options is

Options Indexes FollowSymLinks

You removed the Indexes entry from the Options directive in the first step of the preceding customization procedure. These entries all apply to the directory the Options field appears in. The valid entries for the Options directive are:

All	All features enabled.
ExecCGI	cgi scripts can be executed from this directory.
FollowSymLinks	Allows httpd to follow symbolic links.
Includes	Include files for the server are enabled.
IncludesNoExec	Include files for the server are enabled but the exec option is disabled.
Indexes	Enables users to retrieve server-generated indexes (doesn't affect precompiled indexes).

None	No features enabled.
SymLinksIfOwnerMatch	Follows symbolic links only if the user ID of the symbolic link matches the user ID of the file.

The AllowOverride variable is set to All by default, and this should be changed. There are several valid values for AllowOverride, but the recommended setting for most Linux systems is None. The valid values for AllowOverride are as follows:

All	Access controlled by a configuration file in each directory.
AuthConfig	Enables some authentication routines. Valid values: AuthName (sets authorization name of directory); AuthType (sets authorization type of the directory, although there is only one legal value: Basic); AuthUserFile (specifies a file containing user names and passwords); and AuthGroupFile (specifies a file containing group names).
FileInfo	Enables AddType and AddEncoding directives.
Limit	Enables Limit directive.
None	No access files allowed.
Options	Enables Options directive.

After all that, the configuration files should be properly set. While the syntax is a little confusing, reading the default values shows you the proper format to use when changing entries. Next, you can start the Web server software.

Starting the Web Software

With the configuration complete, it's time to try out the Web server software. In the configuration files, you made a decision as to whether the Web software will run as a daemon (standalone) or will start from inetd. The startup procedure is a little different for each method (as you would expect), but both startup procedures can use one of the following three options on the command line:

-d	The absolute path to the root directory of the server files (used only if the default location is not valid).
-f	The configuration file to read if not the default value of httpd.conf.
-v	Displays the version number.

If you are using inetd to start your Web server software, you need to make a change to the /etc/services file to permit the Web software. Add a line similar to this to the /etc/services file:

```
http    port/tcp
```

where *port* is the port number used by your Web server software (usually 80).

Next, modify the /etc/inetd.conf file to include the startup commands for the Web server where the last entry is the path to the httpd binary:

```
httpd stream tcp nowait nobody /usr/web/httpd
```

Once this is done, restart `inetd` by killing and restarting the `inetd` process or by rebooting your system, and the service should be available through whatever port you specified in `/etc/services`.

If you are running the Web server software as a daemon, you can start it at any time from the command line with the command:

```
httpd &
```

Even better, add the startup commands to the proper `rc` startup files. The entry usually looks like this:

```
# start httpd
if [ -x /usr/web/httpd ]
then
 /usr/web/httpd
fi
```

substituting the proper paths for the `httpd` binary, of course. Rebooting your machine should start the Web server software on the default port number.

To test the Web server software, use any Web browser and type in the URL field:

```
http://machinename
```

where *machinename* is the name of your Web server. If you see the contents of the root Web directory or the `index.html` file, all is well. Otherwise, check the log files and configuration files for clues as to the problem.

If you haven't installed a Web browser yet, you can still check to see if the Web server is running by using `telnet`. Issue a command like this, substituting the name of your server (and your Web port number if different than 80):

```
telnet www.wizard.tpci.com 80
```

You should get a message similar to this if the Web server is responding properly:

```
Connected to wizard.tpci.com
Escape character is '^]'.
HEAD/HTTP/1.0
HTTP/1.0 200 OK
```

You'll also see some more lines showing details about the date and content. You may not be able to access anything, but this shows that the Web software is responding properly.

Setting Up Your Web Site

Having a server with nothing for content is useless, so you need to set up the information you will share through your Web system. This begins with Uniform Resource Locators (URLs), which are an address to file locations. Anyone using your service only has to know the URL. You don't need to have anything fancy. If you don't have a special home page, anyone connecting to your system will get the contents of the Web root directory's `index.html` file, or failing that, a directory listing of the Web root directory. That's pretty boring, though, and most users want fancy home pages. To write a home page, you need to use HTML (HyperText Markup Language).

> **NOTE**
>
> A copy of World Wide Web Worm can be obtained from
> `http://www.cs.colorado.edu/home/mcbryan/WWWW.html`.
> WebCrawler is available from
> `http://www.biotech.washington.edu/WebCrawler/WebCrawler.html`.

A common problem with HTML documents as they age is that links that point to files or servers may no longer exist (because either the locations or the documents have changed). It is therefore good practice to validate the hyperlinks in a document on a regular basis. A popular hyperlink analyzer is HTML_ANALYZER. It examines each hyperlink and the contents of the hyperlink to ensure that they are consistent. HTML_ANALYZER functions by examining a document for all links, and then creating a text file that has a list of the links in it. HTML_ANALYZER uses the text files to compare the actual link content to what it should be.

HTML_ANALYZER actually does three tests: It validates the availability of the documents pointed to by hyperlinks (called validation); it looks for hyperlink contents that occur in the database but are not themselves hyperlinks (called completeness); and it looks for a one-to-one relation between hyperlinks and the contents of the hyperlink (called consistency). Any deviations are listed for the user.

HTML_ANALYZER users should have a good familiarity with HTML, their operating system, and the use of command-line driven analyzers. The tool must be compiled using the make utility prior to execution. There are several directories that must be created prior to running HTML_ANALYZER, and when it runs, it creates several temporary files when that are not cleaned up, so this is not a good utility for a novice.

Summary

Setting up your home page requires you to either use an HTML authoring tool or write HTML code directly into an editor. The HTML language is beyond the scope of this book, but you should find several good guides to HTML at your bookstore. HTML is rather easy to learn. With the information in this chapter, you should be able to set up your Web site to enable anyone on the Internet to connect to you. Enjoy the Web!

IN THIS PART

Advanced Programming Topics

Use a different device driver, if necessary, to place it somewhere else on the hard drive file system. Alternatively, if you plan to use LILO to boot the operating system, you can install the new kernel by running a setup program or the utility /usr/lilo/lilo. See Chapter 4, "Using LILO."

Now all that remains is to reboot the system and see if the new kernel loads properly. If there are any problems, boot from a floppy, restore the old kernel, and start the process again. Check the documentation supplied with the release source code for any information about problems you may encounter or steps that may have been added to the process.

Adding Drivers to the Kernel

You may want to link in new device drivers or special software to the kernel without going through the upgrade process of the kernel itself. This is often necessary when you add a new device to the system (such as a multiport board or an optical drive) that should be loaded during the boot process. Alternatively, you may be adding special security software that must be linked into the kernel.

The add-in kernel software usually has installation instructions provided, but the general process is to locate the source in a directory that can be found by the kernel recompilation process (such as the /usr/src directory). To instruct the make utility to add the new code to the kernel, you often need to modify the Makefile. These modifications may be performed manually or by an installation script. Some software has its own Makefile supplied for this reason.

Then, it's time to begin the kernel recompilation with the new software added into the load. The process is the same as shown in the preceding section; the kernel is installed in the boot location or is set by LILO. Typically, the entire process takes about 10 minutes and is quite trouble-free, unless the vendor of the kernel modification did a sloppy job. Make sure that the source code provided for the modification will work with your version of the Linux kernel by reading any text files that accompany the code as well as the software compatibility files included with most distributions of Linux.

Upgrading Libraries

Most of the software on a Linux system is set to use shared libraries (a set of subroutines used by many programs). When you see the message

```
Incompatible library version
```

displayed after you have performed an upgrade to the system and you try to execute a utility, it means that the libraries have been updated and need to be recompiled. Most libraries are backward-compatible, so existing software should work properly even after a library upgrade.

Library upgrades occur less frequently than kernel upgrades, and you can find them in the same places. There are usually documents that guide you to the latest version of a library, or there may be a file explaining which libraries are necessary with new versions of the operating system kernel.

Most library upgrades are gzipped `tar` files, and the process for unpacking them is the same as for kernel source code—except that the target directories are usually /lib, /usr/lib, and /usr/include. Usually, any files that have the extension .a or .aa belong in the /usr/lib directory. Shared library image files, which have the format libc.so.version, are installed into /lib.

You may have to change symbolic links within the file system to point to the latest version of the library. For example, if you are running library version libc.so.4.4.1 and upgrade to libc.so.4.4.2, you must alter the symbolic link set in /lib to this file. The command would be

```
ln -sf /lib/libc/so/4/4/1 /lib/libc.so.4
```

where the last filename in the link command is the name of the current library file in /lib. Your library name may be different, so check the directory and release or installation notes first.

You would also need to change the symbolic link for the file libm.so.version in the same manner. Do not delete the symbolic links because all programs that depend on the shared library (including ls) would be unable to function without them.

An Introduction to the Linux Source Tree

You will need to look at the source code if you want to make enhancements to the kernel. The Linux source code can be found in the /usr/src/linux directory. For the reader interested in kernels, this directory is a very good reference.

The first place to start is to see what header files you have available in the include directory. This way, you can tell what system services are available. (See Table 52.1.) I have deliberately left out redundant or unused header files. By examining the header files, you can see what files and hardward configurations are available for you in Linux.

Table 52.1. Linux header files in `/usr/src/linux/include/linux`.

File	Description
a.out.h	Generated for the GNU C compilers.
atalk.h	Appletalk network structures and definitions.
autoconf.h	Automatically generated C config file. Don't edit it!
ax25.h	Definitions for the AX.25 protocol.
aztcd.h	Definitions for a AztechCD268 CD-ROM interface.
binfmts.h	Binary formats for the files.
bios32.h	BIOS32, PCI BIOS functions and defines.
blkdev.h	Block device information.
busmouse.h	Header file for Logitech Bus Mouse driver.

continues

Table 52.1. continued

File	Description
mtio.h	Definitions for magnetic tape I/O functions.
net.h	Implementation file for the networking portion of the Linux kernel.
optcd.h	Definitions for the Optics Storage 8000AT CD-ROM drive.
param.h	Internal Linux parameters header.
pci.h	PCI bus defines and function prototypes.
personality.h	Linux file personality declarations.
pipe_fs_i.h	For use with Linux file pipes.
ppp.h	For use with Point-to-Point Protocol with Linux.
proc_fs.h	The proc file system constants/structures.
ptrace.h	Defines to help the user use the ptrace system call.
resource.h	Resource control/accounting header file for Linux.
route.h	Global definitions for the IP router interface.
sbpcd.h	For Panasonic CD-ROM drives.
sched.h	The Linux task scheduler.
scsicam.h	SCSI CAM support functions, use for HDIO_GETGEO, and so on.
sem.h	For use with semaphores on Linux.
serial.h	Linux serial I/O definitions.
serial_reg.h	For the UART port assignments.
shm.h	For shared memory use on Linux.
signal.h	For Linux signal information.
sjcd.h	Definitions for a Sanyo CD-ROM drive.
skbuff.h	Definitions for the struct sk_buff memory handlers.
socket.h	More declarations of the socket-level I/O control calls.
sockios.h	More declarations of the socket-level I/O control calls.
sonycd535.h	Defines all of the commands for the CD-ROMs by Sony (CDU-531-5).
soundcard.h	For interfacing with soundcards.
stat.h	Standard C and UNIX definitions.
stddef.h	Standard C definitions.
string.h	String functions declarations for C programmers.
symtab_begin.h	Symbol table entries.
symtab_end.h	Symbol table entries.
sys.h	System call entry points.

File	Description
sysv_fs.h	The SystemV/Coherent file system definitions.
tasks.h	For specifying the maximum number of tasks at one time in Linux.
tcp.h	Definitions for the TCP protocol.
termios.h	Terminal I/O declarations.
time.h	Standard declarations for use with timers.
timer.h	Do not modify this timer declarations file.
times.h	For use with Linux kernel timers.
timex.h	For TIMEX devices.
tpqic02.h	include file for the QIC-02 driver for Linux.
tqueue.h	The task queue handling information for Linux.
tty.h	Defines some structures used by tty_io.c
tty_driver.h	Defines interface between low-level tty driver and its routines.
types.h	Standard Linux variable type definitions.
udp.h	Definitions for the UDP protocol.
ultrasound.h	For Ultrasound CD-ROM devices.
umsdos_fs.h	The UMSDOS file system header.
un.h	Linux header for socket programming.
unistd.h	Standard UNIX file header.
user.h	For use with core dumps and user segments.
utime.h	Time information.
utsname.h	Time information and structures.
version.h	Linux version information.
vfs.h	Virtual file system headers.
vm86.h	Virtual memory management routines.
vt.h	For use with virtual terminals.
xd.h	Definitions for the I/O ports, and so forth, for XT hard disk controllers.
modules/	Contains the file ksyms.ver, a symbol version table generated by genksyms.

Let's give an example of how you would use this header file information. Suppose that using the default kernel for the sbcpd (Panasonic CD-ROM) drive takes a long time to boot because it probes the I/O ports to see where the drive is in the I/O port memory space. You know you have set your jumpers on the drive to 0×260, so why not just have it look there and keep going? You are sick of typing in the sbpcd=0x260,SoundBlaster sequence every time you boot.

Sounds good. Let's look at the sbpcd.h file in /usr/src/linux/include/linux.

First, log in as root and make sure that you have write privileges to this header file to save your changes. Look at the part of the file where it says to define your CD-ROM port base I/O address as CDROM_PORT and specify the type of your interface card as SBPRO. You can change the address lines in file after line 90 as the following:

```
#undef CDROM_PORT   /* get rid of previous declarations. */
#undef SBPRO        /* get rid of previous declarations. */
#undef SOUND_BASE   /* get rid of previous declarations. */

/* override these values. */
#define CDROM_PORT 0x230 /* port address                       */
#define SBPRO      0     /* interface type                     */
#define SOUND_BASE 0x220 /* sound address of this card or 0    */
```

Now exit the editor after making the changes. Rebuild the kernel and install it as discussed earlier in this chapter. Reboot, and there you have it—a fast boot.

This is only a quick example of how to use this valuable resource of information to customize your Linux system. I am sure that with some exploring, you can come across some more examples.

Making Loadable Modules for Linux

We briefly covered modules in Chapter 5, "Odds and Ends." This section describes the basic strategy for making dynamically loadable modules in the Linux kernel. Let's look at how to use them. However, how modules work is really beyond the scope of this book. Sorry.

In this kernel version (1.2.13 or later), you can also create modules by enabling CONFIG_MODVERSIONS when making a kernel. Also, you have to install the latest module support package modules-1.2.13.tar.gz (or later version.) Next, compile and install the kernel (as explained earlier).

When you have made the kernel, create the modules by typing the following command:

```
make modules
```

This compiles all modules and updates the modules directory. In this directory, you can then find a bunch of symbolic links, pointing to the various object files in the kernel tree.

The set of modules is rapidly increasing, and you have the following list of items with this CD-ROM. You can find descriptions for each of these modules by following each of the links in the files in the directory usr/src/linux/modules:

- 3c501
- 3c509
- BLOCK_MODULES
- FS_MODULES
- NET_MODULES
- apricot

- arcnet
- aztcd
- de4x5
- de600
- de620
- depca
- eexpress
- ewrk3
- plip
- sonycd535
- sysv
- wavelan
- xiafs

As soon as you have rebooted the newly made kernel, you can install and remove modules, at will, with the utilities `insmod` and `rmmod`.

Now, after you have made all modules, you can also type the following command:

```
make modules_install
```

This copies all newly made modules into subdirectories under `/lib/modules/kernel_release/`, where `kernel_release` is something like 1.2.13, or later.

Using the `modprobe` utility, you can load any module like this:

```
/sbin/modprobe module
```

To use `modprobe` successfully, you should place the following command in your `/etc/rc.d/rc.S` script:

```
/sbin/depmod -a
```

This computes the dependencies between the different modules. Then type the following line, for example:

```
/sbin/modprobe umsdos
```

Now you automatically load *both* the MSDOS and UMSDOS modules, because UMSDOS runs piggyback on MSDOS.

A Brief Introduction to ELF

The Executable and Linking Format (ELF) has become a hot topic for Linux users lately. All major releases of the Linux kernel and libraries will support the ELF format in the future. The general idea is that ELF will be the common object file format for all Linux binaries. The public release of all ELF file format compatible compilers are with the kernel on the CD-ROM, and hopefully with future releases of Linux. (The default is *no* support, but you can build your kernel with the support.)

First of all, the current shared libraries are a bit bulky to manage. When you are dealing with large packages that span multiple directories, such as the X Windows System, building and maintaining such a library is a formidable task. Second, the current a.out shared library scheme does not support the dlopen() function. The dlopen() function enables you to tell the dynamic loader to load additional shared libraries.

So what's the big deal about ELF? The general UNIX programming community seems to like this file format. In fact, several commercial versions of UNIX, such as Solaris and UNIXware, already use ELF. More vendors, such as SCO and HP, are moving toward supporting it in the future. (By the way, Microsoft's NT is not based on ELF.) There is no reason why the Linux community should get left behind.

There are three basic types of ELF files: object (.o) files, regular executables, and shared libraries. Even though, functionally, the three types of files perform different functions, internally, they are very similar in structure.

One common part in all different ELF file types (including a.out and other executable file formats) is the idea of a "section." A section represents a portion of the file containing a set of related information. A file consists of many sections. For example, executable code is always placed in a section known as .text, all data variables initialized by the user are placed in a section known as .data, and uninitialized data is placed in a section known as .bss (historically known as "Below Stack Segment").

Dividing executables into sections has many important advantages. For example, once you have loaded the executable portions of an executable into memory, these memory locations need not change. Unless, of course, you happen to be of the twisted mentality that actually modifies code while it's executing. Executable code which could modify itself is considered a despicable programming practice in most cases.

Given this set of code segments, the memory manager on a machine can mark portions of memory read-only. Thereafter, any attempt to modify a read-only memory location will result in the program dying, even printing unprintable epithets and dumping core. So any attempt to modify a read-only memory location is a fatal error indicating a bug in the application.

Usually, you cannot individually set the read-only status for each byte of memory. It would slow the computer down too much. Instead, you can set the protections of regions of memory known as pages. On the i386 architecture, the page size is 4096 bytes. So, for example, on PCs you could indicate that addresses 0-4095 are read-only, and bytes 4096 and up are writeable.

It follows that we want all executable portions of an executable in read-only memory and all modifiable locations of memory (such as data) in writeable memory. It's efficient to group all of the executable portions of an executable into one section of memory (the .text section), and all modifiable data areas together into another area of memory (.data).

One more distinction exists between data variables the user has initialized and data variables the program has not initialized. If the program has not specified the initial value of a variable, there is no sense wasting space in the executable file to store the value. So, initialized variables are grouped into the `.data` section, and uninitialized variables are grouped into the `.bss` section. The `.bss` section is different from `.data` because `.bss` doesn't take up space in the file; it only tells how much space is needed for uninitialized variables.

When the kernel starts to load and run an executable, it looks at the image header on how to go about loading the image. First, the kernel locates the `.text` section within the executable, then loads it into the appropriate portions of available memory, and marks these pages as read-only. The kernel then locates the `.data` section in the executable and loads it into the user's address space; this time in read-write memory. Finally, it finds the location and size of the `.bss` section from the image header and adds the appropriate pages of memory to the user's address space. Even though the user has not specified the initial values of variables placed in `.bss`, by convention, the Linux kernel initializes all of this memory to zero.

In most cases each `a.out` or ELF file also includes a symbol table. A symbol table is a list of all of the symbols in the program. A symbol can be a program entry point, addresses of variables, and so forth. Symbols are defined or referenced within the file. Information about a symbol in the symbol table contains the address associated with the symbol and some kind of tag indicating the type of the symbol at the minimum. ELF files have considerably more information per symbol.

Symbol information is critical when you need to debug files. However, the size of the executable file is greater than it has to be. You can remove symbol tables with the `strip` utility. The advantage to this is that the executable is smaller once stripped. The disadvantage is that you lose the ability to debug the stripped binary. With `a.out`, it is always possible to remove the symbol table from a file, but with ELF, you typically need some symbolic information in the file for the program to load and run. Thus, in the case of ELF, the `strip` program removes a portion of the symbol table, but it never removes all of the symbol table.

Now let's see the topic of relocation. First compile a simple "hello world" program:

```
main( )
{
        printf("Hello World\n");
}
```

The compiler generates an object file which contains a reference to the function `printf`. Since you have not defined this symbol, it is an "external reference." The executable code for this function contains an instruction to call `printf`, but in the object code, you do not yet know the actual location to call to perform this function. The compiler generates assembler code which is passed to the assembler portion for conversion into machine-readable instructions. The assembler portion of the compiler also notices that the function `printf` is external and generates a relocation reference.

A relocation reference contains several components. One is an index into the symbol table, so the kernel loader will know which symbol is being referenced. Two, it contains an offset into the `.text` section, which refers to the address of the operand of the call instructions. Third, it contains a tag that indicates what type of relocation is actually present. When `gcc` links this file, the linker will walk through the relocations, look up the final address of the external function `printf`, and then patch this address back into the operand of the call instruction so the call instruction points to the actual function `printf`.

The output from this process, after the linker, is the `a.out` file (unless you specified a different name with `-o name` option). The `a.out` executables have no relocations. The kernel loader cannot resolve any symbols and rejects any attempt to run such a binary. An `a.out` object file will, of course, have relocations, but the linker must be able to fully resolve these to generate a usable executable.

So far, everything described here applies to both `a.out` and ELF. Now let's look at the differences. You have to understand two concepts: the `a.out` file format and exactly what a shared library is. Let's look at `a.out` formats first.

Exploring *a.out* Formats

First, the header of an `a.out` file contains limited information (see `struct exec`, defined in `/usr/src/linux/include/linux/a.out.h`). It only supports the `.text`, `.data` and `.bss` sections and does not directly support any additional sections. Secondly, `a.out` contains only the sizes of the various sections and does not directly specify the offsets within the file where the section starts. Therefore, the linker and the kernel loader have some unwritten understanding about where the various sections start within a file. Finally, it has no built-in shared library support. The `a.out` format was developed before shared library technology was developed, so as a result, implementations of shared libraries are crude. It is not impossible to design shared library implementations that work with `a.out`. However, ELF allows you to discard some of the hacks that were required to piggyback a shared library implementation onto `a.out`.

Around November 1994, the default file `a.out` format switched from ZMAGIC to QMAGIC files. The only real difference was the different set of "undocumented" understandings between the linker and kernel. Both formats of executables have a 32-byte header at the start of the file, but with ZMAGIC, the `.text` section starts at byte offset 1024, while with QMAGIC, the `.text` section starts at the beginning of the file and includes the header. Thus, ZMAGIC wastes disk space. Also, the 1024 byte offset used with ZMAGIC makes for less efficient buffer cache management within the kernel. With a QMAGIC binary, the mapping from the file offset to the block representing a given page of memory is easier because it's at a 1KB boundary. This enabled some performance enhancements in the kernel. ELF binaries are also formatted in a natural way that is compatible with possible future changes to the buffer cache.

Defining the Shared Library

Now let's look a little bit at what a shared library is. Non-shared libraries (also known as static libraries) contain useful procedures that programmers make use of. A programmer does not need to do everything from scratch, but can use a set of standard well-defined functions. This enables the programmer to be more productive. Unfortunately, when you link against a static library, the linker must extract all library functions you require and make them part of your executable, which can make the executable very large.

The idea behind a shared library is that you take the contents of the static version of a library and pre-link it into some kind of special executable. When you link your program against the shared library, the linker merely makes note of the fact that you are calling a function in a shared library, so it does not extract any executable code from the shared library.

Instead, the linker adds instructions to the executable which tells the startup code in your executable that some shared libraries are also required, so when you run your program, the kernel starts by inserting the executable into your address space. However, once your program starts up, all of these shared libraries are also added to your address space. Neat. Obviously, some mechanism must be present for making sure that when your program calls a function in the shared library, it actually branches to the correct location within the shared library. Now let's see how shared libraries are implemented under ELF.

To begin with, ELF-shared libraries are *position independent.* This means that you can load them more or less anywhere in memory, and they still work. The current a.out-shared libraries are known as *fixed address* libraries. Each a.out library has one specific address where it must be loaded to work. It will not work if loaded anywhere else.

ELF-shared libraries achieve their position independence in a couple of ways. You should compile everything you want to insert into the shared library with the compiler switch -fPIC. This switch tells the compiler to generate code that is designed to be position independent. The compiler then avoids referencing data by absolute address as much as possible. When you compile something to be fPIC, the compiler reserves one machine register (Register ebx on the i386) to point to the start of a special table known as the *global offset table* (GOT). The cost is that this register is reserved by the compiler and results in less flexibility in optimizing code. The performance hit is minimal in practice because the ebx register in an i386 machine is not as heavily used as once thought.

Another ELF feature is that its shared libraries resolve symbols and externals at runtime. This resolution is done using a symbol table and a list of relocations and is performed before the image executes. The ELF support in Linux makes it very efficient. Everything is referenced by the same global variable for the ELF library, rather than a fixed location in memory.

When you reference global data within a shared library, the assembly code cannot load the value from memory the way it would do with non-PIC code. If it tried this, the code would not be position independent, and a relocation would be associated with the instruction where you were attempting to load the value from the variable. With the GOT, you have one pointer for each global variable defined or referenced in the shared library. Each time the library needs to reference a given variable, it first loads the address of the variable from the GOT and adds it to ebx, and there you have the address!

The advantage of doing it this way is to establish the address of a global variable (ebx) in only one place and reference off this one variable.

A similar setup is used for functions with the use of a Procedure Link Table (PLT). The use of the PLT enables the programmer to redefine (override) functions which might be in the shared library. Then the PLT entry for the function can be used instead of the regular library entry. In this way, a PLT is nothing more than a *jumptable*—an array of jump instructions, one for each function that you might need to go to. Therefore, if a particular function is called from thousands of locations within the shared library, control still always passes through one jump instruction. This way, you need only one relocation to determine which version of a given function is actually called—efficient and clean.

This chapter cannot possibly cover all you need to know about the ELF format. For more information about the ELF file format, you can obtain the ELF specifications from a number of sources—you can try `ftp.intel.com` in `pub/tis/elf11g.zip`.

The specifications are also available in a printed format. See *SYSTEM V Application Binary Interface* (ISBN 0-13-100439-5) and *SYSTEM V Application Binary Interface, Intel386 Architecture Processor Supplement* (ISBN 0-13-104670-5).

Summary

Recompiling kernel source and adding new features to the kernel proceeds smoothly, as long as you know what you are doing. Don't let the process scare you, but always keep boot disks on hand. Follow instructions wherever available because most new software has special requirements for linking into the kernel or replacing existing systems.

Writing Device Drivers

53

by Tim Parker

IN THIS CHAPTER

```
/* if not open, initialize by calling ttinit() */
if((tp->t_state & (ISOPEN|WOPEN)) == 0)
{
    ttinit(tp);
    /* initialize flags, and call tdparam() to set line */
    tdparam(device);
}

/* if a modem is used, check carrier status */
/* if direct, set carrier detect flags */
/* set interrupt priority to avoid overwrite */
/* wait for carrier detect signal */
/* code eliminated from example */
```

Closing the Device

The close() routine is used only after the process is finished with the device. The routine disables interrupts from the device and issues any shut-down commands. All internal references to the device will be reset. close() routines are not usually required in many device drivers because the device is treated as being available throughout. Exceptions are removable media and exclusive-use devices. Some modems require closing (close()) to allow the line to be hung up.

Again, the terminal device example is used for the close() routine sample:

```
tdclose(device)
{
    register struct tty *tp;
    tp = &td_tty[UNMODEM(device)];
    (*linesw[tp->t_line].l_close)(tp);
    if(tp->t_cflag & HUPCL)
        tdmodem(device,TURNOFF);
    /* turn off exclusive flag bit */
    ip->t_lflag & =~XCLUDE
}
```

Strategy Functions

Strategy functions (block mode devices only) are issued with a parameter to the kernel buffer header. The buffer header contains the instructions for a read or write along with a memory location for the operation to occur to or from. The size of the buffer is usually fixed at installation and varies from 512 to 1024 bytes. It can be examined in the file param.h as the BSIZE variable. A device's block size may be smaller than the buffer block size, in which case, the driver executes multiple reads or writes.

The strategy function can be illustrated in a sample device driver for a hard disk. No code is supplied, but the skeleton explains the functions of the device driver in order:

```
int hdstrategy(bp)
register struct buf *bp;
{
    /* initialize drive and partition numbers */
    /* set local variables */

    /* check for valid drive & partition */
    /* compute target cylinder */
```

```
                /* disable interrupts */
                /* push request into the queue */
                /* check controller: if not active, start it */
                /* reset interrupt level */
        }
```

Write Functions

Character mode devices employ a write() instruction that checks the arguments of the instruction for validity, and then copies the data from the process memory to the device driver buffer. When all data is copied, or the buffer is full, I/O is initiated to the device until the buffer is empty, at which point the process is repeated. Data is read from the process memory using a simple function (cpass) that returns a -1 when end of memory is reached. The data is written to process memory using a complementary function (passc). The write() routine is illustrated for the terminal device:

```
tdwrite(device)
        {
                register struct tty *tp;
                tp=&td_tty[UNMODEM(device)];
                (*linesw[tp->t_line].l_write)(tp);
        }
```

Large amounts of data are handled by a process called copyio which takes the addresses of source and destination, a byte count, and a status flag as arguments.

Read Functions

The read() operation for character mode devices transfers data from the device to the process memory. The operation is analogous to that of the write procedure. For the terminal device, the read() code becomes:

```
        tdread(device)
        {
                register struct tty *tp;
                tp=&td_tty[UNMODEM(device)];
                (*linesw[tp->t_line].l_read)(tp);
        }
```

A small buffer is used when several characters are to be copied at once by read() or write(), rather than continually copying single characters. clist implements a small buffer used by character mode devices as a series of linked lists that use getc and putc to move characters on and off the buffer respectively. A header for clist maintains a count of the contents.

start and *ioctl* Routines

A start routine is usually used for both block and character mode devices. It takes requests or data from device queues and sends them in order to the device. Block mode devices queue data with the *strategy* routine, while character mode devices use clist. The start routine maintains busy flags automatically as instructions are passed to the device. When a device has finished its process, it executes an intr routine which reinitializes the device for the next process.

The character mode `ioctl()` routine provides a special series of instructions to drivers. These include changes in the communications method between the driver and the operating system, as well as device-dependent operations (tape load or rewind, or memory allocation, for example).

The `ioctl()` function can be illustrated with the terminal device example. The `ioctl()` routine, in this case, calls another function that sets the device parameters. No code is supplied for the called function, but the skeleton explains the process of the device driver in order:

```
tdioctl(device,cmd,arg,mode)        int device;
int cmd;
int mode;
faddr_t arg;
{
     if(ttiocom(&td_tty[UNMODEM(device)],cmd,arg,mode))
          tdparam(device)
}

tdparam(device)
{
     /* initialize variables */
     /* get address and flags for referenced line */
     addr=td_addr[UNMODEM(device)];
     cflag=td_tty[UNMODEM(device].t_cflag;

     /* check speed: if zero hang up line */
     /* set up speed change */
     /* set up line control */
     /* manage interrupts */
}
```

Using a New Device Driver

Drivers are added to Linux systems in a series of steps. First the interrupt handler is identified, and then the device driver entry points (such as open) are added to a driver entry point table. The entire driver is compiled and linked to the kernel, and then placed in the /dev directory. (See Chapter 52, "Working with the Kernel," for more information on adding to the Linux kernel.) Finally, the system is rebooted and the device driver tested. Obviously, changes to the driver require the process to be repeated, so device driver debugging is an art that minimizes the number of machine reboots!

CAUTION

Two basic don'ts are important for device driver programming. Don't use `sleep()` or `seterror()` during interrupt suspensions, and don't use floating-point operations.

Interrupt suspensions must be minimized, but they must be used to avoid corruption of `clist` (or other buffer) data. Finally, it is important to minimize stack space.

You can simplify debugging device drivers in many cases by using judicious `printf` or `getchar` statements to another device, such as the console. Statements like `printf` and `getchar` enable you to set up code that traces the execution steps of the device driver. If you are testing the device when logged in as root, the `adb` debugger can be used to allow examination of the kernel's memory while the device driver executes. Careful use of `adb` allows direct testing of minor changes in variables or addresses, but be careful as incorrect use of `adb` may result in system crashes!

One of the most common problems with device drivers (other than faulty coding) is the loss of interrupts or the suspension of a device while an interrupt is pending. This causes the device to hang. A time-out routine is included in most device drivers to prevent this. Typically, if an interrupt is expected and has not been received within a specified amount of time, the device is checked directly to ensure the interrupt was not missed. If an interrupt was missed, it can be simulated by code. You can use the `spl` functions during debugging usually helps to isolate these problems.

Block mode-based device drivers are generally written using interrupts. However, more programmers are now using *polling* for character mode devices. Polling means the device driver checks at frequent intervals to determine the device's status. The device driver doesn't wait for interrupts but this does add to the CPU overhead the process requires. Polling is not suitable for many devices, such as mass storage systems, but for character mode devices it can be of benefit. Serial devices generally are polled to save interrupt overhead.

A 19,200 baud terminal will cause approximately 1,920 interrupts per second, causing the operating system to interrupt and enter the device driver that many times. By replacing the interrupt routines with polling routines, the interval between CPU demands can be decreased by an order of magnitude, using a small device buffer to hold intermediate characters generated to or from the device. Real time devices also benefit from polling, since the number of interrupts does not overwhelm the CPU. If you want to use polling in your device drivers, you should read one of the books dedicated to device driver design, as this is a complex subject.

Summary

Most Linux users will never have to write a device driver, as most devices you can buy already have a device driver available. If you acquire brand new hardware, or have the adventurous bug, you may want to try writing a driver, though. Device drivers are not really difficult to write (as long as you are comfortable coding in a high-level language like C), but drivers tend to be very difficult to debug. The device driver programmer must at all times be careful of impacting other processes or devices. However, there is a peculiar sense of accomplishment when a device driver executes properly.

Network
Programming

54

*by Kamran
Husain and
Tim Parker*

IN THIS CHAPTER

Unfortunately, this technique is not good when you must have several processes access the same information quickly because the delays waiting for file opening and closing can grow to be appreciable. Also, if one process doesn't release the file properly, other processes can hang there, waiting for access.

For this reason, record locking is sometimes implemented. With record locking, a single part of a larger file is locked to prevent two processes from changing its contents at the same time. Record locking enables many processes to access the same file at the same time, each updating different records within the file, if necessary. The programming necessary to implement record locking is more complex than file locking, of course.

Normally, to implement record locking, you use a file offset, or the number of characters from the beginning of the file. In most cases, a range of characters are locked, so the program has to note the start of the locking region and the length of it, and then store that information somewhere other processes can examine it.

Writing either file locking or record locking code requires a good understanding of the operating system, but is otherwise not difficult, especially because there are thousands of programs readily available from the Internet, in networking programming books, and on BBSes to examine for example code.

Interprocess Communications

Network programming always involves two or more processes talking to each other (interprocess communications), so the way in which processes communicate is vitally important to network programmers. Network programming differs from the usual method of programming in a few important aspects. A traditional program can talk to different modules (or even other applications on the same machine) through global variables and function calls. That doesn't work across networks.

A key goal of network programming is to ensure that processes don't interfere with each other. Otherwise, systems can get bogged down or lock up. Therefore, processes must have a clean and efficient method of communicating. UNIX is particularly strong in this regard, because many of the basic UNIX capabilities, such as pipes and queues, are used effectively across networks.

Writing code for interprocess communications is quite difficult compared to single application coding. If you want to write this type of routine, you should study sample programs from a network programming book or a BBS site to see how they accomplish the task.

Summary

Few people need to write network applications, so the details of the process are best left to those who want them. Experience and lots of examples are the best way to begin writing network code, and mastering the skills can take many years.

Adding Server Support for PEX

55

by Kamran Husain

IN THIS CHAPTER

This chapter is really two chapters in one. I will discuss two topics here:

- Building a new server for X.
- To build this new server, we will add PEX support to it. This will serve as an example of how to add more capabilities to the X server.

After you read this chapter, you will have an idea of how to draw to an X drawable, and use Motif and PEX together. This chapter is not a tutorial on PEX, nor will you become the world's expert on writing additions to X servers. This chapter will introduce you to techniques that you can use to add features to the X server. You will also learn where to look for more information about PEX and X servers.

What is PEX?

The X Window system is primarily a two-dimensional graphical system. Due to the lack of standards in the three-dimensional (3D) area, there hasn't been an evolution of good 3-D developmental tool libraries. However, PEX is supposed to alleviate this problem by providing a consistent set of toolkit calls, which enables a user to support 3-D software with little effort.

PEX originally stood for *PHIGS Extensions to X.* PHIGS stands for *Programmer's Hierarchical Interactive Graphics System.* PEX has been adopted by the Common Open Software Environment (COSE) for X11 releases that are later than 2.2.

However, PEX is simply historical at this point, because the last version of the PEX protocol (Version 6.0) is not designed specifically for PHIGS at all. PEX is now designed to support 3-D application programs. PEX is an extension to the Core X Protocol to provide 3-D graphics support within the X Window environment. Included in the X11R5 distribution is code for the Sample Implementation of the extensions to the X Window server, which implements the functionality defined by the PEX Protocol Extensions.

In order to access the PEX functional extensions to the X server, one must use an application that generates PEX Protocol. The application can either generate the Protocol bytestream itself, or use something called an Application Protocol Interface (API). One such API provided with the X11R5 distribution is the PHIGS 3D graphics standard. This is a port of the PHIGS C language binding onto an internal layer, which generates the PEX Protocol enabling this particular PHIGS implementation to work within the X Window environment. Other alternate APIs are available via anonymous FTP from `export.lcs.mit.edu`.

When discussing PEX, it is important not to confuse the protocol with the API. The API is the conceptual model of 3-D graphics that the application developer sees when developing a client program. The PEX protocol is generated by the API, and is interpreted by the X server to perform graphics requests on behalf of the client program.

One API provided with the R5 PEX-SI is a PHIGS/PHIGS-PLUS API. The PHIGS/PHIGS-PLUS standards are specified in two parts. First, a functional description explains each operation conceptually, in a language-independent manner. Second, language bindings are used to bind the particular PHIGS functions to the semantics of the language. The PEX-SI comes with an application programmer interface that conforms to the latest revision of the PHIGS/PHIGS-PLUS C language binding.

If your version of R5 is patched through patch number 22, you have a second MIT-supplied API called PEXlib. PEXlib is to the PEX protocol what Xlib is to the core X protocol. PEXlib provides an interface that is as close as possible to a one-to-one correspondence between functions and protocol requests. It is intended to be a systems programming interface (so, people developing graphics toolkits and graphics systems will implement their system on top of PEXlib). It is proposed that the PHIGS API be ported to PEXlib when PEXlib is finalized. This change would not affect programs written to the existing PHIGS API.

However, because PEXlib is intimately tied to the protocol, it is expected that there will be changes between the current PEXlib (which supports Version 5.0 and 5.1 of the PEX protocol) and the PEXlib that supports the next major version of the PEX protocol, Version 6.0. Naturally, every attempt will be made to make the changes to the API minimal. The nature of the changes from 5.1 to 6.0 are not such that every primitive will be affected; rather the changes deal with the sticky problems of subsets, multibuffering, and other issues of global rendering semantics.

PEX Server

Find out whether you have PEX available on your X server first. By default, PEX support is *not* built into the servers you received for Linux. The xdpyinfo command displays all the extensions supported by a server.

Output from the PEX command should contain strings of the following form:

```
number of extensions:    7
XTestExtension1
SHAPE
MIT-SHM
X3D-PEX        (<— This is the line you are looking for)
Multi-buffering
MIT-SUNDRY-NONSTANDARD
```

If one of the extensions listed is X3D-PEX, your server supports PEX. If you do not see this line, you must build the server yourself.

Building a Server

To build a server that only includes the drivers you need, use the LinkKit instead of compiling the complete X system. Using the LinkKit package is much easier. The LinkKit package can be found in /usr/X386/lib/Server.

The LinkKit package contains a file called site.def for you to edit. The site.def file contains the site-specific information for your system. Edit the site.def file to define which servers you want to build, and the drivers and font *renderers* (programs that generate fonts for display) you want to include.

> **NOTE**
>
> You must run all the commands in this section as root.

Let's examine the site.def file in a bit of detail. See Listing 55.1 for the site.def file that I used to create a PEX server for my machine.

Listing 55.1. Sample site.def file.

```
XCOMM $XFree86: mit/server/ddx/x386/LinkKit/site.def.LK,v 2.11
      1994/04/10 05:49:56 dawes Exp $

/* Configuration file for Server Link Kit */

#ifdef BeforeVendorCF

/*
 * Change these definitions if you need to override the defaults:
 */

/*
 * HasGcc: defaults:
 *         SVR3,4:             YES
 *         Mach, 386bsd:       YES
 */
/* #define HasGcc          NO */

/*
 * HasGcc2: (should also set HasGcc)
 *       defaults:
 *         SVR3,4:           YES
 *         Mach:       YES
 *         386bsd:           NO
 */
/* #define HasGcc2          NO */

/*
 * If the link kit you are using was built with gcc2, and you are using
 * a different compiler:
 *    1. Install libgcc.a in a directory searched by your 'ld'
 *    2. Set NeedLibGcc to YES
 */
#define NeedLibGcc          NO

/*
 * Uncomment this if you want to link with the Gnu malloc library
 */
/* #define GnuMalloc    YES */

/*
 * GnuMallocLib: link-time flags to include the Gnu malloc library.
 * this is only used when GnuMalloc is set to YES.
 *       defaults:
 *         386bsd:               -lgnumalloc
```

```
*          others:               -lgmalloc
*/
/* #define GnuMallocLib          -L/usr/local/gnu -lmalloc */


/*
 * Server configuration parameters
 */

#define FontRenderers          Speedo Type1
#define X386Vga2Drivers        et4000 et3000 pvga1 gvga tvga8900 ncr \
                        compaq oak generic
#define X386Vga16Drivers       et4000 tvga8900 generic
#define X386Vga256Drivers      et4000 et3000 pvga1 gvga ati tvga8900 cirrus \
                        ncr compaq oak
#define X386Hga2Drivers        /**/
/* To enable the hga2 driver, replace the above line with the following */
/* #define X386Hga2Drivers          hga6845 */


/*
 * To include the generic banked monochrome driver in the monochrome server,
 * uncomment this with one of the following low level drivers
 *    hgc1280        [Hyundai HGC-1280 1280x1024]
 *    sigma          [Sigma L-View]
 *    visa           [???]
 *    apollo         [???]
 *    ...
 *    (list is subject to grow)
 */
/* #define X386Bdm2Drivers    hgc1280 sigma visa apollo */

/* #define XF86S3Drivers            mmio_928 s3_generic */
/*
 * Set which servers to build.  Change the YES to NO for servers you don't
 * want to build.
 */

/* The SVGA color server */
#define XF86SVGAServer         YES

/* The 16-color VGA server */
#define XF86VGA16Server        NO

/* The VGA mono server */
#define XF86MonoServer         NO

/* The S3 server */
#define XF86S3Server           NO

/* The IBM 8514/A server */
#define XF86I8514Server        NO

/* The Mach8 server */
#define XF86Mach8Server        NO

/* The Mach32 server */
#define XF86Mach32Server       NO

/* Set the default server (ie the one that gets the sym-link to "X") */
```

continues

This section covers the basic act of combining PEXlib with Motif. This way, you can get a drawable area under Motif and be able to use PEX functions on it. In addition to this, you still have the Motif framework to add your own menus to it. The steps to combine Motif and PEXlib are as follows:

- Initialize an X Window, and get the best visual you can for PEX.
- Initialize PEX with a call to PEXInitialize.
- Create a top-level shell.
- Create a drawing area interface for PEX.
- Map the drawing area to the screen.
- Create a PEX renderer (just like the GC) for this drawing area.
- Draw to your heart's delight.

Initializing the Toolkit

For initializing the toolkit, you must use a long method instead of XtAppInitialize. This long method enables you to select the best visual you can get for PEX. The following code segment will suffice:

```
XtToolkitInitialize();
app_context = XtCreateApplicationContext();
cp_argc    = argc;
argv_sz = argc * sizeof(char *);
cp_argv = (char **)XtMalloc(argv_sz);
memcpy(cp_argv, argv, argv_sz); /* copy the pointers */

display = XtOpenDisplay(app_context,
            argv[0], argv[0],
            "pEX", /* Class Name */
            NULL, 0, /* no resource options */
            &argc, argv);


if (display == (Display *) NULL)
        abort("Unable to open display");
```

You are making a copy of argc and argv to preserve their values, because the call to XtOpenDisplay() mangles these original values. It's necessary to check whether the display pointer is set to a valid value when you return from XtOpenDisplay() because the display may not have been opened for a variety of reasons, and you do not want to work a NULL pointer for the display.

Initialize the PEXlib functions with a call to the function PEXInitialize(). The syntax for this call is as follows:

```
#include <X11/PEX5/PEXlib.h>

int PEXInitialize(Display *dp,
        PEXExtensionInfo *info_ptr,
        int message_length,
        char *msg);
```

The PEXExtensionInfo pointer should point to a structure to which you want this function to return information about the PEX server. The message array should be about 80 characters long, and contain the text for any returned error messages. The function returns 0 if no errors occurred; otherwise, it returns one of the following values:

- PEXBadExtension if the X server does not support PEX
- PEXBadProtocolVersion if your X server and the PEXlib you are using are of different versions
- PEXBadLocalAlloc if you are out of memory
- PEXBadFloatConversion if the X server does not support the PEX floating point

Also, note that I used PEX5 as the location of the include files. When PEX 6.0 comes along, you may have to change this PEX5 reference to PEX6 in all the code you have to date. A bummer indeed, but necessary for an upgrade.

The returned PEXExtensionInfo structure is of the following form:

```
typedef struct {
unsigned_short     major_version;
unsigned_short     minor_version;
unsigned long release;
unsigned long subset_info;
char *vendor_name;
int    major_opcode;
int    first_event;
int    first_error;
} PEXExtensionInfo;
```

The major version is usually 5 or 6, and the minor version either 0 or 1. The vendor name and release are vendor-specific. The subset information contains information about the features in your PEX server, and can have the following values:

PEXImmediateMode   Enables drawing primitives that are sent directly to the display.

PEXWorkstationOnly   Enables workstation resources.

PEXStructureMode   Enables drawing primitives to be stored in a structure before being sent to the display.

PEXCompeleteImplementation   Enables all of these functions.

Check this value to see what features your X server supports. If your server does not have either the complete or Immediate mode graphics, (the Linux server is and should be complete), you should exit the application with an error message.

Creating the Window

Now create the window with the colormap and the best visual for PEX. The way to do this is as follows:

```
XStandardColormap        colormap;
Colormap     PEX_colormap;
```

```
/* open display as before */

screen = DefaultScreen(display);
visual = DefaultVisual(display,screen);
depth  = DefaultDepth(display,screen);
status = GetStdColormap(display, screen,
                visual, depth,
                &colormap);
if (status == True)
     PEX_colormap = colormap;


blue = AllocNamedColor(display, PEX_colormap,
     "Blue", 0L);

white = AllocNamedColor(display, PEX_colormap,
     "White", 0L);


n = 0;
XtSetArg(args[n],XmNvisual, visual); n++;
XtSetArg(args[n],XmNdepth, depth); n++;
XtSetArg(args[n],XmNcolormap, colormap); n++;
XtSetArg(args[n],XmNallowResize, True); n++;
XtSetArg(args[n],XmNmapWhenManaged, False); n++;
XtSetArg(args[n],XmNbackground, blue); n++;
Xt3etArg(args[n],XmNforeground, white); n++;
XtSetArg(args[n],XmNargc, cp_argc); n++;
XtSetArg(args[n],XmNargv, cp_argv); n++;
XtSetArg(args[n],XmNheight, 400); n++;
XtSetArg(args[n],XmNwidth, 400); n++;

toplevel = XtAppCreateShell(NULL, "peX",
     applicationShellWidgetClass, display, args, n);


mainWindow = XmCreateMainWindow(toplevel, "mainWin", NULL, 0);

drawMe = XmCreateDrawingArea(mainWindow,
             "pexdraw", args, n);
```

TIP

If you are unfamiliar with programming in Motif or X, please refer to Chapter 32, "Motif for Programmers."

The application requires the toplevel shell. For this shell, you have to manually set its visual, screen, display, and colormap. Note that the resize resource is set to True and mapWhenManaged is set to False. You have to set these values via the XtArgs args array at creation time for this to work. The toplevel shell is where you create the main window to place your Motif widgets. After you have created the main window with the XmCreateMainWindow function call, you create the drawing area called drawMe on top of this window.

Next, you add callbacks to the drawing area widget to allow for redrawing. Add the callbacks to the drawing area for the following types of events: resize, expose, and input.

The complete code for a very simple application is shown in Listing 55.2.

Listing 55.2. A sample PEX application with Motif.

```
#include <Xm/Xm.h>
#include <Xm/DrawingA.h>
#include <Xm/MainW.h>
#include <Xm/RowColumn.h>
#include <X11/PEX5/PEXlib.h>
#include <stdio.h>

int bailout(char *str)
{
printf ("\n %s", str);
exit(1);
}

int pex_set_line_color(Display *dpy, PEXRenderer p,
      float r, float g, float b)
{
PEXColor pc;

pc.rgb.red = r;
pc.rgb.green = g;
pc.rgb.blue = b;

PEXSetLineColor(dpy, p, PEXOCRender, PEXColorTypeRGB, &pc);
}

void doSamplePEX( Display *dpy, Window win, PEXRenderer ren)
{
PEXCoord    coords[10];

PEXBeginRendering(dpy, win, ren);

PEXSetLineWidth(dpy, ren, PEXOCRender, 8.0);

pex_set_line_color(dpy, ren, 0.5, 0.5, 1.0);

coords[0].x = 0.3; coords[0].y = 0.3; coords[0].z = 0.0;
coords[1].x = 0.3; coords[1].y = 0.6; coords[1].z = 0.0;
coords[2].x = 0.6; coords[2].y = 0.6; coords[2].z = 0.0;
coords[3].x = 0.6; coords[3].y = 0.3; coords[3].z = 0.0;

PEXPolyline(dpy, ren, PEXOCRender, 4, coords);

pex_set_line_color(dpy, ren, 1.5, 0.5, 1.5);

coords[0].x = 0.3; coords[0].y = 0.3; coords[0].z = 0.5;
coords[1].x = 0.3; coords[1].y = 0.6; coords[1].z = 0.5;
coords[2].x = 0.6; coords[2].y = 0.6; coords[2].z = 0.5;
coords[3].x = 0.6; coords[3].y = 0.3; coords[3].z = 0.5;
```

continues

Listing 55.2. continued

```
n = 0;
XtSetArg(wars[n], XmNvisual, visual); n++;
XtSetArg(wars[n], XmNdepth, depth); n++;
XtSetArg(wars[n], XmNcolormap, colormap); n++;
XtSetArg(wars[n], XmNbackground, bkg); n++;
XtSetArg(wars[n], XmNborderColor, fore); n++;
XtSetArg(wars[n], XmNargc, cp_argc); n++;
XtSetArg(wars[n], XmNargv,cp_argv); n++;
XtSetArg(wars[n], XmNallowResize, True); n++;
XtSetArg(wars[n], XmNmappedWhenManaged, False); n++;
XtSetArg(wars[n], XmNwidth, 300); n++;
XtSetArg(wars[n], XmNheight, 300); n++;
parent = XtAppCreateShell(NULL,"pexSample",
        applicationShellWidgetClass, dpy, wars, n);

n = 0;
mainw = XmCreateMainWindow(parent, "mainwindow", wars, n);

n = 0;
XtSetArg(wars[n], XmNresizePolicy, XmRESIZE_ANY); n++;
XtSetArg(wars[n], XmNbackground, bkg); n++;
XtSetArg(wars[n], XmNborderColor, fore); n++;

drawme = XmCreateDrawingArea(mainw, "da", wars, n);

XtAddCallback(drawme, XmNexposeCallback,
(XtCallbackProc)drawBtn, (XtPointer) &ren);
XtAddCallback(drawme, XmNinputCallback,
(XtCallbackProc)drawBtn, (XtPointer) &ren);
XtAddCallback(drawme, XmNresizeCallback,
(XtCallbackProc)drawBtn, (XtPointer) &ren);

XtManageChild(drawme);
XtManageChild(mainw);
XtRealizeWidget(parent);

pex_set_color_approx(dpy,XtWindow(drawme), &std_cmp, &pex_attr);

XtMapWidget(parent);

ren = PEXCreateRenderer(XtDisplay(mainw), XtWindow(drawme),
        PEXRAColorApproxTable, &pex_attr);
if (ren == 0) {
        printf("\n Bad renderer \n"); exit (1);
}

XtAppMainLoop(app_context);
return(0);

}
```

A few points to note about Listing 55.2 are that the immediate mode was used for rendering on the screen. PEX-SI provides no support for double buffering. This is a serious bug because lack of double buffering hinders performance.

Even worse, the PEX-SI API assumes that the client desires an XClearArea on the window before each frame is drawn. This causes unnecessary flickering while the screen is cleared and redrawn on all primitive drawing calls. What should have been done was to provide an end-of-render procedure hook, with the default hook installed to do a clear area function call.

Individual vendors (because of market pressure) have provided their own solutions to the double buffering problem. (Most PHIGS workstations do double buffering. If you do immediate mode you get single buffering along with the PEX-SI's XClearArea call.)

A final word about adding too many features in an X server. The more you add to the X server, the more memory it chews up in your system. Unless you absolutely require PEX (or other) support, do not add it to your X server, especially if RAM is 8MB or less. The PEX support for Linux added about 420KB on my system, which is not a lot, but it does start adding up. Also, the overhead of PEX applications tend to make my 8MB, 486/33 somewhat slow when running PEX demos, which leads me to believe that PEX on Linux with less than 16MB is not worth the hassle. If you are serious about PEX on Linux, get a faster machine and put gobs of memory on it. The performance improved very dramatically on a 486/66 with 32MB of RAM.

Where To Look for More Information

If you would like more information and examples of source code for PEX, check out these FTP sites:

- export.lcs.mit.edu in /R5contrib/contrib-R5fixes has several tar files of source code for PHIGS and PEX including a 3-D drawing program.
- http://www.x.org is a good place to start looking for more information on X.

Summary

This chapter has been a whirlwind tour of PEX. The topic of PEX could be a book in itself. In fact, there are several texts available that go into excruciating detail about PEX. You should have learned the following information from this chapter:

- How to create a new X server with your specifications. Building your own server with LinkKit is far easier than trying to re-create the entire X distribution. There are fewer memory requirements, and the build takes up less disk space and time to compile and link.
- How to install the new server. The LinkKit does this for you automatically and gives you options to clean your directories, and so on.
- How to check for the extensions in the current server.
- How to interface Motif with PEX.
- The trade-offs of having too many extensions in X server, such as loss of memory and speed for added functionality.
- Where to look for more information about PEX and Linux.

Using Mosaic and Netscape

56

by Kamran Husain

IN THIS CHAPTER

This chapter is a brief introduction to the World Wide Web and Mosaic and Netscape. We will cover the following topics in this chapter:

- A brief introduction to the Web.
- How to get Mosaic for Linux.
- How to set up Mosaic on your Linux machine.
- How to get and set up Netscape for your Linux machine.
- How to configure a SLIP connection for dialup and dedicated lines using Linux.
- Getting started with an HTML document. You will learn the basics of writing your own Web documents.

Introduction to the Web

The World Wide Web (WWW) is a fairly new invention. In 1989, researchers at CERN (a European Lab for Particle Physics) wanted to share information between nodes on their network. The researchers automated the process of locating files on remote machines and then copying the required information to their local machines. This retrieval process had to be done with a standard interface, regardless of the type of data or the means of getting this data. This meant that the interface had to include almost all the data retrieval tools such as FTP, Gopher, and so on, and be able to handle graphical, text, and binary files with a consistent interface.

The resulting network was such a success that the method caught on with users worldwide and gave us the World Wide Web. The letters *WWW* are now synonymous with the word *Internet*. The number of sites offering Web services is growing every day.

Introduction to Mosaic

To access the services on the Web, you need a browser. A browser is an application that knows how to interpret and display documents it finds on the Web. Documents on the Web are encoded in the HyperText Markup Language (HTML). Hypertext documents contain special codes that tell the browser how to locate information on the Web. How the browser interprets the codes is left as a local issue. Some browsers such as Lynx ignore any requests for inline images; some older Mosaic browsers ignore the interactive Forms that a user can fill in while online.

NOTE

The hypertext Home Page about NCSA has the following information:

"Established in 1985 with a National Science Foundation grant, the National Center for Supercomputing Applications (NCSA) opened to the national research community in January 1986. NCSA is a high-performance computing and communications facility designed to serve U.S. computational science and engineering communities. Located on the campus of the University of Illinois at Urbana-

Champaign (UIUC), NCSA is funded by the National Science Foundation, the
Advanced Research Projects Agency, other federal agencies, the state of
Illinois, the University of Illinois, and industrial partners."
Enough said.

Mosaic includes the following features:

- The capability to display plain text, HTML documents, and audio
- The capability to display inline graphics and images
- A customizable graphical user interface
- The capability to track previous sites with lists in a History and Hotlist
- The capability to find items via search commands within a document and over the Internet
- Extendability via third-party viewers for a type of graphical data format

Where to Get Mosaic for Linux

The latest version is available from the Internet at the following FTP sites:

- `Sunsite.Unc.Edu` in the directory `/pub/Linux/system/Network/info-systems/Mosaic`.
- There are several files in here with version numbers 2.0 and higher. The 2.2 version was the most recent stable one on my system at the time I wrote this chapter. Your mileage may vary. I used the file `Mosaic-2.2.bin.tar.gz` as my starting point. FTP to this site and get the latest version for yourself.

TIP

For some reason, the 2.4 version of Mosaic did not work with my modem, a cheap "no name" 28.8 clone. The application hung for some inexplicable reason, requiring a full reboot.

That's what I get for not going with a name brand modem, I know.

You too may experience similar problems. My choices were to get a nicer modem or continue to work with Version 2.2. I chose the latter alternative until I can get a better modem.

- ■ `tsx-11.mit.edu` is a mirror site for `sunsite`. Use this site if `sunsite` appears to be very busy.

- ■ Another excellent site for Web documents is the FTP site `ftp.ncsa.uiuc.edu`. Look under the `/Web` directory tree for a whole forest of documents on the Web, source code, and versions of Mosaic.

- ■ If you have access to the Web already through another source, you should look at `http://www.w3.org` for information about the Web, latest source code, and other Web-related documents.

After you get the files from these sources, you have to unzip the files via GNU's `gunzip` program. The `gunzip` program removes the `.gz` extension after it unzips a file.

The commands to do this are shown next. Substitute the name of the Mosaic version you get for the word *myfile* here.

```
$ ls myfile*
myfile.tar.gz
$ gunzip file.tar.gz
$ ls myfile*
myfile.tar
$ tar -xf myfile.tar
...
```

After the dust settles from the `tar` extraction command (the `-x` option is for extract), you have the file `Mosaic` in your directory. Along with these files, you also have some `app-defaults` files that you can use to customize your copy of Mosaic. As with other X applications, almost all of Mosaic's features can be customized using the `Xdefaults` file with the `Mosaic` resource. For example, to set the home page use this line:

```
Mosaic*HomePage : "http://www.another.nicer.site.com/myfile"
```

Alternatively, you can set the `WWW_HOME` environment variable to the path shown above. Using the environment variable is more consistent with other UNIX platforms.

The distributions from NCSA include the `app-defaults` files for each version of Mosaic. After you have installed Mosaic on your machine, edit these files to customize your own files. Read the `app-defaults` files for all the resources that are available to you for your version of Mosaic.

Now, you can fire up Mosaic from within an `xterm` with the command `Mosaic`. (It's probably best to have Mosaic run in the background so as not to tie up your `xterm`.) When Mosaic is up, it attempts to load its default hypertext document called the Home Page. Basically, the Home Page is the first document you start off with and the one document that you know that you can always load if you get lost while browsing the Web.

Before you go browsing the Web, let's first talk about hypertext documents. Once you know how hypertext documents work, you'll find it easier to browse the Web. Be patient; the next section is worth your time to read.

Hypertext Document and HTML Basics

Hypertext documents contain links to other documents on the Web. Links are often called hyperlinks. They enable you to access other documents and services on the Internet. You *surf the Net* by accessing other documents through these links. It's fairly easy to create these hypertext documents with links, so you can create your own documents with sites that you regularly visit and find interesting.

To create a hypertext document for display on a Web server, you have to learn the HyperText Markup Language (HTML), which is a collection of styles that define the various components of a document. HTML is based on SGML (Standardized General Markup Language), a superset standard of marking documents.

> **NOTE**
>
> So why write your own Web page?
>
> There are many reasons that you would want to create your own HTML documents. The first reason is for exposure. Your own document on the Internet can have information about you or topics that you find interesting. You can have a page about your business, because a Web address on a business card does look cool. Just remember not to *spam* your page's address on the Internet; it's not polite. (*Spamming* is the slang word for posting multiple copies of a message to many unrelated newsgroups.)
>
> Second, a Web page can be a repository of your favorite sites on the Internet. While cruising the Net, if you come across a decent page or two, you can simply edit your own Web page to add this site. Then, it's simply a matter of bringing up your favorite page to get back to the old sites again.
>
> Last, you may decide to dump Mosaic and go with a newer, better browser that doesn't read the hotlists you created from Mosaic. For example, you have to jump through hoops to get your Windows browsers' hotlists into UNIX Mosaic, or vice versa. When all your data is in a Web document, all you have to do is load the document in there, and you are done—no formats, hoops, and magic potions.

Mosaic can display ASCII text files. Therefore, you really don't need to know HTML to write up an HTML document. Any old file will do. However, if you want to have a document formatted when accessed by a viewer such as Mosaic, you must code it with HTML. HTML documents are also called source files. Source files are in plain text format and can be created using any text editor.

Let's get into a bit more detail about HTML formatting codes, called tags. HTML tags consist of a left angle bracket (<), followed by some coding (called the directive), and closed by a right angle bracket (>). HTML tags are generally paired, as with <H1> and </H1>. The ending tag looks just like the starting tag except a slash (/) precedes the directive within the brackets. For example, <H1> tells the viewer to start formatting a top-level heading, and </H1> tells the viewer that the heading is complete.

HTML tags are inserted in the source files to tell Mosaic (or some other Web viewer) how to inter-pret or display the coded information. For example, citation tags are defined by Mosaic to be displayed in italics. Each time you enclose a book title between <cite> and </cite> tags, Mosaic automatically displays the text in italics. This is known as a logical style, because it is configured by the viewer. Viewers can interpret a logical style in different ways.

Hyperlinks

The chief power of HTML comes from its capability to link regions of text (and also images) to another document (or an image, movie, or audio file). These regions are highlighted to indicate that they are hypertext links. To create a hyperlink, a special HTML code is entered that includes the Uniform Resource Locator (URL). A URL is the way of telling your Web Browser where and how to get the information. You can jump directly to URLs to see whether they are valid by using the URL command from the File menu. Enter the URL in the dialog box, and Mosaic attempts to get it for you. (See Figure 56.1.)

FIGURE 56.1.

*Jumping hyperlinks
via URLs.*

At the same time, text or a graphic is designated to serve as the anchor (the information that is dis-played in color or underlined and clicked on). A hyperlink may be made to a remote or local server, depending on how the URL is encoded.

You can keep a history of information space navigation, which tracks where you've been. You now have quick access to frequently used documents via a personal list. (See Figure 56.2.) History lists are valid for a current session only. Hotlists are those lists that you want to keep for all future ses-sions. (See Figure 56.3.) You should enter those places here that you may like to visit in a future session.

FIGURE 56.2.

*The Mosaic History
dialog box.*

FIGURE 56.3.

The Mosaic Hotlist dialog box.

Inline Images

Mosaic can display images inside documents, making it a highly visual medium for your information. However, each image requires processing time, which slows down the initial display of the document. Using a particular image multiple times in a document causes very little performance degradation compared to using the image only once.

An image is sized before it is included in a document. Images can fill a screen. Or, they can be small images that save time when Mosaic displays the document, but are still large enough to present information and be a teaser for the larger image displayed in a separate window.

An image tag is coded into the source file to tell Mosaic that an image is to be displayed. The image tag is an HTML extension, first implemented in Mosaic. You can test your Web pages by loading this file locally to see how it looks. You don't necessarily have to be connected to the Internet to do this.

Where To Get More Help on HTML

When you have Mosaic, you have access to online help for writing your own HTML documents. To get *The Beginner's Guide to HTML* select On HTML... from the help menu. You have to be on the Internet for this to work, because Mosaic accesses the Web to get the latest copy for you. This file provides up-to-date information in far greater detail than what you are reading right now. You should print this guide out for future reference. See also *Teach Yourself Web Publishing with HTML in 14 Days* (Sams Publishing).

Netscape

The authors of the first NCSA Mosaic have formed their own company called Netscape Communications. Their new brainchild is called Netscape, and you can get a Linux version of it for yourself.

The format for using Netscape is very similar to that of Motif. You can use URLs to type your destination name or use the point-and-click method to navigate HTML documents.

The options buttons include the ability to turn on and off the button bar, URL locator, and the bottom status bars. This way, you can customize your screens to suit your preferences. A sample of the preferences file is shown in Listing 56.1

Listing 56.1. A sample Netscape preferences file.

```
# Netscape Preferences File
# Version: 1.1N
# This is a generated file!  Do not edit.
SHOW_TOOLBAR:      True
SHOW_URL:      True
SHOW_DIRECTORY_BUTTONS:      False
AUTOLOAD_IMAGES:      True
FTP_FILE_INFO:      True
SHOW_SECURITY_BAR:      False
TOOLBAR_ICONS:      False
TOOLBAR_TEXT:      True
HOME_DOCUMENT:      http://www.ikra.com/
FONT_SIZE:      2
UNDERLINE_LINKS:      True
HISTORY_FILE:      /home/khusain/.netscape-history
HISTORY_EXPIRATION:      30
BOOKMARKS_FILE:      /home/khusain/.netscape-bookmarks.html
TMPDIR:      /tmp
TN3270:      xterm -e tn3270 %h
TELNET:      xterm -e telnet %h %p
RLOGIN:      xterm -e rlogin %h
RLOGIN_USER:      xterm -e rlogin %h -l %u
NNTPSERVER:      news
NEWSRC_DIR:      /home/khusain
NEWS_MAX_ARTICLES:      100
REAL_NAME:      Jonathan Doe Husain
EMAIL_ADDRESS:      khusain@ikra.com
ORGANIZATION:      Hardly any mps inc.
SIGNATURE_FILE:      /home/khusain/.signature
SIGNATURE_DATE:      0
8BIT_MAIL_AND_NEWS:      True
MAILHOST:      localhost
SOCKS_HOST:
FTP_PROXY:
HTTP_PROXY:
HTTPS_PROXY:
GOPHER_PROXY:
WAIS_PROXY:
NO_PROXY:
MEMORY_CACHE_SIZE:      2000
DISK_CACHE_SIZE:      5000
SOCKET_BUFFER_SIZE:      32
MAX_CONNECTIONS:      4
CACHE_DIR:      /home/khusain/.netscape-cache
```

```
LICENSE_ACCEPTED:    501 1.1N
DITHER_IMAGES:    True
STREAMING_IMAGES:    True
VERIFY_DOCUMENTS:    0
MIME_TYPES:    /usr/local/lib/netscape/mime.types
PERSONAL_MIME_TYPES:    /home/khusain/.mime.types
MAILCAP:    /usr/local/lib/netscape/mailcap
PERSONAL_MAILCAP:    /home/khusain/.mailcap
WARN_ENTER_SECURE:    False
WARN_LEAVE_SECURE:    False
WARN_MIXED_SECURE:    False
WARN_SUBMIT_INSECURE:    False
ADD_URLS:
BOOKMARK_MENU:
PRINT_COMMAND:    lpr
PRINT_REVERSED:    False
PRINT_COLOR:    True
PRINT_LANDSCAPE:    False
PRINT_PAPER:    0
```

Even though this file states "do not edit," you can get away with a few changes via a text editor. Keep in mind though, that any changes you make through the preferences dialog in the main screen may override what you edited manually.

The "N" display at the top right-hand corner of your display shows shooting stars as files are downloaded. If you want to stop any further transfers, you can click your mouse on this icon.

The bookmark feature is a bit more intuitive than for Mosaic. In fact, for some people, it's a bit easier to use and edit.

Netscape creates a .netscape_cache directory in your home directory, primarily for keeping track of images for HTML files. The size of this directory can get quite big after a few sessions of Netscape. Once in a while, if you are short of disk space, delete the files in this directory and the history file called .netscape-history file.

Another file of interest would be the .netscape-history file. This file can get large, too, after a few months of Web browsing, because this is where Netscape tracks where you have been. You can use this file as a guide to hunt for that special location that you just cannot remember now. If only my memory were this easily accessible.

Where To Get Netscape

You can get netscape from www.netscape.com, the home site for Netscape Communications. Read the license agreements carefully. All you get is a 90-day evaluation period if you are not a student or are using it for commercial, as opposed to personal, reasons.

Installation is easy. Get the file from the www.netscape.com site and un-tar it. You will have all the executables and associated files in a subdirectory.

> **NOTE**
>
> If you are using Netscape Version 1.1, you will get an error or warning message that the environment variable XNLSPATH does not contain the correct config files. This causes the program to crash if you cut and paste text in its text fields. The included files have to be placed in /usr/X386/lib/X11/nls, or you should set XNLSPATH to the nls subdirectory where you installed netscape.
>
> Your best course of action would be to get Netscape 2.0 from the web site at http://www.mcom.com/comprod/mirror/index.html.

SLIP Connections

Setting up a SLIP connection is necessary if you are not already on the Internet. To get a dialup SLIP connection you have to use the /sbin/dip program. The dip stands for Dialup Internet Protocol. For a dedicated connection you should use the slattach program.

If you are already connected to the Internet through another means, skip this section entirely.

dip

The dip program uses a script file to connect you to a SLIP account. You need a SLIP account to use Mosaic. Using dip with a -t option can also let you run in interactive mode for debugging, but in most cases you use it with a script file.

A script file is basically a file that handles your login and setup for you. You invoke /sbin/dip with the script name as an argument. A sample script file to work with my Internet SLIP account is shown in Listing 56.2. Your Internet provider should provide a script for you. If it does not provide one, ask for it.

Let's look at this sample script file in Listing 56.2.

Listing 56.2. A sample dip script file.

```
main:
#
# Get the local and remote names for the network
#
get $remote remote

#
#
#
default
get $mtu 1500
port cua1
speed 38400
modem HAYES
flush
```

```
reset
send +++
sleep 1
send ate1v1m1q0\r
wait OK 2
if $errlvl != 0 goto error
send atdt5551212\r

if $errlvl != 0 goto error
# wait CONNECT 60

login:
sleep 3
wait login: 30
if $errlvl != 0 goto error
send johndoe\r

wait ord: 5
send  doa+sol!\r

wait TERM 10
send  dumb\r

wait $ 10
send dslip\r

wait Your 10
#
# get $remote remote
#
get $local remote
#
# Ask for the remote site's IP address interactively from the user
#
get $remote ask

# cannot do this dec $remote

done:
print LOCAL address is $local
print CONNECTED to $remote
print GATEWAY address $remote
default
mode CSLIP
goto exit

error:
        print SLIP to $remote failed
exit:
```

Listing 56.2 shows how to access an Internet service provider via a dialup SLIP account. This script gives you an example of how to log into the remote system and get your local address, and even asks you for the remote IP address.

Normally, you run the SLIP script as root. You can set the permissions on the files in /etc/dip for all user access and not have to run as root. For debugging purposes, the -v option echoes all the script lines as they are executed. The echo on and echo off commands in script files turn the echoing on or off while executing. The -v option is like having the echo on command set as the first line in the script file.

The modem command in the scripts for dip only supports the HAYES parameter. You can set the speed with the speed command. For other parameters of your modem, use the Hayes command set. For example, send ate1v1m1q0\r sends the accompanying string to the modem to initialize it.

You can send output to the modem (and remote host) with the send command. To wait for a specific string, use the wait command with part of the string you are waiting for. Beware though, that if the string you are waiting for never appears, you can hang forever. The sleep command simply pauses the shell execution for the specified number of seconds. All variables for dip must be lower-case and preceded with a dollar sign. The dip program recognizes the following special variables:

```
$remote for remote host name
$rmtip        for remote host IP address
$local for local host name
$locip        for local host IP address
$mtu   contains the MTU value for the connection.
➥ You get this value from your internet provider.
```

The get command is dip's way of setting a variable. The following line requests the name of the remote host from the user. The ask parameter tells dip to prompt the user for the input.

```
get $remote ask
```

The local address for this script is derived when you log into your service provider. The remote host prints out a string of the form *Your IP address is zzz.yyy.xxx.www*. So the script waits for the Your string and then gets the last word on the line. Some SLIP service providers assign you a different address every time you log in, so you have to do this. The way to do this is as follows:

```
#
# Get local address from this string.
#
wait Your 10
get $local remote
```

The default command tells dip to route all default message traffic points to the SLIP link. The default command should be executed just before the mode command.

The mode command recognizes either SLIP or CSLIP as a parameter. CSLIP is the compressed SLIP mode. If all goes well, the dip program goes into daemon mode. The dip program executes the ifconfig program to automatically configure your interface as a point-to-point link.

Finally, to kill an existing dip process, you can use /sbin/dip with the -k option. You should do this when you turn off your machine or log out to free up your phone line.

> **NOTE**
>
> Read Chapter 42, "Networking," to set your /etc/hosts file. Also, if you are not familiar
> with the ifconfig and traceroute commands, read the man pages for them. The
> ifconfig program configures and maintains kernel resident network interfaces. The
> traceroute command is useful in tracking messages as they come and go from your
> machine on the SLIP link. It is an invaluable tool for debugging.

slattach

The slattach file is used to connect on a dedicated line to a remote server. If your modem is on
/dev/cua2, the command to configure a CSLIP connection is run as root:

```
# slattach /dev/cua2 &
```

You can put this in your rc.inet files if you like. If your service provider does not support CSLIP,
you can use the -p slip option to get the uncompressed SLIP mode. Just make sure that you run
the same mode as your service provider.

Then, you execute the following commands:

```
# ifconfig sl0 localhost pointtopoint myrichISP
# route add myrichISP
# route add default gw myrichISP
```

The first command connects you as a point-to-point to a SLIP connection. (The sl0 is *ess el zero*.)
The next two commands add the node myrichISP (the Internet service provider) as the default route.

To kill this connection, you must issue the following commands:

```
# route del default
# route del myrichISP
# ifconfig sl0 down
# kill -9 (slAttachPID)
```

In this case, slAttachPID is the process ID of the slattach process. For more information on setting up SLIP connections, see Chapter 42.

Using Mosaic

The Mosaic Document View screen is where you see all the HTML documents on the Web. (See
Figure 56.4.)

Forward	Returns to the document that preceded the current document. This button is dimmed if you have not moved backward yet. For example, if you move from Document 1 to Document 2 and return to Document 1 with Back, Forward brings up Document 2 again. Also available on the Navigate menu.
Home	Moves to your home document or home page. The default home document is the Mosaic Home Page. Also available on the Navigate menu.
Reload	Reloads the current document from the server, thus displaying any file changes made and saved since the last loading. (This is particularly useful if you are editing a document file.) Also available on the File menu as Reload Current.
Open	Opens the Open Document window to enter the URL for a file to be viewed. Also available as Open URL... on the File menu.
Save As	Opens the Save Document window that lets you save the current document to your local system in different formats. Also available on the File menu.
Clone	Opens a duplicate of the window being viewed. This is a useful choice if you want to keep a window open for reference but also want to select another hyperlink or open another file. Also available on the File menu as Clone Window.
New Window	Opens a new Document View window. The content of the new window is your default home page. There is no limit on the number of windows you can open. Also available on the File menu.
Close Window	Closes the current Document View window. If you only have one window open, the entire application exits. Also available on the File menu.

The Cursor and Displaying Hyperlink URLs

The cursor in Mosaic is generally a standard short arrow pointing slightly to the left of twelve o'clock. The cursor changes its configuration depending on where you are in the Document View window. It is the arrow configuration unless it is pointing to a hyperlink.

When the cursor rests on a hyperlink, it changes to a small hand icon pointing to the left. At the same time that the cursor changes its configuration, the hyperlink's URL is displayed in the information line. This tells you what will be retrieved if you select the hyperlink. The URL may also tell you the format of the document.

For example, suppose the URL http://www.ncsa.uiuc.edu/Pubs/access/accessDir.html is displayed in the information line. This tells you that the document will be retrieved from the NCSA WWW server (www.ncsa.uiuc.edu).

If you see the CERN WWW server (`info.cern.ch`) and an image file extension (`.gif`), you can surmise that the hyperlink is an image being retrieved from Switzerland and might take longer to download than a local text file. (Of course, your access to the Internet plays a part in the retrieval speed; but in general, you should expect links from overseas, as well as image files, to take slightly longer to display.)

Shortcuts and Keyboard Options

Each underlined letter is a shortcut to the same action as the corresponding menu item after the menu is open on your screen. You must have first selected a menu for the underlined shortcuts to work.

While your mouse pointer is in the hypertext viewing area, the following hotkeys (keyboard shortcuts for common actions) are active. As Table 56.1 shows, in most instances Mosaic accepts either case for the hotkey.

Table 56.1. Mosaic hotkeys.

Equivalent	Action
a or A	Annotate this window
b or B	Back to previous URL
c or C	Clone this window (make a new copy for reference)
d or D	Document source; shows the HTML document
f or F	Forward to next URL
H	Show the Hotlist
m or M	Mail to; you are better off using `mailx` or `pine`
n or N	New window starts a new session
l or L	Open a local HTML file
o or O	Open URL
p or P	Print
R	Refresh
r	Reload
s or S	Search/find in document
h	Window history
EXC	Close current window

You can select text from the viewing area as though you are in a normal workstation or editor window. Cut and paste into other X Window system windows as usual by pressing the left mouse button to begin selecting text, and then holding the button down and dragging. Alternatively, release the left mouse button and use the right mouse button to complete the selection.

The Fancy Selections setting under the Options menu causes the paste function to imitate the formatted display in the NCSA Mosaic viewing area.

Writing a Hypertext Document

Writing a document in HTML is fairly easy if you are a programmer. All you need is a text editor to create and edit a file. From then on, it's a matter of putting the Uniform Resource Locators (URLs) in the file and testing it out.

URLs

A URL is a way of specifying where a resource exists in the Internet. A resource can be a file, FTP site, database, image, newsgroup, archive, and other such goodies. Pointing to a document means telling your local program, such as Mosaic, the location and name of a resource and how to get it. See Appendix A, "Linux FTP Sites and Newsgroups," for a list of Web pages for Linux.

> **TIP**
>
> Try to edit an existing HTML document instead of writing one from scratch. Save an interesting Web document with the File menu and then edit it with your favorite text editor. You'll save a lot of time writing an HTML document this way.

A URL is composed of three parts:

`action://sitename/pathname`

The `action` part can be at least one of the following. It's not limited to these, of course, but these are the most common ways of getting the files that you see:

`http`	For HTML documents
`gopher`	For starting a `gopher` session
`ftp`	For starting an `ftp` session
`file`	For getting a raw file that may or may not be an HTML file

A browser program then attempts to use this action on the `sitename` and `pathname` in the URL. Given this information, you can also write your own HTML documents.

You use text anchors to attach links to an HTML document. An anchor is simply a region of text that is reserved as a pointer to another place. In Mosaic these anchors are displayed as underlined text. Other Web viewers may display a link in a different font, a different color, or both. The beauty of HTML is that different viewers can show an HTML document in their own style. You are not limited to one type of display with all viewers.

HTML anchors take the following form:

`<a href="htmlfile">GoDocument</a>`

In this form, <a and /a> are tags that mark the location pointed to by this HTML anchor. Tags are usually paired, with the ending tag having an extra /. The href token specifies the file to get, and the text between the > and < is what you see in dashed boxes. Tags are not case-sensitive, so <a> is equal to <A>.

In a Hypertext document, you can use the following example to mark a link to the "official" list of WWW servers at CERN:

```
For List servers at CERN, <a
href="http://www.w3.org/hypertext/DataSources/WWW/Servers.html"
>GoCERN</a>
```

With a browser you see the following line:

```
For List servers at CERN, GoCern.
```

In this example, the GoCERN text is underlined when it appears on-screen.

An HTML document uses tags to specify special areas of the text. The format of an HTML document is loosely described as follows:

```
<HTML>
        <HEAD>
     <TITLE>This is a Home Page</TITLE>
     <HEAD>
     <BODY>
             .... tags ... text .... etc. etc.
     </BODY>
     </HTML>
```

There can be only one pair of <BODY> and </BODY> tags in the entire HTML document. These are used to store the text for the HTML document. The <HEAD> and </HEAD> tags show the title in the heading section of a viewer. You generally have only one such pair in an HTML document because the text in the </HEAD> applies to the whole document.

For example, to show the title in an HTML document, use the following tag:

```
<TITLE>This is a Home Page For Mosaic!</TITLE>
```

Tags are not case-sensitive, and any formatting in between the tags is almost always ignored. So the previous title could also be written as follows:

```
<TITLE>
This is

     a Home

Page
For
        Mosaic!
</TITLE>
```

Paragraphs in an HTML document are introduced with a <P> tag and ended with a </P> tag. To break a line in the middle, you use the <BR> tag to add a line break.

HTML enables you to use up to six levels of headings, numbered H1 through H6; H1 is the leftmost (highest) heading, and H6 is the lowest heading. To define a heading use the following:

```
<H1>heading 1</H1>
```

Most Mosaic servers define a different point size for the level of heading you are supposed to be on. Don't skip heading titles when writing a document (for instance, don't use level 5 after level 1). It's not considered a good writing style and does not show up well on Mosaic viewers. You won't get any errors, but the document will look sloppy.

The following tags can be used to specify how to display the text on a viewer:

```
<I> </I>  italicize the text in between
    <B> </B>  bold face the text in between
    <U> </U>  underline the text in between
```

HTML supports unordered lists of items with the <UL>, <LI>, </LI>, and </UL> tags. To specify such a list, use the following construct:

```
<UL>
    <LI> Eat the  cake</LI>
    <LI> Swim with the fish</LI>
    <LI> Start the BBQ </LI>
    <LI> Write a chapter </LI>
    </UL>
```

This list is displayed with each item between the <LI> and </LI> as a bulleted item. Unordered lists are generally used as menu items from which a user can choose an item.

To display a numbered list, use an ordered list with <OL> and </OL> to enclose the list. Technically, you do not need to use the </LI> for each item, but some browsers may not support it. The previous list could be shown as follows:

```
<OL>
    <LI> Eat the  cake</LI>
    <LI> Swim with the fish</LI>
    <LI> Start the BBQ </LI>
    <LI> Write a chapter </LI>
    </OL>
```

HTML documents enable you to keep a glossary between <DL> and </DL> tags. Each glossary item contains a pair of <DT> and <DD> tags. The syntax for the glossary is as follows:

```
<DL>
    <DT>Item<DD>Description of this item in one line.
    <DT>Another item <DD>Another One Line Description
    </DL>
```

The <DT> tag indicates the beginning of an element within a glossary, followed by the description after the <DD> tag. The glossary item is displayed flushed left on a line by itself, followed by the description with a tab in front of it.

If you really want to include source listings and the like, you can put the text between <PRE> and </PRE> tags. The text between these two tags is displayed literally by your browser.

Other types of tags supported by Mosaic include the following:

```
<BR>       Produce a line break
   <HR>        Draw a horizontal line
   <EM> </EM> Emphasize in different font (italics in Mosaic)
   <STRONG> </STRONG>  Boldface in Mosaic, another font with other browsers.
```

You can also place images in your document with the `<IMG>` tag. For example, the construct

```
<IMG SRC=http://dont.inhale.com/graphics/billy.gif>
```

gets the image `billy.gif` from the site `dont.inhale.com` and has the browser display it for you. (If you want to get a better image editor for HTML documents, try `mapedit` at `sunsite.unc.edu` in the `/pub/packages/info-systems` directory.) If you do not specify a full address for the image, the browser uses the current page's directory and site.

Images that are declared one after another are placed side by side on the user's screen. You can introduce line breaks with the `<BR>` or `<P>` tags. You can also annotate the images with the text `ALIGN` keyword:

```
<IMG SRC="local.gif" ALIGN="bottom"> annotation
```

The keywords for the `ALIGN` keyword are `top`, `middle`, and `bottom` for aligning the annotation text position. In the previous example, the text will be shown on the bottom of the figure.

Some text-based browsers are not capable of displaying images that enable you to specify a special character that is displayed instead of the image. The attribute for this special character is the `ALT` keyword.

```
<IMG SRC="local.gif" ALIGN="middle" ALT="$"> annotation
```

This shows a dollar sign where the image would be shown on a graphic browser.

You can link images to actions within a link pair. For example, the following action gets you an HTML document by clicking or selecting the figure:

```
<A HREF="bozo.html" <IMG SRC="clown.gif"> </A>
```

That's about all I can put in this space about writing HTML documents. You can always find more interesting documents on the Web as you surf. Save these and see how others do their documents. Most of the information on the Web is very helpful in teaching you how to write your own Web documents.

TIP

Avoid the temptation to put large GIF images in your HTML documents. The time needed to download these large GIF files on 14.4 modems (still a limitation for a lot of dialup users) is very long. No one wants to wait 12 minutes or so for a pretty 1MB image to come down, when he or she could be looking at other sites with a faster download. Be considerate of your reader's time and keep the sizes of any included images to a reasonable size, say not more than 20KB. You'll still have enough resolution to put your pictures in there.

Using Other Browsers

If you can use Mosaic, you can use just about any other browser. All browsers are based on the same basic principles of retrieving and displaying a file by checking the type of data in it. Once you know how to navigate using URLs, surfing the Net becomes a task of learning how to use the special keys for your browser to help you customize its functions to best suit your needs.

There are many browsers already available for surfing the Net. Also, enhancements are being made to those that already have been out for a while. For example, as we go to print the Netscape 2.0 port to Linux is being completed. You will then have access to more features, including Sun Microsystems' JAVA language with multimedia support.

Summary

After a brief introduction to the Web, the following items were covered in this chapter:

- ■ Where to get Mosaic for Linux, which versions to use, and how to debug common problems in Mosaic.
- ■ How to install Mosaic on your machine after you have FTPed it.
- ■ How to surf the Web with Mosaic and use its controls to get around documents.
- ■ A brief introduction to connecting your Linux node via SLIP to an Internet service provider.
- ■ Some of the basics on HTML and how to write your own HTML documents for the Web. After reading this chapter, you should be able to write your own files and read HTML documents from other sites.

Happy surfin'.

DOSemu

57

*by Robert Pfister
and
Kamran Husain*

IN THIS CHAPTER

DOSemu stands for DOS emulator. This is a bit of a misnomer, because DOSemu does not actually emulate MS-DOS. Instead, it provides an environment in Linux under which MS-DOS and MS-DOS applications can be run. DOSemu enables you to run MS-DOS sessions

- On a virtual console
- Within an `xterm`
- As an X Window application
- Over a serial or network connection

The development of DOSemu is not yet complete. A small but growing number of MS-DOS applications will run under DOSemu. The most impressive application reported to run under DOSemu is the real mode of MS-Windows 3.0.

MS-DOS applications will not run as fast under DOSemu as they would under native MS-DOS, but most applications are fast enough. You have the added advantage of being able to run Linux and MS-DOS applications side by side.

The design of DOSemu will always cause some speed degradation, but the same design also provides the capability to virtualize a PC. The disk drives, serial ports, and memory configurations configured under DOSemu do not need to match the hardware that actually exists on your PC.

CAUTION

There are a few things you need to be wary of when you first start using DOSemu. DOSemu is considered to be alpha software. Major disk corruption is unlikely to happen when you run DOSemu, but you should take normal precautions. You should back up anything valuable on your DOS and Linux hard-drive partitions before actually running DOSemu.

Although DOSemu is strictly user-level code, some unexpected results may occur. When you first configure and test DOSemu you should shut down any critical Linux applications and be prepared to reboot your machine. This may seem like an unnecessary precaution for an experienced Linux user. However, my first attempt at DOSemu caused my modem to hang up because DOSemu reset the configured serial ports.

Installing DOSemu from Source Distributions

DOSemu is available on some CD-ROM distributions and on most major Linux BBSs and FTP sites such as `sunsite.unc.edu` (in directory `/pub/Linux/system/Emulators/dosemu`). The latest version available as of this writing was 0.53pl39 (pre-release 0.53, patch level 39). DOSemu is dependent on the version of the Linux kernel installed. Version 0.52 will not work with kernels newer than 1.1.30, nor will version 0.53 work with Linux kernels prior to 1.1.30.

For the truly adventuresome, the latest development version of DOSemu is available on the Internet via anonymous FTP at `dspsun.eas.asu.edu:/pub/dosemu/`. As with the development version of any software, it is not as thoroughly tested, and may have some serious bugs. Stick to the released versions if at all possible.

The latest released version at the time of writing that is stable was `/pub/Linux/ALPHA/dosemu/ dosemu0.60.3.tgz` from `tsx-11.mit.edu`. Be cautious with later releases.

The DOSemu distribution needs to be installed in a directory under `/usr/src`. DOSemu will not build correctly if the distribution is installed elsewhere. A DOSemu distribution consists of a compressed `tar` file that is unpacked by a shell command such as

```
bash# tar -zxvf filename.tar.gz
```

DOSemu is undergoing constant revisions. Review the QuickStart and other README files before proceeding.

Building an Executable Version of DOSemu

DOSemu is distributed as source code that needs to be compiled and linked before you use it. This is not a very complicated task because the process is automated. To build DOSemu, you need the following software installed:

- GNU C compiler version 2.5.8 or later
- GNU make
- `libc` 4.5.21 or later
- `ncurses`

To build DOSemu, log in as `root`, change directory (`cd`) to the directory created by unpacking the `tar` archive and type the following commands:

```
bash# make config
bash# make depend
bash# make most
```

The DOSemu distribution includes a reference manual written in `TeX`. If you have `TeX` installed and want to create a typeset version of the manual, use `make everything` instead of `make most`.

To properly compile DOSemu, you need to be logged in as `root`, and have approximately 12MB of virtual memory free. Use the `top` command to check how much free memory is available. You can increase the free memory by either installing an additional swap file or by killing unnecessary processes. Fortunately, you only need excess memory to compile DOSemu.

The full build of DOSemu takes approximately 10 minutes on a 90 MHz Pentium. When the build is complete, you are ready to configure and run DOSemu.

Configuring DOSemu

DOSemu can be configured to boot MS-DOS from a floppy or hard drive. As when configuring a real PC, you usually start by booting from a floppy and work up to booting from a hard drive.

How To Build Wine

To build Wine, simply type

```
make
```

You're done with the hard part of configuring Wine. However, building Wine seems like the longest part. To build Wine from scratch takes approximately eight minutes on a 90MHz Pentium. You will also need the -lXext libraries for the final link to work, so install it from your CD-ROM first.

Using Wine

Using Wine can be as simple as typing wine *filename*. Wine can be configured and used with a number of different options—including a debugger for tracking down internal errors in Wine itself.

Specifying Configuration Parameters

Wine's global configuration file is typically /usr/local/etc/wine.conf. The configuration parameters match mostly with the above questions and are organized in the format of MS-Windows .ini files. A sample file follows, with some comments on the usage of each section.

The following statements map MS-DOS drive letters to the matching subdirectory under Linux:

```
[drives]
A=/a
C=/c
```

These parameters tell Wine where to find Windows- and Wine-specific DLLs and directories:

```
[wine]
Windows=c:\windows
System=c:\windows\system
Temp=c:\temp
Path=c:\windows;c:\windows\system
SystemResources=/users/wine/wine950122/sysres.dll
```

The following section applies to the mapping of MS-Windows fonts to X font (note that the * is used for wildcard matching of X fonts):

```
[fonts]
system=*-helvetica
mssansserif=*-helvetica
msserif=*-times
fixedsys=*-fixed
arial=*-helvetica
helv=*-helvetica
roman=*-times
default=*-*
```

The following section maps serial ports available under Wine with corresponding Linux serial port identifiers:

```
[serialports]
Com1=/dev/cua0
Com2=/dev/cua1
```

The following section maps printer ports available under Wine with the corresponding printer port under Linux

```
[parallelports]
Lpt1=/dev/lp0
```

These parameters determine the amount of logging and the destination:

```
[spy]
File=CON
Exclude=WM_SIZE;WM_TIMER
```

Using Command-Line Options

The Wine command line has the following format: `wine wine_options program program_options`. For example:

```
bash# /usr/wine/wine -debugmsg +all /c/windows/winmine.exe
```

Table 58.1 shows command-line options available with Wine.

Table 58.1. Wine command-line options.

Option	Meaning
-depth n	Change the depth to use for multiple-depth screens. This configures Wine to use other than the default number of colors. (8 bitplanes is 256 colors and usually the only acceptable answer.)
-desktop geom	Run an MS-Windows application with a desktop of the size specified. For example, 850×620 would create a window of 850 by 620. Running with a desktop also eliminates the modal, or stuck-on-top, behavior of Wine applications.
-display name	Use an X display other than the default. This enables users to run an MS-Windows application on another X device over an attached network.
-iconic	Start application as an icon rather than full-screen. This is same functionality as run minimized from the Program Manager under native MS-Windows.
-debug	Enter debugger before starting application
-name name	Set the application name. This is useful for telling the X Windows manager a meaningful name for the application. The default name is `wine`.
-privatemap	Use a private color map. This is useful for applications that make extensive use of color. Running an application this way causes the colors of other X applications to look weird while the Wine session is the selected window.

continues

Table 58.1. continued

Option	Meaning
-synchronous	Turn on synchronous display mode. This can severely slow down applications, as it causes X Windows to wait for the completion of each command before sending the next one. X applications can send commands to an X server that may or may not be on the same machine. Under some applications, synchronization is necessary so that graphics operations do not get optimized away by the X server.
-backingstore	This is an optimization that enables an X server to handle expose events without interrupting the client program.
-spy *file*	Turn on message spying to the specified file. This can also be done by output redirection.
-debugmsg *name*	Turn specific debugging information on or off. To get a current list of debug message types, type the following command: wine -debugmsg help help.

The Wine Debugger

Wine has a built-in debugger that is useful for uncovering problems within the program. When an MS-Windows program exits due to a problem, the debugger starts in the xterm from which Wine was started. If you are not interested in troubleshooting Wine, you need only type quit at the prompt and skip to the next section of this chapter.

The Wine debugger is similar to the GNU debugger gdb. Breakpoints can be set; examination and modification of registers as well as memory locations are possible. However, this is a minimal debugger that includes only the commands listed in Table 58.2.

Table 58.2. Wine debugger commands.

Command	Meaning
break	Set a breakpoint at a specified address or symbolic value. Wine will stop before executing instructions at this address. For example, break * GDI_Ordinal_24 sets a breakpoint at the start of Windows *Ellipse* function known internally as GDI.24.
bt	Backtrace, or show the history of Wine calls leading to the current place. The addresses shown are the return addresses, not the calling addresses.
cont	Continue program execution until a breakpoint or error condition is reached.
define	Equates a symbol to a value. For example: define *myproc* 0x000001c6.

Command	Meaning
disable	Disable a specific breakpoint. Breakpoints defined by the `break` command are stored by breakpoint numbers. To disable a breakpoint, you need to find the breakpoint number with the `info` command. To disable breakpoint number 1, simply type `disable 1`.
enable	Enables a breakpoint number, the opposite of `disable`. To enable the previously disabled breakpoint number 1, simply type `enable 1`.
help	Prints a help text of the available commands.
info	Provides information on the following:
	`reg` registers information.
	`stack` dumps the current stack.
	`break` shows the current breakpoints and if they are enabled.
	`segments` shows information about memory segments in use.
mode	Switches between 16- and 32-bit modes.
print	Prints out values of expressions given.
quit	Exits debugger and ends any MS-Windows program in progress.
set	Enables depositing of values in registers and memory.
symbolfile	Loads a symbol file containing symbolic values. The file `wine.sym` is created as part of the Wine build.
x	Examines memory values in several different formats. The format of x is `x / format address`, where *format* can be one of the following:
	x longword hexadecimal (32-bit integer)
	d longword decimal
	w word hexadecimal
	b byte
	c single character
	s null-terminated ASCII string
	I i386 instruction
	A number can be specified before the *format* to indicate a repeating group. For example, listing 10 instructions after a given address would be `x / 10 I 0x000001cd`.

In order to benefit from using the Wine debugger, an understanding of debugging i386 assembly is essential. If you are serious about debugging Wine, an assembly language output from GCC is essential.

How Wine Works

Wine is composed of a MS-Windows program loader and a library of MS-Windows functions.

How Wine Loads Programs

Wine's first duty is to load an MS-Windows executable image into memory. This also includes any DLL files and other resources that the application needs. MS-Windows uses a different executable image type than does DOS that is called NE, or new executable. DLLs and font files also use this NE format, which makes Wine's job easier.

Individual segments of the NE image must be load into memory, and references to other DLL and Windows calls need to be resolved. Calls to functions outside an image are referred to by the module name and function number. A call to *Ellipse* is actually stored as GDI.24.

After an executable image is loaded into memory, Wine simply jumps to the WinMain() function defined in the image. A call to MS-Windows graphics function *Ellipse* is stored as *GDI.24. GDI* is the name of the MS-Windows graphics library, and 24 is the position in that DLL where *Ellipse* starts. Wine does not need to do any instruction emulation because both Linux and MS-Windows use the i386 instruction set. When an MS-Windows primitive function is called, Wine intercepts that call and passes it to a matching library routine.

The Wine Library

Wine converts the MS-Windows API to the matching X or UNIX API calls. A call to the MS-Windows Ellipse function to draw an ellipse in a window has the following format:

```
Ellipse (hdc, xLeft, yTop, xRight, yBottom);
```

The definitions are of xLeft, yTop, xRight, and yBottom are a bounding box for an ellipse as shown in Figure 58.2.

FIGURE 58.2.

MS-Windows Ellipse coordinates.

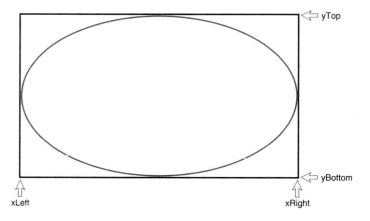

The same ellipse is drawn under the X API XDrawArc function:

```
XDrawArc(display, d, gc, x, y, width, height, angle1, angle2);
```

The definitions of x, y, width, height, angle1, and angle2 are shown in Figure 58.3.

FIGURE 58.3.
XDrawArc coordinates.

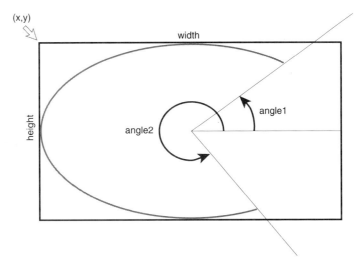

Wine needs to do a little math to convert the coordinates from an Ellipse call to that of an XDrawArc call. Other parameters of the XDrawArc call are a bit easier to map. The *d* refers to a drawable area, which is typically a handle to a window. Under MS-Windows, this is contained in the *hdc* structure. The *gc* is a graphics context and is analogous in functionality to the *hdc* under MS-Windows. As X is capable of displaying on different machines over a network, the *display* parameter describes which display to use. The *display* parameter remains constant over the life of a Wine session. The last thing Wine has to consider is that an MS-Windows Ellipse call can also specify a filled ellipse. Wine checks the *hdc*, and possibly uses XFillArc instead.

There are nearly 300 graphics primitives available under MS-Windows that need to undergo similar translations. While this might seem to be a bit of work, the graphics conversions are among the simpler things to emulate under MS-Windows.

Where Does Wine End and MS-Windows Begin?

As Wine currently requires parts of MS-Windows to operate, it is a bit confusing to know where Wine ends and MS-Windows begins. Wine currently provides API calls for the following parts of a typical MS-Windows installation:

commdlg	Common Windows Dialogs
gdi	Graphics Device Interface

kernel	Kernel Interface
keyboard	Keyboard Interface
mmsystem	Multimedia System Interface
mouse	Mouse Interface
shell	Windows 3.1 Shell API Library
sound	Windows sound system
toolhelp	Debugging and tools helper calls
user	Microsoft Windows User Interface
win87em	Coprocessor/Emulator Library
winsock	Windows Socket interface (TCP/IP)

Wine requires access to some parts of MS-Windows to use features that are not implemented by Wine. One example is the MS-Windows dynamic link library OLECLI, which implements the OLE client. The Wine team has made significant headway in reducing the amount of files needed. The Wine project charter includes removing any dependency on MS-Windows files. This includes utilities and file organizations to install MS-Windows applications.

Some of the simplest MS-Windows applications run today under Wine without need of any MS-Windows code or access to any MS-Windows directories. WINMINE.EXE and SOL.EXE are examples of such applications. Although no suggested directory organization exists to support this, a quick example of doing this is the following:

1. Copy winmine.exe and win.ini to a Linux directory such as /users/windows.
2. Change the Windows path options in wine.conf, such as to /users/windows.
3. Dismount your MS-DOS partition.
4. Run Wine.

Limitations of Wine

Only a few MS-Windows software packages run correctly under Wine. Luckily it is possible to estimate how likely a program is to run correctly without actually running it. Unfortunately there are some classes of applications that are unlikely to ever run under Wine.

Software That Works

The most recent versions of Wine support a good number of the MS-Windows applets and games included with the stock MS-Windows 3.1. There are considerable variations between each release of Wine. Changes that help some applications often break others. But here are some of the accessories and games that work reasonably well under Wine:

- calc.exe
- clock.exe
- cruel.exe
- golf.exe

- notepad.exe
- pipe.exe
- pegged.exe
- reversi.exe
- winmine.exe

Using *winestat* To Analyze Windows Programs

Part of Wine is the winestat utility. This is actually the same program as Wine, but instead of running an MS-Windows executable, winestat simply attempts to load a Windows executable and reports on how successful the load was. In loading an executable, winestat also loads any DLLs necessary, and reports if any are missing. winestat looks for Windows API calls that are used by either the executable or any DLL, and verifies their existence. A sample winestat run on the MS-Windows Paintbrush applet pbrush yields the following:

```
KERNEL.1 not implemented
KERNEL.54 not implemented
KERNEL.113 not implemented
KERNEL.114 not implemented
KERNEL.121 not implemented
KERNEL.154 not implemented
KERNEL.178 not implemented
KERNEL.207 not implemented
KERNEL: 52 of 60 (86.7 %)
USER: 150 of 150 (100.0 %)
GDI.151 not implemented
GDI.307 not implemented
GDI.366 not implemented
GDI.439 not implemented
GDI: 80 of 84 (95.2 %)
SHELL: 9 of 9 (100.0 %)
KEYBOARD: 2 of 2 (100.0 %)
TOTAL: 293 of 305 winapi functions implemented (96.1 %)
```

winestat calls out the individual functions by number and module that are not implemented by Wine. If you are curious as to the function name, rather than number, look at the Wine sources in the if1632 directory for the given module name's spec file. A sample kernel.spec file is as follows:

```
#1 FATALEXIT
#2 EXITKERNEL
3   pascal GetVersion() GetVersion()
...
...
...
#54 pascal16 GETINSTANCEDATA
```

Any line in a .spec file that starts with a # is considered a comment, not an implemented function. In this example, both 1 and 54 are commented, with the respective names of FATALEXIT, and GETINSTANCEDATA. FATALEXIT is used for debugging MS-Windows programs under error conditions and is not important for most MS-Windows users. GETINSTANCEDATA copies configuration data from a previous instance of an application. If you are running only one instance of an application, this does not apply.

The final percentage shows which MS-Windows API calls are implemented. This is often a good measure of how much of an application could work under Wine. Unfortunately, if a single, unimplemented API call is needed to initialize your MS-Windows application, anything less than 100 percent is not good enough.

MS-Windows applications to which `winestat` gives an overall implementation rating over 95 percent are worth a try. Unlike DOSemu, Wine is not as prone to leaving Linux in an unusable state. However it is not always a trivial matter to kill an errant Wine session. The easiest thing to do is to start Wine with a separate desktop: `wine -desktop 800×600 filename`. Normal methods of killing a Windows process from your window manager should work.

> **TIP**
>
> When all else fails trying to stop an errant Wine session, switch to a free virtual console and kill the errant Wine process.
>
> For example, Alt-Ctrl and F2 would switch to virtual console number 2. You can log into a virtual console and use `ps -ax ¦ grep wine` to find your Wine sessions. Use `kill -15 pid` where `pid` is the process id returned by `ps` to stop the process. You can return to your X session by switching to the virtual console that is running X. If you don't know what console number that is, hold down the Alt and Ctrl keys, and press F1 through F8 until you find it.

Major Pieces That Are Missing from Wine

Perhaps the most obvious omission from Wine is the lack of a printer interface. As this is a complex process, work on a printer interface is little more than a few ideas. It would be a huge task to support all of the types of printers supported under MS-Windows. Wine will likely implement only a PostScript driver. Existing Linux utilities such as `GhostScript` are already capable of converting PostScript to other types of printer types, such as HP laser and inkjet printers.

The 32-bit Windows API (`win32`) is mostly unsupported. This is the executable image format for Windows NT and Windows 95, and is known as PE (portable executable). Wine currently supports the loading of resource files, such as fonts, that are in PE format, but is unable to handle executables or DLLs.

Software Unlikely to Ever Work

The Wine project has no plans to support Windows Virtual Device Drivers. (VDDs). VDDs use a different image format, called LE for linear executable, that the Wine loader is unable to handle. Because VDDs do things like direct hardware manipulation, coexistence of a VDD with Linux device drivers would be a tough problem indeed. One of the uses of VDDs in commercial MS-Windows is for TCP/IP stacks. Wine supports TCP/IP through the `winsock` DLL, which uses the TCP/IP inherent in the Linux kernel.

History of Wine

The first parts of Wine were made available in July 1993. The first versions had problems running the MS-Windows Solitaire game, and were quite limited. Notably missing was support for menus. Since then a huge number of changes have been made by many dedicated people. Some of the more notable milestones are the following:

- Dec 1993   Communications port support
- Feb 1994   Winsock interface added
- May 1994   `clock.exe` working, backing store optimizations added
- Aug 1994   Win 32 resource loading support started
- Oct 1994   `commdlg.dll` support started
- Nov 1994   Multiple language support added
- Jul 1995   ipc, DDE, shared memory support,

It would be nearly impossible to mention everyone who contributed to Wine, or to parts of Linux that make Wine possible, but here is a list of people anyway:

Bob Amstadt, Dag Asheim, Martin Ayotte, Erik Bos, John Brezak, Andrew Bulhak, John Burton, Paul Falstad, Peter Galbavy, Jeffrey Hsu, Miguel de Icaza, Alexandre Julliard, Jon Konrath, Scott A. Laird, Martin von Loewis, Kenneth MacDonald, Peter MacDonald, David Metcalfe, Michael Patra, John Richardson, Johannes Ruscheinski, Yngvi Sigurjonsson, Rick Sladkey, William Smith, Jon Tombs, Linus Torvalds, Carl Williams, Karl Guenter Wuensch, and Eric Youngdale.

Using HylaFAX, sendfax, and mgetty

59

by Kamran Husain

IN THIS CHAPTER

Listing 59.1. The output from the `configure` command.

```
$ configure
...(Extraneous text deleted here)...
this means that only a crummy built-in font will be available for imaging text.

Warning, /usr/local/bin/gs does not seem to be an executable program;
you'll need to correct this before starting up the fax server.

HylaFAX configuration parameters are:

Directory for applications:     /usr/local/bin
Directory for lib data files:   /usr/local/lib/fax
Directory for lib executables:  /usr/local/lib/fax
Directory for servers:          /usr/local/etc
Directory for manual pages:     /usr/local/man
Directory for documentation:    /usr/local/doc/HylaFAX
Directory for spooling:         /usr/spool/fax
Type of uucp lock files:        ascii
Directory for uucp lock files:  /usr/spool/uucp
Mode for uucp lock files:       0444
Type of PostScript imager:      gs
PostScript imager program:      /usr/local/bin/gs
Default page size:              North American Letter
Default vertical res (lpi):     98
Directory for font metrics:     /usr/local/lib/afm
Location of sendmail program:   /usr/lib/sendmail

Are these ok [yes]?
```

It's important to maintain the locations of all the listed files. Changing these locations is not a good idea because they are the default values for other applications. For example, the sendfax command did not work with any other location of the afm tree other than at /usr/local/lib/afm. Changing the location via configure did not help at all.

The make install process takes a while because the make install script has to traverse several directories and build source files in each sub-directory. The files are placed in different parts of your system based on the output of the configure command.

You may have to copy the files mkfifo, chown, and chgrp from the /bin directory to the /usr/local/bin directory. The make files exclusively use these files to set the file permissions. You have to edit the location of the echo command in the make files to reflect the correct location for your echo command. If you see /usr/local/bin/echo not found error messages, either copy echo to /usr/local/bin, or edit the make files to point to the correct location. To get rid of the message Warning, /usr/local/bin/gs does not ... in the previous listing, you create a link to gs from /usr/local/bin/gs.

After the installation is done, check /usr/local/bin/fax for executable files. At a minimum, you should have faxcover, faxd, and sendfax in this directory.

Once you have HylaFAX installed, you can add modems with the faxaddmodem shell script. This script is interactive and steps you through the configuration and installation of a new or existing modem.

> **TIP**
>
> Even if you have a previous version of this software installed, run the `faxaddmodem` script to update the configuration information for your modems. Running `faxaddmodem` twice will not ruin anything.

> **TIP**
>
> If your modem is configured to communicate to the host at a fixed baud rate, use the `-s` option with `faxaddmodem`. See the `faxaddmodem` manual page for details.

A sample configuration session for my machine is shown in Listing 59.2. Note that I ran as root while I did this. I pressed the Enter key after each [yes] command to accept the default responses. If you do not like what you see, type n and then press Enter.

Listing 59.2. Sample configuration for HylaFAX.

```
# faxaddmodem
Verifying your system is set up properly for fax service...

There is no entry for the fax user in the password file.
The fax software needs a name to work properly; add it [yes]?

  Added user "fax" to /etc/passwd.
  Added fax user to "/etc/passwd.sgi".

There does not appear to be an entry for the fax service in
either the yellow pages database or the /etc/services file;
should an entry be added to /etc/services [yes]?

There is no entry for the fax service in "/usr/etc/inetd.conf";
should one be added [yes]?

Poking inetd so that it rereads the configuration file.

There does not appear to be an entry for the FaxMaster in
either the yellow pages database or the /usr/lib/aliases file;
should an entry be added to /usr/lib/aliases [yes]?
Users to receive fax-related mail [root]?

Rebuilding /usr/lib/aliases database.
41 aliases, longest 81 bytes, 823 bytes total

Done verifying system setup.

Serial port that modem is connected to []? cua1
```

continues

Listing 59.2. continued

```
Ok, time to set up a configuration file for the modem.  The manual
page config(4F) may be useful during this process.  Also be aware
that at any time you can safely interrupt this procedure.

No existing configuration. Let's do this from scratch.

Phone number of fax modem []? +1.713.265.1539

This is the phone number associated with the modem being configured.
It is passed as an "identity" to peer fax machines and it may
also appear on tag lines created by the fax server.
The phone number should be a complete international dialing specification
in the form +&ltcountry code&gt; &ltarea code&gt; &ltlocal part&gt;.
Any other characters included for readability are automatically
removed if they might cause problems.

Area code []? 713
Country code [1]?
Long distance dialing prefix [1]?
International dialing prefix [011]?
Tracing during normal server operation [1]?
Tracing during send and receive sessions [11]?
Protection mode for received fax [0600]?
Rings to wait before answering [1]?
Modem speaker volume [off]?

The server configuration parameters are

    FAXNumber:              +1.713.265.1539
    AreaCode                713
    CountryCode             1
    LongDistancePrefix:     1
    InternationalPrefix:    011
    ServerTracing:          1
    SessionTracing:         11
    RecvFileMode:           0600
    RingsBeforeAnswer:      1
    SpeakerVolume:          off

    Are these ok [yes]? n

Phone number of fax modem [+1.713.265.1539]?
Area code [713]?
Country code [1]?
Long distance dialing prefix [1]?
International dialing prefix [011]?
Tracing during normal server operation [1]?
Tracing during send and receive sessions [11]?
Protection mode for received fax [0600]?
Rings to wait before answering [1]?
Modem speaker volume [off]? low

The server configuration parameters are

    FAXNumber:              +1.713.265.1539
    AreaCode                713
```

```
CountryCode              1
LongDistancePrefix:      1
InternationalPrefix:     011
ServerTracing:           1
SessionTracing:          11
RecvFileMode:            0600
RingsBeforeAnswer:       1
SpeakerVolume:           low

Are these ok [yes]?

Now we are going to probe the tty port to figure out the type
of modem that is attached.  This takes a few seconds, so be patient.
Note that if you do not have the modem cabled to the port, or the
modem is turned off, this may hang (just go and cable up the modem
or turn it on, or whatever).

Hmm, this looks like a Class 1 modem.
Product code is "1444".
Modem manufacturer is "USRobotics".
Modem model is "Courier".

Using prototype configuration file config.usr-courier...

The modem configuration parameters are:

ModemRate:               19200
ModemFlowControl:        xonxoff
ModemFlowControlCmd:     &H2
ModemSetupDTRCmd:        S13=1&D2
ModemSetupDCDCmd:        &C1
ModemDialCmd:            DT%s@
ModemResultCodesCmd      X4

Are these ok [yes]?

Startup a fax server for this modem [yes]
/usr/etc/faxd -m /dev/cua1
#
```

HylaFAX requires that a fax user exist in the password file on the server machine. This user should have the same user ID as uucp so that lock files can be easily shared.

Client applications communicate with the server machine via the faxd.recv program. This program is designed to be started by the inetd program. If the appropriate entry is not present in inetd's configuration file, confirming this prompt causes it to be added. Note that there must also be a fax service already set up for this step to succeed (see above).

A fax server entry must exist so that the inetd program can set up the fax job submission server, faxd.recv, on the appropriate port. If the server machine is running NIS (formerly known as Yellow Pages), it may be necessary to create the entry in the appropriate map. Otherwise the entry is installed in the /etc/services file.

The fax server sends mail notices to a well-known user called the FaxMaster when certain events occur. Some examples are when faxes are received or when modems appear to be on the blink. This step sets up a mail alias for this the FaxMaster. The alias lists those system administrators that handle HylaFAX-specific problems. I chose root because I have a small system and I usually wind up doing all my administrative stuff as root anyway. If you have a large user base, perhaps a specific user could handle all the fax-related problems.

This completes the collection of server-related parameters. The remaining steps identify and configure the modem. Note that if you do not specify a fixed rate for modem communications, faxaddmodem will probe for a good speed. The faxaddmodem command is good at finding what type of modem you have and configuring it. Unless you have a compelling reason to change the responses to settings other than the defaults, leave them.

The fax daemon is now started for you. This is done with /usr/etc/faxd -m /dev/cua1. You may want to put this command in your /etc/rc.d file for subsequent boots so that you don't have to remember to start it yourself.

Troubleshooting

You are bound to run into difficulties while installing HylaFAX. Despite my assertions in the last section about two simple steps to complete the installation, you still have the potential of running into problems. Here is a brief list of problems and their solutions. The list is by no means complete, nor is it guaranteed the examples will apply to you, but at least it will give you an idea of what could be wrong.

- You need the afm-tar.Z file for the Adobe Font Metric (AFM) fonts required by the sendfax program. You can get this file via FTP from sgi.com. Some HylaFAX distributions do not include these Metric files. A subset of these fonts is available via FTP from sgi.com in the file /sgi/fax/afm-tar.Z. If you do not install the AFM files, you get error messages about fonts not found.

- Add a user called fax to the same group as uucp. The faxaddmodem call may not work and bomb with errors about too many arguments. If this happens, make sure your modem works. If you cannot use cu on your modem, fix that problem first. Check the cables, initialization strings, and so on. For external modems, check to see whether the cable has the relevant signals for doing hardware flow control if necessary and that it passes the DCD and DTR signals appropriately.

- If you have a Class 1 modem, you cannot use hardware flow control. Class 2 modems do support hardware control. Ensure that you have the correct cables for the type of external modem you plan to connect to.

Setting Up a Send and Receive Daemon

The faxd daemon is the main processing agent of the HylaFAX package. You need one faxd process and FIFO for each fax modem on your system. faxd listens to its own FIFO for all its command directives. When you start faxd, you can use the following options:

- ▪ -m to specify the terminal device the fax modem is attached to. For example, /dev/cua1 is a mandatory argument to faxd.

- ▪ -q to specify a spooling area in which to operate other than /var/spool/HylaFAX.

- ▪ -i to specify the interval in seconds that a job should be held between transmission attempts. By default, this interval is 900 seconds.

- ▪ -g option can be used to indicate that faxd should act like the getty program if it receives a call from a data modem. See the getty man page for details. If this option is not specified and the server is not configured to support incoming data connections, incoming data connections will be rejected.

- ▪ -d stops faxd from detaching itself from the terminal. This is useful for debugging.

- ▪ -1 option causes faxd to generate only 1D-encoded fax when sending.

CAUTION

There is no way to abort an incoming fax. Just sit back and wait until it's over.

The faxd.recv daemon is the program that implements the server side of the fax job submission protocol. It also implements extensions to this protocol to support job removal and the return of status information. faxd.recv is normally invoked by inetd with a line in the following form:

```
fax stream tcp nowait fax /usr/libexec/faxd.recv  faxd.recv
```

The faxd.recv daemon accepts requests for transmitting faxes and creates the appropriate queue and document files in the HylaFAX spooling area. If a job is received properly, a request to process the job is then sent to a fax server by writing to a FIFO special file named FIFO in the spooling directory. The faxd.recv daemon then returns a message to the sender indicating the Job ID (an integer number associated with the job). This Job ID can be used later to remove the job from the queue and to query the job's status.

Diagnostics generated by faxd.recv are logged with the syslog facility. The user is always informed of any problem that affects the status of the queued job. Check the man pages for a list of these error messages.

Sending a Fax

To send a fax, you will use the sendfax program. The syntax for this command from the man page is

```
sendfax [ -a transmit-time ]
             [ -c comments ]
             [ -r regarding ]
             [ -x to-company ]
             [ -y to-location ]
             [ -d destination ]
             [ -f from ]
```

```
[ -h host[:modem] ]
[ -i identifier ]
[ -k kill-time ]
[ -lm ]
[ -n ]
[ -p ]
[ -s pagesize-name      ]
[ -t tries ]
[ -v ]
[ -DR ]
[ files...   ]
```

sendfax queues up fax requests to a faxd server. These requests normally are processed immediately, although they may also be queued for later transmission using a syntax identical to the at command. For each job that is queued, Sendfax prints on the standard output a job identifier. This number can be supplied to the faxrm command to remove the job or to the faxalter(1) command to alter some of its parameters.

Fax documents are made from the concatenation of files specified on the command line. If no files are supplied, sendfax reads data from the standard input unless polling is requested. sendfax passes PostScript and TIFF documents directly to the fax server for transmission and attempts to convert other file formats to either PostScript or TIFF. In normal operation, sendfax automatically converts ASCII-text or troff output before transmission.

By default, sendfax will generate a cover page for each fax that is transmitted. This cover page is created by the faxcover program using information determined by sendfax and by information supplied on the command line. The -x option is used to specify the receiver's company; the -y option to specify the receiver's geographical location; the -c option to specify a comments field; and the -r option to specify a Re: subject. If a destination is specified as user@fax-number, the user string is passed to faxcover as the identity of the recipient.

NOTE

The preceding options must precede the -d option on the command line. Note also that multiword names must be enclosed in quote marks (").

TIP

If you don't want a cover page, specify the -n option.

Here are a few other things about sending faxes:

- You can use *70, on the -d parameter of sendfax when you want to disable call waiting.
- By default, a fax is sent at low resolution (98 lines per inch). Medium resolution (196 lines per inch), often called *fine mode*, is requested with the -m option. Low resolution is requested with the -l option.

■ Faxes are on 8.5×11 pages unless otherwise configured. Other sizes include A3, ISO A4, ISO A5, ISO A6, ISO B4, North American Letter, American Legal, American Ledger, American Executive, Japanese Letter, and Japanese Legal.

■ By default, `sendfax` uses the `FAXSERVER` environment variable to identify the fax server to which the job should be directed. This can be overridden with a `-h` option. The server specified with the `-h` option, and by the environment variable, is a host name or address and optionally, a modem identifier. The syntax for the latter is either `host:modem` or `modem@host`. For example, `cua2@no.inhale.edu`. If no modem is specified, the job will be submitted to any available modem.

If the first attempt to send a fax is unsuccessful, HylaFAX periodically tries to resend the fax. By default, HylaFAX tries to transmit the fax for one day from the time of the initial transmission. The `-k` option is used to specify an alternate time for killing the job. This time is specified using notation compatible with `at` and as a time relative to the time of the initial transmission attempt.

If an error is encountered while HylaFAX is processing a job, the fax server sends an electronic mail message to the account submitting the job. If the `-D` option is specified, HylaFAX also notifies the account by mail when the job is completed. In addition, if the `-R` option is specified, notification also is returned any time the job must be queued for retransmission.

Notification messages identify a job by its job identifier.

An arbitrary identification string can be specified instead with the `-i` option.

If the `-v` option is specified, `sendfax` prints information on the standard output about what `sendfax` does. If you specify `---v -v`, even `faxd.recv` displays its status messages as it works.

See the man pages for more information on the options available with this `sendfax` command.

Only two types of files are accepted by the fax server for transmission: PostScript files or TIFF Class F (bi-level Group 3-encoded) files. All other types of files must be converted to one of these two formats. The `sendfax` program applies a set of rules against the contents of each input file to identify the file's type and to figure out how to convert the file to a format that is suitable for transmission. These rules are stored in the `/usr/local/lib/HylaFAX/typerules` file, an ASCII file similar to `/etc/magic`. See the man pages on type rules for a detailed look at how these type rules work.

Receiving Faxes

Server processes can be configured to answer incoming phone calls and automatically receive faxes. Received documents are placed in the `recvq` subdirectory as TIFF Class F files. The server can be configured to make these files publicly accessible, or they can be made private, in which case an administrator must manage their delivery.

When a fax is received, the server process invokes the `bin/faxrcvd` command. The default command is a shell script that sends a mail message to a well-known user, the `FaxMaster`, but you might also, for example, automatically spool the document for printing.

Actually the man pages for HylaFAX are well written (for man pages). In the man pages for `faxd`, you get a lot of detailed information about how received faxes are handled.

Special Features

HylaFAX comes with several features from creating cover pages and receiving incoming data calls to handling polling requests. In each of these cases you can get more information for the man pages for each command discussed in the remainder of this chapter.

Cover Pages

You generate PostScript cover sheets for your outgoing faxes with the `faxcover` command. The syntax for this command from the man page is

```
$ faxcover [ -t to-name ]
           [ -l to-location ]
           [ -x to-company ]
           [ -v to-voice-number ]
           [ -c comments ]
           [ -r regarding ]
           [ -p page-count ]
           [ -s pagesize-name ]
           [ -C  template-file ]
           -f from-name -n fax-number
```

To generate the cover page for each outgoing fax, `faxcover` is invoked by the `sendfax` program. `Faxcover` generates a PostScript cover-page document on the standard output. The cover page fills the entire area of the default page and is created according to the information supplied on the command line and a cover sheet template file. The default template file is named `faxcover.ps`. You can override the default cover sheet with the `-C` option by specifying a file in the `FAXCOVER` environment variable.

If the cover sheet's filename is not an absolute path, `faxcover` looks first for this file in the sender's home directory. If no such file is present, `faxcover` looks in the library directory where the HylaFAX client application data is installed. If no template file is located, `faxcover` terminates without generating a cover page.

Polling

HylaFAX supports the polled retrieval of fax documents. Documents received because of a poll request are stored in the `recvq` subdirectory and also delivered directly to the requester using the `bin/pollrcvd` command. This script typically encodes the binary fax data and returns it to the recipient via e-mail.

Receiving Data Calls

Most fax modems also support non-fax communications. HylaFAX uses the locking mechanism employed by `uucp` and `cu`. Therefore, HylaFAX transparently relinquishes the serial port when an application uses the modem for an outgoing call. In addition, HylaFAX attempts to deduce whether an incoming call is for fax or data use. If an incoming call comes from a data modem and the -g argument is specified in the configuration file (or on the command line when the fax server process is started), HylaFAX invokes the getty program so that the caller may log in to the system.

Checking Status

HylaFAX maintains status information in several forms. General status information for each server process can be displayed by the faxstat(1) program. The server processes may also be configured to log various kinds of debugging and tracing information. For more information about configuration, see the section entitled "Installation Steps" in this chapter. The faxstat utility provides information such as the remote status of jobs queued for transmission, jobs received, and the general status of server processes. See Listing 59.3.

Listing 59.3. Output of the `faxstat` command.

```
# faxstat
Server on localhost:cua1 for C: Running and idle.

Job  Modem Destination    Time-To-Send    Sender      Status
2    any   5551212                        root        Queued and waiting
1    any   5551212                        kamran      Being processed
Server on localhost:cua1 for C: Sending job 1 to 5796555.
```

Any problems encountered during fax transmission are reported to the user by e-mail. A user may also request notification by mail when a job is requeued. The server process uses the /bin/notify command to inform the user via e-mail.

The file etc/xferlog contains status information about all faxes sent and received. This file is in a simple ASCII format that is easy to manipulate with programs such as vi or emacs.

To get more accounting information, use the following commands.

- ▪ xferlog—A log file of all transmitted files
- ▪ xferstats—Accounting information about all faxes sent or received

E-Mail Setup

It is easy to set up a simple mail-to-fax gateway facility with HylaFAX. If your system uses sendmail to deliver mail, follow the instructions in the faxmail/mailfax.sh-sendmail document. If your system uses smail (Linux users), follow the instructions in faxmail/mailfax.sh-smail. Restart your mail software.

Now, mail to user@dest.fax will be formatted and submitted as a facsimile job to user at the specified destination. By writing a more involved mailfax script, you can add options and display parameters such as different resolutions by parsing the user string. See the faxgateway documentation on www.vix.com in HylaFAX/faxgateway.html or the /sgi/fax/contrib/dirks-faxmailer/README on sgi.com for more information.

Files Used

HylaFAX stores its data, configuration, and faxes in several places on the file system in Linux. Here is a list of the important files and directories:

- HylaFAX uses a spool area on the disk for sending and receiving faxes. The spooling area is located under the directory /var/spool/HylaFAX.
- The /usr/local/bin directory has the commands used by the HylaFAX package. The commands are fax2ps, faxaddmodem, faxalter, faxanswer, faxcover, faxmail, faxquit, faxrm, faxstat, and sendfax.
- The ./etc directory stores all the configuration, access control, and accounting information.
- The ./sendq directory has all the outgoing fax jobs.
- The ./recvq directory contains a copy of all received faxes.
- The ./docq and ./temp subdirectories are used in fax transmission also.
- The info subdirectory contains files that describe the capabilities of fax machines called by HylaFAX. This information is used in preparing documents for transmission.
- The cinfo subdirectory contains files with per-machine control parameters to use when sending faxes.
- The status subdirectory contains files to which server processes write their current status.
- The log subdirectory contains logging information about send and receive sessions.

Multiple Modems

HylaFAX supports multiple fax modems on a single host. Associated with each modem is a server process that handles transmission and asynchronous reception. Server processes operate independently of each other and use file-locking to avoid conflicts when handling jobs submitted for transmission. All modems are treated equally at the same priority. A HylaFAX server process accepts messages and commands through FIFOs. A FIFO is basically a communications data channel where the first data in (FI) is the first data out (FO).

Another Fax Solution

The mgetty+sendfax+vgetty package is a set of programs to send and receive faxes in a UNIX environment. The package only supports Class 2 modems. The filename is called mgetty+sendfax-0.98.tar.gz, and you can get it from tsx-11.mit.edu in the /pub/linux/sources/sbin directory. There are three parts to this package: sendfax, vgetty, and mgetty. The program mgetty is for receiving faxes and handling external logins without killing any outgoing calls. sendfax is a program that sends fax files. vgetty is an extended version of mgetty that can answer the telephone like an answering machine and record voice-mail messages in addition to mgetty's fax or data call handling capabilities. The entire package lets you manage faxes and voice messages.

So what's the difference between mgetty and the regular versions of getty? Unlike traditional versions of getty or uugetty, which will put a modem into auto-answer mode, mgetty does not. When a call comes in, mgetty tells the modem to answer and tell mgetty what kind of call is being received. If it is fax, mgetty will receive the fax itself. If the modem is getting data, mgetty prompts for a user ID, and then hands the open line off to login for a normal data login.

It's the modem's job to distinguish a fax call from a data call. Not all fax modems can do this, so if yours does not do this, there is no way for mgetty to do this for you. mgetty can be used with modems that cannot distinguish a fax call from a data call, but you must tell it ahead of time what type of call to expect. You can configure mgetty to allow for uucp and other connections.

> **NOTE**
>
> Note that mgetty also supports caller ID and can be programmed to deny connections based on originating telephone number.

If you have a voice-capable modem, then you can use vgetty. The vgetty program is an extension to mgetty that provides additional call-handling capabilities. When the modem reports an incoming call, vgetty has the modem pick up the line and play a greeting. Then, as with mgetty, the modem reports the type of call. If it hears "human voices" (stuff it can't identify), the modem reports a voice connection and vgetty records the noise as an incoming voice message. If the modem reports that it identifies a fax tone, vgetty acts like mgetty and receives a fax or answers a poll. If instead, the modem hears nothing following the greeting (a certain level of silence that continues for a certain number of seconds), the modem assumes the caller is a data modem and attempts a data connection.

> **TIP**
>
> Do not use vgetty if you expect a large number of voice calls and very few data calls on the phone line you hook up. Most modems will hang up during the incoming message.

Basically the sendfax portion does the following:

- Send faxes directly or using shell scripts.
- Do fax polling. The *polling* means that you can call another fax machine and request data from it.
- Create a fax queue: outgoing faxes get sent automatically, and the user is informed by mail about the result.

You will need the Portable Bitmap Toolkit (pbmplus) for converting from the standard G3 fax format to printable images. The reason is that mgetty itself can only send or receive G3 (raster) format. However, the distribution includes tools to convert raw G3 files to or from the format used by pbmplus. The pbmplus toolkit is available from tsx-11 or sunsite archives. You will have to use the pbmtog3 and g3topbm utilities in mgetty to convert between PBM and G3. Also, the Ghostscript interpreter can convert PostScript to G3, but not vice versa.

To compile the package, copy the policy.h-dist over to the policy.h file. Then run make all to make all the packages.

To enable logins with fax capability, replace the getty with mgetty (or vgetty if your modem can handle voice) for the /dev/tty device you have configured for incoming calls. To send faxes, you have to use sendfax. The syntax for the command is:

```
sendfax  [-p]   [-xdebuglevel]   [-v]   [-lmodemlines]
[-minitstring]] [-dpolldirectory] [-Cmodemclass] [-S]
[-n] phone-number [g3file]
```

The options for this command are as follows:

- -p   Tells sendfax to try fax polling, that is, get any documents queued in the remote fax machine for you.

- -x   Uses the given level of verbosity for logging—0 means no logging, 5 is really noisy.

- -v   Gives some progress report on stdout.

- -l   Uses the given modem lines. Multiple lines can be separated by a colon. Example: sendfax -l tty1a:tty2a

- -m   Sends an additional init string. This string is sent right after initializing the modem and setting it into Class 2 mode. You can use this to set the speaker value, some special registers, and so on.

           The modem must return "OK." If it returns "ERROR," sendfax prints an error message and aborts. You do not have to prepend the "AT" prefix, but it won't do any harm either.

- -d   Specifies the directory where polled fax files should go to. Defaults to the directory from which the program was invoked for the current directory. Unused if not polling a fax.

- -C   The values for class are the type of modem: "auto" (the default), or "cls2."

- -S   Assumes modem connection on stdin, do not try to lock or initialize anything. To take over existing connections use with a dial string of T1. The T1 command sends out a short beep and no phone number at all. Such a behavior would confuse many modems. In the case of a pulse dialed number, this action may confuse the telco switch. You may also use the -m ATX1 option with the -S option if you do not wait for dial tone.

- -n   Tells sendfax to send the fax pages in "normal" (204×98 dpi) mode. Default is "fine" mode (204×196 dpi).

Now that we have discussed all these options, you may be happy to know that none of these options are required to send a fax. So the following commmand by itself will send out a fax:

```
$ sendfax 5551212 sample.g3
```

will send the G3 encoded file fax to the number 5551212. For sending graphic images in the popular PBM format, you can also pipe the output of the pbm2g3 command to sendfax:

```
$ pbm2g3 sample.pbm | sendfax 555-1212
```

The Sticky Copyright Issue

From the FAQ, the note about copyrights is as follows:

"The mgetty +sendfax package is Copyright © 1993 Gert Doering. You are permitted to do anything you want with this program—redistribute it, use parts of the code in your own programs, ..., but you have to give me credit—do not remove my name.

"If the program works for you, and you want to honour my efforts, you are invited to donate as much as you want.

"If you make money with mgetty, I want a share. What I mean by that is: it's perfectly OK with me to get paid for mgetty installation or support, but if you want to actually sell mgetty, or pack mgetty with a modem and sell it as "UNIX FAX package," contact me first."

> **WARNING**
>
> This package is still BETA software. Use it at your own risk, there is NO warranty. If it erases all the data on your hard disk, damages your hardware, or kills your dog, that is entirely your problem. Anyway, the program works for me and quite a lot of other people.
>
> For more info on the copyright issue, please contact Mr. Doering directly.

Troubleshooting the Modems

The FAQ has some interesting questions and answers to the commonly found bugs, "features," and fixes. In most cases, if your modem is not supported, twiddling with a few files here or there will not do the trick. I tried four different types of known name-brand modems before a cheap clone modem worked. I have no idea why this modem, which by the way has no visible markings, worked whereas the others did not. You may have better luck than I did.

In short, trying to fax out of Linux may not be as easy as you think. It's possible, but will take time and effort on your part.

Summary

This is a brief introduction to HylaFAX, a complete fax-handling package for UNIX and Linux. I covered the following items in this chapter.

- How to get HylaFAX for your machine.
- HylaFAX installation involves untarring the source files in a local directory. Then it's a matter of running `configure` to customize the program for your machine and running `make install`. You have to be `root` to install HylaFAX.
- How to check the `MODEMS` file to see whether your modem is supported.
- HylaFAX requires a background daemon `faxd` to handle incoming and outgoing faxes. You have to start the daemon with the `-m` option to specify where your modem exists. You need a FIFO and daemon for each modem on your system.
- The sendfax program requires the Adobe Font Metric files (in `/usr/local/lib/afm`) for converting from text to fax.
- Install Ghostscript before you install the HylaFAX package. This saves you a lot of time and gets rid of most installation problems.
- How to check the status of received or sent faxes with the `faxstat` program.
- The fax daemon, `faxd`, can be configured to answer either data or fax transmissions if `faxd` is invoked with the `-g` argument.
- HylaFAX supports polling via fax machines.
- How to get more information about HylaFAX via the WWW by accessing the Web page `http://www.vix.com/HylaFAX`.

The source code for HylaFAX is available for public FTP on `ftp.sgi.com` as `/sgi/fax/source/hylaFAX-v3.0.pl0-tar.gz`.

I have also introduced you to `sendfax`, `mgetty`, and `vgetty`. These three programs enable you to send faxes, receive faxes, and even set up voice mail on your Linux box, provided your modem is supported.

Linux Games

60

by Ed Trejis

IN THIS CHAPTER

A variety of games comes with Linux. The games can be roughly divided between those that require the X Window system to run and those that will run in plain text mode. In this chapter, you will learn about both types. The chapter provides a reasonably complete list of both X- and character-based games.

This is the final chapter in the book. We decided to save the most fun and addictive Linux programs for last!

Which Games Have You Installed?

The games listed in this chapter come in several different installation packages, so you might not have one or more of these games on your system. For instance, the graphical version of Tetris, GNU Chess, and Xfractint are each installed separately.

If one of the listed games sounds intriguing, you might want to install it if you haven't done so already.

> **NOTE**
>
> Many more games are available from Internet sites.

X Games

The following games require X Window to run.

As X Window is a graphical, windowing environment, you might guess that X games are graphically oriented. You would be right! Almost all of the following games use color and bitmapped graphics. Often, you can specify the palette of colors the game will use.

However, you should keep in mind the following:

- Arcade games, and home video game systems, have dedicated hardware that is designed specifically for running games. X Window is a generic environment. Even today's powerful personal computers can't match the speed and smoothness of movement of a game machine.

- Games work your hardware and operating system software harder than any other application. For best performance, games are often programmed to run "close to the edge" and do various software and hardware tricks. You might find that one or more of these games will crash your system or have strange side effects.

- The X games that come with Linux are personal efforts. The individuals who wrote the games, and allowed free distribution, appreciate suggestions and help in further development. Don't hold these games to commercial standards—they are not commercial products.

■ The Slackware version on the CD-ROM will let you install two types games. The "Y" set contains the BSD games collection and the other set "XAP" contains the games with X Window support. Install both versions and then remove the ones you don't like.

> **NOTE**
>
> It's tempting to put new games in /usr/games, though the most common area for user installed games is in /usr/local/games. The /usr/games directory is usually reserved for games that come with the system.

Following is a discussion of the X games you should find on your system. Keep in mind that installation differences might mean that you have more or fewer games.

Games in the *xdm* Root Menu

If you use the X display manager xdm, the xdm Root menu (usually accessed by holding down the right mouse button while the cursor is in the root screen area) has a Games submenu choice. From the Games menu, you can then choose a Demo/Gadgets submenu. If you use a different window manager, such as Motif, your menus will be correspondingly different.

The menu choices are listed here. The games they start are described in detail later in this chapter.

The Games menu features the following entries:

■ Spider (small)
■ Spider (large)
■ Puzzle
■ GNU Chess using xboard
■ Xtetris
■ Xlander
■ Xmahjongg
■ Xvier

The Demos/Gadgets submenu contains the following:

■ Ico
■ Maze
■ Xeyes
■ Xgas
■ Xlogo
■ Xroach

X Games Not in the Menus

The following games can be started by typing the appropriate command at the Linux prompt in a command-line window. These, and any other games you may install, can be added to the Games menu if you desire. See Chapter 21, "Installing X Window on Linux," for more information.

- Xhextris
- Xbombs
- Xpaint
- Xfractint

Spider (Small and Large)

This is double-deck solitaire. There is no difference in the play of Spider (small) and Spider (large). The difference is that the small Spider game uses smaller cards, and therefore fits into a smaller window than the large Spider game.

To see this game's man page, type man `spider`.

To start this game, type `spider` in a command-line window.

This game requires a fair bit of thought, planning, and skill. The aim is to arrange cards of the same suit in descending order. You can also, however, have cards of different suits arranged in descending order. Sometimes this can help you immediately, but hinder you in the long run! Note that, if you do have two or more consecutive cards of the same suit, the cards will move as a group. Spider is challenging; don't try to play it just to pass the time!

Puzzle

This is a superior version of the game, usually a cheap party favor at a child's party, in which you push around 15 numbered tiles on a 16×16 grid, trying to get the numbers in order.

To see this game's man page, type man `puzzle`.

To start this game, type `puzzle` in a command-line window.

The reason the X version of Puzzle is superior is because the pieces move very smoothly. Let's face it, the party-favor plastic versions kept jamming and sticking. This is a vast improvement.

If you click on the left box, the game will give you a random starting position. Click on the right box and watch the game solve itself! (Try clicking on the right box when the numbers are already in order.)

GNU Chess

This is a graphical version of GNU Chess that uses the xboard display system.

WARNING

Running GNU Chess under xboard is very resource-intensive. It may crash your system.

Adding more swap space may correct an agonizingly long response time. Do not worry, it's not your system, it's GNU Chess.

Xtetris

If you've never been hooked on Tetris, here's your chance. This is a nice X implementation of a game that always seems to suffer when taken from the video arcade and placed on a home computer.

To see this game's man page, type `man xtetris`.

To start this game, type `xtetris` in a command-line window.

The colors are nicely done, and the movement is relatively smooth. However, if you're used to the arcade version of Tetris, watch out for the following:

- Left and right arrow keys move from side to side; up and down arrow keys rotate clockwise and counterclockwise. Most people have a preferred direction of rotation for the pieces; experiment to find out which way is right for you.

- The spacebar, as is usual on home-computer implementation, slam-dunks the piece to the bottom rather than just hauling it down faster.

- The colors of the pieces, though attractive, are sometimes confusing. For instance, the L-shaped piece that is yellow in the arcade version is purple in xtetris, and the L-shaped piece that is purple in the arcade version is light blue in xtetris. Again, very confusing if you're used to the arcade version.

The purpose of the game? Arrange the pieces so they interlock without gaps. As soon as you create a (horizontal) row that's completely filled, it vaporizes. This is good, because when the pieces stack up to the top, the game is over. (Pity the Cossack doesn't come out and tap his feet when things start to get a little out of control.)

Xlander

This is an update of the old arcade game, Lunar Lander. You get a bird's-eye view from the window of your lunar lander. By operating the main and directional thruster engines, you attempt to touch down softly on the landing pad. If things go wrong, instead of a bird's-eye view, you get a meteorite's-eye view!

To see this game's man page, type `man xlander`.

To start this game, type `xlander` in a command-line window.

You may have problems getting the game to respond to your keyboard input. In that case, the moon's surface is only a short plummet away.

Xmahjongg

This is an implementation of the old Chinese game. The graphics are attractively done; the ideograms on the pieces are very nice. The game builds your castle for you, of course. This alone speeds things up considerably.

There is no man page for xmahjongg.

Xvier

Xvier is a relative of tic-tac-toe. On a 5×5 grid, you and the computer take turns placing your pieces; the first to get four pieces in a row, horizontally, diagonally, or vertically, wins. Xvier differs from tic-tac-toe in that you can only select the column where you want to place your playing piece; your piece then falls down the column to the lowest unoccupied row.

To see this game's man page, type `man xvier`.

To start this game, type `xvier` in a command-line window.

You can change the level of the computer's play by typing a number between 0 and 9 while in the game. However, in the higher levels, the computer thinks for a *long* time. Increase the level of play only one at a time. The default level of play is 0; you might not want to exceed 3.

Ico

Ico sets a polyhedron (a solid, multisided geometric shape) bouncing around your screen. Depending on the options specified, this three-dimensional polygon can occupy its own window or use the entire root window.

To see this game's man page, type `man ico`. It can be started from the command line (within X Window) by typing `ico`. In fact, you *should* start it from the command line because of the options available. If you start it from the Demo/Gadgets menu, you will only get a wireframe polygon in its own, small window.

One interesting option you can use from the command line is `-colors`. If you specify more than one color, you get a multicolored polyhedron, with each face a different color.

With the `-colors` option, you must type in the colors to be used in the following format: `rgb:<red intensity>/<green intensity>/<blue intensity>`. The intensities have to be specified in hexadecimal notation; `000` is the lowest value and `fff` is the highest. For example, the complete command might be

```
ico -color rgb:000/888/fff rgb:e00/400/b80 rgb:123/789/def
```

This program is fairly resource-intensive and might slow down your system.

Maze

This draws a maze, and then solves it. There is no way you can solve it for yourself. Maze is a demo, not a game. On a fast system, it solves it too quickly to follow!

Xeyes

Not really a game, but cute anyway. Whenever you start Xeyes, you get a large pair of bodiless eyes that follow your cursor's movements. Running four or five copies of Xeyes at once gives your system a surrealistic touch.

To see this game's man page, type man xeyes.

To start this game, type xeyes in a command-line window.

Xgas

This is a demo of how perfect gases behave, but you don't need a degree in thermodynamics and statistical mechanics to find this fun to watch. You have two chambers side-by-side, with a small opening in the wall between them. The chambers can be set to different temperatures. The neat part is when you place your cursor in one of the chambers and click the left mouse button—every click launches another gas particle in a random direction!

To see this game's man page, type man xgas. Online help also is available.

To start this game, type xgas in a command-line window.

Xlogo

This displays the official X logo.

Xroach

This is halfway between a game and a demo. Don't start this up if insects give you the shivers!

If you have ever lived in a roach-infested building, this will bring back fond (or not-so-fond) memories. Every time you start another copy of Xroach, a new set of roaches goes scurrying around your screen, looking for windows to hide under. Eventually you don't see them—until you move or close some windows!

To see this game's man page, type man xroach.

To start this game, type xroach in a command-line window.

If you start Xroach from the command line, you can add -squish. You can then try to swat the insects by clicking on them. Be warned, however: they're fast. You can also specify what color the roach guts will be, should you succeed in squishing some.

Xhextris

This is a version of Tetris that uses pieces made up of hexagons. To start the game, type xhextris on an X Window command line. No man page is available.

Xbombs

This is an X version of Minesweeper. You are given a large grid. Some of the squares contain mines. Your job is to flag all of the mines.

This game is started by typing xbombs at the Linux prompt in a command-line window. No man page is available.

Starting Xbombs brings up the playing field, which is a dark gray grid, and a Score window.

You uncover a square by clicking on it with the left mouse button. If you uncover a mine, you are blown up and the game is over!

It's more likely, though, that you will either uncover a number or open up several light gray, blank squares (with no numbers or mines). The number tells you how many mines are found adjacent to that square, horizontally, vertically, or diagonally. For example, a "1" means there is only one mine adjacent to that square. If you've already determined the location of one mine adjacent to a "1" square, then it's safe to uncover all other squares next to the "1" square because they can't possibly contain a mine! In this fashion, you try to deduce the location of the mines. If you happen to un-cover a square that has no number (and therefore no mines next to it), the game will automatically uncover the entire numberless area and its border.

When you think you've located a mine, you "sweep" or mark it by clicking on it with the *right* mouse button (if you click the left button accidentally, and there is indeed a mine there, the game is over). The right button toggles on and off a flag marker. Note that the game does not tell you whether you have correctly placed the flag.

You will soon discover that certain patterns of numbers let you place a mine without any doubt; other times, you have to make an educated guess.

Of course, sometimes you miscalculate and blow up. To restart the game, click with either mouse button in the Score window. If you complete the game successfully, your time will be recorded.

Xpaint

This is a color drawing-and-painting program. Start it from the Linux prompt in a command-line window by typing xpaint. A Tool menu will appear. Start a new canvas from the File menu. The Tool menu holds your drawing and painting implements (brushes, pencils, spray cans, and so on); the palette of colors and patterns is found underneath the canvas.

To see the man page, type man xpaint.

Xfractint

Xfractint is an easy way to get started with fractals. If you're not sure what a fractal is, try this program! It's almost certain that you've seen fractals before.

To see this game's man page, type man xfractint.

To start this game, type xfractint in a command-line window.

This program has an excellent setup; you can immediately generate many different fractals without getting into their detailed specifications or mathematics.

When you start Xfractint, two windows appear: one that will hold the fractal image (initially empty), and another in which you enter your commands. You can go into the Type selection and choose the type of fractal to generate; or you can click on Select video mode, which starts drawing a fractal in the image window. The default fractal is one of the Mandelbrot types.

When the image has been fully generated (it can take some time), you can go to the command window, type t, and select another type of fractal from the large list of available choices. At this point, you shouldn't have to change the defaults the program gives you. There are enough different types available.

To exit Xfractint, press the Esc key twice from the command window.

Character-Based Games

There is a long history of games being written for the UNIX operating system. Your Linux /usr/games directory contains a number of these games, from various time periods.

Many of these games were written before color, bitmapped windowing systems became common. All the games in /usr/games, except for Sasteroids, are character-based. This means that all graphics (if there are any!) are displayed on your screen using standard screen characters: A, *, ¦, x, and so on. In addition, all input is from the keyboard (again, Sasteroids is an exception).

An advantage of character-based games is that they do not require a graphical or windowing environment to run. A monochrome display is fine.

The character-based nature of some games, such as Hangman or Bog (Boggle), takes nothing away from the play; you don't really wish for fancy color graphics when playing them. Other character-based games might strike you as interesting historical curiosities: they show you what their ingenious programmers could manage with such a simple display system, but clearly would be better served by color graphics.

A Summary of Games in /usr/games

The games found in /usr/games can be roughly categorized into the following types:

- Text adventure: Battlestar; Dungeon; Paranoia; Wump
- Word games: Bog (Boggle); Hangman

- Card games: Canfield; Cribbage; Go Fish
- Board games: Backgammon and Teachgammon; GNU Chess; Mille Miglia; Monop (Monopoly)
- Simulations: ATC (air traffic control); Sail; Trek
- Character-based "video" games: Robots, Snake, Tetris, Worm
- Math games/utilities: arithmetic; bcd, Morse, and ppt; Factor; Primes
- Multiplayer games: Hunt
- Full graphics games: Sasteroids
- Miscellaneous demos and utilities: Caesar; Fortune; Number; Pom; Rain; and Worms

> **TIP**
>
> Two of the more interesting character-based games, Rogue and Hack, do not come with the Linux distribution. These games use the screen to display the rooms and corridors of a dungeon. You (and, in Hack, your trusty dog) move around the dungeon, mapping out the corridors, entering the rooms (be careful when you explore dark, unlit rooms), picking up treasure and magical items—and, last but not least, fighting monsters (or running from them!). After you have fully explored the level you're on, you can descend to a lower, more difficult level.
>
> Every time you run Hack or Rogue, the dungeons are different. Every monster has different fighting skills, and some monsters have special talents. The magical items, which include rings, wands, scrolls, and potions, have a variety of effects. Some of the items you find, such as armor, might be enchanted or magically enhanced; but if you find a cursed item, you may have been better off not picking it up at all!
>
> Both Rogue and Hack have their enthusiasts, but Hack is a later, more elaborate version that is generally preferred. If you come across either game on the Internet, pick it up and try it! There are also versions of Hack available for MS-DOS-based computers.

Text Adventure Games

These games follow the classic text-based formula: the system informs you that "you are in a maze of small twisty passages, all alike" or something similar; you type in your actions as go forward, east, take sword, and so on. If you like solving puzzles, these games will appeal to you. With text-based games, the adventure follows a defined path, and your responses are usually limited.

The following example is the start of the text-based game Battlestar, which you will learn about in the next section. Your commands are typed at the >-: prompt:

```
Version 4.2, fall 1984.
First Adventure game written by His Lordship, the honorable
Admiral D.W. Riggle
```

```
          This is a luxurious stateroom.
The floor is carpeted with a soft animal fur and the great wooden furniture
is inlaid with strips of platinum and gold.  Electronic equipment built
into the walls and ceiling is flashing wildly.  The floor shudders and
the sounds of dull explosions rumble though the room.  From a window in
the wall ahead comes a view of darkest space.  There is a small adjoining
room behind you, and a doorway right.

>-: right
          These are the executive suites of the battlestar.
Luxurious staterooms carpeted with crushed velvet and adorned with beaten
gold open onto this parlor. A wide staircase with ivory banisters leads
up or down. This parlor leads into a hallway left. The bridal suite is right.
Other rooms lie ahead and behind you.

>-: up
          You are at the entrance to the dining hall.
A wide staircase with ebony banisters leads down here.
The dining hall is to the ahead.

>-: bye
Your rating was novice.
```

Battlestar

Type `battlestar` at the command prompt. A sample session is shown in the code in the previous section. A man page is available by typing `man battlestar`.

Dungeon

Type `dungeon` at the command prompt. Typing `help` at the game prompt gives you useful information. You start out-of-doors, and have to find the dungeon entrance. There is no man page for Dungeon.

Paranoia

Type `paranoia` at the command prompt. In this humorous game, you play a secret agent on a desperate mission. Unlike most text-based adventure games, Paranoia lets you choose your actions from a menu. This is useful if you hate having to find a command that the game will understand. There is no man page for Paranoia.

Wump

Type `wump` at the command prompt. You are out hunting the Wumpus, armed with some custom arrows and relying on your wit and sense of smell. When you start the game, you are given the choice of seeing the instructions.

Type `man wumpus` to see the man page.

Word Games

The following two games are versions of popular word-finding and word-guessing games.

Boggle

Type `bog` at the command prompt. This is a version of the Parker Brothers game Boggle Deluxe. You are given a 5×5 grid of letters. In the allotted time of three minutes, you type in words made up from the given letters. By default, you must use letters that adjoin horizontally, vertically, and diagonally, without reusing any letters. Plurals and different tenses count as different words—for instance, "use," "uses," "used," and "user" are all allowed in your word list. This follows the official Boggle rules. You can change these defaults, if you want.

At the end, the computer displays the list of words which it found. You can never beat the computer, because it only allows you to type in real words. You will discover that the Boggle dictionary has some odd omissions; this can be annoying, but it isn't very serious.

This game works well without color graphics, although the small size of the letter grid makes your eyes blur after a while.

A man page is available by typing `man bog`.

Hangman

Type `hangman` at the command prompt. You won't miss the color graphics. The game is self-explanatory, but just in case, a man page is available; type `man hangman`. Hangman picks its words at random; sometimes the choices seem quite impossible to guess.

Card Games

Because of the lack of graphics, the following games are not as successful as the character-based word games.

Canfield

Type `canfield` at the command prompt. This is a version of solitaire. A man page is available by typing `man canfield`. This game does not have the time-wasting potential of graphics and mouse-based solitaire games.

Cribbage

Type `cribbage` at the command prompt. If you're a cribbage fan, this game is for you. A man page is available by typing `man cribbage`.

Go Fish

Type `fish` at the command prompt. It's you against the computer at Go Fish. A man page is available by typing `man fish`. One confusing aspect is that sometimes several actions are displayed all together on the screen (for instance, you have to go fish, the computer has to go fish, and it's back to you, all in one block).

Board Games

These are character-based versions of board games. The play quality is variable; Backgammon is probably the best of the lot.

Backgammon

Type `backgammon` at the command prompt; or, for an easy-to-follow tutorial on how to play Backgammon, type `teachgammon`. These games don't suffer from lack of graphics, but the lack of a pointing device such as a mouse means that specifying your moves is a cumbersome task, requiring entries such as 8-12,4-5. Typing ? at the game prompt gives you help on entering your moves.

Typing `man backgammon` will give you the manual entry for both Backgammon and Teachgammon.

Chess

Several chess and chess-related programs come in the GNU Chess package. Type `gnuchess` at the prompt to play chess against the computer. There is an analysis program, gnuan. The game utility prints the chessboard position to a PostScript printer or file.

Enter your moves using standard algebraic notation—for instance, e2-4.

This is an elaborate package; you should start by reading the man page.

> **NOTE**
>
> There seem to be some problems with startup messages overwriting parts of the chessboard.

Mille Miglia

Type `mille` at the command prompt. This is the Linux version of a Parker Brothers racing game. You should read the man page before starting, because the game's commands are not very intuitive. To see the man page, type `man mille`.

Monopoly

Type `monop` at the command prompt. This is a character-based version of the Parker Brothers game Monopoly. The computer does not actually play; it simply keeps track of who owns what and how much money each player has. You can play by yourself, but it's pretty obvious that you will, eventually, win! Unfortunately, the board is not displayed in any form, making it quite difficult to keep track of what's happening. This is an interesting effort, but the play is poor. A man page is available.

Simulations

The following games let you try your hand at being in charge. They are open-ended, in that each game is different and does not follow a canned plot. They combine character graphics, for instance a radar display, with text readouts and text-based commands.

Air Traffic Control

Type atc at the command prompt. Type man atc and read the man page first; otherwise, you will be responsible for one or more air tragedies! This game runs in real time. A good supply of caffeine will probably help you do well.

Sail

Type sail at the command prompt. You have a choice of over 20 scenarios, mainly historical battles involving sailing ships. You are the captain, and determine what course to sail and what weapons to use. A man page is available by typing man sail; it's worth reading beforehand, because some commands are obscure or confusing.

Trek

Type trek at the command prompt. You can "go where no one has gone before," hunt (and be hunted by) Klingons, and so on. A man page is available by typing man trek; read it before playing to avoid being a disgrace to the Federation.

"Video" Games

The following games all rely on a full-screen display, although all graphics are assembled from the standard character set.

Robots

Type robots at the command prompt. Robots on the screen pursue you; your only hope is to make two robots collide, at which point the robots explode. The resulting junk heap destroys any robots that run into it. You move about the screen using the hjkl keys, as used by the vi editor (diagonal movement is allowed, using yubn). Moves are simultaneous: each time you move, so do the robots. Sometimes, though, you have to teleport to get out of an impossible situation. You die if a robot touches you; otherwise, after clearing the screen, you go on to a bigger and better wave of robots. A man page is available by typing man robots.

> **NOTE**
>
> Some Linux distributions might include a version of Robots that has been hacked or modified so that you can't make a misstep that brings you in contact with a robot (thus leading to your demise). This takes away from the challenge of the game.

Snake

Type `snake` at the command prompt. Use the `hjkl` keys to move around, picking up money (the $) while avoiding the snake (made up, appropriately, of s characters). The snake gets hungrier as you get richer. Escape the room by running to the # character, or be eaten by the snake! You can also type `w` in an emergency to warp to a random location. A man page is available by typing `man snake`.

Tetris

Type `tetris` at the command prompt. The Tetris play screen is drawn with clever use of various characters. Ironically, although it does not look anywhere near as professional as Xtetris or other full-graphics versions, it plays very well—especially if you're used to the arcade version of Tetris. The movement keys consist of , to move left, / to move right, and . to rotate (counterclockwise!). The spacebar drops the piece. You can vary the control keys by using options with the `tetris` command. See the man page (type `man tetris`) for details.

Worm

Type `worm` at the command prompt. You are a worm, moving about the screen and eating numbers. As you eat the numbers, you grow in length. Do not run into yourself or into the wall! How long can you get before you (inevitably) run into something? Note that you still slowly crawl forward, even if you don't enter a move command.

A man page is available by typing `man worm`.

Math Games and Utilities

The following programs are small and interesting, although perhaps not that exciting.

Arithmetic

Type `arithmetic` at the command prompt. You are asked the answer to simple addition questions. This goes on until you type Ctrl-C to exit. A man page is available by typing `man arithmetic`.

BCD Punch Card Code, Morse Code, Paper Tape Punch Code

Type `bcd` at the command line to convert text you type to a punched card, type `morse` to see your text converted to Morse code, or type `ppt` for paper punch tape output. If the command line doesn't contain any text to encode, the programs go into interactive mode. Note that the Enter character you must use to finish each line of input gets coded as well. The `bcd` man page covers all three programs.

Factor

Type `factor` at the command line. This command provides you with the prime factors of any number you supply. You can type `factor <number>` to factor just the one number, or `factor` without any number to go into interactive mode. Numbers can range from –2,147,483,648 to 2,147,483,648. The following is a sample run of Factor:

```
darkstar:/usr/games$ factor
123
123: 3 41
36
36: 2 2 3 3
1234567
1234567: 127 9721
6378172984028367
factor: ouch
darkstar:/usr/games$
```

Primes

Type primes at the command prompt. If you include a range on the command line, Primes displays all prime numbers in the range. If no range is included, Primes waits for you to enter a number, and then starts displaying primes greater than that number. The program is surprisingly fast! A man page is available by typing man primes.

Multiplayer Game: Hunt

This game requires several players. You have to hook up other terminals to your system (for instance, a character-based terminal to your serial port).

Full Graphics Game: Sasteroids

You must have a VGA or better color display for this game. Type sasteroids at the command prompt. The game takes over the screen, switching you to color graphics mode. This is a relative of the arcade game Asteroids. The following keys control your ship:

Left arrow key	Rotate counterclockwise
Right arrow key	Rotate clockwise
Up arrow key	Thrust
Down arrow key	Enables the shield (one per ship)
Left Ctrl key	Fire
Left Alt key	Hyperspace

It takes a while to get the hang of the controls. The layout is very different from the standard arcade control layout. There is no man page available.

Other Thinking Games

The following programs might actually be a bit frustrating to play with initially, but they can also provide hours of addiction!

Sokoban

Imagine yourself in charge of a warehouse containing a maze and lots of bales of cotton. Each bale is so heavy that you can only push it and not pull it. So don't push a bale into a spot where you cannot push it out. Each level in this game gets more and more challenging as you attempt to collect all the bales into a loading area where you can move to the next level. The source code is available from `sunsite.unc.edu` in the file `sokoban-src.tar.gz`.

DOOM

This exciting, though controversially gory, game is now ported to Linux as well. Complete with sound support and exquisite graphics, this Linux port does its DOS counterpart justice. One problem to keep in mind though, is that your colormaps in X may be mixed up once your cursor moves out of the X terminal you run DOOM under. Two other things to keep in mind—you have to rebuild your kernel to add the sound support, and the version 1.666 of DOOM will not run external WAD files. (I recommend that you get the registered version.)

Conquest

This is an elaborate game of global conquest with equally complex instructions and display. At least the files are in an executable form, and you do not have to build them. One thing to remember is to use the `xconq` file and run `xset fp rehash` to bring up the correct fonts. A comparable game, called Empire, is also available in source from `tsx-11.mit.edu`, but you need a network connection to run this game.

Miscellaneous Demos and Utilities

The following programs might interest you. If you're a werewolf, the fourth one will be particularly useful!

Caesar

Type `caesar` at the command line. This program attempts to decrypt encoded words. Type `man caesar` to see the man page.

Fortune

Type `fortune` at the command line for your Linux fortune-cookie message.

Number

Type `number <number>` at the command line. Converts the Arabic number given as `<number>` (for example, 41) to its equivalent in English (forty-one).

Phase of the Moon

Type pom at the command prompt. The program tells you the current phase of the moon. As the man page mentions, this can be useful in predicting the behavior of others, and maybe yourself, too! Type man pom to see the man page.

Rain

Type rain at the command prompt. Your screen becomes rippled like a puddle in a rainstorm. On most Linux console screens, the program runs too fast to look even remotely convincing. Press Ctrl-C to exit.

Worms

Type worms at the command prompt (do not confuse with the Worm program, above). This fills your screen with squirming worms. Like Rain, the program runs much too fast on a Linux console screen. A man page is available by typing man worms.

Summary

You should now be able to while away the time by sitting at your machine and playing your favorite games. If you haven't installed the X Window system yet, maybe this is an extra incentive!

PART

IN THIS PART

Appendixes

Linux FTP Sites and Newsgroups

The other newsgroups tend to change frequently, primarily because they are either regional or populated with highly opinionated users who may lose interest after a while. The .alt (alternate) newsgroups are particularly bad about this. Only one .alt newsgroup was in operation when this book was written:

alt.uu.comp.os.linux.questions

There are also regional newsgroups that usually are not widely distributed, or that have specific issues which may be in a language other than English. Some sample regional newsgroups carried by Usenet are

    dc.org.linux-users

    de.comp.os.linux

    fr.comp.os.linux

    tn.linux

If you do have access to Usenet newsgroups, it is advisable to regularly scan the newsgroup additions and deletions to check for new Linux newsgroups or existing groups that have folded. Most online services that provide access to Usenet maintain lists of all active newsgroups, which can be searched quickly.

The traffic on most of these Linux newsgroups deals with problems and issues people have when installing, configuring, or using the operating system. Usually, there is a lot of valuable information passing through the newsgroups, so check them regularly. The most interesting messages that deal with a specific subject (called *threads*) are collected and stored for access through an FTP site.

Commercial Vendors for Linux

This appendix lists all the commercial vendors that sell Linux distributions. See Appendix A, "Linux FTP Sites and Newsgroups," for a list of FTP sites that have Linux for free. The advantage of getting Linux from a commercial vendor is that you get a lot of software bundled in one package instead of having to do it yourself. You can also get a list of these vendors from the *Linux Journal*, a monthly periodical:

> *Linux Journal*
> P.O. Box 85867
> Seattle, WA 98145-1867
> Phone: (206) 527-3385
> Fax: (206) 527-2806

The Linux Distribution-HOWTO file contains up-to-date information on Linux vendors that bundle packages together for sale. This list is maintained by Matt Welsh, mdw@sunsite.unc.edu. The HOWTO file can be found in /pub/linux/docs/HOWTO/Distribution-howto at tsx-11.mit.edu.

Debian Linux Distribution

> The Debian Linux Association
> Station 11
> P.O. Box 3121
> West Lafayette, IN 47906

Beta releases are available to the general public at sunsite.unc.edu in the directory /pub/Linux/distributions/debian.

Yggdrasil Plug-and-Play Linux CD-ROM and the Linux Bible

> Yggdrasil Computing, Incorporated
> 4880 Stevens Creek Blvd., Suite 205
> San Jose, CA 95129-1034
> Toll free: 800 261-6630
> Phone: (408) 261-6630
> Fax: (408) 261-6631
> E-mail: info@yggdrasil.com

Linux from Nascent CD-ROM

> Nascent Technology
> Linux from Nascent CD-ROM
> P.O. Box 60669
> Sunnyvale, CA 94088-0669

Phone: (408) 737-9500
Fax: (408) 241-9390
E-mail: nascent@netcom.com

Unifix 1.02 CD-ROM

Unifix Software GmbH
Postfach 4918
D-38039 Braunschweig, Germany
Phone: +49 (0)531 515161
Fax: +49 (0)531 515162

Fintronic Linux Systems

Fintronic USA, Inc.
1360 Willow Rd., Suite 205
Menlo Park, CA 94025
Phone: (415) 325-4474
Fax: (415) 325-4908
E-mail: linux@fintronic.com
http://www.fintronic.com/linux/catalog.html

InfoMagic Developer's Resource CD-ROM Kit

InfoMagic, Inc.
P.O. Box 30370
Flagstaff, AZ 86003-0370
Toll free: 800 800-6613
Phone: (602) 526-9565
Fax: (602) 526-9573
E-mail: Orders@InfoMagic.com

Linux Quarterly CD-ROM

Morse Telecommunication, Inc.
26 East Park Avenue, Suite 240
Long Beach, NY 11561
Orders: 800 60-MORSE
Tech Support: (516) 889-8610
Fax: (516) 889-8665
E-mail: Linux@morse.net

Linux Systems Labs

Linux Systems Labs
18300 Tara Drive
Clinton Twp, MI 48036
Phone: 800 432-0556
E-mail: dirvin@vela.acs.oakland.edu

Sequoia International Motif Development Package

Sequoia International, Inc.
600 West Hillsboro Blvd., Suite 300
Deerfield Beach, FL 33441
Phone: (305) 480-6118

Takelap Systems Ltd.

The Reddings
Court Robin Lane, Llangwm
Usk, Gwent, United Kingdom NP5 1ET
Phone: +44 (0)291 650357
E-mail: info@ddrive.demon.co.uk

Trans-Ameritech Linux Plus BSD CD-ROM

Trans-Ameritech Enterprises, Inc.
2342A Walsh Ave.
Santa Clara, CA 95051
Phone: (408) 727-3883
E-mail: roman@trans-ameritech.com

The Linux
Documentation Project

You may charge a fee for the physical act of transferring a copy, and you may at your option offer warranty protection in exchange for a fee.

2. *You may modify your copy or copies of the Program or any portion of it, thus forming a work based on the Program, and copy and distribute such modifications or work under the terms of Section 1 above, provided that you also meet all of these conditions:*

    a. *You must cause the modified files to carry prominent notices stating that you changed the files and the date of any change.*

    b. *You must cause any work that you distribute or publish, that in whole or in part contains or is derived from the Program or any part thereof, to be licensed as a whole at no charge to all third parties under the terms of this License.*

    c. *If the modified program normally reads commands interactively when run, you must cause it, when started running for such interactive use in the most ordinary way, to print or display an announcement including an appropriate copyright notice and a notice that there is no warranty (or else, saying that you provide a warranty) and that users may redistribute the program under these conditions, and telling the user how to view a copy of this License. (Exception: if the Program itself is interactive but does not normally print such an announcement, your work based on the Program is not required to print an announcement.)*

These requirements apply to the modified work as a whole. If identifiable sections of that work are not derived from the Program, and can be reasonably considered independent and separate works in themselves, then this License, and its terms, do not apply to those sections when you distribute them as separate works. But when you distribute the same sections as part of a whole which is a work based on the Program, the distribution of the whole must be on the terms of this License, whose permissions for other licensees extend to the entire whole, and thus to each and every part regardless of who wrote it.

Thus, it is not the intent of this section to claim rights or contest your rights to work written entirely by you; rather, the intent is to exercise the right to control the distribution of derivative or collective works based on the Program.

In addition, mere aggregation of another work not based on the Program with the Program (or with a work based on the Program) on a volume of a storage or distribution medium does not bring the other work under the scope of this License.

3. *You may copy and distribute the Program (or a work based on it, under Section 2) in object code or executable form under the terms of Sections 1 and 2 above provided that you also do one of the following:*

    a. *Accompany it with the complete corresponding machine-readable source code, which must be distributed under the terms of Sections 1 and 2 above on a medium customarily used for software interchange; or,*

    b. *Accompany it with a written offer, valid for at least three years, to give any third party, for a charge no more than your cost of physically performing source distribution, a complete machine-readable copy of the corresponding source code, to be distributed under the terms of Sections 1 and 2 above on a medium customarily used for software interchange; or,*

    c. *Accompany it with the information you received as to the offer to distribute corresponding source code. (This alternative is allowed only for noncommercial distribution and only if you received the program in object code or executable form with such an offer, in accord with Subsection b above.)*

The source code for a work means the preferred form of the work for making modifications to it. For an executable work, complete source code means all the source code for all modules it contains, plus any associated interface definition files, plus the scripts used to control compilation and installation of the executable. However, as a special exception, the source code distributed need not include anything that is normally distributed (in either source or binary form) with the major components (compiler, kernel, and so on) of the operating system on which the executable runs, unless that component itself accompanies the executable.

If distribution of executable or object code is made by offering access to copy from a designated place, then offering equivalent access to copy the source code from the same place counts as distribution of the source code, even though third parties are not compelled to copy the source along with the object code.

4. *You may not copy, modify, sublicense, or distribute the Program except as expressly provided under this License. Any attempt otherwise to copy, modify, sublicense, or distribute the Program is void, and will automatically terminate your rights under this License. However, parties who have received copies, or rights, from you under this License will not have their licenses terminated so long as such parties remain in full compliance.*

5. *You are not required to accept this License, since you have not signed it. However, nothing else grants you permission to modify or distribute the Program or its derivative works. These actions are prohibited by law if you do not accept this License. Therefore, by modifying or distributing the Program (or any work based on the Program), you indicate your acceptance of this License to do so, and all its terms and conditions for copying, distributing, or modifying the Program or works based on it.*

6. *Each time you redistribute the Program (or any work based on the Program), the recipient automatically receives a license from the original licenser to copy, distribute, or modify the Program subject to these terms and conditions. You may not impose any further restrictions on the recipients' exercise of the rights granted herein. You are not responsible for enforcing compliance by third parties to this License.*

7. *If, as a consequence of a court judgment or allegation of patent infringement or for any other reason (not limited to patent issues), conditions are imposed on you (whether by court order, agreement, or otherwise) that contradict the conditions of this License, they do not excuse you from the conditions of this License. If you cannot distribute so as to satisfy simultaneously your obligations under this License and any other pertinent obligations, then as a consequence you may not distribute the Program at all. For example, if a patent license would not permit royalty-free redistribution of the Program by all those who receive copies directly or indirectly through you, then the only way you could satisfy both it and this License would be to refrain entirely from distribution of the Program.*

    If any portion of this section is held invalid or unenforceable under any particular circumstance, the balance of the section is intended to apply and the section as a whole is intended to apply in other circumstances.

It is not the purpose of this section to induce you to infringe any patents or other property right claims or to contest validity of any such claims; this section has the sole purpose of protecting the integrity of the free software distribution system, which is implemented by public license practices. Many people have made generous contributions to the wide range of software distributed through that system in reliance on consistent application of that system; it is up to the author/donor to decide if he or she is willing to distribute software through any other system and a licensee cannot impose that choice.

This section is intended to make thoroughly clear what is believed to be a consequence of the rest of this License.

8. *If the distribution and/or use of the Program is restricted in certain countries either by patents or by copyrighted interfaces, the original copyright holder who places the Program under this License may add an explicit geographical distribution limitation excluding those countries, so that distribution is permitted only in or among countries not thus excluded. In such case, this License incorporates the limitation as if written in the body of this License.*

9. *The Free Software Foundation may publish revised and/or new versions of the General Public License from time to time. Such new versions will be similar in spirit to the present version but may differ in detail to address new problems or concerns.*

Each version is given a distinguishing version number. If the Program specifies a version number of this License which applies to it and "any later version," you have the option of following the terms and conditions either of that version or of any later version published by the Free Software Foundation. If the Program does not specify a version number of this License, you may choose any version ever published by the Free Software Foundation.

10. *If you wish to incorporate parts of the Program into other free programs whose distribution conditions are different, write to the author to ask for permission. For software which is copyrighted by the Free Software Foundation, write to the Free Software Foundation; we sometimes make exceptions for this. Our decision will be guided by the two goals of preserving the free status of all derivatives of our free software and of promoting the sharing and reuse of software generally.*

NO WARRANTY

11. *BECAUSE THE PROGRAM IS LICENSED FREE OF CHARGE, THERE IS NO WARRANTY FOR THE PROGRAM, TO THE EXTENT PERMITTED BY APPLICABLE LAW. EXCEPT WHEN OTHERWISE STATED IN WRITING, THE COPYRIGHT HOLDERS AND/OR OTHER PARTIES PROVIDE THE PROGRAM "AS IS" WITHOUT WARRANTY OF ANY KIND, EITHER EXPRESSED OR IMPLIED, INCLUDING, BUT NOT LIMITED TO, THE IMPLIED WARRANTIES OF MERCHANTABILITY AND FITNESS FOR A PARTICULAR PURPOSE. THE ENTIRE RISK AS TO THE QUALITY AND PERFORMANCE OF THE PROGRAM IS WITH YOU. SHOULD THE PROGRAM PROVE DEFECTIVE, YOU ASSUME THE COST OF ALL NECESSARY SERVICING, REPAIR, OR CORRECTION.*

12. *IN NO EVENT, UNLESS REQUIRED BY APPLICABLE LAW OR AGREED TO IN WRITING, WILL ANY COPYRIGHT HOLDER, OR ANY OTHER PARTY WHO MAY MODIFY AND/OR REDISTRIBUTE THE PROGRAM AS PERMITTED ABOVE, BE LIABLE TO YOU FOR DAMAGES, INCLUDING ANY GENERAL, SPECIAL, INCIDENTAL, OR CONSEQUENTIAL DAMAGES ARISING OUT OF THE USE OR INABILITY TO USE THE PROGRAM (INCLUDING BUT NOT LIMITED TO LOSS OF DATA OR DATA BEING RENDERED INACCURATE OR LOSSES SUSTAINED BY YOU OR THIRD PARTIES OR A FAILURE OF THE PROGRAM TO OPERATE WITH ANY OTHER PROGRAMS), EVEN IF SUCH HOLDER OR OTHER PARTY HAS BEEN ADVISED OF THE POSSIBILITY OF SUCH DAMAGES.*

END OF TERMS AND CONDITIONS

How To Apply These Terms to Your New Programs

If you develop a new program and you want it to be of the greatest possible use to the public, the best way to achieve this is to make it free software that everyone can redistribute and change under these terms.

To do so, attach the following notices to the program. It is safest to attach them to the start of each source file to most effectively convey the exclusion of warranty. Each file should have at least the "copyright" line and a pointer to where the full notice is found:

```
<one line to give the program's name and a brief idea of what it does.>
    Copyright (C) 19yy  <name of author>
```

```
This program is free software; you can redistribute it and/or modify it under
the terms of the GNU General Public License as published by the Free Software
Foundation; either version 2 of the License, or (at your option) any later
version.
```

```
This program is distributed in the hope that it will be useful, but WITHOUT ANY
WARRANTY; without even the implied warranty of MERCHANTABILITY or FITNESS FOR
A PARTICULAR PURPOSE. See the GNU General Public License for more details.
```

```
You should have received a copy of the GNU General Public License along with
this program; if not, write to the Free Software Foundation, Inc., 675 Mass
Ave, Cambridge, MA 02139, USA.
```

Also add information on how to contact you by electronic and paper mail.

If the program is interactive, make it output a short notice like this when it starts in an interactive mode:

```
Gnomovision version 69, Copyright (C) 19yy name of author Gnomovision comes
with ABSOLUTELY NO WARRANTY; for details type '  show w'  . This is free software,
and you are welcome to redistribute it under certain conditions; type '  show c'
for details.
```

The hypothetical commands ' show w' and ' show c' should show the appropriate parts of the General Public License. Of course, the commands you use may be called something other than ' show w' and ' show c' ; they could even be mouse-clicks or menu items—whatever suits your program.

You should also get your employer (if you work as a programmer) or your school, if any, to sign a "copyright disclaimer" for the program, if necessary. Here is a sample; alter the names:

> *Yoyodyne, Inc., hereby disclaims all copyright interest in the program ' Gnomovision' (which makes passes at compilers) written by James Hacker.*
>
> *<signature of Ty Coon>, 1 April 1989*
>
> *Ty Coon, President of V.*

This General Public License does not permit incorporating your program into proprietary programs. If your program is a subroutine library, you may consider it more useful to permit linking proprietary applications with the library. If this is what you want to do, use the GNU Library General Public License instead of this License.

Copyright Information

E

The Linux kernel is Copyright 1991, 1992, 1993, 1994 Linus Torvalds (others hold copyrights on some of the drivers, file systems, and other parts of the kernel) and is licensed under the terms of the GNU General Public License (see COPYING in /usr/src/linux).

Many other software packages included in Slackware are licensed under the GNU General Public License, which is included in the file COPYING.

This product includes software developed by the University of California, Berkeley and its contributors:

Copyright © 1980, 1983, 1986, 1988, 1990, 1991 The Regents of the University of California. All rights reserved.

Redistribution and use in source and binary forms, with or without modification, are permitted, provided that the following conditions are met:

1. Redistributions of source code must retain the above copyright notice, this list of conditions, and the following disclaimer.

2. Redistributions in binary form must reproduce the above copyright notice, this list of conditions, and the following disclaimer in the documentation and/or other materials provided with the distribution.

3. All advertising materials mentioning features or use of this software must display the following acknowledgment:

   This product includes software developed by the University of California, Berkeley and its contributors.

4. Neither the name of the university nor the names of its contributors may be used to endorse or promote products derived from this software without specific prior written permission.

THIS SOFTWARE IS PROVIDED BY THE REGENTS AND CONTRIBUTORS "AS IS" AND ANY EXPRESS OR IMPLIED WARRANTIES, INCLUDING, BUT NOT LIMITED TO, THE IMPLIED WARRANTIES OF MERCHANTABILITY AND FITNESS FOR A PARTICULAR PURPOSE ARE DISCLAIMED. IN NO EVENT SHALL THE REGENTS OR CONTRIBU-TORS BE LIABLE FOR ANY DIRECT, INDIRECT, INCIDENTAL, SPECIAL, EXEMPLARY, OR CONSEQUENTIAL DAMAGES (INCLUDING, BUT NOT LIMITED TO, PROCURE-MENT OF SUBSTITUTE GOODS OR SERVICES; LOSS OF USE, DATA, OR PROFITS; OR BUSINESS INTERRUPTION) HOWEVER CAUSED AND ON ANY THEORY OF LI-ABILITY, WHETHER IN CONTRACT, STRICT LIABILITY, OR TORT (INCLUDING NEGLIGENCE OR OTHERWISE) ARISING IN ANY WAY OUT OF THE USE OF THIS SOFTWARE, EVEN IF ADVISED OF THE POSSIBILITY OF SUCH DAMAGE.

The Slackware distribution contains Info-ZIP's compression utilities. Info-ZIP's software (Zip, UnZip, and related utilities) is free and can be obtained as source code or executables from various anonymous-FTP sites, including ftp.uu.net:/pub/archiving/zip/*. This software is provided free—there are no extra or hidden charges resulting from the use of this compression code. Thanks, Info-ZIP! :^)

Zip/Unzip source can also be found in the `slackware_source/a/base` directory.

The Slackware Installation scripts are Copyright 1993, 1994, Patrick Volkerding, Moorhead, Minnesota, USA. All rights reserved.

Redistribution and use of this software, with or without modification, is permitted provided that the following condition is met:

1. Redistributions of this software must retain the above copyright notice, this list of conditions, and the following disclaimer.

THIS SOFTWARE IS PROVIDED BY THE AUTHOR "AS IS" AND ANY EXPRESS OR IMPLIED WARRANTIES, INCLUDING, BUT NOT LIMITED TO, THE IMPLIED WARRANTIES OF MERCHANTABILITY AND FITNESS FOR A PARTICULAR PURPOSE ARE DISCLAIMED. IN NO EVENT SHALL THE AUTHOR BE LIABLE FOR ANY DIRECT, INDIRECT, INCIDENTAL, SPECIAL, EXEMPLARY, OR CONSEQUENTIAL DAMAGES (INCLUDING, BUT NOT LIMITED TO, PROCUREMENT OF SUBSTITUTE GOODS OR SERVICES; LOSS OF USE, DATA, OR PROFITS; OR BUSINESS INTERRUPTION) HOWEVER CAUSED AND ON ANY THEORY OF LIABILITY, WHETHER IN CONTRACT, STRICT LIABILITY, OR TORT (INCLUDING NEGLIGENCE OR OTHERWISE) ARISING IN ANY WAY OUT OF THE USE OF THIS SOFTWARE, EVEN IF ADVISED OF THE POSSIBILITY OF SUCH DAMAGE.

Slackware is a trademark of Patrick Volkerding. Permission to use the Slackware trademark to refer to the Slackware distribution of Linux is hereby granted if the following conditions are met:

1. In order to be called "Slackware," the distribution may not be altered from the way it appears on the central FTP site (`ftp.cdrom.com`). This is to protect the integrity, reliability, and reputation of the Slackware distribution. Anyone wishing to distribute an altered version must have the changes approved by `volkerdi@ftp.cdrom.com` (in other words, certified to be reasonably bug-free). If the changed distribution meets the required standards for quality, then written permission to use the Slackware trademark will be provided.

2. All related source code must be included. (This is also required by the GNU General Public License.)

3. Except by written permission, the Slackware trademark may not be used as (or as part of) a product name or company name. Note that you can still redistribute a distribution that doesn't meet these criteria; you just can't call it "Slackware." Personally, I hate restricting things in any way, but these restrictions are not designed to make life difficult for anyone. I just want to make sure that bugs are not added to commercial redistributions of Slackware. They have been in the past, and the resulting requests for help have flooded my mailbox! I'm just trying to make sure that I have some recourse when something like that happens.

Any questions about this policy should be directed to Patrick Volkerding <`volkerdi@ftp.cdrom.com`>.

Copyright notice for XView3.2-X11R6:

©Copyright 1989, 1990, 1991 Sun Microsystems, Inc. Sun design patents pending in the U.S. and foreign countries. OPEN LOOK is a trademark of USL. Used by written permission of the owners.©

©Copyright Bigelow & Holmes 1986, 1985. Lucida is a registered trademark of Bigelow & Holmes. Permission to use the Lucida trademark is hereby granted only in association with the images and fonts described in this file.

SUN MICROSYSTEMS, INC., USL, AND BIGELOW & HOLMES MAKE NO REPRESEN-TATIONS ABOUT THE SUITABILITY OF THIS SOURCE CODE FOR ANY PURPOSE. IT IS PROVIDED "AS IS" WITHOUT EXPRESS OR IMPLIED WARRANTY OF ANY KIND. SUN MICROSYSTEMS, INC., USL AND BIGELOW & HOLMES, SEVERALLY AND IN-DIVIDUALLY, DISCLAIM ALL WARRANTIES WITH REGARD TO THIS SOURCE CODE, INCLUDING ALL IMPLIED WARRANTIES OF MERCHANTABILITY AND FITNESS FOR A PARTICULAR PURPOSE. IN NO EVENT SHALL SUN MICROSYSTEMS, INC., USL OR BIGELOW & HOLMES BE LIABLE FOR ANY SPECIAL, INDIRECT, INCIDENTAL, OR CONSEQUENTIAL DAMAGES, OR ANY DAMAGES WHATSOEVER RESULTING FROM LOSS OF USE, DATA OR PROFITS, WHETHER IN AN ACTION OF CONTRACT, NEG-LIGENCE OR OTHER TORTIOUS ACTION, ARISING OUT OF OR IN CONNECTION WITH THE USE OR PERFORMANCE OF THIS SOURCE CODE.

***Various other copyrights apply. See the documentation accompanying the software packages for full details.

Although every effort has been made to provide a complete source tree for this project, it's possible that something may have been forgotten. If you discover anything is missing, we will provide copies—just ask!

NOTE

We are required to provide any missing source to GPLed software for three years, per the following section (E.2.3.b) of the GNU General Public License.

> b. *Accompany it with a written offer, valid for at least three years, to give any third party, for a charge no more than your cost of physically performing source distribution, a complete machine-readable copy of the corresponding source code, to be distributed under the terms of Sections 1 and 2 above on a medium customarily used for software interchange;*

Furthermore, if you find something is missing (even if you don't need a copy), please point it out to volkerdi@ftp.cdrom.com so it can be fixed.

The Slackware
CD-ROM

F

The CD-ROM accompanying this book contains the latest Slackware Linux 3.0 distribution from InfoMagic. This includes the latest versions of the kernel (1.3.18), XFree86 3.1.2, and most utilities, as well as some collections from the Linux archives.

The CD-ROM is readable directly by DOS, Windows, and Linux. The root directory contains a number of text files that relate to the disc's contents and installation instructions. Beneath the root directory are a number of directories used to install Linux for the first time.

NOTE

See Part I, "Introduction," of this book for detailed instructions on installing Linux.

The directories on the CD-ROM have the following contents:

- `bootdsks.12`   1.2MB floppy kernel images.
- `bootdsks.144`   1.44MB floppy kernel images.
- `contents`   Lists of files comprising each installable software package used during the installation routines. You don't need to use this directory.
- `contrib`   Software packages not a part of the basic Linux distribution. These packages include the Andrew User Interface System, GNU Fortran 77, GNU Common LISP, GNU gnat (Ada), GNU Pascal, NCSA httpd, ircII, Lucid Emacs, SLiRP, and more.
- `docs`   Subdirectories contain Linux man pages, FAQs, and some Linux Documentation Project documents.
- `fixes`   Contains fixes for various problems (from InfoMagic).
- `howto`   Subdirectories contain the Linux HOWTO files.
- `install`   Installation utilities, including RAWRITE, GZIP, and FIPS. FIPS lets you shrink the size of an existing MS-DOS partition to make room for a Linux partition without damaging existing files. (But make backups!)
- `kernels`   Many precompiled Linux kernels (used during installation).
- `lininst`   Contains a Microsoft Windows–based installation utility (see XREADME.1ST for more information).
- `live`   Live Slackware /USR filesystem.
- `patches`   Contains Slackware patches.
- `rootdsks`   Root file system images for initial floppy installation.
- `slaktest`   Files used to let you run Linux from a CD-ROM using the least amount of hard drive space.
- `slakware`   The Slackware Linux distribution that is installed to your hard drive. This includes other software, such as XFree86, X applications, development tools, networking tools, and more.
- `source`   Source code for much of Slackware 3.0 and utilities.

The CD-ROM can be used as an installation source with most of the needed files copied to your hard drive, or you can run your Linux system with the CD-ROM as part of the file system. The latter approach reduces the amount of hard disk space you need for Linux, but the speed of the system is slower because a CD-ROM is inherently much slower than a hard drive. Also, you must keep the CD-ROM in the drive at all times with this approach.

Sams Publishing Support

If you have a damaged CD-ROM, or if you're having a problem with the book, you can contact our support department.

E-mail:	support@mcp.com
Mail:	Macmillan Computer Publishing Support Department 201 West 103rd Street Indianapolis, IN 46290
Telephone:	(317) 581-3833
Fax:	(317) 581-4773

InfoMagic Support

Support for installing and running Linux is available through InfoMagic, Inc. Limited support for configuring X Window is available only through e-mail, due to the overwhelming number of combinations of video cards and monitors.

If you need support for specific Linux utilities and programs, you need to contact the author of the program. InfoMagic's support is available only for purchasers of this book and CD-ROM. When contacting tech support, have the following information available:

- Manufacturer and model of your computer
- Number, type, capacity, and "geometry" of your hard drives
- Manufacturer, model, I/O port, and IRQ information on all installed cards (especially sound cards and SCSI interfaces)
- Complete text of any error messages
- Manufacturer and model of your CD-ROM drive and interface details (dedicated card, sound card, IDE, SCSI, and so on)

Support via E-Mail

Send Internet e-mail to support@infomagic.com for free technical support. There is no charge for e-mail support, but you may not get an immediate response. No response-time guarantees are made for support via e-mail.

Support via Phone

Call (900) 786-5555 for immediate technical support. You will be charged $2.00 per minute for calls to this number. It will be helpful if you can be near your system when you call because you will often be asked to check configuration details or to manually adjust system startup files.

INDEX

SYMBOLS

"" (double quotation marks)
  gawk pattern-action pairs, 494, 496
  shell programming, 240-241
  Tcl scripts, 568
' (single quotation marks)
  Perl strings, 550
  shell programming, 240-241
!= (not equal to; gawk pattern-action pairs), 494
(pound sign)
  gawk comments, 505
  Tcl comments, 572
$ (dollar sign)
  gawk pattern-action pairs, 500
  Perl variables, 547
% (percent sign; gawk remainder operator), 495
& (ampersands; menus), 432
* (asterisk)
  gawk multiplication operator, 495
  gawk pattern-action pairs, 501
* (asterisks)
  widgets, 420
  wildcards, 138-139, 158
    bourne again shells, 189
    public domain korn shells, 204-205
    tcsh shells, 221

Index

Index

Index

Index

Index

Index

Index

Index

PLUG YOURSELF INTO...

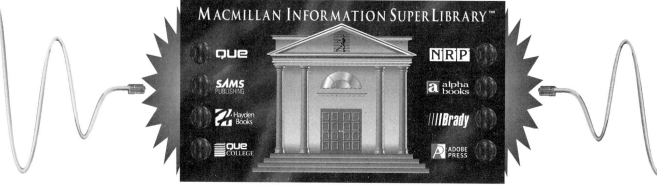

MACMILLAN INFORMATION SUPERLIBRARY™

que   SAMS PUBLISHING   Hayden Books   que COLLEGE

NRP   alpha books   Brady   ADOBE PRESS

THE MACMILLAN INFORMATION SUPERLIBRARY™

Free information and vast computer resources from the world's leading computer book publisher—online!

FIND THE BOOKS THAT ARE RIGHT FOR YOU!

A complete online catalog, plus sample chapters and tables of contents give you an in-depth look at *all* of our books, including hard-to-find titles. It's the best way to find the books you need!

- **STAY INFORMED** with the latest computer industry news through our online newsletter, press releases, and customized Information SuperLibrary Reports.

- **GET FAST ANSWERS** to your questions about MCP books and software.

- **VISIT** our online bookstore for the latest information and editions!

- **COMMUNICATE** with our expert authors through e-mail and conferences.

- **DOWNLOAD SOFTWARE** from the immense MCP library:
    - Source code and files from MCP books
    - The best shareware, freeware, and demos

- **DISCOVER HOT SPOTS** on other parts of the Internet.

- **WIN BOOKS** in ongoing contests and giveaways!

TO PLUG INTO MCP: →   **WORLD WIDE WEB: http://www.mcp.com**

GOPHER: gopher.mcp.com

FTP: ftp.mcp.com

Home Page   What's New   Bookstore   Reference Desk   Software Library   Macmillan Overview   Talk to Us

Add to Your Sams Library Today with the Best Books for Programming, Operating Systems, and New Technologies

The easiest way to order is to pick up the phone and call

1-800-428-5331

between 9:00 a.m. and 5:00 p.m. EST.
For faster service please have your credit card available.

ISBN	Quantity	Description of Item	Unit Cost	Total Cost
0-672-30850-9		Linux System Administrator's Survival Guide (Book/CD-ROM)	$49.99	
0-672-30840-1		Understanding Local Area Networks, Fifth Edition	$29.99	
0-672-30537-2		The Waite Group's UNIX Communications and the Internet, Third Edition	$35.00	
0-672-30584-4		Networking UNIX	$35.00	
0-672-30542-9		X Window System Programming, Second Edition (Book/Disk)	$39.99	
0-672-30540-2		Teach Yourself the Unix C Shell in 14 Days	$29.99	
0-672-30586-0		Teach Yourself Perl in 21 Days	$29.99	
0-672-30402-3		UNIX Unleashed (Book/CD-ROM)	$49.99	
0-672-30714-6		The Internet Unleashed, Second Edition	$35.00	
0-672-30737-5		The World Wide Web Unleashed, Second Edition	$39.99	
1-57521-014-2		Teach Yourself Web Publishing with HTML in 14 Days, Premier Edition	$39.99	
1-57521-005-3		Teach Yourself More Web Publishing with HTML in a Week	$29.99	
0-672-30745-6		HTML & CGI Unleashed	$49.99	
❏ 3 ½" Disk		Shipping and Handling: See information below.		
❏ 5 ¼" Disk		TOTAL		

Shipping and Handling: $4.00 for the first book, and $1.75 for each additional book. Floppy disk: add $1.75 for shipping and handling. If you need to have it NOW, we can ship product to you in 24 hours for an additional charge of approximately $18.00, and you will receive your item overnight or in two days. Overseas shipping and handling adds $2.00 per book and $8.00 for up to three disks. Prices subject to change. Call for availability and pricing information on latest editions.

201 W. 103rd Street, Indianapolis, Indiana 46290

1-800-428-5331 — Orders   1-800-835-3202 — FAX   1-800-858-7674 — Customer Service

The Slackware
CD-ROM

The companion CD-ROM contains InfoMagic's complete Slackware Version 3.0 distribution of Linux. It includes a variety of Linux kernels, including version 1.3.18. Plus, you'll find hundreds of additional programs and tools for Linux. See Part I, "Introduction," of this book for detailed instructions on installing Linux.

Sams Publishing Support

If you have a damaged CD-ROM, or if you're having a problem with the book, you can contact our support department.

E-mail:	support@mcp.com	*Telephone:*	(317) 581-3833
Mail:	Macmillan Computer Publishing	*Fax:*	(317) 581-4773
	Support Department		
	201 West 103rd Street		
	Indianapolis, IN 46290		

InfoMagic Support

Support for installing and running Linux is available through InfoMagic, Inc. Limited support for configuring X Window is available only through e-mail, due to the overwhelming number of combinations of video cards and monitors.

If you need support for specific Linux utilities and programs, you need to contact the author of the program. InfoMagic's support is available only for purchasers of this book and CD-ROM. When contacting tech support, have the following information available:

- Manufacturer and model of your computer
- Number, type, capacity and "geometry" of your hard drives
- Manufacturer, model, I/O port, and IRQ information on all installed cards (especially sound cards and SCSI interfaces)
- Complete text of any error messages
- Manufacturer and model of your CD-ROM drive and interface details (dedicated card, sound card, IDE, SCSI, and so on)

Support via E-Mail

Send Internet e-mail to support@infomagic.com for free technical support. There is no charge for e-mail support, but you may not get an immediate response. No response-time guarantees are made for support via e-mail.

Support via Phone

Call 900 786-5555 for immediate technical support. You will be charged $2.00 per minute for calls to this number. It will be helpful if you can be near your system when you call because you will often be asked to check configuration details or to manually adjust system startup files.